THE PARIS PEACE CONFERENCE
HISTORY AND DOCUMENTS

Published for

THE CARNEGIE ENDOWMENT FOR INTERNATIONAL PEACE
DIVISION OF ECONOMICS AND HISTORY

———

HUNGARY AT THE PARIS
PEACE CONFERENCE

Hungary at the Paris Peace Conference

The Diplomatic History Of the Treaty of Trianon

By FRANCIS DEÁK

NEW YORK: MORNINGSIDE HEIGHTS

COLUMBIA UNIVERSITY PRESS

1942

To My Wife

FOREWORD

THIS VOLUME records one of the most important chapters in the diplomatic history of Europe. Although its central theme is the history of the negotiations which resulted in the Treaty of Trianon, Professor Deák has not confined himself to the technique of diplomacy. Instead he has conceived of his subject as one with deep roots in the past and fateful consequences for the future, and in judging the decisions taken and registered in the Treaty, he has not lost sight of the political forces which conditioned the whole structure of the State system of Europe and the catastrophic blow which that structure suffered as a result of the first World War.

The issues today in Southeastern Europe were shaped in the iron crucible of the last war out of the raw materials of history into forms which not only retained but accentuated ancient antagonisms. Although in the heart of the land-mass of the oldest civilized areas of the Western world, the Danube valley remained until the nineteenth century a political frontier with a history of its own. It also served as one of the principal battlegrounds of empires seeking to control this gateway connecting the East with the West. From the tenth century, when following the defeat of the Magyar invaders at the Battle of Lechfeld (933 A.D.) the Germans settled on the farms of Upper Austria, they never gained foothold farther east than a few miles beyond the citadel of Vienna—not because they did not wish to, for the *Drang nach Osten* is by no means a policy invented by Imperial Germany of the late nineteenth century. The Magyar's state, which dates from the early eleventh century, when St. Stephen established his sovereignty on the rocky cliff of Buda, rising like a bastion in the center of the Danubian plain, had the strength which lay in a single coherent people islanded in the midst of populations that had been broken up in earlier migrations. This gave Magyar feudalism of the Middle Ages a political quality beyond that of the Germanic feudalism of the same period. Never too large in numbers for a common consciousness of their nationality, and strengthened in that consciousness by a language unintelligible to their neighbors, the Magyars preserved a continuity of history which has left an ineradicable impress upon them to the present.

This consciousness was not impaired even by a long affiliation with the Germanic empire of the Habsburgs. Although ruled for centuries by a single dynasty, the two centers of power—Vienna and Budapest —never coalesced. Indeed, it is doubtful if Austria and Hungary would have accepted even the degree of partnership which was symbolized in the Dual Monarchy had it not been for the Turkish invasion of the Danube valley and the imminent peril of annihilation by the militant imperialism of the Ottoman empire. The nations of Western Europe have forgotten how much their fate was settled on the battlefields along the Danube whence the Turks were ultimately driven back into the Balkans. But the effect on the economic and political evolution of the Danubian peoples was to maintain a monarchy which was held together chiefly by a common army and bureaucracy, the influence of the clergy, and the prestige of the court.

When the nineteenth-century movement for constitutional government spread to the realm of the Habsburgs, it encountered not only the opposition of an absolutist tradition on the part of the court, but an adequate preparation on the part of its citizenship. Moreover, the concept of the national state, emphasized by the French Revolution, accentuated the conflicting national aspirations of the mixed population comprising the Monarchy and became an obstacle to necessary compromises such as successfully resolved the problem of Switzerland. Under these conditions, nationalism tended to become a disruptive force, both in the Austrian part of the Empire and in that ruled by the Magyars. It was natural, therefore, that the ruling section of the population, the Germanic element in the Austrian portion and the Magyar element in Hungary, should both increase their efforts to strengthen their positions and should meet with added opposition from those of different nationalities.

These contending forces were in full conflict when the World War tested the vitality of the Habsburg structure and revealed its inherent weaknesses. Both in Vienna and in Budapest it was the subjects of the Emperor King, and not an invading enemy, who overthrew the Monarchy whose ruling elements were discredited by defeat. It is true that the victory of the Allied and Associated Powers supplied the opportunity for the revolution in both states; but the fact that the action was taken by the peoples themselves in the absence of occupying troops left no alternatives for the makers of the Peace Treaty. They had to recognize the breakup of the Habsburg Monarchy as the fundamental condition of the peace settlement. There is much popular misunderstanding on this point. It would have been impossible, and indeed inconceivable, for British and American troops, for example, to have been sent into the Habsburg realm to restore the dynasty under such conditions.

This much history is necessary for an understanding of the narrative which follows. For there has been a widespread belief—some of it still subsisting—that most of the ills which befell the world, particularly Europe, are attributable to the peace treaties of 1919. This, of course, is a shortsighted and untenable view. The origins of the social, economic, political, and moral deterioration of Europe, leading to the present war, are not to be found in the peace treaties alone—however unfortunate some of their stipulations were—but also in the inability of statesmen and of men of affairs of the late nineteenth and twentieth centuries to direct and keep within bounds the conflicting forces of awakened nationalism and to respond to the new influences set into motion by the Industrial Revolution. Nowhere except in this heart of Europe had the forces of history retained such vitality as that which expressed itself in the almost tribal loyalties of the peoples within the Habsburg Monarchy; and yet even before 1914 the political frontiers were rapidly ceasing to be the economic frontiers of these peoples. Isolation was giving way to an European economy, and it required farsighted statesmen to control the operation of these forces so as to ensure that truer sense of nationality which is rooted in the sense of common interest as well as of common outlook. This kind of statesmanship was unfortunately lacking. Instead of wise guidance, canalizing these forces in evolutionary operation, they were directed by the levity of a Berchtold—overcoming the opposition of Tisza by falsehood and intrigue—toward the war of 1914–1918.

The war, of course, accentuated the political, economic, and social disequilibrium; and since leadership after the war was incapable of restoring the balance, the process of disintegration was bound to continue at an accelerated pace—not solely, not even predominantly because of the defects of the peace treaties, but because of the failure or lack of constructive statesmanship in the postwar years. This failure was partly due to inexperienced leaders of the Succession States after 1919. But a larger share of responsibility must be borne by the Great

Powers of Europe and, to some extent at least, by the United States. To apportion this blame with exactness is a difficult—perhaps impossible—undertaking; nor is it very important at this juncture. But it may be useful, as an illustration, to refer to the part played by France in this section of the peace settlement.

It must be admitted that there was a failure on her part to measure up to the generous ideals which from the days of the philosophers of the eighteenth century had made France a leader in forward-looking political and social thinking. Instead of maintaining this proud tradition, conservative elements in the political life of the Third Republic linked nationalism with reactionary policies, based not on the understanding of the fundamental issues of an European polity, but on a narrowly conceived idea of the interests of France. It is, of course, true that this trend, represented by men like Delcassé before the war, by Poincaré, Millerand, and Tardieu after it, was a wholly natural reaction to the aggressive and bullying policy of Imperial Germany after the Franco-Prussian war. It must also be remembered that opposing this trend was a group of statesmen who gained prominence after the Dreyfus affair, denouncing militarism in all its forms and envisaging an European polity which, while loyal to France's interests, conceived of the policy of power as a pacific rather than a military doctrine. Such men as Jaurès, Briand, and Herriot were the true representatives in the twentieth century of that eighteenth-century France which gave inspiration to those everywhere struggling for freedom. Unfortunately, after 1919 the fear of the return of the war haunted France to such an extent as to obscure the liberal movement of French opinion, and Europe suffered in consequence from the lack of that leadership upon the part of French statesmanship which might have helped to solve the greater problems confronting the continent. It had been primarily the French genius, with its inimitable logic and ingenuity, which until the end of the last century devised the basic formulae for the balancing of revolutionary forces. These formulae were generally acceptable and, after adjustment to local peculiarities, applicable to the similar problems of the other European nations. But the flower of the French people had fallen on the battlefields, and the minds of those who survived were patterned, with but rare exceptions, on the processes of past generations, processes which failed to offer the solutions for poblems of our days. The other great nations were apparently incapable of supplanting France's leadership in this respect with their own.

It is in complex and evanescent factors like these rather than in any single document, even one as important as the Treaty of Trianon or that of Versailles, that one finds the fundamental clue to the inequities of the postwar world. Nevertheless, as Professor Deák shows in this volume, diplomacy did register statesmanship or the lack of it in the terms of the Peace Treaty in ways that were fateful not only for Southeastern Europe but also for the peace of the world. Diplomacy has also its responsibilities, which cannot be explained away by the analysis of preëxisting conditions. Just as the action taken by the Vienna Cabinet in July, 1914, was the primary cause of the World War, in spite of all the antecedent history in the alliances and counteralliances, so the Treaty of Trianon must face the judgment of history for the way in which the peace settlement created a new state system and registered with ruthless definiteness the consequences of the war.

The present volume is the result of years of study by Professor Deák, who has the double advantage of mastery of the whole field of documentary evidence and intimate acquaintance with the chief personalities involved in this story of diplomacy and policy. In keeping with the purpose of this series, the documents furnish the heart of the text; but the volume also furnishes a narrative which, while serving a ready guide for the researcher, is in itself an illuminating and authoritative history of the whole period with which it deals.

JAMES T. SHOTWELL

Columbia University
June 1, 1942

PREFACE

A STUDY of one of the peace treaties concluded at the end of the first World War may appear incongruous today when the flames of another war envelop the globe. The explanation of this book at this date, if one is needed, lies in the fact that work on it was begun several years ago when, although storm clouds had begun to gather on the horizon, the hope had not yet vanished that armed conflict might be avoided through the application of statesmanship. Even though this hope has not been fulfilled,—even though events have demonstrated that this generation, like those preceding it, had ignored the teachings of history—I have not abandoned the task of recording as faithfully and completely as possible the diplomatic history involved in the treaty of peace between the Allied Powers and Hungary. The political and economic structure of Europe—indeed of the world—as set up by the peace treaties of 1919 and 1920 has disappeared; all that remains is pure history. Yet it seems to me that an examination of the principles and methods of the Paris Peace Conference may be instructive and useful when a new peace conference shall attempt to build a new and perhaps more durable edifice on the ruins left in the wake of this war.

Upon Professor Shotwell's suggestion I began to collect material for this book in 1935, fully realizing that the dearth of published documentary sources is the principal handicap confronting students of recent history and that this handicap would, in the case of the Hungarian peace treaty, be particularly heavy. To overcome this handicap, to discover and to gain access to unpublished records, constituted my main objective. Realizing further that documents themselves very often do not tell the whole story and may even give a false impression of what actually transpired, I deemed it my duty to obtain, through personal interviews with such participants in the work of the Peace Conference as could be reached, as much of the atmosphere and the spirit behind the lifeless letters, memoranda, and minutes as was possible. Above all, I have endeavored to present my findings and my analysis of the events not merely in coherent and integrated form, but also as objectively and dispassionately as I was capable of doing, despite my Hungarian heritage.

The accomplishment of my task was made possible by the generous assistance extended to me from many quarters, which I gratefully acknowledge. The Hungarian Foreign Minister, Mr. Koloman de Kánya, gave me permission, in 1935, to roam freely in the archives of the Foreign Office. It was as a result of these researches among the dust-covered files of 1919 and 1920 that, following the example set by the United States, the Hungarian Foreign Office began the publication of Hungary's diplomatic correspondence. Members of the Hungarian Peace Delegation gave valuable information in personal interviews; and, in particular, I should like to record my gratitude to a Hungarian statesman now dead, Count Stephen Csáky, who gave me every help I could ask for. I also was able to use information which the late Count Apponyi gave me during conversations with him long before I started work on this book. As for the living, I owe a great deal to Count Stephen Bethlen, who spared neither time nor effort to fill in the lacunae in the Hungarian records.

I was also fortunate in obtaining assistance from members of the American Commission to Negotiate Peace. President Charles Seymour, of Yale University, Colonel Lawrence Martin, of the Library of Congress, Major Douglas Johnson, Professor of Geology in Columbia University, Mr. Nicholas Roosevelt, and Mr. Allen W. Dulles were kind enough to read portions of the manuscript relating to events of which they had personal knowledge while exercising their respective functions during the Peace Conference period. Their suggestions and criticism have contributed to the accuracy of my narrative.

The Department of State of the United States, through the kindness of Mr. E. Wilder Spaulding, Chief of the Division of Research and Publications, gave me permission to study several important memoranda and made it possible for me to check the accuracy of the identification of, and quotations from Peace Conference documents obtained from various sources.

My thanks are also due to the Hoover Library on War and Revolution for permission to examine a collection of manuscript documents —awaiting publication by the Library—relating to the Hungarian peace treaty and to refer to or cite some of them.

I gratefully acknowledge Mr. D. Hunter Miller's generosity in having allowed me to reprint, in the documentary section of this book, a number of other documents relating to the Hungarian peace treaty, which are available only in his *Diary at the Conference of Paris.*

I wish to express my appreciation also for the permission granted by the following authors, publishers, and copyright owners to quote from the books indicated: Mr. Ray Stannard Baker and Doubleday, Doran and Company, Inc. *Woodrow Wilson and World Settlement;* Mr. Harold Nicolson and Harcourt, Brace and Company *Peacemaking, 1919;* Professor Ralph H. Lutz and Miss Nina Almond and the Stanford University Press *The Treaty of St. Germain. A Documentary History of Its Territorial and Political Clauses;* the Rt. Hon. David Lloyd George and the Yale University Press *Memoirs of the Peace Conference;* Professor F.-K. Krüger and Mrs. H. H. Bandholtz and Columbia University Press *An Undiplomatic Diary;* Professor F. J. Vondracek and Columbia University Press *The Foreign Policy of Czechoslovakia, 1918–1935.*

To complete this record, I ought to say that I also endeavored to obtain material and information from countries, other than Hungary and the United States, which were directly concerned in the making of the Treaty of Trianon. These efforts, however, remained either wholly fruitless or brought only inconsequential results.

I have left it to the last gratefully to acknowledge the help I have had from those most intimately connected with my work. First, I should like to pay my debt to the late Count Paul Teleki. He not only sacrificed a great deal of his time to give me valuable information regarding the work of the Hungarian Peace Delegation, of which he was the moving spirit, but he also encouraged me to proceed in the face of what seemed at times to be insurmountable obstacles. Next, I owe most to Dr. James T. Shotwell, editor of the series of which this volume is a part, for the time he spent in reading the manuscript, for his unceasing advice and his constructive criticism as an expert historian, which alone enabled me to overcome the limitations of a strictly legal point of view. Miss Katharine K. McGee has been an efficient, generous, and uncomplaining assistant in preparing the manuscript and typing many thousand pages of the various revisions thereof. Mr. Kurt E. Lowe, of the Department of Geology of the College of the City of New York, is responsible for the draftsmanship of the maps appended to this volume. The staff of Columbia University Press has been generously coöperative and helpful in solving the many problems encountered in transforming a manuscript into a printed book. Last but not least, I wish to thank my wife for her patient help and inspiration, without which this book would have never been finished.

But I alone am responsible for the narrative, analysis, and conclusions herein contained.

FRANCIS DEÁK

Columbia University
School of Law
June 1, 1942

Contents

Part One

Introduction

The Armistice of November 3, 1918, and the disintegration of the
Austro-Hungarian Monarchy; The Belgrade Armistice of November 13, 1918; Post-Armistice developments; The Coolidge mission: Conditions in Hungary at the opening of the Peace Conference

Part Two

The Hungarian Question at the Peace Conference in Hungary's Absence

The American recommendations; The presentation of territorial claims by Hungary's neighbors; The proposal of a neutral zone between the Hungarians and the Rumanians; The proceedings in the Territorial Commissions; The establishment of the communist regime in Hungary; The recommendations of the Territorial Commissions before the Council of Foreign Ministers and the Council of Four; Autonomy for Ruthenia; The final consideration of Hungary's frontiers with Rumania and Czecho-Slovakia by the Council of Foreign Ministers and by the Council of Four; The allocation of Western Hungary to Austria

Part Three

The Collapse of the Communist Regime in Hungary and the Rumanian Occupation

Prelude to the renewal of hostilities between Hungary and Rumania; The war between Hungary and Rumania and the col-

CONTENTS

Maps 1–5 of Hungary at end of volume

Abbreviations Used in Parts One to Four

AD, *Bulletin:* Bulletins issued by the American Commission to Negotiate Peace, and printed in Miller, *My Diary at the Conference of Paris.*

AD, SH Bulletin: Bulletins issued by the American Commission to Negotiate Peace, MSS.

Almond and Lutz, *The Treaty: The Treaty of St. Germain. A Documentary History of Its Territorial and Political Clauses.*

ARA: American Relief Administration. Manuscript collection relating to its European operations, in the Hoover Library on War and Revolutions, Stanford University, Cal.

CHD: Minutes of the Meetings of the Council of Heads and Delegations. MSS.

Bandholtz, *Diary: An Undiplomatic Diary.*

HFR: *Papers and Documents Relating to the Foreign Relations of Hungary,* Vol. I, 1919–20.

HPN: *The Hungarian Peace Negotiations.*

HWL: Hoover Library on War and Revolutions, Stanford University, Cal.

Lapradelle, *La Paix de Versailles: La Documentation internationale: La Paix de Versailles,* edited by G. de Lapradelle.

Lloyd George, *Memoirs: Memoirs of the Peace Conference.*

Miller, *Diary: My Diary at the Conference of Paris.*

"Political Diary": "Political Diary of the Hungarian Peace Delegation," printed in an English translation in *Papers and Documents Relating to the Foreign Relations of Hungary,* Vol. I, Appendix 1.

Temperley, *History: A History of the Peace Conference of Paris.*

PART ONE

Introduction

I. INTRODUCTION

The Armistice of November 3, 1918, and the Disintegration of the Austro-Hungarian Monarchy

THE TECHNICAL END of active warfare, as far as the peoples of the Austro-Hungarian Monarchy were concerned, came with the signing of the armistice between the Italian High Command, representing the Allied and Associated Powers, and the representatives of the Austro-Hungarian High Command, in the Villa Giusta, at Padua, on November 3, 1918. The curious thing about this armistice is that it was signed by the general staff of a disintegrating army belonging to an empire in the process of dissolution.

The consensus of expert opinion is that the military fate of Austria-Hungary was sealed by the defection of Bulgaria and the collapse of the Balkan front. The signing of a separate armistice between that country and the Allies, on September 29, 1918, seems to have given the signal for open manifestations of that dissatisfaction and unrest which, for some time, had been seething below the surface throughout the Monarchy. It lies beyond the scope of this study to inquire into the causes of its disintegration—whether it was really so antiquated internally that it was bound to disappear; whether it was crushed under the terrific burdens imposed by four-and-a-half years of war; and whether the process was accelerated, and if so to what extent, by Allied efforts to weaken the enemy by sowing discontent among the various nationalities of the Monarchy and actively supporting separatist movements. The disintegration of this once great empire, wholly unexpected by the Monarchy itself, and largely so by Allied governmental circles, concerns us only as being the factual background of the peace settlement in Central Europe and insofar as it had a direct bearing on the formulation of the peace treaties, more particularly the Treaty of Trianon between Hungary and the Allied and Associated Powers. For this reason no attempt is made here either to record the political movements which in the fall of 1918 led to revolution and independence in various parts of the Monarchy, including Hungary, or to analyze their whys and wherefores, or assess their historical significance.[1]

The relevant events that led to the Padua Armistice of November 3, 1918, may be briefly stated. The growing restlessness which the collapse of Bulgaria brought to the surface throughout the Monarchy made it clear to her statesmen and military leaders that the war could not be continued. An offer of peace was sent, on October 4, 1918, to the President of the United States, stating the willingness of the Austro-Hungarian Government to enter into peace negotiations on the basis of President Wilson's Fourteen Points as later amplified.[2] The reply of President Wilson, dated October 19, 1918, did not augur well for the future of the Monarchy. It stated that the United States could no longer negotiate for peace on the basis of Point Ten, which sought to safeguard and assure the autonomous development of the peoples of the Monarchy, because meanwhile the United States had recognized the Czecho-Slovak National Council as a *de facto* belligerent government on the Allied side and had also recognized "the justice of the nationalistic aspirations of the Jugo-Slavs for freedom." [3]

[1] Despite the sizable literature on this subject, a dispassionate and objective inquiry into the disintegration of Austria-Hungary is still a task to be undertaken by historians. Much useful information relating to the effect of the war is contained in the studies published under the direction of Professor James T. Shotwell by the Carnegie Endowment for International Peace in the "Social and Economic History of the World War" series. See particularly Gratz and Schüller, *The Economic Policy of Austria-Hungary during the War*, and, by the same authors, *Der wirtschaftliche Zusammenbruch Österreich-Ungarns*; Pap, *Hungarian Social Policy in the World War* [in Hungarian]. The account of the collapse as given in Temperley's *A History of the Peace Conference at Paris*, Vol. IV, Part II, chap. i, suffers from an absence of historical perspective. Treatises and memoirs written largely by those who played greater or lesser parts in this drama are of course not objective. Thus Jászi's otherwise scholarly endeavor in his *Dissolution of the Habsburg Monarchy*, is strongly flavored by the personal prejudices and antagonisms of the author. *Cf.* also Burián, *Austria in Dissolution;* Czernin, *In the World War;* and Andrássy, *Diplomacy and the War*. Perhaps the best, though by no means adequate works are von Glaise-Horstenau's *The Collapse of the Austro-Hungarian Empire*, and Gratz's *The Era of Revolutions* [in Hungarian]. Reference should also be made to Strong's *Austria (October 1918–March 1919): Transition from Empire to Republic*, which contains a brief and useful summary of events in Austria which led to the revolutions of Oct.–Nov., 1918. Other accounts dealing with this problem are, in most instances, colored by the pseudo-liberalism of their respective authors, who proceed from an imaginary blue print and shape the causes of events to fit the preconceived pattern.

[2] For the text of the Austro-Hungarian peace offer transmitted through the Swedish Minister at Washington on Oct. 7 see *Foreign Relations of the United States*, 1918, Supplement 1, Vol. I, p. 341.

[3] *Ibid.*, p. 368.

When President Wilson's reply reached Vienna, the Government of the Monarchy was no longer in a position to bargain. The last-minute efforts of the emperor-king to federalize the Empire came too late to satisfy the increasingly loud clamor for independence by the various nationality groups. Conversations aiming at some compromise solution within a federal framework, to which Emperor Charles invited party leaders in the Austrian Parliament on October 12, produced no results. A general strike which began in Bohemia on October 14 [4] and, on October 15, a declaration of Croatia's independence by the recently formed Southern Slav Council, at Zagreb, foretold the shape of things to come. Nevertheless, on October 16 the Emperor issued a Manifesto which, with certain reservations, authorized the transformation of the Monarchy into a federal state. The most important reservation which the Manifesto contained was the proviso that the contemplated federalization should not affect the integrity of the lands of the Hungarian Crown—a reservation which Charles inserted in observance of the oath he had taken as King of Hungary. In the light of events the reservation had a purely theoretical value. The promise of federalization no longer satisfied the ambitions of the dissident elements, and its effect on the armed forces appears to have been demoralizing. The declaration of Czecho-Slovakia's independence in Washington on October 18, the day before President Wilson's discouraging reply to the Austro-Hungarian peace offer was handed to the Swedish Minister, was followed by a similar declaration by the Czech National Council at Prague on October 20.

The situation in Hungary also went from bad to worse. The government headed by Mr. Alexander Wekerle resigned in the middle of October, and efforts to form an acceptable cabinet failed, due to the unwillingness of the radical and leftist elements, who rallied around Count Michel Károlyi, to participate in any government except their own. The result was confusion which subversive elements were quick to exploit to their own advantage. Opposition members in Parliament demanded the return of Hungarian army units from the front. [5] A Hungarian National Council, similar to those formed in Croatia, Bo-

---

[4] On the same day the establishment of a Czecho-Slovak Government was announced in Paris. France recognized this government on the following day.

[5] It is, however, incorrectly stated in Temperley, *History,* IV, 55, that the Hungarian Parliament demanded, on Oct. 20, 1918, the repatriation of Hungarian troops. Resolutions to this effect were presented on Oct. 17 and 19 by individual deputies, but Parliament did not act on these resolutions. There was no session of the House on Oct. 20.

hemia, among the Poles in Galicia and, on October 21, in Vienna for the German lands of Austria, was established in Budapest on October 23, and was composed, with a few exceptions, of obscure politicians and radical leaders. On the day following, King Charles came to Hungary in the hope that the crisis might be averted through personal contact with the leaders of the contending factions. Large-scale demonstrations calling for Hungary's independence and immediate peace were organized by the National Council, which gained another ally in the Soldiers' Council formed in Budapest next day.

It was under these circumstances that Count Andrássy was appointed to succeed Count Burian as the Monarchy's Minister for Foreign Affairs, and to him was entrusted the task of severing the alliance with Germany and of securing a separate armistice.

Despite the discouraging reply of President Wilson, Count Andrássy was urged to act without delay, since, in addition to the threatening internal revolt, the military situation of the Monarchy had become hopeless. The Italians had begun an offensive on October 24 to which the exhausted Austro-Hungarian troops, weakened by the collapse of the home front, could offer, after two days of bitter fighting, only desultory resistance. Even if the morale of the army had been better, the chances of successful resistance would have been slight, in view of the fact that the army's supply lines and lines of communication with the hinterland had been virtually severed, as a result of the revolutionary activities of the Slavic population in the southern provinces of Austria and in Croatia, activities under full headway when the Italian offensive began. There can be no doubt that the collapse of the Austro-Hungarian front in Italy was due primarily to the collapse of the home front. To regard the Italian victory of October, 1918, as a battle fought under the same conditions as those preceding it in the war of 1914–18 is certainly one of the great fictions of modern history.

Thus Count Andrássy had no choice but to ask for peace. The request of the Monarchy for a separate armistice on the terms set forth in President Wilson's note of October 19 was delivered in Washington on October 29; [6] this was followed on October 30 by a personal appeal by Count Andrássy to the American Secretary of State, Mr. Lansing, for his intercession in the interest of immediate armistice negotiations. [7] The United States Government immediately submitted the Austro-

[6] See *Foreign Relations of the United States,* 1918, Supplement 1, Vol. I, p. 404.
[7] *Ibid.,* p. 429.

Hungarian request to the Allied governments. The terms of the armistice were approved at a meeting of the British, French, and Italian prime ministers, Field-marshal Foch, and Colonel House on October 31 and were communicated on the same day to General Diaz, Commander in Chief of the Italian Army, for transmission to the Austro-Hungarian High Command.[8] On November 3, the armistice was signed in Padua. But by that time the Austro-Hungarian Empire no longer existed. The Hungarian Government, in particular, took the position that the union with the other half of the Monarchy had been dissolved and refused to recognize the competence of the Austro-Hungarian High Command to represent Hungary in the armistice negotiations.[9]

The visit of King Charles to Hungary did not succeed in bringing the government crisis nearer to a solution. On October 27 the King returned to Vienna and named Archduke Joseph as *homo regius*, or regent, with full powers to handle the political crisis. The Archduke had been chosen for this delicate task because he belonged to that branch of the Habsburg family which for several generations had lived in Hungary and actively participated in Hungarian public life. After two days of feverish negotiation with party leaders, Archduke Joseph appointed Count John Hadik, a moderate, to form a coalition cabinet. This gave the signal to the radical elements, pressing for Count Károlyi's appointment as premier, openly to espouse the cause of revolution. The first move came from the Social-Democratic Party, which addressed an appeal to the army to make common cause with the National Council and to refuse to obey any orders directed against the revolution. By the morning of October 31 the Council succeeded, with the coöperation of revolting troops, in establishing control in the capital, and Archduke Joseph had no choice but to appoint Count Károlyi

[8] *Ibid.,* p. 430.

[9] There is some dispute among Hungarian historians and constitutional lawyers as to the precise date at which Hungary became independent. Mr. Wekerle, then Prime Minister of Hungary, announced in Parliament on Oct. 16 that the dualism with Austria had come to an end, but the personal union was upheld by him. Count Károlyi received his appointment from, and took the oath of office for King Charles. He was relieved of that oath by the King, the day following his appointment, and he then swore allegiance to the National Council. Although the King did not renounce the exercise of the royal prerogative until Nov. 13 and although the Republic was not proclaimed until Nov. 16, Count Károlyi's Government appears to have proceeded as wholly independent of Austria and as no longer subject to the Habsburg sovereign from the moment when it was released from its oath of loyalty by the King on Nov. 1.

as prime minister. The cabinet which he formed took the oath of office on the evening of the same day, and at almost the same moment that saw a roving band of soldiers assassinate Count Stephen Tisza, who, as the Hungarian premier, had been the one member who, at the fatal Crown Council of July 11, 1914, opposed the war. Count Károlyi's Government was strongly leftist; it consisted of representatives of the left wing of the Independence Party, of the Radical Bourgeois Party, and the Social-Democratic Party—the two latter being even more radical than the Independence Party. The next day the King under pressure from Károlyi and his followers relieved Károlyi of his oath, and the government no longer pledged loyalty to the Sovereign, the bearer of the Holy Crown of St. Stephen, but to the National Council. On the following day the army was required to pledge loyalty to the Council. After the ceremony Béla Linder, Minister of War in Károlyi's new "Peoples' Government," addressed the assembled troops, ending his exhortation with these words: "Never again do I wish to see a soldier."

The Minister of War took pacifism seriously. Almost his first act after he assumed office was the issuing of an order to Hungarian army units at the front to lay down their arms, an order which the Austro-Hungarian High Command refused to forward to the field. On the following day Linder addressed a proclamation to the soldiers, announcing the government's intention to cease fighting on all fronts. When the High Command advised Budapest that negotiations for the cessation of hostilities were progressing satisfactorily and that an armistice would be signed within a few hours, Linder replied that the men negotiating with General Diaz were not recognized as representing the Hungarian Government and insisted that Hungarian troops must be ordered to return home at once.

Whether or not Károlyi and his government were informed of the terms of the armistice, the position they took with respect to the termination of hostilities can be explained only by a total lack of comprehension and responsibility on the part of the men who took control of Hungary's destinies. To order an army to lay down its arms when the nation was threatened by external enemies and internal disorder is obviously inexcusable. To believe that by mere declarations of peaceful intentions at the end of four-and-a-half years of bitter warfare, the enemy would suddenly turn into a protecting friend is evidence of an unbelievable degree of naïveté. And yet this was the policy which

Károlyi and his associates followed. The armistice terms which they refused to recognize were rather favorable to Hungary in that they did not foresee specifically the occupation of any Hungarian territory. The Padua Armistice, concluded on the false assumption that the Monarchy still existed, indeed took account solely of Italy's interests and provided exclusively for the military *desiderata* of the Italian front, for which it was subsequently severely criticized. It is true that it gave the Allies a blanket authority "to occupy at any moment any strategic points of Austria-Hungary, deemed by those Powers necessary to render any military operations possible or to maintain order." [10] There can be no doubt that if the necessity had arisen the Allies would have proceeded to occupy Hungarian territories, either by invoking such blanket authority or by otherwise forcing Hungary to acquiesce in the implimentation of the armistice convention. The unfortunate thing, from Hungary's point of view, was the almost incredible fact that the leaders of Hungary took the initiative for the conclusion of a far less advantageous armistice, thus relieving the Allies of the moral responsibility which any extension of the armistice would have involved. Their responsibility to the nation is further aggravated by the voluntary handing over of even the few weapons which the homecoming Hungarian troops could have salvaged from the revolting Croatians, Slovenes, and Austrians, through whose hostile territories they had to pass, although the mere existence of a small, disciplined, armed force might have saved the country from as extensive an occupation as it finally had to accept.[11]

[10] Art. 4, par. 2. For the complete text of the Armistice of November 3, 1918, see *infra*, Doc. 1, p. 355.

[11] At the end of Oct., 1918, the bulk of the Austro-Hungarian Army, consisting of about 70 infantry and 12 cavalry divisions, with the necessary artillery, technical, and supply equipment, was on the Italian front, which was held by 53 infantry and 5 cavalry divisions. Of these 58 divisions, 27 were either Hungarian *Honvéd* divisions or divisions of the Imperial and Royal Army recruited from Hungary. The rest of the fighting units were in line in France (4 divisions, 3 of which were Hungarian), on the Ukrainian front (6 divisions, 3 of which were Hungarian), and in the Balkans (14 divisions, of which 7 were Hungarian). With the exception of the army in the Ukraine, Hungarian troops returning home had to pass through hostile lands and often to face disarmament by former enemies or fellow nationals turned enemy. Illuminating details of the disintegration of the Austro-Hungarian Army and of the return journey of Hungarian army units to their homeland came to light recently in a series of articles based on authentic military documents preserved in the archives of the Hungarian War Office. See Szende, "Les Derniers Jours de l'armée austro-hongroise en 1918," *Nouvelle Revue de Hongrie*, LX (Jan., 1939), 88 ff.; "Une armée qui rentre et ne trouve pas sa patrie," *ibid*. (April, 1939), pp. 376 ff. It is also evident that non-

The Belgrade Armistice of November 13, 1918

The most effective appeal which Count Károlyi seems to have made for the support of the Hungarians was the assertion that he was known as a friend of the Allies and that therefore Hungary under his leadership would be better treated than otherwise. Possibly Count Károlyi himself sincerely believed that this claim was well founded and it was for that reason that he decided to negotiate a separate armistice for Hungary with General Franchet d'Esperay, Commander in Chief of the Allied Armies of the East. This army, which after the conclusion of an armistice with Turkey on October 30 gained control over the whole Balkan Peninsula, moved rapidly northward and had already reached the Danube, Hungary's southern border, at several places. Although by this time negotiations with Germany for an armistice had begun and there was no particular reason for immediate changes in the armistice terms of November 3 with Austria-Hungary, the Allied command in the East doubtless welcomed such an unexpected opportunity to secure the evacuation of Hungarian territories in the south for the benefit of the Serbian ally and also for Rumania, who chose to reënter the war on November 8 and had already invaded Transylvania at several points.

The Hungarian Delegation, under the leadership of Count Károlyi himself, left for Belgrade on November 7. Their reception was anything but cordial—according to some accounts, humiliating—and the terms which Hungary was compelled to accept provided for the occupation by Allied, primarily Serbian and Rumanian, troops of large portions of territory in southern Hungary. Article I of the Belgrade Armistice, signed on November 13, provided for the withdrawal of Hungarian troops north of a line following the upper valley of the

---

transportable heavy equipment of all sorts was left at the fronts. According to a confidential compilation made by the Hungarian Ministry of National Defense early in 1920, which the author was allowed to consult, there was comparatively little reserve stock of military matériel stored in Hungary proper; the returning Hungarian army units, despite the difficulties referred to, succeeded in bringing back a considerable quantity of light weapons, such as rifles and machine guns, and other equipment easily transportable. But the bulk of really valuable matériel was left behind, either in compliance with armistice conditions or because of the difficulties of transportation. These facts ought to be taken into account in considering Hungary's war potential in the turbulent months following the armistice, when her neighbors claimed to be so apprehensive of possible aggression on her part. The value of this lost matériel, representing an investment of no mean portion of the nation's wealth, has also a bearing on the financial status of postwar Hungary.

rivers Szamos and Beszterce, to their confluence with the Tisza River,[12] thence a line through the cities of Szabadka, Baja, and Pécs (these to be free of Hungarian troops), then the course of the Drava River to its junction with the boundary of Croatia-Slavonia. The civil administration of the evacuated territories was to remain in the hands of the Hungarian Government, which was authorized to maintain in the country the police and gendarmerie indispensable for the maintenance of public order and the safety of railroad lines.[13]

Post-Armistice Developments

The disappointment caused by the harsh terms of the Belgrade Armistice was temporarily eclipsed by the Eckertsau declaration of King Charles, whereby, without renouncing the Crown, he agreed to refrain from exercising the royal power and prerogatives in Hungary. On November 16, after both Houses of Parliament had dissolved, Hungary was proclaimed a republic, and the Hungarian people were promised extensive political, social, and economic reforms. But conditions were such that none of these promises could be fulfilled. Even if Hungary had not been subjected to increasing pressure from without, men of greater wisdom and ability than that possessed by Count Károlyi and his associates would have been required to cope with the social upheaval and economic dislocation which was the result of the lost war and the revolution. The occupation of ever larger sections of Hungary made wholly impossible the creation of even a semblance of order in the chaos which followed. The Belgrade Armistice was violated almost from the moment of its signature, and during the two months which elapsed between its conclusion and the assembly of the Peace Conference in Paris in the middle of January, 1919, the demarcation line established at Belgrade was constantly extended to include more and more Hungarian territory in the south and in the east as well as in the north. Despite the confusion and demoralization which reigned in Hungary following the revolution, the Károlyi Government endeavored to check the extension of the occupied zone and protested daily against the conduct of the occupying authorities and troops. But having disbanded its army because of its reliance on the presumed generosity of the Allies, its protests lacked the authority which even a

[12] Better known to American and English readers as the Theiss.

[13] For the complete text of the Armistice of Nov. 13, 1918, see *infra*, Doc. 2, p. 359. For the demarcation line see Map 1 at the end of this volume.

small potential force would have given them, and they were completely ignored.

It would serve no useful purpose to review in detail the steps taken by the Hungarian Government to safeguard Hungary's interests in the face of the excessive claims of her neighbors and to protect the population from mistreatment. The documents fill several large cases in the archives of the Hungarian Foreign Office. Here, the course of events can be traced only in its barest outline. The situation is perhaps best illustrated by pointing out that the Hungarian Government was not even able to obtain a precise tracing of the demarcation line. In reply to numerous requests, word was finally received on December 19— five weeks after the signature of the Belgrade Armistice—that the details of the demarcation line would be communicated by the General in Command of the Allied Armies in the East "as soon as he shall have collected the material bearing on the subject." [14]

Hungary's neighbors, of course, took advantage of this uncertainty. In the middle of December the Chief of the Rumanian General Staff gave orders to cross the demarcation line laid down in the Belgrade Armistice and to advance to the Szatmárnémeti-Nagykároly-Nagyvárad-Békéscsaba line. The order was asserted by the Rumanians to have the approval of the Principal Allied Powers, who were said to have consented to the extension of the occupied zone "to protect the life and fortunes of Rumanian peasants." The claim of Allied approval was supported by a communication from the head of the Allied Military Mission in Budapest, the French Lieutenant-Colonel Vyx, to the Hungarian Government, dated December 16, informing it of the contemplated Rumanian advance and requesting the Hungarian Government to avoid bloodshed by ordering its troops not to resist.[15] Hungary at once protested against such action by the Rumanians which, in its opinion, constituted a violation of the armistice terms. Two days later General Berthelot requested the Hungarian Government to evacuate Kolozsvár, the capital of Transylvania, which, he said, was to be occupied on his orders by the Rumanians temporarily, until French troops could be sent.[16] Hungarian protests were of no avail, and, apart from sporadic and spontaneous resistance in isolated sections, Hun-

---

[14] For the text of this communication see *The Hungarian Peace Negotiations* (cited hereafter as *HPN*) I, 359.

[15] *Ibid.*, p. 371. See also Map I at the end of this volume.   [16] *Ibid.*, p. 372.

garian troops fell slowly back toward the center of the country. The replacement of Rumanian by French troops never took place.

In the north no provision had been made for the occupation of Hungarian territory in either the Padua or the Belgrade Armistices. But on December 3 the Hungarian Government was notified that Czecho-Slovakia had been recognized as an Allied state and was authorized to occupy Slovak territories in Northern Hungary in execution of the armistice. Hungary was requested to withdraw its troops, but no indication was given as to the territory to be evacuated.[17] And, only three weeks later, on December 23, when Czech troops had already invaded Hungary through the Vág valley, Lieutenant-Colonel Vyx communicated to the Hungarian Government a request from the General in Command of the Allied Armies in the East to withdraw its troops to the south of a line claimed by the Czechs as the "historic boundaries" of the Czecho-Slovak state. This line, as laid down in this communication, followed the course of the Danube to the mouth of the Ipoly River. From there it followed the Ipoly to the industrial city of Rimaszombat, the town to be occupied by the Czechs. From there it went in a straight line to the mouth of the Ung River, and thence followed the course of the Ung to the Uzsok Pass. Lieutenant-Colonel Vyx stated that the exact boundary line would be fixed by the Peace Conference.[18] To a bitter protest and a refusal of the Hungarian Government, General Franchet d'Esperay replied by wire on January 10, 1919, that the armistice, upon which the Hungarian Government relied, had reference exclusively to the front of the Eastern Allied Armies, that is, to the demarcation line in the south and east of Hungary, facing the Serbs and the Rumanians, and in no way prejudiced Allied decisions respecting other fronts. "In consequence, the Czecho-Slovak State, which has been recognised by the Allies, *possesses absolute sovereign authority* over the territories *reoccupied* by it within the provisional boundaries fixed for it." [19] By the time this communication was received in Budapest, the greater part of Northern Hungary was already in Czech hands; and about the middle of January the Czechs crossed even the demarcation line and occupied territory south of the Ipoly River, against which the Hungarians vainly protested.[20]

Similar difficulties arose also in the south. Shortly before Christmas,

[17] *Ibid.*, p. 383.   [18] *Ibid.*, p. 384. See Map 1 at the end of this volume.
[19] *Ibid.*, p. 385. Italics added.   [20] *Ibid.*, pp. 388–90.

Serb troops crossed the Drava River which, under the Belgrade Armistice, constituted the demarcation line, and occupied the town of Csáktornya, north of the river. To several Hungarian protests against this and other violations of the armistice terms the Allied Military Mission finally replied on January 18, 1919. Denying the Hungarian contention that Hungary ought to be heard in decisions regarding the final tracing of the demarcation line, the Mission informed the Hungarian Government that the line had now been defined with greater precision, at least west of the Tisza River. This line, although it left Szeged, Hungary's second largest city, free of Serbian occupation, pushed the occupied zone further north into Hungary, including in the occupied zone, for strategic reasons, the cities of Baja, Pécs, Szigetvár, and Barcs. The demarcation line east of the Tisza was not mentioned. To Hungary's specific complaint, the reply stated that the occupation of Csáktornya and Alsólendva by the Serbs is "a question wholly different" from the determination of the demarcation line and cannot be solved until the "justice" of the Hungarian protest has been established.[21] By the time this answer reached the Hungarian Government the Serbs had extended their occupation further north of the demarcation line and had taken possession of the coal mines around Pécs, thus depriving Hungary of her last source of anthracite coal.

This gradual extension of the occupied zone rendered any effort of the Hungarian Government to cope with the situation impossible. The economic life of the country, already badly shaken by the disintegration of the Monarchy, was completely paralyzed. First, the territories occupied were, from the point of view of supplies and raw materials, far more valuable than the unoccupied, chiefly agricultural, center of the country. Secondly, the hundreds of thousands of refugees streaming into unoccupied Hungary, some of them expelled by, and most of them fleeing from the occupying armies, put a burden on the country which its weakened economy could not possibly sustain. Politically, the continued shrinkage of Hungarian territory caused growing resentment among the population. The relief felt over the termination of the war and the unthinking enthusiasm which greeted the revolution gave way swiftly to disillusionment and despair.

[21] HPN, I, 361. See Map 1 at the end of this volume.

The Coolidge Mission: Conditions in Hungary at the Opening of the Peace Conference

A few days before the first session of the Peace Conference in Paris, Professor Archibald C. Coolidge, of Harvard University, member of the American Peace Commission, arrived in Budapest to investigate and report on conditions in Southeastern Europe. Apart from strictly military matters connected with the execution of the armistice, this was the first contact the Hungarians had with a representative of one of the Allied and Associated Powers, and Professor Coolidge's reports are the first known documents emanating from a nonmilitary authority recording conditions in post-armistice Hungary. Although Professor Coolidge and the small staff accompanying him on this wholly unofficial mission stayed only six days in Hungary, his reports deserve full consideration. During his short visit he had an opportunity to talk with every member of the government and with many leaders in various walks of life; moreover, being an outsider, his impressions may be taken as giving an objective picture of the Hungarian scene two months after the armistice and on the eve of the opening of the Peace Conference.[22]

The first thing which impressed Professor Coolidge was the universal dissatisfaction in Hungary, generated by the repeated violations of the armistice terms. In his first report, of January 16, 1919, he succinctly stated the Hungarian point of view, gathered from interviews with Count Károlyi (by that time President of the Republic of Hungary) and other Hungarian public figures, as follows:

The Hungarians feel that they have a great and legitimate grievance. They accepted an armistice on certain definite terms. . . . These terms they claim have been violated in several respects. Under the armistice a certain territory in the southern part of the country was to be occupied by the Allies, but no acts of sovereignty were to be performed in it until its legitimate fate had been decided by the Peace Conference. Since the conclusion of the Armistice and

[22] Professor Coolidge arrived in Budapest on the morning of Jan. 15, 1919, and left Hungary on Jan. 20. The results of his interviews and observations are incorporated in eight reports sent to the American Peace Commission, the first being dated Jan. 16, and all the remaining seven dated Jan. 19. The first of these reports is printed in Miller, *Diary*, IV (Doc. 218), 6–8, without its four enclosures, whence its contents and quotations are taken. The other reports and the enclosures of the first report the author obtained from an anonymous source, and the summaries and quotations are from the manuscript.

after the dissolution of the Hungarian army other large tracts have been occupied by the Czechs, the Serbs, and the Rumanians and Ukrainians; and the Hungarians were formally notified by the French Commanding General that they were not to oppose these advances. Also in all the above territories the invaders have deposed officials, changed the language of signs and in other ways acted as if they had every intention of remaining there and of forcing the inhabitants to adopt their nationality. There have been numerous tales of outrages, particularly on the part of the Rumanians, but the conduct of the Serbs is praised. There has also been received a notification from Lt. Col. Vix [Vyx] saying that the Allied Powers and the United States have authorized the Czechs to act in full sovereignty in the territories occupied by them.[23]

The report, however, went further than a mere summation of Hungary's complaints. An independent examination of the economic consequences of the occupation—the severing of communications between the occupied and unoccupied territories, the fact that Hungary had suddenly been deprived of many of its most valuable resources, and, particularly, the acute shortage of coal—led Professor Coolidge to the conclusion that the continuation of these conditions would cripple industry and bring about unemployment, thus increasing the danger of a bolshevik uprising against a government which had no armed forces with which to meet it. Unfortunately, events proved the accuracy of this apprehension.

The report stated that the greatest single issue in the minds of the Hungarians was the threatened dismemberment of their country, but Professor Coolidge found that the Hungarians would be perfectly willing to submit the fate of disputed territories to plebiscites. Interesting light is thrown on the attitude of the Hungarians toward their ex-enemies; the report stated that the Hungarians "rest their whole appeal on the Fourteen Points of President Wilson and say that their only hope is in the sense of justice of the United States and its leader." In this respect, also, Professor Coolidge gauged correctly the feelings in Hungary, where throughout the Peace Conference period there was more confidence in the United States than in the other Allies.[24]

As appears from interviews which Count Károlyi had on January 15

[23] The last sentence apparently refers to the communication of General Franchet d'Esperay, cf. *supra*, p. 13, transmitted through the Allied Military Mission in Budapest just a day or two before Professor Coolidge's arrival.

[24] In an interview which Count Károlyi had on the morning of Jan. 15, 1919, with Lt. Philip L. Goodwin (United States Army), a member of Professor Coolidge's mission, the Hungarian President emphasized the point that "Hungary must look to Eng-

with members of Professor Coolidge's mission, his confidence in the Allies by this time was shaken. He explained to Lieutenant Goodwin that he had refrained from opposing Hungary's neighbors with force pending the determination of new frontiers by the Peace Conference. Later on the same day he told Mr. Storey, another member of Mr. Coolidge's staff, that the policy of nonresistance had been adopted in the belief that Hungary's just claims would be recognized by the Allies and that such recognition would net Hungary more than resistance or bargaining with her neighbors. Count Károlyi told his interviewer that he would continue to adhere to this policy until he was reasonably sure that his hopes for justice at the Peace Conference were unfounded or that "if justice is to be done it will be a justice so different from what he anticipated that it will be more worth his while to look out [for] himself than to trust in others." [25] Mr. Storey's impression was that Károlyi felt he had made a "colossal blunder" in trusting to persons and nations outside Hungary for help—an impression apparently created by repeated exclamations of the Hungarian President: "I have

land's sense of justice and especially to America, who desires nothing but a just settlement with no new Alsace-Lorraines in Europe, to get her fair treatment at the Peace Conference." Lieutenant Goodwin (his report on this interview was an enclosure in the first Coolidge report) quoted Károlyi as saying that Hungary's policy was "Wilson, Wilson, and again Wilson."

In the first of several reports by Professor Coolidge, all dated Jan. 19, 1919, the trust of the Hungarians in the United States is further emphasized. "I have continually insisted on the fact," the report reads, "that there was nothing diplomatic in my mission, and that all official things must go through the regular channels. Nevertheless, I have not been able to prevent what seems to be a general feeling that this is the first chance that the Hungarians have had of putting their views before the Allied powers and especially before America. As they look primarily to America for their salvation, I have been overwhelmed with visits, appeals, memoranda and attentions. . . . Their faith in America, and particularly in President Wilson, is touching; and their expressions are I believe for the most part genuine. . . . There are many placards in the streets with President Wilson's picture and the statement 'We are for a Wilson peace only.' Today one of the ministers said to me, 'Our only hope is in God and President Wilson.' "

[25] In this respect Mr. Storey commented that if Hungary's neighbors persisted in their present attitude Count Károlyi would not be able to pursue for long the policy of nonresistance; he would have to change or be thrown out of office by the Bolsheviks. "The best solution would be interference by the Entente. Such interference could take two forms.—Either a suggestion to some of the rapacious neighbors that they hold their hand in Hungarian territory, or a direct public answer by the United States to some of Károlyi's notes and requests in a tone leading clearly to the belief that Károlyi's faith in the Entente is not misplaced." Quoted from Mr. Storey's typewritten report to Professor Coolidge on his interview with Count Károlyi on Jan. 15, 1919, enclosed with Mr. Coolidge's report of Jan. 16, 1919.

put my trust in the Entente! Was I right?" But in the United States, Count Károlyi's faith was unshaken. He emphasized, as in his earlier interviews with Professor Coolidge and Lieutenant Goodwin, that he looked to the United States for help and trusted President Wilson's ability to see that Hungary got a "square deal" at the Peace Conference.

Concerning internal politics Count Károlyi apparently had some difficulty in explaining to his American visitors the position of his government. While it was a "people's government," he had to admit that it exercised both executive and legislative powers by virtue of an undefined grant from the self-constituted National Council. Since the holding of elections appeared impossible until the determination of Hungary's frontiers, his intention was to continue this form of government until after peace was concluded.

Interesting also are Count Károlyi's comments to Lieutenant Goodwin concerning the future of Europe. He expressed the belief that the Pan-German idea and the *Drang nach Osten* would be revived if Austria and Hungary, dismembered, were left to German support. According to him, the German influence should be checked by a confederation of Central European states, no one of which should be so weak as to be at the mercy of the others.

The subsequent reports of Professor Coolidge, although more detailed, merely confirmed the general impressions received by him and his associates during the first day of their sojourn in Hungary.

On foreign questions [writes Mr. Coolidge in the first of the seven reports (No. 21) written on January 19] opinions are practically unanimous. There were very different views as to the past, the origin of the war, and the advisability of the policy followed by the Hungarian Government. But, on the burning question of the day, the integrity of Hungary, there are almost no differences, except a greater or less insistence on the principle of a fair plebiscite and a willingness to abide by its result.

The arguments for the country's integrity, upon which the Hungarians "dwell upon with passionate insistence," formed the subject of the second report (No. 22). Whether the Hungarian arguments were historically, economically, or from any other point of view correct, Professor Coolidge summarized them with such precision that his report may be regarded as a forecast of the platform upon which Hungary's case at the Peace Conference was argued and upon which that country's foreign policy subsequently was based. For that reason it will here be quoted in full.

No country in Europe has been more genuinely and historically united for the last thousand years than has Hungary. Her boundaries have been so well marked out by nature that except for the period when the greater part of her territory had been conquered by the Turks her frontiers have changed but little since the days when the Magyars first entered into this land. The only considerable accretion has been Croatia and Slavonia, whose union has never been complete and whose separation is now accepted.

The Hungarian State has had a long, and in many respects a glorious, history, with the usual variations of prosperity and decay, but always with a lively sense of its national existence. In the age when most of Hungary was in the hands of the Turks, Hungarian national life took refuge in portions of their land under Hapsburg rule or under that of the semi-independent Hungarian princes of Transylvania. It is to be noted that precisely these territories in the west, north and east, dear to Hungarian traditions, are the ones where the non-Magyar nationalities predominate in numbers. There is much dispute as to whether the Rumanians are the older or the later comers in Transylvania. The Germans mostly settled at various times in the middle ages. The mixed populations, Germans, Serbs, Rumanians, etc. in the Banat of Temesvar were welcomed in the 18th Century by the Hapsburg sovereigns as immigrants into a region which had formerly been Magyar and most of whose population disappeared under Turkish rule. Just as the fact that there are Alsatians, Bretons, Basques and other elements who do not speak French does not impair the recognized unity of France, so the Hungarians feel that their unity of a thousand years is not affected by the existence within their borders of people who do not in ordinary life make use of the national language. That the land should now be partitioned after the fashion of Poland seems so incredible to them that many even now cannot realize it is possible. They declare that, however unable to resist at the present moment, the Hungarians will never submit to being permanently divided up among neighboring states, leaving them but a helpless fragment of territory, one incapable of economic existence. If the boundaries of Hungary in the future should correspond to the present lines of foreign occupation which are continually being changed to her disadvantage, she would be left with 31 percent. of her previous extent and less than 40 percent. of her previous population. Thirty-four percent of the Magyars of today, or more than three and three quarters millions of people, would be subjected to foreign rule. . . . This population, a proud, determined and enduring one, thus subjected to nationalities whom it has for centuries regarded as inferior to itself would constitute a number of Irredentas which could not be absorbed in any time that it is now possible to foresee. One Hungarian statesman and former prime minister put it to me thus: "It looks as if the policy of the Allies was to create at the same time an Ulster (the Seckler region in Transylvania) and an Alsace-Lorraine (the

Magyar speaking regions now occupied by the Czechs) in this part of the world." To compel what has been since a thousand years a unified country to accept such an arrangement as permanent would be only to condemn it to a future of hatred and strife with every probability of violent outbreak before many years have elapsed. . . .[26]

Another of the reports (No. 23) dealt briefly with the delicate question of nationalities. With some exceptions Mr. Coolidge's interlocutors conceded that the treatment of non-Magyar nationalities in the preceding fifty years had not been satisfactory. He found, however, that the government was then willing to transform Hungary into a sort of Switzerland by granting wide autonomy to the various nationalities, and Ruthenian leaders assured him that they were perfectly satisfied with the laws already promulgated for the benefit of the Ruthenian people.

The Hungarians are convinced [reported Mr. Coolidge] that if arrangements of this sort can be made, the great majority of the non-Magyar peoples who have until now been in the Hungarian state will prefer to remain in it rather than be absorbed by their neighbors; and they claim in the name of justice and particularly in the name of the 14 points and the principles enunciated by President Wilson that these peoples should be given a fair chance to express their wishes.

It was pointed out that no such fair chance could be given as long as the contested territories remained under occupation by Hungary's neighbors.

The question of autonomy for the non-Magyar nationalities was also discussed in connection with the fate of Slovakia, to which problem one of Mr. Coolidge's reports (No. 27) was devoted. Apparently the Hungarians were particularly agitated at the time of Mr. Coolidge's visit over the occupation of Northern Hungary and the somewhat exaggerated language of General Franchet d'Esperay supporting Czech claims to Hungarian territories.[27] This may explain why only the

[26] Arguments with respect to the geographic and economic unity of Hungary were summed up in another of this series of reports (No. 25). The essence of these arguments was that Hungary's unity could never have been preserved through all the ups and downs of her history for a thousand years, despite the variety of nationalities that have lived within her borders, if her continuity had not been in the nature of things in obedience to geographic law. For the complete text of this report see *infra*, Doc. 3, p. 362.

[27] It will be remembered that his message was communicated to the Hungarian Government just before Mr. Coolidge's arrival in Budapest; see *supra*, p. 13. It was during his sojourn that news reached the Hungarian capital that the Czechs, not satis-

Slovak question was made the subject of a special report by Mr. Coolidge—although the fate of Transylvania loomed equally large in Hungarian preoccupations. Referring to the occupation of almost the whole of Northern Hungary by Czechs and to fears that the capital itself might be exposed to danger from the steadily advancing Czech troops, then only a few miles from Budapest, Mr. Coolidge reported the bitter feeling in Hungary against the Czechs who had immediately cut off occupied territories from the rest of Hungary and had proceeded to denationalize such territories. While contesting claims as to the identity of the Czech and Slovak languages, the Hungarian spokesmen recognized the aspirations of the Slovaks for autonomy and greater privileges than they had theretofore enjoyed; and they had assured Mr. Coolidge of their willingness to satisfy Slovak demands and their readiness to abide by the decision of the Slovak people as to whether they preferred autonomy within Hungary or union with Bohemia. It would seem that the Hungarians were already acquainted with the bases of the Czech claims, since they impressed upon Mr. Coolidge the inconsistency of the Czechs in claiming Bohemia on historical and geographical grounds, Slovakia on the basis of ethnographic, and Magyar-inhabited lands north of the Danube on the basis of economic considerations. Mr. Coolidge reported that the Hungarians regarded this as imperialism in its most naked form and that they "cannot believe the allies and especially America can countenance such a violation of the principles of justice and self-determination."

The last of Mr. Coolidge's reports (No. 26), which completes the picture, recorded his impressions of the internal situation, the position of the government and of the various political parties. He judged that the Károlyi Government was weak and bitterly opposed by the conservatives because of the fear that this weakness would lead the country to ruin and bolshevism. The only well-organized party appeared to him to be the Social-Democrats, whose leaders were, in the opinion of Mr. Coolidge, men of ability.

There may be truth in the charge brought against them [Mr. Coolidge commented] that they live in the domain of theory and not of fact. They are patriotic enough and dread the partition of their country as much as do the conservatives, though they admit errors in the past and appeal to the doctrine of self-determination rather than to history.

---

fied even with the recognition of their "historic boundaries," crossed the Ipoly River and extended their occupation south of the demarcation line.

The admitted weakness of the government was explained by Coolidge as caused by the disappointment of the people that Count Károlyi, who assumed power as the man who opposed the war, had not only been unable to establish contact with the Allies, but had seen a great part of the country occupied contrary to the armistice terms. Mr. Coolidge found the financial situation very bad and suspected that only the printing press kept the government going. The economic life of the country had been disrupted by the occupation of the industrial portion of Hungary; and while the food situation was found to be less alarming than in Austria, the scarcity of coal and clothing was judged by Mr. Coolidge to be most serious.[28]

These, then, were general impressions of conditions in Hungary on the eve of the opening of the Peace Conference as recorded by an objective and impartial observer who apparently came to Hungary with no more prejudice than is inevitable in any person's outlook on the world, and who clearly had no axe to grind or interests to defend. The points which stand out in Professor Coolidge's reports may be summed up as follows: (1) the gradual extension of occupation of Hungarian territory had emphasized the grave economic and social problems which the country would have had to face in any event as a result of a revolution; it also had adverse political repercussions by weakening a not-too-strong and not-too-competent government; (2) the uppermost consideration in the minds of the Hungarians, irrespective of party politics, was clearly the threatened partition of their country; (3) despite the country's isolation Hungarian leaders appear to have had sufficient information as to the extent of the claims of Hungary's neighbors to realize the seriousness of the danger of partition, although there was only speculation concerning the attitude of the Principal Allied Powers toward such claims and their plans and policy for the general post-war order; (4) and, last but not least, the apparent Allied support of Hungary's neighbors in what the Hungarians considered repeated violations of the armistice terms had obviously shaken their confidence in the fairness of the Principal Allied Powers, while they still retained, unimpaired, their confidence in the United States, and particularly in President Wilson.

[28] For the complete text of this illuminating report see *infra*, Doc. 4, p. 365. Concerning the occupation of Hungary by the neighboring countries following the armistice see Szende, "La guerre contre la Hongrie, après la guerre," *Nouvelle Revue de Hongrie*, LXI (Aug., 1939), 181 ff.

With this brief sketch of events and developments in and around Hungary preceding the assembly of the Peace Conference, we may now turn to our main task, namely, the story of the making of the peace treaty itself between the Allies and Hungary.

PART TWO

The Hungarian Question at the Peace Conference in Hungary's Absence

II. The Determination of Hungary's Frontiers

The American Recommendations

THE FIRST concrete and recorded plan for the new frontiers of Hungary seems to have been formulated by members of the American Peace Delegation. It is perhaps superfluous to point out that this plan did not consider Hungary alone, but envisaged the whole peace settlement. The Intelligence Section of the Delegation prepared a comprehensive outline of various problems, territorial, political, economic, and social, which were likely to be dealt with by the Peace Conference. This report, dated January 21, 1919,[1] also dealt with the new order in Southeastern Europe and made tentative recommendations as to the boundaries of the Succession States of the Austro-Hungarian Empire. As far as Hungary was concerned the report recommended a frontier with Czecho-Slovakia which, except for one important difference, followed substantially the line ultimately laid down in the Treaty of Trianon [2] and which proposed, as an alternative, either the incorporation of Ruthenia into Czech state or a protectorate over that province by Czecho-Slovakia as a mandatory of the League of Nations.[3]

[1] Miller, *Diary*, IV (Doc. 246), 209 ff. Outline of a Tentative Report and Recommendations prepared by the Intelligence Section, in accordance with instructions, for the President and the Plenipotentiaries. This document was prepared by some of the division chiefs of the Intelligence Section of the American Commission to Negotiate Peace. The procedure was to request the division chiefs to submit memoranda. These were reduced to brief and undocumented recommendations. After being reviewed by the division chiefs, the recommendations were assembled, illustrated with maps, and brought together in what was called "The Black Book." Later, too, some non-American plenipotentiaries were also supplied, upon request, with copies of this document. The author is indebted for the information concerning its origin to Dr. Isaiah Bowman, President of Johns Hopkins University, who was executive officer of the Intelligence Section of the American Peace Delegation.

It should be noted that "The Black Book" was in substance a summary of preliminary reports on various phases of the peace settlement, reports which had been in the course of preparation for about a year before the Armistice. Consequently, the recommendations contained in "The Black Book" were the result of careful studies.

[2] See Map No. 8, in Miller, *Diary*, IV, facing 232. The American proposal would have left the city of Ungvár in eastern Slovakia to Hungary.

[3] *Ibid.*, pp. 230–31.

The important difference was that the American plan would have left the island of Csallóköz (or Grosse Schütt), with its overwhelmingly Magyar population, to Hungary. The report stated that the suggested frontier would run south of the linguistic border and would include more than half a million Magyars in the new Czecho-Slovak state. This departure from the ethnic principle proclaimed by President Wilson in his Fourteen Points was explained by the necessity of giving landlocked Czecho-Slovakia a commercial outlet along the Danube. "Moreover," the report continued, "were the ethnic lines to be followed, it [the frontier] would cross at right angles the main northern tributary valleys of the Danube in the region, and seriously derange the economic relations of the people." [4] The recommendation concerning the fate of Ruthenia was explained by the "desirability of freeing Ruthenians from Magyar oppression"; in addition, the report pointed out, "it is undesirable that a Hungarian wedge be thrust between the Rumanians and the Czecho-Slovaks."

In the east, the report recommended allotting to Rumania all of Transylvania, the ethnic Rumanian zone in Hungary proper, and about two-thirds of the Bánát, but called attention to the necessity of providing for the protection of Magyar minorities in eastern Transylvania.[5] The proposed frontier was substantially the same as that finally laid down in the peace treaty, although it was somewhat more favorable to Hungary than the Trianon frontier.[6] Indeed, the American report regarded it as essential that the frontier should be carefully defined "so as to do full justice to delicate questions of commercial outlets that affect dense groups of both Rumanian and Magyar population."

In the south, the Hungarian-Yugoslav frontier proposed by the American report was materially different and was more favorable to Hungary than that ultimately laid down in the Trianon Treaty. The

[4] The report does not give the reasons which induced the proposed departure from the ethnic line east of the Danube and in Czecho-Slovakia's favor.

[5] Ibid., pp. 233–34.

[6] See Map No. 10, in Miller, Diary, IV, facing 234. The proposal to divide the Hungarian province of Bánát between Rumania and Yugoslavia did not directly concern Hungary, since she was to be deprived, in any event, of that territory. It may be noted, however, that this region was claimed both by Rumania and Yugoslavia (see infra, pp. 30 ff.) and remained a bone of contention between the two countries for several years. Final agreement concerning the definite boundaries was not reached until the signature of the frontier agreement at Belgrade, on Nov. 24, 1923. See Martens, Nouveau Recueil général des traités (3 sér.), XVII, 342.

towns of Zenta, Topolya, Magyarkanizsa, and Szabadka, together with compact masses of Magyar populations, would have been left under Hungarian sovereignty.[7]

Finally, in the west, the report envisaged the maintenance of the historic frontier between Austria and Hungary. "These historic boundaries leave about 2,500,000 Germans in Western Hungary, but the adjustment of the frontier to include them [in Austria] would result in a disturbance of long-established institutions, and until it becomes clear that it is sincerely desired by the people in question it seems unwise to include them." [8]

The report indicated that the new Hungary would have only half of her prewar area and population—and even this is decidedly an understatement of Hungary's losses. The placing of large compact masses of Magyar population under alien sovereignties was explained on the ground of their geographical separation from the central mass of Magyars (as in the case of Transylvania) or (as in the case of Slovakia) from necessity, in order to "satisfy vital economic needs of neighboring states." [9] It may be noted that there is no indication in the report that the vital economic needs of Hungary were considered. The author has been given to understand by members of the American Peace Commission whom he has interviewed that Hungarian interests were carefully examined and that an earnest effort was made to exclude alien populations on either side of the proposed frontiers.[10] But the task was a difficult one, and under the circumstances it was perhaps inevitable that the solution favored the non-Magyar claimant. On the other hand, it does not appear from the report that the conclusions of the American experts concerning Hungary's new frontiers were motivated by strategic considerations.

[7] See Map No. 11, in Miller, *Diary*, IV, facing 238. For the frontiers recommended by the American report see Map 2 at the end of this volume.

[8] *Ibid.*, p. 243. The figure quoted is apparently an error since the whole population of the Burgenland district, subsequently claimed by Austria, can be counted in hundreds of thousands rather than in millions. The Austrian note of June 16, 1919, claiming Western Hungary for Austria, estimated the number of Germans living in that territory at 300,000. The total German population in pre-Trianon Hungary was barely over 500,000.

[9] Miller, *Diary*, IV, 245.

[10] It is fair to say that the starting point of the American argument was in most instances ethnic rather than economic.

The Presentation of Territorial Claims by Hungary's Neighbors

The first formal discussion of territorial questions affecting Hungary took place when the question of the Bánát came before the meeting of the Supreme Council on January 31, 1919.[11] This territory, enclosed between the Maros River on the north, the Tisza River on the west, and the Danube on the south, had belonged to Hungary throughout the existence of that country and had constituted for several centuries a protective zone against the onslaught of the Turkish armies. Its population was strongly mixed, however, as a result both of a continued infiltration of Serbs and Rumanians seeking and finding refuge from the Turks and of a systematic colonization by the Habsburgs, who invited Germans (Schwabs) to settle there, partly to fill the ranks of Hungarians decimated while defending the southeastern outpost of their empire and partly to prevent a predominance of the Magyar stock. Now both Rumania and Yugoslavia claimed all or part of this region. At this meeting of the Supreme Council, Rumania was represented by Messrs. Bratianu and Misu, and Yugoslavia by Messrs. Pasić, Trumbić, and Vesnić.

The Rumanians rested their claim to the whole of the Bánát on the secret treaty of August 17, 1916, between the Allied Powers and Ru-

[11] For the minutes of this meeting of the Supreme Council see Miller, *Diary*, XIV, 138 ff., reprinted *infra*, Doc. 5, p. 368. In view of the complexity of and the repeated changes in the organization of the Peace Conference, the following information concerning its directing bodies, may be helpful. The highest authority in the Conference was the Supreme Council, or Council of Ten, consisting of two representatives from each of the Principal Allied and Associated Powers (the United States, the British Empire, France, Italy, and Japan). When it was found that the Supreme Council was too large to act effectively, it was divided into two councils, the Council of Four, consisting of the ranking delegates of the United States, the British Empire, France, and Italy; and the Council of Five, or Council of Foreign Ministers, composed of the Foreign Ministers of the five Principal Allied and Associated Powers. Following the signature of the peace treaty with Germany on June 28, 1919, the functions of these Councils were taken over by the Council of the Heads of Delegations, composed, again, of representatives of the five principal powers. A detailed account of the organization of the Peace Conference and of the relations between the central authority and the various subordinate commissions and committees is found in Temperley, *History*, I, 247 ff.; also *ibid.*, 497 ff. See also Almond and Lutz, *The Treaty*, pp. 1–14. For a more or less complete outline of the composition and organization of the Peace Conference and its various branches, including the personnel of the various delegations, committees, and so forth, see *La Documentation internationale: La Paix de Versailles,* ed. by G. de Lapradelle (cited hereafter as *La Paix de Versailles*), I, 201–311.

mania.[12] Mr. Vesnić, refusing to recognize the validity of the secret
treaty so far as Yugoslavia was concerned, claimed only that part of
the Bánát to which his country had a right on ethnological grounds,
i.e., the sections where the Serbs claimed to be in a majority over the
Germans, the Hungarians, and the Rumanians. As later specified by
Mr. Trumbić, this claim included the counties of Torontál and Temesvár and a small part of the county of Krassó-Szörény.[13] Mr. Trumbić
admitted the presence in this territory of a large Magyar and German
population and conceded the desirability of ascertaining their wishes
as well as those of the Serbs and the Rumanians, "because the question
of future peace was involved and it was essential to ensure contentment
to all peoples." However, Mr. Trumbić contended that the Germans,
"who were very numerous," would prefer incorporation into Serbia
rather than into Rumania and he rested his claims not merely on
nationality, a claim admittedly weak,[14] but also on the "will of the
people." He expressed Serbia's willingness to agree to a referendum.
Mr. Bratianu, when asked by M. Clemenceau whether he would agree
to such a referendum, stated that he considered the question as already

[12] See the Rumanian memorandum, Annex A to the Minutes of the Supreme Council meeting of Jan. 31, 1919, *infra*, Doc. 5, p. 368. By Art. 3 of the secret treaty the
Allies recognized the right of Rumania to annex territory of the Austro-Hungarian
Monarchy within the frontiers described in Art. 4 as follows: "La ligne de délimita-
tion . . . suivra la frontière . . . de la Galicie et de la Hongrie jusqu'au point Stog
coté 1655. De là elle suivra la ligne de séparation des eaux de la Tisza et du Viso,
pour atteindre la Tisza au village de Trebusa en amont de l'endroit où elle s'unit
au Viso. A partir de ce point elle descendra le Thalweg de la Tisza jusqu'à 4 kilom.
en aval de son confluent avec le Szamos, en laissant le village de Vasaros-Nameny
à la Roumanie. Elle continuera ensuite dans la direction du sud-sudouest jusqu'à
un point à 6 kilom. à l'est de la ville de Debreczen. De ce point elle atteindre le
Crish à 3 kilom. en aval de la réunion de ces deux affluents (le Crisch blanc et le
Crish rapide). Elle joindra ensuite la Tisza à la hauteur du village Algyö au nord
de Szegedin, en passant à l'ouest des villages d'Oroshaza et de Bekessamson, à 3 kilom.
duquel elle fera une petite courbe. A partir d'Algyö la ligne descendra le Thalweg de
la Tisza jusqu'à son confluent avec le Danube, et enfin suivra le Thalweg du Danube
jusqu'à la frontière actuelle de la Roumanie. . . ." For the complete text of the secret
treaty, see Martens, *Nouveau Recueil général des traités*, X (3 sér.), 342 (including the
text of the military convention); Temperley, *History*, IV, 516–17 (the political agreement only).

[13] The Yugoslav claims were in conflict with the recommendations of the American
experts; cf. *supra*, n. 6.

[14] According to Hungarian statistics which Mr. Trumbić claimed to cite, the population of the two counties of Torontál and Temesvár, sought by the Serbs, was composed as follows: Rumanians, 266,000; Germans, 328,560; Magyars, 251,000; Serbs,
272,000.

settled and that he could not agree to any partition of the area. He did not expressly reject the idea of a plebiscite but said that he would require time for consideration, should the Allies insist on a referendum.

The territorial claims of Rumania were fully presented to the Supreme Council by Mr. Bratianu on the following day, February 1, 1919.[15] Denying any aspirations of an imperialistic character and asserting that the Rumanians merely wished the incorporation of the ethnical territory historically theirs, Mr. Bratianu first defined what he claimed as "Transylvania." He stated that in that term he included "not only the Bánát but all the counties extending as far as the Galician Carpathians and the Theiss [Tisza River] . . ." He claimed that, according to Hungarian statistics, Rumanians constituted 55 percent and the Magyars only 23 percent of the population and suggested that the true proportion would be 72 and 15 percent respectively. To an inquiry by Mr. Lloyd George as to whether Rumania was asking the Allies purely and simply to proclaim the annexation of Transylvania and other territories or was asking the Peace Conference to declare that in these regions regularly constituted assemblies should have power definitely to declare for union with Rumania, Mr. Bratianu replied that he was asking for the recognition of the already-proclaimed union of these provinces. When Mr. Lloyd George suggested that certain minorities had not taken part in the elections of the assemblies which proclaimed the union, Mr. Bratianu expressed doubt that the Hungarians would vote in favor of union with Rumania, since she had gone to war "to impose her national will on the Hungarian minority in Transylvania." Giving assurances that the rights of minorities would be recognized and respected, he asked authorization to occupy immediately all territories claimed by Rumania, with the exception of the Bánát, which,

---

[15] Miller, *Diary* XIV, 154 ff., and especially, 162 ff., reprinted *infra*, Doc. 6, p. 380. See also Map 3 at the end of the volume. Concerning the Rumanian claims upon Hungary, the following Peace Conference documents prepared by the Rumanian Delegation are relevant: (1) La Roumanie devant le Congrès de la Paix: Le Territoire revendiqué par les Roumains au nord-ouest de la Transylvanie proprement dite (undated); (2) La Roumanie devant le Congrès de la Paix: Ses Revendications Territoriales (Mémoire présenté à la Conférence dans la séance du 1er Février 1919; Résumé de l'exposé verbal fait par le Premier Délégué de Roumanie), especially, pp. 6–8, with Annexes. Annex I contains the text of the secret treaty of Aug. 4–17, 1916, between the Allies and Rumania, referred to *supra*, n. 12. The French texts of memoranda presented to the Peace Conference by the delegations of Rumania, Czecho-Slovakia, and Yugoslavia concerning territorial claims of their respective governments are conveniently collected in de Lapradelle, *La Paix de Versailles*, Vol. IX (*Questions territoriales*).

he suggested, should be evacuated by the Serbs and occupied by Allied troops.

After the presentation of the Rumanian claims and the withdrawal of the Rumanian delegation, Mr. Lloyd George, referring to the extreme difficulty of deciding questions of boundaries, suggested the submission of such questions to a body of experts, not for decision but for preliminary investigation and recommendation.[16] There followed an interesting discussion before Mr. Lloyd George's proposal was finally accepted. President Wilson, who expressed the belief that decisions concerning questions which require the exercise of tact and compromise, including specifically the protection of minorities, ought to be reserved to the representatives of the Great Powers, wished to restrict the jurisdiction of the expert committee to the consideration of territorial and racial problems. Mr. Balfour thought that the experts might also consider strategic questions. Signor Orlando's insistence on the binding character of the secret treaty with Rumania was challenged both by M. Clemenceau, who drew attention to the agreement of the Allies to regard the secret treaty as canceled by Rumania's conclusion of a separate peace with the Central Powers, and by Mr. Lloyd George, who pointed out that Rumania was now claiming more than she was entitled to under the secret treaty. Signor Orlando was perhaps on surer ground when he pointed out that frontier problems are entirely political and that therefore "the whole responsibility for the settlement must rest with the representatives of the Great Powers." He also expressed some apprehension, shared by the other Italian representative, Baron Sonnino, concerning the practicability of working through experts. He asked whether these experts should be geographers, historians, ethnologists, or strategists. If the representatives of the peoples concerned were consulted (and Baron Sonnino pointed out that, in the case of Rumania, the Magyar and Ukrainian minorities would have to be consulted on the spot since they were not represented in Paris), the expert committee would function as a court of first in-

[16] The resolution moved by Mr. Lloyd George read: (Miller, *Diary,* XIV, 177): "It is agreed that the questions raised in Mr. Bratiano's statement on the Roumanian territorial interests in the Peace Settlement shall be referred for examination in the first instance by an expert Committee composed of two representatives each of the United States of America, the British Empire, France and Italy. It shall be the duty of the Committee to reduce the questions for decision within the narrowest possible limits, and to make recommendations for a just settlement. The Committee is authorized to consult the representatives of the peoples concerned."

stance and the delegates of the Great Powers as a final court of appeal. In Signor Orlando's opinion, this procedure would not expedite the business of the Peace Conference. President Wilson agreed that it might be wise to omit the paragraph authorizing the experts to consult the representatives of the peoples concerned. It is not clear whether the President had in mind the representatives of the claimant nations alone, or also those of the absent former enemies at whose expense these claims were advanced; he was of the opinion, however, that the delegates presenting claims were merely advocates and might present claims not supported by facts. Signor Orlando also conditioned his acceptance of Mr. Lloyd George's resolution on the assurance that it was not to create a precedent, an assurance which was suggested by Mr. Lloyd George himself in introducing the proposed resolution, but which was subsequently overlooked or disregarded so far as the Succession States of the Austro-Hungarian Monarchy were concerned.

It was in pursuance of this resolution that the "Committee for the Study of Territorial Questions Relating to Rumania" [17] was appointed. The Committee consisted of Dr. Clive Day and Dr. Charles Seymour (the United States), M. Tardieu (who served as chairman) and Ambassador Laroche (France), Sir Eyre Crowe and Mr. A. W. A. Leeper (the British Empire), Signor de Martino and Count Vannutelli-Rey (Italy).

A few days later, on February 5, 1919, the claims of the Czecho-Slovaks were presented to the Supreme Council by Messrs. Beneš and Kramarcz.[18] Prefacing his explanation of the newly born state's territorial claims with the assurance that the Czechs must be prudent,

---

[17] The name of the committee was subsequently changed to "Committee for the Study of Territorial Questions relating to Rumania and Yugoslavia." See *infra*, p. 38.

[18] For the minutes of this meeting, see Miller, *Diary*, XIV, 211 ff., reprinted *infra*, Doc. 7, p. 389. See also Map 3 at the end of this volume. Concerning the Czecho-Slovak claims against Hungary, see Memoire No. 2 presented by the Czecho-Slovak Delegation to the Peace Conference: "The Territorial Claims of the Czecho-Slovak Republic," especially pp. 11–30; Memoire No. 5, "Slovakia: Territory Claimed"; Memoire No. 6, "Problem of the Ruthenians of Hungary." A devastating criticism of the Czecho-Slovak memoranda, from the point of view of accuracy and objectivity, is contained in the monograph of Dr. Hermann Raichhofer, *Die tschechoslovakischen Denkschriften für die Friedenskonferenz von Paris 1919/1920*. With respect to the controversy as to the accuracy of ethnic maps and other information presented by the Succession States to the Peace Conference see also Teleki, "A propos d'une carte ethnique," *Nouvelle Revue de Hongrie*, LVI (January, 1937), 21 ff.; Both, "La Tchéchoslovaquie à la Conférence de la Paix: Les Cartes et mémoires . . . présentés par la Délégation Tchéque," *ibid.* (Feb. 1937), 102 ff.

reasonable, and just to their neighbors and that they must avoid provoking jealousy and renewed struggles, Dr. Beneš claimed the provinces
of Bohemia, Moravia, Austrian Silesia, and Slovakia on ethnographical
grounds. Of these, only Slovakia belonged to Hungary and this examination of the arguments advanced by Czecho-Slovak delegates in
support of their claims may be restricted to that province alone.[19]
Dr. Beneš claimed that Slovakia had, before the tenth century, formed
part of a "Czecho-Slovak" state when it had been overrun by the Magyars. According to him, the population still considered itself Czech;
it wished to belong to the new Czecho-Slovak state; and the prevailing
language and religion were the same in Slovakia as in the Czech provinces proper.[20] Mr. Lloyd George stated that the Supreme Council had
no doubts as to the claims relating to Slovakia proper and suggested
that Dr. Beneš confine his remarks to the doubtful points, i.e., the
frontiers with Hungary. Dr. Beneš said that the Danube frontier was
claimed as a matter of principle, Slovakia being a Danubian country;
also for economic reasons, because thereby the landlocked Czecho-
Slovak state would have direct access to the sea. Upon Mr. Lloyd
George's inquiring as to the composition of the population, Dr. Beneš
said that about 350,000 Magyars would come under Czech sovereignty
in the region between Pozsony and Vác (i.e., in the western part of
Slovakia); but, in compensation, many scattered communities of Slo-

[19] It is noteworthy that in claiming the former Austrian provinces of Bohemia,
Moravia, and Silesia, Dr. Beneš emphasized the exposed situation of the Czecho-
Slovak nation, which, he said, was the advance guard of the Slav world in the West,
and therefore constantly threatened by German expansion. He said that the Czechs
always felt they had a special mission to resist the Teutonic flood and that they
were the protectors of democracy against Germanism. Miller, *Diary,* XIV, 212–13.

[20] It should be noted that Dr. Beneš's claims regarding the existence of a "Czecho-
Slovak" state in the tenth century and the identity of the Czech and Slovak languages are historically and scientifically untenable. There was from about 830 to
906 A.D. a Moravian empire roughly coterminous with the territory of Bohemia and
Moravia, which under the reign of Szvatopluk expanded so as to comprise parts of
the then duchy of Austria and, perhaps, some districts inhabited by Slovaks on the
southern slopes of the Carpathians. This Moravian empire disappeared soon after the
death of Szvatopluk and was followed by the Bohemian state. *Bohemia and Moravia,*
p. 14 [Handbook prepared under the Direction of the Historical Section of the
(British) Foreign Office. No. 2]. Cf. also Krofta, *A Short History of Czechoslovakia,*
p. 3. The Czechs and the Slovaks both belong to the Western Slavs and are closely
akin racially. This racial affinity served as a basis of the claim by certain authorities
that they are identical. However, "a closer examination of their language . . . sug-
gests that they were a separate and perhaps older branch of the Slav family than
the Czechs." *Slovakia,* pp. 10–11 [Handbooks prepared under the Direction of the
Historical Section of the (British) Foreign Office. No. 3].

vaks on the right bank of the river would be abandoned.[21] As far as the sector of the frontier between the Danube and the Ung Rivers was concerned, the line claimed by the Czechs was dictated, according to Dr. Beneš, by railway communications. Since the mountains ran from north to south, it was necessary to include within the new state the only railway offering lateral communication, although that would admittedly bring a considerable Magyar population into Czecho-Slovakia.[22]

In addition, Dr. Beneš submitted suggestions for the consideration of the Peace Conference which, he said, were not to be considered claims made on behalf of Czecho-Slovakia. The first of these suggestions related to the Ruthenes in the northeastern corner of what had previously been Hungary, estimated by Dr. Beneš to number about 450,000. These people, said Dr. Beneš, neighbors of the Slovaks, socially and economically similar to them, proposed to form an autonomous state in close federation with Czecho-Slovakia. He made no claim on their behalf, but had undertaken to put their case before the Peace Conference. Such a federation would impose a burden on Czecho-Slovakia, said Dr. Beneš, but would afford the advantage of a common frontier with Rumania.

The second suggestion related to direct communication with the Adriatic, the sea nearest to Czecho-Slovak territory, by means of a small corridor through Hungary, either under Czech or Yugoslav sovereignty or under the administration of the League of Nations.

Although, a few days before, an expert committee for the examination of Rumania's claims had been appointed with the understanding that such action would not serve as a precedent, the Supreme Council again decided to refer the territorial claims to a special "Committee on

[21] Dr. Beneš suggested in this connection that in the region of Budapest there were some 150,000 Slovaks.

[22] According to Dr. Beneš, the number in this eastern part of Slovakia was about 250,000; but, he said, about 350,000 Slovaks would remain within Hungary. Altogether, he asserted, about 650,000 Magyars would be included in Czecho-Slovakia, while some 450,000 Slovaks would remain Hungarian subjects. Subsequently Dr. Beneš disclosed that the Czech memoranda for the Peace Conference had been prepared by him without any source-material and largely from memory. This fact, according to him, explains "some errors of facts" which occurred therein. See Beneš, *Der Aufstand der Nationen, der Weltkrieg und die tchechoslowakische Revolution*, pp. 687–88. Dr. Beneš argued that these errors had no effect on the decisions of the Supreme Council; but at least one distinguished scholar came to the conclusion that this argument "hardly seems to be borne out by the actual course of events." Macartney, *Hungary and Her Successors*, 84n.

Czecho-Slovak Questions." [23] The membership of this Committee was as follows: Dr. Charles Seymour and Mr. A. W. Dulles (the United States); Sir Joseph Cook, Mr. Harold Nicolson, Sir Eyre Crowe, the latter as technical adviser (the British Empire); M. Jules Cambon, M. Laroche, and General Le Rond, the latter as technical adviser (France); and Marquis Salvago Raggi and Signor Stranieri (Italy).

Finally the Yugoslav claims were presented by the Serbian representatives, Messrs. Pasić, Vesnić, Trumbić, and Zolger, at the meeting of the Supreme Council on February 18, 1919.[24] After a brief survey of the causes of the war, which he saw in the German *Drang nach Osten*, Mr. Vesnić declared that his delegation regarded the right of self-determination as inviolable and any treaty disposing of the Yugoslav people without its consent as null and void. With respect to the frontiers of Yugoslavia, Mr. Vesnić reiterated the suggestion made during the discussion of the Rumanian-Yugoslav claims concerning the Bánát on January 31, namely, to allow the population to choose their allegiance. In the north, that is to say toward Hungary, the Serbs proposed a frontier which "corresponded not only to ethnic, but to geographical realities," Dr. Zolger explaining that this boundary was drawn to include all Croats, Slovenes, and Serbs "along" the Drava River.

After the withdrawal of the Serbian representatives, the Supreme Council discussed the difficulties presented by the delimitation of the Italian-Yugoslav boundary. Baron Sonnino frankly stated that Italy would not agree to the examination by any committee of the questions outstanding between his country and the South-Slav state; but he had no objection to referring the question of the other frontiers of Yugoslavia to an expert committee, as had been done in the case of Czecho-

[23] The following is the text of the resolution adopted: ". . . the questions raised in the statement by M. Beneš on the Czecho-Slovak territorial interests in the Peace Settlement shall be referred for examination in the first instance to an expert Committee composed of two representatives each of the United States of America, the British Empire, France and Italy. It shall be the duty of this Committee to reduce the question for decision within the narrowest possible limits and make recommendations for a just settlement. The Committee is authorized to consult representatives of the peoples concerned." Miller, *Diary*, XIV, 225.

[24] For the minutes of this meeting, see Miller, *Diary*, XIV, 487 ff., reprinted *infra*, Doc. 8, p. 395. See also Map 3, at the end of this volume. Concerning the Yugoslav claims against Hungary, the following documents prepared by the Serbian Delegation and presented to the Peace Conference in Paris are relevant: "Memorandum Concerning the Claims of the Kingdom of the Serbians, Croatians and Slovenes" (n.d.); memorandum concerning the "North Frontier" (n.d.). See also the memorandum concerning "Delimitation between the Serbians and the Roumanians in the Banat" (n.d.).

Slovakia and Rumania. Upon Mr. Lansing's suggestion, the Council decided to refer the Yugoslav territorial claim to the Committee which had already been appointed to examine the Rumanian claims.[25]

Thus within a month of the formal opening of the Peace Conference, the territorial claims of three of Hungary's four neighbors were presented to the Principal Allied and Associated Powers and were referred in each instance to an expert committee. It should be noted that the task of these committees was to examine the claims advanced and to formulate recommendations for a just settlement. The decision was reserved for the Great Powers, who therefore were technically free to change or even to disregard these recommendations. Their reservation to themselves of the final decision also made it indisputable that the ultimate responsibility for whatever new boundaries were laid down would rest primarily with the Great Powers. Whatever responsibility might be charged to the expert committees could be only vicarious— a responsibility inverse in proportion to the thoroughness and objectivity with which their task was accomplished. It should also be noted that the resolutions appointing these expert committees authorized them "to consult the representatives of the peoples concerned." There is no evidence that the Supreme Council gave any instructions to the committees as to the nature and extent of such consultations, should any take place. But the discussion in the meeting of January 31, 1919, seems to indicate that some members of the Supreme Council at least had appreciated the desirability of consulting not only the representatives of the claimants but also those of groups alien to the claimants in race, nationality, language, or religion.

The Proposal of a Neutral Zone between the Hungarians and the Rumanians

While the representatives of Hungary's neighbors presented their claims in Paris for Hungarian territories and while expert committees began the examination of these claims with a view to formulating

[25] The resolution, moved by Mr. Balfour, reads: ". . . the questions raised in the statements made by MM. Vesnitch, Zolger and Trumbitch, on behalf of the Serbian Delegation on the Serbian territorial interests in the peace settlement (excepting only the question in which Italy is directly concerned) shall be referred for examination in the first instance to an expert Committee similar to that which is considering the question of the Banat. It shall be the duty of this Committee to reduce the questions for decision within the narrowest possible limits and to make recommendations for a just settlement. The Committee is authorized to consult the representatives of the peoples concerned." Miller, *Diary*, XIV, 501.

recommendations for the decision of the Supreme Council, the situation in Hungary progressed from bad to worse. As indicated in the Introduction, the gradual pushing of the line of demarcation laid down in the armistice conventions of November 3 and November 13, 1918, deeper into Hungarian territory caused growing resentment among the Hungarian people. It should be repeated that technically the Allies were entitled to change the line of demarcation and to occupy points of strategic importance throughout the country.[26] It proved, nevertheless, to be unfortunate that the necessity for extending the line of occupation, if such there was, was discovered by the Allies only little by little and that fresh instructions to evacuate were given to the Hungarian Government weekly.[27] The fact that the evacuated territories were occupied by Hungary's neighbors, rather than by troops of the Principal Allied Powers, did not make the Allied decisions more palatable to the Hungarians. Their dissatisfaction was heightened by the conduct of the occupying authorities, who, disregarding the express provisions of the armistice terms, constantly interfered with and for all practical purposes took over the civil administration of the occupied territories.[28] The cautiously expressed apprehensions of Professor Coolidge, summarized in the Introduction, as to the future course of events [29] proved unfortunately to be quite accurate. It was particularly the action of Rumania and the support given to her by the Allies which brought to a head the situation anticipated by the American observer. The continued advance of the Rumanians in Transylvania was viewed with increasing concern and growing bitterness in Hungary. Such advances occurred without Allied approval and more often than not without prior notification to Hungarian authorities; frequently they were accompanied by conflicts between the resisting Hungarian and the advancing Rumanian troops.[30]

[26] Cf. supra, p. 9.

[27] For a criticism of the armistice conventions of Nov. 3 and 13, although from a different point of view and offering at the same time an explanation of the successive extension of the occupied areas, see Temperley, History, I, 351–52.

[28] The conventions of both armistices provided that civil administration of the evacuated territories should remain in the hands of the Hungarian Government. See Art. 6 of the armistice of November 3 (Military Clauses) and Art. 1, par. 2, of the armistice of November 13, in Docs. 1 and 2, pp. 355, 359. Many, although by no means all documents relating to Hungarian complaints concerning violations of the armistice terms are incorporated in Annex I of Note XI presented by the Hungarian Peace Delegation to the Peace Conference on Jan. 18, 1920. See HPN, I, 342 ff.

[29] See supra, pp. 15–16.

[30] It may be pointed out that soon after the formal opening of the Peace Conference the Conference took note of recurring local armed conflicts in the Danu-

It was only after the presentation of the Rumanian claims to the Supreme Council that the Rumanian Government brought to the attention of the Peace Conference its desire to occupy at once all the Hungarian territories she claimed. In two communications, dated February 8 and 9, 1919, addressed to M. Clemenceau, the chief Rumanian delegate, Mr. Bratianu, urged the modification of the armistice terms in favor of Rumania. He specifically requested permission for the Rumanian Army to occupy territories which Rumania claimed in Hungary, where, according to Bratianu, "the Budapest Government is encouraging Bolshevist propaganda." In the second of these communications the Rumanian statesman complained about Hungarian activities in Transylvania, such as alleged incursions of armed Hungarian bands "spreading terror" and "forcing the defenceless population" to join their ranks.[31] No proofs were offered to substantiate these allegations, which, it may be noted incidentally, concerned territory claimed by Rumania but not yet legally under her sovereignty.

The matter also came up before the Committee for the Study of Territorial Questions Relating to Rumania, which meanwhile had held several meetings pursuant to the task entrusted to it by the Supreme Council's resolution of February 1. At the fourth session of the Committee, held on February 17, there was before it a report from General Franchet d'Esperay, dated February 14, on the advance of Rumanian troops toward the territories whose allocation was under the Committee's consideration; the report further stated that Hun-

---

bian area as well as in other parts of Europe. The Supreme Council broadcast a declaration, prepared by President Wilson, on Jan. 24, 1919, to the effect that its members were "deeply disturbed by the news which comes to them of the many instances in which armed force is being made use of, in many parts of Europe . . . to gain possession of territory, the rightful claim to which the Peace Conference is to be asked to determine. They deem it their duty to utter a solemn warning that possession gained by force will seriously prejudice the claims of those who use such means. It will create the presumption that those who employ force doubt the justice and validity of their claim and purpose to substitute possession for proof of right and set up sovereignty by coercion rather than by racial or national preference and natural historical association. . . ." Minutes of the Supreme Council, Jan. 24, 1919, reprinted in Almond and Lutz, *Treaty*, p. 26. See also Thompson, *The Peace Conference Day by Day*, pp. 138–39. It is of course common knowledge that this solemn warning was not heeded by those powers to which it was addressed. According to Mr. Thompson, *loc. cit.*, it was "more particularly directed against the warring elements in Central Europe—Poles, Czechoslovaks, Roumanians and Jugo Slavs—which are reaching out to grab territory." Neither did its disregard adversely affect claims advanced by such powers.

[31] Miller, *Diary*, V (Docs. 382, 383), 246–47.

garian troops were being massed to oppose such an advance, which had already reached the line Mármarossziget, Zilah, Csucsa, Nagyszeben. The Committee decided to make two recommendations to the Supreme Council: first, that the four Principal Allied Governments advise Rumania "that any military aggression by her would serve to prejudice her claims in that region"; second, that "a neutral zone be established between the Rumanians and the Hungarians, possibly to be occupied by Allied troops to prevent any Bolshevistic activities pending the final settlement of the territorial questions involved." [32] At the next session, held on February 19, the Committee decided to submit a proposal concerning the suggested neutral zone, accompanied by recommendations of the French General Staff, to the next meeting of the Supreme Council. [33] Curiously, the suggestion that Rumania should be warned, agreed upon at the Committee's previous meeting, was not examined, [34] nor was it mentioned when M. Tardieu, as chairman of the Committee, presented the proposal at the Supreme Council on February 21. [35] The concrete suggestion of the Committee was that there should be established two lines, beyond which Hungarian and Rumanian troops respectively might not penetrate, thus setting up a zone free of military occupation by the contestants which might be occupied by Allied troops for the maintenance of order, if deemed necessary by the Supreme Council. The lines proposed by the Committee were to run as follows: ten kilometers (about six miles) west of the line from Vásárosnamény; the confluence of the Körös and the Algyö Rivers for the Hungarians and ten kilometers east of the line Szatmárnémeti-Nagy-

[32] American Commission to Negotiate Peace, *Bulletin* [cited hereafter as AD, *Bulletin*], 23, Feb. 18, 1919, in Miller, *Diary, XVII*, 13–14. For an explanation of the daily bulletins issued by the American delegation see the Prefatory Note in Volume XVII of Mr. Miller's *Diary*. According to Mr. Temperley, the proposal to extend the Rumanian line of occupation to the west so as to include the cities of Arad, Nagyvárad, and Szatmárnémeti was made by General Franchet d'Esperay "in deference to a strong Rumanian protest." See Temperley, *History, I*, 353. For the French text of the minutes of this meeting, see de Lapradelle, *La Paix de Versailles, IX*, 341 ff.

[33] AD, *Bulletin* 25, Feb. 19, 1919. Miller, *Diary, XVII*, 18–19.

[34] A memorandum prepared by Dr. Day, American member of the Committee, for General Bliss and for the information of the American Peace Commission refers only to the recommendation of a neutral zone and makes no mention of any suggestion to issue a warning to Rumania. According to Dr. Day's memorandum, the Committee felt it to be "of direct interest to the prosecution of its work on territorial claims that districts within a debatable area should be preserved from armed occupation by either side." Miller, *Diary, XVII*, 23, reprinted *infra*, Doc. 9 (II), p. 403.

[35] The minutes of this meeting are printed *infra*, Doc. 9 (I), p. 401.

várad and Arad for the Rumanians.[36] After a brief discussion the Supreme Council decided to refer the recommendations for the establishment of such a neutral zone to the Military Representatives of the Supreme War Council at Versailles.

The report of the military advisers was presented to the Supreme Council at a meeting held on February 26.[37] After hearing several Rumanian representatives (specifically General Coanda, Colonel Dimitrescu, and Dr. Vaida), General Henrys, commander in chief of the French Army of the Orient and General Charpy, the military representatives concluded that the creation of a neutral zone in Transylvania was desirable. The zone proposed was as follows: The Rumanian line to be the main highway from Arad to Nagyszalonta, thence the railway from Nagyvárad to Nagyszalonta, and thence the railway via Nagyvárad, Nagykároly to Szatmárnémeti. The above cities were to be free of Rumanian military occupation, but available, together with the railway, for the use of Rumanian troops for economic purposes under Allied control. The Hungarian line was to leave the Tisza River five kilometers (about three miles) northwest of Vásárosnamény, passing five kilometers to the west of Debrecen and three kilometers west of Dévaványa; continuing slightly to the west of Gyoma, thence five kilometers west of Orosháza, Hódmezövásárhely, and Szeged, and rejoining the southern frontier south of Szeged. For the maintenance of order in the neutral zone, occupation by a small Allied force was suggested. The preamble of the report stated that the proposals "relate only to provisional measures of occupation, without prejudice in any manner to the final attribution of the occupied regions."

Comparing the recommendations made by the Committee for the Study of Territorial Questions Relating to Rumania with the proposals

[36] According to Dr. Day's comment accompanying his memorandum, cited *supra*, n. 34, there were military objections to the proposed limit upon the Rumanian advance, the opinion of the military experts consulted being that "it was necessary to allow the Rumanians to occupy" the towns of Szatmárnémeti, Nagykároly, Nagyvárad, and Arad. From explanations given by M. Tardieu to the Supreme Council, it appears that the Committee received reports and advices on this point from General Alby, the French chief of staff, from the military advisers of the Italian Peace Delegation, from General Charpy, chief of staff to General Franchet d'Esperay, and from Mr. Bratianu.

[37] For the minutes of this meeting containing the verbatim report of the military advisers, see *infra*, Doc. 9 (III), p. 404. See also Map 4 at the end of this volume. The report was signed by General Belin (France), Signor Cavallero (Italy), Major General Sackville West (the British Empire), and Mr. Lochridge (the United States), military representatives on the Supreme War Council.

of the military representatives of the Supreme War Council, one is forced to the conclusion that the compromise solution took greater account of strategic desiderata pressed upon the Allies by the military and political spokesmen of Rumania than the considerations of a different nature which guided the Committee.[38] In fact, the eastern demarcation line was pushed ten kilometers further west into Hungary, even though the important cities through which the line was traced were technically freed from outright military occupation, while the Hungarian side of the demarcation line was even more disadvantageous for Hungary than the one proposed by the Committee. Considering that the Allied military representatives arrived at their conclusions largely on the basis of information from only one of the interested parties and that it is unlikely that the French officers of the Eastern Allied Army, whose advice was sought, had put forward any arguments in the interest of Hungary, the astonishing thing is not the harshness of their proposal, in the light of all the facts and their consequences, but that, from the point of view of Hungary, the outcome was not worse.

After a brief discussion which related to the size and the location of the small Allied force needed for the occupation of the neutral zone,[39] the Supreme Council adopted these proposals, and the French Government at once instructed General Franchet d'Esperay, as commander in chief of the Allied Armies in the East, to take the necessary action.[40]

The establishment of this neutral zone has been described in some detail because it was this decision which later brought about the resignation of Count Michael Károlyi's already strongly leftist government and made possible the assumption of power in Hungary by a small group of irresponsible Communists, with far-reaching consequences for Hungary herself and for the future relations of the Danubian states.

[38] Dr. Seymour, American member of the Committee, confirms this conclusion. Both he and Dr. Day were strongly opposed to the pushing of the zone farther west, but the American objections were summarily overruled, chiefly on French pressure. Obviously the members of the Committee were experts in other than purely military matters and did not feel competent to argue about the strategic necessities of the moment.

[39] It is not without interest that the Allied military representatives thought two Allied battalions sufficient, on the ground that "there was not between the Hungarians and Roumanians any very notable tension. . . ."

[40] See M. Pichon's statement at the meeting of the Supreme Council on Feb. 27, 1919. Miller, *Diary*, XV, 119.

The Proceedings in the Territorial Commissions

The complete record of the manner and methods by which the two territorial committees arrived at their recommendations concerning the frontiers of three of Hungary's four neighbors has not as yet been disclosed. Available contemporary evidence, together with the *ex post facto* observations of some of the participants, nevertheless throws some light on the processes by which conclusions were reached. It should be observed at the outset that however vitally their recommendations were to affect Hungary, the task of these committees was to inquire into claims put forward by Hungary's enemies; their problem was to determine the future frontiers of Czecho-Slovakia, Rumania, and Yugoslavia, rather than those of Hungary. Consequently, their approach was inevitably predetermined by the positing of the issues in those terms. It should also be remembered that these committees began their work almost immediately after four and a half years of war, which of necessity generated a great deal of bitterness and hatred; and therefore it should not be expected that the effects of years of enmity could at once be erased from their minds and that they would decide with objectivity and impartiality between the conflicting claims of their own nations and allies and those of the ex-enemy countries. Another point to be emphasized is the *de facto* situation which confronted these committees—the actual disintegration of the Austro-Hungarian Monarchy and the control of considerable portions of Hungarian territory by the claimants. It is not my task to inquire into the causes or the process of this disintegration or to examine the legality of the occupation; I merely wish, in the interest of historical accuracy and objectivity, to call attention to the various factors which to a greater or less extent probably influenced the conclusions of the territorial committees.

Finally, it is important to note that the committees completed their work in a comparatively short time.[41] The report of the "Committee

[41] The speed with which the recommendations were arrived at should not be overemphasized, since each Allied delegation came to Paris with fairly definite ideas. The work of the territorial committees consisted largely—as was bound to be the case—in working out compromise solutions. Also, generally speaking, the Peace Conference proceeded on the assumption that immediate decisions were desirable, even though more thorough deliberation and reflection might have resulted in more prudent ones. No doubt, too, the expectation of future rectifications through the League of Nations played its part in the ready acceptance of compromises.

on Czecho-Slovak Questions" was submitted to the Supreme Council on March 12, 1919, exactly five weeks after its appointment. During this time its subcommittee charged with the elaboration of Czecho-Slovakia's future frontiers [42] held, according to the Committee's final report, seven meetings, and the only witness heard was the Czech representative, Dr. Beneš. Apparently there was some difference of opinion between the members of the Committee as to the Czech-Hungarian frontiers, but the differences of opinion were "only matters of detail." The second meeting of the Committee also decided, over Italian opposition, "to advocate in principle the formation of an autonomous state to include the Ruthenians of Hungary, which should be under Czecho-Slovak protection, with guarantees, however, for the freedom of transit across Ruthenian territory between Hungary and Poland as well as between Rumania and Czecho-Slovakia." [43] The Czech-Hungarian frontiers were discussed at the third and fourth meetings, held on March 3 and 5. As reported in Bulletin 61 (March 6, 1919) of the American Delegation, [44] the Americans and Italians regarded it as "a vital consideration to include the smallest possible number of Magyars" within Czecho-Slovakia, while in the opinion of the British and the French that consideration was "secondary to that of finding a line which will insure all the possible lines of railway communications and the best geographic frontiers to the Czecho-Slovak State." Judging from the final report, the British and the French point of view ultimately prevailed, not with respect to Hungary alone, but generally. The report states that the Committee had been "principally" guided by ethnical considerations, but found it necessary "in certain cases to take into account certain important considerations other than those of nationality."

It became evident, indeed [the report continues], that whereas it was extremely desirable to give to the new Tchecho-Slovak State the greatest possible ethnic unity, it was above all essential to provide for the new State conditions which would satisfy its economic needs; and for this purpose it was considered important, on the one hand, not to destroy the existing unity

---

[42] The subcommittee consisted of General Le Rond (France) as chairman, Mr. Allen W. Dulles assisted by Maj. Douglas Johnson (the United States), Mr. Harold Nicolson, assisted by Lt. Col. J. H. M. Cornwall (the British Empire) and Signor Stranieri, assisted by Captain Romagnoli (Italy). As appears from AD, *Bulletin* 49, Feb. 28, 1919 (Miller, *Diary*, XVII, 94), the subcommittee held its second meeting on Feb. 28, less than two weeks before the submission of its final report.

[43] AD, *Bulletin* 49, cited *supra*, n. 42.   [44] Miller, *Diary*, XVII, 134.

of economic life, and on the other hand to assure to the Tchechs such means of communication as were indispensible to their economic development, as well as a frontier line providing the necessary guarantees for their national security.[45]

The substance of the Committee's recommendations will be examined later in connection with the decisions of the Supreme Council on Hungary's frontiers, when the question to what extent the Committee's report was decisive in the ultimate determination of these boundaries can also be answered. For the moment, attention is called to the division of opinion among the members as to the fundamental concepts which ought to have guided the Committee in reaching its conclusions and to the absence of any consideration, at least so far as the record shows, of the economic needs, the indispensable means of communications, and the security of one of the states to be vitally affected, namely Hungary. It may also be noted that the Committee's report was completed before the Communists took over the Hungarian Government, and therefore it may be assumed that fear of the spread of communism was not decisive in the Committee's conclusions.

The other territorial committee did not accomplish its task as speedily as did the Czecho-Slovak Committee. Its two reports, one on the frontiers of Rumania, the other on the frontiers of Yugoslavia, were not submitted to the Supreme Council until April 6, 1919. Its deliberations lasted almost twice as long as those over the Czecho-Slovak frontiers. This may be explained by the fact that it had to define the frontiers of two countries instead of one; moreover, its task was complicated by the delimitation of boundaries not only between an ally and an ex-enemy, but also between two allied states. Finally, the magnitude of the claims put forward by Rumania required perhaps more consideration than the relatively slighter pretensions of the Czechs and the Yugoslavs. This last point seems to be borne out by the fact that the division of opinion among the committee members was both greater and more persistent than in the Czecho-Slovak Committee.

At the very first meeting of the "Committee for the Study of Rumanian Territorial Questions," although the Committee reached an

---

[45] Quoted from the original "Report Submitted to the Supreme Council by the Committee on Tchecho-Slovak Questions," Paris, March 12, 1919, p. 4. The complete text of this Report, as far as it concerns Hungary's frontiers, is printed *infra*, Doc. 10, p. 411. See also Map 3 at the end of this volume.

agreement that the whole of Rumania's claim to Transylvania should not be allowed, each of the members proposed different boundaries; that proposed by the French was furthest west, giving the largest slice of Hungarian territory to the Rumanians, while the line suggested by the Americans was furthest east.[46] The discussion of the Transylvanian frontier was continued into the fourth meeting of the Committee, held on February 17, without any agreement being reached, the frontier favored by the British and the French still being "considerably" to the west of the American line. The Italians refrained from offering a concrete proposal, but intimated that their line would approximate that of the Franco-British rather than that of the Americans.[47] The main contention seems to have been between the Americans and the French, the latter laying great stress upon military and strategic considerations. To solve the impasse, a meeting was arranged between the American members of the Committee and French experts to examine in detail the basis for the French suggestion.[48] At the fifth meeting of the Committee, held on February 19, it was decided to defer the question until the delegations could reëxamine the alternative compromise lines suggested, based on conflicting data; the Committee also decided to hear the Rumanian representatives.[49] The Rumanian delegation, consisting of Prime Minister Bratianu, Dr. Vaida-Voevod, and Mr. Misu, Rumanian Minister in London, appeared before the Committee and presented their arguments at the meeting held on February 22. Inasmuch as the Committee was also charged with the task of recommending Yugoslavia's frontiers, it also invited the Serbian representatives to appear, especially since Rumania and Serbia were making con-

[46] AD, *Bulletin* 23, Feb. 18, 1919 (Miller, *Diary,* XVII, 13–14).

[47] The Italian attitude in this instance seems to have been determined not only by Italy's friendship for Rumania, but also by the fact that Italy rested her own claims on the secret London treaty of April 26, 1915; hence she felt compelled, in order to be consistent, to support Rumanian claims based on another secret treaty. As has been indicated (*supra,* p. 33), Signor Orlando alone among the representatives of the Principal Allied and Associated Powers took the view at the Supreme Council meeting of Feb. 1 that the secret treaty of Aug., 1916, between the Allies and Rumania was still binding. It cannot be denied that in the case of the Czech-Hungarian or the Yugoslav-Hungarian frontiers, the Italian representatives on the territorial commissions were inclined to be fair and objective, or even to espouse absentee Hungary's interests, while with respect to the Hungarian-Rumanian frontier they rather favored Rumania.

[48] AD, *Bulletin* 23, Feb. 18, 1919 (Miller, *Diary,* XVII, 13–14).

[49] AD, *Bulletin* 25, Feb. 19, 1919 (Miller, *Diary,* XVII, 18–19).

flicting claims to the Bánát.[50] The Serbian delegation, composed of Mr. Pašić, Minister for Foreign Affairs Trumbić, Mr. Vesnić, Serbian Minister at Paris, Dr. Zolger, Professor Tsvyić, and General Pešić, Assistant Chief of the Serbian General Staff, attended the seventh meeting of the Committee held on February 25.[51] By February 28 the American, the British, and the French members were more or less agreed on a Hungarian-Yugoslav boundary, in the Bácska region, which would follow "substantially" the line proposed by the Serbs, and a partition of the Bánát leaving Szeged and a limited area surrounding it to Hungary. The Italians reserved decision.[52] By March 2 agreement was reached concerning the frontiers of Rumania and Yugoslavia in Transylvania, the Bánát, the Bácska, and west of the Danube as far as the confluence of the Dráva and the Mur Rivers, and the tracing of the line was entrusted to a subcommittee.[53] The subcommittee was to draw up a report on the entire Rumanian frontier by March 6, this to be reviewed by the whole Committee on the following day. But it was not until March 11 that the draft of the report on Transylvania and a portion of the Bánát was accepted. The report of the subcommittee on the part of the Hungarian-Yugoslav frontier in Baranya was reserved for further discussion.[54] There were other disagreements among members of the Committee, and meanwhile events had occurred in Hungary which caused further delays, so that the final reports of the Committee were not submitted to the Supreme Council until April 6, 1919.[55]

As in the case of Czecho-Slovakia, an analysis of the concrete recommendations of the Committee will be presented later, in connection

[50] The Committee was as much divided concerning the Rumanian-Yugoslav boundary in the Bánát as with respect to the Hungarian-Rumanian frontier in Transylvania. As in the latter case, the Committee agreed that the whole of Rumania's claim should not be allowed, but each Delegation proposed a different line. See AD, *Bulletins* 23 and 25 (Miller, *Diary,* XVII, 13, 18).

[51] AD, *Bulletin* 40, Feb. 25, 1919 (Miller, *Diary,* XVII, 67 ff., especially 71–72).

[52] AD, *Bulletin* 49, Feb. 28, 1919 (Miller, *Diary,* XVII, 95).

[53] AD, *Bulletin* 53, March 3, 1919 (Miller, *Diary,* XVII, 104). The subcommittee was composed of General Le Rond (France), chairman, Dr. Seymour (the United States), Mr. Leeper (the British Empire) and Count Vannutelli-Rey (Italy). AD, *Bulletin* 57, March 5, 1919 (Miller, *Diary,* XVII, 111). According to the Final Report of the Committee to the Supreme Council, a number of other people also took part in the work of the subcommittee.

[54] AD, *Bulletin* 72, March 11, 1919 (Miller, *Diary,* XVII, 163 and especially 164).

[55] Committee for the Study of Territorial Questions Relating to Rumania and Yugoslavia: Report No. 1, Rumanian Frontiers; Report No. 2, Frontiers of Yugoslavia. Both reports are dated April 6, 1919.

with their consideration by the Supreme Council. An attempt will be made here to evaluate the processes, in the light of the Committee's own pronouncements, by which its conclusions were reached.

As far as Rumania was concerned, the Committee observed that it could not pass over certain questions which, "though foreign to the territorial claims of Rumania, are still likely to present themselves in a critical aspect in the territories bordering on that kingdom, and might compromise the relations of Rumania with the neighboring States." [56] The Committee also called attention to the necessity of guaranteeing the rights of ethnical or religious minorities in Rumania. These preliminary observations would seem to indicate that the Committee must have had some apprehension as to the consequences which might ensue from the recommended new frontiers, although, it stated, its inquiries and conclusions were guided by "an examination of the facts and the justice of the case." Another *caveat* voiced by the Committee is also worthy of notice, namely a disclaimer "to pronounce on the juridical bases of the claims presented—bases the evaluation of which belongs to the Council of the Allies, and which in any case, are inapplicable in themselves to the sum of the demands at the present time submitted to the Conference." [57]

The recommendations of the Committee concerning the Hungarian-Rumanian frontier in Transylvania were based, according to the Committee's report, on the ethnical principle, by virtue of which it proposed to allot to Rumania not only Transylvania proper, but also adjacent territories "where the majority of the population is Rumanian." [58] The Committee frankly acknowledged, however, that it did not always apply the ethnical principle, but was guided concurrently by other considerations. Specifically: (1) When on the linguistic frontiers Magyar cities were surrounded by Rumanian rural districts, the Committee, save for the Italians, thought that the nationality of the rural district should be given more weight than that of the towns, this conclusion being supported by the Committee's statement that in towns the Hungarian administration had "created artificial majorities"; (2) lest the

---

[56] Report No. 1 (cited *supra*, n. 55) p. 5. All quotations are from the original report. For the complete text of the report as far as it concerns Hungary's frontiers, see *infra* Doc. 11, p. 419. See also Map 3 at the end of this volume.

[57] *Ibid.*

[58] *Ibid.*, p. 6. There is no indication in the report of the data on the basis of which the Committee decided in what areas the Rumanians constituted the majority of the population.

economic unity of Transylvania be destroyed, Rumania should not be refused possession of the outlets of the valleys to the plain and a railway connecting these outlets with one another and with the Danube; and (3) the Committee deemed it advisable, "in the general interests of peace," to facilitate the junction of the railway referred to in section 2 with the railways of other Allied countries, so as to make it a great connecting artery between those countries and the Danube.

Despite its breadth of view, the Committee did not find it possible to accede to all claims put forward by Rumania. An Italian proposal aiming to place Western Transylvania in direct contact with Poland, "in the interest of peace," by assigning to Rumania the two railways running north from the Tisza River, was not approved because the Committee felt that the cutting in half of Ruthenia, which had been already assigned to Czecho-Slovakia, would impede the homogeneous development of the Ruthenian people. Taking into account the exclusively Magyar population of the district traversed by the Nagykároly-Csap railway, the Committee decided to put the frontier east of the railway, although its inclusion in Rumania would have facilitated communciations between that country and Czecho-Slovakia.[59] In the Bánát the area at the confluence of the Maros and the Tisza Rivers was found by the Committee to depend ethnographically and economically on the immediate surroundings of Szeged, and the Committee recommended that it should remain, with Szeged, in Hungary. In several places the Committee insisted on the advisability of providing for the protection of minority rights. It also suggested the operation of several railway lines connecting territories which were to be separated by the new frontiers under a temporary Allied supervision.

The recommendations of the Committee concerning the Yugoslav frontiers were arrived at after taking into account "all the elements of fact and all the considerations of equity which have come to its knowledge so far as ethnographical, historical, geographical, economic and political questions are concerned." [60] But it is also stated that the Yugoslav claims with respect to the frontier with Hungary were considered

[59] The American members of the Committee strongly opposed the Italian proposal and succeeded finally in keeping the frontier east of the railway line. The bitter struggle over this point does not appear in the records, and the author is indebted for this information to Dr. Seymour, an American delegate on the Committee.

[60] Report No. 2 (cited *supra*, n. 55), p. 3. All quotations are from the original report. For the complete text of the report as far as it concerns Hungary's frontiers, see *infra* Doc. 12, p. 426. See also Map 3 at the end of this volume.

"with the most benevolent attention." [61] Despite the divergence of language and religion in the case of the Serbs, Croats, Slovenes, and other peoples in Southern Hungary, the Committee found that they tended to form a homogeneous mass which would unite without difficulty with the new Yugoslav state. Where the mixture and confusion of races made it impossible to ascertain the ethnic line or where that line could not be made to coincide with any natural frontier, the decisive consideration was to be the avoidance of any disturbance of the normal economic life of the population. As in the Rumanian report, the Committee suggested, although with less emphasis, the protection of minorities' rights. While in the Rumanian report there is no indication as to the information and data upon which the ethnic character was determined—that is to say, in those instances where other considerations did not induce the Committee to recommend a line different from the ethnic frontier, the Yugoslav report indicates that the Committee's conclusions were reached on the basis of "properly corrected" or "rectified" official Hungarian statistics.[62] Unfortunately, the methods whereby the "correction" and "rectification" of Hungarian statistics were accomplished are not indicated either in the final report or in the available records of the proceedings of the Committee.

The reports on the Rumanian and Yugoslav frontiers were completed only after the assumption of power by the Communists in Hungary had caused considerable uneasiness in Paris. However, there is no evidence that the Committee's conclusions were influenced thereby.

As already suggested, in judging the merits of these reports account should be taken of the fact that both territorial committees were composed of representatives of Powers which were enemies of Hungary and that they reached their conclusions without the advantage of constant consultation with the representatives of the ex-enemy states. The Hungarians, at whose expense the recommendations were made, may find little solace in this; but, from the point of view of the objective historian, it is surprising that any account was taken of the Hungarian absentee. Nevertheless, the contemplated territorial dispositions caused

[61] *Ibid.,* p. 6.

[62] Thus the frontier line suggested in the Bácska allotted to Yugoslavia territory where the Yugoslavs of all categories were, according to the report, in a "relative" majority "if the official Hungarian statistics be properly corrected." The inclusion of Szabadka and Zombor in this region was supported by the Committee's finding that these cities, "for centuries centers of Yugoslav civilization," possess an "absolute" Slav majority "according to rectified statistics." *Ibid.,* p. 7.

uneasiness in the minds of at least some of the Allied statesmen. Conclusive proof thereof can be found in Mr. Lloyd George's Fontainebleau memorandum, "Some Considerations for the Peace Conference before they Finally Draft Their Terms." This highly interesting document bears the date of March 25, 1919. In other words, it was written after the final report of the Czecho-Slovak Committee had been placed in the hands of the "Big Four," and when the work of the Rumanian-Yugoslav Committee was in a fairly advanced stage, about which, it may be presumed, the respective chief delegates were more or less informed.

After expressing his objection to the proposed transfer of large German populations to alien rule, Mr. Lloyd George wrote:

. . . What I have said about the Germans is equally true of the Magyars. There will never be peace in South-Eastern Europe if every little state now coming into being is to have a large Magyar Irredenta within its borders. I would therefore take as a guiding principle of the peace that as far as humanly possible the different races should be allocated to their motherlands, and that this human criterion should have precedence over considerations of strategy or economics or communications, which can usually be adjusted by other means. . . .[63]

The significance of Mr. Lloyd George's suggestion lies in the fact that it is contemporary. The preceding analysis of the proceedings of the territorial committees indicates that the human criterion urged by the then British Prime Minister was not always the guiding principle in their deliberations; neither was it taken into account, as will be shown later, by the Supreme Council when that body decided the frontiers of the new states, on the basis of the recommendations of its territorial committees.

Attention may be called in this connection to the subsequent judgments passed by Mr. Lloyd George upon the procedure whereby the new frontiers of the Succession States were defined. It is impossible to say to what extent these *ex post facto* observations were based on contemporary records; therefore their significance for the historian is not conclusive. Nevertheless, coming from one of the chief figures of the Peace Conference, they cannot be ignored. After pointing out that the task was by no means an easy one, in view of the intermingling of races and the Allied distrust of the statistics of the Monarchy, statistics which, according to Lloyd George, were "vitiated by the obvious bias of the

[63] Lloyd George, *Memoirs*, I, 266–67.

Imperial bureaucracy either for or against any particular race," Mr. Lloyd George goes on to say:

The witnesses who came before us, or supplied us with written statements, belonged to the rival claimants, and their testimony was naturally prejudiced. Events have proved that, as far as the disputed areas are concerned, the statistical evidence as to racial majorities furnished to us in many cases was grossly erroneous and misleading.[64]

Interesting light is also thrown on the attitude of the Allied representatives in the territorial committees by certain passages in Mr. Lloyd George's volumes. He quotes a characteristic remark of the French representative on the committee defining the Rumanian and Yugoslav frontiers: "Having a choice to make between an Allied and an enemy country, the Commission must not hesitate, however strong its desire of legitimate impartiality may be, to favour the Allied side," while Sir Eyre Crowe, British representative on the same committee, stated at the meeting of February 25, 1919:

When we come to face these ethnographical difficulties it makes a great difference whether they arise between the Roumanians and the Hungarians who are our enemies, or between the Roumanians and the Serbs, who are our Allies. In the first case if it were found to be impossible to do justice to both sides, the balance must *naturally* be inclined toward our ally Roumania rather than toward our enemy Hungary. At the same time this principle must not be carried too far, for our ultimate duty is to produce a condition of things likely to lead to permanent peace.[65]

[64] *Ibid.*, II, 587.

[65] *Ibid.*, II, 597. Italics added. If this statement correctly indicates Sir Eyre's attitude, Mr. Lloyd George did not fairly represent the British attitude when he asserted that while Britain "leaned" toward the Allies, the British representatives on the territorial committees were "free from any antipathies or apprehension which would interfere with the balance of their judgment between the litigants." *Ibid.*, II, 598. See in this connection the minutes of the meeting of the Rumanian territorial committee held on Feb. 17, 1919, de Lapradelle, *La Paix de Versailles,* IX, 341 ff. At this meeting an attempt was made to reconcile the Franco-British proposal regarding the future frontier between Hungary and Rumania with the line proposed by the Americans and the Italians. The French and the British favored a line which would leave the Szatmárnémeti-Nagykároly-Nagyvárad railway to Rumania, while the American-Italian line was drawn farther east because in the opinion of their experts the Franco-British proposal would subject a considerable number of Hungarians to Rumanian sovereignty. (The figures were admittedly unverified, the French estimate being around 40,000, the American and the Italian estimates ranging from 225,000 to 360,000.) In the course of the discussion Sir Eyre remarked (de Lapradelle, *La Paix de Versailles,* IX, 348): "I suggest, however, that if, in order to secure a better line of

The conclusions drawn by Mr. Lloyd George as to the attitude of the
Allied representatives deserve attention. Concerning the French he
writes:

. . . Wherever there was any conflict of evidence between Poles, Czechs,
Yugoslavs or Roumanians on the one hand, and Germans and Magyars on
the other, the French members of the Boundary Commission showed a distinct and obvious bias in favour of the former and against the latter. They
leaned as far in that direction as any plausible argument or testimony would
afford support to propensity, or as far as America, Britain and Italy would
allow.

The Italians, owing to their antagonism to the Serbs, gave "eager support to Hungary; as between Hungary and Rumania, they were sympathetic to both" and "helped in arriving at a fair decision." [66] The
Americans, according to Mr. Lloyd George, were not "altogether unbiased" because of the large body of Polish, Czech, Slovak, and Croatian voters in the United States, who brought organized pressure on the
government and, through it, on the Peace Delegation.[67]

---

communication [for Rumania], we should have to sacrifice a few hundred thousand
Hungarians, that ought not to stop us" ("Je suggère cependant que s'il fallait, pour
obtenir une meilleure ligne de communication, sacrifier quelques centaines de milliers
de Hongrois, cela ne devrait pas nous arrêter"). Comparing Sir Eyre's position with
that of the French representative, one may find a shade of a difference in emphasis
but not in substance. Dr. Seymour, who served as American representative on one
of the territorial committees and who has been one of the staunchest defenders of
the peace treaties, summed up the situation as follows: "With certain exceptions, the
boundaries finally approved conform roughly to the distribution of the several peoples, although in all matters of doubt the balance turns slightly against the former
dominant nationalities—the Germans and Magyars." House and Seymour, *What
Really Happened at Paris,* pp. 101 ff. Among the exceptions Dr. Seymour noted particularly Czecho-Slovakia, the political boundaries of which did not even "roughly"
correspond with the ethnic or linguistic line. *Ibid.,* pp. 103 ff. Concerning the attitude
of the Principal Allied representatives on the territorial committees, see also Temperley, "How the Hungarian Frontiers Were Drawn," *Foreign Affairs,* VI (1928),
432 ff., especially 434–35. Mr. Temperley in this article defends generally, though
with certain important reservations, the frontiers recommended for Hungary.

[66] The record does not bear out Mr. Lloyd George as far as the Hungarian-
Rumanian boundary is concerned. Whatever sympathy Italy may have had for
Hungary, it was outweighed by her inclination to support Rumanian pretensions
based on the secret treaty of Aug., 1916. See *supra,* n. 47.

[67] Lloyd George, *Memoirs,* II, 597–98. This observation of Mr. Lloyd George is
of course somewhat exaggerated. Any one familiar with political life in the United
States can easily appreciate that whatever may have been the size of the vote of the
Poles, Czechs, and similar groups, no effective pressure could have been brought to
bear on the members of the Peace Commission, who, at the time of the Conference,

Attention may be called to criticism, voiced by Harold Nicolson, of the method adopted by the Peace Conference of referring territorial claims advanced by small Allied countries to committees and of the proceedings of the committees themselves. Although this criticism is *ex post facto,* it comes from one who served on several of these committees—among others the Czecho-Slovak—and, as such, it commands respect. Mr. Nicolson pointed out first the unfortunate consequences of the fact that the Conference approached the territorial problems not in terms of the ex-enemy powers, but of respective claims of the smaller Allies, and that these committees were appointed *ad hoc* to examine specific claims. This resulted not only in overlapping and lack of coordination, but also precluded the various committees from realizing the aggregate of what was taken away from the ex-enemy states.[68] Secondly, the committees were given to understand that their recommendations would be discussed by the Supreme Council, when the "interested parties" (presumably including the ex-enemy powers) would have their say.

We were never for one instant given to suppose [wrote Mr. Nicolson] that our recommendations were absolutely final. And we thus tended to accept compromises, and even to support decisions, which we ardently hoped would not, in this last resort, be approved.[69]

---

were quite independent of Congress. Thus even if we assume for the sake of argument that organized pressure by voters may have influenced Congress, this pressure could not have made itself felt in Paris. Cf. Dr. Seymour's view that the American proposals in the territorial committees were characterized by greater generosity toward the defeated nationalities than those put forward or supported by the other Allied representatives. House and Seymour, *What Really Happened at Paris,* pp. 87 ff., especially 97. This view is borne out by the available records of the Peace Conference.

[68] See Nicolson, *Peacemaking, 1919,* p. 117, and also p. 127: "This empirical and wholly adventitious method of appointment produced unfortunate results. The Committee on Rumanian Claims, for instance, thought only in terms of Transylvania, the Committee on Czech claims concentrated upon the southern frontier of Slovakia. It was only too late that it was realized that these two entirely separate committees had between them imposed upon Hungary a loss of territory and population which, when combined, was very serious indeed."

[69] *Ibid.,* pp. 122–23, 128–29. Members of the American Peace Delegation question this statement by Mr. Nicolson. Professor Douglas Johnson, of Columbia University, doubts that there was any expectation among the members of the territorial committees that their recommendations would be rejected. It is of course quite possible that Mr. Nicolson personally was motivated by such a hope. Dr. Seymour expressed the view that members of the territorial committees not only believed but also desired that their recommendations would be approved by the Supreme Council —not because they believed such recommendations to be by any means ideal, but be-

As against contemporaneous and subsequent criticism of the proceedings of the territorial committees, account should be taken of the opinion of those who defended these proceedings. Among the latter the views of Dr. Seymour, the distinguished American historian and participant in the work of one of the territorial committees affecting Hungary, deserves respectful consideration. According to Dr. Seymour, the territorial committees

took their responsibility seriously and spared neither time nor effort in endeavoring to secure ideal frontiers. In general, it is fair to say that their decisions resulted from honest study and were only slightly affected by selfish political considerations. . . . The commissions spent long hours in studying the conflicting claims of nationalities and in comparing them with the host of statistics which were available.[70]

A somewhat detailed analysis of the work of the territorial committees has been deemed appropriate, in view of the fact that their recommendations, as far as Hungary was concerned, were, as will be shown, almost without exception integrally adopted by the Supreme Council, practically without further discussion and certainly without any hearing given to the representatives of that country.[71] Before the reports of the territorial committees were considered by the Supreme Council, events had taken place in Hungary to which we shall now turn our attention.

The Establishment of the Communist Regime in Hungary

As indicated above, the Supreme Council decided, upon the recommendation of the Committee for the Study of Territorial Questions

---

cause they regarded them as the best that could then be secured. For an interesting analysis of the relation of the various commissions and committees of the Peace Conference to the Supreme Council, see Binkley, "New Light on the Paris Peace Conference," *Political Science Quarterly*, XLVI (1931), 509 ff., especially 519 ff.

[70] House and Seymour, *What Really Happened at Paris*, pp. 97–98. The proceedings of the Peace Conference are eloquently defended and the earnestness and thoroughness of its work are emphasized—though primarily with regard to the treaty with Germany—by Tardieu in *The Truth about the Treaty*, pp. 77 ff.

[71] Attention may be called in this connection to the views of one of the most authoritative interpreters of the Peace Conference. Mr. Temperley points out that the territorial committees working on the problem of the frontiers of Austria, Hungary, and the other states south of Germany, "are of transcendent importance for they had to deal with questions, not of paring off provinces, but of creating and constructing new states. They decided on the amount of air, space, and freedom necessary to the life of the new peoples." Temperley, *History*, IV, 130–31.

Relating to Rumania and Yugoslavia and after consultation with the Military Representatives of the Principal Allies, to fix a demarcation line for Rumanian occupation of Hungarian territory in Transylvania and to establish, west of that line, a neutral zone of about twenty kilometers, or some fourteen miles, in order to avoid conflict between Rumanian and Hungarian troops. The decision taken by the Supreme Council on February 26, 1919, was communicated for execution to the Commander in Chief of the Allied Armies in the East, General Franchet d'Esperay; but it was not until March 19 that General de Lobit, from Belgrade, instructed his representative in Budapest, Lieutenant Colonel Vyx, to make known the decision to the Hungarian Government. According to the note which Lieutenant Colonel Vyx handed to the Hungarian officials on the following day, the withdrawal of Hungarian troops to the line laid down by the Supreme Council was to begin on March 23 and was to be completed in ten days. The neutral zone, as defined by the Supreme Council on February 26, would be occupied by Interallied troops under General Gondrecourt's command, but the civil administration was to remain in the hands of the Hungarian authorities, under Allied control. Hungary was also advised that the Peace Conference authorized Rumanian troops to advance to the eastern boundary of the neutral zone after Hungarian troops had crossed its western boundary.

Count Károlyi's reply, dated March 21, informed Lieutenant Colonel Vyx that the Hungarian Government "finds itself unable to take note of the decision of the Peace Conference and to safeguard its execution." The Hungarian note stated that in the opinion of the Government the decision was opposed to the Belgrade Armistice of November 13, 1918, and took no account of Hungary's vital interests. Since the Government could not assume responsibility for carrying out a decision in the formulation of which it had had no opportunity to participate, it felt obliged to resign.[72]

On the same day Béla Kun, with a handful of communist sympathizers and supporters—many of whom until the preceding day had been kept in jail—took over the government, thereby inaugurating a regime of terror in Hungary and marking the beginning of a period of open defiance of the Allies by the Hungarian bolshevik government. According to a report to Marshal Foch by General Franchet d'Esperay, from Constantinople, dated March 22, the representatives of the bour-

[72] The text of these notes is printed *infra,* Docs. 9 (IV) and 9 (V), pp. 407, 409.

geois parties in Hungary made a last attempt to save the situation
before surrendering power to the bolsheviks. They proposed to Lieutenant Colonel Vyx an alliance with the Entente against bolshevik
Russia, on condition that the demarcation line, as it then stood, be
maintained and that the Allies send troops to Hungary to assist the
government in maintaining order; if the proposal was rejected, they
would make an alliance with the bolsheviks.[73]

The situation created by the establishment of a communist regime
in Hungary was discussed at a meeting of the American Delegation on
March 27, 1919. Messrs. Lansing, White, Herter, and General Bliss had
an opportunity to listen to first-hand reports from Capt. Nicholas
Roosevelt, United States Army, who as a member of Professor Coolidge's special mission left Budapest after the Communists took over the
government. Captain Roosevelt explained the reasons which, in his
opinion, had lead the Károlyi Government to resign. Successive steps of
the Allies had aroused much resentment among the Hungarians; "the
final delineation of the neutral zone between Hungarians and Rumanians marked the breaking point," he reported. "When Col. Vix
handed to Károlyi the notice that Hungarian troops should withdraw
behind the line in question, Károlyi stated that no Government in
Hungary could be found that would agree to such conditions." Mr.
Roosevelt exonerated Lieutenant Colonel Vyx of all personal responsibility, indicating that in his opinion Vyx had handled the matter with
tact.[74]

To Mr. Lansing's inquiry as to what action would be proper, Captain
Roosevelt suggested that an Allied division of ten thousand men could
deal with the situation. Should this not be feasible, the Czechs and the
Rumanians might be allowed to take action; but in that case, he said,
"a very cruel and bloody war would undoubtedly ensue." Mr. Lansing
thought both courses bad: the first, because of past experiences, when
small Allied units were sent to establish order in restless localities; the

[73] Miller, *Diary*, XVII, 281, reprinted *infra*, Doc. 9 (VI), p. 410.

[74] There was, among the Hungarians, much complaint about the manners of Lieutenant Colonel Vyx. Doubtless the conduct of the Allied military authorities in
Hungary was, in the early months of the armistice, not always characterized by
consideration and tact; but this is not surprising in view of the widespread bitterness
generated in the course of four and a half years of war. In any event, the French
army officer or his manners should not be made responsible, as some have sought to
do, for the resignation of Count Károlyi or for his transference of power to the
Communists. It is believed that the new demarcation line would have been unacceptable, irrespective of the manners of M. Vyx.

second, because "it would merely mean the beginning of a series of wars in central Europe which would antagonize the peoples to a greater extent than they were antagonized already."

It is from the remarks of General Tasker Bliss during this discussion that, for the first time, it appears that the Americans at least were not convinced of the justice of the decision concerning the boundaries of the proposed neutral zone. General Bliss was of the opinion that the Allies had no reason to change their attitude toward Hungary because of a change of government in that country. At the same time, he took the position that if the bolshevik government should refuse to obey the order of the Peace Conference to retire its troops behind the designated line and should prefer to fight,

we [apparently meaning the United States, rather than the Allies in general] should then refuse to give any assistance to the Rumanians regardless of how greatly such a step might be misinterpreted by the other nations. The line of the neutral zone which had been drawn was absolutely unjust, and we should not make matters worse by enforcing an extremely unjust decision by force of arms.[75]

General Bliss was not the only American plenipotentiary to hold this view, for, according to the records of this meeting, "the Commissioners realized how difficult it would be to revoke a decision which had formerly been reached by the Peace Conference, but felt that whereas we had once been fooled into agreeing to a rotten decision, we should no longer have the injustice of backing it up by force of arms." [76]

[75] Miller, *Diary*, VII (Doc. 627), 259-61.

[76] *Ibid.* There is no evidence in the available records that the American members of the Rumanian committee objected to the demarcation line recommended, or that such objections were made by the American military experts who, with their Allied colleagues, advised the Supreme Council. The minutes of the meeting of the Supreme Council of February 26, which decided to establish the neutral zone, reveal no objection on the part of the American plenipotentiaries. The statement that the Americans were "fooled into" agreeing indicated that their conclusion as to the injustice of the decision must have been reached subsequently, either on the basis of new information or of a more careful examination of the evidence on which the recommendation was based. It should be noted that the criticism was not directed toward the establishment of the neutral zone as such, but at the line of demarcation.

Dr. Seymour, in a memorandum with which he kindly supplied the author, confirmed the belief that the conclusion as to the injustice of the decision was reached subsequently, on the basis of new information and a careful examination of new evidence. Dr. Seymour believes that it was quite improper to put this matter before the territorial committee, which did not—and perhaps could not—appreciate the implications of the proposal. If any blame falls on the territorial committee, it is on account of failure to insist on its incompetence to deal with this matter.

The American objections to the neutral zone, as approved by the Supreme Council on February 26, 1919, were stated as follows in a memorandum prepared by General Bliss for President Wilson on March 27: (1) the entire neutral zone lies within territory that is ethnically Hungarian; (2) through sanctioning a further and extended advance of Rumanian troops beyond the demarcation line laid down in the Belgrade Armistice, it subjects the Associated Powers to a charge of breach of faith; (3) it has been interpreted by the Hungarians as a recognition by the Supreme Council of the secret treaty of 1916 between the Allies and Rumania. Referring to the result, in Hungary, of the communication of the decision relating to this neutral zone (i.e., the resignation of the Károlyi Government and the assumption of power by the bolsheviks), General Bliss squarely laid the blame at the door of the Supreme Council.

The present conditions in Hungary [the memorandum reads] are the direct result of the action of the Supreme Council on February 26, 1919. That act, therefore, was politically unwise. It cannot be justified morally before the people of the United States.

General Bliss's conclusion was that the United States should decline categorically to participate in any armed intervention to enforce this decision.

It is believed also [he wrote to President Wilson] that if the United States is to continue to act with the Associated Powers in the determination of territorial and economic questions relating to the former Austro-Hungarian Empire, it insist upon the immediate reversal of the action of the Supreme Council of February 26, 1919; upon the issuance of orders to the Commanding General of the Army of the Orient and all other representatives of the Associated Powers in the countries bordering on Hungary, that no action will be taken by them with respect to the Hungarian people or territory that is not clearly within the scope of the terms of the armistice concluded with Hungary; and that meanwhile every effort be made by the Supreme Council to reopen communication with the Hungarian people and to assure them that it is the purpose of the Associated Powers to conclude a peace with Hungary on a basis of the declarations of President Wilson contained in his address of January 8, 1918, and subsequent addresses.[77]

---

[77] Baker, *Woodrow Wilson and World Settlement,* III, 239–41. It should be noted in this connection that the Americans were not alone in disapproving the line approved by the Supreme Council. General Charpy, chief of staff of General Franchet d'Esperay, was of the opinion that the Rumanians should remain at the line held by them when the neutral zone was discussed in Paris. According to General Bliss's

In any event, the Allies were confronted with an unexpected situation. While the Communist government did not openly refuse to abide by the decision of the Supreme Council, it certainly gave no indication that Hungarian troops would be withdrawn to the new demarcation line. Indeed, reports reached Paris that the Hungarians planned to attack their neighbors. After some hesitation,[78] the Supreme Council decided on April 1 to send General Smuts to Budapest to ascertain the true situation in Hungary and, if possible, to induce Béla Kun to comply with the decision relating to the neutral zone. General Smuts, accompanied by a small retinue, left Paris on the same evening and arrived in Budapest on April 4. During his one-and-a-half-day sojourn in Budapest he had several interviews with Kun and his associates. These conferences took place in the railway carriage, which General Smuts never left, lest his presence in the Hungarian capital should be seized upon as implying recognition of Kun's Government by the Allies. The substance of General Smuts's proposal was that the Hungarians should withdraw in the east behind a new demarcation line, which, as laid down by him, was somewhat more favorable to Hungary than the line determined by the Supreme Council and communicated to Károlyi on March 21;[79] he also requested that the bolshevik government acknowledge as binding the armistices of November 3 and November 13, 1918. In exchange, the Allies would occupy the neutral zone with their own troops and would lift the blockade against Hungary.[80] On the morning of April 5 a draft agreement embodying the

memorandum, General Charpy reported on Feb. 25, 1919, when the question was before the Allied military advisers (see *supra*, p. 42), that "the Hungarians had carried out all the conditions of the armistice but that the Roumanians had not, as, without informing Gen. Franchet d'Esperay, they had crossed the demarcation line and advanced into Hungarian territory." *Loc. cit.*

[78] According to Major General Sir George Aston, "At the end of March proposals by Foch to deal forthwith by military action with Bolshevism in Hungary were discussed, the decision arrived at being that military action was not the answer to Bolshevism." *The Biography of the Late Marshal Foch,* p. 423.

[79] See Gratz, *The Era of Revolutions* [in Hungarian], pp. 160–61.

[80] As is well known, the armistice conventions did not provide for lifting the Allied blockade against the former Central Powers, and the blockade was maintained for a considerable time after Nov., 1918, as a weapon with which the Allies forced Germany and her former partners to comply with their demands. At the beginning of April, 1919, the raising of the blockade against both Austria and Hungary was in contemplation, but no action was taken with regard to Hungary, on account of the assumption of power by the Communists. On May 9, the day after it approved Hungary's future frontiers as recommended by the various territorial committees (see *infra,* pp. 66–70), the Council of Foreign Ministers examined an inquiry from the

terms of the Smuts proposals was handed to Kun, to which he promised a reply by 7:00 P.M. that day, after consultation with his associates. The reply accepted the proposal, but on condition that the Rumanians, on their side, withdraw behind the Maros River. Courteously but firmly Smuts told the bolshevik leaders that he could not accept reservations and, after ushering them out of his railway carriage, he gave orders for the train to leave at once, to the chagrin and bewilderment of Kun and his associates, who had believed that they could haggle with him over details.[81] The Hungarian reply was not intended as a rejection of Smuts's proposals—indeed Kun was most anxious to come to an agreement, a proceeding which would have carried, by implication at least, *de facto* recognition of his regime by the Allies and would have bolstered his authority at home, something which he badly needed. He may have been stalling for time, in order to ascertain the views of his allies in Moscow; he may also have hoped to secure a more favorable demarcation line. What he failed to take into account was that Smuts and his retinue had contacts also with a few Allied and neutral observers resident in Budapest and that from their reports Smuts, rightly or wrongly, had come to the conclusion that Kun's regime was not sufficiently stable to be seriously reckoned with.

While the Smuts mission did not accomplish its objective, its presence in Budapest was, by adroit manipulation, turned to advantage by the bolshevik leaders. Kun, without revealing that General Smuts had

---

Supreme Economic Council as to whether the blockade against Hungary should be lifted. The discussion indicated that the Allies were unwilling to aid Kun's Government by lifting the blockade; Baron Sonnino even suggested that information should be allowed to leak out that the blockade would be lifted as soon as Kun's Government was overthrown. It may be noted that this discussion took place a few days after Rumania's successful attack on the Hungarian Red Army, which was expected to put an end to the Communist regime in Hungary; indeed Kun's Government stood in those days on a ledge too narrow for safety. The decision of the Council of Foreign Ministers, reached after a brief discussion, authorized the Supreme Economic Council to prepare for lifting the blockade and to act as soon as the General Staff was satisfied that order had been reëstablished in Hungary. Miller, *Diary*, XVI, 233 ff., especially 255, reprinted *infra* Doc. 15, p. 442. In fact, the blockade against Hungary was maintained for several months longer.

[81] Nicolson, who accompanied General Smuts on his mission to Budapest, gives a dramatic description of these events in his *Peacemaking, 1919,* pp. 292–304. Cf. also Ashmead-Bartlett, *The Tragedy of Central Europe.* The author, a British journalist, divided his time between Vienna and Budapest during these weeks and gave a detailed report to General Smuts on his experiences and observations with regard to events in Hungary.

terminated conversations with him, published the proposed draft agreement and the Hungarian reply, giving the Hungarian public the impression that negotiations for a settlement were in course between the Allies and Kun. The mistaken belief doubtless gave a new lease of life to the tottering bolshevik regime, as well as a breathing space during which to build into better shape its disorganized and leaderless red army.

While Smuts was on his way to Budapest, the Rumanians continued to press their claims on the diplomatic front. Availing himself of renewed Russian attacks on Rumanian troops near Odessa, Prime Minister Bratianu, in a communication dated April 3, requested the Peace Conference to take urgent measures to hasten the withdrawal of Hungarian troops beyond the now-famous neutral zone and to force the complete disarmament of Hungary, in order to protect Rumania, then engaged in fighting bolshevism, from the rear.[82] The argument advanced by the Rumanian statesmen appears to have been one of convenience, since a few days after General Smuts left Budapest, the Rumanian Army, under the pretext of provocations by Hungarian army units and of bolshevist propaganda, suddenly attacked the Hungarian lines along the whole length of the frontier between the Szamos and the Maros Rivers. As will be described more fully later, the Rumanian troops, superior in number and equipment, easily overcame any resistance and advanced in a few days to the Tisza River. The success of the Rumanians encouraged the Czechs also to push their lines deeper into Hungary; the war was on on two fronts. But, before considering the renewal of hostilities between Hungary and two of her neighbors, let us return to the proceedings of the Peace Conference, still faced with the problem of determining Hungary's frontiers.

The Recommendations of the Territorial Commissions before the Council of Foreign Ministers and the Council of Four

Owing to the pressure of work, the Supreme Council was superseded at the end of March, 1919, by the "Council of Four," i.e., the chief delegates of the Principal Allied and Associated Powers (President Wilson, Mr. Lloyd George, M. Clemenceau, and Signor Orlando). Since the drafting of the treaty with Germany occupied the center of

[82] AD, *Bulletin* 135, April 4, 1919 (Miller, *Diary*, XVII, 374).

attention, questions deemed to be less important and matters of detail were turned over to the "Council of Five" or the "Council of Foreign Ministers," consisting of the Foreign Ministers of these powers and of Japan.[83] The reports of the territorial committees affecting the Succession States were among the matters which were referred in the first instance to the Council of Foreign Ministers.

Curiously, the Hungarian frontiers came up for discussion for the first time in consequence of a memorandum from General Smuts dated April 9, 1919, pressing for a modification of the Czech-Hungarian frontier as recommended by the Czecho-Slovak Territorial Committee in its report of March 12, 1919.[84] After leaving Budapest on April 5, General Smuts proceeded through Vienna to Prague, where, on the morning of April 7, he had a long interview with President Masaryk. According to Smuts's notes on this conversation, the future frontiers of the new Czecho-Slovak state were also discussed. General Smuts pointed out to President Masaryk the undesirability of including a very large purely Magyar population, living north of the Danube between Pozsony and Komárom, in order to give Czecho-Slovakia a Danube frontier. President Masaryk was said in the memorandum to have agreed and to have remarked that "he would prefer to waive all claims to this Magyar territory and withdraw the Czech frontier to the north, so as to leave all this ethnologically Magyar territory to Hungary," if, in exchange, a small strip of Hungarian territory on the south bank of the Danube opposite Pozsony were assigned to Czecho-Slovakia. This claim was made for economic reasons, i.e., to enable the Czechs to build in safety proper harbors and docks along both banks of the river. "For this economic advantage," read General Smuts's notes, "Masaryk would be prepared to surrender his claim to a large area with an alien population." Smuts concluded:

With some millions of Germans already included in Bohemia in the north, the further inclusion of some 400,000 or 500,000 Magyars in the south would be a very serious matter for the young State, besides the grave violation of the principle of nationality involved. I would therefore press very strongly for effect being given to this exchange, as I am sure it would be both to the advantage of Bohemia, and immensely please the Hungarians, who already look upon this part of their Magyar population as lost to them. In fact the

[83] Concerning the organization of the Peace Conference see Temperley, *History,* I, 236–78, 499.
[84] *Supra,* pp. 45–46.

Great Powers thus obtain a valuable bargaining counter in any dealings with the Hungarian Government.[85]

General Smuts's report came before the Council of Foreign Ministers on May 3, when M. Pichon (Mr. Lansing concurring) proposed that the question be referred to the Czecho-Slovak Committee for report.[86] Lord Hardinge submitted a draft resolution, prepared by the British Delegation, which would have instructed the Czecho-Slovak Committee "to proceed from the assumption that the island of the Grosse Schütt [Csallóköz] shall be excluded from Czecho-Slovak territory provided that in return a small enclave opposite Presbourg [Pozsony] is ceded to the new Republic." Mr. Lansing, with whom M. Pichon concurred, opposed the instruction part of the British resolution on the ground that the Council should not prejudge the case. M. Pichon also expressed the fear that General Smuts had misunderstood President Masaryk. Ambassador Laroche, also present at the meeting, explained the source of M. Pichon's fear. Dr. Beneš, having learned of General Smuts's suggestion, referred the matter to President Masaryk, who replied that Smuts had seriously misunderstood him. According to Dr. Beneš, as related by Ambassador Laroche, President Masaryk had merely stated during the conversation that "certain parties in Bohemia held the view that the island of Grosse Schütt might be exchanged for a small enclave opposite Presbourg," but he himself did not support that view. Rather, he maintained that the island was indispensable to the free navigation of the Danube. Upon Mr. Lansing's inquiry whether Dr. Beneš had submitted a written statement concerning President Masaryk's explanation, M. Laroche replied that he had obtained the information in a personal interview with the Czech representative, but Beneš would no doubt be prepared to give a written statement if required. In view of the reported misunderstanding, Lord Hardinge withdrew his resolution and the Council decided simply to refer the matter for report to the Czecho-Slovak Committee.[87]

The records of the committee meeting of May 5, when General

[85] The Smuts memorandum is printed *infra*, Doc. 13 (I), p. 431. It is interesting to compare General Smuts's estimate of the Magyar population of this territory (some 400,000 or 500,000) with that of Dr. Beneš at the Supreme Council meeting on Feb. 5 (some 350,000). See *supra*, p. 35.

[86] The minutes are printed *infra*, Doc. 13 (II), p. 432. No Italian representative attended this meeting.

[87] Mr. Nicolson claims that it was he who begged General Smuts in Prague to urge Masaryk not to claim the island and who induced Lord Hardinge to introduce

Smuts's memorandum was examined, are not available.[88] The evidence supplied by Mr. Nicolson as to what happened there is not conclusive, since he states in his diary that he was in the adjoining room and was not present during the conversation when apparently the Committee sought to have Smuts's understanding of Masaryk's statement corroborated.[89]

The reports of the territorial committees again came before the Council of Foreign Ministers on May 8.[90] After deciding to defer consideration of the Rumanian frontiers bordering on Russia, the latter not being represented at the Conference, the Council examined first the proposed Hungarian-Rumanian frontier. M. Tardieu, explaining the

the resolution above referred to, which Nicolson himself drafted. As to the explanation of the misunderstanding, Mr. Nicolson, who attended this meeting of the Council of Foreign Ministers, recorded in his diary: ". . . This, I fear, is untrue. It increases my dislike of Kramarsh, who is behind everything nasty that Beneš does. They are in the pockets of the French. The French will now tell them that they have 'déjoué' an anti-Czech intrigue on my part. Yet it wasn't an intrigue. It was an eleventh-hour attempt to right a palpable injustice. . . ." *Peacemaking, 1919*, p. 324. Miss Gertrude Millin, in her authorized biography, *General Smuts,* describes the General's journey to Budapest and Prague largely on the basis of Mr. Nicolson's diary (II, 184 ff.). General Smuts's own brief unofficial account of his mission, quoted by Miss Millin on pp. 193–94, does not refer to his conversation with President Masaryk on the proposed territorial readjustment between Hungary and Czecho-Slovakia.

[88] Dr. Seymour kindly gave the author some information on this point. According to Dr. Seymour's recollection (he could offer confirmation that there are no records of the debates concerning this issue which were conducted largely outside of formal committee meetings), the suggestion of Dr. Masaryk's willingness to give up the Grosse Schütt was brought forward and waved aside rather casually. The Committee did not consider the matter seriously because, first, Masaryk's suggestion and General Smuts's interpretation were contradicted by Mr. Beneš; secondly, the whole Committee and particularly the American members were unwilling to grant to the Czechs the *quid pro quo.* Both Dr. Seymour and Mr. Allen W. Dulles advised the author that the Americans alone insisted on leaving this territory in Hungary. The British delegates stood firmly in favor of allotting the Grosse Schütt to the Czechs. The Americans felt that they had been worsted by the French in this matter and received little active support from Mr. Harold Nicolson, who claims to have sympathized with the American position. Dr. Seymour regards it as a mistake that no minority report was made on the Grosse Schütt question; such a minority report was omitted in order to present a unanimous report.

[89] According to Nicolson, Ambassador Laroche produced a note from Dr. Beneš which contradicted Smuts's interpretation. "We are forced to give way," writes Nicolson. "The Czechs will have their Magyars and their Island. I do not feel this to be a wise decision; but I have done my best. Evidently Masaryk committed a gaffe and has been forced to deny it by his Government." *Peacemaking, 1919*, p. 325.

[90] The minutes of this meeting are printed *infra,* Doc. 14, p. 434. By this time the Italians, who earlier bolted the Conference, had returned, and Baron Sonnino attended the meeting.

recommendations of the territorial Committee over which he presided, pointed out that the acceptance of the Rumanian claims would have resulted in alloting a "very large number" of aliens to both sides. After discussing the matter through twelve meetings, his Committee agreed upon a frontier which, he said, halved the number of aliens included within the new frontiers, and he thought that this result was ethnologically satisfactory. The Committee also thought it reasonable to give Rumania a main line of communication running from northeast to southwest (i.e., the railway from Szatmárnémeti to Nagyvárad), while leaving a parallel line to Hungary (i.e., the railway connecting Debrecen with Szeged).

Mr. Lansing inquired where the true ethnic line would be. M. Tardieu replied that the population was very mixed. A truer line might be drawn "in some cases" about twenty kilometers to the east but the Committee's recommendations represented an equitable compromise; a more accurate ethnic line would cut the railway and suppress continuous communications. Pressed further on the ethnic question, M. Tardieu said that some 600,000 Hungarians would come under Rumanian rule, while some 25,000 Rumanians would remain within Hungary.[91] This distribution did not appear very just to Mr. Lansing, who expressed the view that "in every case the decision seemed to have been given against the Hungarians." M. Tardieu retorted that any other adjustment would have been in favor of Hungary and to the detriment of Rumania. He emphasized the fact that the solutions recommended by the Committee were adopted unanimously and represented the best that could be done in very difficult circumstances. Thereupon Mr. Lansing withdrew his criticism and stated that he had no objection to the recommendations of the Committee. Mr. Balfour and Baron Sonnino also agreed, after Balfour stated that the Council of Foreign Ministers could not possibly go over in detail the whole work of the Committee. Since the Council was satisfied that the Committee had done everything in its power to find an equitable solution and since there had been no disagreement within the Committee itself, Mr. Balfour felt that nothing could be done to improve the frontiers recommended. Reserving the Rumanian-Yugoslav frontier in the Bánát for

[91] It does not appear clearly whether M. Tardieu's estimate referred only to Hungarians living outside of Transylvania or those in all the Hungarian territories which it was proposed to allocate to Rumania. If the latter, he grossly underestimated their number, which was well over 1,500,000.

future discussion, the Hungarian-Rumanian frontier as recommended by the territorial Committee was accepted by the Council of Foreign Ministers without further debate.

The frontier between Hungary and Yugoslavia was accepted without any discussion at all. Baron Sonnino then raised the question whether anything had been done regarding the frontier between Hungary and Austria. Mr. Lansing questioned whether any change there need be considered. Mr. Balfour said that he understood there was a German population in Hungary which might wish to join Austria. So far as can be ascertained from the available records, this was the first time that the possibility of changing the historic boundary between Austria and Hungary was raised at the Peace Conference.[92] Baron Sonnino took the position that neither of the countries had raised any question in this connection, and both he and M. Pichon expressed that view that it was unnecessary for the Council to deal with the matter at that time. Mr. Lansing, on the other hand, felt that it would be desirable to appoint a committee to be charged with the task of collecting information regarding any possible modification which might be proposed by either Austria or Hungary. Thus the Council would be placed in a position of rapidly settling any trouble that might arise between these two countries. Sonnino objected that he saw no reason for stirring these countries up by thrusting upon them a controversy over a boundary which had been uncontested for fifty years. Finally the Council decided to appoint a commission to collect information concerning possible rectifications of the Austro-Hungarian frontier; but it was understood that no action would be taken unless the question were raised by Austria or Hungary.

Finally, the Czech-Hungarian frontier was considered. Ambassador Laroche, speaking for the Committee on Czecho-Slovak Questions, stated that its recommendations had been adopted unanimously. The reasons for giving the Danube frontier to Czecho-Slovakia were, according to M. Laroche, obvious—namely, to give her access to the international waterway. M. Laroche also referred to General Smuts's suggestion to leave to Hungary the island of Grosse Schütt, in exchange for a bridge-head across the Danube at Pozsony; but, he said, the Committee

---

[92] The Central Committee on Territorial Questions agreed at its meeting of March 5, 1919, that "the frontier between German-Austria and Hungary need not be considered." Almond and Lutz, *Treaty*, pp. 272–73. This meeting was attended by Dr. Mezes (the United States), Sir Eyre Crowe (the British Empire), M. Tardieu (France), and Marquis Salvago Riggi (Italy).

had rejected this unanimously. Upon Mr. Lansing's inquiry as to the population of this island, M. Laroche replied that it was partly Hungarian and partly German, but that the area was closely connected economically with the territories alloted to Czecho-Slovakia. According to him, the people desired to maintain connection with Czecho-Slovakia in order to protect their economic interests. Mr. Lansing objected that as a result of the recommendations of the territorial committees, some 2,000,000 Magyars were to be placed under Rumanian and Czecho-Slovak rule. M. Laroche observed that his Committee had so reduced the Czech claims that only 855,000 instead of 1,300,000 Magyars would be included in Czecho-Slovakia, while, according to Dr. Beneš figures, 638,000 Slovaks would be left in Hungary. M. Laroche admitted that this figure might be exaggerated, but the number was considerable and might be regarded as a guarantee for good treatment of the Magyar minorities by the Czechs. After a brief discussion, the Czech-Hungarian frontier, as recommended by the territorial Committee, was also accepted.

There followed an exchange of views concerning the unsettled problem of "some form of autonomy" which the Ruthenians were to enjoy within the new Czecho-Slovak state. Mr. Balfour suggested that this question be referred to the committee dealing with the rights of minorities. On the other hand Mr. Lansing expressed a preference for a committee with a knowledge of the area and proposed the Committee on Czecho-Slovak Questions. M. Laroche said that his Committee would ask the Czecho-Slovak Government to submit proposals; should they not be approved by the Committee, experts could be consulted and the Ruthenes could be invited to make suggestions. The Council decided to request the Committee on Czecho-Slovak Questions to make recommendations regarding the status of the Ruthenians within Czecho-Slovakia.[93]

Thus Hungary's future frontiers were disposed of during a single meeting of the Council of Foreign Ministers, on the basis of the reports before them. With respect to the frontiers with Czecho-Slovakia, Rumania, and Yugoslavia, the recommendations made by the territorial committees were approved without any change and without much discussion. The American Secretary of State, Mr. Lansing, alone voiced apprehension concerning the preponderance of economic and other considerations over ethnic principles and the resulting allocation of

[93] See *infra*, pp. 72 ff.

large Magyar populations to the neighboring states. Beyond his remarks, no criticism was made of the reports of the territorial committees, and there was no attempt to examine the merits or justice of
their recommendations. In this connection it should be noted that the
recommendations of the committees were without exception unanimous. Had there been any dissent with respect to any of the new frontiers proposed, it may be assumed from Mr. Balfour's remark that the
Council of Foreign Ministers would have examined more carefully the
points at issue. On the other hand, the fate of General Smuts's suggestion concerning the rectification of a section of the Czech-Hungarian frontier seems to indicate that the ultimate decision, in fact
if not in law, rested with the technical committees rather than with
the supreme councils of the Peace Conference. This was, under the
circumstances, perhaps inevitable. Mr. Balfour was realistic when he
said that the Council of Foreign Ministers (or the Council of Four, for
that matter) could not subject to detailed and minute examination
every report and recommendation made by two score or more technical
committees, especially since the pressure for the completion of the
work of the Peace Conference was steadily increasing in all Allied
countries. Moreover, the various technical committees, including those
charged with determining the frontiers of the Succession States, were
composed of representatives of the same powers whose prime ministers
or foreign ministers constituted the supreme councils of the Peace
Conference. It is logical to assume that Messrs. Balfour, Pichon, and
Lansing had full confidence in the British, French, and American
representatives on the technical committees and did not feel it necessary to reëxamine findings in which these representatives concurred.
The process of approving new frontiers in the Danubian area without
examination on their merits can be criticized only on the grounds that
the territorial committees were not advised from the beginning that
their recommendations would not be reëxamined by the supreme councils of the conference; that there was inadequate coördination between
the several committees, and insufficient consideration of the aggregate effect of their respective recommendations; finally, and above
all, that these recommendations were approved as final without giving
an opportunity to the ex-enemy states (in this instance, Hungary) to
present their side of the points at issue.[94]

[94] There is an ironic description of the May 8, 1919, meeting of the Council of
Foreign Ministers in Nicolson, *Peacemaking, 1919,* pp. 328–29. On the other hand,

Even more perfunctory was the proceeding of the Council of Four. During its meeting of May 12, President Wilson again raised the question of the Austro-Hungarian frontier. He said that he was informed that the Austrians (already invited to send a delegation to receive the peace conditions) would raise the question and he wanted to know whether the commission to investigate the matter had been appointed, as decided at the May 8 meeting of the Council of Foreign Ministers. It appeared that no nominations had been made, and Baron Sonnino repeated the suggestion made in the Council of Foreign Ministers a few days earlier that the frontier question should not be raised at all. After some discussion, the Council of Four decided to require from Austria the recognition of the 1867 frontier with Hungary; should difficulties arise, the Allied and Associated Powers would arbitrate. The report of the Council of Foreign Ministers, approving Hungary's future frontiers as recommended by the territorial committees, was then accepted without discussion.[95]

It may be noted parenthetically that there is no indication of the source from which President Wilson and Mr. Balfour obtained information concerning the alleged desire of the German population of Western Hungary to be joined with Austria. The Austrian Peace Delegation had not yet reached Paris, but the issue may have been raised by an Allied representative in Central Europe. It is also possible that the suggestion came from quarters which feared a possible reunion of Austria and Hungary and believed that in this manner a permanent rift could be created between the two countries. As to the desire of the population concerned, there appears to be no evidence of disaffection on the part of the German-speaking inhabitants of Western Hungary, who for centuries had been among the most loyal of the minority groups. It is conceivable that intense dislike of Béla Kun's communist regime might have induced them to seek salvation elsewhere; but it is unlikely that

---

Dr. Seymour points out that "It is important to emphasize the fact . . . that the technical aspects of the treaties were not drafted hastily by the statesmen of the great powers, who obviously must have been ignorant of many details, but resulted, rather, from the labors and application of a body of experts who had taken pains to go into all phases of the situation." House and Seymour, *What Really Happened at Paris*, p. 99. Another student of the Peace Conference process also is of the opinion that the peace treaties by and large were written according to the text proposed by the various technical and expert committees. See Binkley, "New Light on the Paris Peace Conference," *Political Science Quarterly*, XLVI (1931), 509 ff.

[95] Miller, *Diary*, XVI, 268 ff., especially 272; also Almond and Lutz, *The Treaty*, p. 414. See *infra*, Doc. 16, p. 444.

the social-democratic government of Vienna would have appealed to the strongly conservative Germans of Western Hungary as a haven from bolshevism.

A comparison of the report of the Council of Foreign Ministers on Hungary's frontiers, approved by the Council of Four on May 12,[96] with the draft articles annexed to the final reports of the Czecho-Slovak, Rumanian, and Yugoslav territorial committees respectively,[97] shows that the recommendations of these committees were incorporated bodily, with insignificant verbal changes only, in the former report and were approved by the supreme councils of the Peace Conference. These became in fact the frontiers of Hungary, with the exception of a modification of the Czech-Hungarian frontier in favor of Czecho-Slovakia and of the Austro-Hungarian boundary, subsequently altered in favor of Austria. Both these changes will be discussed presently.

Autonomy for Ruthenia

As indicated above,[98] the Council of Foreign Ministers decided, at its meeting of May 8, 1919, to request the Committee on Czecho-Slovak Questions to make recommendations regarding the status of the Ruthenians who were to be incorporated into the new Czecho-Slovak state, but were to enjoy some autonomy. Pursuant to a request of the Committee, the Czecho-Slovak Foreign Minister, Dr. Beneš, submitted a memorandum, dated May 17, setting forth the extent of autonomy which the Czecho-Slovak Government was prepared to grant to the Ruthenians south of the Carpathians—i.e., in territory which belonged to Hungary. According to Dr. Beneš's memorandum, Ruthenia was to be given a special name, to be determined by agreement between the Czecho-Slovak Government and the Ruthenian Diet; and a legislative body competent to deal with linguistic, scholastic, and ecclesiastical questions, as well as with "all other questions which the laws of the Czecho-Slovak Republic may attribute to it in accordance with particular needs." Laws enacted by the Diet were to be approved by the President of the Republic and countersigned by the Governor of Ruthenia, appointed by the President, who was to be responsible to the Diet. In other matters, legislative power would be exercised by the

[96] See *infra*, Doc. 16, p. 444.

[97] See *infra*, Docs. 10, 11, 12, pp. 411, 419, 426. See also Map 3 at the end of this volume.

[98] *Supra*, p. 69.

Czecho-Slovak legislature, which would contain deputies elected by the Ruthenians. The Governor of Ruthenia would be the final authority in all linguistic, scholastic, and ecclesiastical questions and in all internal matters. For all other questions, the supreme authority was vested in the Government of the Republic, and the Ministries were to have special Ruthenian sections. No special court system was foreseen for the territory of Ruthenia; but a special Ruthenian higher court was to be provided, to which appeals might be taken. Government officials of lower rank in Ruthenia were to be appointed by the Governor; higher officials by the President, upon recommendation either of the Governor or the Czecho-Slovak Government, which was to include a native of Ruthenia, chosen by the President, as minister without portfolio.[99]

The request for the written memorandum summarized above was made after Dr. Beneš appeared personally before the Committee on May 15 and explained the views of the Czecho-Slovak Government. As appears from the Committee's report to the Council of Foreign Ministers, Dr. Beneš in his oral statement made some reservations, especially as to the time element involved, which do not appear in the written memorandum submitted two days later. According to Dr. Beneš (as stated in the Committee's report), the general policy of his Government would "tend to encourage in the Republic every form of evolution towards a federal union"; for this reason it would be premature to accept a complete plan of decentralization until the various provinces acquired "a more pronounced national sentiment and have attained a certain degree of culture and economic development." Dr. Beneš said that this applied "very specially" to the Ruthenians, their country being poor and the population relatively undeveloped. The Czecho-Slovak Government would have to furnish a large amount of capital to improve the conditions of agriculture, roads, and education; and it would also have to administer this capital, "since the Ruthenians will not for long years be capable of managing these operations." "With these reserves," the report stated, "M. Beneš declared that his Government was anxious to accord to the Ruthenians the most generous local autonomy possible."

On the basis of Dr. Beneš's oral statements and written memoran-

---

[99] Dr. Beneš's memorandum is printed as the Annex to the Report of the Czecho-Slovak Committee, dated May 20, 1919, to the Council of Foreign Ministers. Miller, *Diary*, XIII, 93; *ibid.*, XVI, 360 ff.; *infra*, Doc. 17 (I), p. 449.

dum, the Committee unanimously recommended that the plan proposed by Dr. Beneš be adopted as a basis for the future relations between
Czecho-Slovakia and the Ruthenians and be referred for final formulation to the special Committee on New States.[100]

When the report came before the Council of Foreign Ministers on
May 23, the Secretary of State of the United States, Mr. Lansing, made
two concrete suggestions in order better to safeguard the rights of the
Ruthenians. First he suggested, with respect to the nomination of
public officials, that they—particularly police and other minor officials
—be chosen wherever possible from the Ruthenians. According to Mr.
Lansing, the curse of these regions had been that their officials had
hitherto all been Hungarians, the people therefore never acquiring the
habit of self-government. Secondly Mr. Lansing pointed out that the
Ruthenians, although given some form of autonomy, would nevertheless be subject to a state the majority of whose population would be
alien to them. He questioned, therefore, whether it would not be desirable to include a provision enabling them to appeal to the League of
Nations if Czecho-Slovak sovereignty was exercised in a manner regarded by the Ruthenians as in conflict with their rights. Mr. Lansing's
second suggestion was thought by Baron Sonnino to be too dangerous
to be stated openly, since he felt that it would be preferable to have the
League intervene, if necessary, on its own initiative. Ambassador Laroche also opposed the insertion of such a provision in that treaty, because, he said, that "might encourage immediate trouble in Ruthenia."
He alluded to the fact that there were already Ukrainians in Paris,
claiming that territory. After Mr. Balfour's suggestion that a decision
on the question might be deferred until the Committee on New States
made its final report on the draft articles to safeguard minorities' rights
in Poland, the meeting decided to refer the matter to that Committee.[101]

When the Ruthenian matter was referred to the Committee on New
States, that Committee already had before it the general question of

[100] For the complete text of the Committee's report, see *infra*, Doc. 17 (II) p. 450.
The Committee on New States was set up on May 1, pursuant to an agreement between
M. Clemenceau, President Wilson, and Mr. Lloyd George "to consider the question
of international obligations to be accepted by Poland and other new States to be
created by the Treaties of Peace, including the protection of racial and religious minori-
ties." Miller, *Diary*, XIII, 13. The Committee was composed of Messrs. Berthelot
(France), David Hunter Miller (the United States), and Headlam-Morley (the British
Empire). Subsequently Italy also was represented on the Committee.

[101] For the minutes of the meeting of Foreign Ministers on May 23, 1919, see *infra*,
Doc. 17 (III), p. 452.

minorities' protection in Czecho-Slovakia. At the tenth meeting of the Committee, held on May 20, 1919, it considered a memorandum from Dr. Beneš setting forth the privileges which Czecho-Slovakia proposed to accord to her minorities. This memorandum did not refer to Ruthenia, but dealt with minorities generally; [102] and the draft treaty which was considered by the Committee at that meeting contained no provisions referring specifically to Ruthenia. On the following day, however, the Committee, while approving the draft treaty, decided not to submit it to the Council of Four, pending a decision as to whether the question of Ruthenian autonomy would be dealt with by the Committee. [103] The question was discussed by the Committee at its meeting of May 27, in the light of Dr. Beneš's above-summarized memorandum of May 17, [104] and draft articles to be inserted into the minorities treaty with Czecho-Slovakia were tentatively approved at the meeting of May 29. [105] The final draft was approved by the Committee at its twenty-second meeting, held on June 16. In its report the Committee explained the articles proposed for the safeguarding of Ruthenian autonomy as follows:

In addition to the general clauses there will be found in the draft Treaty a special chapter providing autonomous rights for the territory south of the Carpathians inhabited by Ruthenians. The Council of Foreign Ministers had decided that this territory shall be assigned to Czecho-Slovakia, but determined on the recommendation of the Czecho-Slovak Delegation that there should be secured for it special autonomous rights. The question of the precise nature of the rights to be secured was the subject of discussion before the Council of Foreign Ministers, and was referred to the Committee on New States.

The Committee have had before them the proposals put forward by M. Benes on behalf of the Czecho-Slovak Government. These proposals are very far-reaching and seem of such a nature as to fulfil the intentions of the Conference. The Committee in their draft clauses have followed very closely the proposals, and to a large extent the actual words of M. Benes; in some cases, however, his proposals went into considerable detail, and the Com-

---

[102] The memorandum stated that the Czech Government intended to make the Republic into a sort of Switzerland; to grant universal suffrage under the proportional system; to maintain schools from the public funds, and to establish schools for various nationalities; to have mixed courts and to carry on local administration in the language of the majority of the population, and so forth. As the Committee noted, "these facilities would be considerably more far-reaching than any obligations which would be imposed on Czecho-Slovakia by the Treaty." Miller, *Diary,* XIII, 68–70.

[103] *Ibid.,* p. 74.   [104] *Ibid.,* p. 89.   [105] *Ibid.,* pp. 96, 98.

mittee thought it was neither necessary nor desirable to bind the Czecho-Slovak State in a treaty too closely as to details.

The clauses submitted herewith are believed by the Committee to give the fullest guarantees for Ruthene autonomy.[106]

The divergence between Dr. Beneš's memorandum of May 17 and the draft treaty proposed by the Committee is considerable. The omissions from the draft of concessions originally offered by Dr. Beneš whittled away much of the guarantees of Ruthenian autonomy.[107] Whether the Committee came to the conclusion by its own reasoning or by outside persuasion that it was desirable to make Czecho-Slovakia's obligations less definite, is not known. There is some evidence that the Czecho-Slovak Delegation was reluctant to make a far-reaching commitment.[108]

The draft of the treaty, although submitted to the Council of Foreign Ministers, was apparently not acted upon by that body, because on July 4 the Committee addressed a communication to the Secretary General of the Peace Conference, requesting that, in the absence of any information with regard to the decision of the Foreign Ministers, the draft and the accompanying report be submitted to the Council of Four for approval.[109] The draft was finally approved by the Council of Five on August 6 and communicated to the Czecho-Slovak Delegation.[110] The treaty was signed at St. Germain on September 10, 1919, the same day that the treaty of peace with Austria was signed. A comparison between the draft proposed by the Committee on New States and the

[106] Miller, *Diary*, XIII, 160, 163.

[107] The following guarantees, originally suggested by Dr. Beneš, were omitted from the draft: that the Governor of Ruthenia shall represent the final authority in all linguistic, scholastic, and ecclesiastical matters and in questions affecting internal administration; that subordinate officials be appointed by the Governor; that in the ministries of the central government special Ruthenian sections would be created; that Ruthenia would be represented in the central government by a cabinet officer without portfolio; that a special Ruthenian appellate court be established. See *infra*, Doc. 17 (IV), p. 453.

[108] On Aug. 6, 1919, the Czecho-Slovak Delegation suggested to the Committee on New States that the language of the treaty provision granting the Ruthenian Diet legislative powers "in questions of *local* administration" be changed to *"communal* administration." The change, which would have made possible complete evasion of autonomy, was rejected by the Committee at its forty-fifth meeting, held on Aug. 12, 1919. De Lapradelle, *La Paix de Versailles*, X, 288 ff.

[109] Miller, *Diary*, XIII, 241, 244. For the text of the draft as finally approved by the Committee on New States see *ibid.*, pp. 245 ff. The provisions relating to Ruthenia are reprinted *infra*, Doc. 17 (IV), p. 453.

[110] Miller, *Diary*, XIII, 378, 380.

text of the treaty as signed shows, with one exception, only insignificant stylistic changes.[111]

The original proposals made by the Czech representative were such as to promise, on their face, a fair chance for autonomy. Acquiescence by the Allied experts and statesmen in the vague language of the treaty ought to be viewed in the light of repeated and emphatic assurances of the good intentions of the Czech representatives, as well as in that of the belief in the effectiveness of the League of Nations guarantee. To what extent the original intentions were carried into practice subsequently by the Czech Government and how effective the League's guarantee proved to be, are matters which are beyond the scope of this study.

The Final Consideration of Hungary's Frontiers with Rumania and Czecho-Slovakia by the Council of Foreign Ministers and by the Council of Four

Since the draft of the peace terms with Hungary—particularly those dealing with the new frontiers—had already been approved by the Supreme Council early in May, it is likely that in the normal course of events Hungary would have been invited to send a delegation to receive the peace conditions at about the time that such an invitation was sent to Austria.[112] However, conditions in and around Hungary had changed from bad to worse during the weeks in which Hungary's future frontiers were drawn up in Paris. Following the failure of General Smuts's mission in Budapest,[113] the tension on the eastern front

---

[111] British Treaty Series No. 20 (1919) Cmd. 479. The significant change was from the designation of Ruthenia in the draft as "the *country* of the Ruthenes" to "Ruthenian *territory*" in the treaty. The provisions relating to Ruthenia are reprinted *infra*, Doc. 17 (IV), p. 453.

[112] It is possible that an invitation to Hungary was in contemplation. On May 1, 1919, M. Clemenceau telegraphed to General Haller, chief of the French military mission in Vienna, requesting him to transmit a message to the Hungarian Government inviting it to send plenipotentiaries to Saint-Germain on May 15 to receive the peace conditions. See AD, *Bulletin* 252, May 9, 1919 (Miller, *Diary*, XVIII, 175–76). Whether or not the invitation was meant for Austria only and was erroneously transmitted as including Hungary also, it is impossible to say. As a matter of fact, the invitation had not been delivered in Budapest; however, news regarding it leaked out and was utilized by Béla Kun to strengthen the position of the communist government, which, in those days, was badly shaken in consequence of successful Rumanian attacks against the line held by the Hungarian Red Army.

[113] *Supra*, pp. 61–63.

increased considerably. The Rumanians were determined to extend the lines of occupation; the Hungarians were equally determined to oppose such efforts; the result was constant skirmishes along the demarcation line. Rumanian representatives in Paris spread rumors of an impending Hungarian attack on their lines. In view of the general apprehension over bolshevism in Allied circles, it is not surprising that some credence was given to these rumors. About the middle of April, a few days after General Smuts's return, the Rumanians received confidential advice from Paris that should the Hungarians attack, Rumania might advance to the eastern boundary of the neutral zone established at the end of February by the Supreme Council.[114] Although there was no attack by Hungarian troops, the Chief of the Rumanian General Staff, General Presan, construed the advice as a blanket permission and ordered the Rumanian Army to advance. The attack began on April 16 along the whole front between the Maros and the Tisza Rivers. The badly equipped Hungarian Red Army, controlled by inexperienced political commissars, was no match for the numerically superior enemy. Despite valiant resistance by some units of the Hungarian Army (e.g., the Szekler division), whose morale was not yet undermined by Béla Kun's emissaries, the front was broken through at Csucsa on Good Friday, April 18, and the Rumanians advanced rapidly. In a few days they were beyond the neutral zone, which should have been the limit of their advance, and on May 1 they crossed the Tisza River at Szolnok. Meanwhile the Czechs also began to advance from the direction of Miskolc, an important rail junction and industrial town in northeastern Hungary. In the face of impending disaster, the government in Budapest abandoned the preaching of world revolution and substituted an appeal to patriotism. The response to this appeal was much more effective than the "general mobilization of the proletariat" which Kun's Government had attempted a few days earlier. Thanks to patriotism, many thousands of Hungarians, loving their country more than they despised the communist regime, volunteered their services to fight the invaders. The Army was quickly reorganized under the leadership of active and reserve officers of the former Austro-Hungarian Army, and political interference with discipline and operations was eliminated. The advance of the Rumanians and the Czechs, however, was halted in the opening days of May not merely because of the stiffening

[114] See *supra*, pp. 38–43. This line ran somewhat east of Arad-Nagyszalonta-Nagyvárad-Nagykároly-Szatmárnémeti, leaving the towns named in the neutral zone.

resistance of the reorganized Hungarian Red Army, but also because of energetic representations by the Principal Allied aand Associated Powers to Rumania and Czecho-Slovakia.[115]

But on May 18 the Czechs again attacked in the north, threatening Eger and the coal mines around Salgotarján.[116] The Hungarians replied by a counter attack on May 20, which succeeded beyond expectation. Within twenty-four hours they reoccupied Miskolc and, driving a wedge between the Czech and the Rumanian lines which met just at the outskirts of this city, began a triumphant march northward. On June 6 they entered Kassa, and three days later Eperjes was in their hands. The Czech Army was in full retreat. Consternation was great, both in Prague and Paris. On June 7 M. Clemenceau, in the name of the Allied and Associated Powers, requested the immediate cessation of hostilities; but this first warning was not heeded by the Hungarians. It was against the background of these events that the frontiers of Hungary once more came before the Peace Conference, Hungary herself still being absent.

The success of the Hungarian Red Army and apprehension as to the possible extension of the area of warfare induced the Supreme Council to make public its decision concerning the frontiers of Hungary. Accordingly, the frontiers with the two countries with which Hungary was in open warfare were communicated to the Rumanian and Czech representatives, and on June 11 several questions raised by their obser-

[115] It seems that the Americans at least were not misled as to the true objective of the Rumanians. A few days after the attack began it was reported to the American Delegation that the operations were intended "to drive back the Hungarians to the approximate frontier which it is expected will be granted to Rumania by the Peace Conference." Bulletin 81 of the American Information Section, April 21, 1919. MSS. A later report stated that the purpose of the Rumanians appeared to be to occupy desired territory and in no way to attack bolshevism. Bulletin 84 of the American Information Section, April 24, 1919. MSS. Apparently the British and French also disapproved the Rumanian attack; they received reports of the Rumanian point of view, which was that since military coercion by the Allies was unlikely, they ought to seize the opportunity and take by force the territory which they desired. Bulletin 82 of the American Information Section, April 22, 1919. MSS.

[116] Subsequently Dr. Beneš, in a communication dated June 16, in reply to M. Clemenceau's telegram of June 13, demanding the cessation of hostilities in Northern Hungary (see infra, pp. 82–83), protested against reports that the offensive was begun by the Czechs. He alleged that the attack upon Czecho-Slovakia was planned by the Hungarian Communists, in order to affect a junction with Russian and German troops. Dr. Beneš also claimed that the Czechs had occupied Hungarian territory beyond the demarcation line upon the request of the local population and in order to protect the security of Czecho-Slovakia. Text in AD, SH Bulletin 447, July 7, 1919. MSS.

vations were referred by the Supreme Council to the Council of Foreign
Ministers. The Foreign Ministers met on the following day to consider
these questions.[117]

Concerning the Rumanian-Hungarian frontier, M. Pichon informed
the Council that Mr. Bratianu, the Rumanian representative, had raised
certain objections and had stated his inability, without consulting his
government, to accept two sections of the proposed boundary line,
namely, the sections between Csap and Nagykároly and between Nagyvárad and Szeged respectively. According to M. Tardieu, the Rumanians desired that the railway line between these towns should be
included in Rumania. Moreover, said M. Tardieu, Mr. Bratianu supported his opposition to the proposed boundary line by strategic reasons—namely, that the frontier between Nagykároly and Nagyvárad
would run within two or three kilometers (about a mile and a half or
two miles) of an important railway line. As a result, M. Tardieu
thought that the Rumanian representative was disputing the whole of
the proposed boundary line. The meeting decided to inform the Supreme Council that Mr. Bratianu expressed his inability to accept or
to discuss the proposed frontier without first consulting his government, a process which would require ten or twelve days. In addition,
upon the suggestion of Mr. Lansing, the meeting expressed the opinion that the Rumanian-Hungarian frontier, as approved by the Foreign
Ministers and the Supreme Council in May, should not be altered.

Certain alterations proposed by the Czecho-Slovak Delegation were
also considered. While the Rumanians apparently contested the whole
of the proposed boundary line, the Czechs accepted in principle the
line approved by the Supreme Council on May 12,[118] but asked for two
specific modifications, characterized as "slight" by Dr. Kramarcz. According to M. Cambon's report to the Foreign Ministers, the first
modification related to the district of Edor, a small strip of territory
situated on the right, or southern bank of the Danube, opposite Pozsony.
Evidently the Czechs sought to include this territory within Czecho-
Slovakia for strategic reasons. The unanimous recommendation of the
Committee on Czecho-Slovak Questions—that the Danube formed an
excellent boundary and that no reason existed for any alterations in the

[117] For the minutes of the meeting of Foreign Ministers, held on June 12, 1919, see
infra, Doc. 18, p. 455.

[118] See supra, p. 71.

line already decided upon—was approved by the Foreign Ministers, apparently without discussion.[119]

The second claim of the Czechs concerned the railway line between Kalondo and Komárom, including the junction at Ipolyság. In its final report the Committee on Czecho-Slovak Questions recommended that this line be left to Hungary, since otherwise a large number of Hungarians would have to be included in Czecho-Slovakia. On the other hand, M. Cambon advised the Foreign Ministers that the railway between Ipolyság (left to Hungary) and Korpona (allotted to the Czechs) served an important extension of Czecho-Slovak territory which was accessible only from the south. Therefore the allocation of the rail junction to Hungary would cause very grave inconvenience to Czecho-Slovakia. In view of these facts, M. Cambon, as President of the Committee on Czecho-Slovak Questions, strongly recommended that the line approved on May 8 and May 12 be altered, in order to place this rail junction inside the Czech boundaries.

The Italian Foreign Minister, Baron Sonnino, reminded the meeting that the boundary line, as recommended by the Czecho-Slovak Committee and approved by both the Council of Foreign Ministers and by the Supreme Council, had been the result of a compromise. M. Cambon conceded this and explained that for that reason his Committee did not recommend an alteration of the approved boundary between Kalondo and Csap, but suggested merely "a very slight modification" at the railway junction, which would be "essential in order to obtain full use of the Korpona railway line" serving exclusively Czecho-Slovak territory. According to M. Cambon, no material alteration in the agreed boundary line was intended. After a further inquiry by Baron Sonnino, the Foreign Ministers agreed in principle to include the rail junction of Ipolyság in Czecho-Slovak territory and requested the Committee on Czecho-Slovak Questions to submit definite proposals without delay.

Finally the Foreign Ministers considered a proposal made by General Pelle, commanding officer of the Czech Army, who, in view of the armed conflict in Northern Hungary, suggested the fixing of a tempo-

---

[119] It may be noted that this claim for a bridgehead on the right bank of the Danube opposite Pozsony was again put forward by the Czecho-Slovak Delegation although a few weeks earlier a proposal by General Smuts to leave the Grosse Schütt in Hungary in exchange for this desired strategic foothold was rejected by the Peace Conference, due to the strenuous opposition of Dr. Beneš. See *supra*, pp. 64–66.

rary military demarcation line. This proposal had already been discussed in the meeting of the Foreign Ministers held on June 11, when the conclusion was reached that it would be undesirable from the political point of view to fix a demarcation line divergent from the frontiers approved by the Supreme Council and already accepted by the Czecho-Slovak Delegation. M. Pichon pointed out that the demarcation line proposed by General Pelle would lie deeper within Hungarian territory than the proposed permanent frontiers. Another disadvantage was pointed out by M. Tardieu, namely that General Pelle's line coincided with the frontiers originally claimed by the Czechs. The Foreign Ministers agreed to recommend that the permanent boundaries of Hungary with Czecho-Slovakia (including, obviously, the modification relating to the rail junction of Ipolyság just agreed to), as approved previously by the Supreme Council, should forthwith be laid down and that Hungary should be required to withdraw her troops at once behind such frontiers.

Action upon these decisions was taken the following day, June 13, at the meeting of the Supreme Council.[120] The Council discussed the military situation in Hungary and resolved to send a telegram to the warring nations, in the name of the Principal Allied and Associated Powers. The first part of this message was addressed equally to Hungary, Rumania, and Czecho-Slovakia. Reminding the addressees of the determination of the Allies, expressed in the warning dispatched on June 7, "to put an end to all useless hostilities," the Allies stated that the frontiers of the Succession States would not be modified by the temporary accidents of military operations. Therefore the Allies declared that the frontiers communicated therewith would be the permanent boundary between Hungary, on the one hand, and Czecho-Slovakia and Rumania respectively, on the other. The telegram further stated that the armed forces of all three states must immediately cease hostilities and withdraw without delay within the national frontiers thus laid down, without prejudice to possible local rectifications necessitated by economic and other considerations.

This common part of the telegram was followed by a specific admonition addressed to each of the three states involved.

Hungary was requested to withdraw her troops at once behind the

---

[120] The minutes of this meeting are reprinted *infra,* Doc. 19 (I), p. 461. The meeting was attended by President Wilson, Mr. Lloyd George, M. Clemenceau, Baron Sonnino, Baron Makino, and, later, by Mr. Balfour.

assigned frontiers. If the Allies were not informed within four days —that is to say, by midday, June 18, 1919—that this request was being effectively complied with, the Allies reserved the right to occupy Budapest "and to take such other steps as may seem desirable to secure a just and speedy peace." The telegram concluded with the assurance that "the Rumanian troops will be withdrawn from Hungarian territory as soon as the Hungarian troops have evacuated Czecho-Slovakia," but admonished the Hungarian Government that the Rumanian troops should not be molested during such withdrawal, nor should the Hungarians follow them across the new permanent frontier.

The closing paragraph of the communication to Czecho-Slovakia outlined the request addressed to Hungary and expressed the "fullest confidence" of the Allies that the Czechs would not interfere with the withdrawal of the Hungarians and would keep their troops within their own borders.

A final paragraph was added to the communication addressed to Rumania, again stating the request for the evacuation of Czecho-Slovakia and the conditions attached to the withdrawal of Rumanian troops from Hungary and expressing confidence that Rumania "will carry out its share of this common policy." [121] The detailed delimitation of the frontiers between Hungary and Czecho-Slovakia and Hungary and Rumania were dispatched simultaneously to all three countries, in separate telegrams.[122] As will be seen later, these frontiers were incorporated without change in the Treaty of Trianon. To this extent Mr. Temperley was correct in asserting that "the Hungarian frontiers were in fact settled by the Four on the 13 June 1919." [123] He was not

[121] For the text of these communications, see *infra,* Doc. 19 (II), p. 461.

[122] For the text of these telegrams, see *infra,* Docs. 19 (III) and 19 (IV), pp. 463, 466. See also Map 3 at the end of this volume.

[123] Temperley, *History,* IV, 130. It is here also that Mr. Temperley assigns the authorship of both the Austrian and the Hungarian peace treaties in the main to the representatives of the Principal Allied and Associated Powers. "It is of importance to realize this," he states, "because the Small Powers were never allowed to take part in the decision either of the 'Five' or the 'Four.'" This statement appears to be correct and is borne out (at least as far as frontiers are concerned) by the discussion which took place at the outset of the June 12 meeting of the Foreign Ministers discussed above (see *supra,* p. 80; *infra,* Doc. 18, p. 455). The Supreme Council, having found that Hungary's new frontiers, as approved on May 12, were not communicated to the Rumanian representative "or, presumably, to the other States concerned," inquired of the Council of Foreign Ministers why this had not been done. From the discussion and from M. Pichon's explanation, it appears that the practice followed in the case of both Germany and Austria was to communicate decisions regarding frontiers to

correct so far as Hungary's frontiers with Austria were concerned, for those were materially altered subsequently, as will be shown.

It should be noted that the delimited frontier between Hungary and Yugoslavia, although also approved both by the Foreign Ministers and by the Council of Four, was not made public at this time. In fact, the description of this frontier was not communicated to the governments concerned until several months later.[124]

The request for the withdrawal of Hungarian troops from Czecho-Slovakia was accompanied by express and unequivocal assurance that upon compliance with that request the Rumanians would withdraw from the Hungarian territory then occupied by them. This is important, because this assurance was one of the main reasons why the Hungarian Government called a halt to the successful march against the Czechs and proceeded to withdraw its troops behind the lines laid down by the Supreme Council.[125] Moreover, the failure of the Allies to make good this assurance and to bring about the withdrawal of the Rumanian troops was the direct cause of the renewal of warfare between Hungary and Rumania a month later,[126] which in turn precipitated a chain of events producing irreparable effects upon the rela-

the small Allies only the day before the peace terms were presented to the ex-enemy state. Under normal circumstances the same procedure would have been followed in Hungary's case. Thus the small Allied states had, prima facie, slight opportunity to object to the decisions of the Supreme Council. However, taking account of processes previously described, whereby these decisions were reached, the conclusion seems inevitable that the authorship or the finality of the Supreme Council's determination is more apparent than real. It cannot be sufficiently emphasized that decisions were reached upon the basis of the presentation of claims by the small Allied representatives, without giving a hearing to the ex-enemy states, which was hardly counterbalanced by even the most solicitous consideration of Austrian or Hungarian interests by the Principal Allied representatives who composed the territorial commissions; and that the recommendations made by the territorial commissions were approved by the Supreme Council more or less perfunctorily. Perhaps the clearest proof of the influence of the small Allies can be found in the few changes made—as, for example, the allocation of Ipolyság to Czecho-Slovakia—in the approved frontiers, without exception in favor of an ally who succeeded in persuading the competent territorial commission of the necessity of such change.

[124] See *infra*, p. 164.

[125] The other reason was Béla Kun's hope and expectation that by complying he might gain Allied recognition of his government and thus strengthen his position at home. It may be noted that military operations in Northern Hungary were not suspended until June 23d. At that time the Hungarians had advanced to the line Bártfa-Igló-Besztercebánya. The withdrawal of Hungarian troops to the line laid down in the Supreme Council's communication of June 13 was completed by the end of June.

[126] See *infra*, Part Three.

tions of these two countries and consequently upon the future of the peace of Europe.

The Allocation of Western Hungary to Austria

The only major change in Hungary's frontiers approved by the Foreign Ministers and the Supreme Council respectively on May 8 and May 12 was the allocation of Western Hungary, or Burgenland, to Austria. In comparison with the area which Hungary was to lose to her other neighbors, the significance of this territory, from the economic or any other point of view, was indeed negligible. Yet of all the decisions of the Peace Conference relating to Hungary this was beyond doubt the most unexpected.

As pointed out before,[127] originally there was no intention on the part of the Principal Allied Powers in any way to modify the historic frontier between Austria and Hungary. The issue involved in this frontier was formally raised in a note of the Austrian Peace Delegation to the Peace Conference, dated June 10, 1919, commenting upon the peace conditions handed to the Austrians on June 2. In protesting against the territorial clauses of the draft treaty, the note observed that "the desire repeatedly manifested by the German population of the districts of Western Hungary to be allowed a plebiscite on the question of its adjunction to German-Austria, has been passed over in discouraging silence." [128] The matter was discussed in greater detail in an Austrian note dated June 16, 1919, transmitting a memorandum on the frontiers of Austria. After suggesting that the Morava and the Leitha Rivers should form the frontier between Austria, on the one hand, and Czecho-Slovakia and Hungary, on the other, the Austrian note proceeded to justify the proposed changes with respect to Hungary. Admitting that the Leitha had for a long time formed the frontier between the two countries, the note asserted that the river had become, as a result of the establishment of the Monarchy, a purely administrative line of demarcation. From political, military, and economic points of view, that frontier had lost all importance centuries ago. To leave such a frontier between two states "which have become foreign to each other" was objected to, because it was only forty-eight kilometers (about thirty-one miles) from Vienna and one day's march from Graz. Labor for the great industries in Wiener-Neustadt was

[127] *Supra*, pp. 68, 71.
[128] Almond and Lutz, *The Treaty*, pp. 204–5. Miller, *Diary*, XVIII, 496.

largely recruited from Western Hungary. The Oedenburg (Sopron) district supplied Vienna with vegetables, dairy products, and fresh meat. Graz was also supplied with foodstuffs largely from Western Hungary. The note continued:

By transforming these regions into foreign countries through the creation of a political and customs frontier, the draft reëstablishes a barrier from which commerce had been free since the time of the discovery of America, and separates our three most important industrial centers from their vegetable gardens, from their farms and from their agricultural land. This delimitation, so to speak, places the most sensitive points of our country within the range of the artillery of our neighbors, a state of affairs which gives rise, at this moment, to inconveniences and to serious apprehensions. . . .

German-Austria has the right to claim these territories for geographic, national and economic reasons; however she does not aspire to any arbitrary annexation that does not place her cause, here as in every other territorial question, under the self-determination of nations. This is why we ask that the right be granted to the inhabitants of these territories themselves deciding by a free plebiscite whether or not they wish to be joined to German-Austria.[129]

It is important to note that Austria put forward no claim other than what might be established by the holding of a plebiscite to determine whether or not Western Hungary should become part of Austria. Irrespective of whether or not she was justified in claiming any territory at all from her former partner in the Monarchy, who had loyally stood shoulder to shoulder with Austria throughout the war which they had both lost, it should be admitted that the Austrian attitude in

[129] Almond and Lutz, *The Treaty*, pp. 276, 278–79. In the memorandum annexed to this note it is again stated that "Desiring only those territories where the will of the population to remain united in the same country has been clearly and plainly established, German-Austria bases her claims on certain territories only under the strict reservation of the result of a plebiscite. . . ." With reference to Western Hungary the memorandum specifically claims "large coherent territories" extending east of the former Austro-Hungarian frontier, "inhabited for centuries by a fixed population of pure German race and speech," these territories comprising, according to the Austrians, some 5,000 square kilometers and a population of about 300,000 Germans. "Without demanding in advance the incorporation of the districts in question (Odenburg, Eisenburg, and Wieselburg), we must insist in declaring that it would be in agreement with the principles of international justice to grant the inhabitants of these districts a plebiscite, through which the will of the people to join their co-nations beyond the Hungarian boundaries would be clearly expressed." *Ibid.*, pp. 281, 282–83. Annexed to the memorandum concerning the frontiers of Austria was a draft convention to regulate the modalities of plebiscites to be undertaken in the territories claimed by Austria. *Ibid.*, pp. 291 ff.

this respect was in marked contrast to that of Czecho-Slovakia, Rumania, and Yugoslavia, each of which in turn seized large sections of Hungarian territory by outright annexation. Nevertheless, the Austrian claims did not pass unchallenged, and curiously this challenge came from Czecho-Slovakia. On July 3, 1919, the Czech Delegation addressed a note to M. Clemenceau, signed by Dr. Beneš and Mr. Kramarcz, protesting against the Austrian claim to Western Hungary and requesting that the Czech Delegation be given an opportunity to be heard in support of a solution other than the allocation of this territory to either Austria or Hungary.[130]

However, at the meeting of the Supreme Council of July 7, 1919, the American, British, French, and Japanese delegates agreed to ignore the Austrian request for a plebiscite, as well as the Czech protest, and decided to assign Western Hungary to Austria without a plebiscite.[131] Hungary was to retain the railway line from Pozsony to Zagreb (Agram), through Szentjános, Csorna, and Nagykanizsa. The Italian delegate dissented from this decision.[132] The decision of the Council defining the new Austro-Hungarian frontier was communicated by the Secretariat General of the Peace Conference to the Chairman of the Drafting Committee on July 19 and was incorporated in the revised peace conditions handed to the Austrian Peace Delegation on the following day.[133]

The Observations of the Austrian Delegation, dated August 9, 1919, concerning the territorial clauses in the revised peace conditions of July 20, acknowledged the decision concerning Western Hungary as follows:

It is with a sincere gratitude that the undersigned Delegation must recognize the decision made by the Conference on the subject of the German

---

[130] *Ibid.,* p. 415. The solution envisaged by Dr. Beneš was the creation of a Czecho-Yugoslav corridor; an earlier proposal made by him to this effect was disapproved by the Czecho-Slovak Territorial Commission. See *infra,* Doc. 10, p. 411.

[131] In Temperley, *History,* IV, 384–85, this decision is explained by circumstances, both physical and emotional, which would have rendered it exceedingly difficult to ascertain the true wishes of the population concerned. These were the impracticability of sending Allied forces for the supervision of a plebiscite and the confusing effect of the bolshevik revolution upon the minds and opinions of the inhabitants. To what extent these considerations did, in fact, influence the Principal Allied and Associated Powers must, despite their plausibility, be left to conjecture.

[132] Almond and Lutz, *The Treaty,* pp. 416–17. Miller, *Diary,* XIX, 510.

[133] *Ibid.,* p. 418. See also Maps 2 and 3 at the end of this volume.

regions of Western Hungary. By extending the frontiers of the young German Austrian Republic beyond these districts, the Peace Conference has effectively contributed to make German Austria viable as well as to attain the realization of the principle of the right of peoples to self-determination. German Austria desires, however, to execute scrupulously said principle which, for that matter, has been adopted as the basis of her national organization. In order to remove every suspicion of a measure which might have disposed of a territory contrary to the will of its population, German Austria takes the liberty of insisting with the Supreme Council to the end of having gathered, by way of a plebiscite under the supervision and direction of one of the principal Allied and Associated Powers, the explicit declarations of the inhabitants of Western Hungary on the subject of the State to which they desire their native soil attached. It is only this will formally declared by the people itself which may serve, in right and in fact, as a basis for the incorporation of Western Hungary in German Austrian territory.[134]

It should again be noted that although the Peace Conference, ignoring the original Austrian request for a plebiscite, allocated to Austria most, if not all, of the Hungarian territory claimed by her, the Austrians nevertheless continued to insist upon holding a plebiscite. A faint shadow is cast on the sincerity of this insistence—a perhaps unparalleled exhibition of high standards of international morality—by the simultaneous request of the head of the Austrian Delegation, Chancellor Renner, for permission from the Supreme Council to send Austrian forces into Western Hungary, ostensibly to maintain order.[135] Nevertheless, the conclusion is inevitable that the Austrian suggestion that territories should not be transferred by simple fiat was passed over by the Peace Conference, without its giving even lip service to the principle of self-determination. As stated in the final reply to the Austrian Delegation, dated September 2, 1919:

The Allied and Associated Powers have deemed it just to affect to Austria the districts of western Hungary inhabited by a German population and whose agricultural products form an important element of the food supply of Vienna and other centers. . . . Within the frontier so fixed, the ethnic character and the national sentiment of the population indicate too positively their attachment to Austria for the Allied and Associated Powers to believe it necessary to have recourse to a plebiscite, or, in any case, to par-

[134] Almond and Lutz, *The Treaty*, pp. 310, 312–13.
[135] This was a few days after the collapse of the communist regime in Hungary and the occupation of that country by the Rumanians. For the resentment caused in Hungary by this request and its effect on Austro-Hungarian relations, see *infra*, pp. 190–91.

ticipate in the organisation and the surveillance of this consultation if Austria should proceed to one.[136]

It was of course inevitable that the allocation of Hungarian territory to Austria had an adverse effect on subsequent relations between Austria and Hungary. The depth of Hungary's resentment against Austria was not wholly justified, since the Austrian claim was for a plebiscite and not for outright annexation, and the Austrians could not logically be held responsible for the decision of the Allies simply to assign the territory claimed, rather than to bother about a plebiscite. While it is true that in their final reply the Allies left it to the discretion of Austria to proceed with some sort of popular referendum in Western Hungary if she deemed this desirable, one can hardly blame Chancellor Renner and his successors in office for rejecting Hungarian suggestions for a plebiscite to decide the fate of territory which the Allies had so magnanimously assigned to Austria. On the other hand, the feeling of the Hungarians—disproportionately intense, considering the area and wealth of Western Hungary in relation to that of other territorial losses—can be explained by the fact that while they knew the Czechs, the Rumanians, and the Yugoslavs to be enemies, they did not so regard the Austrians and could not understand why a country which stood in the same relation to the Allies as they themselves should be rewarded at Hungary's expense.

As will be explained elsewhere, the question of Western Hungary was an important factor in Austro-Hungarian relations for several years to come. It was also largely instrumental in aligning Austria, for the time being at least, with Czecho-Slovakia against Hungary, at the expense of which country both benefited and whose opposition to their gains supplied them with a common cause.

The Allied reply of September 2, 1919, marks the last step taken by the Peace Conference regarding Hungary's frontiers until several months later, when the peace conditions were presented to the Hungarian Delegation. The outstanding facts to be noted from this detailed narrative are: first, that these frontiers were fully determined without hearing any Hungarian representative; secondly, that this determination became final—not because of any particular ill will on the part of the Peace Conference toward Hungary, but because the

---

[136] Almond and Lutz, *The Treaty*, pp. 423–24. For a brief survey of the proceedings of the Peace Conference with respect to Western Hungary, see the notes of Mr. P. W. Slosson concerning the Austro-Hungarian frontier in Miller, *Diary*, XIX, 509–11.

treaty of peace with Austria and other treaties signed with the other Succession States in St. Germain on September 10, 1919, committed the Principal Allied and Associated Powers to a structure of Central and Southeastern Europe which they felt could no longer be disturbed even in small details, however persuasive the arguments the Hungarians may have advanced when, several months later, they finally came to Paris.

Before taking up the second phase of the history of the Hungarian peace treaty—namely the direct dealings between the Peace Conference and the Hungarian Delegation—we must turn our attention to the tragic events in Hungary which delayed until January, 1920, the presentation of the peace terms to the representatives of that country. A brief history of these events serves as an indispensable background for the postwar relations of Hungary with her neighbors, particularly with Rumania, and for an understanding of the atmosphere in which the peace treaties in Southeastern Europe were to operate.

PART THREE

The Collapse of the Communist Regime in Hungary and the Rumanian Occupation

III. The Collapse of the Communist Regime in Hungary and the Rumanian Occupation

Prelude to the Renewal of Hostilities between Hungary and Rumania

THE ULTIMATUM which M. Clemenceau addressed to the Hungarian Communist Government on June 13, in the name of the Principal Allied and Associated Powers, did, after some difficulties, bring about the cessation of warfare between Hungary and Czecho-Slovakia. But far from ending the troubles in the Danube valley, this move of the Allies, despite its seeming success, was rather the starting point for new and unforeseen complications, carrying, as will be seen presently, the seeds of another war.

The problems which confronted the Allies with reference to Hungary were indeed confusing and disquieting. Had they been in a position to devote more attention to the situation, they might have been able to devise defter methods of dealing with it. But at the time when the events related in the preceding chapter were taking place, the primary concern of the Allies was the treaty with Germany, then ready to be signed. Considering the issues at stake in this respect, it is indeed remarkable that the Allies paid even as much attention as they did to Southeastern Europe.

The picture as it appeared to the statesmen assembled in Paris was in no way reassuring. That Béla Kun's Communist Government did not inspire much confidence in Hungary goes without saying. That they would have been glad to see bolshevism driven out of Central Europe is understandable, considering the ever-present danger that Hungary—in herself weak—might receive support from Soviet Russia and infect her neighbors with the poison of communism. Whether or not these dangers were exaggerated in the minds of the Peace Conference leaders and whether the power of Soviet Russia was overestimated is immaterial. What matters is the fact that the attitude of the Peace Conference to bolshevism was undeniably dominated by grave apprehension. Hence consideration in Paris during this period of the problems of Hungary was colored by the more or less outspoken hope or desire of putting an end to the communist regime which seemed at that moment to be firmly entrenched in Budapest and the unoccupied parts of Hungary.

The military and economic aspects of the situation, both of which had far-reaching political implications, affected not only Hungary but her neighbors as well.

Herbert Hoover, in charge of Allied relief operations, was one of the first to call attention to the pressing economic problems of Southeastern Europe, which, he argued persuasively, could not be solved until Hungary's position was clarified. In a communication to the American Secretary of State, Mr. Lansing, on July 1, 1919 (two days after the signature of the peace treaty with Germany at Versailles), Mr. Hoover pointed out that, because of Hungary's geographical and economic position, the economic destiny of the surrounding states was "almost absolutely" in the hands of the government at Budapest. In order to reëstablish international traffic and public order, Mr. Hoover suggested alternative policies. First, military occupation of Budapest under Allied control and expulsion of the communist government; secondly, informal economic negotiations for removing the blockade, without, however, recognition of Kun's Government; thirdly, the opening of international traffic to Hungary by means of an agreement with Kun under which Hungary would be policed by troops, under Allied direction, to maintain order and ensure observance of the agreement; or, finally, recognition of the communist government and the submission to it of the final peace terms. In his note to Lansing, Mr. Hoover urged that immediate action pursuant to one or the other of these policies was imperative, lest Austria be completely disorganized and the surrounding states collapse economically.[1] Mr. Hoover's apprehensions were supported by reports from Allied observers stationed in or traveling through the Danubian states, which uniformly emphasized a serious coal shortage and breakdown of transportation in and around

---

[1] Text of Mr. Hoover's letter, in AD, SH Bulletin 484, July 19, 1919. MS. The present chapter is based largely on heretofore unpublished documents. The Hoover Library on War, Revolution and Peace (cited hereafter as HWL) is preparing for inclusion in its Publication Series a collection of documents relating to the peace settlement with Hungary. The Directors of the Library have been kind enough to allow the author to see the list of documents the Library intends to publish. Some of these documents have been placed at the author's disposal for the preparation of this chapter. A large number of documents were obtained from an anonymous source. The author is glad to acknowledge his indebtedness and appreciation to those who have furnished this material.

Hungary. Several Allied observers suggested that Béla Kun's Government could be overthrown by taking account of rising Hungarian nationalist sentiment. This could be best accomplished by promising the new government a hearing on the territorial question; for, as one report pointed out, the fate of any territory with a mixed population had been decided against Hungary.[2]

The military solution was apparently under earnest consideration in Paris. While the Hungarians were evacuating recently occupied territories in Northern Hungary, pursuant to M. Clemenceau's communication of June 13, Rumanian statesmen and military leaders were busy behind the scenes preparing the ground for a breach of the definite and unequivocal assurance given to Hungary by the Principal Allied Powers that Rumanian troops would withdraw behind the frontiers, as announced by the Supreme Council on June 13, as soon as Hungary evacuated the territory awarded to Czecho-Slovakia.

During the progress of this evacuation, the Commander in Chief of the Allies, Marshal Foch, presented a report to M. Clemenceau on June 25, urging the President of the Peace Conference to delay the withdrawal of Rumanian troops from the Tisza River to the new frontiers until Hungary carried out integrally the armistice terms relating to disarmament. Expressing his belief that Rumania would scrupulously abide by the decision of the Allies, Marshal Foch stated that under the circumstances Rumania then would be placed in a difficult position because she would have to maintain a large army on her eastern frontier to keep Russian bolshevism in check. According to Marshal Foch, Rumania could protect herself effectively at the Tisza line against an attack from the west; but the frontier fixed for her on June 13 would not enable her to resist a Hungarian offensive. "In order to protect Roumania against the Hungarian peril and to avoid jeopardizing the work of the Entente in South-Eastern Europe, it is important to subordinate the withdrawal of Roumanian forces east of the Theiss [Tisza], to the integral application to Hungary of the clauses of the Armistice of November 13th,[3] that is, to impose on her an immediate demobilization, the reduction of her army to six divisions on a peace footing and the distribution of these divisions on her territory in such conditions as to exclude any measure of an offensive against her neighbors." [4]

[2] MS report of an Allied representative from Vienna, dated July 4, 1919.
[3] *Infra,* Doc. 2, p. 359.
[4] Text of Marshal Foch's report in AD, SH Bulletin 431, July 3, 1919. MS.

To what extent this proposal was the result of the independent conclusions of Marshal Foch and his military aides, who were doubtless very well informed of the situation on the Rumanian-Russian border, is impossible to say. But if there were no communications on this subject between the Allied military leadership and the Rumanians, it is an extraordinary coincidence that in a communication, dated July 2, from the chief Rumanian delegate, Mr. Bratianu, to M. Clemenceau, the maintenance of the Rumanian occupation line at the Tisza River was supported by the same line of argument as that advanced by Marshal Foch himself.[5]

The enforcement of the disarmament terms of the armistice, in accordance with Marshal Foch's suggestion, was considered by the Supreme Council at its meeting of July 5. The Council decided to request the Allied military representatives at Versailles to examine, in consultation with Marshal Foch, "the possibilities of enforcing on Hungary respect for the Armistice conditions" and to make a report in forty-eight hours. The Council also asked for a report on the arms and ammunition at the disposal of the Hungarian Government.[6]

From the report of the military representatives, dated July 8, 1919,[7] it appears that as early as June 7, the date on which M. Clemenceau first requested Hungary and Czecho-Slovakia to cease hostilities, military measures against Hungary were in contemplation, at that time, apparently, solely with a view to putting an end to the Czech-Hungarian war. The report noted first that, pursuant to the intervention of the Supreme Council, the evacuation of Czecho-Slovakian territory by the Hungarian troops had been carried out within the time limit prescribed. As to the disposition of the Hungarian Army, it was reported that Hungarian troops withdrawn from Slovakia were being concentrated in regions whence they could threaten Rumanian forces in the east and French and Yugoslav troops in the south; that new divisions then in formation would bring the Hungarian Army to from 100,000 to 120,000 well-disciplined, well-equipped troops, "animated by a very strong national feeling," and capable of offering "considerable" re-

---

[5] Text of this communication in AD, SH Bulletin 464, July 10, 1919. MS. It will be remembered that similar arguments were put forward by the Rumanians earlier in the spring when they sought to push their line of occupation deeper into Hungarian territory. See *supra*, p. 63.

[6] Text in American Relief Administration (cited hereafter as ARA), European Operations, HWL, VI. MSS.

[7] The complete text of this report is in AD, SH Bulletin 479, July 12, 1919. MS. *Infra*, Doc. 20, p. 467.

sistance. The conclusion was that in case of an offensive action against Hungary in the east and in the south, the Allied forces would be faced by at least 90,000 to 100,000 good Hungarian troops. "It must be added," the report continued, "that Buda-Pesth, the seat of the Hungarian Government and the final objective of the Entente Armies, appears now to have been transformed into a veritable fortress provided with successive lines of defence extending to a great distance and a strong defensive organization, the capture of which would without doubt entail a great effort if the Hungarian Government had not beforehand asked for peace."

The report then considered the available Allied forces which, conditional on the agreement of the Rumanian and Yugoslav Governments, amounted to some 84,000 men, of which about two-thirds belonged to the Rumanian Army. If the Czecho-Slovak Government should consent to participation, the report noted, after the previous month's reverses the Czechs would be able to reorganize at the most two divisions of about 20,000 men; the remainder of the Czecho-Slovak Army would probably not be available for action for two months, so that the Allies could muster against Hungary's 100,000 to 120,000 men only some 100,000 or 110,000.

The conclusions of the military representatives were that while military action against Hungary was possible, it presented grave risks unless the Allied troops were reinforced. The report called attention to the fact that the undertaking of military action depended absolutely upon the coöperation of Hungary's neighbors, Czecho-Slovakia, Rumania, and Yugoslavia; that serious difficulties might be expected in the course of operations; and that if action was contemplated, withdrawal of the Rumanians from the Tisza line must be postponed.

The report summarized above, as also the report of June 7, the text of which is not available, indicate clearly that military action against Hungary was seriously contemplated from the beginning of June. It can also be stated that such action would have been carried out almost exclusively by the armies of Hungary's neighbors, although under Allied command.[8] It appears, finally, that the military move against Hungary, which was originally meant to halt hostilities between that country and Czecho-Slovakia, included later the more general objec-

---

[8] There were only two French divisions—about 16,000 men—in and near Hungary. The report of July 8 proposed that the direction of any military action should be entrusted to General Franchet d'Esperay, Commander in Chief of the Allied Armies of the East.

tive of enforcing the armistice terms. It is not clear whether this was the sole objective or whether the aim was more far-reaching, namely, the elimination of a disagreeable bolshevik outpost in the heart of Europe—that of the communist government of Hungary. Marshal Foch's report of June 25 contains no indication that he had in mind a military offensive to force compliance with the armistice terms; his proposal was wholly negative in that respect. Is it possible that the action was envisaged pursuant to one of Mr. Hoover's alternative suggestions? The answer to this question may never be found. But subsequent developments indicate that whatever the original objective may have been, the elimination of the communist government in Hungary became the thing uppermost in the minds of the Allied statesmen.

It cannot be said with certainty whether Béla Kun had any inkling of what was being discussed in Paris with reference to Hungary. The archives of the communist government were not kept with a view to lightening the task of the historian. What is certain is that the Hungarians, having completed their withdrawal from Slovakia as requested by the Allies, were impatiently awaiting in their turn the fulfillment of the promise of evacuation of Hungarian territory by the Rumanians. This impatience was understandable, since the communist leaders had tried to sugar-coat the bitter pill of the withdrawal of a victorious army by emphasizing the fact that more territory would be regained from Rumania than would be given up to the Czechs. Instead of an evacuation, there were new skirmishes along the demarcation line. On July 1, the day on which the evacuation of Slovakia was completed, Rumanians crossed the Tisza at Tiszaluc and attacked Hungarian troops in process of withdrawal.[9] As days passed without any sign that the Rumanians would withdraw, the Hungarian public became restive. On July 11 Kun sent another telegram to Paris, complaining of the failure of the Rumanians to carry out the promise contained in M. Clemenceau's communication of June 13 and demanding the withdrawal of the Rumanians.[10] Kun's protest and the report of the Allied military representatives came before the Supreme Council at the meeting held on July 12. To the Hungarian protest, the Supreme Council replied by wire that the Peace Conference would not enter into any discussions with

[9] Kun telegraphed a protest to Clemenceau against this attack on July 1. Text in the archives of the Hungarian Foreign Office, MS; also in AD, SH Bulletin 509, July 18, 1919. MS.

[10] Text in the archives of the Hungarian Foreign Office. MS.

Kun's Government until the armistice terms had been carried out.[11] As to the latter, the Supreme Council instructed Marshal Foch to report on the observance or violation of the armistice by either side and to formulate a plan of operations after consultation with the governments of Hungary's neighbors, who were expected to coöperate therein.[12]

From an objective point of view, the attitude thus taken by the Supreme Council was a breach of an obligation toward Hungary. The evacuation of Hungarian territory occupied by the Rumanians had been unequivocally promised upon compliance with a single condition, namely the withdrawal of the Hungarian Army from Slovakia. This condition the Hungarian Government fulfilled. In M. Clemenceau's communication of June 13 to Kun there was no indication that Hungary must fulfill other conditions before the above unequivocal promise would be carried out. If Hungary was derelict in observing the armistice terms, her dereliction was existent in June as well as in July. If the Allies desired to call her to account for such dereliction, as they had the privilege and power to do, they could have done so on June 13 as well as on July 12. Subsequent events must be appraised in the light of this background.

At the time Kun's protest was received and considered, plans for military action against Hungary were examined by Marshal Foch, pursuant to the request of the Supreme Council. It is not without interest to note the transformation of the objectives behind the contemplated move. At the beginning, early in June, the move seems to have been conceived solely with a view to putting an end to the triumphant march of the Hungarian Army against the Czechs. In its second phase the action seems to have been directed toward disarmament in Hungary, in accordance with the armistice terms. But when Marshal Foch reported to the Supreme Council on July 17 [13] on the plan of military operations against Hungary, he spoke of "the liberation of Hungary from communism." [14] The plan suggested apparently contemplated a whirlwind action, to be finished in one week by an army of eight infantry divisions and one cavalry division, assisted by a hundred airplanes and a fleet of armored cars, all under a single command. Marshal

---

[11] *Ibid.* See also CHD, July 12, 1919 (H.D. 6), MS.

[12] CHD, July 15, 1919 (H.D. 7), MS.

[13] At this time, the highest committee of the Peace Conference was the "Council of Heads of Delegations."

[14] For the record of the meeting, see *infra*, Doc. 21, p. 471.

Foch suggested that the Allied Powers should inform the commanding officer of their desires "regarding the form of government which should be established by him" in Hungary. Steps were suggested for equipping and provisioning the Czech and the Rumanian Armies, but there is no evidence that the coöperation of the Yugoslav Army was contemplated.[15]

The meeting discussed at length the necessity for establishing a government in Hungary with which peace could be concluded. The Italian delegate, Signor Tittoni, proposed that contact be established with the counter-revolutionary Hungarian Government established at Szeged; but both the Czech and the Rumanian representatives opposed negotiations with any Hungarian faction and urged that the Allied Armies ought to march under the banner of "respect for the Armistice." The representative of the United States, General Bliss, with characteristic American honesty, pointed out that if action was to be based on the pretext of a breach of the armistice by Hungary, "the Allies must be quite clear that the fault was on the side of Hungary." He said that there was considerable doubt as to whether the Hungarians had violated the armistice, and suggested that a careful examination of the matter would show that the Hungarian Army was reconstituted in view of the violation of that armistice by the Rumanians.

Mr. Balfour protested against General Bliss's suggestion that the breach of the armistice was merely a pretext for attacking the communist government. According to the records of the meeting, Mr. Balfour stated that he was not animated by any considerations of Hungarian internal politics, little though he might approve of Béla Kun; but he agreed with the Czech representative, Mr. Kramarcz, that the Allies must not allow Hungary to become a military stronghold from which economic and political disturbances could radiate over Central Europe.

The disagreement must have been somewhat sharper than the summary record of the meeting indicates, for it was decided to postpone

[15] The explanation may be found in the rather tense relations between Rumania and Yugoslavia, due to their conflicting claims to the Bánát. See *supra,* pp.30–32. An indication of the seriousness of this tension is a complaint made by the Rumanian delegates, Messrs. Misu and Vaida-Voivoda, of the attitude of the Yugoslav army units during an alleged Hungarian attack against the Rumanian line, which was said to have occurred on July 17. The Rumanians characterized as "flagrant hostility" the conduct of the Yugoslav army command, which, so the Rumanians claimed, instead of helping, sought to prevent urgent military operations. The communication of the Rumanian delegates to M. Clemenceau is in AD, SH Bulletin 675, Aug. 11, 1919. MS.

further discussion until the following morning. Unfortunately no records of the next day's meeting of the Council are available, and the conclusions ultimately reached, if any, remain unknown. But whatever the conclusions may have been, it is not likely that they anticipated the turn of events.

An explanation of Signor Tittoni's reference to the counter-revolutionary government at Szeged appears necessary before we return to the renewal of the war between Hungary and Rumania. Although circumstances were anything but favorable for counter-revolutionary movements, the Hungarians did not wait to be saved by the Allies. The nucleus of a counter-revolutionary government was formed on May 5 in the Rumanian-occupied city of Arad, under the premiership of Count Julius Károlyi. Owing to the hostility of the Rumanians, this group decided a few days later to move to Szeged, which was occupied by the French. After having been intercepted and interned for two weeks by Rumanian military authorities, they finally reached their destination at the end of May. Soon afterwards, on June 7, 1919, Count Károlyi wrote to General de Lobit, commander of the French Army in Hungary, informing him of the formation of this government, stating that its aims were to combat communism and to reëstablish order, and asking recognition by and assistance from the Allies. The Szeged Government availed itself of every means at its disposal—but unluckily they were very small—to attract the attention and enlist the support of the Allies. A summary of its efforts to do this, as recorded by its Foreign Minister, Count Paul Teleki, shortly after the collapse of the communist regime, shows clearly a complete lack of support or even of understanding on the part of the Allies in the case of this handful of Magyar patriots who sought to deliver their country from the scourge of bolshevism.[16] This may have been due to any one of several factors. Possibly the French, who were on the spot, and through them the Allies, were influenced by the obvious limitations under which this group labored. They may have taken the position that with Kun entrenched in unoccupied Hungary and the rest of the country in the hands of Hungary's enemies, these few men could not rally enough support to carry out their plans. It may be that Count Teleki appraised the situation correctly when he concluded that the French did not wish the Szeged Government, representing a renascent national party, to succeed, and gave their support to an opposition group. "By playing

[16] For the text of this report, see *HFR,* Vol. I, Doc. 1.

the two parties against each other," he wrote, the French "prevented effective action by us, without rendering our existence impossible." Whatever the reason may have been, the fact remains that in the consideration of Hungary's problems, the first evidence that the Allied statesmen noted the existence of a counter-revolutionary movement in Hungary was Signor Tittoni's above-mentioned suggestion that contact ought to be established with the Szeged Government.[17]

The War between Hungary and Rumania and the Collapse of the Communist Regime

The reply of the Allies on July 12, that they would not deal with Budapest until Hungary disarmed, was a bitter disappointment to Béla Kun and his associates. But Kun's decision to take matters in his own hands was not solely due to the Allied refusal to request the withdrawal of Rumanian troops from Hungary, as had been promised in M. Clemenceau's communication of June 13. By this time Kun knew that the Allies sought to put an end to the communist regime in Hungary. He was cognizant of the activities of Allied representatives in Central Europe that had been undertaken with that end in view and of the simultaneous consideration of military action in Paris. Whether the initiative to oust Kun's Government came from Allied circles or from members of his own entourage who saw the handwriting on the wall is impossible to say. The fact is that William Böhm, formerly

---

[17] Thus, from the point of view of the peace settlement, the activities of the Szeged Government may not deserve much attention. Yet its significance transcends the seeming absence of concrete accomplishment. For it cannot be gainsaid that it was this group at Szeged which roused the Magyar people from the stupor into which they seemed to have fallen after the armistice. The vitality of the movement is perhaps best demonstrated by the fact that the spirit which inspired the Szeged Government in June and July, 1919, survived the emergency and continued to guide the Hungarian people, and its members have provided Hungary's leadership ever since. Its Minister of War, Admiral Horthy, became the Regent of the country. Three of Hungary's prime ministers since 1920—and Hungarian cabinet changes have been infrequent during the last twenty years—were members of or closely associated with the Szeged Government, namely, Count Paul Teleki, Count Stephen Bethlen, and Count Julius Károlyi. The same may be said of many public men who played prominent parts in the political, economic, or cultural life of postwar Hungary. This chapter of Hungarian history is nowhere discussed in the English language; the best concise survey of its activities is to be found in Gratz, *The Era of Revolutions* [in Hungarian], chap. vii, pp. 187 ff. See also Ashmead-Bartlett, *The Tragedy of Central Europe,* for a journalistic account of the origin of the counter-revolutionary movement in Vienna and the difficulties of the Szeged Government.

Commissar of War in Kun's Government, who had recently been made envoy to Austria, on July 15 approached the Austrian Foreign Secretary, Herr Bauer, with a request that he ascertain whether the Allies would deal with a socialist government and raise the blockade. Bauer agreed to act as intermediary and to make confidential inquiries through Colonel Cunninghame, the British military representative in Vienna. The latter at once reported the move to Paris and established direct contact with Böhm.[18]

But before this move could have borne fruit, Kun decided to act and to drive the Rumanians out of the occupied territories. Doubtless he hoped to bolster up his position by a successful military action, which he expected would strengthen his hold on the starving and harassed population, then becoming increasingly restive. Upon Kun's orders, the Hungarian Red Army on July 20 attacked the Rumanian lines along the Tisza and succeeded in crossing the river at several points. The Allies were informed of the attack by a telegram which Kun sent to Clemenceau, in which he stated that in view of the provocative attitude of the Rumanians he had been compelled to resort to arms and promised to "enforce compliance by the Rumanians with the wishes of the Allies." [19] The Supreme Council discussed the turn of events at its meeting of July 21 and agreed in principle to send an Allied Committee of Inquiry to Hungary. Mr. Balfour consented to the appointment of Brigadier General Gorton as the British member of such a committee; but the Council deferred its appointment, pending an expression of views on the contemplated action by the United States Government, which Mr. White agreed to obtain.[20]

On the Hungarian-Rumanian front the initial successes of the red offensive were of short duration. At the southern flank of the Hungarian Army several units, whose leaders had established contact with the Szeged Government, stopped fighting, thus enabling the Rumanians to throw their whole weight against the middle and northern sections of the front. After several days of bitter fighting, the Hungarian lines were broken in various places and the Rumanians began to ad-

[18] Communication from Colonel Cunninghame to Mr. Hoover, dated Vienna, July 16, 1919. ARA, European Operations, VI. MSS. in HWL. An account of Böhm's move and Herr Bauer's inquiry is also found in a report sent on the same date by the Italian representative in Vienna, Signor Cerutti, to Signor Tittoni. AD, SH Bulletin 500, July 17, 1919, Annex A. MS.

[19] Text in the archives of the Hungarian Foreign Office. MS.

[20] CHD, July 21, 1919 (H.D. 12). MS.

vance, crossing the Tisza on July 29. The Red Army, not too well led or fed, could no longer offer serious resistance; the end of the war was only a matter of days. On August 1 Kun's Government resigned and fled to Austria, after handing over its powers to a socialist government headed by Julius Peidl. On August 3 the Rumanians marched into Budapest.

It should be noted that while the collapse of the communist regime in Hungary was doubtless precipitated by the Rumanians, the flight of Béla Kun and of his associates cannot be attributed solely to the success of Rumanian arms. When the retreat of the Red Army began the communists were already doomed by reason of the restlessness of the starving population of Budapest and the increasingly active hostility of the peasants.

Once more the slow-moving machinery of the Peace Conference was faced with a *fait accompli*. While the war was being fought on the Hungarian plains, the course initiated by Böhm and Bauer in Vienna proceeded serenely. On July 22 Mr. Böhm informed Colonel Cunninghame that Kun had expressed willingness to withdraw if the socialists were acceptable to the Allies. If Böhm really was authorized to convey such information, it is more than likely that Kun was merely playing for time, because on that date he was still confident that he would be able to cope with the Rumanians. On the following day the American Relief representative in Vienna, Captain Gregory, reported the bases of an agreement proposed by Böhm. A temporary dictatorship of the more moderate members of the communist government was to replace Kun, repudiating bolshevism and terminating all communist propaganda. This dictatorship would at once end all confiscation of private property and would be replaced by a government representative of all classes, which would decide the question of socialization. It would invite an Allied advisory body. The agreement foresaw the raising of the blockade, the opening of the Danube to international traffic, and the supply of food and coal by the Allies to Hungary.[21]

This proposal was forwarded to the Supreme Council by Colonel Cunninghame and the chief of the Italian mission in Vienna, Prince Borghese, who, fearing further bloodshed through either revolution or by the continuation of the war, tried to find a way to bring about a painless liquidation of the communist regime in Hungary. It came

[21] The text of Captain Gregory's report to Colonel Logan in ARA, European Operations, Vol. VI. MSS. in HWL.

before the Supreme Council on July 25, but discussion was postponed until the following day, when Marshal Foch and Mr. Hoover were invited to attend.[22] At the meeting held on the morning of July 26 the Council decided that the Allies would not consider Böhm's proposal and entrusted Messrs. Balfour and Hoover with the preparation of a statement.[23] Mr. Hoover at once wired this decision to Captain Gregory in Vienna.[24] At the afternoon meeting the Council accepted the Balfour-Hoover draft and decided not only to send it to Hungary but to make it public to the world.

The statement of the Allies, issued to the press late in the afternoon of July 26 and wired to Hungary at the same time, was designed to make clear to the Hungarian people that they could not expect an end of their tribulations until they got rid of their present government. It was frankly an appeal to a nation over the head of its government, a customary procedure of postwar diplomacy. The text of the statement follows:

The Allied and Associated Governments are most anxious to arrange a Peace with the Hungarian People and thus bring to an end a condition of things which makes the economic revival of Central Europe impossible and defeats any attempt to secure supplies for its population. These tasks cannot even be attempted until there is in Hungary a Government which represents its people, and carries out in the letter and the spirit the engagements into which it has entered with the Associated Governments. None of these conditions are fulfilled by the administration of Bela Kun, which has not only broken the Armistice to which Hungary was pledged, but is at this moment actually attacking a friendly and Allied Power. With this particular aspect of the question it is for the Associated Governments to deal on their own responsibility. If food and supplies are to be made available, if the blockade is to be removed, if economic reconstruction is to be attempted, if peace is to be settled it can only be done with a Government which represents the Hungarian people and not with one that rests its authority upon terrorism. The Associated Powers think it opportune to add that all foreign occupation of Hungarian territory, as defined by the Peace Conference will cease as soon as the terms of the armistice have in the opinion of the Allied Commander-in-Chief, been satisfactorily complied with.[25]

At the same meeting the Supreme Council also requested Marshal Foch to continue negotiations with the Czechs, Rumanians, and Yugo-

[22] *Ibid.* [23] *Ibid.* [24] *Ibid.*
[25] From the archives of the Hungarian Foreign Office. MS.

slavs regarding the guarantees they would require in case of military intervention in Hungary. Apparently the Allies were dubious as to the effectiveness of their appeal to the Hungarian people to oust Kun and believed that military intervention might have to be resorted to. We do not know how accurate their information was concerning the status of the war in Hungary; but it should be remembered that on that day, July 26, the outcome of the Rumanian-Hungarian conflict was by no means certain. Although the Red Army already had suffered reverses, it was not yet evident, even to Kun and his associates and perhaps much less to the experts in more distant Paris, that the tide, if it had not yet turned, was about to do so.

The report of Marshal Foch to M. Clemenceau, dated July 29, indicates that the Czechs were prepared to make available to the Allies "the totality of the forces at their disposal" for possible action against Hungary, without asking for special guarantees. The Yugoslav Government conditioned its coöperation upon Allied support to obtain (1) the elimination of causes of friction with Italy and (2) the protection of Yugoslav territory from the Bulgarians. Finally, the Rumanian Army was prepared "to give the most complete coöperation to the Allies" in restoring order in Central Europe and asked, in addition to desiderata of a military nature not specified in Marshal Foch's report, (1) the immediate shipment of munitions and equipment ordered in France and England and (2) the sending into Rumania of locomotives to improve transportation facilities and make possible the moving of reserves from the Russian front to the Tisza.[26]

On the day Marshal Foch filed the above report the Rumanians crossed the Tisza and began their advance against the capital of Hungary; the military intervention contemplated in Paris since early June was in the course of realization, but in a very different manner from that envisaged by Marshal Foch.

On July 31 the Rumanian Peace Delegation in Paris submitted to M. Clemenceau proposals "for the Pacification of Hungary."[27] The Rumanian memorandum appealed to the President of the Peace Conference "to make possible finally the pacification of Hungary," in the expectation that Rumania might achieve with Hungary "a situation of friendly neighborliness." It said further that after the cruelties and

---

[26] Text in AD, SH Bulletin 604, July 31, 1919. MS.
[27] The text of this memorandum is in AD, SH Bulletin 618, Aug. 2, 1919. MS.; and is printed *infra*, Doc. 22, p. 473.

bloodshed of the bolshevik regime, the Allies had "the humanitarian and moral duty of making it possible for the Magyar people to determine freely its own fate." Pointing out that Hungary's pacification was of vital interest to the neighboring states and to the Allied Powers generally, the Rumanian memorandum proposed the following immediate measures:

1. Complete disarmament and demobilization of all Hungary, including the dismantling of all munition plants and the placing of all means of communication under Allied control. To assure the execution of this measure, all Hungary should be provisionally occupied by troops of Allied countries bordering upon Hungary, i.e., Rumania, Yugoslavia, and Czecho-Slovakia.

2. The issuance of a manifesto to the Hungarian people, signed by Marshal Foch and by the commanders of the Allied Armies, assuring the Hungarians that the Allied Armies were coming to free them from the bolshevist terror, to enable them to establish a new constitution on freely determined democratic bases, and to further inform them of the desire of Hungary's neighbors that she be happy and friendly, "a free State among free States."

3. The formation of a government during the provisional occupation which would be controlled by the Allied military chiefs, assisted by a commission of "political counsellors," chosen from among Czecho-Slovaks, Rumanians, and Yugoslavs of the former Hungary who were thoroughly acquainted with the Hungarian way of life and thought and who understood political conditions there. "It is not admissible," the memorandum stated, "that the Allies should exercise open and direct management of the formation of the new Hungarian Government. It was necessary to aid tactfully the elements likely to succeed and to prevent, on the contrary, the success of men and groups who might hinder a happy issue." Under the Rumanian plan, all assemblies would be prohibited until "discreet negotiations" with the selected Magyar politicians led to the formation of a new government which would then convoke an assembly to "elect" it by acclamation. Before allowing the formation of any government, the men "judged capable of forming it" should undertake formally to accept all conditions imposed upon Hungary by the Allies and to sign and ratify the peace treaty "without discussion." Elections for a constituent assembly would take place after the withdrawal of the Allied Armies.

4. The new government would be permitted to organize a police

force for the maintenance of order. The organization of an army would be allowed only after Hungary had signed the peace treaty, and within the limitations of that treaty.

5. The Allies would arrest communist leaders, but leave their trial and punishment to Hungarian authorities.

6. The expenses of the occupation would be borne by Hungary.

These Rumanian proposals for the pacification of Hungary have been set forth in detail because when they were presented Rumania was very near the point—which, in fact, she reached within two days— where she could carry out some or all of the suggestions submitted to M. Clemenceau. It will be shown how Rumanian conduct was guided by these proposals after she became master in Hungary.

As already indicated, the communist government resigned on August 1, when it became clear that further resistance to Rumania was impossible. This resignation and the formation of the new socialist government was reported at once to M. Clemenceau by Lieutenant Colonel Romanelli, chief of the Italian Military Mission in Hungary and the only Allied representative in Budapest during the last few weeks of the communist regime. Romanelli informed the Allies that the new government was ready to accept proposals worked out in Vienna with Colonel Cunninghame and the Italian diplomatic representative, Prince Borghese,[28] and transmitted new Hungarian proposals to suspend all hostilities between Hungary and the Allied Armies as soon as possible, to stop the advance of the Rumanians pending the decisions of the Supreme Council, and to conclude an armistice with a provisional line of occupation until the decision of the President of the Peace Conference on this matter. The Hungarians asked that the armistice line for the Rumanian Army be fixed at the Tisza River.[29]

The reply of the Allies, dated August 2, 1919, and signed by M. Clemenceau, was not wholly negative. It first stated that the proposals

[28] The reference is to the project which was discussed between the British and the Italian representatives, pursuant to Böhm's above-described attempts to replace Kun's Government before the Allied attitude became known through the statement of July 26; see *supra*, p. 104. While the British and the Italian representatives in Vienna were inclined to accept Böhm's suggestions, the French representative had little confidence in the plan. Nevertheless, M. Allizé reported to Paris on July 28 that in his opinion no risk would be taken by dealing with Böhm, since a government such as he proposed would offer less resistance to the peace terms than an anti-revolutionary and nationalistic government like that at Szeged. AD, SH Bulletin 601, July 31, 1919. MS.

[29] The text of this telegram is reprinted from AD, SH Bulletin 633, Aug. 5, 1919. MS.; see *infra*, Doc. 23, p. 477.

worked out by Colonel Cunninghame and Prince Borghese had not been seriously considered, since the Supreme Council believed that it ought not to interfere in the internal politics of Hungary. Next, it pointed out that the only basis of relations between the Allies and Hungary was the Padua Armistice of November 3, 1918,[30] and the communication of the Supreme Council of June 13, establishing frontiers with Czecho-Slovakia and Rumania, behind which Hungarian troops were to be maintained.[31] As to the Hungarian request to stop the advance of the Rumanians and to fix the demarcation line at the Tisza, the telegram stated that the Supreme Council would only request the Rumanian Government "to stop its troops on the positions which they now occupy" and would not ask for their retirement to the line fixed on June 13 "until the new Government at Budapest has conformed strictly with the terms of the armistice."[32]

This telegram reached Lieutenant Colonel Romanelli in Budapest on the morning of August 3; perhaps while he was reading it the advance patrols of the Rumanian Army were entering the outskirts of the capital. It was also on August 3 that the French Foreign Minister, M. Pichon, pursuant to M. Clemenceau's request, instructed the French minister in Bucharest "to demand urgently of the Rumanian Government that it halt its troops in the position which they then occupied." Whether or not the dilatory intervention of the Allies was due to lack of information concerning the true military situation in Hungary or was designed to permit the Rumanians to occupy Budapest cannot be answered. The fact is that the Peace Conference moved exceedingly slowly. At the meeting of the Supreme Council on August 4, when news of the occupation of Hungary's capital reached Paris, it was decided to send a Mission of Allied Generals to Budapest, accompanied by a small escort of Allied troops;[33] the preparation of written instructions for the mission was entrusted to Marshal Foch and Mr. Balfour.

The Supreme Council also considered the desirability of addressing a warning to the Rumanian Government and calling attention to its responsibility as an occupying power. During the discussion, the United States representative, Assistant Secretary of State Polk, expressed anx-

[30] Infra, Doc. 1, p. 355. [31] See supra, pp. 82 ff.

[32] The text of this telegram is reprinted from AD, SH Bulletin 633, Aug. 5, 1919, MS.; see infra, Doc. 24, p. 478.

[33] It may be noted that while the General's mission was dispatched in a few days, no Allied escort was ever sent to Hungary.

iety as to the possible consequences from unfortunate incidents and raised the question whether it should not be intimated to Rumania that disregard of the instructions of the Supreme Council would be visited with economic sanctions. He was prepared, however, to forego a threat of economic measures if the Council would make clear that it would hold Rumania responsible for any such incident. Finally a carefully worded communication, drafted by Mr. Balfour, was accepted and wired to the French minister in Bucharest for transmission to the Rumanian Government, the first of a series of dispatches which the Peace Conference had to address to Rumania in the ensuing weeks.[34]

The dispatch of the Mission of Allied Generals to Hungary was finally decided upon, and written instructions, drafted by Mr. Balfour and Marshal Foch, were issued at the meeting of the Supreme Council held on the following day, August 5. The Council appointed as members of the mission Major General Harry H. Bandholtz (the United States), Brigadier General Reginald St. George Gorton (Great Britain), General Jean Césare Graziani (France), and General Ernesto Mombelli (Italy).[35] The instructions to the Mission outlined its tasks as follows: to establish contact with the Hungarian Government, with a view to insuring compliance with the disarmament clauses of the armistice; to report on the present status of and outlook for disarmament; to contact the Rumanian and Yugoslav Army Commands in order to prevent, on their part, any measure likely to excite national resentment in Hungary or to cause any trouble likely to retard the conclusion of peace; and to determine the number and placement of Rumanian and Yugoslav occupation troops necessary to guarantee order and

[34] The text of this telegram was as follows: "The Conference has received assurances from the new Government of Hungary that they are prepared to disarm in accordance with the terms of the Armistice and are anxious to work in harmony with the Allied and Associated Powers. Under these circumstances the Conference have resolved to send a mission of Allied Generals to Budapest to see that these promises are fulfilled. The Rumanian Government are requested to give orders to the General commanding their troops in Hungary to conform to the policy laid down by the Mission, which represents the Conference and will act by its authority. The Conference do not conceal from the Rumanian Government their great anxiety lest some untoward incident in Budapest or elsewhere in Hungary should mar the success of the Rumanian army. Any such incident might destroy the prospects of a speedy peace in Central Europe, cause infinite sufferings to its population, and indefinitely postpone the hopes of its economic reconstruction. Those whose unconsidered action was the occasion of so great a calamity would not easily be forgiven and could no longer count on the goodwill of the peoples of the Entente, whose assistance and coöperation are so necessary if the disasters which have overtaken European civilization are to be speedily remedied." CHD, Aug. 4, 1919 (H.D. 23). Appendix "C." MS.

[35] CHD, Aug. 5, 1919 (H.D. 24). MS.

the execution of the armistice and to regulate the withdrawal of troops not needed for that purpose. To carry out Hungary's disarmament, the Mission was charged with fixing the maximum number of effectives necessary solely for the maintenance of order; disarming demobilized units; insuring the delivery to the Allies of arms and ammunition in excess of war matériel necessary for the units kept under arms; regulating the distribution among the interested Allied Powers (i.e., Hungary's neighbors) of the war matériel thus surrendered; and stopping the manufacture of war matériel by Hungary.

As a guide for its conduct in the political field, the Mission was advised: first, that, since the Hungarian frontiers had been defined by the Peace Conference and communicated to all the governments concerned, the policy of the Conference was to withdraw all foreign troops without unnecessary delay (the instructions noted a Rumanian promise to withdraw their army "as soon as the disarming of the Hungarians is accomplished"); secondly, that the blockade had been raised and that Hungary was to be allowed to import urgently needed foodstuffs at once; [36] thirdly, that these new conditions would be maintained as long as the conduct of the Hungarian Government toward the Allies was satisfactory; and fourthly, that the Allies had no desire to interfere with Hungary's internal affairs and with the choice of her government, but they could not deal with any government which could not be trusted to carry out fairly its international obligations.[37]

The appointment of the Interallied Mission and a summary of its duties were communicated by wire to the Hungarian, Rumanian, and Yugoslav Governments; [38] the communication to the two latter closed with a request that they at once instruct the commanding officers of their respective armies in Hungary to conform to the instructions of the Mission, whose members represented the Peace Conference.[39] Some

[36] The Supreme Council on Aug. 4 decided to raise the blockade against Hungary, which had been maintained throughout the nine months which had elapsed since the armistice.

[37] The Supreme Council's Instructions to the Interallied Mission of Generals is printed in full in *An Undiplomatic Diary* by General Bandholtz, the American member of that Mission, pp. 368–69. The daily notes of this distinguished American soldier during these critical weeks in Hungary's history are indispensable to anyone desiring to recapture the atmosphere in which the events here recorded occurred.

[38] Text of the telegram to Hungary in the archives of the Hungarian Foreign Office. MS.

[39] Text of the telegrams to the Rumanian and the Yugoslav Governments (the first two paragraphs being identical with those in the communication to Hungary) in Appendix "A" to CHD, Aug. 5, 1919 (H.D. 24). MS.

of the Allied Generals were already en route to Hungary to take up their duties there; but by the time they reached their destination, the international political scene in Hungary was in process of fundamental change and the Rumanian Army of occupation had begun to indulge in conduct quite contrary to the ethical and humanitarian principles enunciated in its proposals, cited above, for the pacification of Hungary, and submitted to M. Clemenceau on July 31. The auspices for the accomplishment of the tasks entrusted to the Interallied Mission were anything but favorable.

The Rumanian Occupation: The Struggle for the Reëstablishment of Constitutional Government in Hungary

When the Rumanian troops entered Budapest on August 3, proclamations were issued by the Rumanian High Command stating that the Rumanian Army came not as a foe but as a friend to free the Hungarian people from the yoke of bolshevism. Active and reserve officers of the former Austro-Hungarian Army were urged to present themselves at the Rumanian headquarters in order that a militia, or temporary police force, might be organized for the maintenance of order and discipline. Taking these professions of good will at their face value, Hungarian officers flocked in great numbers to Rumanian Army posts in Budapest and in the provinces. They were at once arrested and herded into freight cars, and within the first forty-eight hours of Rumanian occupation several thousands of Hungarian officers of all ranks were on the way to Transylvania as "prisoners of war." [40] Having thus got rid of a group of young men who might have formed the nucleus of discipline and order, the Rumanian Army then proceeded without delay to engage in Hungary's "pacification."

While the Supreme Council in Paris was deliberating the appointment and dispatch of the Mission of Allied Generals to Hungary, the Rumanian Army Command confiscated, on the morning of August 5,

[40] Most of these men reported at Rumanian Army posts wearing light summer uniforms and without equipment. They were not even allowed to communicate with their families or friends and were carried away without a change of clothes or the most essential equipment and were kept in barracks or other temporary shelters until the beginning of December, when they were finally allowed to return to Hungary, following the intervention of Sir George Clerk (special envoy of the Supreme Council to Central Europe) and energetic representations by the British Government. The apprehension and treatment of these Hungarian officers was a dark chapter in the military annals of modern history.

all hospital supplies in Budapest. Colonel Causey, Chairman of the Interallied Railway Mission for Central Europe, telegraphed from Budapest to Mr. Hoover that although the Hungarians were badly in need of such supplies, he would hold up all Red Cross supplies, kept in readiness in Vienna for just this anticipated emergency, since they would also be confiscated by the Rumanians.[41]

On the evening of August 5 the Rumanians presented an ultimatum to the already tottering Peidl Government which said that it must agree to an armistice, without discussion, by ten o'clock that night. The terms called for the delivery of all war matériel, except that necessary for an army to be organized under Rumanian supervision and not to exceed 15,000 men, including officers; the dismantling of all munitions factories, the equipment to be handed over to Rumania; the delivery to Rumania of equipment for an army of 300,000; also, of 50 percent of Hungary's rolling stock, machinery, and material for the construction, maintenance, and equipment of railways and rolling stock; of 200 touring cars and 400 trucks with accessories; of 30 percent of Hungary's live stock and agricultural machinery; of 20,000 carloads of barley and fodder; of all shipping alleged to have been taken from Rumania during the war, plus 50 percent of Hungary's own shipping. The terms also demanded the immediate release of all Rumanian prisoners of war and hostages, the payment of the expenses of the Rumanian Army throughout the period of occupation, and the supplying of coal for transportation. The ultimatum concluded with the threat that the Rumanians would withdraw to the Tisza only after all these conditions had been fulfilled.[42]

The Hungarian Government at once turned this ultimatum over to General Gorton, the only Allied General who had already reached Budapest, and also communicated it to Lieutenant Colonel Romanelli and Colonel Causey, who in turn reported immediately to Paris by wireless.[43] The Rumanian ultimatum also precipitated a government crisis, which came to a head on the following day when a group of Hungarians, representing strongly nationalistic elements, forced the resignation of Peidl's Government, preparatory to the assumption of a regency by the Archduke Joseph, a member of the Habsburg family.

The Rumanian armistice terms came before the Supreme Council

[41] Colonel Causey's telegram is in ARA, European Operations, Vol. VI. MSS. in HWL.

[42] Text of the Rumanian ultimatum in the archives of the Hungarian Foreign Office. MS.

[43] See AD, SH Bulletin 677, Aug. 11, 1919. MS.

at its meeting on August 6.[44] After discussing the situation, the Council decided to send another warning to the Rumanian Government, again through the French diplomatic representative in Bucharest.[45] On the morning of the same day, the American, British, and Italian members of the Allied Mission, who had meanwhile reached Budapest (the French group did not arrive until several days later), addressed a communication to the commanding officer of the Rumanian Army, requesting suspension of execution of the new armistice terms offered Hungary by Rumania, pending advice from the Supreme Council. The communication pointed out that these terms were "in direct conflict with the promises made by the Allied and Associated Powers which induced the Hungarian people to change their government on August 1." [46]

[44] CHD, Aug. 6, 1919 (H.D. 25) MS. It is not clear whether the information came to the Council only through the Allied representatives in Budapest or whether the Rumanians also communicated the terms of the proposed armistice to Paris.

[45] The text of this communication, signed by M. Clemenceau and dated Aug. 7, reads in part: "The Supreme Council learned on August 6th that the military authorities of Roumania at Budapest desired to impose on the Hungarian Government an armistice that contravened that concluded with Hungary in November by the Allied Powers, thereby acting in violation of the prerogative of the Allies as regards reparations. The Supreme Council therefore on that very day informed the Roumanian Government that it refused to recognize the right of the Roumanian Generals to conclude an armistice without the authorization of the Allied Powers. At the same time, the Roumanian Government was warned against any action contrary to humanity or justice which might be committed by Roumanian forces. The Roumanian Government was requested to order the commander-in-chief of the Roumanian forces in Hungary to act in conformity with the direction of the commission of Generals who represent the Conference and who act by authority delegated from it.

"The Peace Conference has as yet received no direct reply from the Roumanian Government and learns that the Roumanian Generals refuse to defer to the directions of the Allied Generals, opposing the publication of the telegram addressed by the President of the Conference to the Hungarian Government, allowing their soldiers to pillage private property, requisitioning and sending into Roumania cattle and rolling stock, subjecting Budapest to a useless blockade that is starving out the city, destroying the railways especially that from Budapest to Vienna, and finally committing a series of acts that are both violations of decisions of the Conference, of the rights of the Allied and Associated Powers and also of common humanity. . . .

"In the presence of these facts the Conference is obliged to believe that the Roumanian Government intends to defy the Conference and to separate itself from the Allied and Associated Powers.

"If the Conference is mistaken in this regard the Roumanian Government is requested to immediately destroy this impression not by words but by acts which will publicly prove that Roumania accepts and is ready to execute in good faith the policy determined upon by the Conference." AD, SH Bulletin 680, Aug. 11, 1919 (Annex XX). MS. For the French text see CHD, Aug. 7, 1919 (H.D. 26), Appendix "B." MS.

[46] ARA, European Operations, Vol. VI, MSS. in HWL.

In the afternoon four Allied officers, led by General Gorton, called at the Rumanian headquarters to protest in person against the growing excesses of the occupation troops. The Rumanian commanding officer, General Holban, not only declined to accept the protest but was most discourteous to the Allied officers. As Captain Gregory, representing the American Relief Administration in Central Europe, who was present at the interview, wired to the American Delegation: "There is nothing to be done with this situation except to settle whether Roumanians are going to loot this country [Hungary] under one guise or another and if France is going to back them; [47] then to determine whether other members of the Entente are going to have a voice in determining the future policy of Central Europe." [48] General Gorton made his report to the Allied Supreme War Council. He stated that General Holban prohibited the publication of M. Clemenceau's telegram of August 5 to the Hungarian Government, announcing the appointment of the Interallied Mission,[49] and he expressed his disapproval of the conduct of the Rumanian Army.

The Rumanians continue to perpetrate acts [he wired] which are most discreditable to a power associated with the Entente. Harmless individuals are assaulted, food, live stock, agricultural implements and rolling stock are requisitioned and sent to Rumania and through the purposeless blockade and destruction of railways, Budapest is on the verge of starvation. The latest act of wanton destruction is the demolition of the railway between Budapest and Vienna. Unless instant measures are taken to compel the Rumanians to evacuate Budapest and cease their predatory operations in Hungary, the confidence of the Hungarians in the good will of the Entente will be destroyed.[50]

These reports, together with confirmatory reports coming from other sources,[51] were received with various degrees of dismay by the

[47] The charge that France was inclined to support the Rumanians was repeatedly made from various sources. Thus according to the report of the American Commissioner in Austria, Mr. Halstead, from Budapest, dated Aug. 6, 1919, to the American Delegation, Budapest was occupied upon the advice of the French general attached to the Rumanian Army. *Ibid.* General Bandholtz recorded his suspicions of the French more than once in his diary.

[48] *Ibid.*   [49] See *supra*, p. 111.

[50] Appendix to CHD, Aug. 7, 1919 (H.D. 26). MS.

[51] For instance, Captain Gregory reported to Mr. Hoover on Aug. 7 from Vienna that the situation in Hungary was very bad. "The Rumanians continue to conduct their occupation in the most harassing manner and their attitude towards Entente representatives who are there is distinctly hostile and puts us in a humiliating position." ARA, European Operations, Vol. VI. MSS. in HWL.

Delegations of the Principal Allied Powers, and by none with greater disgust than by the Americans. A summary of these reports was submitted to the Supreme Council, at its meeting on the late afternoon of August 7, by the American representative, Mr. Polk; he also informed the Council that in view of this information, Mr. Hoover had ordered all supplies destined for Hungary held up, since the Americans did not propose to supply the Rumanians with food and medicine intended for Hungary. After hearing these reports, M. Clemenceau expressed the view that the conduct of the Rumanians could not be tolerated and he moved the dispatch of an energetic telegram to the Rumanian Government. The motion was seconded by Mr. Balfour, and it was decided to send a copy of this communication to General Gorton for transmission to his colleagues on the Interallied Mission and to the Rumanian commander in Budapest, General Holban. The original—as already indicated—was sent through the French Legation in Bucharest.[52] This was the third warning sent by the Peace Conference to Rumania in as many days.

Meanwhile the Peidl Government, as already mentioned, had been forced out of office by a coup d'état engineered by a group recruited largely from middle-class representatives, some of whom had never before played any role in political life. For several days they had been in communication with the Archduke Joseph, whom they had chosen for the role of provisional head of the state; their objective was to eliminate all traces of the leftist regime which had ruled Hungary since the October revolution. Whatever criticism may be made of the unconventional method whereby they took over the government and of their selection of a member of the Habsburg family as the head of the state, it cannot be denied that they were acting in conformity with popular sentiment. The Peidl Government, despite some halting, conciliatory gestures, failed to gain the confidence of the majority of the Hungarian people, who had difficulty in perceiving the dividing line between socialism and communism. The Archduke Joseph came to Budapest on August 7, accepted the role of provisional Governor of Hungary, and entrusted the formation of a government to Stephen Friedrich, who had begun his political career as a revolutionary under Count Michael Károlyi less than a year before, but had now emerged as the extreme right leader of the counter-revolution. The Archduke telegraphed to M. Clemenceau on August 8 concerning the political

[52] *Supra,* n. 45.

change which had occurred: "Our most urgent task for the moment is the preparation and convocation of a National Assembly as soon as possible in order that, on a constitutional basis, it may later make a definite decision on the form of the state." Until that time, the provisional government's program was the complete elimination of bolshevism, the execution of the armistice terms, the reëstablishment of internal order, and the early conclusion of peace with the Allies.[53]

Considering the complete disorganization of Hungary's political, economic, and social life after more than four months of communism and under enemy occupation, it is not surprising that Mr. Friedrich had great difficulties in forming a government; indeed it was not until August 16 that the Archduke Joseph was able to inform M. Clemenceau in a second telegram that a provisional arrangement representing more or less the bourgeois parties, with seats reserved for representatives of labor, had finally been formed under Friedrich's premiership.[54] Nor did Friedrich and his associates anticipate the opposition which the presence of a member of the Habsburg family, even as temporary head of the state, provoked in the neighboring states.

These unsettled conditions and the lack, for all practical purposes, of a government enabled the Rumanians to continue undisturbed their "pacification" of Hungary. A written protest addressed on August 8 by the Allied officers in Budapest to General Holban, requesting him to reëstablish communications by rail and water, to permit food to be brought into the capital, to reduce the number of troops in the disarmed city, and to cease requisitioning, was ignored.[55] Colonel Causey reported on the same day to Mr. Hoover that requisitions by the Rumanians were being continued, although the food situation in Budapest was worse than in Vienna at the beginning of 1919, when the famine there was at its height.[56]

On August 10 the American member of the Interallied Mission, General Bandholtz, arrived in Budapest; but though the Mission's authority was strengthened by the addition of this unusually fearless personality, it was not sufficient to give decisive weight to the Mission, which was striving valiantly to keep the Rumanian authorities within bounds. The looting of the Royal Palace was forestalled by the action of General Bandholtz on August 11, when he quartered the Allied

[53] Text in the archives of the Hungarian Foreign Office. MS. English text quoted from AD, SH Bulletin 687. Aug. 12, 1919. MS.
[54] Text of this communication in HFR, Vol. I, Doc. 5.
[55] ARA, European Operations, Vol. VI. MSS. in HWL.   [56] Ibid.

Mission there. But not having even a single company of French, Italian, or British soldiers at its disposal, the Mission was powerless to do much against the apparent determination of the Rumanians to strip the country to the bone. The Rumanians proceeded on the assumption that since the Allies were unable to enforce their will on Hungary, they would not be able to do so with respect to Rumania.[57] So the looting of Hungary continued unabated.

But the Rumanians were not the only ill which plagued Hungary. The southern demarcation line was crossed by Yugoslav troops a few days after the Rumanians occupied Budapest, and the Yugoslavs proceeded to make themselves at home in Hungarian territory. When news of this reached Budapest, Generals Bandholtz and Gorton reported to Paris and, on August 11, requested the Commander in Chief of the Yugoslav Army immediately to withdraw his troops behind the demarcation line;[58] for the time being, this request was ignored. In the north, the Czechs proceeded at about the same time to occupy the neutral zone—including the coal mines around Salgotarján—established at the end of June when the Hungarians evacuated Slovakia. The Interallied Mission requested the withdrawal of the Czech troops and the Rumanians also protested; but the Czechs replied that their occupation of the neutral zone was necessary because of the advance into Hungary of Rumanian troops and of the confused situation in Hungary. The commanding officer of the Czechs, General Mittelhauser, advised General Holban that he would maintain the provisional occupation until the receipt of orders from the Peace Conference or from the Interallied Mission in Budapest. On August 15 the Mission

[57] Erdélyi, a Rumanian from Transylvania, attached to Rumanian headquarters in Budapest as political adviser, in a conference with Prime Minister Friedrich on Aug. 11, during which he urged a union of Hungary and Rumania under King Ferdinand I, stated that Rumania did not trust the Allies. He accused the Allies of wanting to humiliate Rumania because she "refused the domination of American and British capital." According to him, Rumania did not care what the Allies or M. Clemenceau thought or did; Rumanians would follow their own policy. Memorandum of this interview in the archives of the Hungarian Foreign Office. MS. The substance of this conversation was reported on Aug. 12 by Captain Gregory to Colonel Logan. ARA, European Operations, Vol. VI. MSS. in HWL. Rumanian attempts to force a union of Hungary with Rumania were confirmed by a report of General Gorton to the Military Section of the British Peace Delegation under date of Aug. 16. Gorton reported that the Rumanians were doing their best to shake Hungary's confidence in the Allies by spreading rumors about the inability of the Allies to intervene and through a whispering campaign about revolutions in the United States and Great Britain. *Ibid.*

[58] *Ibid.*

renewed the request that the neutral zone and the coal mines be evacuated, but the Czechs again failed to obey.[59] The occupation of the
neutral zone was announced in a communication, dated August 17,
from Dr. Beneš to M. Clemenceau, giving the above reasons as the
excuse and asking the approval of the Peace Conference for Czech
troops in that zone.[60] The matter was then referred to Marshal Foch,
who returned, on August 26, a somewhat inconclusive report. After
reciting the circumstances of the occupation and the inability of the
Interallied Mission in Budapest to obtain from the Czechs the evacuation of the neutral zone, the report pointed out that such an occupation presented not only problems of a military and political but also
of an economic nature, since the exploitation of the mines in that region, on which all Hungarian railroads depended, must be insured.
The question before the Supreme Council was, according to Marshal
Foch, whether or not such a continued occupation by the Czechs was
necessary, either as security for the Czechs against Hungary or for the
maintenance of order and for the insurance of the operation of the
mines. If the question were resolved in the negative, the Supreme
Council would invite the Czech Government to withdraw its troops;
otherwise, the Supreme Council ought to fix the conditions and mode
of occupation, specifically: the forces of occupation, the state to which
it should be entrusted, i.e., Czecho-Slovakia or Rumania, and the distribution of the coal, it being understood that the satisfaction of Hungary's needs should have priority. The report concluded with the recommendation that the Interallied Mission in Hungary be invited to
submit proposals as to what ought to be done.[61] But the Salgotarján
area was, in fact, not evacuated by the Czechs for several months.[62]

In the west both Austria and Czecho-Slovakia sought to profit by
the general confusion. The Czechs sought permission to occupy the
bridgehead opposite Pozsony on the right bank of the Danube, while
Chancellor Renner on August 12 requested authorization from the
Peace Conference to occupy Western Hungary, which, as indicated
above, the Peace Conference had already decided to allot to Austria.
Both of these requests were supported by the French representative in

[59] See General Bandholtz's report of Aug. 15 to M. Clemenceau. Text in AD, SH
Bulletin 680, Part III, Aug. 19, 1919. MS.

[60] Mr. Beneš's communication is in AD, SH Bulletin 750, Aug. 21, 1919. MS.

[61] The text of Marshal Foch's report is printed *infra*, Doc. 30, p. 490.

[62] It was not until the beginning of Nov. that the Interallied Mission succeeded in
bringing about the evacuation of this region. See *HFR*, Vol. I, Doc. 35.

Austria, M. Allizé, on the ground that otherwise the Rumanians might occupy those territories.[63] Neither request was granted by the Peace Conference; but the action of Chancellor Renner evoked particularly bitter feelings in Hungary and brought forth a sharp protest to the Austrian Government, to which the Austrians replied in an acrimonious note.[64]

On the political front the assumption of Hungary's governorship by the Archduke Joseph evoked a chorus of protest from the neighboring governments. The first cry was raised by Czecho-Slovakia, whose Foreign Minister, Dr. Beneš, addressed to M. Clemenceau a long memorandum, dated August 12, setting forth the point of view of his government toward political developments in Hungary. Expressing the fear that it would not be long before the monarchy in Hungary were restored if the Archduke Joseph were permitted to manage her affairs, the note stated the irreconcilable opposition of the Czechs to the Habsburgs. "It is a Germanic dynasty," wrote Dr. Beneš; "it never will be anything else; it is a proud, absolutist and anti-liberal dynasty the very name of which is deeply hated . . . by every Czech." He said that every Czecho-Slovak entertained feelings of profound hostility toward everything which recalled the Habsburgs and that the Archduke Joseph's accession to power in Hungary evoked "astonishment, surprise and fright" among the Czechs, whose opposition to Béla Kun's regime was not greater than that to Archduke Joseph. Dr. Beneš flatly stated that no peaceful collaboration between Czecho-Slovakia and a Habsburg-governed Hungary would be possible, a warning which he felt in duty bound to utter when the Peace Conference was about to take up the Hungarian question. The reasons for this attitude of the Czechs were not merely sentimental:

For the Habsburg Dynasty would never give up regions out of which it has been driven, even if it signed the Treaty; it would never give up Slovakia, as it believes itself heir to the throne of St. Stephen which should, according

[63] The communication of M. Allizé is in AD, SH Bulletin 707, Aug. 14, 1919. MS.

[64] For the text of these notes, dated Aug. 16 and 20 respectively, see *HFR*, Vol. I, Docs. 4 and 7. The rumors spread by Austria concerning alleged persecution of the German-speaking inhabitants of Western Hungary induced the Hungarian Government to propose to the Interallied Mission the dispatch of a fact-finding commission composed of Allied and neutral representatives to be chosen by the Supreme Council. This proposal was also communicated to the Austrian Government. For the text of these communications, both dated Aug. 27, see *HFR*, Vol. I, Docs. 11 and 13. No action was ever taken on this proposal.

to its opinion, include entire former Hungary. Filled with Germanic spirit, it will try by every means to intrigue among the Germans in Czecho-Slovakia to make trouble for us and to unite again some day under its sceptre the territories of former Austria-Hungary. The same problem arises for the Transylvanians and for the Serbo-Croats in the South. If the Habsburgs reign at Budapest, it will not be long before Vienna is undergoing the influence of the intrigues of this dynasty.

In short, Dr. Beneš considered the reappearance of a Habsburg in Hungary as extremely dangerous for the peace of Central Europe and, expressing regret that the Allies did not intervene in Hungary to help in the establishment of a democratic government, he implored the President of the Peace Conference not to recognize or to support the regime established under the Archduke, who, he concluded, "on the day following the signature of the peace will combine with all the former German Pan-Germanists and imperialists to begin again the policy of revenge." [65]

The importance of this communication lies less in the influence which it may have exerted on the decision of the Allies with respect to the Archduke Joseph's provisional regime than in the full disclosure of Dr. Beneš's own attitude, which, owing to the dominant position which he occupied during the existence of the Czecho-Slovak Republic, became a corner stone of Czech foreign policy and a determining factor in Czecho-Slovak-Hungarian relations. [66]

The next protest came two days later, on August 14, from Rumania, in the form of a note from the Rumanian legation in Paris addressed to the French Foreign Minister, M. Pichon, who transmitted it to the Supreme Council. [67] It is likely that this move was the result of Dr. Beneš's influence in Paris, for the Rumanian authorities in Budapest seem at that moment to have been supporting to some extent both the Archduke and Prime Minister Friedrich, in the hope that through them they might achieve the union of Hungary and Rumania. The third protest from the Yugoslav Delegation, dated August 15 and signed by Prime Minister Pasić, followed the Czech note closely in its

[65] Dr. Beneš's note is printed in full, *infra,* Doc. 27, p. 483.

[66] In a conversation which the author was privileged to have with Dr. Beneš in Geneva in early Sept., 1935, the Czech statesman stated emphatically that in his opinion a Habsburg restoration either in Vienna or in Budapest would threaten the existence of Czecho-Slovakia infinitely more than any plan or move by National-Socialist Germany.

[67] Text in ARA, European Operations, Vol. VI. MSS. in HWL.

line of argument, though not in phraseology, and may have been drafted after consultation with the Czech representatives in Paris. The fear was expressed that the Archduke Joseph's administration would be a first step toward Habsburg restoration in Hungary, which, in turn, would be a serious threat to the surrounding countries. Therefore the Yugoslav note asked the Peace Conference not to recognize the government headed by the Archduke Joseph.[68]

These protests found sympathetic hearing in the Supreme Council. The reply dispatched on August 18 in answer to the Archduke Joseph's request for the recognition of Friedrich's Government stated that the Allies could not recognize and conclude peace with a government which, as far as they could judge, did not represent the country. "The mere fact that the head of the State is a Habsburg, diminishes the possibility of feeling confidence in the administration which has in any case been established by a *coup d'état* during a foreign occupation." The message, signed for the Supreme Council by M. Pichon, concluded with the usual protestation that of course the Allies did not wish to intervene in Hungary's domestic affairs, but wished to be assured that her government represented her people. A legislature elected by universal secret suffrage seemed to the Supreme Council a necessary preliminary to any satisfactory arrangement and any stable peace.[69]

Just how these necessary preliminaries could be accomplished, under conditions with which both the Supreme Council and the Interallied Mission in Budapest were apparently quite unable to cope, was not indicated in M. Pichon's message. It must have been evident to the Allied statesmen that Rumania intended to do what she pleased in Hungary, irrespective of what the Allies did; and her plans did not seem to include, for the time being at least, the creation of a stable peace or an atmosphere suitable for universal, secret suffrage. While the Supreme Council was patiently awaiting a reply to its several communications from Bucharest, reports were pouring in from Allied officers in Budapest about the refusal of the Rumanians to recognize the authority of the Interallied Mission and to heed its requests. The Mission finally asked the Supreme Council to define its authority and to inform the Rumanian Government accordingly.[70] When this matter came before the Supreme Council on August 13, no reply had been received as yet

[68] Mr. Pasić's note is printed in full, *infra,* Doc. 28, p. 486.

[69] Text in the archives of the Hungarian Foreign Office, MS.

[70] Telegram from the Interallied Mission at Budapest to the Supreme Council, Aug. 12, 1919, in AD, SH Bulletin 680, Part II, Aug. 14, 1919. MS.

from Bucharest to the three urgent communications sent to the Rumanian Government on August 5, 6, and 7.[71] The Supreme Council then resolved to inform the Rumanian Government and the Allied generals in Budapest that the Mission was invested with the authority conferred upon it by the Supreme Council's instructions issued on August 5.[72] It was not authorized to give direct orders of a military character to the Rumanian generals; but it was qualified to communicate to them the view of the Allied Powers. Unless the Rumanian Government intended to break away from the Allies, it would give to its generals the necessary orders to conform to the decisions of the Peace Conference. "The Conference cannot believe," the telegram concluded, "that the Rumanian Government will, by refusing to conform to the views of the Allied Powers, take a decision so serious in its consequences." [73]

Finally, on August 14, a reply from Rumania was received and submitted to the Supreme Council. It is to be noted that the reply was dated August 9; but the reason why its transmission from Bucharest to Paris took five full days has never been explained. Even in those turbulent days telegraphic and wireless communications traveled at a somewhat faster pace. Acknowledging the above detailed communications from the Peace Conference, the Rumanian note expressed painful surprise over the undeserved reproaches and accusations contained therein. Rumania intended to work in harmony with the Allies in Hungary as elsewhere and orders were issued to the Rumanian military command to collaborate with the Interallied Mission at Budapest. To facilitate this collaboration, the Rumanian Government had appointed Mr. Diamandi as High Commissioner in Hungary. Concerning the occupation of Budapest, the note stated that the city was already occupied when the request of the Peace Conference to halt the advance of its troops was presented to the Rumanian Government in the afternoon of August 9.[74] Concerning requisitions, the note stated:

[71] Supra, pp. 110, 111, 114.   [72] Supra, pp. 110–11.

[73] CHD, Aug. 13, 1919, (H.D. 30). MS. Text of the Supreme Council's telegram to the Interallied Mission in Budapest, in AD, SH Bulletin 680, Part II, Aug. 14, 1919. MS.

[74] No explanation has been found anywhere for the delay of various communications of the Peace Conference in reaching the Rumanian Government. It will be remembered that all these communications were sent through the French legation in Bucharest. It is possible that the delay occurred in transmission; but suspicions were expressed in Allied circles, both in Paris and in Budapest, that the messages were deliberately delayed at the French legation in Bucharest or were allowed to go serenely on their way through the bureaucratic routine of the Rumanian Foreign Office.

Rumania could not conceive that, after the bloody combats which resulted in the surrender of all the enemy's organized forces to the Rumanian army, she would not have the right to take possession of the war material that the former had used to attack her, without being prevented by the situation created by the previous armistice [that of November 13, 1918]. As to the other requisitions, they were levied only in proportions that assured, in addition to the needs of the population, large quantities for exportation, and did not compromise the economic activity of the country.

Requisitions were claimed to be further justified as a measure to recoup losses suffered by Rumania during the World War, when Rumania was occupied by German and Austro-Hungarian armies; the note alleged that the greater part of the spoils were left in Hungary. With respect to the conduct of the occupying troops, the note continued:

The Rumanian Government regrets that the Allies should have taken into consideration the slanderous accusations preferred by an unscrupulous enemy.[75] Far from encouraging pillaging, the Rumanian troops, by their very presence, reëstablished order and checked anarchy and devastation. The presence of the Representatives of the Allied Powers at Budapest is a testimony to such a state of affairs. The Rumanian Command, from the very first days, adopted measures to insure the provisioning of the Hungarian Capital which it had found completely deprived of provisions. Railroad transportation was interrupted only temporarily in the strict interest of military security. Concerning the Governments which have succeeded Bela Kun, they have been neither established, nor replaced, nor interfered with by the Rumanian troops.[76]

The note closed by expressing Rumania's conviction that "she has rendered an eminent service towards the work of peace which is the object of the Peace Conference."

However, the testimony of Allied representatives in Hungary in no way supported the flat denial by the Rumanian Government of the

[75] It should be noted that all complaints against the conduct of the Rumanians from the opening days of the occupation came to the Peace Conference exclusively through Allied representatives in Hungary, who presented their reports on the basis of occurrences which they witnessed. It was only after the middle of August that the political situation in Hungary was sufficiently clarified to enable Hungarian authorities to present complaints to the Interallied Mission. Although verbal protests were doubtless made galore by those in charge of Hungarian government departments, as well as by individuals, the first formal written protests to the Interallied Mission by the Hungarian Foreign Office found in the archives bear the date of Aug. 16, 1919. *HFR*, Vol. I, Docs. 2 and 3.

[76] The complete text of the Rumanian note of Aug. 9 is printed *infra*, Doc. 25, p. 479.

excesses charged against the occupying authorities. It is possible of course that the Government in Bucharest was uninformed or misinformed by its military leaders as to the true state of affairs in Hungary and protested its innocence in good faith. But the reports coming from Budapest were so weighty that they more than counterbalanced the claim of the Rumanian Government that its army in Hungary "has never lost sight of the duties towards humanity and civilization which were incumbent upon it." The Supreme Council's reply, dated August 14, sent under M. Pichon's signature after consideration of the Rumanian communication, noted with satisfaction the declaration of the Rumanian Government "that it has decided to act in accord with the policy which the [Peace] Conference shall fix regarding Hungary." This declaration was interpreted as indicating Rumania's intention to conform to directions already forwarded to Bucharest as well as to the decisions to be communicated through the Allied representatives in Budapest. The Supreme Council reiterated its position that Rumania alone might not requisition war matériel, railway stocks, agricultural equipment, and the like, since all Hungarian properties constituted a common security of the Allies and their distribution among the various claimant states and Rumania's share therein could be determined only by them in common.[77]

The Rumanians then made another gesture toward the Peace Conference in Budapest. The Rumanian High Commissioner, Mr. Diamandi, accompanied by General Mardarescu, the Commander in Chief of the Rumanian Army in Hungary, appeared at the meeting of the Interallied Mission and acknowledged the authority of the Mission as the representative of the Conference. The Mission requested the Rumanian representatives to cease immediately all requisitioning except in zones authorized by the Mission and only to the extent needed for the army as reported to the Mission; to return at once to the owners all private property taken by the Rumanians; to return to the Hungarian Government all railway, post-office, and telephone equipment; to suspend the requisitioning of buildings and to evacuate as rapidly as possible all schools and other public buildings; to stop at once the shipment of rolling stock and Hungarian property of whatever

---

[77] The complete text of the Supreme Council's communication to the Rumanian Government is printed *infra*, Doc. 26, p. 482. A copy of this telegram, together with the text of the Rumanian note, was also wired to the Interallied Military Mission in Budapest. See Bandholtz, *Diary*, p. 9.

kind to Rumania and to return whatever was already en route to Budapest; to limit supervision over public and private life in Budapest to
the extent approved by the Mission; to furnish the Mission, at the
latest by August 23, with a complete list of all war matériel, railway
and agricultural equipment, live stock, and any other property that
had been seized in Hungary by Rumanian forces; and finally, to cease
further occupation of Hungarian territory. The Rumanian representatives gave assurances that there would be full coöperation with the Mission.[78]

However good the intentions of the Rumanian Government and of
the Rumanian Army Command may have been, the promises of good
behavior were not fulfilled. The requisitions continued on an even
larger scale, despite the incessant efforts of the Interallied Mission to
prevent them.[79] Reports continued to pour into Paris and induced the
American Assistant Secretary of State, Mr. Polk, to demand an urgent
consideration of the situation in Hungary by the Supreme Council. In
a letter dated August 20, addressed to M. Clemenceau—copies were
also sent to Messrs. Balfour, Tittoni, and Matsui—he called attention to
the systematic and wholesale seizure of Hungarian assets by the Rumanians, confirmed by the reports of eyewitnesses, which was likely
to jeopardize the possibility of securing reparations from Hungary.
Rumania, by appropriating to her exclusive use enemy assets which
were the common security of all the Allies, was destroying the principle
of joint and several liability of the ex-enemy states, laid down in the
treaty with Germany as the fundamental basis of reparations and previously accepted as such by Rumania.[80]

It is true that while Mr. Polk's argument puts the emphasis upon fear
that Allied interests in reparations were adversely affected, rather than
upon humanitarian considerations for Hungary and her people, it is
obvious that the attempt to save Hungary's assets would, if successful,
redound to her benefit. The result of Polk's intervention was a decision

[78] Bandholtz, *Diary*, pp. 10–13. General Bandholtz's report on this meeting to the
American Peace Delegation is in ARA, European Operations, Vol. VI. MSS. in HWL.

[79] General Bandholtz noted in his diary on Aug. 19: "It is not possible to describe
conditions in a city or country occupied by an enemy, but judging from conditions in
Budapest and Hungary while occupied by the Roumanians, we Americans should
promptly take every measure possible to avoid any such catastrophe. Universal training
should be adopted without further parley." *Diary*, p. 18. Had this advice been heeded
at that time, the second World War might never have occurred.

[80] Mr. Polk's letter is printed in full, *infra*, Doc. 29, p. 488.

of the Supreme Council on the following day (August 21) to refer the matter to the Organization Committee of the Reparation Commission and to request a report from the Interallied Mission in Budapest as to the practicability of posting Allied officers at frontier points to prevent the exportation from Hungary of goods requisitioned by the Rumanians. The Mission was authorized to put such a plan, if feasible, into effect.[81] Nothing came of it, since the Mission did not have sufficient personnel at its disposal, and it so informed the Supreme Council on August 30.[82] Thus there appeared to be no effective means at the disposal of the Allies to stop Rumania from carrying away whatever she could lay hands on.[83] The only thing which the Rumanians could not touch was the shipping on the Danube. The head of the Allied Danube Commission, Admiral Troubridge (Great Britain), firmly told the Rumanians to keep their hands off; since he was in a position to back up his admonition by armed patrol vessels anchored off Budapest, the Rumanians obeyed.

The Rumanian attitude toward the position of the Allies with respect to requisitions was conveyed to the Interallied Mission by Mr. Diamandi on August 23. According to the Rumanian point of view, the rolling stock taken from Hungary did not constitute assets to which all the Allies had a claim; therefore Rumania believed herself entitled to requisition not only what was indispensable for her army, but also 30 percent of all equipment found in Hungary. The Mission at once reported this to the Supreme Council, adding that requisitions and the shipping of goods of all kinds into Rumania would continue. The Mission was contemplating the sending of Allied officers to the main transshipment point, Szolnok, to supervise shipments, but it had no power to prevent requisitions. "As far as the Rumanians are concerned," the report concluded, "the Mission has been practically valueless and consequently the Mission considers that it would be useless to continue negotiations with the local Rumanian authorities who follow a course of procrastination with the evident intention of getting possession of

[81] CHD, Aug. 21, 1919 (H.D. 35) MS; cf. Bandholtz, *Diary,* p. 26.

[82] AD, SH Bulletin 680, Part V, Sept. 3, 1919. MS.

[83] General Bandholtz reported on Aug. 20 to the American Delegation that no action had been taken by the Rumanians with respect to the demands presented by the Mission on Aug. 16 to Mr. Diamandi and General Mardarescu (*supra,* pp. 125–26), and that requisitions continued. In particular, a great quantity of telephone and telegraph equipment had been carried away. Text in ARA, European Operations, VI, 379. MSS. in HWL.

everything of value that remains in Hungary and who constantly fail to carry out their promises." [84]

The situation which confronted the Allied statesmen in Paris was indeed disconcerting. On the one hand, their small allies bombarded them with protests and descriptions of the dire consequences which would ensue if a Habsburg were allowed to direct, even temporarily, Hungary's affairs. On the other hand, their own representatives in Hungary kept the wires hot with reports of defiance by the Czechs, Rumanians, and Yugoslavs of every order issued by the Peace Conference. How could peace, so ardently desired by everyone, be concluded under such circumstances?

As to the internal political situation in Hungary, the Allies decided that a regime under the leadership of the Archduke Joseph was not acceptable; [85] this decision was communicated to the Interallied Mission in Budapest by M. Clemenceau in a telegram dated August 22. [86]

[84] The text of this report was before the meeting of the Supreme Council at its meeting held on the day following. CHD, Aug. 24, 1919 (H.D. 38). MS. A much more strongly worded report from General Bandholtz to the American Delegation, also dated August 23, indicates that it was primarily the American and British members of the Mission who stressed the point that there was no use in dealing with the local Rumanian authorities. See Appendix "B" to the Minutes cited above. The next day, August 24, Bandholtz reported that General Graziani, the French member of the Mission, did not want this view communicated to the Supreme Council. The telegram, originally drafted by Graziani in French, did not contain the passage quoted in the text. Bandholtz was then asked to draft it in English; but when that was translated into French, the translator had changed it into what he called "better French" and again left out the statement upon which both Bandholtz and Gorton insisted. Finally the literal French translation of Bandholtz' draft was turned over to General Mombelli for incorporation in the Mission's report. For a description of this incident by General Bandholtz himself, see Bandholtz, *Diary,* pp. 31–32, 35.

[85] To what extent this decision was the result of the protests of the Succession States (see *supra,* pp. 120–22) cannot be ascertained.

[86] The full text of this telegram is printed in Bandholtz, *Diary,* pp. 30–31. See also CHD, Aug. 22, 1919 (H.D. 36), Annex "G." MS. The telegram stated that while the Allies were most anxious to conclude a lasting peace with the Hungarian people, they did not feel that this could be done with the existing government, established by a coup d'état and headed by a member of the Habsburg family. Were the Archduke Joseph willing to submit to a popular election, the Allies would not regard the result of an election carried out under an administration controlled by him as satisfactory. "In the interest, therefore, of European peace the Allied and Associated Governments must insist that the present claimant to the leadership of the Hungarian State should resign, and that a Government in which all parties are represented should appeal to the Hungarian people." The message concluded with the statement that the Allies would be prepared to negotiate with "any government which possessed the confidence of an Assembly so elected," and instructed the Mission to publish the message in Hungary.

The Mission transmitted the message to the Archduke Joseph on the following afternoon, giving him two hours in which to reply and advising him that in case of noncompliance with the wishes of the Supreme Council, the message would be released to the public. At eight o'clock that evening the Mission was informed that the Archduke and the government had resigned and that the Mission might take over the administration of the country. This the Mission refused to do, on the ground that the Allies had no intention whatever of interfering with Hungary's internal affairs, and it suggested to Prime Minister Friedrich that he and his associates continue in office until a government, acceptable to the Allies, had been formed.[87]

Thus, by the fiat of the Allies, Hungary was plunged into another government crisis which was to last for several weeks, until, despite repeated protestations that they did not desire to interfere with internal affairs, the Allies sent Sir George Clerk to disentangle the political situation in Hungary.[88] A share of the responsibility for this crisis must be allocated to the Hungarian leaders who failed to sense and to comprehend the distrust and hostility felt by the heretofore subject peoples toward the name of Habsburg. Whether this distrust and hostility had any foundation or justification in fact is immaterial;

[87] Bandholtz, *Diary,* pp. 32–33. The Mission's report on this incident was laid before the Supreme Council at its meeting of Aug. 25. CHD (H.D. 38), Annex "B." MS.

[88] Mr. Friedrich tried to obtain temporary recognition for a newly formed government after the Archduke Joseph's resignation. He announced the formation of this government in a communication dated Aug. 28 and addressed to M. Clemenceau. Pointing out the impossibility of forming a government satisfactory to the Allies, the Hungarian political parties, and the Rumanian occupying authorities, Mr. Friedrich claimed that his reconstituted cabinet enjoyed the confidence of the Hungarian people. He stated that he intended to hold elections within four weeks, on the basis of universal secret suffrage, which, he requested, should be supervised by an Allied mission, including a Social-Democratic representative, and asked for the support of the Allies. (Text of this communication in MS in the archives of the Hungarian Foreign Office.) In transmitting this communication to Paris, the Interallied Mission commented that in their opinion the reconstituted Friedrich Government did not meet the requirements of the Supreme Council, as set forth in the message of Aug. 22 which brought about the retirement of the Archduke Joseph. (The report of the Mission to the Supreme Council, containing the text of Mr. Friedrich's letter, is in AD, SH Bulletin 680, Part VI, Sept. 4, 1919, MS.) Friedrich's Government stayed in office for several weeks, and although the Interallied Mission dealt with it as the *de facto* authority exercising governmental powers and functions, it was never recognized by the Allies. Technically, of course, this, as well as the succeeding government of Charles Huszár, formed itself and did not take office pursuant to an election or other expression of popular will. Sir George Clerk's mission and his efforts to bring about the formation of a government acceptable to the Allies will be described below.

political wisdom would have dictated a realistic appraisal of the reaction likely to follow the appearance of any member of the former ruling dynasty as the present ruler of Hungary.

However, in addition to the question of the Habsburgs, there were other obstacles to that "free expression of popular will" which the Allies desired as the foundation of a government with which they were prepared to conclude peace. It was evident that the popular will could hardly be expressed freely while the Rumanians were roaming and looting the country. So after disposing of the Habsburg question, for the time being at least, the Allies had to turn their attention again to Rumania.

At the meeting of the Supreme Council held on August 23 it was decided to send another energetic note to Rumania, pursuant to the position outlined in Mr. Polk's letter to the Heads of Delegations.[89] The first part of this note set forth, in almost identical language, Mr. Polk's reasoning with respect to the established principles of reparations and their violation by Rumania. It then called attention to the possible consequences of Rumania's conduct, which were regarded as "so serious and fraught with such danger to the orderly restoration of Europe, that the Allied and Associated Powers would, if necessity arose, feel constrained to adopt a most vigorous course of action to avoid these consequences." If the collection of reparations were allowed to degenerate into competitive action by the several Allied Powers, injustices would result and cupidity would be aroused, resulting in confusion advantageous only to the enemy. Refusing to believe that the Rumanian Government would wish to create such a situation, the Peace Conference requested Rumania to make an "immediate and unequivocal" declaration to the effect that her government (1) recognizes the principle that the assets of enemy states constitute a common security for all the Allies; (2) that it recognizes the Reparation Commission as the exclusive agency for the collection of enemy assets for reparation; (3) that it will account for in detail and hold at the disposal of that Commission, or of an agency designated by the Peace Conference, all Hungarian property seized by Rumania since the armistice of November, 1918 (Rumania retaining the right of disposal of only such property as could be definitely identified to the satisfaction of the Reparation Commission as having been taken from Rumania by the enemy); (4) that it will cease at once all shipments of Hungarian

[89] See *supra,* p. 126.

property into Rumania; and (5) that it will ratify the reparation agreement, signed at the end of June by the Rumanian representative. The Rumanian Government was advised that the Interallied Mission in Budapest had been authorized to act as the agent of the Peace Conference in the accounting of Hungarian properties. The Supreme Council also resolved to halt immediately and until further notice the delivery of all war matériel to Rumania, including war matériel to be delivered under contract, whether paid for or not.[90] Two days later, on August 25, no reply having been received from Bucharest, a more peremptory message was dispatched to the French chargé d'affaires in Bucharest for transmission to the Rumanian Government. M. Clemenceau put it in these words:

Reports from the Interallied Mission of Generals at Budapest indicate that despite assurance given both by the Rumanian Government and by its representatives in Paris, the Rumanian military authorities continue to remove from Hungary all her assets of every description. The Peace Conference takes note of this information with the most painful surprise. It awaits with the greatest impatience the reply of the Rumanian Government to the telegram addressed to it by the Supreme Council on the 23rd inst. which confirmed the Supreme Council's views which on various occasions have already been repeatedly expressed. The Supreme Council feels bound to notify the Rumanian Government that if the conduct of the Rumanian authorities in Hungary is not entirely and immediately modified, such attitude would bring forth for Rumania the most serious consequences.[91]

Most conveniently, the Rumanian Government seems never to have received the first of the above-mentioned communications, that of August 23. Equally conveniently, M. Clemenceau's telegram of August 25 reached the Rumanian Prime Minister only on August 31, in the afternoon, as appears from a note, dated September 5, from the Rumanian Peace Delegation in Paris to M. Clemenceau. Mr. Bratianu's reply, addressed through the French chargé d'affaires in Bucharest, M. Saint-Aulaire, to the Peace Conference, claimed that the communication of August 23 was never received and for that reason was never answered. Mr. Bratianu also claimed that Rumanian authorities had in the past and would in the future respect instructions given by the Rumanian Government and that information furnished to the Supreme

[90] See AD, SH Bulletin 767, Aug. 23, 1919. MS; also CHD, Aug. 23, 1919 (H.D. 37), Appendix "A." MS.
[91] CHD, Aug. 25, 1919 (H.D. 38), Appendix "C." MS.

Council in this respect was "surely erroneous." The reply concluded with an expression of painful surprise that as a result of such "erroneous" information the Supreme Council had stopped the shipment of war matériel allotted or due to Rumania.[92]

In the meanwhile, the magnitude of the plunder of Hungary was unfolded before the Allied representatives in Paris. When Major Borrow, of the British Army, visited Szolnok about August 24, he found the railway tracks from Budapest to Szolnok choked with cars, partly empty, partly loaded, and a great number of engines, awaiting the opening of the bridge over the Tisza River, which had been destroyed during hostilities.[93] On August 28 General Bandholtz sent a detailed report, in which the British member of the Mission, General Gorton, concurred, to the American Delegation in Paris concerning Rumanian requisitions since August 16. According to this report, on August 16 106 railway cars were seized and on the next day 24 engines and 74 cars. The Rumanians broke into the Ministry of War and removed telescopes, cameras, typewriters, and telephones. On August 18 they took from an estate near the capital cattle valued at 700,000 crowns, and left 20,000 crowns in payment; on the same day, they took from a warehouse 140,000 flour bags, the property of the Austrian Government, and relieved the Siemens-Schuckert factory of several hundred coils of insulated wire. The machinery of munitions factories was dismounted and removed and all airplanes were seized, despite protests that some of these planes were for the use of the Allied forces. Stallions and breed-

[92] The text of Mr. Misu's communication to M. Clemenceau is in AD, SH Bulletin 680, Part VII, Sept. 8, 1919. MS. The Rumanian Peace Delegation had already protested on Sept. 2 to the President of the Peace Conference against the order of the Supreme Council stopping the transport of food and war matériel to Rumania. The text of the communication, signed by Messrs. Misu and Vaida-Voivoda, is in AD, SH Bulletin 849, Sept. 6, 1919. MS. On Sept. 3 Mr. Misu informed M. Clemenceau that, according to telegraphic advice from Bucharest, the Rumanian Prime Minister had not received, up to the morning of August 31, any communication from the Peace Conference. Mr. Bratianu desired that Mr. Misu call the attention of the Peace Conference to the "pernicious and dangerous" character of its policy toward Rumania, i.e., the stoppage of delivery of food and war matériel; and claimed that Rumania had rendered a great service to the Allied cause by the occupation of Budapest and the destruction of bolshevism. The communication closed with the statement that since the Peace Conference did not take account of Rumania's sacrifices, the Rumanian Government was considering the desirability of withdrawing its army east of the Tisza River, "declining all responsibility for the chaotic state into which it will plunge this region of Europe, disputed by the Bolshevists and the monarchical reactionaries." AD, SH Bulletin 928, Sept. 22, 1919. MS.

[93] See Bandholtz, Diary, p. 39.

ing animals from the government breeding stations were taken, throughout the territory under Rumanian occupation. Machinery, tools, cloth, and electrical apparatus, amounting in value to many millions of crowns, were taken from the warehouses and depots of government departments and private industrial establishments. Visiting several places in Budapest with General Gorton, Bandholtz found that about 2,400 carloads of goods had been carted away from the warehouses of the Hungarian Discount and Exchange Bank. At the central depot of the Postal Administration, they found several cars loaded with shoes, uniforms, and rags, and the Rumanians were engaged busily in removing machinery from the repair shop. From the Central Sanitary Depot 132 carloads of material was removed, the Rumanians having stripped the building to the walls. "If the Rumanians continue at the present rate," the report concluded, "they will soon leave Hungary as a charge upon the Allies instead of in a condition to pay an indemnity." [94]

As to the possibility of any Hungarian resistance to or attack upon Rumania, the Interallied Mission reported by wire to the Supreme Council on August 29 that, apart from some 8,000 ill-equipped men under the command of Admiral Horthy, stationed in unoccupied territory west of the Danube, the Hungarian Army had ceased to exist and, in the opinion of the Mission, had been reduced for some time to come below the number of effectives foreseen in the armistice of November 13, 1918. [95]

Thus the Supreme Council was confronted on the one hand by reports pouring in from its own trusted representatives in Budapest, picturing the continued and systematic looting of Hungary by the Rumanians; and on the other hand by occasional but belated denials from

[94] Text of this report in ARA, European Operations, Vol. VI. MSS. in HWL. Cf. Bandholtz, *Diary*, pp. 42–43. Bandholtz noted in his diary on Aug. 30: "Our beloved Roumanian allies are continuing merrily with their requisitions and seizures, and apparently have not the slightest intention of letting up until they have cleaned Hungary out of everything worth taking." *Ibid.*, p. 48. And on the next day he wrote: "The Roumanians are paying not the slightest attention to the last ultimatum sent them and are going right along with their looting, which has become a habit." *Ibid.*, p. 50.

[95] Text of this report in AD, SH Bulletin 680, Part V, Sept. 3, 1919. MS. During the first days of August Admiral Horthy, Minister of War in the counter-revolutionary government, had moved with the handful of men, mostly commissioned and noncommissioned officers, whom he had organized at Szeged during June and July, to the region of Lake Balaton west of the Danube. There he had at once began to recruit volunteers and to organize a force large enough to take over at least the policing of the country. These troops became the nucleus of the Hungarian National Army.

the Rumanian Government that anything improper had happened, coupled with noncommittal assurances of Rumania's devotion to the Allies. Desire to create conditions which would make the conclusion of peace with Hungary possible, together with a growing realization of the danger that Hungary's economic assets would be irrevocably lost for whatever reparation she would be required to pay, finally overcame procrastination, and the Supreme Council decided at its meeting on September 5 to send a special envoy to Rumania. The person chosen for the task of bringing the recalcitrant Rumanian Government back into the Allied fold was Sir George Clerk. While this step did not end the unprecedented conduct of the Rumanian occupation authorities in Hungary, the appointment of Sir George marks the beginning of the process of clarification which led to the partial evacuation of Hungary, to the formation of a Hungarian Government acceptable to the Allies, and ultimately to an invitation to send Hungarian plenipotentiaries to Paris to receive the peace terms.

Sir George Clerk's Mission to Rumania

The Supreme Council's instructions to Sir George regarding his mission to Rumania, issued over M. Clemenceau's signature and dated September 5, outlined his tasks as follows: he was to carry to Bucharest and to deliver to the Rumanian Government a note restating the views of the Supreme Council regarding the position of Rumania in relation to the Allied and Associated Powers. Sir George was not directed to make orally any official comment upon the Allied note; but he was empowered "to reply, semi-officially, to any request for enlightenment" which the Rumanian authorities might require and in general to be available for such exchanges of opinion as he might judge necessary.[96]

The declaration of the Supreme Council which Sir George was to deliver to the Rumanian Government was drafted by Mr. Balfour. It expressed, at the outset, the "deepest concern" of the Allies over Rumanian policy in Hungary, which seemed to indicate that Rumania proposed to follow her course independently of the Allies. Rumania's failure to withdraw behind her new frontiers, i.e., those made public on June 13, as requested by the Peace Conference, had been excusable under the allegation of self-preservation as long as the communist gov-

[96] The text of Sir George Clerk's instructions is in AD, SH Bulletin 863, Sept. 8, 1919. MS.

ernment in Hungary, disposing of an army in excess of that authorized in the armistice, was attacking or was threatening to attack Rumania. But this argument had no longer any force, when "assuredly no considerations of national security can any longer be urged by the Rumanian Government in defence of their recent action." If Hungary should fail fully to conform to the armistice terms, the remedy was to be administered collectively by the Allies and not by way of individual action by Rumania, which she had taken "in a manner which seems wholly without excuse." The declaration continued:

Hungary, suing for peace, already partially disarmed, in the throes of revolution, without allies and without food, has been overrun by troops, who under order from Bucharest, systematically strip it of every species of movable wealth, alive or dead, which seems worth the labour of transportation. Cattle, horses, agricultural implements, raw material, machinery, railway equipment, even the outfit of a children's hospital, choke the lines which lead from Buda Pesth to Roumania. Wherever there are Roumanian soldiers, and Hungarian prisoners to work for them, everything is being taken that can be taken, however necessary it may be to provide employment in the towns or to raise food in the country. . . .

While Rumanian soldiers may have believed that since they were only taking back what presumably the Central Powers, Hungary included, had taken from Rumania, their conduct needed no defense; but the Rumanian Government must have known that the "rough and ready method of exacting reparation" was neither just nor expedient in the common Allied interests. The Rumanian Government, when organizing the plunder of Hungary, must have known that the principles of reparation, to which the Rumanian representatives had assented, were being violated. As the note further stated,

These considerations are so obvious in themselves, and have been so earnestly pressed upon the Roumanian Government, that the Associated Powers are reluctantly compelled to ask themselves whether Roumania still counts herself among their number. None of the events that have occurred during the last few weeks are of a nature to reassure them. Remonstrances addressed to Bucharest have remained without reply. Remonstrances addressed to Roumanian representatives in Paris have been of no effect. Remonstrances made in the name of the Conference by the Allied generals at Buda Pesth have been met with fair promises. But the promises have not been kept. Roumania has persistently treated Hungary as a conquered province, and herself as its conqueror, sole and irresponsible. There is no sign that she still deems herself a member of an Alliance, or that in her judgment the Five Great Powers who mainly won the war have any predominant claim to settle the terms of peace.

In order to determine without delay, "for good or for evil," where Rumania stood, the Peace Conference demanded a "clear reply" to the questions of whether Rumania was prepared (1) to withdraw her troops from Hungary on a date to be fixed by the Conference; (2) to cease requisitioning in Hungary immediately; (3) to turn over to the Reparation Commission Hungarian property already taken; and (4) to coöperate loyally with the Allies and under their direction to restore order in Hungary, thus enabling a responsible government to conclude peace.[97]

With this statement of the Allied position in his brief case, Sir George Clerk left for Bucharest on September 7; but the news which reached Paris while he was en route did not augur too well for the success of his mission. This news created the conviction among the Allied statesmen that while the tone of the communication which Sir George was then carrying to Bucharest was stern, it was not stern enough to cope with the provocative attitude adopted by Rumania toward the Allied Powers. For the Peace Conference had received further evidence of Rumania's defiant attitude in the form of a memorandum from that country's Prime Minister, Mr. Bratianu, stating the position of his government with respect to the peace treaty with Austria, the signature of which was then imminent.[98] This memorandum began by calling attention to the great services which Rumania claimed to have rendered to the Allied cause and by protesting against the draft treaty which "seriously injures her rights and interests," specifically by imposing on

[97] The complete text of this communication is printed *infra*, Doc. 31, p. 492. The decisive tone of the Supreme Council's note was, in all likelihood, attributable to the growing impatience of the American Delegation. In informing General Bandholtz of the mission of Sir George Clerk to Bucharest, General Bliss wrote from Paris in a letter dated Sept. 4, 1919: "If this [i.e., the note] is not promptly effective and if the Entente then shows inability or unwillingness to apply further pressure upon the Roumanians, I think it very likely that our Government may relieve you from the Mission of Generals at Budapest, although it may leave you there as an independent observer. We shall think that the time has come to make everybody in Europe understand that if they expect further coöperation and assistance from the United States they must play the game properly or we will show them at once that we intend to withdraw completely and leave them to their own resources." Bandholtz, *Diary*, pp. 87–88.

[98] This memorandum was transmitted by the Rumanian Delegation in Paris to the Peace Conference on Sept. 9, one day before the Austrian treaty was signed at Saint-Germain-en-Laye. See AD, SH Bulletin 882, Sept. 11, 1919. MS.

Rumania obligations to accept in advance the decisions of the Allies in regard to the treatment of minorities, transit, and trade. "In form and content this stipulation is incompatible with the dignity, the internal security and the economic interests of a sovereign state." The memorandum also protested against the "arbitrary and artificial" division of the Bánát, to the detriment of political and economic interests of the first importance to Rumania and contrary to the sentiments of the great majority of the inhabitants. Bitter complaints were also raised against the frontiers laid down between Hungary and Rumania and against the Allied injunctions against Rumanian requisitions in Hungary.[99] "The Rumanian Government felt obliged to declare," the memorandum concluded, "that, for the above cited reasons, it is impossible to adhere to certain clauses inserted in the Treaty with Austria and cannot agree to sign the Treaty if the Supreme Council thinks it unnecessary to revise certain stipulations which attack the dignity and the interests of Rumania." [100] In fact Rumania did not participate in the signing of the Austrian peace treaty on September 10 at Saint-Germain-en-Laye; nor did she sign the minorities treaty which she was requested to sign at the same time.[101]

In addition, reports were received from the Interallied Mission in Budapest that requisitions in Hungary continued on a large scale, despite promises made to the Mission by Rumanian authorities in Hungary and denials to the Peace Conference by the Rumanian Government.[102] Neither had any progress been made toward clearing up the confused political situation. The unrecognized Friedrich Government, harassed by the Rumanians and unable to cope with the problems pre-

[99] This part of the Rumanian memorandum is printed in full, *infra,* Doc. 33, p. 497.

[100] The text of the rather lengthy Rumanian memorandum is in AD, SH Bulletin 882, Sept. 11, 1919. MS.

[101] Rumania's signature was not obtained to either of these treaties until several weeks later, following the replacement of Mr. Bratianu's Government by that presided over by Mr. Vaida-Voivoda. The Supreme Council's growing irritation with Rumania is thus to be explained not merely by her attitude toward the Hungarian question, but also by her defiance of the Allies with respect to the peace settlement in Southeastern Europe in general. See in this connection Temperley, *History,* IV, 231–36.

[102] Up to and including Sept. 8, the Rumanians had requisitioned in railway equipment alone 1,160 passenger coaches, 62 private Pullman cars, including the royal train, 21 sleeping cars, 281 service and postal cars, 15,161 box and 7,713 flat cars, 1,767 oil tanks, and 678 engines. Already 8,877 cars and 245 engines had passed through Szolnok and 4,391 cars through Csongrád on their way to Rumania. From the report of the Interallied Mission at Budapest to the Supreme Council, dated Sept. 12. AD, SH Bulletin 680, Part X, Sept. 15, 1919. MS.

sented by a penniless country and a starving population, threatened
in desperation to place the government of Hungary in the hands of the
Interallied Mission, unless the Allies were prepared to extend moral
and material assistance to Hungary.[103]

It was under these circumstances that Sir George Clerk arrived in
Bucharest on September 11. On the following morning Mr. Bratianu's
Government resigned, presumably in protest against the minorities
clauses of the Austrian peace treaty.[104] Sir George had his first interview with Bratianu on September 12, after the resignation, and Bratianu
was in the comfortable position of being at the head of a government
remaining in office temporarily in order to carry on the administration
until the formation of a new government and, as such, being able to
assure the special envoy of the Supreme Council that he wished to
work in "complete harmony" with the Allies. This assurance in no
way committed Rumania, since Mr. Bratianu, as he himself pointed
out to Sir George Clerk, no longer held a political position qualifying
him to give a formal and final reply to the Allied declaration which
Sir George handed to him.[105] After studying the Supreme Council's
communication, Mr. Bratianu explained his position to Sir George, in
an interview which took place on the morning of September 16. Mr.
Bratianu thought the Allied statement was unjust to Rumania, both
in form and substance, and was founded on uncorroborated evidence.
He claimed that Rumania never intended to separate herself from the
Allies. While admitting that isolated acts of abuse might have occurred

[103] Communication from Mr. Friedrich to the Interallied Mission, dated Sept. 6, 1919.
MS in the archives of the Hungarian Foreign Office. The English text of this communication, transmitted to the Supreme Council by General Gorton, was reproduced
in AD, SH Bulletin 680, Part XII, Sept. 18, 1919. MS and is printed in full, *infra*, Doc.
32, p. 495. The issue thus raised was considered at the meeting of the Council of Heads of
Delegations held Sept. 11, 1919; M. Clemenceau said that he was not prepared either
to extend credits to Hungary or to see the government handed over to the Allied Generals. See Miller, *Diary*, XVI, 508.

[104] When the American member of the Interallied Mission in Budapest, General
Bandholtz, visited Bucharest from Sept. 7 to Sept. 9, complaints about the minorities
clauses and Rumanian resentment in this connection loomed large in the interviews
he had with the King, Prime Minister Bratianu, and the Minister of War, General
Vaiotanu, who succeeded Bratianu at the end of September and held the office of
Prime Minister during the elections which were called following Bratianu's resignation. See Bandholtz, *Diary,* pp. 64–78. General Bandholtz undertook this trip in the
hope that, by personal contact with the Sovereign and the head of the government,
he might succeed in putting an end to Rumanian requisitions in Hungary.

[105] Sir George Clerk's first reports from Bucharest, dated Sept. 12 and 13, are in
AD, SH Bulletin 863, Sept.—(n.d.). MS.

during the advance of the Rumanian Army, Mr. Bratianu claimed that they were against his policy and instructions and would be punished, if proved. For the occupation of Budapest, without the consent of the Allies, Mr. Bratianu assumed full responsibility, expressing the belief that for both the security of Rumania and of Europe such a step had been essential.

With respect to the four specific questions addressed by the Supreme Council to Rumania in the declaration of September 5,[106] Mr. Bratianu said that (1) Rumania was not only disposed but anxious to withdraw her army from Hungary, the maintenance of which was a heavy drain on Rumanian finances; since the Allies suspected and hindered measures taken in the "general interest" by the Rumanian Army, Mr. Bratianu had given orders for immediate withdrawal. As for points (2) and (3), only requisition of war matériel, railway equipment, and supplies for the occupation army were authorized, and orders had been given to pay either by money or by requisition orders for supplies requisitioned. Mr. Bratianu agreed to the taking of an inventory of all requisitions for the Reparation Commission, provided that Rumania was represented on the Commission. (4) The maintenance of order and the existence of a responsible government in Hungary were more essential to Rumania than to any other outside power; but Mr. Bratianu insisted on the necessity for real collaboration and claimed that Rumania should not be asked to carry out orders without previous consultation.

In reporting this interview to the Supreme Council, Mr. Bratianu's reply to the last point which, in Sir George's opinion, was a "somewhat obscure phrase," was understood by him to mean that Rumania's interests with respect to future relations with Hungary were so great that a Hungarian Government must give guarantees satisfactory not only to the Allied Powers but also to Rumania.[107]

A separate report was sent by Sir George concerning the explanation which Mr. Bratianu gave him, during the same interview, on the subject of Rumanian requisitions in Hungary. Sir George was assured that the Rumanian Government was careful not to injure Hungary's economic life; from the beginning, it made it a rule to requisition only

[106] *Supra,* p. 136.

[107] Sir George Clerk's report of Sept. 16, transmitted through Budapest, is quoted in full in the minutes of the meeting of the Council of Heads of Delegations, held on Sept. 23, 1919. Miller, *Diary,* XVI, 534 ff.; also in AD, SH Bulletin 929, Sept. 22, 1919. MS.

30 percent of the articles the army was authorized to seize, the requisitions being based on the armistice conditions which Rumania wished to impose on Hungary.

Mr. Bratianu also stated that, having learned from the newspapers of the Allied note of August 23,[108] the Rumanian Government decided to recognize the principle that the property of enemy states constituted a common security for all the Allied Powers and that of the exclusive competency of the Reparation Commission to allocate enemy property to cover reparation claims; but Rumania demanded representation on the Commission and insisted that war matériel and railway equipment captured during hostilities could not be included among property constituting common Allied assets. Rumania also reserved the right to regard as her own property that identified as having been taken from her by the Central Powers during the World War. Finally the Rumanian Government had ordered the occupying forces at once to halt all removal of Hungarian property into Rumania, except with the consent of the Peace Conference, and had since ordered the cessation of all requisitions except those necessary for the maintenance of the army of occupation.[109]

The Rumanian point of view with respect to the situation in Hungary was further elaborated by Mr. Bratianu in another interview with Sir George Clerk on September 20, a few days before Sir George left Bucharest.[110] Mr. Bratianu again asserted that all requisitions of private property in Hungary had been stopped; therefore he thought that there would be no difficulty in reaching a mutually satisfactory agreement on this point, in principle at least, between the Supreme Council and Rumania. On the other hand, an agreement had still to be reached concerning the conditions of the Rumanian evacuation of Hungary. Mr.

---

[108] As indicated above, the Rumanian Government claimed that it never received this note from the Supreme Council, which had been wired to the French diplomatic representative at Bucharest for transmission to the Rumanian Government. See *supra,* p. 131.

[109] This report of Sir George Clerk, also dated Sept. 16, is in AD, SH Bulletin 945, Sept. 25, 1919. MS.

[110] On Sept. 19 Sir George reported to Paris that he intended to leave Rumania on the twenty-second since a prolongation of his stay might be used by political parties, jockeying for position in the still-unsolved government crisis, to further their own interests; Sir George also reported that he would stop at Budapest to consult with the Interallied Mission and the Rumanian diplomatic representative, Mr. Diamandi. See Miller, *Diary,* XVI, 537. In fact, Sir George did not receive the Supreme Council's instructions which he had asked for until Sept. 28 and he did not leave Rumania until the twenty-ninth.

Bratianu felt that the evacuation should take place only when a government guaranteeing order in the evacuated territories had been formed, one which would be supported by the Peace Conference and by the Rumanian military authorities. Mr. Bratianu felt that the declaration of the Peace Conference that the choice of such a government was the exclusive concern of the Hungarian people was a "theoretical formula," inasmuch as the Allies could not be indifferent to either the domestic or the foreign policy of this government. He summed up Rumania's desiderata as involving a renunciation by Hungary of all claims with respect to Rumania's new frontiers, and further territorial concessions in Rumania's favor, namely that (1) the mouth of the Maros River, (2) the Békéscsaba railway junction, and (3) a zone sufficient to insure the safety of the Nagyvárad-Szatmár railway be included within the Rumanian frontiers.

In support of this renewed claim for further extension of territorial gains, Mr. Bratianu observed that: (1) possession of both banks of the Maros to its mouth was an economic necessity of the greatest importance for Rumania, since the river "is the only navigable waterway that penetrates to the center of the Kingdom"; (2) the economic life of the region of Arad depended on the Békéscsaba railway junction, and the majority of the inhabitants were Slovaks who repeatedly had expressed a desire to be united with Rumania; (3) the life and security of Western Transylvania depended on the Nagyvárad-Szatmár railway, which should therefore be protected by a zone of at least 20 kilometers (about fourteen miles) in width.

Mr. Bratianu thought that the Peace Conference had rejected his proposals with respect to the tracing of Rumania's western boundaries as above described only because of fear of Magyar hostility and opposition; but he claimed to know that Budapest could be induced to accept the frontier he proposed. He told Sir George that Hungarian statesmen of all political parties had made proposals for an understanding with Rumania; but the Rumanian Government did not wish to enter into any agreement without the knowledge and consent of the Peace Conference. "Without such agreement," Mr. Bratianu stated, "the Rumanian Army could not help to set up a Hungarian Government which, after having been made master of the situation would not give the guarantees necessary for peace in Central Europe and tranquillity in Rumania." He expressed the hope that the Allies would recognize Rumania's vital interests in this matter; if not, he or his successor would have only two courses. One would be to adopt an individual policy toward Hungary, irrespective of what the Allies desired; this he would not do. The other would be to evacuate Hungary immediately, leaving her to her own fate.[111]

Although Mr. Bratianu appeared conciliatory and full of good intentions in his dealings with Sir George Clerk, the fact remains that as far as concrete accomplishments were concerned, Sir George's endeavors to bring Rumania into line with the Allied Powers were as complete a failure as the notes of the Supreme Council which had been dispatched to Bucharest since the beginning of August. Assurances, promises, and denials he got galore; but one looks in vain for the fulfillment of these promises or for evidence in support of the denials. While Mr. Bratianu told Sir George that the Rumanian Government had ordered the stopping of requisitions, when the newspapers had brought to its attention the Supreme Council's protest of August 23 against such requisitions, the Interallied Mission in Budapest reported to Paris that requisitions and the removal of seized property continued unabated.[112] One cannot fail to notice certain contradictions in the Rumanian Prime Minister's own statements. On September 16 Mr. Bratianu told Sir George Clerk that orders had already been given to the Rumanian Army to withdraw from Hungary, while on September 20 he proposed such withdrawal as a threat, destined to turn Hungary into chaos should the Allies fail to pay due attention to Rumania's interests. It may

[111] The above summary is based on Sir George Clerk's memorandum to the Supreme Council on this interview, dated Sept. 20, 1919, reproduced in full in AD, SH Bulletin 1001, Oct. 4, 1919. MS.

[112] On Sept. 17 the Mission reported that parts of Hungary were being evacuated, but the Rumanians were taking with them everything they could lay their hands on, without paying for the seized property. They took everything, whether jewelry or a farmer's only team of oxen. Fodder and live stock in great numbers were taken by Rumanian army units moving eastward. According to the Mission's report, 684 engines, 16,153 railway cars, including 201 private saloon coaches and 946 passenger coaches, had so far crossed the Tisza. Thousands of carloads of munitions, guns, autos, airplanes, other war matériel, railway equipment, and agricultural machinery had already been carried away, and the contents of over 4,000 cars could not be ascertained. AD, SH Bulletin 680, Part XIV, Sept. 19, 1919. MS. Cf. Bandholtz, Diary, pp. 90, 95. On Sept. 20 the Mission reported the volume and seizures of exportations up to noon of Sept. 18. According to this report, 75 percent of the eastbound trains were loaded with horses, cattle, and forage, under the escort of Rumanian soldiers. The central freight yard at Budapest was crowded with trains loading confiscated property, and 212 carloads of machinery, tools, and electric motors, to an estimated value of 65,000,000 crowns, were removed from the Arms and Machine Factory of Budapest. The total of rolling stock previously seized grew to 800 engines and 19,800 cars. AD, SH Bulletin 680, Part XVIII, Sept. 25, 1919. MS.

also be noted that Mr. Bratianu had used Sir George Clerk's presence to renew Rumanian claims, previously considered and disallowed by the Peace Conference, for further extension of her frontiers westward at Hungary's expense.[113] Mr. Temperley's criticism of Mr. Bratianu's attitude and policy [114] is more than borne out by contemporary and incontrovertible evidence.

The failure of Sir George Clerk's mission to Rumania is best illustrated by two important documents: One is a memorandum dated September 23 on Hungary's economic situation resulting from Rumanian requisitions, which Sir George was sent to stop; the other is Sir George's final report on his mission, dated October 7, after his return to Paris. These two documents bring out in sharp relief the events which took place in both Hungary and Rumania during those weeks and they deserve careful analysis.

The first of the two documents was prepared by the American representative on the Organization Committee of the Reparation Commission; [115] its origin may perhaps be traced to the concern expressed by the Assistant Secretary of State of the United States, Mr. Polk, in his letter of August 20 to the Heads of Delegations, in which he pointed out that the wholesale seizure of Hungarian property by the Rumanians would jeopardize the common Allied interests in securing reparations from Hungary.[116] Although the report was primarily written from the point of view of the reparations problem and proposed certain steps chiefly in order to re-acquire from the Rumanians what was considered common assets of the Allies, the facts upon which its conclusions were based indicate the extent to which Hungary had been injured during the six weeks since the Rumanian occupation had begun.

The report stated at the outset that Rumania had removed property from Hungary far in excess of her share under the reparation policies agreed upon by the Allied and Associated Powers, thus prejudicing the

[113] The rectification of frontiers proposed by Mr. Bratianu, together with additional demands along the Rumanian-Ruthenian border and with certain claims of an ecclesiastical nature, were further urged in a lengthy note addressed by Mr. Vaida-Voivoda on behalf of the Rumanian Peace Delegation in Paris to M. Clemenceau. This note, dated Oct. 10, 1919, is printed in full, *infra,* Doc. 36, p. 513.

[114] Temperley, *History,* IV, 230–35, *passim.*

[115] The American representative on the Organization Committee of the Reparations Commission was Mr. E. L. Drexel, assisted by two secretaries, Major Tyler and Captain Morris. The author was unable to ascertain which of these American officials journeyed to Hungary and prepared this report.

[116] See *supra,* pp. 126–27.

claims of the other Succession States, i.e., Italy, Czecho-Slovakia, Poland and Yugoslavia. As a result of the stripping of Hungary of all its seed grain, live stock, agricultural machinery, and so forth, the minimum needs of the Hungarian population would soon have to be supplied by Rumania's allies. Rumania had a substantial surplus of foodstuffs before she began emptying Hungarian warehouses; she would now be in the "curious position" of supplying, at a profit, foodstuffs and other classes of requisitioned property to her allies, particularly Poland and Czecho-Slovakia, from stocks in which those states had a joint ownership. Hungary would have to be taken care of by the Allies, in the same way in which they had been forced to help Austria, although this would not have been necessary had Rumania awaited the orderly disposition of her claims by the Reparation Commission. "However," the report stated, "by her systematic stripping of Hungary, without preoccupation as to leaving the minimum necessities for the Hungarian population during the coming year, Rumania has thrown this burden on her Allies." It was further pointed out that since the Allies had not approved the removal of Hungarian property and no Allied representatives had been present at the time of its removal, there was no basis for determining what part of the property taken was identifiable as having been taken from Rumania by the Central Powers and thus due to Rumania under the policy of restitution adopted by the Allies. Therefore it must be assumed that none of the property sequestered by Rumania in Hungary fell within the so-called "restitution" categories, and hence the total value of this property must be charged to Rumania's reparation account until she successfully proved to the Reparation Commission that all or part of such property originally belonged to her.

A proposal, today, on the part of Rumania [concluded the report], to abide, in the future, by the terms of her engagements with the Allied and Associated Powers could not be accepted as an equitable solution of this matter. An agreement to any such proposal would be to the sole interest of Rumania with an entire disregard of the other Allied interests, as such agreement could only be construed as a "quitclaim" or approval of all Rumania's appropriations of Hungary's values and property to date. Any agreement entered into today with Rumania should be predicated upon her admission of the right to [of] her allies to make a joint inquiry into what has happened in the past and to fix their own and Rumania's interests in all Hungarian values and property in the manner hereinafter set forth.

The recommendations to be proposed to the Supreme Council were as follows:

First, That a Special Commission, including representatives of the Allied and Associated Powers having property and financial interests in Hungary under the Reparation clauses, which interests have been either partially or wholly appropriated by Rumania, be established at once in Budapest for the purpose of listing and valuing the property removed by Rumania in contravention to Rumania's engagements with her allies and in contravention of the direct and specific instructions of the Supreme Council.

Second, That this Special Commission will establish the value of the various Allies' equities in Hungarian values and property appropriated by the Rumanians, in accordance with the reparation policies adopted by the Allied and Associated Governments, and that these values will be at once reported to the Committee on Organization of the Reparations Commission, so that upon the establishment of the Reparations Commission, they may be appropriately entered against the Rumanian accounts, under the various treaties of peace which have or are to be formulated.

Third, That this Special Commission investigate and report to the Supreme Council the fiscal and other effect on Rumania's Allies of Rumania's appropriation of foodstuffs, grain seeds, live stock, agricultural machinery, etc., with reference to its effect on future purchases by them of Rumanian food and other surpluses and the similar direct or indirect effect of Rumania's action so far as it affects benefits accruing to Rumania's Allies from Austrian and Hungarian reparations.

Fourth, That this Special Commission is empowered to give proper credit to Rumania for values and property returned to Hungary up until the time of the closing out of its operations and to make appropriate cancellations on this account on reports submitted to the Supreme Council or to the Organization Committee of the Reparations Commission, as provided for in the preceding paragraph.

In conclusion, the report suggested that the proposed special commission should include, in addition to the Principal Allied and Associated Powers, representatives of Yugoslavia, Poland, and Czecho-Slovakia (no representation for Rumania was proposed) and should have its first meeting at Budapest on September 28.[117]

The second document, Sir George Clerk's final report on his mission to Bucharest, is dated October 7. As far as Allied-Rumanian relations are concerned, this report is complementary to the earlier reports, summarized above, which Sir George had sent to the Supreme Council from Bucharest, and merely relates developments during the last five days of his sojourn in the Rumanian capital. On the other hand, it gives a full account of the situation in Hungary as he found it during a short

[117] The complete text of this report is printed *infra,* Doc. 34, p. 499.

stop-over in Budapest, when he conferred with the Interallied Mission as well as with Hungarian political leaders. Since it was due to his observations and suggestions that Sir George was sent on a second mission, this time to Budapest to unravel the political confusion in Hungary, his report may properly be regarded as one of the most important Peace Conference documents relating to Hungary, aside from those determining Hungary's frontiers.

As far as the conclusion of his mission to Bucharest was concerned, Sir George's report stated that he had decided to await the instructions of the Supreme Council outside of the capital, lest his presence in Bucharest be exploited by one of the political parties. The first attempt to solve the political crisis precipitated by Mr. Bratianu's resignation, the formation of a pro-Bratianu cabinet under Mr. Manolescu, failed because of the refusal of Transylvanian politicians to serve in such a government. Thereupon the King invited Mr. Take Jonescu to form a government with the Transylvanian leader, Mr. Maniu, and Mr. Jonescu agreed. Following this interview, the King received Mr. Bratianu, whereupon, instead of a government headed by Jonescu, a military government under the premiership of General Vaiotoianu, Minister of War in Bratianu's cabinet, was appointed, comprising six generals on the active list, with Mr. Misu, a member of the Rumanian Peace Delegation, as Foreign Minister. This government, which took office on September 28, the day preceding Sir George Clerk's departure from Bucharest, was, as Sir George reported, merely a continuation of Bratianu's regime in another form. Upon taking leave, Sir George was assured both by the new prime minister and Mr. Bratianu that Rumania intended to coöperate fully with the Allies, but that she could not yield on the question of the minorities treaty, which they would keep "floating" until after the elections. "I wondered," reads Sir George's report, "what would happen if the Allies, who were perhaps less interested in the skillful moves of Mr. Bratiano's internal policy, could not keep their decision waiting for the Roumanian elections, which have, I think, been successfully postponed since last January, and should demand a definite answer from Rumania in the near future." The answer of the Rumanian statesmen was that a "very serious" situation would arise. As regards Hungary, Sir George received "the most satisfactory assurances." All requisitions, beyond those of railway and war matériel and food for the army of occupation had been stopped, and Rumania was anxious to establish, in her own interests, harmonious relations with

Hungary as soon as a Hungarian Government was found with which both the Allies and Rumania could work.[118]

On his arrival in Budapest on the morning of October 1, Sir George first visited the Rumanian High Commissioner, Mr. Diamandi, who again assured the Supreme Council's envoy that requisitions had been stopped and that the needs of the local population had been cared for. However, Mr. Diamandi claimed that the dismantling of factories and the removal of machinery were justified, because Rumania thus prevented her enemy from manufacturing war matériel; and he said that since practically every Hungarian factory turned out war matériel, Rumanian action was necessarily "on a large scale." On his part, Mr. Diamandi expressed dissatisfaction with the Friedrich Government and complained of lack of support from the Interallied Mission, whose members, he claimed, "tended to look on themselves as protectors of the Hungarians against the Rumanian oppressor."

Sir George Clerk's meeting with the Allied Generals gave a slightly different picture. He was informed that the Mission was obstructed in every way by the Rumanians. They got promises but nothing else, lived in a "cloud of polite lies," and the Rumanians made it impossible for the Mission to discharge its task. Since there was no prospect of an Allied force strong enough to make the Mission's advice respected by the Rumanians, the Mission strongly urged immediate evacuation; the Allied Generals believed that Friedrich, strengthened by provisional recognition of the Supreme Council, could maintain order. With respect to requisitions, the Mission expressed the view that the Rumanians, by the "persistence, extent and stupidity" of their requisitions, forfeited, perhaps irretrievably, whatever gratitude the Hungarians may have initially felt for having been freed from bolshevism. Sir George, who was by no means prejudiced in Hungary's favor, stated that the evidence accumulated by the Mission on the subject of requisitions could not possibly be ignored. While official orders had been given to stop requisitions except for railway stocks, war matériel, and food for the army of occupation, in practice requisitioning of all sorts continued. There was the additional fact, as Sir George remarked, that the Rumanian definition of "war matériel" was very broad. Complaints registered with the Rumanian authorities were promptly ordered to

[118] It may be noted that there is no mention in the report of the withdrawal of Rumanian troops from Hungary, which Mr. Bratianu had informed Sir George on Sept. 16 had already been ordered and which, on Sept. 20, Mr. Bratianu threatened to order. See *supra*, pp. 139, 142.

be investigated and, if necessary, punished, but the matter usually ended with the issuance of the orders. The Interallied Mission had neither the personnel nor the time to see that the large number of complaints daily registered were fully investigated.

In fact, the Roumanian, who is after all a Balkan and therefore an Oriental [reads Sir George's report], and who has been pillaged and looted by the enemy and by his Russian ally, sees here, in the occupation of Hungary, an opportunity which he will consider himself a lunatic to forego. From the private soldier who "requisitions" the umbrella of a passenger leaving the station, to the officer who "requisitions" a motor car or a carpet to be sold for cash to a Jew and re-sold by the latter at a higher price to its original owner, they intend to leave this country with their pockets full. . . . While the Rumanian higher authorities may realize that this procedure is inimical to Rumania's own interests, they have apparently neither the authority nor the energy to suppress the misconduct of their subordinates.

While Sir George did not concur in the findings of the report prepared by the American Representative on the Organization Committee of the Reparation Commission as to the extent to which the Rumanians had stripped Hungary,[119] "there is no shadow of doubt," he wrote "that the common property of the Allies has been diminished by Roumanian action, and that owing largely to that action, the Allies have the additional burden of helping Hungary to regain her economic existence." [120]

Sir George also reported the interviews he had held with Prime Minister Friedrich and Mr. Garami, the leader of the Hungarian Social-Democratic party. He paid tribute to Mr. Friedrich for having shown "strength and courage in holding on to an office which is neither lucrative nor comfortable" and expressed the belief that Friedrich had established himself as a political leader for a great mass of the Hungarians. The Prime Minister, Sir George reported, sought help from the Allies not in the form of recognition but in the form of permission to hold

[119] See *supra,* pp. 143–44. "After all, the Hungarian peasant is as good as others in hiding his possession from the looter, and the Roumanian has many more accomplished rivals in the art of looting," wrote Sir George Clerk.

[120] For an account of Sir George Clerk's meeting with the Interallied Mission in Budapest on Oct. 1 and a somewhat critical appraisal of his conduct while in the Hungarian capital, see also Bandholtz, *Diary,* pp. 125–30, 132–34. The minutes of this meeting were attached to Sir George's report, summarized above, and were reproduced in full in AD, SH Bulletin 1027, Part II, Oct. 10, 1919. MS. Sir George acquainted the Allied Generals with his mission in Bucharest and expressed the opinion that the Supreme Council would not agree to the frontier changes proposed by Mr. Bratianu.

elections under Allied supervision in order to preclude charges of pressure. Friedrich also assured Sir George that he could maintain order in Budapest when the Rumanians left.

On the other hand, Mr. Garami advised the representative of the Supreme Council that the Friedrich Government could not assure either domestic order or an early peace with the Allies, both of which Hungary badly needed. Since Mr. Garami did not wish to see Friedrich eliminated by another revolution, he thought that the Supreme Council ought to repeat the message sent a month before, demanding the resignation of the Archduke Joseph.[121] "It was no longer possible to be rigid about non-intervention in the internal affairs of Hungary," Mr. Garami told Sir George. He urged the necessity of a clear statement from the Allies of their intentions, and of the formation of what Mr. Garami called a representative government.

The problems to be solved with respect to the Hungarian question were, Sir George concluded, two in number, namely, the stopping of requisitions by Rumania and the selection of a government in Hungary with which both the Allies and Rumania could deal.

The question of requisitions had two aspects, the cessation of requisitions and the restoration of property already taken. Sir George expressed the belief that orders from the Rumanian Government to stop requisitions, however sincerely given, would be evaded as before; therefore the only real solution would be evacuation. In order to check what was being taken away, Sir George suggested a method of effective control by Allied officers, in collaboration with the Rumanians, of every shipment going from Hungary to Rumania by way of the bridges at Szolnok and Csongrád, the only two roads available for transportation.[122]

As to the restoration of property already removed, Sir George took

---

[121] See *supra*, p. 128.

[122] Sir George Clerk proposed *in concreto* that substantially increased Allied personnel should be given copies of bills of lading covering the contents of every train and authority to verify such freight by opening and inspecting sealed cars. He pointed out that the Allied officers merely checked some 6,000 sealed cars passing from Hungary to Rumania, without being able to ascertain their contents. The procedure suggested would be an improvement, in that it "would at least check and put on record the depredations that are being committed; it would facilitate the making up of the bill against the Roumanians; it would be a test of the good faith of the Roumanian government; it might even, by exposures and their consequences, deter some of the looters in their proceedings." Objections against the delay caused by the inspection of sealed cars, which were raised by Mr. Diamandi (although otherwise these suggestions were assented to by him), would have to be overruled, stated Sir George.

issue with the proposals made by the American Representative of the Organization Committee of the Reparation Commission.[123] While saying that the proposal was useful and practical "so far as it goes," he believed that Rumania should be allowed to collaborate to a greater extent than was foreseen in that report.[124] Moreover, the American plan provided only for the restoration of common property to the Allies, or for making good its value; no proposal was made for helping the Hungarians.

Even more difficult of solution were, in Sir George's opinion, the internal political problems of Hungary. After stating the conflicting views of the Interallied Mission on the one hand and of the Rumanians and "democratic Hungary" on the other hand, with respect to the recognition of Mr. Friedrich's Government, Sir George submitted the following suggestions: the Rumanians should be clearly informed of the Supreme Council's decision in regard to the territorial changes sought by Mr. Bratianu. Whatever such a decision might be, the Rumanians would no longer have any reason to flirt with Hungarian political factions in the hope of obtaining territorial concessions or an alliance in exchange for recognition and so could be induced to evacuate.[125] But before taking steps to secure Hungary's evacuation, a type of government must be set up acceptable to the Allies. Perhaps Mr. Friedrich could be induced, by appropriate pressure, to place his government on a wider basis; should he refuse, the support of the Supreme

[123] See *supra,* p. 145.

[124] The Rumanian attitude was summed up in the report as follows: "What the Roumanians feel, and feel very deeply, is that from the outset they have been prejudged by the Allies as criminals and put into the dock. They ask for collaboration and coöperation, and, instead, are haled before the tribunal for sentence. This does not make them any more ready to sink their own interests in the common stock, and if they were treated more as Allies, who have fought and suffered, and less as criminals, things would probably go far more easily. They feel bitterly such implications as that their action alone has turned Hungary into a burden on the Allies. They ask that allowance should be made for other factors: Bolshevism, moderate harvest, the peasant's general mistrust of the future, the general dislocation of economic life in Europe; all these are factors in the Allies' disappointment at Hungary proving to be not self-supporting but the whole sin is visited upon Roumania."

[125] The report on this point reads: "It is, I think, the hope of finding a more pliant Hungarian administration that is a main cause of the Roumanian objections to Friedrich and one of their principal reasons for not leaving Hungary. If the Roumanians knew that they have nothing to hope for in this respect, they might be more ready to carry out immediate evacuation. The only plea the Roumanian Government could urge for remaining would be the maintenance of order, and that could be met by insisting on the provision of sufficient arms to the Hungarian Police."

Council might be offered to a coalition government without Friedrich, prepared to meet the Allies' conditions. In that alternative, the technically still existent Parliament might be summoned to provide for an election and a plebiscite to determine Hungary's form of government.

Sir George Clerk's report concluded by urging the imposition of some solution on Hungary from the outside.

On that point all parties are agreed: that Hungary can only be saved, if the Allies intervene and by their recognition of some Government, enable that Government to exhort the authority necessary to preserve the country from ruin and anarchy. This is an interest of all Europe.[126]

The Hungarian and the Rumanian Problems before the Supreme Council

Both the memorandum of September 23 by the American representative on the Organization Committee of the Reparation Commission [127] and Sir George Clerk's final report were discussed in the meeting of the Council of Heads of Delegations held on October 10, 1919. The Council agreed to send a special committee to Budapest, charged with the duty of determining the reparation value of the property which the Rumanians had removed from Hungary. It was decided at this meeting that the special committee should consist of representatives of the Principal Allied and Associated Powers and of a Rumanian representative who would sit in an advisory capacity.[128] This arrangement was changed, over the objections of the American representative, Assistant Secretary of State Polk, at the meeting held three days later, when the French representative, M. Loucheur, insisted that the Rumanian representative should have the right to vote.[129]

Sir George Clerk was invited to attend the meeting of October 10 while his report was discussed. As far as the internal situation in Hungary was concerned, he repeated the suggestion incorporated in the report, that Mr. Friedrich be required to broaden the basis of his government; Sir George also proposed the appointment of a commission to deal with Hungary in the name of the Supreme Council. M. Berthe-

---

[126] Sir George Clerk's report, with his letter of submission, was included in AD, SH Bulletin 1027, Oct. 9, 1919. MS. The report is printed in full, *infra,* Doc. 35, p. 503.

[127] *Supra,* pp. 143–45.

[128] CHD, Oct. 10, 1919 (H.D. 67). MS.

[129] *Ibid.,* Oct. 13, 1919 (H.D. 69). MS.

lot, the French representative, opposed the recognition of Friedrich, and no conclusions were reached at this meeting.[130]

The Rumanian situation was also examined and discussion of Allied-Rumanian relations was continued at the meeting held on the following day, when an agreement was reached on the text of a note to be addressed to the Rumanian Government. The communication, dispatched the same day to Allied diplomatic representatives in Bucharest for transmission, noted "with great satisfaction" assurances of the Rumanian Government's intention to adhere to the alliance, as reported by Sir George Clerk, and proposed to deal with perfect frankness and definiteness with the three questions in regard to which differences and misunderstandings existed between the Allies and Rumania, namely, frontiers, the Minorities Treaty, and Hungary.

Concerning the changes in the Hungarian-Rumanian frontiers sought by Mr. Bratianu,[131] the Supreme Council expressed regret that "they are unable to modify in favour of Roumania their original decision taken after the closest examination of all the relevant factors and made known as definite to all the parties interested."

Concerning the Minorities Treaty, the communication stated the determination of the Supreme Council to uphold the underlying principle, but expressed willingness to examine, in common with Rumania, a modification of those clauses to which her government expressed opposition, as soon as Rumania indicated that she was prepared to sign the peace treaty with Austria without reservations.

With respect to the Hungarian question, the Supreme Council's views were set forth under two main headings.

As to requisitions by the Rumanian army of occupation, the communication noted the absence of any difference of opinion as to the general principle, previously expressed by the Council, that the property taken by Rumania formed part of the common reparation stock of all the Allied Powers. As regards the application of that principle, i.e., the determination of what should be allocated to Rumania and what part, or its value, assigned to the common stock, the note suggested the dispatch to Budapest of the Interallied Committee agreed upon at the meeting held on October 10,[132] and requested the appointment of a Rumanian representative with full authority to sit on this Committee. Adverting to the evasion by the Rumanian Government of orders re-

[130] CHD, Oct. 10, 1919 (H.D. 67). MS.
[131] See *supra*, p. 141.   [132] *Supra*, p. 151.

stricting requisitions, the Allies also proposed, in conformity with Sir George Clerk's suggestion, the establishment of an Interallied control, which would include Rumanian officials, at Szolnok and Csongrád, to check all shipments into Rumania.

With respect to the establishment of an acceptable Hungarian Government, the note stated the Supreme Council's opinion that the Friedrich Government, as at present constituted, would not fulfill the requirements sought by the Allies, namely, the maintenance of order, the holding of free and impartial elections, and the negotiating of peace. Therefore the Council felt that Prime Minister Friedrich ought to broaden his government by including representatives of the various political parties; should he be unwilling or unable to do this, "the Hungarian people must realize that the Allies can only recognize and deal with a Government which fulfills these conditions." The Supreme Council expressed the hope that this view of the situation was shared by Rumania.

In conclusion, the Council requested assurances that arms already promised for the Hungarian police would be immediately released and that the Rumanians would at once evacuate Hungary.[133]

The discussions which had taken place in the Supreme Council with respect to Hungary and Rumania and the text of the communication to the Rumanian Government, summarized above, indicate that the Council was, to a considerable extent, influenced by Sir George Clerk's suggestions. While previous communications to the Rumanians show growing irritation under the evasive tactics of Bucharest, the note of October 11, although maintaining a firm attitude, was considerably milder in tone and more conciliatory than previous admonitions. Sir George's point of view concerning full-fledged Rumanian representation on the special reparation committee prevailed over the proposal made by the American representative in his report of September 23. Also, the Supreme Council disregarded the proposal of the Interallied Mission in Budapest that the Friedrich Government be recognized and gave preference to Sir George's suggestion that a more representative government on a broader basis be formed. The evacuation of Hungary by the Rumanians, although urged, was not pressed too much. On one point, however, the Supreme Council was definite and unequivocal:

---

[133] The complete text of the Supreme Council's communication is contained in AD, SH Bulletin 1051, Oct. 13, 1919. MS; also CHD, Oct. 11, 1919 (H.D. 68), Appendix "D." MS; reprinted in part *infra,* Doc. 37, p. 517.

the Rumanian claims for further adjustment of the Hungarian-Rumanian frontier in Rumania's favor were rejected.

There remained the question of dealing with the Hungarian internal situation. Obviously, and as pointed out by Sir George Clerk, this problem was closely related to and complicated by the presence of the Rumanian army of occupation, whose conduct did not by any means improve.[134] Originally the plan was to send a telegram to Prime Minister Friedrich demanding the reorganization of his government along the lines indicated by Sir George Clerk, but Mr. Polk questioned the wisdom of such a step. When the matter was further discussed at the Supreme Council's meeting on October 13, it was decided that instead of sending a written communication to Hungary, the Council would send Sir George himself to Budapest. Any doubts which may have existed as to the necessity of such action were dispelled by the receipt of a distressing telegraphic report from the Interallied Mission of the same date, in which they reported on the situation in Hungary and requested prompt action. This report, which came before the Supreme Council at its meeting on October 16, laid the blame for Hungary's plight unequivocally on the shoulders of the Rumanians. It called attention to the serious food and coal shortage, due both to the requisitioning of these commodities and to the scarcity of railway rolling stock, which made transportation well-nigh impossible. The Mission reported interference with the opening of schools, the seizure of machinery and the consequent loss of employment by thousands of workers, attempts to arrest Prime Minister Friedrich, such maltreatment of prisoners of war as called forth strong censure by representatives of the International Red Cross,[135] atrocities committed upon the population, and in general

[134] A few days after Sir George Clerk left Budapest for Paris, or on Oct. 5, General Serbanescu, upon orders of General Mardarescu, commanding officer of the occupation army, and of the Rumanian High Commissioner, Mr. Diamandi, tried to ransack the Hungarian National Museum. This was prevented by the personal intervention of the American member of the Interallied Mission, General Bandholtz. See his *Diary*, pp. 136–38. The next day the Mission reported to Paris that it had taken the Museum under its protection. AD, SH Bulletin 680, Part XIX, Oct. 9, 1919. MS.

[135] On Oct. 20 the Interallied Mission addressed a note to the Rumanian command in Budapest relative to the deplorable condition of the prisoners of war and civilians interned at Arad, and their immediate liberation was recommended. No reply having been received in ten days' time, the Mission addressed another communication, on Oct. 31, to the Commander in Chief of the Rumanian Army in Transylvania, calling attention to the inhuman conditions found by a Committee of Allied officers and of Red Cross representatives when visiting prisoners' camps, at Arad, Brassó, Fogaras, and other places under Rumanian occupation. The Mission expressed the view that the

a "condition of affairs difficult for a Western European to realize who has not seen and heard evidence."

In general [the telegram ended], Roumanian conduct has been such that this Mission been almost wholly unable carry out its instructions and there apparently no prospect immediate improvement. It is unanimous opinion of Mission that unless Roumanians immediately evacuate Hungary and make at least partial restitution in particular of rolling stock, machinery and much other property seized here, there will result in short time extreme suffering from lack food and fuel and recrudescence of Bolshevism. The Mission therefore of unanimous opinion that either Roumanians should be forced to evacuate Hungary at once and make restitution outlined or this Mission should be relieved.[136]

With this report before it, the Supreme Council confirmed its decision that Sir George Clerk should proceed immediately to Budapest as the special representative of the Principal Allied and Associated Powers. He was directed to communicate with the Hungarian political parties, with a view to the formation of a government acceptable to the Allies; and to inform the Interallied Mission in Budapest of the discussion which took place in the Supreme Council and of the Council's determination to do all that was necessary to compel the Rumanian Government to follow the line decided upon by the Allies.[137]

Sir George Clerk's Mission to Hungary

When Sir George Clerk arrived in Budapest on the morning of October 23, the situation in Hungary was very much as pictured in the

report of this committee, forwarded to the Peace Conference, "will arouse the resentment of the Great Powers, as an Associated Power has taken no account of the rules of humanity which govern the Alliance, and furthermore has exposed the Alliance to being accused of abusing defenseless prisoners of war." The Mission requested that civilians under eighteen and over sixty and all invalid prisoners incapable of service be immediately freed; that sick prisoners be sent to hospitals for necessary treatment; that prisoners not freed receive pay, sufficient food, and more decent treatment; and that the places of detention should satisfy elementary sanitary requirements. The text of this communication is in AD, SH Bulletin 1333, Nov. 20, 1919. MS. For a telegraphic report to the Supreme Council, dated Oct. 30, giving detailed information on the conditions of prisoners, see Bandholtz, Diary, pp. 187–89.

[136] The complete text of this important report, which gives a graphic picture of the situation of Hungary in the middle of Oct., 1919, is reprinted infra, Doc. 38, p. 521. A study of this report emanating from the representatives of the Principal Allied and Associated Powers is indispensable for an understanding of Hungarian-Rumanian relations from that time to the present.

[137] CHD, Oct. 16, 1919 (H.D. 71). MS.

report of the Interallied Mission dispatched to Paris ten days earlier.[138] The problems which the special representative of the Supreme Council had to meet were anything but simple or easy of solution. The day after his arrival, Sir George had conversations with Prime Minister Friedrich and also with Count Somssich, the Minister for Foreign Affairs in the Friedrich Government. He informed the Prime Minister quite bluntly of the attitude of the Supreme Council as laid down at the Council's meeting on October 16, namely, that the Allies would not recognize even provisionally any Hungarian Government unless satisfied that such government really represented the various political factions. Prime Minister Friedrich contended during this interview that his was a representative government. But Sir George insisted on the necessity of reorganization on a broader basis and told him frankly that the Allies did not trust him.[139] By "broader basis," Sir George Clerk as well as the Allies meant the inclusion of the leftist parties—particularly the Social Democrats—which it was believed would have a restraining influence on the strongly nationalistic tendencies of the Friedrich Government.[140] In view of the fact that the war was conducted with the slogan, to "make the world safe for democracy," and that, for better or for worse, "democracy" was conceived to be in opposition to nationalism, the preference of the Allies for a coalition government in which so-called liberal elements would predominate is fully understandable.

Sir George himself realized within a week that a number of concrete obstacles stood in the way of the theoretical aspirations of his principals in Paris. A study of the situation in Hungary and a realistic grasp of the temper of public opinion, as expressed in conferences he had held with representatives of various political parties and leaders in different walks of Hungarian life, induced him to warn the Supreme Council that "it is impossible to ignore popular sentiment which, unless handled

---

[138] *Supra*, pp. 154-55.

[139] Sir George's first report from Budapest, dated Oct. 25, is in AD, SH Bulletin 1178, Oct. 30, 1919. MS.

[140] The representative of the Hungarian Government at The Hague, Alexis Nagy, reported an interview he had on Oct. 16 with Ambassador White, member of the American Peace Delegation, who visited The Hague that week-end. Ambassador White was reported to have advised Mr. Nagy that Hungary would be invited to the Peace Conference only when she had a government which the Allies could recognize. Mr. White said that Prime Minister Friedrich was not recognized because he was regarded as supporting a restoration of the Habsburgs and as a believer in the monarchical form of government; moreover, his government was not representative. *HFR*, Vol. I, Doc. 28.

with great care, will break out in violence and unrest throughout the country." In his telegraphic report, dated November 1, Sir George summed up the conclusions reached during his first week in Budapest as follows:

1. Immediate evacuation of all Hungary by the Rumanians is essential, because while they occupy the country nothing can be accomplished. Since Mr. Diamandi's telegraphic request urging Bucharest to withdraw, sent immediately upon Sir George's arrival, was unanswered, Sir George asked the Supreme Council to exercise "all possible pressure" in Bucharest "to secure the earliest possible withdrawal." Sir George expressed the hope that with a definite assurance of Rumanian evacuation, he could induce Prime Minister Friedrich to make way for a government acceptable to the Allies.

2. Private negotiations with a view to the formation of such a government convinced Sir George that the Christian-National party, which supported the Prime Minister, must be given full representation. In view of the strong anti-Jewish feeling, the inclusion of a Jew in the government was deemed practically impossible by Sir George,[141] but he reported that he would endeavor to secure a government so composed as to be satisfactory to the Jewish elements. In view of the delicacy of the situation, Sir George asked for authority to extend to a new government the provisional recognition of the Supreme Council.

3. An interview with Admiral Horthy, commander of Hungary's small armed forces assembled west of the Danube, resulted in an assurance from Admiral Horthy, accepted by Sir George, that the former would maintain discipline among his troops and insure order, when the Rumanians withdrew.

4. Reports from Transylvania left little doubt in Sir George's mind that the Rumanians were acting there "not only with great harshness but in flagrant violation of conditions of the peace treaty," and he urged the dispatch of an Interallied commission to report on the situation.[142]

[141] Following the collapse of the communist regime, in which Jews had occupied many of the leading positions, a strong anti-Semitic feeling was evident throughout Hungary, and excesses committed against Jews by isolated and irresponsible groups caused anxiety in Paris and considerable agitation among the public in Western Europe and in the United States. This tendency was pretty much in evidence during the first two years following the fall of Kun's Government and was in no small measure responsible for hostility against Hungary in early postwar years.

[142] Sir George's report of Nov. 1 is contained in Appendix "B" to the Minutes of the Meeting of the Supreme Council held on November 4 (H.D. 83). MS; also in AD, SH Bulletin 1212, Nov. 4, 1919. MS. The situation in Transylvania was the sub-

Simultaneously with Sir George's report, another proposal from an unidentified source came before the Supreme Council in the form of a note, passed on by the French Delegation, purporting to be a report on the situation in Hungary. This undated "report" was considered by the Council at its meeting on November 3. It proposed that an Interallied force of two divisions, composed of Rumanian, Czech, and Yugoslav contingents, under the orders of Allied officers and under the command of a general selected by the Peace Conference, should replace the Rumanian troops, which would retire to the Tisza River.[143] This suggestion was directly contrary to the views both of the Interallied Mission in Budapest and of Sir George Clerk, who urged evacuation— the former repeatedly—by the Rumanians without asking for the replacement of Rumanian by other Allied troops. As will appear presently, the sender of this proposal, whoever he may have been, did not consult any of the Allied representatives in Hungary, who, upon learning of this proposal, objected to it vigorously and unequivocally. Fortunately the Supreme Council decided before acting to inquire of its representatives in Budapest what they thought of the proposal. The Council also noted the absence of a reply to its note of October 12 to the Rumanian Government[144] and decided to send another note, insisting on a prompt reply.[145]

---

ject of another report to the Supreme Council. On Nov. 6 Sir George wired to Paris that he had received evidence from reliable and impartial sources that the Rumanian authorities "are using every means to suppress Hungarian element in country and so during their occupation Roumanize whole province by unscrupulous and arbitrary acts in such a manner as to present a false situation to Allies when moment comes for final decision of Conference in regard to attribution of these regions." "Their measures include," the report continued, "every form of personal pressure; persons and families are being arbitrarily turned out of their homes. Arrests and personal distraints on no reasonable grounds are frequent; a land reform scheme is actually being enforced for express purpose of falsifying whole system of land ownership to prejudice Hungarians and of facilitating an arbitrary Roumanian colonization. Schools, university and hospitals are being closed; oaths of allegiance to Roumania are being extorted by compulsion everywhere. Roumanian officials, doctors, teachers, etc. are being substituted for Hungarians. . . ." Sir George's wire concluded that the Rumanians were "thus befouling name of Allied and Associated Powers, diminishing their prestige and destroying faith in their justice and impartiality." Complete text of this telegram in AD, SH Bulletin 1245, Nov. 8, 1919. MS.

[143] CHD, Nov. 3, 1919 (H.D. 82), Appendix "C." MS; also in AD, SH Bulletin 1207, Nov. 3, 1919. MS.

[144] *Supra*, pp. 152–53.

[145] Pursuant to this decision, M. Pichon sent telegraphic instructions to the French minister in Bucharest to make, jointly with the Allied representatives there, formal representations to the Rumanian Government to obtain, without delay, a clear reply

The above outlined anonymous proposal was communicated to Sir George Clerk in a telegram from the Supreme Council dated November 5. The Council first acknowledged Sir George's reports of October 25 and November 1 [146] and approved, in general, his suggestions. Specifically, the Council expressed the view that Hungary must be completely evacuated by the Rumanians and that the Friedrich Government must be replaced by one "comprising the democratic element." Sir George was authorized to guarantee to such a government recognition by the Allies. The rest of the communication dealt with the proposal for replacing Rumanian troops by Allied forces, as follows:

This Council was presented with a suggestion tending to emphasize the necessity, in order to prevent the elections and the Hungarian Government being subject to the influence of the local police which is in the power of Friedrich, and by the small army of Admiral Horthy whose tendencies are openly reactionary, of replacing the Rumanian military force by an Allied military force capable of inspiring confidence in the population and strengthening the moral authority of the Commission of Generals and of the Conference itself. . . . On [the] one hand, the fact that the Allies do not in any wise wish to impede the expression of the free will of the Hungarians must be clearly understood, but on the other hand they have decided to prevent the restoration of the fallen dynasty, in any form, either direct, or indirect.

The Council requested Sir George to consult with the Interallied Mission in Budapest and to report whether in his opinion the Rumanians should be replaced by an Interallied force or whether assurances given by Admiral Horthy to maintain order could be trusted. The Council pointed out that since the Principal Allied Powers had no effectives available, an Interallied force of about two divisions to be sent to Hungary would have to consist of Czech and Yugoslav troops commanded by English, Italian, American, and French officers. Sir George was advised also that the Italian Delegation, in view of the state of mind of the Hungarians, objected to sending any Yugoslavs to Hungary; and that all the Delegations realized the inconveniences which might result from the presence in Hungary of troops of Hungary's neighbors, all hostile to her, even though under a firm Allied command. "The Su-

---

to all points raised in the Supreme Council's note. The text of this communication forms Appendix "D" in CHD, Nov. 3, 1919 (H.D. 82). MS. The Rumanian reply, dated Nov. 2, did not reach Paris until several days later. See *infra,* p. 167.

[146] *Supra,* pp. 156–57.

preme Council," the communication concluded, "confident in your judgment and your local information, asks you for prompt and precise advice."[147]

The attitude of Sir George Clerk and the Allied Generals toward these suggestions was made unequivocally clear, even before the receipt of the communication from the Supreme Council, summarized above. News of the discussions which took place in the Supreme Council on November 3 and 4 apparently leaked out and reached Allied representatives in Budapest through unofficial channels before the dispatch of the Supreme Council's telegram to Sir George. The news was received in all quarters with the gravest apprehension, if not with consternation, since any such plan would obviously have nullified whatever progress had been made by the Interallied Mission and by Sir George Clerk toward an acceptable and workable clearing up of the Hungarian tangle. Indeed Sir George had just reported on the previous day, November 4, an official announcement made to him by Mr. Diamandi that the Rumanian troops would begin an evacuation of Budapest that would be completed by the eleventh.[148] In the same communication Sir George reported that while Prime Minister Friedrich was still adamant and threatened to go into opposition if the Allies insisted on his relinquishing the premiership, he was still hopeful that the Prime Minister "may be induced to see reason."[149] On the following day, having been informed of the proposals affecting Hungary which were being considered by the Supreme Council, Sir George wired the Supreme Council his views concerning each of the three steps contemplated in Paris. As to the demand for Prime Minister Friedrich's immediate resignation, Sir George asked for a delay of two or three days, in the hope of securing the agreement of all the political parties to a coalition government. As to the withdrawal of the Rumanians, he expressed the hope that the Allies would insist upon their evacuation of *all* Hungarian territories. Sir George deemed this important primarily because elections could not be held until the country was cleared of foreign troops.

[147] A complete text of the Supreme Council's telegram of Nov. 5 to Sir George Clerk is in Appendix "B" to CHD, Nov. 5, 1919 (H.D. 84). MS; also in AD, SH Bulletin 1227, Nov. 6, 1919. MS. See *infra,* Doc. 40, p. 526.

[148] These dates were subsequently changed to Nov. 12 and 15 respectively, according to telegraphic report of the Interallied Mission to the Supreme Council, dated Nov. 7. AD, SH Bulletin 1256, Nov. 10, 1919. MS.

[149] The complete text of Sir George Clerk's wire of Nov. 4 is in CHD, Nov. 6, 1919 (H.D. 85), Appendix "A." MS; also in AD, SH Bulletin 1224, Nov. 6, 1919. MS.

Finally, concerning the replacement of the Rumanians by an Interallied force, he expressed his

"earnest hope that under no circumstances will Jugo-Slav and Czecho-Slav [*sic*] divisions be sent into Hungary even under Allied officers. Result in country [he continued] would be indescribable and I am convinced that Hungarians would at once sink all their differences and resist with such arms as they have to the last man.[150]

In similar vein was a telegram of the same date from the Interallied Military Mission.

Against this third proposition the Interallied Military Mission unanimously and urgently protests. Such procedure it is believed would stir Hungary into revolution and would destroy all prospects for an early solution of the Hungarian question. It is further urged that the Roumanians, the Yugo-Slavs and the Czecho-Slovaks be all required to retire at once behind their respective lines of demarcation.[151]

In view of the fact that the Interallied Mission had been urging Hungary's evacuation for several weeks, its opposition to the proposed replacement of one occupying army by another was both logical and understandable. The attitude of the Mission gains significance by the adoption of exactly the same point of view by Sir George Clerk, who was in Hungary for a much shorter time than any of the Allied Generals.

With reference to the last sentence of the Mission's telegram, it should be noted that the Mission had made several unsuccessful attempts, even before Sir George Clerk's arrival, to secure the withdrawal of foreign troops from Hungary. On October 15 the Mission requested the Rumanians to begin the evacuation of Hungary and to withdraw at once to a line at least fifty kilometers (about thirty-two miles) east of Budapest.[152] General Mardarescu in his reply, received by the Mission on October 20, refused to comply with this request, saying that the Rumanian Command reserved to itself entire liberty of action in regard to military operations.[153] In order to relieve the pressing coal shortage,

[150] The complete text of Sir George Clerk's wire of Nov. 5 is in CHD, Nov. 6, 1919 (H.D. 85), Appendix "B." MS; also in AD, SH Bulletin 1224, Nov. 6, 1919. MS.

[151] The complete text of this telegram is in CHD, Nov. 6, 1919 (H.D. 85), Appendix "C." MS. Also in Bandholtz, *Diary,* pp. 203–4.

[152] Bandholtz, *Diary,* pp. 157–58.

[153] *Ibid.,* pp. 169–70. In ordering the evacuation of Budapest, the Interallied Military Mission acted strictly within the powers conferred upon it by the Supreme Council

which on October 22 was becoming increasingly threatening with the approach of winter, the Mission also requested the Yugoslavs to evacuate the mining region around Pécs, in the county of Baranya. A similar request for the evacuation of the Salgótarján coal region was sent to the Czechs. Both these territories were within Hungary's frontiers, as determined by the Supreme Council on June 13, and were occupied by the Yugoslavs and the Czechs without the authorization of the Allies.[154] Neither of these requests of the Interallied Mission had, however, been complied with when the news reached Budapest that the Supreme Council contemplated sending Czecho-Slovak and Yugoslav divisions into Hungary to replace the withdrawing Rumanians.[155]

With these reports and protests of Sir George Clerk and of the Interallied Mission concerning various aspects of the situation in Hungary before it, the Supreme Council met on November 6. Several steps were decided on and communicated to Sir George by wire on the same date. He was advised that the Supreme Council would formally invite the Czech and Yugoslav Governments to evacuate to the respective frontiers determined for Hungary by the Council on June 13;[156] no such step was contemplated with respect to Rumania since she had already been

---

under paragraph 3(b) of the original instructions of Aug. 5, 1919 (*supra*, pp. 110–11). Its duties were, *inter alia*, "to determine, according to the situation of the moment, the effectives and the emplacements of the Roumanian and Serbian troops that it will be necessary to maintain on Hungarian soil to guarantee order and the execution of the armistice."

[154] See *supra*, pp. 118–19.

[155] On Oct. 27 the Mission reported to the Supreme Council that it had received no reply to its request from Belgrade and begged the Council to exert pressure on the Yugoslav Government to evacuate Pécs. AD, SH Bulletin 1178, Oct. 30, 1919. MS. On Oct. 31 the Mission asked the Supreme Council to bring pressure on Prague to evacuate Salgótarján, since the Czechs had not answered the Mission's request. AD, SH Bulletin 1218, Nov. 4, 1919. MS. A reply from the Czech Government arrived on Nov. 3, but, as reported by wire on the same date to the Supreme Council, subordinated evacuation to conditions, namely, that the Hungarians would maintain order, would not attack the Czechs, and would reimburse the Czech Government for the amounts advanced for feeding the population. The first two conditions were guaranteed by the Interallied Mission (cf. *HFR*, Vol. I, Doc. 35); with respect to reimbursement, the Mission again requested the Supreme Council's intervention in Prague, expressing the view that a new delay "must be avoided at any price." The full text of the Mission's telegram of Nov. 3 is in CHD, Nov. 3, 1919 (H.D. 82), Appendix "D." MS; also in AD, SH Bulletin 1232, Nov. 7, 1919. MS. The Mission reported to the Supreme Council on Nov. 7 that the Czech command issued orders for the evacuation of Salgótarján on Nov. 11. AD, SH Bulletin 1256, Nov. 10, 1919. MS.

[156] *Supra*, pp. 82–83.

invited to begin the evacuation of Hungary in the note which the Supreme Council dispatched to Bucharest on October 12.[157] Sir George was also assured that the Supreme Council envisaged the complete evacuation of Hungary by the Rumanians and that their troops were not to remain at the Tisza River. The Council also promised that it would intervene with the Czech Government to assure indispensable coal supplies to Hungary without a previous agreement concerning payment. Finally Sir George was advised that in view of his protest and of the unanimous opinion of the Interallied Mission, the Supreme Council had abandoned the idea of sending a combined Czech-Yugoslav force under Allied command to Hungary. That the Supreme Council was still apprehensive about the internal situation in Hungary appears from the closing paragraph of the telegram, which again requested Sir George's opinion concerning the necessity of a bona fide Interallied force to support the authority of the Interallied Mission and the orders of the Peace Conference. "The attitude of defiance adopted by Mr. Friedrich," read the communication, "referred to in your telegram of November 4,[158] immediately after the decision calling for the evacuation of the Rumanian troops leads us to fear that the reactionary elements will offer resistance as soon as the Allies will no longer have a sufficient local military force to force respect for their decisions." Pointing out that the dispatch of troops by the Principal Allied and Associated Powers would encounter "serious difficulties," the Council asked whether, in Sir George's opinion, the Hungarian *gendarmerie,* placed under the control of the Allied Generals in Budapest, would be sufficient to maintain order.[159]

At the same meeting the Supreme Council decided to inform the Yugoslav Government that the Council's decisions regarding territorial questions were final, but that the evacuation of Hungarian territories occupied by Yugoslav troops would not prejudice decision on the Yugoslav Government's request for the right of exploitation of the coal mines at Pécs for a period of five years; the matter was referred for

[157] *Supra,* pp. 152–53. It seems, however, that a telegram was sent to the French representative in Bucharest, instructing him to request, jointly with his Allied colleagues, an immediate reply from the Rumanian Government to the three questions raised in the Supreme Council's note of Oct. 12. AD, SH Bulletin 1249, Nov. 10, 1919. MS; cf. also Bandholtz, *Diary,* pp. 207–8.

[158] See *supra,* p. 160.

[159] The complete text of the Supreme Council's telegram to Sir George Clerk, dated Nov. 6, 1919, is in CHD, Nov. 6, 1919 (H.D. 85), Appendix "E." MS.

consideration to the Committee for the Study of Territorial Questions Relating to Rumania and Yugoslavia.[160]

It will be remembered that when the Supreme Council decided on June 13 to make public its decisions concerning Hungary's future frontiers, in the hope that this might put an end to the war between Hungary on the one hand and Czecho-Slovakia and Rumania on the other, the Council made public only the Czech-Hungarian and Rumanian-Hungarian frontiers.[161] The line which was to separate Hungary from Yugoslavia was not communicated to either of the governments concerned. Accordingly, in a telegram addressed on November 7 to the French minister in Belgrade, the latter was instructed to invite the Yugoslav Government, in the name of the Supreme Council, immediately to withdraw its troops behind the new frontiers, which, the instructions said, were to be considered as final and which were described precisely as adopted by the Council on June 13.[162]

The Allied representatives in Budapest were greatly relieved upon learning the decisions of the Supreme Council. Sir George Clerk reported on November 9, with the concurrence of the Allied Generals and of Admiral Troubridge, commander of the Allied naval units stationed on the Danube, that the decision of the Supreme Council to bring about the withdrawal of foreign troops and to ease Hungary's acute coal shortage would greatly help the already improved situation. As evidence of a better atmosphere and less uneasiness, Sir George reported a meeting which took place on November 7 at his house between Admiral Horthy and leaders of the extreme left, when the latter accepted Admiral Horthy's assurances of impartiality and the discipline of his army. He also stated his own, Admiral Troubridge's, and the Allied Generals' "complete confidence" in Admiral Horthy's loyalty, sincerity, and effective control over the Hungarian troops. With respect to the police and the *gendarmerie,* Sir George suggested that in order to prevent any abuse they should be placed under the authority

---

[160] CHD, Nov. 6, 1919 (H.D. 85). MS; also in AD, SH Bulletin 1249, Nov. 10, 1919. MS.

[161] See *supra,* pp. 82–84; *infra,* Docs. 19, (I)–(IV), pp. 461, 463, 466.

[162] The complete text of this communication is printed *infra,* Doc. 39, p. 524. It may be noted that there was no reference in this communication to the question of the exploitation of the Pécs coal mines by Yugoslavia. In fact, despite repeated requests by the Interallied Mission and countless protests by Hungary, the Allied Powers did not succeed in bringing about the evacuation of the Baranya region by the Yugoslavs until after the Trianon Treaty came into force in 1921.

of the Interallied Mission and he requested the immediate dispatch of twenty Allied officers to be attached to army and police units.

As to the political situation, Sir George reported satisfactory progress and the gradual realization among responsible politicians of the necessity for a coalition government. He expressed confidence that in view of the substantial improvement in the atmosphere the remaining difficulties—consisting mainly of the reconciliation of conflicting political ambitions—would be overcome shortly and that law and order would be maintained.[163]

Meanwhile, preparations were made for the often-urged withdrawal of the Rumanian army of occupation. Yielding to increasing Allied pressure, the Rumanians finally informed the Interallied Mission of their plan to begin evacuation with the withdrawal of their troops, for the time being, to the east bank of the Tisza (Theiss) River, on November 11.[164] Details for the organization of a police force in Budapest and the taking over of the evacuated territories by Hungarian troops so as to avoid undesirable incidents were arranged between the Interallied Mission and Hungarian officials. The Rumanian troops left the capital on the morning of November 14, and a few hours later advance units of the Hungarian National Army entered it. Contrary to the fears of some, there were no untoward incidents; and the enthusiastic reception given two days later by a wildly cheering population to Admiral Horthy, who rode into the city with the main body of the army, was clear evidence that, despite the apprehension which doubtless had existed in some quarters, the Hungarians were happy to be freed from the indescribable terror and mismanagement of the Rumanian occupation.

Conversations looking toward the formation of a government acceptable to the Allies progressed with more speed after the Rumanians left the Hungarian capital. Prime Minister Friedrich's unwillingness to relinquish the premiership, which he believed was supported by the overwhelming majority of the people, was overcome by the firm stand of Sir George Clerk and by the very frank description of Allied psychology by General Bandholtz in his conversations with

[163] The complete text of Sir George Clerk's telegram of Nov. 9, 1919, is printed *infra*, Doc. 41, p. 528.

[164] On Nov. 10 the Interallied Mission stressed to the Supreme Council that the Rumanians ought to withdraw from Hungary completely and urged the release of Hungarian prisoners of war held by the Rumanians. Bandholtz, *Diary*, pp. 215, 217.

the Prime Minister.[165] By November 16 the Prime Minister agreed to give way to a coalition government. It remained only to reach an agreement as to the head of the government and the distribution of cabinet posts among the parties which agreed to participate in its formation. A suggestion to entrust the premiership to Count Albert Apponyi, one of the most distinguished figures in Hungary's political life, proved to be abortive. After some jockeying for position, the contending political factions finally chose Charles Huszár as the new Prime Minister. A member of the Christian-Socialist party, he had served as Minister of Education in the Friedrich Government, but he was a comparatively unknown politician. On November 22 Sir George reported to the Supreme Council that the formation of a coalition government was about to be completed [166] and on November 25 he extended, on behalf of the Allies, provisional *de facto* recognition to the new government. This government was composed of representatives of the Christian-Socialist, Small Farmers', National-Democratic (Liberal), and Social-Democratic parties. Mr. Friedrich remained in the cabinet as Minister of War, and Count Somssich, who had served as Minister for Foreign Affairs in the Friedrich Government since September and who did not belong to any party, retained his same post in the Huszár Government. As reported by Sir George, Allied recognition was conditioned upon the holding of free elections without delay, the maintenance of law and order in the country, abstention from any aggressive action, respect for Hungary's provisional frontiers pending their final determination in the peace treaty, and, for all Hungarian nationals, a guarantee of all civil liberties, including freedom of the press, of assembly, and of speech, and free, secret, impartial elections based on universal suffrage. Prime Minister Huszár assured Sir George that he was prepared to send a delegation to Paris to conclude peace as soon as an invitation should be received from the Peace Conference.[167]

Thus, despite many difficulties and complications, Sir George Clerk's mission to Hungary was crowned with success. To whatever extent his earlier visit to Bucharest may ultimately have contributed to Rumania's capitulation to the wishes of the Allies, the results of his mission in Hungary were more evident and concrete than those of his mission in Rumania. Here he accomplished directly what he was asked to do:

[165] Bandholtz, *Diary,* pp. 210–13, 217–18.
[166] AD, SH Bulletin 1357, Nov. 24, 1919. MS.
[167] The complete text of Sir George Clerk's telegraphic report is printed *infra,* Doc. 42, p. 530.

to assist in Hungary, in the creation of a more or less stable internal political condition. The road to the conclusion of a peace between Hungary and the Allies was finally made passable, at least from the point of view of the Allies.[168]

To complete the picture of this phase of the Peace Conference history, the final stages of the controversy between the Principal Allies and Rumania, which, as we have seen, centered primarily around the Hungarian question, must be recorded.

It will be remembered that the Supreme Council, on October 12 addressed a note to the Rumanian Government, which, while comparatively mild in tone, called for unequivocal replies to three specific questions.[169] The Rumanian reply, dated November 2 and signed by the Prime Minister, General Vaitoianu, reached Paris only on November 10 or 11, after the Supreme Council had sent at least two reminders to Bucharest that a reply was expected.[170] The Rumanian reply began with a profession of Rumania's firm desire to maintain and develop her alliance and close collaboration and to harmonize her interests with those of the Allied Powers. Rumania, the note stated, gladly accepted the proposal of the Supreme Council to establish an Interallied Commission in Budapest to ascertain the value of the property requisitioned; she also agreed to Interallied control and verification of shipments going through Szolnok and Csongrád en route to Rumania. However, it was thought "inopportune" to authorize these agencies to unload merchandise. The note expressed regret at the Supreme Council's criticism of requisitions in Hungary when such criticism "corresponded neither with the spirit of order or the discipline of the Rumanian army." General Vaitoianu promised that "isolated cases" of any abuse, if proved, would be made good and punished. But he protested against the proposal that the contemplated Interallied Commission be authorized to receive complaints concerning abusive requisitions, for this would subject Rumanian military authorities "to an

[168] The substance of Sir George Clerk's final report on his mission to Hungary, dated Nov. 29, 1919, is printed *infra,* Doc. 43, p. 531. The difficulties which faced him are amply illustrated in selected papers connected with his activities at Budapest, furnished by the British Delegation and collected in AD, SH Bulletin 1413, Dec. 4, 1919. MS. (102 pages). The most important of these documents are the minutes of the conferences held on Nov. 17 and 18 by the representatives of all Hungarian political parties, and called by Sir George in order to bring about a coalition government acceptable to the Allies.

[169] *Supra,* pp. 152–53.

[170] See *supra,* nn. 145, 157.

international treatment to which none of the other Allied armies of occupation [specifically mentioning the Yugoslav army in the Bánát] have been subjected." Finally the Supreme Council was informed that the Rumanian occupation authorities had turned over rifles and ammunition destined for the Hungarian police and that orders had been given to the Rumanian forces to evacuate Hungary as far as the River Tisza. The note stated flatly—and obviously contrary to the truth— that evacuation had been postponed up to that time "only at the request of the Allied representatives." Territories between the Tisza (Theiss) and the new frontiers would be evacuated "as soon as the Hungarian Government is in a position to furnish the necessary guarantees for the security of these territories." The note concluded by stating that the withdrawal of the Rumanian troops would begin on November 10 and by informing the Peace Conference that the Rumanian Government was "preoccupied entirely with the work of reconstructing the Rumanian countries drained and impoverished by the countless extortions effected by the German and Austro-Hungarian armies during their occupation." [171]

The Supreme Council found the Rumanian reply "entirely unsatisfactory" and the draft of a note in the nature of an ultimatum, prepared by M. Berthelot, was tentatively approved at the meeting of November 13, demanding an unconditional reply from the Rumanian Government within six days.[172] The Allied note recited that since the occupation of Budapest at the beginning of August, the Peace Conference had unceasingly requested Rumania to adopt in Hungary an attitude conforming to the principles and engagements of the Allies. Reference was made to the numerous communications addressed by the Supreme Council to Bucharest between August 4 and November 7, in the hope that Rumania would realize that it could not with impunity disregard these principles and escape the reciprocal engagements of the Allies. "All these patient efforts," the note continued, "resulted only in the answer of November 2, conciliatory in words, but, negative in fact; regarding the three questions asked, acceptance of the frontiers determined by the Supreme Council, signature of the Peace Treaty with Austria, and of the Minorities Treaty, adjustment of the situation in

[171] The complete text of the Rumanian note of Nov. 2 is in CHD, Nov. 12 (H.D. 90), Appendix "D." MS; also in AD, SH Bulletin 1268, Nov. 11, 1919. MS.

[172] In the final text dispatched to Rumania, this was changed to eight days from the day of receipt by the Rumanian Government. See the Supreme Council's ultimatum of Dec. 3, printed in Temperley, History, IV, 517-19.

Hungary, the Note postpones the two first ones and answers only to the third." But even insofar as a reply was given, the demands of the Allies were not satisfactorily agreed to. Rumania did not agree to the investing of the contemplated Interallied control agency, with authority to unload merchandise for verification and to inquire into abuses committed by Rumanian military authorities. The withdrawal of Rumanian troops from Hungary was agreed to only insofar as they would withdraw to the Tisza River, although the Allies specifically called for evacuation to the frontiers laid down by the Supreme Council. "In short, the Rumanian Government has continued, for the last three and a half months, to negotiate with the Conference, from Power to Power, taking into consideration no other rights or interests than her own, and refusing to accept the charges of solidarity, although she wishes to enjoy the benefit of them."

In view of these facts, before deciding to sever relations with Rumania the Supreme Council addressed a last appeal to the wisdom of the Rumanian Government and people by inviting Rumania to comply, "without discussion, reservation or conditions," first with the complete evacuation of Hungary; secondly, to the constitution of an Interallied Commission empowered to control and judge all requisitions since the beginning of the Rumanian occupation of Hungary; and, thirdly, to the signature of the peace treaty with Austria and of the Minorities Treaty. Should the Rumanian reply be unsatisfactory, the Allies would recall their diplomatic missions from Bucharest, would request Rumania to withdraw her Delegation from the Peace Conference, and the Peace Conference would no longer "sustain" Rumania's territorial claims. "It would be with the profoundest regret," the note concluded, "that the Supreme Council of the Allies should see itself forced to sever relations with Rumania, but it is confident that it has been patient to the very last degree." [173]

But even the extreme limit of Allied patience was capable of further

[173] The complete text of the draft Allied note is in CHD, Nov. 13, 1919 (H.D. 91), Appendix "F." MS; also in AD, SH Bulletin 1284, Nov. 17, 1919. MS. Obedience to the Allied demands was based expressly on the ground that Rumania owed to the Allied victory the "reconstitution of her national unity." "Without the immense sacrifices of the Allies," the note reads, "Rumania would be decimated, ruined and in bondage. . . . Rumania entered the struggle for her own freedom at the end of the second year of the war, and by dictation of her own conditions; it is true she made great sacrifices, and suffered hard trials, but she finally agreed to treat separately with the enemy and to submit to his law at a time when she still had under arms an army of more than 400,000 men; her liberty and her victory, as well as her future, she owes to the Allies."

stretching. The note, like several preceding ones, although telegraphed to Bucharest, was in transmission for an inordinately long time and was not delivered to the Rumanian Government until November 24. The Government of General Vaitoianu—which continued to hold office despite elections adverse to the Liberal party—promptly resigned and sought to obtain further delay from the Supreme Council, pleading as an excuse the government crisis and the time required for the assemblage of the newly elected Parliament. On the day the Allied note was received, King Ferdinand of Rumania sent a half-plaintive, half-indignant letter to the Kings of Great Britain and Italy and the President of France, protesting against the "violence," inconsistent with friendly relations, with which the Supreme Council treated Rumania and imploring them for a "more friendly and just attitude toward Rumania." [174] Since neither the King's communication nor the government's request for more time could be accepted as replies to the concrete questions contained in the Allied note, the Supreme Council decided, on November 29, to bring further pressure on Rumania by the publication of its last note in the Allied press the next morning. Another note was dispatched to Bucharest on December 3, in which the Supreme Council granted a further and last delay of six days, expiring on December 8, to prove the Allies' "moderation and their extreme regret at the prospect of Rumania separating herself from her Allies." [175] The new Government of Mr. Vaida-Voivoda, formed after considerable difficulties, bowed before the determination of the Allies and acceded unconditionally to the three demands of the Supreme Council. The treaty of peace with Austria as well as the Minorities Treaty—the latter with a slightly altered text to meet Rumanian objections—were signed by the Rumanian delegates in Paris on December 9. But Rumania's agreement to evacuate Hungary was merely theoretical; many weeks passed before the territories east of the Tisza River were free from occupation. However, the major battle between the Allies and Rumania was ended, and we may now proceed to the next phase of our history—the direct dealings between the Peace Conference and Hungary with a view to the conclusion of a peace treaty.

[174] The complete text of King Ferdinand's letter, dated Nov. 24, is in CHD, Nov. 29, 1919 (H.D. 102), Appendix "D." MS.

[175] The complete text of this note is printed in Temperley, *History,* IV, 517–19.

PART FOUR

Hungary at the Peace Conference

IV. The Official Peace Negotiations

The Invitation of Hungary to the Peace Conference

ON THE BASIS OF the report made to the Supreme Council of the Allies by its special representative, Sir George Clerk, the Allies decided finally to invite Hungary to send plenipotentiaries to Paris to receive the peace conditions. This invitation, dated December 1, 1919, was communicated through the American Mission in Paris and the American member of the Interallied Military Mission in Budapest, General Bandholtz, to Prime Minister Huszár. The text of the communication reads as follows:

The Supreme Council of the Allied and Associated Powers, after hearing Sir George Clerk, their delegate at Budapest, have decided to invite the Hungarian Government to send its delegates, furnished with the necessary credentials, to Neuilly (Château de Madrid) to conclude the peace with the Allied and Associated Powers.

The Hungarian Government is consequently requested to be good enough to send its delegates to Neuilly with the shortest possible delay.[1]

The Hungarian Government sent its acceptance through the American Mission in Budapest on December 3. The Prime Minister's communication, addressed to M. Clemenceau, called attention to the fact that several persons whose services were required by the Hungarian Peace Delegation were interned by the Rumanian authorities in occupied Transylvania and sought the intervention of the Supreme Council for their liberation.[2] In another telegram, sent on the same date to the President of the Peace Conference, the Prime Minister called attention to the situation in Hungary and to the exasperated state of public opinion, due to foreign occupation. The communication continued:

The Supreme Council would greatly facilitate the arduous task of the Government if they would order the occupying troops, and more especially

[1] Translation from the original French text in *HFR,* Vol. I, Doc. 45. A slightly different English translation is printed in *HPN,* I, vii.

[2] Original French text of this document in *HFR,* Vol. I, Doc. 46. English translation in *HPN,* I, vii–viii.

those of the Rumanians now standing in the very heart of the country, to retire to a military line to be fixed by the Supreme Council.

The Hungarian Government must also emphasize the deplorable situation of the country resulting from the innumerable requisitions carried out by the occupying troops contrary to all laws. The country which has already sustained the trials of five years of war and the horrors of bolshevism is now deprived of its last resources and reduced to impotence.

Due to the requisitioning of the rolling stock of the railways and the complete exhaustion of our stock of food supplies and of fuel, the very existence of the country is threatened and it is delivered in mid-winter to cold and famine.

In this desperate situation, the Government cannot hope to muster the moral forces necessary for binding the nation, exasperated by these painful events, by a peace treaty which it is now invited to sign.

The Supreme Council could powerfully contribute to the appeasement of public opinion, so necessary for the satisfactory course of negotiations, by despatching commissions to Transylvania, especially to Kolozsvár, Nagyvárad and Marosvásárhely; to Northern Hungary, especially to Pozsony, Rózsahegy and Kassa; and, finally, to Southern Hungary, especially in the neighborhoods of Szabadka and Zombor, in order that such commissions may obtain evidence on the spot regarding the violences to which the Hungarian population has been subjected, and to remedy the ills above referred to.[3]

To these communications the Allies replied on December 10. M. Clemenceau informed Prime Minister Huszár that the Supreme Council did not "consider itself qualified" to interfere with the Rumanians to obtain the release of interned Hungarians whose inclusion in the Hungarian Peace Delegation was desired and repeated the invitation "to send within the shortest time the Hungarian delegates to Paris."[4] The request of the Hungarian Government for the evacuation of Hungarian territories and for the dispatch of Allied missions to the occupied parts of Hungary was ignored. When the Supreme Council declined

[3] Translation from the original French text in *HFR*, Vol. I, Doc. 47. A slightly different English translation is printed in *HPN*, I, viii. Count Somssich, the Minister for Foreign Affairs, had requested, in a communication dated Dec. 4, 1919, and addressed to the Interallied Military Mission in Budapest, the dispatch of an Allied mission to the county of Baranya, to supervise the evacuation of that territory by the Yugoslavs, which it was expected would take place in the near future. *Ibid.*, Doc. 48. In fact, despite repeated urging on the part of Hungary and promises held out by the Allies, Baranya and the city of Pécs were not evacuated until long after the Treaty of Trianon came into force. Cf. *supra*, Part Three, pp. 118, 162–64.

[4] *HFR*, Vol. I, Doc. 50; *HPN*, I, ix.

to interpose for the liberation of these Hungarian experts, the Hungarian Government, on December 12, addressed a direct communication on their behalf to the Rumanian Government,[5] a communication which remained unanswered. To M. Clemenceau, the Prime Minister replied on December 13 that the Hungarian Government would do everything within its power to send the Hungarian delegates to Neuilly immediately after the New Year; at the same time, their request for the evacuation of Hungarian territories by the Rumanians and the dispatch of Allied missions to the occupied territories of Hungary was repeated.[6]

It should perhaps be noted that the requests made by the Hungarians in replying to the invitation to the Peace Conference were amply justified by circumstances and need not be regarded as a manifestation of obstructionist tactics. As far as the dispatch of Allied missions is concerned, there was, as the preceding chapter indicates, abundant evidence to support the complaint that the Hungarian population in the occupied territories was subjected to a variety of mistreatment by the Czech, Yugoslav, and Rumanian occupants.[7] Enough was known in Hungary of the treaties concluded between the Principal Allies and Hungary's neighbors to justify the fear that Transylvania and the greater part of Northern and Southern Hungary were definitely lost. Consequently, the government was anxious to produce evidence at

[5] HFR, Vol. I, Doc. 52; HPN, I, ix

[6] Ibid., Doc. 53; HPN, I, ix.

[7] Apart from the reports of the Interallied Mission and Sir George Clerk, which dealt chiefly with the objectionable conduct of the Rumanians (see supra, Part Three, passim), reference may be made to a number of formal protests lodged by the Hungarian Government against the mistreatment of the population in the territories occupied by Hungary's neighbors. See HFR, Vol. I, Docs. 14, 15, 18, 36, 40, 42, 43. The question of the persecution of non-Rumanian elements in Transylvania was brought up in the House of Lords by Lord Bryce on Dec. 16, 1919, in the form of a question based upon a joint memorandum of the Catholic, Calvinist, and Unitarian Bishops of Transylvania. Lord Bryce suggested an investigation into the allegations of mistreatment contained in the memorandum and the drafting of measures to put an end to the persecutions, if the allegations were found true. He also criticized the methods of the Peace Conference in settling Rumanian territorial claims and urged an impartial investigation to determine the proper boundaries of the two countries. Lord Stanmore, replying for the Government, while expressing the belief that a great part of the evidence concerning Rumanian misbehavior would be found on examination to be true, assured the House that the recent signature of the Minorities Treaty by Rumania put a "new complexion" on the situation. He thought that the British Government ought to give Rumania a chance to put her house in Transylvania in order. Hansard, Parliamentary Debates, House of Lords, 5th ser., Vol. 38, pp. 210 ff.

least to support its claim for the effective protection of Hungarians in these territories. Their claim for the evacuation of those territories—and according to information then available, they were to be left to Hungary—arose from the government's anxiety to end the requisitions made by the occupying troops, which, as had been found by the Allied representatives, had already stripped the country to the bone; moreover, the government desired to hold the scheduled elections in all territories which would remain under Hungary's sovereignty.

The Appointment of the Hungarian Peace Delegation and Hungarian Preparations for the Peace Conference

As soon as the invitation to the Peace Conference was received, the Hungarian Government concentrated its energies on preparing Hungary's case for presentation to the Allied representatives. It was a late beginning, but the delay had arisen from the extraordinary circumstances with which the government was confronted. Prior to the armistice, the foreign relations of the Austro-Hungarian Monarchy were conducted from Vienna and such preparations as were undertaken on behalf of the Monarchy were concentrated at the Ballplatz. A few people in Hungary, prior to the latter part of 1918, did contemplate the possible disappearance of the Habsburg Empire and the consequent necessity for each of its component elements to manage individually their separate problems arising out of the peace settlement. When Hungary became an independent country in November, 1918, the revolutionary governments of Count Károlyi and of Béla Kun were confronted with problems which would have confused men of far greater ability and competence than those who, unfortunately, composed the various cabinets during those unhappy months. The demobilization of the army, the economic needs of the country at the end of four-and-a-half years of war, aggravated by the daily influx of thousands of refugees from the occupied territories, the necessity of organizing new government offices to take care of problems heretofore entrusted to common agencies of the Monarchy—as, for example, the organization of the Foreign Office—were tasks which under the conditions then existing would have baffled almost any government. If one considers in addition the fact that few of the men whom the revolution tossed to the top had much if any experience in administration and the highly complicated art of government, it is not surprising that, apart

from dealing with concrete issues daily presented, no planned preparation of material for the Peace Conference was undertaken during this
revolutionary period.

The counter-revolutionary government at Szeged was fully aware
of the necessity of compiling data for the Peace Conference, but in its
isolated position it was of course unable to undertake the task. The
first step taken by Count Paul Teleki, who served as Minister for Foreign Affairs of the Szeged Government, after the fall of the communist
government, was to order the preparation of documents concerning
Hungary's relations with her neighbors and with France.[8]

The reëstablishment of constitutional order following the collapse
of the communist government in August, 1919, coincided, as we have
seen, with the occupation of the greater part of Hungary, including
the capital, by Rumanian troops. It is evident that the conditions prevailing under a foreign occupation were hardly conducive to the establishment of an agency, such, for instance, as the American "Inquiry,"
to equip the country's plenipotentiaries for a peace settlement of the
magnitude involved. While the governments which followed the short-
lived socialist cabinet under the premiership of Julius Peidl (August 1–
6, 1919) were fully aware of the desirability of preparing the Hungarian
case for submission in Paris, they were overwhelmed by the immediate
issues presented by the Rumanian occupation and by the necessity of
bringing at least a semblance of order into the economic, political,
social, and moral life of the nation, disrupted and dislocated by successive revolutions. Little if anything, therefore, was done in the way of
preparation before Hungary was faced concretely with the issue of
sending plenipotentiaries to plead her case before the Peace Conference.

In the light of these facts the capacity shown by the Hungarians at
the Peace Conference to support their contentions with voluminous
material of no mean scientific value and a fair amount of accuracy was
indeed remarkable. This accomplishment says much for the quality of
the men who composed the Hungarian Peace Delegation and indicates
a self-sacrificing willingness to work and coöperate in the effort to
salvage everything possible from the shambles left in the wake of war,
revolution, and enemy occupation.

[8] See Count Teleki's report on the activities of the Provisional Hungarian Government at Szeged, presented at the end of Aug., 1919, to General Tánczos, Minister for
Foreign Affairs in the Friedrich Government. *HFR,* Vol. I, Doc. 1, entry of Aug. 1,
1919.

The Delegation appointed by the government was in fact composed of men of outstanding ability. It comprised the élite of Hungarian statesmen and scientists, the leaders of Hungarian industry, trade, finance, agriculture and the most intellectual members of the civil and military administration.

Count Albert Apponyi, Hungary's elder statesman, was chosen to head the Peace Delegation. No person could have commanded greater respect or spoken with greater authority in the name of the Hungarian nation than this extraordinary, many-faceted man, whose exceptional ability, knowledge, and wisdom were recognized by friend and foe alike. Whatever accomplishments may be claimed for the Peace Delegation, credit therefor is due in large part to the inspiring leadership, the unlimited capacity for work, and the burning patriotism of Count Apponyi, who was both the mainstay and the driving force of the Delegation in many days of dark despair.

Other leading delegates appointed were Count Paul Teleki; Count Stephen Bethlen; Alexander Popovics, former Minister of Finance and Governor of the Austro-Hungarian Bank; Baron William Lers, Secretary of State; Count László Somssich, President of the Agricultural Association of Hungary; Béla Zoltán, former Minister of Justice; and Iván Ottlik, Secretary of State.

Two of the chief delegates, Count Teleki and Count Bethlen, who did the lion's share of the work of the Peace Delegation during the ensuing months and later were called upon to assume high governmental posts in Hungary, were more or less newcomers to the political scene. Count Teleki was a distinguished scientist, a professor of geography in the University of Budapest, and, although a member of the House of Lords, had devoted his attention almost exclusively to study and research until the misfortunes which befell his country called him from the quiet contemplation of the scholar to the arena of statesmanship. His first experience with practical politics had taken place under exceedingly trying circumstances, when he served as Minister for Foreign Affairs in the Hungarian Provisional Government established at Szeged in May, 1919, to combat the bolshevik regime of Béla Kun. Faced with a thousand difficulties and handicapped by the grudges and suspicions of the occupying authorities, he showed adaptability, determination, and tireless energy in accomplishing his tasks. His knowledge of geography, geopolitics, demography, and history was largely the foundation on which the work of the Peace Delegation was based.

Count Bethlen had been a Member of Parliament before the revolution, but had not gained prominence in political life. His ability to lead, his sagacity, wisdom, and understanding of the forces which underly political currents became evident at an early stage of the counter-revolutionary movement, and Count Bethlen soon became the spiritual leader of the Vienna organization which coöperated closely with the Provisional Government at Szeged. His ability accurately and quickly to appraise a situation, however complicated, and to choose the best road to follow under the circumstances were of course most useful to the Peace Delegation through the trying weeks of isolation in Neuilly.

If the other chief delegates did not make so deep an imprint on the history of the Hungarian peace negotiations, the reason lies in the extraordinary personalities of Apponyi, Teleki, and Bethlen, rather than in any lack of outstanding ability on their part. The same thing may be said of the remaining members of the Delegation who, although occupying the less exalted positions of experts or advisers, were nevertheless without exception the best men to be found in their respective fields. Indeed some of the minor members of the Delegation later played a conspicuous part in the rehabilitation of the country. The name of Dr. Lewis Walkó, who later occupied successively the posts of Minister of Commerce and Minister for Foreign Affairs, is indissolubly connected with the economic reconstruction of Hungary in the late 1920's through the opening of trade channels and the establishment of normal commercial intercourse. Count Emery Csáky, then Councillor of Legation, had an important part in the heretofore undisclosed and confidential conversations between the French and Hungarian Governments, the details of which will be revealed in later pages of this volume, and which by their far-reaching implications and potentialities doubtless constitute the most important part of the Hungarian peace negotiations. A few months after the signature of the Treaty of Trianon, Count Emery Csáky became Minister for Foreign Affairs in the cabinet of Count Teleki. Count Stephen Csáky, then an attaché, after another twenty years of incessant activity in every issue which directly or indirectly concerned Hungary, held the same high office at a time which may be regarded as one of the most critical in Hungary's thousand years of history. Dr. László Bárdossy, a young secretary in the Foreign Office in 1919, had a brilliant career in the foreign service and recently took over the Ministry for Foreign Affairs upon Count Csáky's untimely death.

These men are mentioned here merely to illustrate the quality of the Hungarian Peace Delegation; but the name of practically every member could be mentioned with equal respect. Although in so large a group [9] some persons of course inevitably stand out, no one who has studied the records and who, like the author, has had the opportunity of knowing many of those who made a part of this group, can fail to reach the conclusion that as regards unflagging devotion to the task assigned, a coöperative spirit, and personal disinterestedness no distinctions can be drawn. As Count Apponyi stated at the last meeting of the Delegation, in expressing his thanks "for the unselfish and eager performance by every single one of the delegates of a patriotic duty," "during his long life he had never dealt with an organization so large and heterogeneous whose work had been characterized by so much unqualified selflessness and harmonious coöperation as had been the case with the Hungarian Peace Delegation." [10]

The preparations made by the Delegation prior to its departure for Paris were as thorough and conscientious as time permitted. Assisted by every department and agency of the government, the Delegation collected and compiled information and evidence on every conceivable problem, as if in the hope that these data would in fact be taken into account by the Peace Conference. The truth of the matter is that, whatever may have been the hopes of the nation, Hungary's leading statesmen and the Delegation members had few illusions that the peace conditions would be modified in any material respect. They fully realized that irrespective of the good will of the Allied statesmen, any consideration of Hungary's claims for revision or alteration of the peace conditions was virtually excluded by the fact that she was called to Paris at a time when her position in postwar Europe was in all material respects already determined.

It is important to remember that when the Peace Conference finally

[9] The Peace Delegation proper, i.e., the chief delegates, councillors, experts, and the secretariat, exclusive of the clerical staff, numbered seventy-four. For a complete list, see HPN, I, ix–x.

[10] Minutes of the Plenary Meeting of the Peace Delegation held at Budapest, May 19, 1920, in the "Political Diary of the Hungarian Peace Delegation" [cited hereafter as "Political Diary"]. An English translation of this important document is printed in HFR, I, 848–931, Appendix I.

saw its way clear to dealing directly with Hungary, the major work of the Conference had been completed and the Hungarian peace conditions were, in all essentials, final. The treaties between the Allies and Germany and Austria respectively had been signed and ratified before Hungary was bidden to appear. Indeed the Treaty of Versailles came into force on January 10, 1920, a few days after the Hungarians arrived in Paris. The Treaty of Versailles had no direct bearing on the peace to be made with Hungary, but it had a decided bearing on the psychology of some of the Allied participants in the Peace Conference, who were primarily interested in Germany and who, after the peace with her had been made, exhibited only a perfunctory interest in the other peace treaties. During this period, too, it must be remembered, there was increasing uncertainty as to the position of the United States and growing indications of her ultimate rejection of the Treaty of Versailles and her withdrawal from participation in the work of the Peace Conference.[11] The Treaty of Saint-Germain between the Allies and Austria, on the other hand, was very important in that it served as a pattern for the Hungarian treaty. Most important of all were the treaties which the Principal Allies concluded, prior to the appearance of the Hungarian Peace Delegation in Paris, with Hungary's neighbors, Czecho-Slovakia, Rumania, and Yugoslavia, recognizing the territorial and other claims put forward by those countries and adjudicated by the Principal Allies at Hungary's expense months before Hungary was called to the peace table. Nor was there any doubt as to the attitude of Hungary's neighbors; their hostility to her had been amply demonstrated in the year which had elapsed since the armistice. An indication of what was to be expected from those quarters was found in the refusal of the Czech Government to grant permission, when asked by Count Apponyi to be allowed to spend Christmas on his estate in the occupied part of Northern Hungary, the reason given

[11] On Nov. 17, 1919, the Versailles Treaty, without reservations, failed to obtain the necessary two-thirds vote in the United States Senate, although the treaty was not finally rejected until March 19, 1920. The American members of the Commission to Negotiate Peace sailed from France for home on Dec. 12, 1919 and the American members were withdrawn from all commissions set up by the Peace Conference. Any matter requiring action by the United States Government was thereafter to be referred to the remote State Department in Washington, although the Ambassador to France, Hugh C. Wallace, was authorized to sit on the Supreme Council—not as a participant, but as an observer on behalf of the United States. General Bandholtz, however, was allowed to remain as American representative in Budapest until his successor, Ulysses Grant-Smith, should arrive. See *Foreign Relations of the United States,* 1919, I, 16 ff.

being that "a person chosen to defend Hungary's interests against Czecho-Slovakia at the Peace Conference cannot be allowed to sojourn on Czech soil." [12]

It is therefore no exaggeration to say that Hungary's case was fatally prejudged, before she was called into court, because of the postwar structure of Europe erected in Paris and, in particular, by the prior Allied commitments to Hungary's neighbors. Enough of this general structure and of these commitments was known to Hungarian statesmen, despite the relative isolation of Hungary from all sources of information, to enable them to appreciate the situation which they were to face. If they nevertheless spared no effort to present Hungary's case with the utmost care, it was done not so much in expectation of immediate results as in anticipation of possible future changes. [13]

After a month of feverish work, part of the Hungarian Delegation left Budapest for Paris on January 5, 1920. [14]

[12] Note from Major Hémelot, the Head of the Czecho-Slovak Mission in Budapest, to the Minister for Foreign Affairs, Dec. 22, 1919. HFR, Vol. I, Doc. 60.

[13] Count Teleki, when presenting his program as Foreign Minister to the National Assembly, stated that the Peace Delegation did not expect to accomplish much by means of the voluminous material it presented to the Peace Conference. "As much as we may have wished to," he said, "we could not hope to achieve fundamental and radical changes in the peace conditions. We knew that these conditions were determined by circumstances which would make any change in details difficult. We attacked the Peace Treaty not only in its details but also in its bases as one which [it] is impossible to fulfill and execute. All our arguments, however, and we knew this as well at the time as we know it now, served not so much for the present as for the future. . . ." Translated from the Minutes of the National Assembly, 35th Meeting, April 26, 1920. Records of the National Assembly, II, 299 ff., in HFR, I (Appendix III, No. I), 947.

Again, when the Trianon Treaty was presented to the National Assembly for ratification, Count Teleki, then Prime Minister, stated: "When the Peace Delegation went to Neuilly, we did not expect to find understanding. While I was engaged in the preparatory work for the peace negotiations, I never thought that we would find any real understanding. I was convinced that we were preparing our arguments for the judgment of history and not of those who lacked all the attributes of the judicial function. . . . We realized that the Hungarian peace is a small and unimportant part of a much larger structure. We realized that any change in this small and unimportant part might necessitate changes in the larger structure which was directed against Germany. . . ." Translated from the Minutes of the National Assembly, 128th Meeting, Nov. 13, 1920. Records of the National Assembly, VII, 4 ff., in HFR, I (Appendix III), 989.

[14] The following Delegation members were sent: Count Apponyi, Count Teleki, Count Bethlen, Alexander Popovics, Baron William Lers, and Count László Somssich, chief delegates; Count Emery Csáky, Dr. Lewis Walkó, Richard Bartha, Tibor Kállay, Baron Balthazár Láng, Captain Emil Konek, delegates; Dr. Roland Hegedüs, Dr. Tibor Scitovszky, Béla Török, Alexander Kiss, Emil Walther, Elemér Jármay, Charles

The Arrival of the Hungarians in Paris: Initial Difficulties

After two and a half days of slow travel in an unheated train through Austria and Switzerland, the Hungarian Peace Delegation arrived in Paris in the early morning of January 7, 1920. They were received at the Gare de l'Est by Lieutenant Colonel Henry, chief of the French Military Mission attached to the Hungarian Delegation, and several other Allied officers. The Hungarians were conducted at once to the Château de Madrid in Neuilly. Colonel Henry informed Mr. Praznovszky, who acted as Secretary General of the Delegation, that the peace conditions would be transmitted in eight or ten days and acquainted him with the arrangements made for the Hungarians. Lieutenant Colonel Henry was to serve as liaison officer between the Allies and the Peace Delegation, and all communications and mail were to go through his hands. Reporters might be received only with the permission of the President of the Peace Conference, M. Clemenceau, and the Hungarians were strongly advised against any attempt to inspire articles favorable to Hungary in the French press, because "they would merely call forth a hundred that were hostile." Visitors could be received only with the permission of the Secretary General of the Peace Conference, Ambassador Dutasta. The Hungarians were allowed to go about freely in Neuilly and in the Bois de Boulogne, but they had to have special permission to go to Paris and then must have an escort.[15]

Thus the Peace Delegation found itself in an isolation not unlike that of the Duke of Reichstadt, who, in the words of Rostand, described his position as "pas prisonnier, mais. . . ." The Hungarians were advised in the most polite terms as to the restrictions imposed, but nevertheless the restrictions were there. Even communications with Budapest were difficult, and it was due only to the kindness of the Americans that the Peace Delegation was able to send 7,000 words daily over the American wires. The situation perhaps can best be characterized in Lieutenant Colonel Henry's own words. After explaining the regulations described above, he assured Mr. Praznovszky that he would do

Ottrubay, George Barkóczy, Alexander Kirchner, Arnold Bobrik, Count Stephen Csáky, Baron Zoltán Bánffy, Alexander Erry, and Professor Arthur Yolland, experts and secretaries, Mr. Iván Praznovszky and Dr. John Wettstein constituting the Secretariat. The Delegation took with it a small clerical staff and was accompanied by several Hungarian journalists.

[15] "Political Diary," entry of Jan. 7, 1920.

his best "to make your sojourn as little disagreeable as possible." [16] In fairness to a gallant French officer, it should be said that he fully lived up to his promise. It was not due to any lack of good will on his part that the Hungarian Delegation, in the opening weeks at least, was almost hermetically separated from the world.

A few illustrations will indicate the extent of this isolation. On January 9 Count Bethlen received information from Budapest that Mr. Matsui, the Japanese ambassador in Paris, wished to establish contact with the Hungarian Delegation. After twenty-four hours of vain effort, the Delegation had to report to Count Somssich, the Minister for Foreign Affairs, that it was unable to reach anyone and that the Japanese ambassador must himself take the initiative if he wished to get in touch with the Hungarians.[17] When Count Apponyi sought to establish contact with the delegates of the Principal Allied Powers in order to urge upon them the desirability of oral negotiations, Lieutenant Colonel Henry had to reply that personal relations between the Allies and the Hungarian delegates were impossible until after the signing of the peace treaty.[18] When, after several days of repeated efforts, the Delegation had to record that "every attempt to obtain permission for personal contact has met with absolute refusal," the Delegation decided to urge Count Somssich to ask the British, Italian, and Polish representatives in Budapest to help the Delegation to break through its ring of isolation.[19] It was, however, not till several weeks later that their intervention was crowned with some success.

The first clash between the Allies and the Hungarian Delegation occurred over the participation of the United States in the Peace Conference. The Hungarians knew, of course, before they came to Neuilly that the American Senate had rejected the Treaty of Versailles and that the American Peace Delegation had been recalled from Paris. The relation of the United States to the Peace Conference was not clear to the Hungarians—it may be doubted whether it was quite clear to the Allies themselves—and there was considerable anxiety among the members of the Delegation as to whether the United States would take part in the negotiations with Hungary. For several reasons the Hungarians attributed much importance to the presence of American plenipotentiaries. First of all, the Hungarians had great confidence in the

[16] Code telegram No. 4, from the Peace Delegation to the Minister for Foreign Affairs, Jan. 10, 1920. *HFR*, Vol. I, Doc. 71.

[17] "Political Diary," entries of Jan. 10 and 11, 1920.

[18] *Ibid.*, entry of Jan. 11, 1920. [19] *Ibid.*, entry of Jan. 12, 1920.

Americans and hoped that their sense of fair play would be a moderating influence. This confidence was due not merely to the traditional liking that Hungarians felt for Americans, dating back to the friendly reception given Louis Kossuth by the United States after the unsuccessful struggle for independence in 1848-49, but also to the excellent impression created in Hungary by the correct and helpful attitude of the American representatives, civil and military, who had visited the country since the armistice. The marked contrast between their behavior and the bullying, or at best condescending manners of many of the other Allied officials naturally evoked a response from the Hungarian people.[20] Moreover, because of the large number of Hungarians living in the United States, the government as well as the Delegation felt it important that relations between the two countries should be regulated as soon as possible.

The status of the United States with respect to the Peace Conference was discussed at the very first meeting of the Delegation, on the day of its arrival at Neuilly. Count Bethlen in raising the issue, pointed out that the United States was no longer represented in the Supreme Council and emphasized the importance of informing American public opinion of the course of the peace negotiations with Hungary. But the precise situation was not known,[21] and after it was discovered that the United States was no longer officially represented in the Supreme Council Count Apponyi requested the Minister for Foreign Affairs to ascertain, through General Bandholtz,[22] the relations of the United States with the Peace Conference and to make arrangements through him, if possible, to enable the Delegation to send copies of all communications with the Peace Conference to the American ambassador in Paris.[23] The reply came a few days later. General Bandholtz informed Count Somssich that although Ambassador Wallace was at-

[20] To support this conclusion, it is enough to refer to the conduct of General Bandholtz, the American member of the Interallied Military Mission, whose activities were described in some detail in the preceding chapter. While the French, British, and Italian members of this mission were in no way deficient in their accomplishment of the task entrusted to them, it was General Bandholtz who took the lead, more than once at the risk of his personal safety, in trying to prevent the excesses of the Rumanian troops when occupying Hungary. There his name is worshiped even today.

[21] "Political Diary," entry of Jan. 7, 1920.

[22] Although Ulysses Grant-Smith was appointed as American Commissioner to Hungary, to replace the military representative, on Dec. 4, 1919 (*Foreign Relations of the United States*, 1919, II, 410), he did not arrive in Budapest until the latter part of Jan., 1920, and General Bandholtz did not leave Hungary until February.

[23] "Political Diary," entry of Jan. 9, 1920.

tending the meetings of the Supreme Council, he was doing so merely in the capacity of observer. Bandholtz agreed that it was desirable fully to inform the American ambassador of every move and promised to suggest to the Ambassador that he himself make the desired direct contact possible.[24]

The issue was brought to a head when Ambassador Jules Cambon came to Neuilly on January 14 to present the Allied credentials.[25] The frigid formality of this ceremony was characteristically in keeping with the atmosphere of the Peace Conference. After formally introducing himself and the Allied representatives who accompanied him, M. Cambon informed Count Apponyi that the Hungarian credentials had been accepted by the Allies. In looking over the Allied credentials handed to him, Count Apponyi, seeing that no American representative was listed among the plenipotentiaries, inquired whether the United States was represented. M. Cambon replied that it was not and stated that the peace conditions would be handed to the Hungarians the next day. The ceremony was ended without further conversation, and there was no handshaking.[26]

After that Count Apponyi at once sent a letter to the President of the Peace Conference, requesting a brief postponement while the Hungarians examined the Allied credentials and asking M. Clemenceau's good offices in establishing direct contact with the American ambassador in Paris.[27] The reply came promptly—within a few hours indeed—but its abrupt tone caused a painful impression in the Château de Madrid. Acknowledging Count Apponyi's communication, M. Clemenceau wrote as follows:

The Supreme Council received this answer with surprise: the handing over of the Conditions of Peace cannot be postponed on the pretext of verifying the pouvoirs of the Allied Powers. The verification is only a formality since the pouvoirs have been verified and accepted in turn by the Germans, Austrians and Bulgarians. . . .

[24] HFR, Vol. I, Doc. 73.
[25] The Hungarians sent their credentials through Lieutenant Colonel Henry the day after their arrival. "Political Diary," entry of Jan. 8, 1920.
[26] Ibid., entry of Jan. 14, 1920.
[27] "Having received information from M. Cambon as to the fact that the United States of America will not be represented at the conference to which we are delegated and being commissioned by our Government to prepare the peace with all the belligerent Powers, we beg you, Sir, kindly to furnish us with means of entering into direct relations with the accredited representative of the Government of Washington in Paris." Note No. 14 (adm.), Jan. 14, 1920, from the Hungarian Peace Delegation to M. Clemenceau. HPN, I, 308.

The fact of the Americans not having ratified the Peace of Versailles can have no influence whatever on the handing over of the Conditions of Peace. Besides, the representative of the United States, Ambassador Wallace, has received a plein pouvoir from his Government to sign the Peace with Hungary, and he will be present at the handing over of the Peace Conditions.

Under the circumstances I have the honour to repeat in writing the invitation already presented by M. Jules Cambon for tomorrow, Thursday, at 4 o'clock in the Foreign Office, for receiving the text of the Conditions of Peace.

Please let me know at your convenience your final reply. In case the Hungarian Peace Delegation should not consider it necessary to comply with the invitation of the Supreme Council, the Allies would take this fact as a refusal to accept the Conditions of Peace, and would consider that there would be no further reason for the Delegation of which you are the President to continue their stay in Paris.[28]

The Hungarians had considerable difficulty in finding an explanation for the brusque tone of M. Clemenceau's reply. The Delegation had been in Paris for a full week, and no one had seemed to be, until that moment, in any particular hurry to acquaint them with the peace terms. Nevertheless, Count Apponyi's rejoinder was polite and restrained. He explained that there was no intention of seeking delay, since the Delegation obviously came to Paris to receive the peace conditions. Count Apponyi felt that his duty to clarify the position of the United States was equally obvious and he had been compelled to turn in this matter to the President of the Peace Conference, since the Hungarian Delegation was completely shut off from the world. Since the position of the United States had meanwhile been clarified,[29] Count Apponyi concluded, the Hungarians would appear to receive the peace conditions at the appointed place and hour.[30]

Hungary's Isolated Position

It is perhaps superfluous to point out that Hungary's isolated position in general, and at the Peace Conference in particular, was not wholly of her own making. On the contrary, the various governments in power since the collapse of the bolshevik regime (August 1, 1919) had made every effort to establish channels of communication with the outside

[28] M. Clemenceau to Count Apponyi, Jan. 14, 1920. Ibid., p. 309.

[29] The credentials of the American ambassador were received by the Hungarian Delegation on the afternoon of Jan. 14.

[30] For the text of Count Apponyi's reply, see HPN, II, 468. Cf. "Political Diary," entry of Jan. 14, 1920.

world. In this endeavor the Hungarians, however, had encountered great difficulties.

First, the status of Hungary and of the Hungarian Government was undetermined. Neither the independence of Hungary nor of her government was recognized *de facto* or *de jure* by any of the Allied Powers or by neutral states. Apart from Austria and Germany, no country maintained permanent diplomatic representatives in Budapest. The Rumanian military authorities of course did their best to seal every avenue of contact with the outside world. Thus, for all practical purposes, the only means of communication with the Allied and Associated Powers, including Hungary's neighbors other than Austria, was, at least during the first months following the reëstablishment of constitutional government, the Interallied Mission appointed by the Supreme Council on August 5, 1919, to deal with the problems created by the unauthorized occupation of Hungary by the Rumanians, and other Allied representatives stationed in or visiting Hungary for specific purposes.

The presence of the Interallied Mission in Budapest brought about a decided improvement over the situation which existed prior to its arrival. From the signing of the armistice until August, 1919, the Hungarians had dealings, with rare exceptions, only with officers of the Allied armies of occupation. Neither the circumstances in which these officers had to perform their tasks nor their relations with the officials of a vanquished state were, with a few exceptions, such as to be conducive to normal diplomatic intercourse. Nor did the few Allied officials who intermittently paid short visits to Hungary on special missions end the country's isolation. With the establishment of the Interallied Mission there was at least a permanent representation of the Principal Allies in Hungary and at least a possibility of direct contact between the Supreme Council and the Hungarian Government.

But in fact the presence of the Allied Generals in Budapest did not materially alleviate Hungary's isolation. As the preceding chapter indicates, the Supreme Council and the Principal Allied governments paid little attention to the reports and recommendations of their own representatives—so little, indeed, that the Allied Generals themselves were often exasperated by the ineffectiveness of their intervention. To be sure, this unconcern of the Allies was due not to any sinister design against Hungary but to their preoccupation with other matters which, in their view, took precedence over the Hungarian problem. They were at that time occupied with the Austrian and Bulgarian treaties and, even more, with the difficulties arising out of the Treaty of Versailles. Therefore, irrespective of the best intentions of the Allied Generals— and there can be no doubt that these gentlemen did their very best under the circumstances—their presence in Budapest was not of much help to the Hungarian Government in its endeavor to get a hearing from the statesmen assembled in Paris. Their lack of success in this respect, it should be emphasized, was caused by no omission on their part. In innumerable cases, upon complaints of Hungarian authorities and individuals, they attempted to restrain the occupying Rumanian Army and they urged the evacuation of Hungary, in order to enable the Hungarians to reëstablish order and to form a government sufficiently stable and representative to conclude the peace. They faithfully forwarded the pleas and protests of the Hungarian Government to Paris, there to be buried in most instances in the archives of the Peace Conference. It is useless to burden this narrative with extended quotations and references. It is enough to say that an examination of the voluminous correspondence between the Interallied Military Mission and the departments of the Hungarian Government [31] clearly indicates that between August, 1919, and January, 1920, by far the greater part of the communications consisted of protests against the conduct of the Rumanian occupants and against the treatment of the Hungarian population in Hungary's outlying districts, the loss of which (this the Hungarians well realized) was already a *fait accompli*. While these protests all implied a refusal to acquiesce in the contemplated dismemberment of the thousand-year-old kingdom, their purpose was to seek, through whatever influence the Interallied Mission was capable of exerting, immediate relief from concrete evils, rather than, by enlightening the Supreme Council, to lay the foundation for a frontal attack against the peace treaty. The first real opportunity which Hungary had to acquaint the Peace Conference at first hand with the situation was afforded by the mission of Sir George Clerk. But any opportunity for further elucidation of Hungary's position disappeared with his departure, and Hungary sank back to the status of almost complete isolation in which she had previously found herself.

[31] The confusion characterizing the situation in Hungary during this period is well illustrated by the multiplicity of agencies which carried on correspondence with the Interallied Mission. Besides the Foreign Office, the Inter-Ministerial Armistice Commission, the Prime Minister's office, and the Ministry of National Defence, and still other ministries communicated directly with the Mission.

In considering Hungary's relations with other countries, the obvious starting point is Austria. The fact that diplomatic relations with Austria suffered no interruption during the post-armistice period in no way lessened Hungary's isolation. First, Austria was herself a defeated state, and there were as yet few representatives of foreign countries resident in Vienna through whom communications could be established with the outside world, especially with neutral countries. Moreover, relations between the erstwhile partners of the defunct Empire were far from satisfactory. The traditional animosity between the Austrians and the Hungarians was further emphasized by the unconcealed hostility between the Social-Democratic party, which had held sway in Austria since the armistice, and the conservative and nationalistic regime which established itself in Hungary after the collapse of the bolshevik government. On the other hand, the Hungarians bitterly resented the fact that Austria, with whom they had fought the war side by side, now presented a claim for Hungarian territory. Indeed Austro-Hungarian relations were so strongly colored throughout this period by the claim for the incorporation of Western Hungary into Austria that a full understanding of these relations necessitates a somewhat detailed account of the situation.[32]

A few days after the fall of Béla Kun's Government and after the assignment of Western Hungary to Austria, the Austrian Government asked permission from the Peace Conference to occupy that territory "to maintain order and security." Needless to say, the request created a very bad impression in Hungary. After all, while the decision of the Allies to allocate Western Hungary to Austria had, in fact, been communicated to the Austrian Peace Delegation, the peace treaty with Austria was not yet signed. No sooner was constitutional order in Hungary reëstablished than an exchange of notes took place which set the key, for months to come, for the acrimony which characterized relations between the two countries. Upon instructions of Martin Lovászy, Minister for Foreign Affairs in the second Friedrich Cabinet, the Hungarian chargé d'affaires in Vienna protested to the Austrian Government against the request for the occupation of Western Hungary and against the accusation that the German-speaking population of Western Hungary would be mistreated by Hungarian troops sent there to restore order. Such an accusation, the note pointed out, seri-

[32] The allocation of Western Hungary to Austria by the Peace Conference has been described *supra,* Part Two, pp. 85–90.

ously threatened the friendly relations which the government and people of Hungary earnestly desired to maintain with Austria. As far as the ultimate fate of this territory was concerned, the note stated, while the Hungarian Government might be compelled to bow to the unalterable decision of the Peace Conference, any attempt to prejudice such decision by occupation would be met by armed resistance.[33]

The Austrian reply was bitter and, in places, insultingly sarcastic. It started out by claiming that the population of Western Hungary were "body and soul part of Austria and were only alienated from her artificially through forcible magyarization under the old régime." According to the note, the decision of the Peace Conference allotting this territory to Austria "was dictated by wisdom and justice and must be regarded as unalterable." Austria was merely seeking to protect her own people against requisitions and persecution. Should Hungary send troops into Western Hungary, in disregard of the intentions of the highest international forum and without the consent of the future sovereign of this territory, such conduct would obviously constitute an unfriendly act. Austria made the further accusation that Hungary, by sending troops into Western Hungary ostensibly to maintain order, was really seeking to influence by armed force the free expression of popular will at a plebiscite "in favor of Magyar imperialism." [34]

This brief summary of the exchange, which omits the more acrimonious passages, is indicative of the tone of Austro-Hungarian relations at that period. Efforts of the Hungarian Government to improve them were of no avail. The Austrians continued to spread atrocity stories in their own and in the foreign press. At the end of August the Hungarian Government proposed to the Supreme Council, through the Interallied Military Mission in Budapest, the dispatch of a commission composed of Allied and neutral representatives to Western Hungary to investigate the alleged oppression and mistreatment of the population [35] and communicated this proposal to the Austrian Government as proof of its good faith.[36] The Hungarian proposal produced

[33] The Minister for Foreign Affairs to the Hungarian chargé d'affaires in Vienna, Aug. 16, 1919. *HFR,* Vol. I, Doc. 4.
[34] Note Verbale, dated Aug. 20, 1919, from the Austrian Legation in Budapest to the Hungarian Ministry for Foreign Affairs. *Ibid.,* Doc. 7.
[35] The Ministry for Foreign Affairs to the Interallied Military Mission, Aug. 27, 1919. *Ibid.,* Doc. 11.
[36] The Ministry for Foreign Affairs to the Hungarian Legation in Vienna, Aug. 27, 1919. *Ibid.,* Doc. 13.

no effect, either in Paris or in Vienna. The treaty of peace between the Allies and Austria was signed on September 10, and a few days later the Interallied Military Mission in Budapest requested the Hungarian Government, upon complaint of the Austrian minister to Hungary, to enjoin Hungarian officials not to "encroach" upon "formerly Hungarian territories" which had now been "definitely assigned" to Austria.[37] Another request demanded the evacuation of a Hungarian battalion from Sopron and the withdrawal of all military units west of the frontiers laid down in the Treaty of Saint-Germain, since their presence in a territory which "no longer belongs to Hungary" may give rise to incidents with the Austrians.[38] In replying to these two communications, the Hungarian Government courteously but firmly rejected the suggestions of the Interallied Military Mission. Count Somssich took the unassailable position that the Armistice Convention of Belgrade, signed on November 13, 1918, clearly indicated that even in the territories occupied, the civil administration was to be left in the hands of the Hungarian authorities;[39] as far as future sovereignty over the territory was concerned, that question was to be determined by the peace treaty, and it was difficult to conceive how Hungary could be bound by the unratified Treaty of Saint-Germain, to which she was not a party, which was made without Hungary being heard, and the contents of which had never been communicated to her. In conclusion, the Hungarian Government expressed its willingness to submit the question of Western Hungary to a plebiscite.[40]

Another factor which adversely affected Austro-Hungarian relations was the constant agitation of Hungarian communists who took refuge in Austria and found there not merely asylum but, the Hun-

[37] The President of the Day of the Interallied Military Mission in Budapest, General Bandholtz, to the Minister for Foreign Affairs, Count Somssich, Sept. 16, 1919. *Ibid.,* Doc. 17.

[38] The President of the Day of the Interallied Military Mission, General Mombelli, to Prime Minister Friedrich, Oct. 1, 1919. *Ibid.,* Doc. 24.

[39] *Infra,* Doc. 2, p. 359. The fact that this stipulation was disregarded in no way weakened the Hungarian argument; breaches of the law do not affect its validity.

[40] The Minister for Foreign Affairs, Count Somssich, to the Interallied Military Mission in Budapest, Oct. 1, 1919. *HFR,* Vol. I, Doc. 21. The same stand was taken in the reply to the second communication. The second Hungarian note called attention to the fact that the occupation of Sopron by the Austrian national guard (*Volkswehr*), recruited largely from socialists and communists, might well create a bolshevik propaganda center in the immediate neighborhood of Hungary, which was just beginnng to recover from the nightmare of a communist regime. The Minister for Foreign Affairs to the Interallied Military Mission in Budapest, Oct. 10, 1919. *Ibid.,* Doc. 25.

garian Government claimed, more or less open support. Among these refugees were several of the peoples' commissars in the Soviet Government, including Béla Kun himself; and they were active in trying to prevent the reëstablishment of order in Hungary, in the hope of regaining their own power. The Hungarian Foreign Minister complained to the Interallied Mission of the support received in Austria by Hungarian communists and called attention to the publication of articles by the interned communist leaders in the Austrian press as evidence of coöperation between these Hungarian refugees and Austrian left-wing leaders. Count Somssich reported that rumors had reached the government of plans to invade Hungary with the help of Austrian labor battalions and that the proximity to the Hungarian border of the camps in which the refugee communists were interned was a cause of deep anxiety to the Hungarian Government.[41]

Finally, the obligation undertaken by Austria to assist the Allies in an economic blockade, should they find it necessary to resort to such a weapon in order to force on Hungary the peace conditions, was another cause of estrangement between Austria and Hungary.[42] Although Austria had no choice as to complying with the request to assume this obligation, the possibility of Austria's becoming one of the instruments through which Hungary might be forced to her knees was one more element which created distrust of Austria among Hungarians and, in their eyes aligned her with their hostile neighbors.

In late October, 1919, the Hungarian Government took another step to improve relations with Austria by sending Dr. Gustav Gratz as Hungarian minister to Vienna. Dr. Gratz was known to be a liberal, a strong believer in economic coöperation for the Danubian states in general, and a staunch supporter of friendly Austro-Hungarian relations in particular. He also had a wide circle of acquaintances in Austria, and it was hoped that he might find a way to *rapprochement* between the two countries. But Dr. Gratz's sympathetic understanding

[41] See the communication of Count Somssich dated Oct. 10, referred to in the preceding footnote, and cf. another note of the Minister for Foreign Affairs to the Interallied Military Mission, dated Oct. 14, 1920. *Ibid.*, Doc. 26.

[42] Under the Special Declaration, dated Sept. 10, 1919, supplementary to the Treaty of Saint-Germain, Austria agreed, "in the case of a request by the Governments of the United States, the British Empire, France and Italy, effectively to prohibit the import, export and transit of all articles between Austria and Hungary, and to maintain such prohibition up to the time of the formal acceptance by the Government of Hungary of the terms of peace proposed by the Allied and Associated Governments." *British and Foreign State Papers*, CXII, 501.

of Austrian psychology and his suave diplomacy were not able to overcome a certain distrust of what was believed to be his attachment to
the monarchy and he was powerless against the opposition of Chancellor Renner and his strongly left-wing socialist advisers. The first
conversation between the Chancellor and Dr. Gratz, when the latter
presented his credentials on November 10, 1919, brought out sharply
the divergent points of view. To Dr. Gratz's assurance that he would
do his best to promote friendly relations between the two countries,
Dr. Renner replied that he also accepted the interdependence of Austria and Hungary, but that circumstances rendered it difficult for the
Austrian Government to cultivate intimate and friendly relations with
Hungary. He referred particularly to the political regime in Hungary,
which he designated as "conservative and monarchistic" and which, the
Chancellor stated, was viewed with concern by the Austrian Government because of the deep anxiety of the Austrian labor classes. On this
score great difficulties had been caused by the request of the Hungarian
authorities for the extradition of the communist leaders who had taken
refuge in Austria. Compliance with that request, the Chancellor said,
would hardly be approved by Austrian labor. Another obstacle was
presented by the question of Western Hungary, on which Austria
would not change her attitude. A detailed discussion of these questions
by Dr. Gratz did not succeed in moving Chancellor Renner to a more
coöperative position.[43] Somewhat friendlier in tone but equally inconclusive was the meeting later in the month between Dr. Carl Seitz, the
President of Austria, and Dr. Gratz. Dr. Seitz said that Austria attributed great importance to friendly relations with Hungary and expressed the belief that intimate relations were possible, provided that
neither party attempted to reëstablish the union or to interfere in the
internal affairs of the other. Obviously the fear of a Habsburg restoration must have been paramount in the mind of the Austrian socialist
leaders and supplied the common ground for the anti-Habsburg, Austro-Czech *rapprochement* which began to take shape at this time.

Besides opposition to the Habsburgs, the attitude of the Austrian
leaders was doubtless influenced by the historic antagonism which
existed between the two partners of the defunct Monarchy. The distrust which the Hungarians harbored of Austrian attempts at German-
ization was reciprocated by the Austrians, usually dissatisfied with
Hungary's policy within the Empire. More particularly, much of the

[43] Dr. Gratz to Count Somssich, Nov. 13, 1919. *HFR,* Vol. I, Doc. 39.

resentment over Hungary's food policy during the World War, considered by Austria as unfair and selfish, remained alive in the minds of the Austrians, submerged by want. Whether or not such distrust and resentment had any real foundation is of course immaterial. In order to appraise objectively the attitude of Austria toward the attempts at *rapprochement* made by her former partner, account ought to be taken of the existence of these psychological factors, which doubtless influenced, if not determined, the policy of the Austrian political leaders.

Concerning Western Hungary, Dr. Seitz told Dr. Gratz that Austria had no annexationist policy; by adopting the policy of *"so weit die deutsche Zunge reicht"* ("as far as the German language is spoken") as the basis of territorial claims, Austria had primarily in view the Germans allotted to Czecho-Slovakia. However, since the question of Western Hungary had been settled by the Treaty of Saint-Germain, Dr. Seitz expressed the hope that Hungary, in the interest of friendly relations, would acquiesce.[44] Both Dr. Seitz and Dr. Renner evaded the question of why Austria, abandoning her original position in favor of a plebiscite in Western Hungary, now maintained that under the circumstances—meaning high-pressure Hungarian propaganda—the true will of the population could not be expressed.

While Hungary endeavored to better the atmosphere between Vienna and Budapest, and the leaders of the Austrian Republic gave reluctant lip service to a reciprocal desire for friendlier relations, Austrian foreign policy began to take an even more decidedly anti-Hungarian turn, owing to a gradual *rapprochement* with Czecho-Slovakia. The wooing of Austria by Prague began soon after the Treaty of Saint-Germain was signed in September, 1919. The primary motive of the Czech statesmen in seeking to draw Austria into the Czech orbit was the fear of *Anschluss*. A shrewd politician, Dr. Beneš, realized that Austria alone would inevitably veer toward Germany and that unless she received more effective assistance than the half-hearted injections administered by the Principal Allies, her association with Germany would logically follow. Moreover, Austria could be a useful link in the ring of isolation which Dr. Beneš was determined to forge around Hungary. On the other hand, the desperate economic and financial situation in which Austria found herself forced Chancellor Renner to turn for help to any quarter from which it might be forthcoming. Austria, despite

[44] Dr. Gratz to Count Somssich, Nov. 29, 1919. *Ibid.*, Doc. 44.

some assistance from the Allies, was urgently in need of economic and financial help; an acute coal shortage was paralyzing the already-deteriorated Austrian industries; lack of food and raw materials and the constantly falling rate of exchange rendered the purchase of indispensable supplies in foreign markets increasingly difficult. Czecho-Slovakia was in a position to alleviate these difficulties, to some extent at least, and the Czech statesmen were quick to appreciate the advantages which might be derived from dangling before the downtrodden Austrians the promise of a more abundant life. The mutual hostility of the Czechs and the Austrians was somewhat offset by the fact that the governments in both countries was in the hands, or at least under the control of left-wing parties; the Social-Democrat Dr. Renner and Dr. Beneš, with his decided sympathy for liberal-socialist tendencies, spoke very much the same language. They both distrusted the nationalist regime in Hungary, which, they feared, threatened the undisturbed enjoyment of vast Hungarian territories now under Czech rule, as well as the acquisition of Western Hungary by Austria. They were equally apprehensive of a Habsburg restoration in Hungary. Finally, the Austrian Government appeared to be more willing to acquiesce in the peace treaty than Hungary and presented no such problems to Czecho-Slovak foreign policy as the resurgent nationalism in Hungary. Under these circumstances confidential conversations between Dr. Renner and Prime Minister Tusar, of Czecho-Slovakia, progressed rapidly, and early in December, 1919, rumors began to circulate in Vienna that Dr. Renner would soon visit Prague to conclude an agreement with the Czecho-Slovak Government.

Despite the secrecy which surrounded these conversations, enough information leaked out for Dr. Gratz to realize that should an agreement be reached between Vienna and Prague, it would certainly be directed against Hungary. In order to forestall this, Dr. Gratz decided, on his own initiative and responsibility, to investigate the possibility of arriving at a *modus vivendi* between Hungary and Czecho-Slovakia. On December 10, 1919, he called on Dr. Flieder, the Czech minister in Vienna. Dr. Gratz told his Czech colleague that while the settlement of Czech-Hungarian differences did not fall within the competence of the envoys of these two countries to a third state, they might be able, for the very reason that they were not directly concerned with the issues, to seek a solution with less prejudice and more objectivity. Dr. Flieder was very reserved in response to this overture and replied, according to Dr. Gratz, "with extreme caution and with colorless generalities." He told Dr. Gratz that the Czechs were willing to establish friendlier relations. Gratz pointed out that hostility to Hungary had now taken the form of military preparations, although Hungary had no aggressive intention whatsoever against Czecho-Slovakia; on the contrary, Hungary was anxious to conclude peace and to reëstablish order. Flieder said that unfriendly speeches by Hungarian politicians had created the impression in Czecho-Slovakia that the Hungarian Government did have aggressive intentions. Dr. Gratz referred to the fact that Czech statesmen were also using unfriendly language with reference to Hungary and suggested that it might be possible to bring about an economic *rapprochement,* which in turn might react favorably on the political differences between the two countries.

When he returned the call, two days later, the Czech minister, who had meanwhile consulted his government about the overtures made by Dr. Gratz, adopted a friendlier tone and a less reserved attitude. He denied, first, that Czecho-Slovakia had hostile plans against Hungary, whereupon Dr. Gratz formally assured Dr. Flieder that Hungary did not contemplate war against Czecho-Slovakia. Admitting that the principal issue between the two countries was the territorial question, at present apparently insoluble, Dr. Gratz suggested that an approach to understanding might still be found in the economic sphere. Czecho-Slovakia, he said, more than any of the Succession States, was in need of markets; were Hungary to admit Czech and German goods on an equal basis and to deny the opportunity to Czecho-Slovakia to conclude preferential agreements with Austria and Hungary, as she was entitled under the Treaty of Saint-Germain to do, German industry would doubtless defeat Czech industry in the competitive struggle. To Dr. Flieder's inquiry as to the methods whereby an economic agreement might be arrived at, Dr. Gratz proposed negotiations through expert commissions. The two envoys agreed to refer the matters discussed to their governments and to resume conversations after they had ascertained the attitude of their superiors.[45]

Dr. Gratz, like the Hungarian Government, was fully aware of the difficulties which stood in the way of the proposed economic negotiations. Although the Hungarians had no precise information as to the extent to which Dr. Beneš was willing to go in his policy of isolating Hungary, they had few if any illusions concerning his fundamentally

[45] Dr. Gratz to Count Somssich, Dec. 15, 1919. *HFR,* Vol. I, Doc. 55.

hostile attitude toward the Magyars. Nor did they doubt that despite all protestations of good intentions, Chancellor Renner and his advisers harbored no friendly feelings toward Hungary. Hungary had also to consider the adverse effect which negotiations with the Czechs might have on her relations with Poland, the only country at once friendly to Hungary and whose relations with Czecho-Slovakia were strained.[46] Finally, account had to be taken of the possibility that the Slovaks loyal to Hungary—and their number was not negligible—might consider such negotiations as evidence of Hungary's willingness to abandon them. Nevertheless, the possibility of Czech military action, which the Hungarians, rightly or wrongly, believed to be imminent, and the desirability of neutralizing the effects of the increasing friendliness between Austria and Czecho-Slovakia outweighed these considerations. The Hungarian Government decided to begin economic negotiations along the lines suggested by Dr. Gratz in his conversations with the Czech minister in Vienna. Count Somssich, emphasizing the pacific intentions of the Hungarian Government, instructed Dr. Gratz to continue the conversations with Dr. Flieder, and he himself engaged in an exchange of views with the acting head of the Czech Mission in Budapest, Councillor of Legation Lejhanec.[47] To forestall possible misunderstandings with Poland, the Minister for Foreign Affairs advised the Polish Government that Hungary, compelled by circumstances, planned to engage in economic negotiations with Czecho-Slovakia, without, however, changing the orientation of Hungary's foreign policy.[48]

The initiative taken by Dr. Gratz remained fruitless. Conversations were not resumed prior to Chancellor Renner's departure for Prague early in January, 1920, and the agreement concluded between Austria and Czecho-Slovakia on January 12, 1920, was directed, in part, against Hungary.[49] This fact was openly admitted by Chancellor Renner him-

[46] The controversy between Poland and Czecho-Slovakia arose from the conflicting claims of these countries to the Teschen district in Silesia. For the history of this conflict, which had a decisive influence on Czech-Polish relations throughout the period between 1919 and 1939, see Temperley, *History*, IV, 348 ff.; see also *Recueil des documents diplomatiques concernant la question Jaworzyna, Décembre 1918–Août 1923*, published by the Polish Foreign Office.

[47] Count Somssich to Dr. Gratz, Dec. 21, 1919. *HFR*, Vol. I, Doc. 57.

[48] Count Somssich to Count Csekonics, the Representative of the Hungarian Government in Warsaw, Dec. 21, 1919. *Ibid.*, Doc. 58.

[49] It was only after Dr. Renner's return from Prague that Dr. Flieder renewed the conversations with Dr. Gratz which were left in abeyance in Dec., 1919. Dr. Flieder

self to Dr. Gratz upon his return from Prague. At the diplomatic reception held on January 18, 1920, the Chancellor informed the Hungarian minister that his negotiations had resulted in an agreement of friendly coöperation and mutual assistance, which, he felt it his duty frankly to disclose, might be applied against Hungary should she engage in an aggressive policy or try to force a Habsburg restoration in Austria.[50] The nature of the Austro-Czech agreement must have been clear, even before Dr. Renner's open avowal, from confidential information imparted by the Italian legation to Dr. Gratz, to the effect that the Czechs were concentrating troops near Pozsony to assist Austria in the occupation of Western Hungary.[51]

advised Dr. Gratz that Dr. Beneš would welcome economic negotiations with Hungary, but suggested that the possibilities should be explored through a direct preliminary exchange of views. Dr. Gratz to Count Somssich, Jan. 16, 1920, *ibid.,* Doc. 78. The Hungarian Government followed up this suggestion by appointing, in the middle of February, Mr. Gustav Pechár, an inspector of industry, as unofficial representative to explore in Prague the prospects of economic negotiations. Count Somssich to Dr. Gratz, Feb. 19, 1920, *ibid.,* Doc. 136. When Dr. Gratz informed Dr. Flieder of this appointment, the latter appeared to be "very much pleased." Dr. Gratz, although favoring *rapprochement* with Czecho-Slovakia, counseled caution, lest the initiation of direct negotiations between the two countries while the peace treaty was still under discussion in Paris be represented by the Czechs in Paris to the Allies as a consummated agreement between Hungary and Czecho-Slovakia as to the basis of peace. Dr. Gratz to Count Somssich, March 4, 1920. *Ibid.,* Doc. 162. There is no record in the archives of the Hungarian Foreign Office as to what, if anything, came of Mr. Pechár's mission, and there is no indication that any further move was made, prior to the signature of the Trianon Treaty, to improve relations between Hungary and Czecho-Slovakia. It seems, however, that the possibility of some adjustment of territorial questions was informally discussed between officials of the Czecho-Slovak Foreign Office and the Hungarian representatives sometime in Feb., 1920; see *infra,* p. 269 *n.* Whether such discussion took place as a result of the move of Dr. Gratz, or was connected with the plans of the French military mission in Kassa to bring about a friendly agreement between Hungary and Czecho-Slovakia under French mediation (see on this, *infra,* pp. 254 ff.) or, finally, was wholly independent of either of these moves, cannot be ascertained.

[50] Dr. Gratz to Count Somssich, Jan. 18, 1920. *HFR,* Vol. I, Doc. 81. The terms of the agreement have not been revealed, but according to persistent rumors, Dr. Renner agreed to permit the passage of Czech troops through Austria in case of war with Hungary. *Ibid.,* Docs. 92, 98. Subsequently Dr. Renner qualified this somewhat bellicose announcement by assuring Dr. Gratz that the Prague agreement did not oblige Austria to join a bloc directed against Hungary and that Austria had no intention of so doing. Dr. Gratz to Count Somssich, March 5, 1920. *Ibid.,* Doc. 166. Dr. Gratz told the Austrian Chancellor on this occasion that the intermittent rumors of an alliance of Hungary's neighbors had no influence on Hungarian foreign policy, since such an alliance had been anticipated by his government from the outset.

[51] Dr. Gratz to Count Somssich, Jan. 14, 1920. *Ibid.,* Doc. 75. Colonel Cunninghame, the British military representative in Vienna, assured Dr. Gratz that the Supreme Coun-

The somewhat detailed account given above has been necessary in order to show that throughout the period between the establishment of constitutional order in Hungary and the arrival of the Hungarian Peace Delegation in Paris, Austro-Hungarian relations had been definitely strained. Far from relieving Hungary's isolation, Austria was, for the time being at least, a link in the chain which Prague began to forge[52] with the approval and even with the assistance of France.[53]

cil did not intend to see Western Hungary occupied (*ibid.*) and that under no conditions would they permit the Czechs to do so. Dr. Gratz to Count Somssich, Jan. 15, 1920. *Ibid.*, Doc. 77. Subsequently Dr. Renner denied that any agreement contemplating the occupation of Western Hungary had been concluded at Prague. Dr. Gratz to Count Somssich, March 5, 1920. *Ibid.*, Doc. 166.

[52] There can be little doubt that the efforts of Dr. Beneš to render Hungary impotent by a chain of alliances was called forth by the invitation of Hungary to the Peace Conference. Dr. Beneš feared that the Hungarians might challenge, or rather that they might succeed in challenging the peace conditions and he desired to insure the gains which his country had made by the decisions of the Supreme Council. During his trip to Paris early in Dec., 1919, Dr. Beneš suggested to Mr. Trumbić, the Yugoslav Minister for Foreign Affairs, the conclusion of an alliance between his country and Yugoslavia. In a conversation with Mr. Osusky, the Czecho-Slovak minister to France, Mr. Trumbić told him on Dec. 30, 1919, that the arrangement suggested by Dr. Beneš had been submitted, with the approval of the Yugoslav Peace Delegation, to the Belgrade Government and that he himself approved the plan of collective action in case of an attack by Hungary. *Documents diplomatiques relatifs aux conventions d'alliance conclues par la République Tchécoslovaque,* Doc. 1, p. 13. At about the same time Mr. Cermak, the Czecho-Slovak minister to Rumania, was charged with the task of proposing a similar agreement to Rumania. The nature and objective of the proposed agreement is clearly revealed in a letter which Dr. Beneš addressed on Jan. 5, 1920, to the new Rumanian Prime Minister, Dr. Vaida-Voivoda (translation from *ibid.*, Doc. 2, pp. 15–16):

". . . In view of the situation in Hungary, I believe that our two countries have the greatest possible interest in reaching a full agreement with respect to the problems which concern and the danger which threatens us both. We shall have a difficult job in Paris in defending ourselves. I believe that our interests in this respect are absolutely identical and that we have the strict duty of mutually helping each other.

"We have discussed frequently the idea of mutual collaboration with respect to the Magyar danger. I think the time has arrived when we should put into practice our common ideas and prepare the basis for the tranquillity of our countries. Mr. Cermak will submit to you concrete proposals in this regard.

"I have also questioned the Yugoslav Government concerning this matter and I believe that our interests are identical. Yugoslavia, Rumania and Czecho-Slovakia could very well agree mutually to guarantee each other against danger from whatever quarter.

"In my opinion the solution of this question is very urgent. . . ."

[53] Scarcely had the Austrian-Czech agreement been concluded than the Hungarian legation in Vienna obtained reliable information that the French were working for an Austrian-Yugoslav agreement along similar lines. The objective of the French was reported to be to exert pressure on Hungary and to force her to accept the peace conditions. Dr. Gratz to Count Somssich, Jan. 18, 1920. *HFR,* Vol. I, Doc. 81. Cf. the warn-

Hungary's relations with Poland, which country alone during this time showed any friendliness toward the Hungarians, also deserve consideration. Their foundation lay, in this case, in the traditional sympathy which had existed for centuries between the Polish and the Magyar peoples and which historical accidents had failed to injure. Moreover, the more or less conservative regime of a strongly nationalistic flavor in both countries drew them together, just as the close identity in political outlook of the left-wing governments in Austria and Czecho-Slovakia facilitated the *rapprochement* between those states. There had always been sympathy in Hungary for Polish aspirations for independence, and, now that Hungary appeared to be doomed to partition if not to total extinction, this was fully reciprocated by the newly liberated Poland, despite her as-yet-precarious existence.

Soon after the reëstablishment of constitutional order in Hungary, although circumstances did not permit the Polish-Hungarian friendship to be loudly proclaimed to the world the two countries sent resident representatives to each other's capitals. Poland, whose eastern frontiers were as yet undetermined and who was dependent on Allied supplies and financial assistance in her struggle with Soviet Russia, could not well afford to offend either the Great Powers or Rumania, a potential ally in the war with the Soviet, by openly declaring her sympathy for Hungary. Count Szembek, the representative of Poland in Budapest, therefore deemed it wise to absent himself from the festivities which marked the evacuation of Budapest by the Rumanians and the entrance of the Hungarian National Army; and Mr. Paderewski, when speaking of Polish foreign policy, about the middle of November, abstained from making even a passing reference to Hungary.[54] In order to avoid unpleasantness with the Allies, the Polish Foreign Office cautiously declined to recognize the "diplomatic character" of the representative sent by Hungary to Warsaw, Count Csekonics, and ex-

---

ing of the Italian Commissioner in Hungary, Mr. Cerrutti, in this respect. *Ibid.*, Doc. 65. As will be shown hereafter, French diplomatic circles were divided as to the policy which France should follow in the Danube valley. While efforts were made to isolate Hungary, conversations began which aimed at drawing Hungary within the French orbit. It should be noted that the reception of the Austrian-Czech agreement was not unanimously favorable in Austria. Some officials in the Austrian Foreign Office were apprehensive of the possible effect of a contemplated journey of the Chancellor to Belgrade, which, they realized, could not fail to be interpreted in Hungary as a further step in the policy of encirclement. Dr. Gratz to Count Somssich, Jan. 20, 1920. *Ibid.*, Doc. 84.

[54] Count Somssich to Count Csekonics, Nov. 21, 1919. *Ibid.*, Doc. 41.

tended to him only "diplomatic facilities," a distinction so fine that it may be regarded as nonexistent. The Poles assured Count Csekonics that he was entitled to all diplomatic privileges and immunities, but the formula served the purpose of diverting attention from the growing intimacy of Polish-Hungarian relations.[55]

The political considerations which conditioned the friendly nature of Polish-Hungarian relations deserve brief mention. The precarious situation of Poland, wedged between Germany and Soviet Russia, both hostile to the reborn state, and her open conflict with Czecho-Slovakia, naturally induced her to seek support wherever she could find it. Hungary, of course, shared Poland's dislike of Czecho-Slovakia. On the other hand, Hungary's bitter feelings against Rumania were not shared by Poland, who regarded Rumania as a natural ally against Russia. It is logical that under these conditions the endeavor to bring Hungary and Rumania together became an axiomatic and ever-recurring problem of Polish foreign policy.[56] The fact that this endeavor was unsuccessful became a stumblingblock in later years in attempts to transform the informal Polish-Hungarian friendship into a formal agreement. The antagonism between Hungary and Rumania was also one of the reasons why Poland declined to join the Little Entente, although her aloofness from that coalition was also due to the friction between Poland and Czecho-Slovakia.

Poland's friendship, even if passive and undemonstrative, was important from Hungary's point of view. Since Poland was one of the Allied Powers, in great favor with France, it was hoped that she would exert her influence in support of Hungary. Moreover, it was expected that in view of her cordial relations with Rumania, Poland might induce Rumania to moderate her hostility to Hungary and even to bring about some sort of *rapprochement,* a possibility which Hungarian statesmen seriously considered at that time, despite the intense feeling which the conduct of the Rumanian Army in Hungary and the perse-

[55] Count Csekonics to Count Somssich, Dec. 11, 1919. *Ibid.,* Doc. 51. When Count Csekonics, after returning to Warsaw from a short visit to Budapest, called at the Foreign Office, Mr. Skrzynsky, Secretary of State in the Ministry, told him that no one in Poland could pursue a foreign policy which did not take into consideration close collaboration with Hungary.

[56] Italy also early indicated a desire, though for different reasons, to bring about a reconciliation between Hungary and Rumania. See report of a conversation which took place on Dec. 28, 1919, between an official of the Hungarian Ministry for Foreign Affairs and Signor Cerrutti, Commissioner of Italy in Budapest. *Ibid.,* Doc. 65.

cution of Magyars and Szeklers in Transylvania evoked in the Hungarian people.[57] Finally, the belief, whether or not erroneous, that Czecho-Slovakia was contemplating armed intervention against Hungary and that this might be held in check by the Poles, was an additional reason for the Hungarians to appreciate Poland's friendliness.

To complete the picture, reference should be made to other efforts of Hungary to end her isolation by establishing diplomatic relations with other countries. At the beginning of October, 1919, Count Somssich approached the Holy See, through the Papal Nuncio in Vienna, with a view to an exchange of diplomatic missions between the Vatican and Hungary. He received a courteous but somewhat vague reply from the Papal Secretary of State that the suggestion was sympathetically received but that decision was reserved until the political situation had been clarified.[58] Early in December, 1919, de facto relations were established with the Netherlands, where the Hungarian representative was cordially received.[59] Switzerland extended de facto recognition to the Hungarian representative in January, 1920,[60] but it took some time before he was given the privilege of sending coded messages and sealed diplomatic mail.[61] Hungary also sent a representative to Belgrade to establish at least correct relations with Yugoslavia, but there were difficulties even with his de facto status.[62]

It is against the background of Hungary's position in the European chessboard of international politics that the initial difficulties facing the Hungarian Peace Delegation must be viewed.

[57] The Rumanian minister to Austria made a feeble suggestion for rapprochement between Hungary and Rumania during a courtesy call on Dr. Gratz, the Hungarian minister to Vienna, early in Jan., 1920. Ibid., Doc. 67. Hungary's attitude toward such rapprochement was outlined in a communication from Count Somssich to Dr. Gratz dated Feb. 6, 1920. Ibid., Doc. 119. From this it is evident that Hungary's policy toward Rumania was largely guided by considerations of the threat of bolshevism and by the consequent desirability of a working agreement between Poland, Rumania, and Hungary. It is also obvious that the Hungarian Government looked at the situation realistically and was quite prepared to search for some modus vivendi with all her neighbors, despite the emotional and sentimental feeling against these countries, and without in the slightest receding from her primary objective of regaining as much Hungarian territory as possible, then or later.

[58] Cardinal Gasparri to Count Somssich, Oct. 15, 1919. Ibid., Doc. 27.

[59] Mr. Nagy to Count Somssich, Dec. 13, 1919. Ibid., Doc. 54.

[60] Baron Bornemisza to Count Somssich, Jan. 20, 1920. Ibid., Doc. 83.

[61] Cf. ibid., Docs. 86, 97, 99.

[62] Mr. Wodianer to Count Somssich, Jan. 2 and 10, 1920. Ibid., Docs. 66 and 72.

The First Hungarian Memoranda to the Peace Conference and the Presentation of Peace Conditions to the Hungarian Delegation

It had been decided at the first meeting of the Peace Delegation in Neuilly that immediately after the exchange of credentials the Hungarians would submit to the Allied Powers the elaborate documentation of their case which had been prepared in Budapest and put into the form of notes and memoranda in Neuilly.[63] As soon as Ambassador Cambon submitted the Allied credentials, the already-completed memoranda were, on the afternoon of January 14, handed to Lieutenant Colonel Henry and—for transmission to their respective embassies—to the British and Italian liaison officers, Lord Hay and Lieutenant Jacomony.[64] The next morning, Count Stephen Csáky was allowed to go, accompanied by two French officers, to the Quai d'Orsay to file these documents with the Secretariat of the Peace Conference. He also carried with him, for the representatives of the Principal Allies, Clemenceau, Lloyd George, Nitti, and Matsui, and the American ambassador, private letters from Count Apponyi, in which Apponyi, pointing out the international implications of the Hungarian question, urged the establishment of personal contact and oral negotiations.[65]

Although this elaborate documentation has been printed in full by the Hungarian Ministry for Foreign Affairs,[66] it may be useful to indicate briefly the issues dealt with in the first formal communications presented to the Peace Conference by the Hungarian Delegation.

The first of these notes requested the withdrawal of the Rumanian troops behind the demarcation line determined by the Supreme Council. It was pointed out that while in deference to exasperated public opinion, the Hungarian Government had declared that it would send no plenipotentiaries to Paris until the Rumanians evacuated, the Peace Delegation was nevertheless dispatched as proof of Hungary's desire for peace and in full confidence that the Principal Allied Powers would make their will respected by the Rumanians.

The second, called the "Presentation Note," was a historical survey of Hungary's past and present situation.

Though we are fully conscious of the difficult situation [began this note], created by the reciprocal agreements made between the victorious States

[63] "Political Diary," entry of Jan. 7, 1920.   [64] Ibid., entry of Jan. 14, 1920.
[65] Ibid., entry of Jan. 15, 1920.   [66] HPN, I, 1–307.

and by the treaties of peace already concluded, yet we consider it our imperative duty towards both the peoples of our country and Europe in general, now, at the eleventh hour before the Supreme Council has decided definitively concerning the fate of Hungary and the text of the conditions of peace, to make the said Council familiar with the situation of Hungary in the past and to-day.

What followed—a careful analysis of Hungary's position in the Austro-Hungarian Monarchy, of the nationality question, and of the economic unity of the Carpathian basin—is a brief history of Hungary, perhaps the best written until then. The two score maps and memoranda annexed to the note offer to the scholar a wealth of condensed information in support of the various contentions put forward in the Presentation Note.[67]

The three following notes dealt with damages inflicted on the country's agriculture, industry, and railways by the Rumanian occupation. The return of agricultural implements, animals, and grain, carried away by the Rumanians, was sought, lest the Hungarians be exposed to famine, and the appointment of a mixed commission by the Supreme Council was suggested to supervise the undertaking. Similarly, the return of illegally removed industrial machinery and raw materials was sought, with reference to ameliorating the widespread unemployment in Hungary, which might lead to serious internal troubles. Finally, the Hungarians pressed for the return of railway equipment removed by the Rumanians, in consequence of which Hungary's transportation

[67] The more important of these memoranda deserve mention, since they concern subjects about which there is much confusion among students of history, government, and international relations. Annexes 1 and 26 give an excellent survey of Austrian-Hungarian relations from the point of view of public law and constitutional history. Annex 7 explains in detail the machinery of the Hungarian census, the authenticity of which was repeatedly challenged by Hungary's enemies. Annex 27 itemizes the participation of Hungarians in the civil and military administration of the Monarchy, with reference to the disproportionately small representation in the imperial and royal household, in the direction of the armed forces, in the diplomatic service, and in the Ministry of Finance—in support of the claim that Hungary could not have exerted a decisive influence on the policies of the Monarchy. By far the most important is Annex 30, reproducing textually the reports of July 1 and July 8, 1914, of Count Tisza, then Prime Minister of Hungary, to Emperor-King Francis Joseph, and the minutes of the Crown Council of July 7 and July 19, 1914, which show conclusively that the Hungarian statesman definitely opposed Berchtold's policy which brought on the war. Annex 34 also deals with and refutes Hungary's responsibility for the World War. In view of the insistent accusation of forcible denationalization of minority groups, Annex 44, dealing with elementary schools and education, is also of great importance.

system was paralyzed and the economic problems of the country further aggravated.

The next two notes called attention to the situation of Hungarian prisoners of war in Russia and France and sought their immediate release. The last note, the most elaborate of all, dealt comprehensively with Transylvania and reviewed in great detail the special position of this part of Hungary, both historically and contemporaneously. Like the Presentation Note, the Note on Transylvania was accompanied by maps and supplementary memoranda.

All these notes were dated January 14, 1920. The covering letter expressed the hope that the documents submitted would be studied with "keen attention" and urged the Allies to grant an opportunity for oral discussion.

In fairness it seems impossible [the letter concluded] that this request should not be granted to the spokesmen of a nation to whom the pending questions mean nothing less than life or death. No precedent of procedure in the case of other nations can forbid the fulfillment of this request, since there is a radical difference between those cases and ours. They, too, had to accept hard conditions, implying some losses of territory; but none of them had been brought face to face, as in our case the attitude of the neighboring nations on the occupied territories seems to indicate, with a scheme of dismemberment amounting to wholesale destruction. Is it asking too much to request to be heard before decisions of such importance become final?

The presentation of the peace conditions to the Hungarian Delegation took place on January 15, 1920, at 4 P.M. in the Red Salon of the French Ministry for Foreign Affairs. When Count Apponyi, accompanied by several members of the Delegation [68] and the Allied liaison officers, entered the room, M. Clemenceau briefly greeted the Hungarians, asked them to be seated, and stated that the Supreme Council had acceded to Count Apponyi's request to explain orally Hungary's position. He was very emphatic that no discussion was to take place following Count Apponyi's statement, which he suggested should be made the following day. Of course what the Hungarians had asked for was oral *negotiation* and not an *address,* but under the circumstances this small concession appeared to be better than nothing, and Count Apponyi accepted the suggestion. The peace conditions in French,

[68] The following Delegation members were present at the ceremony: Count Teleki, Count Bethlen, Mr. Popovics, Count László Somssich, Baron Lers, Messrs. Praznovszky, Hegedüs, and Fabró, and Count Stephen Csáky.

English, and Italian were then handed to Count Apponyi, with M. Clemenceau's warning that Hungary's reply must be made within fifteen days, and the session was ended.[69]

Count Apponyi's Address to the Supreme Council

The next day, January 16, at 2:30 P.M., the leading members of the Hungarian Delegation appeared again at the Quai d'Orsay to explain Hungary's position orally to the Supreme Council. Since they had had less than twenty-four hours in which to acquaint themselves with the peace conditions, Count Apponyi could not possibly deal in detail with the mass of political, economic, financial, and military questions therein contained. His address was of necessity confined to an examination of the fundamental principles presumably guiding the framers of the treaty and of the conformity of the peace conditions to those principles. Nevertheless, even a cursory examination of the preliminary draft of the treaty led Count Apponyi to declare at the outset that the peace conditions were such that they could not, without essential modifications, be accepted. Their acceptance, he said, would mean suicide for Hungary. While the stringency of the treaties with Germany, Austria, and Bulgaria indicated what was to be expected, the extreme severity of the Hungarian peace conditions astonished the Hungarian Delegation, since none of the other treaties had involved territorial changes of comparable significance. Did this severity mean that the Allies were passing sentence upon Hungary? If the former Central Powers were guilty of bringing about the war, then the measure of guilt should be divided in proportion to responsibility. If this was the basis of the peace conditions, Hungary should be given a hearing, on the basis of equality —and such she had not been accorded—in determining her share of responsibility.

Concretely, Count Apponyi requested, first, plebiscites in all the territories which the peace conditions assigned to other states, and declared that Hungary would accept unconditionally the results, whatever they might be. Insisting on the necessity of more effective protection of minorities in territories to be detached from Hungary than that provided for in the peace conditions, he further urged the dispatch of Allied missions to the occupied territories to investigate the mistreat-

---

[69] The English text of the peace conditions presented to the Hungarians on Jan. 15 is printed in *HPN,* I, 559 ff.

ment of Hungarians by the occupying troops and authorities. He assured the Supreme Council that Hungary was ready to grant to non-Magyar populations in Hungary the same extensive protection sought for the Magyar minorities in the territories to be detached. He briefly touched upon the fate of Hungarian prisoners of war and pointed out in conclusion that after enduring revolutions and the Rumanian occupation, Hungary could not possibly carry out the financial and economic clauses of the contemplated treaty nor could she supply Austria with iron ore as requested by the peace conditions.[70]

The burden of Count Apponyi's argument, as he frankly admitted, was against the territorial stipulations. As he pointed out, all the objections of Hungary to the contemplated peace could be stated in terms of territorial losses; and, whether rightly or wrongly, Hungary's dissatisfaction with the peace settlement, both during the Peace Conference and in subsequent years, was expressed almost exclusively in those terms.[71] The loss of more than two-thirds of the country's territory, comprising by far the greater part of its natural resources, and the transfer of more than one-third of the Magyar people to alien sovereignties, paralleled in history only by the partition of Poland, explains why the dismemberment of Hungary loomed larger than any other problem created by the peace treaty in the minds of the Magyars at that time and why it has continued to do so throughout the period between the two great wars.

Contemporary records agree that Count Apponyi's address, delivered successively in perfect English, French, and Italian, made a deep impression on the Allied statesmen, especially the British.[72] Despite M. Clemenceau's insistence the previous day that no discussion take place, Mr. Lloyd George, to the great surprise of everybody, began to question Count Apponyi, when he had finished, about the number and con-

[70] The complete text of Count Apponyi's address is printed *infra*, Doc. 44, p. 539.

[71] It has been pointed out, *supra*, p. 182, that the Hungarians had no illusions that their protests would have any effect on the Allied determination of Hungary's boundaries. The Peace Delegation was also informed that the Commander of the Allied Army in the East, General Franchet d'Esperay, when visiting in Budapest at about the time the Delegation left for Paris, advised the Minister for Foreign Affairs that chances for territorial changes were very slim and urged that the Hungarian Delegation concentrate on economic problems, where "valuable" concessions might be hoped for. Count Somssich to the Peace Delegation, Jan. 6, 1920. *HFR*, Vol. I, Doc. 68.

[72] A bid for Italy's friendship in particular was made when, speaking in Italian, Count Apponyi turned to the Italian representatives and reminded them that the desire for freedom and constitutional government was common to both Hungarians and Italians. Temperley, *History*, IV, 416–17.

dition of the Hungarians in the territories to be detached, especially in Transylvania.[73] During the ensuing explanations, the meeting broke up when the members of the Supreme Council, including M. Clemenceau himself, surrounded Count Apponyi, who was seeking to respond to Mr. Lloyd George's request by showing the distribution of nationalities on a huge map prepared by Count Teleki. The exchange of views took place principally between Mr. Lloyd George and Count Apponyi; at the end Lloyd George congratulated Apponyi upon the presentation of Hungary's case. The interest of Mr. Lloyd George and other members of the British Delegation who were present at this meeting of the Supreme Council was evidently sincere, and they were genuinely impressed with Count Apponyi's arguments.[74] Therefore Mr. Lloyd George's subsequent criticism of Count Apponyi's frontal attack upon the treaty is, to say the least, surprising. In his volumes on the peace treaties, while paying tribute to Count Apponyi's eloquence, he dismisses Count Apponyi's arraignment of the peace conditions as too general and too sweeping. "He had not challenged any specific instances of injustice." [75] As has been pointed out, the Hungarians had had little time to examine the peace conditions and thus enable their spokesman to address himself to specific and narrow issues; neither could such issues be effectively presented within the compass of a single address. Mr. Lloyd George thinks it unfortunate that Count Apponyi

did not confine his case to those border areas which, in spite of the fact that the Magyars were in an undoubted majority, the Boundary Commission had decided, for economic and geographical reasons, to assign to other States. Had he devoted his criticism to these areas, he had at his disposal material which would have enabled him to make a powerful and, as regards some districts, an irresistible appeal for redress on behalf of his fellow-countrymen.[76]

Looking back from the vantage point of some twenty years later, the conclusion that Hungary would conceivably have fared better had she narrowed her claims to ethnic boundaries instead of seeking territorial integrity on historical, geographic and economic grounds seems reasonable enough. The fallacy of Mr. Lloyd George's criticism lies in his

---

[73] While Count Apponyi was speaking, Mr. Lloyd George sent a note by his secretary to M. Clemenceau, apparently asking leave to speak; the latter indicated his consent by a "rather reluctant nod." "Political Diary," entry of Jan. 16, 1920. It will be remembered that the attention of the British Government was called formally to the condition of Hungarians in Transylvania by Lord Bryce. See *supra*, p. 175.

[74] *Ibid.*   [75] Lloyd George, *Memoirs*, II, 629.   [76] *Ibid.*, p. 627.

failure to appraise the contemporary psychology of the Hungarians, who, though realizing their situation, were reluctant to accept the finality of the territorial diminution of their land. Had Count Apponyi had any knowledge of the doubts which were expressed in the territorial commissions about the allocation of large areas contiguous to the new frontiers, inhabited by predominantly Magyar populations,[77] or of the prophetic misgivings expressed by Mr. Lloyd George himself in his Fontainebleau memorandum,[78] he might have concentrated more specifically on demanding the return of these contiguous areas. Yet in the light of all the evidence available, it may be doubted whether a more modest approach would have had such an "irresistible appeal" to the Allied statesmen as Mr. Lloyd George assumes.

In conclusion, it may be noted that the dignified presentation of Hungary's case by Count Apponyi had had a decided effect at least on the atmosphere of the Peace Conference, which was, according to those present, very different from the frigidity which characterized the exchange of credentials and the presentation of the peace conditions. According to the Hungarians, even M. Clemenceau was "surprisingly polite" and, when Count Apponyi stated that he would return at once to Budapest to submit the peace conditions to his government and that he might have to ask for an extension of the limit set for Hungary's reply, the French statesman replied, "Mais certainement." [79]

Two days later, on the evening of January 18, Count Apponyi and the greater part of the Delegation left for Budapest to discuss with the Hungarian Government and the Delegation members who remained in Hungary the peace conditions and the reply to be given to the Allies. A few members of the Delegation, including Count Bethlen, Count Emery Csáky, Baron Láng, Dr. Wettstein, and Count Stephen Csáky, with a small clerical staff headed by Mr. Praznovszky as chargé

[77] See *supra,* Part Two, *passim.*

[78] In his memorandum of March 25, 1919, "Some Considerations for the Peace Conference before They Finally Draft Their terms," Mr. Lloyd George said, after expressing objections to the proposed transfer of large German populations to alien rule: ". . . What I have said about the Germans is equally true of the Magyars. There will never be peace in South-Eastern Europe if every little state now coming into being is to have a large Magyar Irredenta within its borders. I would therefore take as a guiding principle of the peace that as far as humanly possible the different races should be allocated to their motherlands, and that this human criterion should have precedence over considerations of strategy or economics or communications, which can usually be adjusted by other means. . . ." Lloyd George, *Memoirs,* I, 266 ff.

[79] "Political Diary," entry of Jan. 16, 1920.

d'affaires, remained in Neuilly to carry on routine work and serve as liaison officers between the Hungarian Government and the Peace Conference.[80] The departure of Count Apponyi from Paris marked the end of the first phase of the Hungarian peace negotiations.

The Hungarian Reaction to the Original Peace Conditions and Diplomatic Steps for Their Amelioration

Count Apponyi correctly anticipated the attitude of the Hungarian people when he told the Supreme Council that the peace conditions were unacceptable to Hungary without substantial modifications. Interest in the national elections (January 21–26, 1920) was completely overshadowed by popular indignation, on the publication of the peace conditions immediately after Count Apponyi's return to Budapest. Despite the wide differences in the platforms of the various political parties contending for the control of the National Assembly, condemnation of the terms of the Allies was unanimous; in this respect there was no difference between the tone of the extreme right and the socialist press.

While the elections were taking place in Hungary as the last step toward the reëstablishment of parliamentary government and while the Delegation was discussing with the cabinet the reply to be given to the Allies, several events occurred abroad which had a bearing on the efforts of the Hungarian Government to enlist good will and sympathy in support of Hungary's opposition to the contemplated mutilation of the country.

On January 17, 1920, the day after Count Apponyi had addressed the Supreme Council, M. Deschanel defeated Clemenceau in the French presidential elections. Thereupon Clemenceau promptly resigned not only the French premiership but also the chairmanship of the Supreme Council, being succeeded in both offices by M. Millerand. Since the Paris Peace Conference formally came to an end a few days later, on January 21, when the Supreme Council held its last regular meeting and its functions were transferred to the Conference of Ambassadors,[81] M. Clemenceau's resignation from the Council was in itself not of great importance. But the significance of the fact that the principal cause of M. Clemenceau's defeat was his opposition to the concordat with the Holy See did not escape the attention of the Hungarians. Although M.

[80] *Ibid.*, entry of Jan. 18, 1920.
[81] See Toynbee, *Survey of International Affairs, 1920–1923*, p. 6.

Clemenceau's opponents also accused him of being "too lenient" with the Germans—an accusation which boded ill for Hungary's claims for some amelioration of her peace terms—the Hungarian Delegation regarded this turn in French internal politics as evidence of increased Catholic influence [82] which might possibly be turned to Hungary's favor. The Delegation at once sent an urgent request to the Minister for Foreign Affairs to mobilize all available Catholic connections that could reach Cardinal Amette, who, it was believed, would have great influence with M. Deschanel and the new French Government. Even if no other concessions could be gained, at least the dispatch of an Allied commission of investigation might put an end to the persecution of Catholics and Protestants in Transylvania, and perhaps the unity of the Catholic Church administration within the historic Hungarian borders might be preserved.[83] Pursuant to this suggestion, discussions took place between Count Somssich and the Prince Primate of Hungary, Cardinal Csernoch. The latter wrote a private letter, transmitted through private channels, to Cardinal Amette, asking his support.[84]

It was also in consequence of this suggestion that the Hungarian Government decided to seek the support of the Holy See directly. Although no formal diplomatic relations existed as yet between the Vatican and Budapest,[85] it was felt that Hungary, the majority of whose population were Roman Catholic, might reasonably expect to find in Rome a sympathetic hearing of her claims and complaints against her more or less anticlerical neighbors. Accordingly Count Somssich sent a letter to Pope Benedict XV through Cardinal Gasparri, Secretary of State to the Vatican. Calling attention to the proposed dismemberment of the country and to the mistreatment of Catholics in general and church dignitaries in particular in the occupied territories, the Minister for Foreign Affairs asked for the assistance and protection of the Holy

[82] M. Briand, leading the opposition against M. Clemenceau, was strongly supported by Cardinal Amette.

[83] "Political Diary," entry of Jan. 19, 1920.

[84] *Ibid.*, entry of Jan. 28, 1920. No reply was received from Cardinal Amette until the beginning of March, when he sent to the Hungarian Delegation, for transmittal to Prince Primate Csernoch, a copy of the letter he had received from M. Cambon, President of the Conference of Ambassadors, in reply to his intervention in favor of Hungary. Ambassador Cambon pointed out that agreements concluded between the Allies, part of which had already been executed, could not be further modified; but he expressed his willingness to convey to the appropriate forum Cardinal Amette's desire to have the points set forth in the Prince Primate's letter examined. *Ibid.*, entry of March 10, 1920.

[85] Cf. *supra*, p. 203.

See and reiterated an earlier request, referred to above, for the establishment of diplomatic relations between the Vatican and Hungary. Reminding His Holiness of the services Hungary had repeatedly rendered
in the defense of Christianity, Count Somssich emphasized the desirability of preserving the administrative unity of the Catholic Church,
even though the allocation to neighboring states of territories heretofore Hungarian could not be successfully challenged.[86]

Besides appealing to the Vatican, the Hungarian Government used
the short breathing space afforded by the two weeks granted for the
reply to the peace conditions—this time was subsequently extended to
February 12—for an intensified search for contacts with the outside
world.

As already indicated, the Swiss Government finally agreed, about the
middle of January, to extend *de facto* recognition to Hungary's diplomatic representative.[87] Despite the limitations imposed upon him by
the excessive caution of the Swiss Government,[88] the presence of a
Hungarian representative in Berne opened up to the Hungarians new
channels of communication, which Baron Bornemisza was quick to
utilize. Following a suggestion from Count Bethlen, he succeeded in
establishing contact with the Italian Prime Minister, Signor Nitti, on
the latter's return to Italy from the Supreme Council meeting. He en-
listed the sympathy of the Japanese chargé d'affaires, Mr. Ito, who
offered to suggest that the Japanese ambassador in Paris get in touch
with the Hungarian Delegation and convey messages from Hungary
to the Japanese Peace Delegation in Paris or to the Japanese Government.[89]

Partly as a result of the contact with Signor Nitti and thanks to
improved relations with Italian officers residing in Budapest, the Italian
Government agreed, toward the end of January, to receive a *de facto*
representative of Hungary in Rome. The extent of the improvement
may be indicated by the fact that when General Mombelli, the Italian
member of the Interallied Military Mission, conveyed the "agrément"

---

[86] *HFR*, Vol. I, Docs. 107, 108. Both letters were dated Jan. 31, 1920, but owing to
various difficulties, they could not be delivered until several weeks later. See Count
Nemes's report, March 5, 1920, and Cardinal Gasparri's reply, April 3, 1920, *ibid.*, Docs.
165, 204.

[87] See *supra,* p. 203.

[88] Poland, although much more dependent on Allied good will than neutral Switzerland, extended all facilities to Count Csekonics for communications with Budapest.
Even the Yugoslavs, an enemy state, permitted diplomatic mail to reach and be sent
by the Hungarian *de facto* representative in Belgrade.

[89] Baron Bornemisza to Count Somssich, Jan. 25, 1920. *HFR*, Vol. I, Doc. 93.

of the Italian Government to receive Count Nemes as Hungarian representative in Rome, he intimated to the Minister for Foreign Affairs the necessity of coöperation between Italy and Hungary.[90] Count Nemes was immediately dispatched to Rome, where he was at once cordially received, in the absence of the Foreign Minister, by the Secretary of State, Count Sforza.[91] Another evidence of Italy's changed attitude was the open advocacy by Signor Nitti of the Hungarian cause at the London meeting of the three Allied Prime Ministers (February 12–23, 1920).[92]

Needless to say, Italy's espousal of Hungary's cause was not due to any abstract belief in justice. An important motive was Italian apprehension over the persistent rumors of the Czech-Austrian secret agreement concerning Czech occupation of Western Hungary.[93] Although Italy had vigorously opposed the allocation of this territory to Austria,[94] once a decision to that effect was taken, the ultimate fate of Western Hungary, had it concerned Austria and Hungary only, would not perhaps have been a matter of concern to Italy. But the issue became of considerable importance the moment that Czech intervention on the

[90] Count Somssich to the Hungarian Peace Delegation, Jan. 29, 1920. *Ibid.*, Doc. 103. Better feeling between the two countries was due partly to the correct and objective attitude of the Italian officers detailed for the discharge of various missions in Hungary, as, for instance, Colonel Vigna, who was sent to Sopron and Szombathely to study the attitude of the population with respect to the incorporation of Western Hungary into Austria and who later became the chief of the Interallied Mission to Western Hungary appointed by the Allied Powers at the end of Jan. See *infra*, pp. 230–31. The desirability of establishing friendly relations was repeatedly emphasized by the Italian Commissioner in Budapest, Signor Cerrutti, in the course of a conversation he had on Dec. 28 with an official of the Hungarian Ministry for Foreign Affairs. *HFR*, Vol. I, Doc. 65.

[91] Count Nemes to Count Somssich, Feb. 28, 1920. *Ibid.*, Doc. 154. In the course of the conversation, Count Sforza emphatically denied rumors that Italy favored the incorporation of Western Hungary into Austria. The question of Fiume still being unsettled (see Carrié, *Italy at the Paris Peace Conference*, pp. 268 ff.), it was only natural that Sforza sought to align Hungary with Italy against the Yugoslavs by assuring Count Nemes that Italy would fully safeguard Hungary's economic interests, should Fiume be under Italian sovereignty. Italy's apprehension as to a possible Habsburg restoration was also briefly touched upon during the conversation.

[92] For Nitti's intervention, see *infra*, pp. 239–41.

[93] *Supra*, p. 199 and n. 51.

[94] Count Teleki reported that he saw the minutes of the Supreme Council meeting in which the allocation of Western Hungary to Austria was discussed (this was probably the meeting held on July 7, 1919). According to Count Teleki, the Italian representative, Count Vannutelli, defended Hungary's interests very ably and with an astounding knowledge of facts. Count Teleki to Count Somssich, Feb. 23, 1920. *HFR*, Vol. I, Doc. 142.

side of Austria conjured up the idea of the Czech-Yugoslav corridor proposed by Dr. Beneš but never seriously considered by the Allies.[95] In view of their extremely strained relations with Yugoslavia, the Italians naturally did not look with favor upon any plan which would strengthen this potential enemy. Italy's support henceforth of Hungary's case on the question of Western Hungary can be easily understood in the light of this background and explains Hungarian suggestions that if the occupation of Western Hungary should become inevitable, it should be undertaken by Italian rather than by Austrian or Czech troops.[96]

Reference has already been made to the existence of friendly relations between Hungary and Poland, even before the Hungarian Delegation departed for Paris.[97] To enlist Poland's active assistance was therefore quite naturally one of the principal objectives of Hungarian diplomacy. Pursuant to a suggestion of the Peace Delegation, the Minister for Foreign Affairs instructed the Hungarian representative in Warsaw, Count Csekonics, to explain to the Polish Government the importance which Hungary attached to direct contact with the Allied representatives, in order somewhat to counterbalance the advantageous position enjoyed at the Peace Conference by her neighbors. Specifically, the Hungarians would appreciate it if the Polish Delegation would itself seek contact with the Hungarian Delegation; the assistance which Poland would thus render to Hungary would powerfully strengthen the traditional friendship between the two countries.[98] Count Csekonics's

[95] When the Italian Commissioner in Budapest, Signor Cerrutti, first broached the desirability of coöperation between Hungary and Italy, at the end of Dec., 1919, he pointed specifically to the danger which the establishment of a Czech-Yugoslav corridor would represent for both Hungary and Italy. HFR, Vol. I, Doc. 65.

[96] "Political Diary," entries of Jan. 19 and 23. That Italy's avowed support of Hungary was primarily tactical, with a view to exerting pressure on Yugoslavia, seems to be shown by Count Sforza's own claim that his policy was coöperation with the Succession States—a claim supported by the subsequent conclusion of agreements with Yugoslavia and Czecho-Slovakia. It may be noted that it was under Italian mediation that Austria and Hungary finally agreed, in Oct., 1921, to submit the question of Western Hungary to a plebiscite.

[97] Supra, pp. 201–3.

[98] Count Somssich to Count Csekonics, Jan. 21, 1920. HFR, Vol. I, Doc. 85. It may be noted that Poland declined to participate in the peace negotiations with Hungary on the ground that the two countries never were at war. In the list of Allied representatives handed to Count Apponyi by Ambassador Cambon, Poland was originally entered as being represented by her Foreign Minister, Mr. Patek; but this was subsequently crossed out. The Hungarians regarded Poland's nonparticipation as a friendly gesture. "Political Diary," entry of Jan. 14, 1920.

representations were sympathetically received in the Polish Foreign Office.[99] Since the Polish Foreign Minister, Mr. Stanislav Patek, was just about to return to Warsaw and the Polish Delegation in Paris was known to be completely under French influence, contact with the Hungarians was established through a confidential assistant of Mr. Patek, Count Orlovszky. Arriving in Paris at the end of January, Count Orlovszky at once sought and obtained information from the Hungarian Delegation concerning a common Polish-Hungarian frontier and the possibility of Hungarian armed assistance against Soviet Russia.[100] However, for reasons indicated below, the mission of Count Orlovszky yielded no immediate results.

Hungary also sought Polish assistance in another matter which then and in subsequent months caused deep anxiety to the Hungarian Government—namely the spread of bolshevism. In that militant and aggressive stage of the Soviet revolution, Hungary was not the only country which was apprehensive of a possible thrust from the East; her fears were shared not merely by Poland and Rumania, both of whom were immediately threatened, but also by the Western Powers. Rumors of the creation of an anti-bolshevik bloc, and even of Germany's inclusion in it, were circulating widely, and the Hungarians, mindful of their recent experience with a communist regime, quite understandably desired to be included in such a bloc. Realizing how she was distrusted by the Principal Allies, a result of the intense agitation by her neighbors, the Hungarians turned to Poland, to whose interest it was primarily to strengthen the anti-soviet front as much as possible, and asked her to advocate, in Paris, Hungary's participation in any contemplated action to meet the bolshevik threat. At the same time Poland was urged to insist in Paris upon the desirability of a common frontier between Poland and Hungary, in order to insure effective and immediate Hungarian assistance in case of a Russian attack upon Poland and incidentally to drive a wedge into the ring which Prague was already beginning to close around Hungary.[101]

Representations to this effect were made by Count Csekonics early in February, when he presented his credentials to the Polish Foreign Minister shortly after the latter's return from Paris. However, circum-

[99] Count Csekonics to Count Somssich, Jan. 23, 1920. *HFR,* Vol. I, Doc. 88.

[100] "Political Diary," entry of Jan. 28.

[101] Count Somssich to Count Csekonics, Jan. 26, 1920, Count Somssich to the Peace Delegation, Jan. 26, 1920, *HFR,* Vol. I, Docs. 94, 96, 116, and cf. "Political Diary," entry of Jan. 23, 1920.

stances did not then favor Poland's pressing for Hungary's inclusion in a defensive front against bolshevism. Poland had begun negotiations with the Soviet Government, and the Western Powers were also inclined to seek peace with Russia. Mr. Patek frankly admitted that arguments along these lines would not carry much weight at the Peace Conference, where, he thought, the bolshevik danger was rather minimized while the importance of Hungary's disarmament was greatly exaggerated. The Polish Foreign Minister, as a believer in and an advocate of Polish-Hungarian friendship, concurred in the desirability of a common border between the two countries, for which he repeatedly argued in Paris. However, Poland could not well take an unequivocal position in favor of the alteration of the peace treaties—in this instance a change of Czecho-Slovakia's boundaries in northeastern Hungary—without endangering the basis of her very existence as founded on those treaties. But, Mr. Patek said, such caution, dictated by circumstances, did not preclude Poland from supporting Hungary's interests indirectly. Thus Mr. Patek assured Count Csekonics that Poland would, despite her delicate situation with respect to the Allies, under no circumstances side against Hungary in case of a conflict between the latter and Czecho-Slovakia.[102] A few days later Count Csekonics was received by the President of Poland, Marshal Pilsudski, who discussed Polish-Hungarian relations with the utmost frankness. He reiterated the assurances of the Foreign Minister that in case of a Czech-Hungarian conflict, Poland would remain neutral and would not, even under Allied pressure, turn against Hungary. Marshal Pilsudski was equally frank in admitting that at present, being threatened by Russia and with undefined borders in the east, Poland could not affirmatively support Hungary at the Peace Conference by openly advocating a common frontier with Hungary or the elimination of the Czech-Russian corridor.[103]

In addition to the circumstances alluded to in the conversations which Count Csekonics had held with the President and the Foreign Minister of Poland, Polish reluctance to support Hungary more actively was also due in part to the fear that by such action she might alienate Rumania. This wariness was perfectly comprehensible if we consider Poland's deep-seated antagonism to Russia and her very real fear of bolshevism, both shared by Rumania, and the further belief that Ru-

---

[102] Count Csekonics to Count Somssich, Feb. 13, 1920. *HFR,* Vol. I, Doc. 126.
[103] Count Csekonics to Count Somssich, Feb. 20, 1920. *Ibid.,* Doc. 140.

mania more than any other of her neighbors was physically capable of rendering her immediate assistance. In fact, there were persistent rumors of a secret agreement between the two countries against Russia, and the Hungarians were realists enough to appreciate the possibility that the price which Poland might have to pay for Rumanian assistance against Russia would be Polish support of Rumania in case of a conflict with Hungary.[104]

Under these circumstances it is not surprising that Hungarian efforts to enlist Poland's support did not produce tangible results. Nevertheless, the steps taken were important, in that they laid the foundation for coöperation between the two countries when Poland, as will be described later, had to turn, in her hour of need, to Hungary for help in her war with the Soviets.

Somewhat more successful was the effort of unofficial Hungarian diplomacy to arouse, in British circles, some sympathy for the country's plight. Apart, too, from the personal interest shown by some American and Italian officers stationed in Budapest, British political circles alone among the Principal Allied and Associated Powers appear to have given any heed to the events taking place in Hungary. Throughout 1919 questions concerning these events were addressed by Members of Parliament to the British Government. It is true that most of these questions, prior to August, 1919, came from representatives of left-wing party groups, in support of what was believed to be the liberal and democratic regime of Count Michael Károlyi or in opposition to measures which were believed to be discriminatory against the soviet government of Béla Kun; and, after the reëstablishment of constitutional government, most of the inquiries related to alleged atrocities committed against liberals and socialists by the new conservative regime.[105] It is also true that in almost every instance the reply of the Government's spokesman was noncommittal and inconclusive. The fact remains, nevertheless, that issues concerning Hungary were brought up in parliamentary discussion—which is more than can be said of the Parliaments of France or Italy or of the Congress of the United States. Considering that news of these discussions did percolate

---

[104] Cf. Count Csekonics to Count Somssich, Feb. 20, 1920. *Ibid.,* Doc. 141.

[105] See Hansard, *Parliamentary Debates, House of Commons,* 5th series, Vol. 114, p. 586; Vol. 115, pp. 594, 1095, 1900, 1901, 1906-7; Vol. 116, p. 1406; Vol. 117, pp. 597, 1135; Vol. 118, pp. 887, 1348; Vol. 119, pp. 174, 518-19, 546, 689, 890, 1091, 1280; Vol. 120, pp. 1114, 1647; Vol. 121, pp. 909, 1103, 1859, 1887; Vol. 122, pp. 185, 579; Vol. 123, pp. 661.

into Hungary; considering further the undeniable liking felt by Hungarians—especially the Hungarian upper classes—for Anglo-Saxons in general and for British political institutions in particular, it is natural that an important objective of Hungarian diplomacy should have been to get a hearing from the British.

Despite the difficulties caused by the stringent restrictions of the Alien Enemy Acts, which were still in force and which so effectively protected the British Isles, long before Hungary was invited to the Peace Conference the Hungarians had succeeded in establishing contacts with several outstanding figures in English public life, among them Lord Bryce, former British ambassador to the United States. This was possible, at least in part, because of the intimate pre-war relations between British and Hungarian Protestant Church circles. The ground was also prepared by Hungarian diplomats and statesmen, who began to seek friendships, or to renew old ones, in neutral territory soon after the armistice. The key men in this diplomatic offensive were Mr. John Pelényi and Count Nicholas Bánffy. Mr. Pelényi, who had served as Austro-Hungarian consul in Cleveland until the entrance of the United States into the war, was in the Netherlands from early in December, 1918. His full understanding of the Anglo-Saxon psychology and his perfect command of the English language enabled him to overcome the obvious obstacles confronting any ex-enemy who tried to obtain a hearing. Count Bánffy, a descendant of one of the most distinguished Transylvanian families and a man of rare charm and capabilities,[106] had a wide circle of friends and acquaintances in England before the war and early in December, 1919, he was allowed to enter England. It was through these men that a joint memorial of the Transylvanian bishops reached Lord Bryce, giving rise, as already indicated,[107] to the first of a series of addresses and questions by members of both Houses of Parliament which called attention to conditions in the territories detached from Hungary.

Although a reply to Lord Bryce by Lord Stanmore, indicating the position of the British Government, was temporizing and inconclusive, it did not in Hungarian eyes lessen the importance of a statement sympathetic to Hungary's claims by an Englishman of the standing of

---

[106] It may truly be said that Count Bánffy was equally familiar with the fine arts and the art of statesmanship. He was as successful as director of the Royal Opera in Budapest as in the position of Minister for Foreign Affairs, which he later held for about two years.

[107] *Supra,* n. 7, p. 175.

Bryce. The Hungarians were further encouraged by a small but influential group of public men in England to intensify efforts to gain British sympathies.

After the peace conditions had been transmitted to the Hungarians, Lord Bryce advised Count Bánffy also to establish contacts in the United States. Bryce believed that since the United States was not bound by the secret treaty which the Allies had concluded with Rumania,[108] she could take a position against the contemplated incorporation of Transylvania into Rumania and could insist upon the determination of the boundaries by a fact-finding commission or plebiscite; should such a demand be put forward by the United States, he could promise that it would certainly be strongly supported by Hungary's British friends.[109] What Lord Bryce overlooked was the fact that although the United States could conceivably have insisted upon the delimitation of Hungary's new frontiers by methods more in accordance with Wilsonian principles than were the secret treaties, the American representatives on the territorial commissions had, albeit reluctantly, acquiesced in the recommendations made to and subsequently approved by the Supreme Council, in accordance with the claims put forward by Hungary's neighbors, which in the case of Rumania were based on such a secret treaty.

Another suggestion put forward by Hungary's British friends was to put off as long as possible any final decision concerning the treaty.[110] Lord Bryce and Lord Robert Cecil recommended to Count Bánffy a strategy of delay, at least until the opening of the British Parliament, hoping that they could muster opposition strong enough to force the British Government to take steps for the revision of the peace conditions in Hungary's favor.[111]

That the recommendation had a more solid basis than wishful thinking is indicated by the speeches made in Hungary's favor both in the House of Lords and in the House of Commons during the sitting that

[108] For the text of this secret treaty, see Temperley, *History,* IV, 516.

[109] "Political Diary," entry of Jan. 14, 1920. It was pursuant to this suggestion that Mr. Pelényi was sent, a few weeks later, to America to enlist Washington's support for Lord Bryce's plan.

[110] *Ibid.,* entry of Jan. 19, 1920.

[111] *Ibid.,* entries of Jan. 20, 21 and 26, 1920. Information also reached the Hungarians that England would look favorably upon the maintenance of free trade among the Succession States and the preservation of the economic unity of the former Austrian-Hungarian Monarchy, even though its political unity was doomed. *Ibid.,* entry of Jan. 19, 1920.

began on February 10.[112] Although the Hungarians were in no position effectively to delay proceedings, circumstances—such as the temporary upset of French internal politics following M. Clemenceau's defeat, the slowing down of the proceedings consequent upon the formal ending of the Peace Conference and the transfer of the functions of the Supreme Council to the Conference of Ambassadors, and the preoccupation of the Allies with other problems—all contributed to the dragging out of the negotiations with Hungary longer than in the case of Germany, Austria, or Bulgaria. But the promised action of Hungary's British friends did not produce the hoped-for results—not because of lack of time and not because of lack of good intentions on their part, but because the postwar structure of Europe had already frozen into a pattern, to change which would have required more courage and more foresight than statesmanship then possessed.

Coming closer home, reference should be made to the Hungarian Government's continued search for a friendly settlement with Austria regarding Western Hungary. The unfavorable impression created by the Austrian-Czech agreement and by Dr. Renner's contemplated visit to Belgrade [113] was further emphasized by a provocative speech of the Austrian Chancellor, delivered on January 23. He accused the Hungarian Government of persecuting those who favored the incorporation of Western Hungary into Austria and of designs to force upon Austria Hungary's own political philosophy, and he specifically expected Hungary from Austria's neighbors with whom he advocated friendlier relations. When Dr. Gratz, pursuant to instructions, protested against the unfriendly content and tone of the speech,[114] Chancellor Renner answered defiantly that Hungary's attitude in the matter of Western Hungary and her unfriendliness toward Austrian domestic policies at the present time rendered *rapprochement* between the two countries impossible. Dr. Renner stated that Austria's economic interests required close coöperation with Czecho-Slovakia, Rumania, and Yugoslavia, rather than with Hungary, which, stripped to the bone and surrounded by enemies, could offer nothing to Austria, her only hope lying in seeking Austria's friendship. Dr. Gratz declined to enter into an argument, saying that an equally unfriendly answer to the Chancellor's statement would be made by his government only if it wished to sever relations with Austria. He emphatically denied any intention on Hun-

[112] See *infra*, pp. 242–50.   [113] *Supra*, pp. 198–200.
[114] Count Somssich to Dr. Gratz, Jan. 25, 1920. *HFR*, Vol. I, Doc. 91.

gary's part to interfere in Austrian domestic affairs and warned Dr. Renner in no uncertain terms that Hungary was not dependent on Austria. If the Hungarians should be forced to make terms with an enemy, then they would pick the strongest, which was certainly not Austria. Dr. Renner immediately changed his attitude and assured Dr. Gratz that Austria, like Hungary, was desirous of maintaining friendly relations. While he was unwilling to retract his address of January 23, he would at an opportune moment make a conciliatory comment, to remove its sting.[115]

Undeterred by these irritating incidents, Dr. Gratz called on Chancellor Renner a few days later and proposed informally that the question of Western Hungary be settled by a plebiscite. Since, according to the Chancellor's own admission, Austria desired to keep this territory for strategic and economic reasons and for considerations of national policy, Dr. Gratz suggested an agreement including assurances on Hungary's part to (1) limit the number of Hungarian forces stationed in Western Hungary; (2) grant autonomy to the German-speaking population; and (3) enter into a preferential customs arrangement with respect to Western Hungary. Contrary to his heretofore intransigent attitude, Chancellor Renner expressed a willingness to take under advisement these suggestions and to engage in conversations after he had consulted the Foreign Affairs Committee of the National Assembly.[116] Although the Hungarian Government approved these informal suggestions and authorized Dr. Gratz to proceed,[117] Chancellor Renner apparently reconsidered his expressed willingness to negotiate. In a private communication to the Hungarian minister, complaining against alleged requisitions and the removal of state property from the contested territory, which, he said, impaired the rights guaranteed to Austria in the peace treaty, the Chancellor suggested the desirability of reaching a friendly agreement—not to determine the fate of Western Hungary—but concerning its evacuation by Hungary.[118]

Dr. Gratz denied that any requisitions were being made in Western Hungary, repeated the proposal for a plebiscite, and expressed the view that any discussion concerning the evacuation of Western Hungary was

[115] Dr. Gratz to Count Somssich, Jan. 28, 1920. *Ibid.*, Doc. 102.
[116] Dr. Gratz to Count Somssich, Feb. 1, 1920. *Ibid.*, Doc. 113.
[117] Count Somssich to Dr. Gratz, Feb. 5, 1920. *Ibid.*, Doc. 117.
[118] Dr. Gratz to Count Somssich, Feb. 8, 1920. *Ibid.*, Doc. 120.

at present premature,[119] a view which was fully endorsed by the Hungarian Government.[120] In a subsequent meeting between the Chancellor and Dr. Gratz, Dr. Renner again complained of the "reign of terror" in Western Hungary, which would make a plebiscite an "empty gesture," and expressed the belief that Hungary would ultimately acquiesce in the loss of that territory. He also told Dr. Gratz that Austria would not interfere with the freedom of elections, once Western Hungary came under Austrian rule, and should the provincial legislature thus elected oppose incorporation into Austria, Austria would not seek to prevent the return of that territory. In view of these exchanges of views, it is not surprising that Dr. Gratz had little hope for the acceptance of the Hungarian proposals.[121]

Nevertheless, upon instructions from the Minister for Foreign Affairs,[122] the proposals heretofore informally discussed between Chancellor Renner and Dr. Gratz were formally communicated to the Austrian Government in a note dated February 14.[123] Knowing that there was a growing sentiment in Austria for reconciliation with Hungary, the offer was released for publication in the Austrian press the day after its delivery to the Austrian Foreign Office, in the hope that public opinion would bring to bear sufficient pressure on the Austrian Government to cause it to accept Hungary's suggestion as the basis of negotiations.

However, Chancellor Renner and his party had a stronger hold on the government than anticipated. Despite the very favorable reception accorded at the outset by the Austrian press to the Hungarian offer, this effort of the Hungarian Government to bring about a change in the peace terms *in limine,* by means of a direct agreement with Austria, came to nothing.[124] This was the last attempt on the part of Hungary, prior to the signature of the Treaty of Trianon, to reach an understanding with Austria on the question of Western Hungary.

To safeguard Hungary's interests abroad as far as possible, the Hun-

[119] Dr. Gratz to Count Somssich, Feb. 9, 1920. *Ibid.,* Doc. 121.
[120] Count Somssich to Dr. Gratz, Feb. 10, 1920. *Ibid.,* Doc. 122.
[121] Dr. Gratz to Count Somssich, Feb. 11, 1920. *Ibid.,* Doc. 124.
[122] Count Somssich to Dr. Gratz, Feb. 12, 1920. *Ibid.,* Doc. 125.
[123] Dr. Gratz to Chancellor Renner. *Ibid.,* Doc. 127.

[124] On Feb. 17, Dr. Ippen, of the Austrian Foreign Office, intimated to the Hungarian minister that Austria would reject the Hungarian offer, despite the fear that this would put a further strain on Austrian-Hungarian relations. Dr. Gratz to Count Somssich, Feb. 17, 1920. *Ibid.,* Doc. 134. A few days later the offer was formally rejected. *Ibid.,* Doc. 139.

garian Government also undertook to make sure that despite the confused international status of the country, Hungarian interests would be protected by the neutral governments which, during the war, performed this service for the Austro-Hungarian Monarchy. The Hungarian minister in Vienna was instructed to convey to the envoys of Spain, Switzerland, Denmark, Sweden, and the Netherlands in Vienna the desire of the Hungarian Government that these neutral states continue to protect the interests of Hungary and of Hungarian nationals in the former enemy countries [125]—a request with which these governments complied.[126]

Owing partly to its preoccupation with the elections, which made it difficult to concentrate upon the examination of the peace conditions and the preparation of the reply thereto; and owing, furthermore, to its desire to gain time for the diplomatic steps described above, the Hungarian Government asked for [127] and secured [128] an extension of the two weeks' limit until February 12. When the government, perhaps following the advice of Hungary's British friends, later contemplated asking for a further delay, so that Count Apponyi and other Delegation members, elected to the National Assembly, could be present at the opening session, the Delegation strongly advised the Foreign Minister against any further delay, as it would be construed by the Allies as obstructionist tactics.[129]

Meanwhile, the outcome of the elections, fully endorsing the nationalist, conservative, and Christian tendency of the Huszár Government, and the intensified activity of the Hungarians abroad caused Hungary's neighbors to increase their pressure on her, in an effort to weaken her opposition to the peace conditions. The most effective way to accomplish that result appeared to be to interfere with the victualing of the

[125] Count Somssich to Dr. Gratz, Jan. 30, 1920. *Ibid.*, Doc. 104.

[126] See, for instance, Switzerland's intervening with the Rumanian Government in the interest of Colonel Csécsy-Nagy and several other Hungarian officers, condemned to death for alleged conspiracy by a Rumanian court martial at Kolozsvár. The Swiss Consul General in Budapest to Count Somssich, Feb. 18, 1920, and Count Somssich's reply, Feb. 19, 1920. *Ibid.*, Docs. 135 and 137.

[127] Instructions of Count Somssich to Mr. Praznovszky (who acted, during Count Apponyi's absence, as chargé d'affaires of the Hungarian Peace Delegation in Neuilly), Jan. 24. *Ibid.*, Doc. 90; cf. "Political Diary," entry of Jan. 26, 1920. For the text of the note to the President of the Peace Conference requesting the delay, dated Jan. 26, see *HPN*, I, 549.

[128] M. Clemenceau to the Hungarian Peace Delegation, Jan. 31, 1920. *HFR*, Vol. I, No. 111.

[129] "Political Diary," entry Jan. 30, 1920.

country, which, after the ravages of revolutions and the Rumanian occupation, was almost entirely dependent on outside assistance, especially since the lowlands east of the Tisza River, Hungary's granary, and the coal mines of Pécs were still occupied respectively by the Rumanians and the Yugoslavs. It was for this reason that, about the middle of January, Rumania suddenly prohibited the exportation of foodstuffs from the trans-Tisza territory to Budapest and to the evacuated parts of Hungary, and both Rumania and Yugoslavia put obstacles in the way of Allied and particularly American relief going to Hungary. When Hungary protested to the Peace Conference against the above Rumanian prohibition,[130] the Rumanians, upon inquiry by the Allied governments, gave as the reason for their action an alleged arrangement under which Hungary was giving the foodstuffs obtained from Rumania to Austria, in exchange for arms and munitions.[131] Considering the strained relations between Austria and Hungary during those weeks [132] and the serious threat of a food shortage in Budapest, the emphatic denial of this allegation by the Hungarian Government [133] may be accepted as having been made in good faith.

Following reports from American Relief officials, rather than as a result of the Hungarian protest, Secretary Lansing intervened and, on February 16, instructed the American minister at Bucharest, Mr. Charles J. Vopicka, to make vigorous representations to the Rumanian Government in view of the threatening food situation in Budapest, which, the Department of State had learned, was becoming critical. In his instructions Mr. Lansing expressed the belief that Rumania would be the first and greatest sufferer, should Hungary fall into chaos; therefore it would be in the Rumanian Government's own interest to do what it could to prevent Hungary's collapse.[134]

Mr. Vopicka reported the results of his representations on February 17. The Rumanian Foreign Minister said that he would immediately make an investigation; if the situation was as bad as stated, Rumania would do all she could to assist and aid Budapest. However, he expressed doubt that the situation was critical; he said that there was

---

[130] Count Somssich to Mr. Praznovszky, Jan. 26. *HFR,* Vol. I, Doc. 95. Cf. "Political Diary," entry of Jan. 27.

[131] This information was given by Lord Robert Cecil to Count Bánffy in London. See *ibid.,* entry of Feb. 6, 1920.

[132] *Supra,* pp. 198–200, 221–23.   [133] "Political Diary," entry of Feb. 9.

[134] *Foreign Relations of the United States,* 1920, I, 253. Similar representations were made to Yugoslavia. *Ibid.*

plenty of food in Hungary, and reports of food shortage were merely propaganda by Austria and Hungary "to make it appear to the world that these ex-partners of Germany are suffering very much."[135]

Thanks to the formal intervention of the United States and to informal representations by the British Government, this form of pressure against Hungary was momentarily relaxed,[136] and this attempt to starve Hungary into submission may have been partially responsible for the willingness of the Allies to press Rumania, after repeated urgings by Hungary, for the evacuation of territories east of the Tisza River.[137]

The national elections also supplied Hungary's adversaries with ammunition with which to obstruct Hungarian efforts to enlist the sympathies of the Principal Allied Powers. During the election campaign, the extreme right, under Stephen Friedrich's leadership, advocated the elimination of the Huszár coalition cabinet and the establishment of a regency with the Archduke Joseph as regent.[138] Although the elections demonstrated the weakness of Friedrich and although at that time the country as a whole, apart from a small group of vocal but uninfluential legitimists, was not interested in the dynastic ques-

[135] *Foreign Relations of the United States*, 1920, I, 258. The American minister was apparently not wholly satisfied with the reply, for he proposed to investigate personally the situation in Budapest; he then would not be obliged to accept the promised report of the Rumanian authorities.

[136] The American Relief Organization subsequently had difficulties again during the Hungarian peace negotiations, chiefly on account of Yugoslavia, when trying to feed Hungary; and several times these supplies had to be sent from Trieste through circuitous routes because the Yugoslavs tore up the rails on the direct line between Pragerhof and Kotor. See the instruction to the American chargé d'affaires at Belgrade, April 6, 1920. *Foreign Relations of the United States*, 1920, I, 278.

[137] The evacuation began at the end of Feb. It will be remembered that the very first communication from the Peace Delegation requested the Allies to cause Rumania to withdraw her troops behind the demarcation line (see *supra*, p. 204). This request was repeated. See the instructions of Count Somssich to Mr. Praznovszky, Feb. 6, 1919, *HFR*, Vol. I, Doc. 118, and for the text of the note, dated Feb. 9, *HPN*, I, 550 (Administrative Note 75). None of these notes were answered.

Hungary's eagerness to obtain prompt evacuation by the Rumanians was partly motivated by confidential information that the Rumanian Prime Minister, Mr. Vaida-Voivoda, was seeking to obtain France's consent to the continued occupation of the Tisza line, in order to guarantee the rear of the Rumanian Army in case of an attack by Soviet Russia. It was reliably reported that subject to British consent, the French were willing to agree to this. Count Somssich to the British High Commissioner in Budapest, Feb. 3, 1920. *HFR*, Vol. I, Doc. 115.

[138] It will be remembered that when Friedrich ousted Peidl's socialist government early in Aug., 1919, he immediately called upon the Archduke Joseph to act, temporarily, as the Head of the State; but, under Allied pressure, the Archduke was forced, on Aug. 23, 1919, to relinquish his position. *Supra*, Part Three, pp. 116–17, 122, 128–30.

tion, the saber-rattling declarations and campaign speeches of Friedrich and his followers raised among Hungary's neighbors the specter of Habsburg restoration in Hungary and the consequent reëstablishment of the Austro-Hungarian Empire. The fear of such a move felt in Prague, Belgrade, Bucharest, and perhaps also in Vienna was apparently communicated to the Principal Allies, and on February 2 the Hungarian Peace Delegation received a note from the Conference of Ambassadors, signed by M. Millerand, denying alleged rumors that the Allies would support Habsburg restoration in Hungary. The note pointed out that the Allies did not regard a Habsburg restoration as compatible either with the ideals for which they had fought or with their accomplishments in liberating peoples theretofore oppressed. While they did not intend to interfere in Hungary's internal affairs, they could not admit that a Habsburg restoration was a matter of purely domestic concern. The note concluded with the categorical declaration that such a restoration was incompatible with the fundamentals of the peace treaty and would be neither tolerated nor recognized by the Allies.[139]

Although the communication created a painful impression and was regarded as wholly uncalled for, the Hungarian Government decided not to reply for the time being, since it did not consider the question of restoration a living issue. Although the injection of the dynastic question had no direct bearing on the peace negotiations, the inspiration of this astonishing step of the Conference of Ambassadors by Hungary's neighbors was important evidence of their general inclination to seize upon every opportunity to embarrass that country. It is perhaps appropriate to remark that this declaration of the Principal Allied Powers later became the basis upon which the Allies proceeded against King Charles when in 1921 he twice attempted, but unsuccessfully, to regain the throne of Hungary.

Meanwhile the persecution of the Hungarian population in the occupied territories went on unabated. It is difficult to say whether or not such persecution was an end in itself or whether it had become a means to bring further pressure upon Hungary. In any event, Hungarians saw in the mistreatment of their co-nationals one ground upon which attacks against the peace conditions might be based and whereby their

[139] For the text of the note, see *infra*, Doc. 45, p. 550. Cf. the similar attitude taken by the Supreme Council with respect to the Archduke Joseph's regency. *Supra*, Part Three, pp. 122, 128.

requests for the evacuation of occupied territories beyond the demarcation line could be supported. It is in this light that the numerous complaints by the Hungarian Government to the Interallied Military Mission in Budapest [140] and of the Hungarian Peace Delegation to the Peace Conference [141] during this period and subsequently should be viewed.[142] At the same time the Hungarians could hardly be reproached for making use of the misfortunes of their co-nationals to

[140] See, for example, the protests against the conduct of the Yugoslav authorities, especially in the unlawfully occupied city of Pécs, dated Jan. 9, 18, 22, 28, 1920, HFR, Vol. I, Docs, 70, 79, 87, 100; the protest against the imprisonment of the chief of the police of the city of Makó by the Rumanians because he ordered the flags half-masted when the peace conditions were published, Jan. 28, 1920 (ibid., Doc. 101); the complaint of the arrest by the Rumanians of Hungarian farmers from Csongrád, who crossed the Tisza to save their property from the flood, on Jan. 31, 1921 (ibid., Doc. 109); the protest against the internment of General Flohr's family in Debrecen and the imprisonment of Hungarian women by the Rumanians, Feb. 17, 1920 (ibid., Doc. 133); and the reply of the American Commissioner in Budapest, Mr. Grant-Smith, dated Feb. 24, 1920 (ibid., Doc. 145); protests against the persecution of Hungarians in territories occupied by Yugoslavia, Feb. 26 and 27, 1920 (ibid., Docs. 148, 150).

[141] See, for example, the instructions of Count Somssich to Mr. Praznovszky, Feb. 1, 1920, to protest against the conduct of Yugoslav authorities in the occupied territories—specifically against the arrest, imprisonment, and expulsion of Hungarians, the support given to the anti-Hungarian communist movement in the occupied parts of Baranya and the terrorization of the Vends (ibid., Doc. 112); Count Apponyi's request, dated Feb. 6, to urge the evacuation of occupied territories by the Rumanians, in view of the continued atrocities against Hungarians, and to put an end to requisitions (ibid., Doc. 118). For the text of the note sent by the Delegation to the Peace Conference, with its Annexes, dated Feb. 15, see HPN, I, 552 ff. (Administrative Note 76). Cf. the instructions of Count Somssich to the Peace Delegation, Feb. 16, HFR, Vol. I, Doc. 130, to protest against the action of the Czechs in requiring, under threat of expulsion, an oath of loyalty from the Hungarians at Rimaszombat and in seizing the property of the historic provostry at Jászó, Feb. 17. Ibid., Doc. 132. See also the notes filed by the Peace Delegation with the Conference of Ambassadors, pursuant to instructions from the Minister for Foreign Affairs, on Feb. 13 and 16 (Administrative Notes 103 and 108), asking for Allied intervention in behalf of Colonel Csécsy-Nagy and seven Hungarian officers condemned to death by the Rumanians (HPN, II, 84, 86); on Feb. 18 (Administrative Note 121) protesting against the arrest of some 600 Hungarians at Temesvár by the Rumanians (ibid., p. 89); on Feb. 24 (Administrative Note 132) urging the dispatch of an Allied mission to Transylvania to investigate the conditions of the Hungarian population (ibid., p. 473).

[142] Besides the complaints made to the Interallied Mission and through the Hungarian Delegation to the Peace Conference, the Hungarian Government made numerous protests to the representatives of the Czecho-Slovak and Yugoslav Governments stationed in Budapest. See, for example, protests against the treatment of Hungarian nationals in territories occupied by the Czechs, Jan. 8 and 18, 1920, HFR (Vol. I, Docs. 69 and 80); protest against violations of the armistice by Yugoslavia, Jan. 14, 1920 (ibid., Doc. 74). Rumania did not have even a de facto representative in Budapest at this time.

discredit as much and as effectively as possible the alien regimes to which they were to be subjected. From Hungary's point of view it is regrettable that their many complaints and protests were almost completely ineffective in arousing the sympathy of the Allies, who did not even deign to reply to most of these communications.

While the Hungarian Government was thus actively seeking to improve Hungary's international position, the Delegation members who remained in Neuilly did not spend their days in idleness. Besides acting upon the instructions of the government in the various matters described above, the Delegation continued to present notes to the Peace Conference explaining Hungary's problems [143] and to seek to better Hungary's standing with the Allies. In this endeavor the Delegation was handicapped by the strictness with which limitations on its freedom of movement were enforced. How closely the movements of the members were watched is illustrated by an incident of which Mr. George Ottlik was the victim. Mr. Ottlik, who was serving as liaison officer between the Delegation and the Hungarian press, tried to slip into Paris one afternoon without permission in order to meet the Paris correspondent of the London *Times*. He was stopped, not far from the Delegation's quarters, by a detective, who escorted him back, and the next day Lieutenant Colonel Henry intimated that it would be desirable if Mr. Ottlik were sent home without delay—a polite command, in fact, with which the Delegation complied.[144] Owing to this strict supervision also, attempts of Señor Quiñones de Leon, the Spanish ambassador in Paris, to meet Count Bethlen were repeatedly frustrated, and it was with great difficulty that information which the Ambassador sought to obtain could be sent to him through intermediaries.[145]

Appreciating the predominance of the French at the Peace Conference, the Delegation was primarily interested in winning their good

---

[143] The documents filed prior to Count Apponyi's return to Budapest have been indicated, *supra*, pp. 204–6. Between Jan. 18 and Feb. 11 (the date of Count Apponyi's arrival in Paris), the Delegation filed, apart from the protest notes referred to above (*supra*, n. 141), several important memoranda, i.e., on Jan. 18. Note X, containing data in support of Count Apponyi's objections to the proposed frontiers voiced in his address to the Supreme Council on Jan. 16 (*HPN*, I, 329 ff.; this memorandum was sent pursuant to Mr. Lloyd George's request); and Note XI, with several annexes, concerning atrocities committed on the occupied territories (*ibid.*, pp. 336 ff.); on Jan. 22, Note XII, concerning Southern Hungary (*ibid.*, pp. 405 ff.) and No. XIII, concerning the Ruthenian question (*ibid.*, pp. 458 ff.), both with a number of annexes; on Jan. 31, Note XIX concerning the limitation which the Allies contemplated imposing on Hungary's armed forces (*ibid.*, pp. 547–48).

[144] "Political Diary," entry of Jan. 20.   [145] *Ibid.*, entry of Jan. 26.

will. With this end in view, the Delegation suggested, upon Count Bethlen's initiative, that the government should offer Hungarian labor for the reconstruction of the devastated regions of Northern France.[146] The suggestion did not appear at the outset a feasible one to the Hungarian Government, but, after further examination, a formal offer to this effect was made by the Minister for Foreign Affairs to the French Military Mission in Budapest, where it was very favorably received and duly communicated to the French Government.[147] However, no reply to the offer was received until the beginning of March, when General Graziani, French member of the Interallied Military Mission in Budapest, informed Count Somssich that the French Government would consider employing Hungarian labor only after Hungary had signed the peace treaty.[148]

The Delegation was more successful in pressing for the dispatch of an Allied mission to Western Hungary—a suggestion which was advanced by the Hungarian Government in September, 1919[149]—to counteract Austrian charges and accusations which had heretofore been ignored by the Peace Conference. Impressed by reports of the opposition of the population to incorporation into Austria and urged thereto informally by the Hungarian Delegation—as it had been in the first place by the Italians—the Conference of Ambassadors decided, in the closing days of January, to send an Interallied Mission, consisting of a British, a French, and an Italian officer, to Western Hungary.[150] The decision of the Allies was communicated to the Hungarian Delegation.[151] In reply, the Delegation expressed the Hungarian Government's gratification at the presence of an Allied body in Western Hungary and its hope that unbiased investigation would show the true situation there and the feeling of the population and would prove that

---

[146] "Political Diary," entry of Jan. 23. [147] Ibid., entry of Feb. 4.
[148] Ibid., entry of March 12. [149] See supra, pp. 191–92.
[150] The members of the Mission were originally Colonel Vigna (Italy), chairman, Major Michel (France), and Lieutenant Atkins (Great Britain). The Mission established its headquarters in Sopron at the beginning of Feb., 1920, and continued to function until Aug., 1921, when it was superseded by the Commission of Allied Generals, entrusted with the transfer of the territory to Austria. The composition of the Mission changed on several occasions. Colonel Vigna was succeeded after a few weeks first by Prince Pignatelli and later by Colonel Ivaldi; Captain de Redon replaced Major Michel, and Captain Gundry White took Lieutenant Atkins's place. Confidential Report on the Sopron Plebiscite by Baron Frederic Villani, Hungarian representative to the Interallied Mission for Western Hungary [in Hungarian, printed for Government use only, 1923], pp. 7–8.
[151] "Political Diary," entry of Feb. 4.

the charges leveled against Hungary were unfounded. In conclusion, the request for a plebiscite and the assurance that Hungary would abide by its results without reservation were reiterated and the dispatch of similar missions to the occupied territories was urged.[152]

Meanwhile sufficient progress had been made in Budapest with the preparation of the Hungarian reply for Count Apponyi to return to Paris. Accompanied by some of the delegates who had returned with him to Budapest and by several experts who had not originally gone to Neuilly, he arrived in Paris on February 11, the day before the expiration of the extended time limit for filing the Hungarian reply.[153] With Count Apponyi's return to Neuilly, the second phase of the Hungarian peace negotiations began.

The Hungarian Replies to the Original Peace Terms

On February 12, Count Apponyi, Mr. Praznovszky, and Count Stephen Csáky delivered to the Peace Conference Secretariat several notes constituting the partial reply of Hungary to the original peace terms handed to the Hungarian Delegation on January 15. Since the shortness of time given the Hungarians did not permit of the preparation and printing of the voluminous material assembled in Budapest, permission was sought and obtained for the subsequent filing of additional notes and memoranda. Between February 12 and February 20 the Hungarian Delegation filed in all eighteen notes, most of them with several annexes, maps, and statistical tables. These notes and memoranda set forth in greater or less detail the observations, criticisms, and objections of Hungary to the original peace terms, chapter by chapter, and included numerous proposals for their modification or amendment. The reaction of the French press to the Hungarian notes filed on February 12 was so hostile that the Delegation on the following day regarded the situation as definitely unpromising and the hope for improvement of the terms very slight. Under the circumstances the desirability of examining the consequences of a refusal to sign the treaty became evident.[154] This hostility of the press was obviously inspired by the French Government, since the press could not possibly

---

[152] *HPN*, I, 558 (Administrative Note 88, Feb. 10). Subsequently, the Conference of Ambassadors gave permission to Austria and to Hungary each to attach two delegates to this Mission. See *HPN*, II, 470, 475.

[153] "Political Diary," entry of Feb. 11.   [154] *Ibid.*, entry of Feb. 13, 1920.

have formed overnight an independent judgment regarding the extensive notes filed by the Hungarians on the preceding afternoon.

The first document filed by the Hungarian Delegation was in the nature of an introductory note, dealing primarily with the territorial question and setting forth the fundamental change which Hungary sought to obtain—namely, that the fate of the territories, with the exception of Croatia, which the original peace conditions proposed to take away by fiat, should be determined by plebiscites. The conditions and machinery for the proposed plebiscites were set forth in draft articles, which the Hungarians desired to have included in the peace treaty. The introductory note also commented on certain specific issues in the original peace terms which the Hungarians considered most objectionable. The first objection was leveled at the violation of ethnic principles by frontiers based upon strategic considerations, and separating large, contiguous groups of Magyars and purely Magyar towns from the mother country. Secondly, the note pointed out the undesirability of disrupting Hungary's natural economic unity and pleaded for its maintenance, even though the country be dismembered politically. Finally, objection was made to what the Hungarians felt was inadequate protection for national minorities. The note also sought the immediate repatriation of prisoners of war.[155]

The other notes delivered on February 12 dealt with the following sections of the peace treaty: [156]

The League of Nations.—The principle of the League was enthusiastically endorsed, but discrimination against the vanquished states in the matter of admission and limitation of armaments, as well as the inadequacy of the machinery for peaceful changes foreshadowed in Article 19 of the Covenant, were criticized.[157]

The frontiers of Hungary.—This, one of the most elaborate docu-

---

[155] For the complete text of the introductory note, see *HPN*, II, 1 ff.

[156] The draft of the Hungarian peace treaty followed the arrangement of the treaty with Germany, which also had served as the pattern for the treaties with Austria and Bulgaria. The sections of the Hungarian draft were the following: I. The Covenant of the League of Nations (Articles 1–26); II. Frontiers of Hungary (Articles 27–35); III. Political Clauses (Articles 36–78); IV. Hungarian Interests outside Europe (Articles 79–101); V. Military, Naval, and Air Clauses (Articles 102–43); VI. Prisoners of War and Graves (Articles 144–56); VII. Penalties (Articles 157–60); VIII. Reparations (Articles 161–79); IX. Financial Clauses (Articles 180–99); X. Economic Clauses (Articles 200–59); XI. Aerial Navigation (Articles 260–67); XII. Ports, Waterways, and Railways (Articles 268–314); XIII. Labor (Articles 315–55). No change was made in the above arrangement in the final peace terms.

[157] Note XXI, *HPN*, II, 8 ff.

ments presented by the Hungarian Delegation, developed the objections briefly summarized in the introductory note to the proposed boundaries and sought to support the pleas (1) for their rectification so that they would be more in conformity with ethnic principles, and (2) for plebiscites elsewhere, by a detailed analysis of those frontiers proposed by the Allies.[158]

Prisoners of war.—Calling attention to the deplorable conditions of Hungarian prisoners of war and of Hungarian nationals interned in Allied countries,[159] the note suggested modifications with respect to the date [160] and costs [161] of repatriation; there was also a request for special treatment for prisoners of war and interned civilians in Siberia and Turkestan.[162]

Objects of art and archives.—This note dealt at some length with the provisions relating to the division of archaeological and artistic objects, scientific and bibliographical material, and official documents between the Succession States of the former Monarchy. The text of the treaty which had been communicated to the Hungarian Delegation was of course modeled on the corresponding provisions incorporated in the peace treaty with Austria. Besides proposing a modification of these articles, the Hungarian note also called attention to the *sui generis* situation existing between Hungary and Austria by reason of the common ownership of the so-called Crown properties and common institutions shared by the former partners in the defunct Empire, and asked for the inclusion of additional provisions to safeguard Hungarian interests.[163]

Military and naval clauses.—The military and naval restrictions

[158] Note XXII and Annexes, *ibid.,* pp. 12–83.

[159] This matter had already been raised in a note presented by the Hungarian Delegation to the Peace Conference soon after its arrival in Paris, early in Jan., 1920; (see *HPN,* I, 126) and in Count Apponyi's oral exposition of the matter before the Supreme Council on Jan. 16. See *infra,* Doc. 44, p. 539.

[160] The original peace terms foreshadowed the release of Hungarian prisoners of war, following the coming into force of the treaty; the Hungarian suggestion was that it should begin "as soon as possible."

[161] The original peace terms imposed the costs of transportation on the Hungarian Government, which was also to provide the means of transport; the Hungarians asked that the Allies should advance both the cost and means, for which Hungary would undertake to reimburse them.

[162] Note XXV and Annexes, *HPN,* II, 150 ff.

[163] Note XXVIII and Annexes, *ibid.,* pp. 238 ff. It may be noted that the division of Crown properties and the liquidation of common offices and institutions remained the bone of contention for years between Austria and Hungary, as well as between these two countries and the other Succession States.

which the peace conditions were designed to impose on Hungary and which were similar to those imposed on Germany, Austria, and Bulgaria, were commented upon in two separate notes.[164] With respect to the army, the Hungarians requested a slight increase, to 10 percent, in the proportion of officers to the total effectives in service, a gradual instead of an immediate reduction to the determined figure, this reduction to be spread over five years. These requests were based chiefly upon the danger of communism, which had so recently engulfed Hungary. With respect to the naval clauses, the relevant note proposed several modifications in the original peace terms to meet three Hungarian desiderata, namely: first, the necessity of leaving the port of Fiume to Hungary, or at least of assuring her full use of this outlet to the sea; secondly, crediting Hungary's reparation account with a sum corresponding to her legal share, as co-proprietor, of all units and material of the former Austro-Hungarian Navy ceded to the Yugoslav National Council; and, thirdly, leaving the Danube flotilla in Hungary's possession.

The hydraulic system.—This note proposed the substitution of elaborate provisions for Article 293 of the original peace terms (in Part XII relating to ports, waterways and railways), which, according to the Hungarians, failed to take account of the nature and character of Hungary's water-control system and to insure the country the necessary services for irrigation, forestry, the prevention of floods, the control of navigation, and the exploitation of water power.[165]

Agricultural questions.—This note did not especially link itself with any particular part of the peace terms, but sought to bring home to how great an extent Hungary's existence depended on agricultural prosperity, which would be made impossible by the intended dismemberment of the country.[166]

Labor.—The section relating to the International Labor Organization was approved by the Hungarian Government; it was suggested that, in view of various labor unions with differing outlooks, they should be allowed equal opportunity for representation, instead of one delegate each for employers' and employees' organizations respectively. The reply also indicated Hungary's belief that this section of the treaty would apply only to industrial workers, since questions of working

---

[164] Notes XXX and XXXI, both with several Annexes, *HPN,* II, 349 ff., 358 ff.
[165] Note XXXII, with Annexes. *Ibid.,* pp. 377 ff.
[166] Note XXXIII, with Annexes. *Ibid.,* pp. 428 ff.

hours, minimum age of employment, and the like would require different treatment in the case of agricultural labor.[167]

Aerial navigation.—This brief note, relating to Part XI of the original terms, accepted the necessity of uniform international regulation, but voiced its objection to obligations imposed, without reciprocity, on the vanquished states alone.[168]

The few remaining notes, filed with the Peace Conference between February 18 and 20, completed Hungary's reply to the original peace terms and dealt with the following parts thereof:

Sanctions.—This brief note, dated February 18, protested against the provisions requiring the delivery to the Allies of persons accused of acts contrary to the laws and customs of war and their trial and punishment by Allied military tribunals, as being provisions so humiliating that they could not be imposed, even on a conquered state, except by force. The Hungarians urged the omission of this part of the treaty or else a substitution of provisions imposing reciprocal obligations on all belligerents to try in their own courts their nationals accused of violating the laws of war.[169]

Legal questions.—The six Annexes to this note, dated February 19, contain observations, criticisms, and numerous suggestions for the modifications of sections of Part X of the draft treaty (Economic Clauses) dealing with the questions of debts; property, rights and interests; contracts, prescriptions, and judgments; mixed arbitral tri-

---

[167] Note XXXIV, *ibid.,* p. 436. Mr. Temperley, in his *History,* IV, 427, berated the Hungarian Delegation for having "alone of all the defeated nations expressed the wish to retard and not to advance the operation of the provisions laid down in this charter of international labour." According to Mr. Temperley, the Delegation stated that "Hungary had a great excess of agricultural labour over industrial, and that, under such circumstances, it was difficult to have an eight-hour day or to equalize conditions and hours of labour." The criticism of this distinguished historian appears to be wholly unwarranted. First, the text of the Hungarian note does not express, even by implication, the position which Mr. Temperley said was taken by Hungary toward the Labor section of the treaty draft. Secondly, the applicability of the labor section of the treaty to agricultural labor, to which the Hungarian note drew attention in very general terms, was open to doubt, as is shown by the raising of this very issue by the French Government subsequently. The question of the competence of the International Labor Organization to regulate the conditions of labor of persons employed in agriculture was submitted, in 1922, by the Council of the League of Nations to the Permanent Court of International Justice, which, in Advisory Opinion No. 2, rendered on Aug. 12, 1922, answered the question in the affirmative. See *Publications of the Court,* Series B, No. 2; Hudson, *World Court Reports,* I, 122 ff.

[168] Note XXXV, *HPN,* II, 437.   [169] Note XXVI, *ibid.,* pp. 163–64.

bunals; industrial property; and special provisions relating to transferred territories (Articles 231–59).[170]

The remaining notes, all filed on February 20, concerned the following:

Reparation and financial clauses.—Naturally, this was one of the more elaborate and perhaps the most revealing of the documentations presented by Hungary to the Peace Conference. The problems raised by the clauses of the draft were divided into three main groups, namely, the question of reparations, the regulation of financial questions arising from the disappearance of the Monarchy among the Succession States, and finally financial obligations, incurred both before and during the war by Hungary.[171]

Economic and trade questions.—The observation contained in the several Annexes to this note concerned the whole treaty draft and dealt with the political clauses, with the provisions relating to Hungarian interests outside Europe, with the economic clauses of the draft, with railways, telegraph, telephones, and shipping, with freedom of navigation and the proposed internationalization of the Danube, with Hungary's merchant fleet, and finally with guaranteeing for Hungary outlets to the sea.[172] The Hungarians proposed a great many modifications of and amendments to the Allied draft; the most elaborate arguments were presented with respect to the economic clauses, which the Hungarian memorandum declared to be unacceptable in their original wording, primarily because of the total absence of reciprocity.

The protection of minorities.—Considering the number of Magyar people who, under the peace conditions, were to become separated from Hungary, it is not surprising that one of the chief concerns of the Hungarian Delegation was to secure more adequate protection for

[170] Note XXXVII, *ibid.,* pp. 440 ff. The observations on debts contained in Annex I to this note are supplementary to the more elaborate representations set forth in the note dealing with reparation and the financial clauses of the draft. See *infra.*

[171] Note XXIX, *ibid.,* pp. 260 ff. The Annexes to this note contain a wealth of information and data relating to Hungary's financial problems at that period. Annex I is a scholarly monograph on Hungary's financial difficulties and its causes. Annex II contains the first official compilation by Hungarian authorities of the loss and damage Hungary suffered during the Rumanian occupation. Annex III gives an accurate picture of Hungary's public debts, while Annex IV endeavors to throw light on the troublesome problems involved in the liquidation of the Austro-Hungarian Bank. Students who wish to inquire into the economic and financial chaos which engulfed Hungary and most of the Succession States in the early 1920's will find these Annexes most useful for their studies.

[172] Note XXVII, *ibid.,* pp. 165 ff.

national minorities than the draft treaty provided. The argument for more effective protection was supported by a number of Annexes, setting forth the religious, educational, and cultural problems involved and summarizing the complaints against the treatment received by the Magyars from the Czech, Rumanian, and Yugoslav authorities in the territories to be allotted to them under the peace terms.[173]

Nationality and option.—This brief note proposed minor modifications in the treaty provisions relating to change of nationality and the right of option. These provisions followed the pattern adopted in the peace treaty with Austria and, as pointed out in this note, took no account of the difference between the laws governing nationality prior to 1919 in Austria, on the one hand, and in Hungary, on the other.[174]

With the filing of these notes, the peace negotiations between the Allies and Hungary came to an apparent standstill on February 20; the final peace conditions and the Allied reply to the Hungarian observations were not handed to the Hungarian Delegation until May 5. The reasons for this delay of two and a half months can only be surmised. One reason was doubtless the preoccupation of the Principal Allied Powers with matters of more immediate concern to them, namely, the execution of the peace treaty with Germany and the contemplated liquidation of the Ottoman Empire. Another contributing factor may have been the confidential conversations between Hungary and France, to be discussed presently, in consequence of which the French may have exerted pressure to delay the final peace terms, in order to suit the development of their plans. But the chief reason undoubtedly was the fact that the Peace Conference itself had largely disintegrated, following the withdrawal of the United States in December, 1919. One of the Hungarian delegates probably came very near it when he said that the Allies were unhappy about and "frightfully bored by the whole Peace Conference." [175]

---

[173] Note XXIII, *ibid.*, pp. 90 ff.   [174] Note XXIV, *ibid.*, pp. 146–49.

[175] Mr. Praznovszky wrote to Count Apponyi on April 7, 1920: ". . . I am reliably informed that the delegates and particularly the representatives of the Western Powers are frightfully bored by the whole Peace Conference. They feel increasingly that they have got into a labyrinth from which they cannot find a way out and that they have created in the peace treaties a great number of new international problems which they will not know how to solve. One of these problems, and perhaps the principal one, is of course the Hungarian question. Especially since we presented our notes and memoranda they have begun to realize that the Hungarian question should be examined from many angles for which they have neither time nor patience. . . ," *HFR*, Vol. I, Doc. 209.

During the weeks which elapsed between the filing of the Hungarian notes and the Allied reply, communications between the Hungarian Delegation and the Peace Conference consisted almost exclusively of protests against the conduct of Czech, Rumanian, and Yugoslav authorities in the occupied territories, of complaints on account of the mistreatment of the Magyar population in these territories, and of efforts to expedite the repatriation of Hungarian prisoners of war. There being little except routine business, it appeared unnecessary to maintain a large staff in Paris, and therefore in the interests of economy members of the Hungarian Delegation who had accomplished their task were sent home. By the beginning of March the staff of the Delegation had been reduced to barely half its original personnel, and on March 31 Count Apponyi himself returned to Budapest, leaving only a skeleton personnel under the direction of Mr. Praznovszky, the Secretary General of the Delegation, to attend to routine matters. At the beginning of April Mr. Praznovszky and his small staff obtained permission from the French to move from Neuilly to Versailles, to save expense while waiting for the Allied reply.[176]

This lull in the Hungarian peace negotiations was, however, more apparent than real. Indeed all through these weeks negotiations of a different character but of vital import were taking place behind the scenes, which, if successful, might have changed the course of European history. Also during this time the Hungarian Government redoubled its efforts in the Allied camp, to gain support for its opposition to the peace conditions where some apprehension over the harsh treatment of Hungary had become evident. Before turning to the secret conversations between Hungary and France, which began soon after the filing of the Hungarian reply notes, we shall make a rapid survey of the diplomatic scene in Europe.

Allied Views on the Hungarian Peace Negotiations

Criticism of the original peace terms presented to Hungary was not confined to Hungarians, but was voiced in some Allied quarters as well. At the very time when the Hungarian reply notes were being filed in Paris, dissatisfaction with the handling of the Hungarian question

---

[176] Mr. Praznovszky to Mr. Simonyi-Semadam, April 5, 1920, *ibid.*, Doc. 205; cf. "Political Diary," entries of April 3 and 10.

was expressed at the meeting of the Allied Prime Ministers held in London (February 13–23, 1920) and also in the British Parliament.

At the Prime Ministers' meeting, attended by Messrs. Lloyd George, Millerand, and Nitti, the Italian Prime Minister apparently sought fairer treatment for Hungary than she had hitherto received. Because of the secrecy which cloaked the proceedings of the Peace Conference committees, the course of the discussions at this meeting must be surmised from circumstantial evidence and cannot be stated with demonstrable accuracy. The session was devoted chiefly to the treaty with Turkey and the question of Fiume; and the Hungarian treaty, in all likelihood, was brought forward because of the presentation of the Hungarian reply notes and the outburst against Hungary in the French press, already referred to. Only sporadic publicity was given in the Allied press to Signor Nitti's intervention, and there is only meager reference to it in contemporary history.[177] However, rumors that the Italian Prime Minister was pressing in London for the revision of the peace treaties in general and the Hungarian peace conditions in particular reached Budapest at the beginning of March. On March 7 the Hungarian Foreign Minister instructed Count Nemes, the Hungarian representative in Rome,[178] to make inquiries as to the accuracy of these rumors.[179] On the same date the Peace Delegation in Paris reported, on the basis of authentic information, that Signor Nitti had made some statement at the meeting of the Supreme Council and that the British reaction had not been unfavorable.[180] To the Hungarian representative's cautious inquiries, Count Sforza confidentially replied that the substance of Prime Minister Nitti's intervention was the opposition to a suggestion advanced, in all likelihood by M. Millerand, that the

[177] Mr. Toynbee, in his *Survey of International Affairs, 1920–1923*, p. 10, merely notes that "the Conference considered the objections of Hungary to the draft treaty of Trianon. . . ."

[178] As indicated above, *supra*, p. 213, Italy agreed at the end of Jan. to receive a diplomatic agent from the Hungarian Government. Count Nemes, appointed to this position, presented his credentials, in the absence of the Italian Foreign Minister, to the Secretary of State for Foreign Affairs, Count Sforza, on Feb. 21. Count Nemes to Count Somssich, Feb. 28, 1920, *HFR*, Vol. I, Doc. 154.

[179] Count Somssich to Count Nemes, *ibid.*, Doc. 169.

[180] Mr. Praznovszky to Count Somssich, March 7, 1920, *ibid.*, Doc. 173. Also in "Political Diary," entry of March 7. The delegation's report to Count Somssich expressed the opinion that the espousal of Hungary's cause by one of the Principal Allied Powers might bring about slight improvements, provided such a Power were prepared to face the opposition of France and of Hungary's neighbors.

Hungarian counter-proposals be disregarded.[181] According to Count Sforza, Nitti took the position that since Hungary had been allowed to submit counter-proposals, it would be unfair to ignore them. He characterized it as a political error to decide the Hungarian question without even knowing or considering what the Hungarian counter-proposals might contain. Signor Nitti also pointed out that the proposed peace terms violated the ethnic principle.[182] Although the Italian intervention was unsuccessful,[183] Count Somssich requested Count Nemes to convey to the Italian Government the thanks of Hungary and to urge the Italians to continue their support of Hungary's interests. He was instructed to state that Hungarian public opinion warmly welcomed Signor Nitti's intervention and regarded Italy's sympathetic attitude as a manifestation of the traditional friendship between the Italians and the Hungarians.[184] At a subsequent interview Count Sforza informed Count Nemes that Signor Nitti had instructed the Italian Foreign Minister, Signor Scialoja, to continue to try to obtain a reconsideration of the Hungarian peace conditions. However, he also said that British and French opposition was so violent that he saw little hope of any success.[185] When, a few days later, Count Nemes had his first interview with the Italian Prime Minister, the latter assured the Hungarian representative that he would continue to act in Hungary's interest, despite opposition. Signor Nitti shared the pessimism of his Secretary of State and regarded the prospects of any measure of success as discouraging; but he expected further discussion of the Hungarian peace treaty at the forthcoming San Remo Conference, where, in a quieter atmosphere, he hoped to make more progress toward the pacification of Europe,

---

[181] That the opposition to Nitti's move came from French sources was confirmed in a conversation Count Nemes held a few days later with a high official of the Italian Foreign Office, who stated that Mr. Lloyd George supported the Italian Prime Minister, while M. Millerand opposed him "energetically," in view of the French commitments to the Czechs and the Yugoslavs. Count Nemes to Count Somssich, March 13, 1920, HFR, Vol. I, Doc. 186.

[182] Count Nemes to Count Somssich, March 9, 1920, ibid., Doc. 177.

[183] The Peace Delegation reported from Paris that according to British and French press reports, the Supreme Council in London rejected Nitti's intervention in Hungary's favor and decided to impose the original peace terms. See "Political Diary," entry of March 10. Cf. Count Somssich to Count Nemes, March 13, 1920, HFR, Vol. I, Doc. 184.

[184] Count Somssich to Count Nemes, March 9, 1920, ibid., Doc. 175.

[185] Count Nemes to Mr. Simonyi-Semadam, March 16, 1920, ibid., Doc. 192. Count Somssich resigned as Foreign Minister on March 15, and the Hungarian Prime Minister temporarily took charge of the Foreign Office until that post was occupied by Count Teleki on April 19.

"which necessarily includes reconsideration of his request to examine the Hungarian counter-proposals."[186]

Signor Nitti's intervention, although unsuccessful, was nevertheless a further evidence of improved relations between Italy and Hungary, already referred to, and gave some measure of comfort to the Hungarian Government.[187] In an interview which Count Nemes held with Count Sforza soon after the presentation of his credentials, the latter declared that he desired coöperation between Italy and Hungary because mutual interests demanded intimate relations between the two countries; for that reason, Count Sforza said, he wished to see Hungary strengthened and he expressed willingness to agree to mutual diplomatic support, without, however, any formal agreement.[188]

The extent to which relations had improved can be gauged by the fact that when Hungary desired to ascertain what attitude the Allies would take should she refuse to sign the unaltered peace conditions, information was sought from the Italian Government. Following the failure of Nitti's intervention in the Supreme Council, speculation arose among members of the Hungarian Delegation in Paris as to

[186] Count Nemes to Mr. Simonyi-Semadam, March 18, 1920, *ibid.*, Doc. 193. It is not known whether the Hungarian peace treaty was discussed at all at the San Remo Conference (April 19–26, 1920), although one of the reasons for the delay in presenting the final peace conditions to Hungary was, in the opinion of Peace Conference circles, the inclusion of the Hungarian question on the conference agenda. Mr. Praznovszky to Count Apponyi, April 7, 1920, *ibid.*, Doc. 209; cf. also "Political Diary," entry of April 12, 1920. In his statement to the House of Commons on the conference on April 29, 1920, Mr. Lloyd George did not even by implication refer to the question of Hungary. Hansard, *Parliamentary Debates, House of Commons,* 5th Ser., Vol. 128, pp. 1459 ff. The same is true concerning M. Millerand's report to the French Chamber of Deputies, made on April 28. *Journal officiel, Débats parlementaires* (*Chambre des députés*), 1920, pp. 1445–46. Certainly the atmosphere was not favorable to any reconsideration of the peace conditions. The agenda of the conference (execution of the Versailles treaty, the Turkish treaty, and the allocation of the Near East mandates) was overshadowed by the controversy between Great Britain and France over France's independent action against Germany, following disturbances in Germany during the latter part of March. It was at San Remo that permission was denied to Germany to double the army allowed her under the Versailles treaty. According to M. Millerand's report, the Allies agreed from the outset to exclude any revision. "Toute idée de reviser le traité de Versailles devait être formellement exclue." Obviously such a categorical attitude must have frustrated any attempt to obtain reconsideration of the Hungarian peace terms.

[187] That the Hungarian Government considered Nitti's intervention significant is shown by the fact that on that basis the Hungarian representative at Warsaw was instructed to try once more to enlist the active support of Poland for the amelioration of peace terms. Mr. Kánya to Count Csekonics, March 20, 1920, *HFR,* Vol. I, Doc. 194.

[188] Count Nemes to Count Somssich, March 2, 1920, *ibid.*, Doc. 155.

whether the intransigent position taken by the Allies might possibly have been motivated by a desire to bring about Hungary's refusal to sign, thus creating a situation which would make concessions to Hungary feasible, despite preëxistent Allied obligations to Hungary's neighbors. The Delegation suggested that inquiries should be made in Rome as to the probable attitude of the Principal Allied Powers in such an eventuality, and especially whether the occupation of Hungary by her neighbors would be authorized.[189] Count Nemes made inquiries during an interview with Count Sforza on March 16, at which time Count Sforza advised the Hungarian representative that, in his opinion, the Allies would not press Hungary's neighbors to moderate their territorial claims and he expressed the belief that Czecho-Slovakia, Rumania, and Yugoslavia would move against Hungary, with or without Allied authorization. He said, however, that Italy would oppose any military action against Hungary.[190]

With reference to Italian support of Hungary, it appears from information given to the Hungarian representative by a high official of the Italian Foreign Office that Signor Nitti's instructions to the Italian Foreign Minister, already referred to, to support Hungary were limited to support against Czecho-Slovak and Yugoslav claims, but did not include Rumania, toward which Italy felt herself committed.[191] It would also seem that when the Rumanian Government, concerned over Italian efforts on Hungary's behalf, instructed its minister in Rome to make representations to the Italian Government, Count Sforza characterized Nitti's action as "an act of courtesy" and apparently gave the impression to the Rumanian minister that Hungarian territory claimed by Rumania did not come within the purview of any effort looking toward the improvement of the Hungarian peace conditions.[192]

In the British Parliament the Hungarian question was adverted to in the course of the debate on the Address. On February 12, 1920, Sir Donald MacLean, speaking in the House of Commons, expressed a fear that the erection of trade barriers by the Succession States of

---

[189] Count Somssich to Count Nemes, March 13, 1920, *ibid.*, Doc. 184.

[190] Count Nemes to Mr. Simonyi-Semadam, March 16, 1920, *ibid.*, Doc. 192. Count Sforza doubted the wisdom of a refusal to sign. He told Count Nemes that by signing the treaty Hungary would not renounce her claims and expressed the opinion that neither Czecho-Slovakia nor Yugoslavia would last very long.

[191] Count Nemes to Count Somssich, March 13, 1920, *ibid.*, Doc. 186.

[192] Count Nemes to Mr. Simonyi-Semadam, March 25, 1920, *ibid.*, Doc. 199.

Austria-Hungary would lead to confusion and chaos.[193] Referring specifically to the treaty with Hungary and to the claims of her neighbors for Hungarian territories, he urged that such claims should be investigated by an impartial commission of experts and the frontiers determined only after the report of such a commission had been considered. Where there was any doubt, he said, there ought to be a plebiscite, such as was held in Schleswig. Sir Donald was particularly critical of the proposed Hungarian-Rumanian boundary, which would put a large Magyar population under Rumanian sovereignty. Replying on behalf of the Government, Mr. Balfour, Lord President of the Council, defended the Peace Conference decisions, saying that Sir Donald was "wholly wrong in his facts" and that the boundary was probably the best that could be found. Mr. Balfour admitted that these questions were "very difficult"; while the main consideration must be that of population, the question of railway communications, of economics, and possibly even of military frontiers could not be entirely disregarded. He said that in proposing to resubmit these frontiers to the consideration of an impartial commission, Sir Donald was perhaps not aware of "how careful and how elaborate were the inquiries into these frontier questions" by experts. Mr. Balfour denied that these frontiers were settled with prejudice and claimed that there was a sincere desire to lay down frontiers which would be fair to all parties.

At the same meeting Sir Samuel Hoare, who could hardly be looked upon as friendly to Hungary,[194] raised the question of charges against the behavior of the Rumanians during their occupation of Hungary and urged that if upon inquiry these charges were found to be correct, then justice ought to be done. "It seems to me to be a cruel paradox," he said, "that after a war that was meant to end war we should

[193] The economic consequences of the disappearance of so large a trading unit as the Austro-Hungarian Monarchy appears to have caused considerable apprehension in England—perhaps more than in any other Allied country. At the meeting of the House of Commons on Feb. 26, 1920, Lord Cavendish Bentinck asked the Prime Minister whether he would urge on the Peace Conference, then considering the treaty with Hungary, the necessity of assuring free trade among the Succession States, "so that Hungary may not, like Austria, be placed in the disastrous position of economic isolation as a result of the Treaty." Mr. Lloyd George agreed on the importance of encouraging free trade between the Succession States; but he said that the economic policy of these states was not a matter which had been or could be settled in a peace treaty. Hansard, *Parliamentary Debates, House of Commons*, 5th ser., Vol. 125, p. 1895.

[194] In rising to take part in the debate, Sir Samuel assured the House that he had "no affection whatever" for the Magyars, whom he had always regarded as an "arrogant people."

see in Central Europe a state of militarism far worse than ever it was before 1914." [195]

A few days later, on February 25, the Hungarian question was discussed in the House of Lords by Lord Newton. He addressed himself primarily to the failure of the Rumanians to evacuate Hungary, pursuant to the direction of the Supreme Council, but he also criticized what he regarded as an extremely harsh peace which the Allies intended to impose upon Hungary. Calling attention to the enormous damage caused to Hungary (estimated by British officials, according to Lord Newton, at £100,000,000), he complained that even at that date the Rumanians still occupied Hungarian territory east of the Tisza River. Turning to the peace treaty, Lord Newton expressed the opinion that Hungary was slated to suffer more than any other ex-enemy country. He also took issue with Sir Samuel Hoare, who had stated a few days earlier in the House of Commons that the Hungarians were to a large extent responsible for the war. Lord Newton said that Hungary had never wanted war and suggested that of all the ex-enemies that country was the one which should make the greatest appeal to British sympathy.

The reply of the Government was made, in the absence of the Foreign Secretary, Lord Curzon—he was attending the conference of Allied Prime Ministers—by the Earl of Crawford. His understatement of the issues is characteristic of the extreme caution with which spokesmen of the British Government usually approach questions of foreign policy. According to the Earl of Crawford, Czecho-Slovak and Rumanian troops were "forced in self-defence" to occupy Hungarian territories. Since Budapest was first occupied by the Rumanians, at the beginning of August, 1919, "the question of the time and manner of their evacuation of the regions beyond the new frontiers laid down in the draft Treaty had been the subject of a long correspondence" between the Supreme Council and Rumania; but definite settlement was hampered by other questions involved, and it required "prolonged

[195] Hansard, *Parliamentary Debates, House of Commons*, 5th ser., Vol. 125, pp. 271–73, 301–7, 327–28. Among the charges specified by Sir Samuel were the looting of the rolling stock of the Hungarian railways; political intimidation and persecution of the non-Rumanian population and of the Roman Catholic and Protestant Churches; the expulsion of teachers and civil servants because they refused to swear allegiance to the Rumanian crown, in a territory that had not yet been transferred to Rumania by the Allies.

negotiations" before the Supreme Council obtained satisfaction of their demands. According to the Earl of Crawford, the difficulties had in the main been removed since the accession of Mr. Vaida-Voivoda as Prime Minister of Rumania, since he had shown a "most cordial desire" to reach a satisfactory solution of all issues and was most anxious to carry out the requested evacuation at the earliest possible date. He explained the fact that the evacuation had not yet been completed as being due to transport difficulties and expressed the confidence of the British Government that Rumania would coöperate loyally and fully in the restoration of peace.[196] The Earl of Crawford also took the position that since the peace treaty was not yet signed, Hungary would have no legal right to appeal to that treaty to obtain the evacuation of Hungarian territory by Allied troops.[197]

More direct and emphatic attacks upon the Hungarian peace terms were made at the meeting of the House of Lords held on March 30, 1920. The discussion, again initiated by Lord Newton, seems to have been prompted by the Italian intervention in Hungary's interest at the Supreme Council meeting held in London some weeks previous and by rumors that a revision of the proposed conditions had been definitely refused. Lord Newton recited, in somewhat greater detail than on the previous occasion, the losses which Hungary was due to sustain and expressed doubt that it was realized in England "how extremely severe and harsh" the proposed peace terms were. He expressed the fear that

[196] It will be remembered that the Supreme Council from the outset insisted on the evacuation of *all* Hungarian territories beyond the line laid down in the Council's resolution of June 13, 1919. *Supra,* Part Three, *passim.* In the final ultimatum to Rumania, approved by the Supreme Council on Nov. 13, 1919, Rumania was invited to "comply, without discussion, reservation or condition" to the *complete* evacuation of Hungary. *Supra,* p. 169. When upon the receipt of this ultimatum, the Rumanian Government resigned, the new government of Mr. Vaida-Voivoda accepted unconditionally all the demands of the Allies, including the request for complete evacuation of Hungary. Yet the evacuation of territories east of the Tisza did not begin until Feb. 24 and was not completed until the latter part of March. See Count Somssich to Mr. Praznovszky, Feb. 24, 1920. *HFR,* Vol. I, Doc. 144. Cf. also Count Somssich to Mr. Praznovszky, March 8, 1920 (*ibid.,* Doc. 174); same to same, March 12, 1920 (*ibid.,* Doc. 182).

[197] Hansard, *Parliamentary Debates, House of Lords,* 5th ser., Vol. 39, pp. 146–50. The Earl of Crawford stood on solid legal ground in asserting that Hungary could not base any claim on a treaty not yet signed. However, the Hungarian Government requested the withdrawal of Rumanian as well as of Yugoslav troops from Hungarian territory not on the basis of the treaty draft but upon repeated promises and assurances of the Supreme Council.

Hungary would be unable economically to exist, as a result of the loss of her natural resources; but he regarded as even worse the subjection of great masses of Hungarians to alien rule.

What has become of the question of so-called self-determination [he asked]? Why should millions of civilised human beings be handed over like so many sheep or cattle without being allowed to express any opinion at all? Why should these people not be allowed a plebiscite as has been allowed in other cases?

Especially was this so, he added, when the Hungarians had given assurances that they were ready to abide by the results of a plebiscite. Or was Hungary so criminal a country, Lord Newton asked, that she must be denied this elementary right? The only crime that the Hungarians could be charged with was that they fought against England; but the Czechs, the Poles, the Yugoslavs, who were now greeted as friends, also fought against England. Lord Newton refused to believe that the British Government was animated by any hostile feelings toward Hungary and expressed the conviction that the Government was averse to any unnecessary mutilation of that country. Apparently referring to Signor Nitti's intervention, he pointed to the "open secret" that the Italians favored a modification of the Hungarian peace terms and concluded:

The confidence felt by Hungary in British impartiality and in British justice is so great that I believe that anything which emanates from us would be willingly accepted, and it is for this reason that I regret that the negotiations with regard to this Treaty are being conducted at Paris instead of in London. The conditions, whatever they are, whatever they eventually turn out to be, will no doubt be severe. . . . But if those conditions were arrived at in this country, and if the Hungarians had an opportunity of putting their case before impartial opinion here, I believe that, whatever the decision was, it would be accepted more or less cheerfully and without protest by the Hungarians.

Lord Newton was strongly supported by Lord Bryce, Lord Montagu, and Lord Sydenham. Lord Bryce called attention to events in Austria which could serve as a solemn warning of the effects of a peace conceived in a spirit of revenge. He admitted that the frontiers of Hungary presented enormous difficulties, but he urged that the problem deserved more careful investigation than, to his knowledge, had yet been given it by the Supreme Council. Lord Bryce stated the obvious truth that the mixture of races, nationalities, and languages made it impossible in all cases to avoid the subjection of a race to alien rule; he felt, however, that every effort ought to be made to arrive at the solution which would be least troublesome and which would produce the minimum of exasperation. He regarded it as particularly important to ascertain the wishes of the populations concerned; for, he said, it is not only important that justice should be done, but that people should have a sense that justice is being done. He warned that any injustice would involve risk for the future peace. And he ended:

A settlement that is made in contradiction of the principles of justice will not be a permanent settlement. If you want to avoid future wars—and who among us is there who does not wish to give Europe some respite from war? —you must carry out the principles of self-determination as far as you can and see that justice is done. We have had trouble enough already, and I think we may urge upon His Majesty's Government that if they wish to have peace, and if they wish that we shall not continually have the flame of war lit up again by nationalities complaining of unjust treatment, they should settle this question upon those principles to which the Allies proclaimed their adhesion when the Armistice was concluded. We pledged ourselves then to the principle of nationality and self-determination. Here is an opportunity in which we can say that we adhere to those principles, and I earnestly hope that His Majesty's Government will take the view that justice is the highest interest and the best guardian of future peace.

Lord Montagu, who had just returned from Hungary, where he went to examine transportation conditions—and he could speak as an expert—stated that in his opinion the division of Hungary as proposed by the peace terms was not only unworkable but extremely harsh. He said that he could not conceive of any division of the countries in Central Europe which could be justified. He, like the preceding speakers, urged careful inquiries on the spot before deciding on the final terms of the peace treaty—for, easy as it might appear on the map to divide these countries and to set up new states, in practice such division might prove to be economically unworkable.[198]

[198] Determination of the frontiers on the basis of locally conducted investigation was also urged by Lord Sydenham and by the Marquess of Crewe, who later criticized the Government's reply *inter alia* because it failed to hold out hope of a future inquiry on the spot, "in lieu of the perpetual examination of maps," or of taking of evidence by committees in the Allied capitals. "I cannot help thinking," he said, "that a comparatively short and limited degree of inquiry on the spot is worth ten times the amount of examination of maps around the table either in Paris or here."

The reply of the Government to these criticisms, again made by the Earl of Crawford, was, as on the previous occasion, one bordering on the unfriendly; indeed the Marquess of Crewe, speaking later, stated that the Government's response left an impression "of something like a particular animosity to Hungarian aspirations" and expressed the wish that the "feeling of special vindictiveness" which appeared to him to exist toward Hungary—an accusation which the Earl of Crawford vehemently denied—could be dispelled.

The Earl of Crawford began by expressing regret that the unsettled condition of the negotiations made it impossible to give in detail the status of the Hungarian peace treaty and he insisted that some of the criticism directed against the proposed terms and against the method whereby decisions were arrived at had no sufficient foundation. He then proceeded to refute the accusation that the Peace Conference drew information exclusively from anti-Hungarian sources. The Peace Conference had had to proceed with the preparation of the draft treaty, even though there was no stable government in Hungary with which the Allies could negotiate, because the questions involved in the settlement concerned not only Hungary but all the neighboring states. It was true that the territorial commissions which prepared the reports on the new frontiers had received masses of documents and had heard the claims of Hungary's neighbors; but this did not mean that the committees ignored the Hungarian point of view. According to the Earl of Crawford, a great deal of written evidence setting forth the Hungarian position was available to the committees and was examined by them, who moreover drew their statistical and geographical information mainly from Hungarian sources; he claimed that with regard to racial statistics, which formed the crux of the territorial question, the committees worked with the official Hungarian figures, although they knew that "in many cases the Hungarian figures had been distorted by the Hungarian authorities in favour of their own nationality." [199] In the light of these facts, the Earl of Crawford denied that the Hungarian point of view was neglected by the Peace Conference and claimed that their case had been fully examined, even though official Hungarian representatives were not present. After the Hungarian Delegation had

[199] This statement of the Earl of Crawford evoked an energetic protest from the Hungarian Delegation to the Peace Conference. For the instructions of the Foreign Office, dated April 6, 1920, see HFR, Vol. I, Doc. 206. For the English text of the protest note, dated April 13, 1920, see HPN, II, 503.

come to Paris, Count Apponyi was allowed to state Hungary's case fully before the Supreme Council, and the Delegation was given ample time to present Hungary's observations and documentation relating to the peace conditions. The Hungarian notes and documentation, he said, had been referred by the Supreme Council to expert committees for "full examination and consideration," in order that "full justice should be done to the Hungarian point of view." These committees had now reported to the Council. He declined, however, to answer Lord Newton's question as to whether a revision of the proposed conditions had been definitely refused, on the ground that the British Government could not make a separate statement without the consent of the Allies.[200]

Addressing himself to the implied charge that Hungary was not listened to and that no justice was done to this small ex-enemy, Lord Crawford said:

I cannot admit for a moment that the Treaty of Peace with Hungary has been drafted in any spirit of injustice towards a beaten enemy with the object merely of conciliating States which have fought and suffered with us in the war; nor do I think it would be fair to charge these States themselves, in spite of their century-old grievances against the Hungarian Government, with any such policy. His Majesty's Government at least trust that Hungary's neighbours intend, on the contrary, to pursue towards her a sane and enlightened policy of friendly relations which will indicate that the past, so far as is possible, is forgotten, and that all the countries concerned are conscious of the necessity of reconstruction in the future. Without such sane and enlightened policy it is hard to imagine how the economic prosperity of South-Eastern Europe which has been shattered by the War . . . can be put on a solid and permanent basis.

His Majesty's Government and the other principal Allied Powers have lost and will lose no opportunity of reminding the Czecho-Slovak, the Austrian, the Rumanian, and the Serb-Croat-Slovene Governments of the necessity for aid on their part in the reconstruction of Hungary and allowing that country every necessary opportunity for development. On the other hand, such a policy on the part of these four States implies reciprocal treatment from the Hungarian Government and people. So long as the Hungarian

---

[200] Answering a question put by Colonel Wedgwood in the House of Commons on March 17, 1920, as to whether the Italian Prime Minister had been urging the Supreme Council to revise the Hungarian treaty, Mr. Bonar Law answered in the affirmative and stated that "the whole subject was very carefully considered." Hansard, *Parliamentary Debates, House of Commons,* 5th ser., Vol. 126, pp. 2198–99.

Government cherish vain dreams of overthrowing by armed force the settlement which the victorious Allies have justly imposed, so long will it be idle to expect that Hungary's neighbours will regard her either as a friend or as a customer.[201]

The statement of the Earl of Crawford has been quoted at some length to enable the impartial student to form his own judgment as to the correctness of the charges of animosity and vindictiveness toward Hungary, subsequently leveled by the Marquess of Crewe. The position of the British Government, as reflected in the cool recital of its spokesman, gave little encouragement from the point of view of any change in the peace terms or for the expectation of any improvement in the atmosphere between Hungary and her neighbors after peace had been concluded.[202]

Contrary to the moral support given to Hungary in her efforts to bring about changes in the peace terms, by the Italians and by some important figures in the British political world, a determined opposition to any change favorable to that country was raised by Hungary's three neighbors who were to be the principal beneficiaries of her dismemberment. Czecho-Slovakia, Rumania, and Yugoslavia, in the latter part of February, presented a joint memorandum to the Supreme Coun-

[201] For the complete text of the discussion of the Hungarian treaty at the meeting of March 30, 1920, see *ibid., House of Lords,* 5th ser., Vol. 39, pp. 776–99.

[202] It should be noted that the questions relating to the Hungarian peace treaty were also raised several times in the House of Commons in March, 1920. See the questions concerning the application of the principle of self-determination in drawing the frontiers of Hungary, and in the incorporation of Ruthenia into Czecho-Slovakia, put by Mr. Raffan and answered, rather inconclusively, by Mr. Bonar Law at the meeting of March 17, 1920. *Ibid., House of Commons,* 5th ser., Vol. 126, pp. 2197 ff. See also the caustic criticism of Hungary's new frontiers by Captain Elliot, at the meeting of March 25, in the course of the debate on the Consolidated Fund Bill. *Ibid.,* Vol. 127, pp. 684 ff. He called Hungary's new frontiers impossible and ridiculous. "No such boundary has ever been seen in the world," he said. "The Peace Conference is full of very great and important gentlemen, but they cannot make rivers run sideways across mountains, because they run downhill and not across. They cannot convince a peasant who has to go ten miles down stream to buy an axe or plough in the county town at the head of a valley where his forefathers have gone before him, that it is to his interest, because he speaks a Slavonic tongue, to leap over eighty miles of mountain tops to get into Bohemia to buy his axe or plough. . . ." (See p. 692.)

Passing reference may be made here to the views of a neutral country on the Hungarian peace terms. The Swedish Minister for Foreign Affairs, Mr. John Hellner, when receiving the credentials of the *de facto* representative of Hungary, voiced the hope that, in the interest of peace in Central Europe, the Allies would make concessions to Hungary and would permit the contemplated territorial changes to be decided by plebiscites. Mr. Barcza to Count Somssich, Feb. 19, 1920. *HFR,* Vol. I, Doc. 138.

cil relative to the Hungarian peace treaty.[203] Like Signor Nitti's intervention in the Supreme Council, the nature and content of this joint memorandum is shrouded in mystery and can only be surmised from meager and in some respects contradictory information.

According to Mr. Lloyd George,[204] the memorandum was dated February 20, 1920, and was in the nature of a reply to the general case of Hungary presented orally by Count Apponyi to the Supreme Council on January 16.[205] On the other hand, the Hungarian Delegation believed, on the basis of press reports, that the joint memorandum was an answer to the Hungarian reply notes to the original peace terms, and Count Apponyi repeatedly asked the Supreme Council to communicate the memorandum to the Hungarian Delegation, in order that an answer might be made to the arguments of Hungary's adversaries.[206] However, the Hungarians did not succeed in obtaining any information concerning the contents of this joint memorandum; in fact, even today, after more than twenty years, the document remains a deep

[203] Coöperation between Czecho-Slovakia, Yugoslavia, and Rumania, with a view to the preservation of their respective gains, had been envisaged by Czecho-Slovakia's Foreign Minister, Dr. Beneš, and discussed with his Yugoslav and Rumanian colleagues as early as the end of 1918. See Vondracek, *The Foreign Policy of Czecho-slovakia, 1918–1935*, pp. 162–63. Dr. Beneš offered alliances to these countries in Dec., 1919, and in Jan., 1920, shortly after Hungary was invited to the Peace Conference. See *Documents diplomatiques relatives aux conventions d'alliance conclues par la République tchécoslovaque*, Docs. 1 and 2. Cf. *supra*, n. 52. Although the alliances were not concluded until several months later, the three countries coöperated closely in Paris throughout the peace negotiations with Hungary. See the evidence cited in support of this fact by Vondracek, *op. cit.*, p. 164, n. 61.

[204] Lloyd George, *Memoirs*, II, 628.   [205] See *supra*, pp. 207–10.

[206] According to Note 129 from the Hungarian Delegation to the Peace Conference, dated Feb. 22, 1920 (*HPN*, II, 471), the Delegation learned from British press reports that thereafter Czecho-Slovakia, Rumania, and Yugoslavia would act jointly in all matters relating to the peace treaty with Hungary and that these countries were planning to present a joint answer to the Hungarian note concerning the new frontiers. (This Hungarian note was filed on Feb. 12; see *supra*, p. 232.) The note concluded by asking the Peace Conference to communicate such a document to the Delegation, in order that it might formulate its observations thereon. A second note—No. 136—was sent on Feb. 27 (*HPN*, II, 477), according to which the Delegation learned, again from press reports, that the joint memorandum had already been presented to the Supreme Council, "to serve as a reply to Hungarian observations concerning the treaty." The request for the communication of the document to the Delegation was renewed. At the same time, this note repeated earlier requests for oral negotiations and pointed out the inequity of denying Hungary access to the briefs of her adversaries while disclosing her arguments to them. It may be noted that at the Delegation's meeting on Feb. 26 the presentation of the joint memorandum was discussed as an impending rather than as an accomplished fact. "Political Diary," entry of Feb. 26, 1920.

secret, despite the fact that at least one authoritative historian of the Peace Conference claims that it had considerable influence on the rejection *in toto* by the Principal Allied Powers of the arguments put forward by Hungary.[207] Mr. Temperley's belief as to the influence of this document is also confirmed, though only *ex post facto,* by Mr. Lloyd George, who characterized it as a "very well reasoned argument" and described its effect as "crushing." According to Mr. Lloyd George, the Allies gave full consideration both to Count Apponyi's arguments and to the joint memorandum of Hungary's neighbors and then decided "to stand by the recommendations of the boundary Commissions which had been approved by the Foreign Ministers." [208] The sections of the memorandum summarized and quoted in part by Mr. Lloyd George seem to be a general indictment of pre-war Hungary, rather than an argument on specific terms of the peace settlement; however, this does not exclude the possibility of the correctness of the belief held both by Mr. Temperley and by the Hungarian Delegation that the memorandum also advocated the maintenance of the original conditions, especially as these related to the new frontiers. Indeed Mr. Lloyd George indicated that his references were to the first part of the memorandum, which consisted of "an arraignment of Magyar domination over the subject races which had been emancipated by the Allied victory" and which answered Count Apponyi's denial of Hungary's responsibility for the war. There is no indication in Mr. Lloyd George's account of what the rest of the memorandum contained, and students of history can only regret that they are still deprived of accurate knowledge of so important a state paper. This much can be said with certainty, even without knowing its precise language or its line of argument: the joint memorandum was opposed unequivocally to any concession to Hungary.

We may now turn our attention to what is undoubtedly the most interesting phase of the diplomatic history of the peace treaty with Hungary—namely, the secret negotiations between that country and France and the connection of these with and their influence on the Peace Conference proceedings.

[207] Temperley, *History,* IV, 421: "Before the Allies replied [to the Hungarian notes], they considered a joint memorandum from Czecho-Slovakia, Yugo-slavia and Rumania, *which doubtless had considerable influence on their answer.* The chief point of this Memorandum, as reported in the Press, was to call the attention of the Powers to the fact that the Hungarian frontiers were definitely delimited on the 13th June 1919, and that any alteration of these would be regarded as a betrayal." (Italics added.)

[208] Lloyd George, *Memoirs,* II, 630.

V. The First Phase of the Franco-Hungarian Secret Negotiations and the Treaty of Trianon: From January, 1920, to the Signing of the Treaty, June 4, 1920

Owing, doubtless, to the secrecy which surrounded them, very little is known of the conversations between Hungary and France which were initiated even before Hungary's Peace Delegation was despatched to Neuilly.[1] These confidential conversations were first carried on wholly unofficially, and later through plenipotentiaries of the two governments, but always secretly, and continued for several months after the signature of the Treaty of Trianon. Inasmuch as Ambassador Paléologue, then Secretary General of the French Ministry for Foreign

[1] There are only a few, rather vague references to the Franco-Hungarian negotiations in the voluminous literature relating to the peace settlements and even these refer only to later stages in the negotiations. Mr. Toynbee, in the *Survey of International Affairs, 1920–1923*, p. 282, refers to rumors that "in July, 1920, when the Russo-Polish war was approaching its crisis, a secret agreement was concluded between Hungary and France, by which Hungary was to grant concessions to French capitalists and to send her army (which was conspicuously in excess of the Treaty limits) to the assistance of the Poles, while she was to obtain, in return, substantial retrocessions of territory at the expense of Jugoslavia, of Rumania, and above all of Czechoslovakia. In the latter case, it was alleged, the common frontier established by the Treaty of Trianon between Czechoslovakia and Rumania was to be wiped out, and, in place of it, Hungary was to recover her common frontier with Poland along the line of the Carpathians by reannexing Carpatho-Ruthenia and portions of Slovakia. Whether or not negotiations were conducted in this sense, no direct results followed; but the rumour of such negotiations undoubtedly delayed the reconciliation of Czechoslovakia and Poland and hastened the formation of the Little Entente."

In his treatise, *The Foreign Policy of Czechoslovakia, 1918–1935*, Professor Vondracek makes a passing reference to secret communications exchanged between France and Hungary during the summer of 1920 "that had been alarming to Hungary's neighbors." He intimates that the reason for the negotiations was believed to be Hungarian assistance to Poland in the war with Soviet Russia and states that Dr. Beneš was aware of these negotiations (pp. 164–65). Mr. C. A. Macartney's excellent book, *Hungary*, states that the Hungarian Government carried on with France a "fairly warm flirtation (mainly unofficial)" in that period, the reasons indicated being the sympathy of certain French circles toward a monarchist restoration in Hungary on the one hand, and on the other, the prospect of a more favorable treaty for Hungary in consideration of her military help to Poland (p. 336).

Affairs, was the central figure in these conversations on the part of France, this phase of the history of the peace treaty is appropriately designated by Hungarian diplomats as the "Paléologue negotiations." Although the negotiations ultimately failed, it seems desirable to record this practically unknown chapter of European diplomacy in some detail because of its effect on the official peace negotiations and on the attitude of Hungary. Moreover, it offers food for thought as to the turn which European postwar history might have taken, had these conversations accomplished the objectives in view.

Private Conversations

The origins of these conversations may be traced to the initiative of a Hungarian lawyer, Dr. Charles Halmos, who proposed to approach leading statesmen in France through pre-war connections with French business circles. Halmos, who, besides being a lawyer, appears to have been also a shrewd business man, had participated in or was in some way associated with several French business ventures in the Balkans prior to 1914, particularly with the building of the Constantinople street railway in 1910. Through these associations, he had become well acquainted with several influential French business men and financiers, among them former Minister of Finance Loucheur. In the middle of December, 1919, Count Teleki sent Halmos, accompanied by a young diplomat, Count Andor Semsey, to Kassa, to establish contact with the French mission in that city and to explore the possibility of obtaining French support for Hungary. Halmos and Semsey were received by Dr. Eck, chief of the political department of the French mission in Kassa, and it appears from Semsey's report of the conversations [2] that the local French representatives were not averse to coming to an understanding with Hungary. At the end of the first interview, Dr. Eck asked the two Hungarians to postpone their return to Budapest because, later on, he would have an important communication to make. Another interview took place a few days afterwards, on December 20, at the request of Dr. Eck, who then informed Halmos and Semsey of the changed attitude of "very influential French circles" toward Hungary. According to Eck, this change was due in large part to the conduct of Rumania during recent months, this having evoked in France widespread criti-

[2] Count Semsey to the Minister for Foreign Affairs, Count Somssich, Dec. 23, 1919. *HFR,* Vol. I, Doc. 61.

cism.[3] Without further preliminaries, he proposed a political and economic alliance between Hungary and Czecho-Slovakia, which would open the door to resistance to Rumania. If this proposal was acceptable to both parties, the simplest method of its realization would be direct, confidential negotiations between the Hungarians and the Czechs, under French mediation, either before or after the peace negotiations. Dr. Eck assured Semsey and Halmos that the idea was not merely his own but was supported by the French Military Mission at Kassa and suggested that at the end of the month Semsey and Halmos accompany him to Paris to discuss the matter with his superiors. It does not appear whether or not Dr. Eck communicated with Paris between the two interviews. It seems to have been understood, as between Eck on the one hand and Semsey and Halmos on the other, that the contemplated arrangement would call for the voluntary cession by Hungary to Czecho-Slovakia of extensive territories—but, according to Semsey's report, less extensive than the losses by proposed frontiers—and that Hungary would be compensated for such sacrifice by territories now allotted to Rumania. Halmos and Count Semsey urged that Eck's suggestion be followed, because, unless Hungary succeeded in gaining a point or two through independent action, she could not hope for concessions from the Peace Conference "which," they said, "will impose on us a dictated peace."

Semsey's suggestion that the solution proposed by Dr. Eck be explored was accepted by the Hungarian Government, and on December 28 Halmos and Semsey, in company with Eck, left Kassa for Paris, where they arrived several days in advance of the Hungarian Peace Delegation. They were joined, about the middle of January, by Baron Adolf Ullmann, an executive officer of the Hungarian General Credit Bank, one of Hungary's most powerful financial institutions. Ullmann, like Halmos and Semsey, went to Paris in an entirely private capacity, with no official or semi-official status, not even as a confidential agent, although with the consent and tacit approval of the Hungarian Government. Utilizing pre-war connections of the Credit Bank with French financial circles, Ullmann helped Halmos to get in touch with

---

[3] Assuming that the information given to the Hungarians concerning the reason for France's changed attitude were accurate, it does not appear from the report of the interview whether the French were influenced by the behavior of the Rumanian army of occupation or by the reluctance of the Rumanian Government to heed the advice and orders of the Supreme Council.

several leaders of the French business world. The most important of these were Loucheur and Count Saint-Sauveur, head of the Schneider-Creusot concern. Whatever may have been the plan which Eck and his superiors had in mind when the first interviews took place at Kassa, the plan which Ullmann and Halmos began to pursue in Paris was that of directing the attention of French business to Hungary, in the hope that, by attracting French capital, Hungary might secure some measure of political support.

As far as it is possible to ascertain—and here one deals obviously with the imponderables of the human mind—the Hungarian statesmen, in consenting to the private action of Halmos, Semsey, and Ullmann, were not influenced by excessive hopes or expectations that substantial concessions would be obtained for Hungary. The decisive consideration was rather the hopelessness of Hungary's case in view of the harshness of the other peace treaties and the intransigence shown by the Allies toward Germany and Austria. It was felt that under the circumstances, the government should leave no avenue of escape unexplored and should disregard no opportunity to break through the circle of isolation.

At Ullmann's first meeting with M. Loucheur, the latter repeated what General Franchet d'Esperay had told Count Somssich in Budapest a few days earlier, namely, that although there was no hope for any changes in the territorial stipulations, the Hungarians might obtain economic concessions, especially in the light of the damage caused by the Rumanian occupation. Loucheur, by his own admission hostile to the Hungarians, told Ullmann that his interest group would be willing to consider making a moderate investment in Hungary. Meanwhile Ullmann established contact with members of the Hungarian Delegation, to whom he conveyed this information.[4]

It is impossible to state whether Ullmann and Halmos acted upon sheer inspiration or whether they were aware of the far-flung ambition of French industrial and financial circles to establish an economic empire in Southeastern Europe—an ambition which the French Government was expected to endorse and support whole-heartedly for political reasons.[5] In any event, whether by chance or on information, they were

[4] "Political Diary," entries of Jan. 23, 24, and 29.

[5] It should perhaps be pointed out that French business men were not alone in seeking to turn to their benefit the military victory and the resulting political dominance of their country. The scramble for markets and outlets for investments was very much

able to approach persons who had great influence and who were, to some extent, the key men, planning and directing French economic penetration into Central and Southeastern Europe.

For a period of about six weeks, or from the end of January until the middle of March, Halmos, Ullmann, and Semsey held intermittent conversations with Loucheur and Count Saint-Sauveur, entirely on their own responsibility and, as far as it is possible to ascertain, without instructions from the Hungarian Government. They did communicate with individual members of the Peace Delegation in Neuilly, with whom they discussed their plans, but the Delegation took no formal notice of their activity until March 16. At its meeting held on that date Count Teleki reported that Halmos and Semsey had been in contact with French financial and business leaders and through them had gained access to Ambassador Paléologue. They informed Paléologue of their discussions with Count Saint-Sauveur and outlined to him the advantages which France could derive by winning over Hungary to her side. The ground for this interview must have been well prepared, because Paléologue agreed to submit the matter to a cabinet meeting to be held that afternoon and to reply to Halmos on the following day. The plan which Halmos and Semsey put before the French—at the outset rather vaguely and by no means in precise terms—broadly envisaged French political support of Hungary's claims for the amelioration of the peace conditions in exchange for economic concessions to French interests in Hungary and the coördination of Hungary's foreign policy with that of France. The Delegation decided, upon Count Teleki's report, to support Halmos's action.[6]

It is of course impossible to say what occurred at the French cabinet meeting, to which Paléologue, true to his promise, presented the suggestions of Halmos and Semsey. But it seems to be beyond doubt that the French Government was definitely interested in the possibility of drawing Hungary into the French orbit, because Halmos and Semsey were on the following day authorized by Paléologue to visit the Château de Madrid in Neuilly freely thereafter and to serve as unofficial liaison officers between the French Government and the Hungarian Peace Delegation. Concerning the concrete issue, Paléologue informed

---

a concern of the British and, to a lesser extent, the Italian business worlds. The United States alone, among the Great Powers, can be said to have been indifferent to securing extraordinary material advantages for capital, commerce, and industry.

[6] "Political Diary," entry of March 16.

Halmos that any alteration of the peace terms would have to be made pursuant to an agreement between Hungary and her neighbors. If the Hungarian Delegation was willing to proceed along this line, France could prepare the ground for negotiations which could be carried on under French leadership; Paléologue even suggested that M. Bignon would be a good person in the chair.

The Informal Participation of the Peace Delegation in the Private Conversations

Paléologue's suggestions, which Halmos promptly conveyed to Count Emery Csáky, indicated that the time had come when the Delegation must, in some form, take into account the heretofore wholly private action of Halmos, Semsey, and Ullmann. It had become clear by this time that no amount of documentation would induce the Peace Conference to listen to the Hungarian arguments and that any change in the peace conditions could be brought about, if at all, only by winning over completely one of the Principal Allied Powers. Nevertheless, the Delegation deemed it wise to proceed cautiously and decided to authorize Count Bethlen and Count Emery Csáky to explore the matter with Halmos and even to take part in subsequent discussions, not as members of the Delegation, but as private individuals.[7]

Pursuant to this decision, Count Csáky remained from that time in constant touch with Halmos; it was through him thereafter that the Delegation was from day to day informed of the moves of Halmos and that Halmos was advised as to strategy. On March 19 Halmos, upon Paléologue's request, inquired of Csáky whether the Delegation would be prepared to enter into separate negotiations; and, if so, with whom and on what basis the negotiations should begin. According to Halmos's statement to Count Csáky, Paléologue, when requesting him to address this inquiry to the Hungarian Delegation, told Halmos that he was authorized by Prime Minister Millerand to assure him, Halmos, that the French Government was friendly to the suggestions made and wished Halmos to continue exploring the possibilities of the arrangements propounded. Like Franchet d'Esperay and Loucheur previously, Paléologue advised Halmos not to expect much in the way of territorial revision but to concentrate on economic concessions.

Upon Count Csáky's report, the Delegation agreed without much

---

[7] "Political Diary," entry of March 18.

difficulty on the principle of separate negotiations. However, there was a difference of opinion as to what states should first be approached in the negotiations and as to the basis upon which to proceed. The preponderance of opinion appeared to be that, from among all Hungary's neighbors, a settlement with Rumania was most urgent. Whether this feeling was due to the presence of several Transylvanians in the Delegation members, to the fact that Hungary would lose most to Rumania, to the belief of the Hungarians that Rumania was the strongest of their neighbors and therefore potentially the most dangerous adversary, or to the fact that Rumania was, excepting Austria of course, the only non-Slavic nation bordering on Hungary, it is impossible to say.[8] In any event, the Delegation requested Count Bethlen and Count Csáky to prepare a memorandum on the contemplated negotiations, which, after having been examined by the Delegation,[9] could be given to Halmos for his guidance.

This memorandum, submitted to the Delegation at its meeting on

[8] Conceivably, the choice of Rumania may have been due in part to Italy's insistence that Hungary should try to improve relations above all with Rumania. As already indicated, some intimation of Italy's aspirations in this respect had been given as soon as relations between Hungary and Italy had begun to grow friendlier. In a conversation with an official of the Hungarian Foreign Office in the closing days of 1919, the Italian Commissioner in Budapest, Signor Cerrutti, had regarded it as "most unfortunate" that there was so little hope for an agreement between Hungary and Rumania. See *HFR*, Vol. I, Doc. 65. When Count Nemes presented his credentials in Rome, he informed Count Sforza that the Hungarian Government was prepared to establish contact with Rumania. Count Sforza offered to have his government make representations in Bucharest, with a view to having a Rumanian plenipotentiary sent to Hungary. Count Nemes to Count Somssich, March 2, 1920, *ibid.*, Doc. 155. Although, apparently, Italy did make such representations and while Hungary was, in fact, prepared to meet Rumania half way (see *supra*, p. 203, n. 57), Italy's efforts failed to bring about the desired results. On at least two occasions Hungary made inquiries in Rome: on March 23 the Secretary General of the Hungarian Foreign Office requested Count Nemes to call Count Sforza's attention to the failure of Rumania to send a mission to Budapest, although the easing of tension would be in the interest of both countries. Mr. Kánya to Count Nemes, March 23, 1920, *HFR*, Vol. I, Doc. 197. A few days later Count Nemes again asked Count Sforza to intervene and bring up the matter in Bucharest. Count Nemes to Mr. Simonyi-Semadam, April 11, 1920, *ibid.*, Doc. 215. The establishment of diplomatic relations was discussed between Count Nemes and the Italian minister to Rumania, Signor Martin-Franklin, who, in the course of the conversation, revealed that he had been instructed by his government to work in Bucharest with Hungary and Rumania, in order to forestall an agreement between Rumania and Yugoslavia. According to the Italian minister, Bucharest would be willing, save for her fear that Hungary would raise territorial questions. Count Nemes to Mr. Simonyi-Semadam, April 9, 1920, *ibid.*, Doc. 214.

[9] "Political Diary," entry of March 19.

the following afternoon, envisaged, from the procedural point of view, bilateral negotiations with each of Hungary's neighbors on subjects which concerned them alone, respectively, and settlement of the more general questions, which concerned all the Powers, by the Peace Conference. For reasons of foreign policy and of relative strength, Rumania was indicated as the state with which negotiations should first be started. As a basis, the memorandum suggested the return of territories to Hungary where the population was wholly or in majority Magyar, the granting of autonomy for other territories in which there were Hungarian minorities, and broad protection where such minorities were scattered. In regard to economic and financial questions and matters of communications, it was suggested that Hungary's interests ought to receive due consideration. After including a request for the return of property carried away by the Rumanians, the Delegation approved the memorandum and authorized Count Csáky to transmit it to Halmos.[10]

Two days later Count Csáky reported that Halmos had seen Paléologue and had read to him the memorandum setting forth the Hungarian proposals. According to Halmos's report to Csáky, which the latter presented to the Delegation at its meeting, Paléologue listened with great attention and after he, Halmos, had finished reading, Paléologue expressed the belief that the proposals would constitute a suitable starting point. Then the following conversation had taken place between Ambassador Paléologue and Halmos:

Paléologue: "We have confidence in you and we understand what you desire. But what can you offer us in exchange?"

Halmos: "A lasting peace and stability." Then seeing that this answer did not wholly satisfy the Ambassador, he added: "Please indicate yourself what you desire."

Paléologue: "Can you offer us an alliance?"

Halmos: "Offer one, no; but accept one, perhaps."

On this occasion Halmos also inquired whether the presentation of the final peace conditions to the Hungarians could not be postponed, lest they prejudice the contemplated separate negotiations. Paléologue answered that the date for their presentation had not yet been set, but that that matter was solely within the competence of the Peace Conference and that the French could not do much to interfere with its proceedings. Paléologue, however, assured Halmos that even if the

[10] "Political Diary," entry of March 20.

Hungarians should shortly be presented with the final treaty text, as had been intimated to them, it would be possible to find a solution.

That the Delegation was still skeptical as to the significance of Halmos's activities is indicated by Count Apponyi's remark, following Csáky's report, that important results from the contemplated negotiations could be expected only if there was some official expression of the French point of view or, at least, if the French would discuss the matter with authorized representatives of Hungary. There was some doubt also whether in asking for an offer of an alliance with "us," Paléologue meant France alone, or France *and* Rumania, or perhaps even other states. In any event, Count Csáky expressed the belief that if a military alliance with Rumania was contemplated, it could be discussed, in view of Hungarian public opinion, only indirectly, and through French mediation.[11]

Paléologue's direct inquiry as to the attitude of the Peace Delegation toward separate negotiations squarely raised the question of what relations, if any, existed between the official peace negotiations entrusted to the Delegation and Halmos's conversations. This matter came up at the meeting of the Delegation a few days later, on March 28, when Count Apponyi prepared to return to Budapest with the greater part of the Delegation, there to await the final peace conditions. As Count Csáky pointed out, Halmos's action was entirely a private matter, was so regarded by the French, who at any moment could disavow all that had taken place; and was also so regarded by the Delegation, which to date had not even formally reported Halmos's activity to the Hungarian Government. In his opinion, the Delegation's task and the conversations of Halmos were, technically, two entirely distinct proceedings; it was only in their results that one might affect the other. He thought that the activities of Halmos should be separate from those of the peace negotiations and the activities of the Delegation members. However, he felt that the point had been reached where a report on Halmos's conversations should be made to the Minister for Foreign Affairs or to the Regent and that the Delegation should ask for precise instructions as to whether he or any other member of the Delegation was to participate in subsequent negotiations.

On the other hand, Baron Lers believed that the two activities should be coördinated, since Halmos's conversations might at least delay the signature of the treaty. Such a delay was most desirable, for signature

[11] "Political Diary," entry of March 23.

"would prejudice our objectives, would weaken our position and strengthen that of our adversaries."

The Delegation finally agreed that Count Apponyi and the delegates returning with him to Budapest should inform the government as to these developments. Pending instructions from Budapest, the matter would be handled as heretofore by letting Halmos carry on conversations, while Praznovszky acted as unofficial spokesman of the Delegation. Count Csáky was authorized to attend, on the following day, a meeting between Paléologue and Halmos. Contemplating the possibility of Hungary's being forced to sign the treaty before the projected negotiations had produced any results, Count Teleki and Count Bethlen advised Csáky to urge upon Paléologue the inclusion in the treaty of an article leaving the door open for the French to press for revision.[12]

The next day, March 29, Count Csáky and Halmos lunched with Ambassador Paléologue and Count Saint-Sauveur. Paléologue stated at the outset that the meeting was to deal chiefly with economic questions; the political issues were to be examined later. Saint-Sauveur went directly to the point by asking what Hungary could offer that would be attractive to French business interests. Halmos then outlined various projects, the most important among them being the lease of the Hungarian State Railways and the exploitation of navigation on the Danube by a French concern. Saint-Sauveur suggested that a memorandum should be prepared concerning Hungary's resources which might be of interest to France. If a study of this memorandum showed worth-while possibilities, an investigation would be made on the spot and on that basis further steps—that is, political support of Hungary by France, in view of French economic interests there—could be discussed with Paléologue. He referred to the far-flung interests of the Schneider-Creusot group in Czecho-Slovakia, Rumania, and Poland and expressed the belief that if Hungary could also be brought into this sphere of interest, the center of this tremendous regrouping would inevitably be in Budapest, and, as a result, Hungary would become the corner stone of French policy in Southeastern Europe.

Count Csáky remarked that France would have to extend political support to Hungary in order to accomplish what Saint-Sauveur had in mind. Paléologue replied that political support would depend on whether a sphere of French economic interest could be created. He

12 "Political Diary," entry of March 28.

said that political good will did exist, as was shown by the fact that he was meeting Count Csáky with Prime Minister Millerand's approval.

The relation between the official peace negotiations and these informal conversations was also examined. Count Csáky pointed out that while a refusal to sign the peace treaty in its present form would doubtless adversely affect Hungary's international position, its signature would surely prejudice the attainment of the objectives which these informal conversations had in view. Paléologue replied that the French could neither noticeably postpone the conclusion of the peace treaty nor insist on changing its terms without displaying their cards to their allies—something they apparently were not prepared to do. He thought that a reference to Article 19 of the League of Nations Covenant would leave the door open for subsequent revision. Csáky expressed fear that Hungary's neighbors—particularly Rumania—would not be likely to enter into negotiations after the treaty was signed, but Paléologue felt confident that France could exert sufficient pressure to make them amenable.

Although the conversations between Paléologue, Saint-Sauveur, Count Csáky, and Halmos dealt with broad questions of policy rather than with details, Csáky came away with the impression that behind the French interest in Halmos's suggestions, there was involved a carefully thought-out politico-economic plan of major significance, which might conceivably serve as Hungary's avenue of escape from the dreaded mutilation and the political and economic servitude which the peace conditions spelled for her.[13]

The following evening Count Apponyi and most of the Delegation members including Count Csáky, Count Teleki, and Count Bethlen returned to Budapest, there to await the final peace conditions, leaving merely a skeleton staff in Neuilly to carry on the routine business of the Peace Delegation.[14] Halmos of course remained in Paris to continue conversations with the French until the Hungarian Government should decide, on the basis of reports made by the Delegation, what attitude it should adopt toward Halmos's action. Praznovszky was requested to remain in contact with Halmos and to report further developments to Budapest.

[13] "Political Diary," entry of March 29.
[14] Mr. Praznovszky was designated as chargé d'affaires, and Councillor of Legation Dr. Wettstein and Consul Bobrik were left behind, with a small clerical staff to assist him. *Ibid.*, entry of March 30.

Arriving in Budapest, the Delegation was confronted with the aftermath of the cabinet crisis which had occurred, as has been said, in March, and which had not yet fully been solved as far as the important post of Foreign Minister was concerned.[15] After a few days of urging, Count Teleki finally agreed to accept the appointment of Minister for Foreign Affairs. Nothing could have been more logical and sensible than to entrust the conduct of Hungary's foreign affairs to Count Teleki. In addition to having participated from the very beginning in the peace negotiations—the paramount issue then facing Hungarian foreign policy—he had also had first-hand knowledge of the informal conversations with the French which were expected to improve Hungary's outlook.

With Count Teleki now in the key position in Hungary, the transition from informal conversations to more or less official *pourparlers* took place easily and speedily.[16]

The Formulation of Hungarian Claims and the First Official French Memorandum

On April 13 Halmos submitted to M. Paléologue a memorandum outlining in some detail the Hungarian claims. Since this memorandum subsequently became the basis upon which the Hungarian Government instructed its plenipotentiaries to proceed, its content should be set forth in detail.[17]

[15] Following the national elections at the end of Jan. and the election of the Commander in Chief of the Hungarian Army, Admiral Horthy, as Regent of Hungary, Huszár's coalition cabinet resigned and a new cabinet under Mr. Simonyi-Semadam had come into power on March 14. The post of Foreign Minister had been offered to Count Teleki but he had declined, on the ground that at the present juncture a change in the post of Foreign Minister would be harmful. "Political Diary," entry of March 15. Despite attempts to induce Count Somssich to remain, he had decided to resign, and the Ministry for Foreign Affairs had been taken over temporarily by the Prime Minister.

[16] The existence of the Franco-Hungarian *rapprochement* was recognized by the Hungarian Peace Delegation when Mr. Praznovszky confidentially inquired of M. Paléologue whether a friendlier tone toward France in the Hungarian press would be agreeable to the French Government. Upon M. Paléologue's affirmative reply, Mr. Praznovszky suggested to Budapest that on appropriate occasions the Hungarian press might express a discreet appreciation of the consideration shown of late to Hungary by the French Government. Mr. Praznovszky to Count Apponyi, April 11, 1920. *HFR*, Vol. I, Doc. 217.

[17] For the complete French text of the memorandum, see *ibid.*, Doc. 242(a). The memorandum was attached to the instructions issued by the Minister for Foreign Affairs on April 23 to the Hungarian plenipotentiaries appointed to conduct the negotiations with the French Government; see *infra*, pp. 272–74.

Starting from the thesis that the imposition of a treaty depriving Hungary of her means of existence could not be in the interest of the Allies, the memorandum suggested the modification of the peace conditions in such a way as to safeguard Hungary's political and economic future, thus enabling her to accept the treaty in good faith. The minimum concessions that would safeguard Hungary's vital interests were summed up as follows:

1. From the political point of view:

(1) Modification of the frontiers leaving to Hungary territories contiguous to the contemplated boundaries and inhabited wholly or in great majority by Magyar populations. This referred specifically to a point on the right bank of the Danube opposite Pozsony, the island of Csallóköz [Grosse Schütt], the Little Lowland of Hungary, the Magyar districts of the counties of Bars, Hont, Nógrád, Gömör, Abauj-Torna, and Zemplén, and the Bodrogköz, all in the north; the Magyar districts of the counties of Szilágy, Szatmár, Bihar, Békés, Arad, and Csanád, on the east; the Bácska between the Danube and the Tisza (Theiss) Rivers and the Francis Canal, and the southern part of the county of Baranya. With these changes, a Magyar population of about 1,722,000 and the cities of Pozsony, Kassa, Szatmár, Nagykároly, Nagyvárad, Arad, and Szabadka would not be detached from Hungary;

(2) Regional autonomy by Rumania for the Magyar, Székler, and Saxon communities in Transylvania and effective guarantees for the protection of Magyar, German, and other minorities which would fall under the sovereignties of Czecho-Slovakia, Rumania, or Yugoslavia, respectively;

(3) Plebiscites in Western Hungary and in the Bánát territory inhabited by Swabs to decide whether these populations desire to remain with Hungary or to be incorporated into Austria, Rumania, or Yugoslavia, respectively.

2. From the economic point of view:

(1) The preservation of territory furnishing the country with the raw materials and water power indispensable for the economic and industrial life of the nation—specifically, Ruthenia and Eastern Slovakia, that is, east of the Csorba Pass. The ultimate fate of Ruthenia could be determined by plebiscite; but, in any event, Hungary would assure to Ruthenia the same autonomy which she would be given by Czecho-Slovakia;

(2) As a temporary measure, or until the economic consolidation of the new states, the preservation of the economic unity of the former kingdom, irrespective of the new political frontiers, that is to say, the unity of communications (railways, post, telegraph, and telephone), flood control, and irrigation;

(3) An equitable distribution of war debts between Hungary and her neighbors, taking into account Hungary's economic losses caused by two revolutions and the Rumanian occupation;

(4) The restitution of a fair proportion of the industrial and agricultural equipment and railway rolling stock carried away from Hungary by the Rumanians, Hungary's reparation account being credited with the value of the equipment retained by Rumania as war booty.

According to Halmos's report to Praznovszky, the conversation with Paléologue on this occasion was cordial and encouraging. Paléologue seemed to be satisfied with the statement of Hungary's claims, he stated to Halmos that Hungary could count on the good will of France, arranged a meeting for Halmos with Prime Minister Millerand on the following day, and indicated the possibility of beginning formal negotiations within a few days.[18]

On April 15 M. Paléologue handed to Dr. Halmos and Count Semsey a note to transmit to the Hungarian Government, setting forth the French point of view with regard to the heretofore informal conversations and the possible bases of the contemplated negotiations. In view of the great importance of this document, it seems appropriate to print the complete text in English translation.[19]

The conversations envisaged in preceding memoranda with a view to a definitive and satisfactory solution of the Hungarian peace must have as their objective all questions which concern directly and solely the states neighboring Hungary. Questions of a general character, such as certain economic and financial questions—e.g., the reparations question—the scope of

[18] Mr. Praznovszky to Mr. Simonyi-Semadam, April 13, 1920. *HFR,* Vol. I, Doc. 218.

[19] Note No. Sec. IX. Ex. IV 1920/6752 of the French Ministry for Foreign Affairs, dated Paris, April 15, 1920, signed by Paléologue. Curiously, the document is entitled "Preliminary Note relative to the conversations entered into between *the Delegates of the Allied Powers* and the representatives of the Hungarian Government," although there is no evidence that at that time any other of the Principal Allied Powers or any of Hungary's neighbors had been informed of these conversations. Indeed, the note itself does not refer to France's allies in the sense that their consent and approval would be necessary or would be sought, and subsequent developments would seem to indicate that at least the nature of the negotiations was kept scrupulously secret. For the original French text of the French note, see *ibid.,* Doc. 226.

which exceeds the special interests of these countries, can be solved only by the Great Powers, representing all these countries and all the Allies.

The present note can have as its only objective proposals concerning the adjustment of special interests which directly concern the neighboring countries.

The questions to be adjusted, those at present dividing Hungary and Rumania, are the most delicate and most difficult of solution of all problems. Hungary would make conclusive proof of her good will by declaring that she is prepared to begin conversations with Rumania with a view to regulating first of all her relations with that state. It is understood, however, that in case it should appear preferable to proceed in a different order, there would be no opposition on the part of Hungary.

There is on Hungary's part a firm determination to reëstablish fully satisfactory relations and to arrive at a complete and lasting appeasement between the Hungarian and Rumanian peoples. Since they are the Hungarians of Transylvania who must live henceforth with the Rumanians of Transylvania, it is evident that the stability of the peace to be concluded depends above all upon friendly relations between these two peoples *in Transylvania.* It is, therefore, of the utmost importance that the accepted and truly qualified representatives of the Hungarians and Rumanians of Transylvania should be heard in the course of these conversations.

In the following, the bases of a direct agreement between Hungary and Rumania are set forth.

1. From the national and political point of view:

(1) Modification of the frontiers, determined in such a way that territories which have a clearly Magyar character and which form a single bloc with the Magyar race should not be detached from Hungary. Authorization for the Swab people, adjoining Magyar territories, or inhabiting territories with a majority of Magyar or Swab population, to decide their fate by plebiscite. Hungary will offer all proofs of her good will respecting communications and other matters which may arise as a result of the new delimitation of frontiers;

(2) Regional autonomy for territories under Rumanian sovereignty where the majority of the inhabitants are Magyar, Székler or Saxon. The extent, the details and the guarantees of such autonomy will be worked out by common agreement;

(3) Freedom of worship, of language and security of economic existence for the Magyar minorities in territories where Rumanians constitute the majority. Effective guarantees will be stipulated in the peace treaty;

(4) Equitable solution of the question of former civil servants and of employees of Hungarian state enterprises;

(5) General amnesty for all political offenses.

2. From the economic point of view:

(1) Immediate restitution, as far as possible, of rolling stock, industrial and agricultural equipment, and raw materials which Rumanian troops transported into Rumanian territory in excess of requisitions provided for in the Armistice Agreement;

(2) Conclusion of agreements concerning the following matters: Mutual free trade for the greatest possible number of commodities and, particularly, of raw materials. Freedom of railway, postal, and telegraphic communications within the widest limits possible. Reciprocal facilities for the flow of capital between the two countries. Agreement for the identical regulation of hydraulic questions;

(3) Proportional allocation of financial obligations contracted by the Hungarian state before and during the war;

(4) Assurance in any event of the Maramaros salt mines to Hungary and of their free development by her.

As far as the basis of agreement between Hungary on the one hand and Czecho-Slovakia and Yugoslavia on the other hand is concerned, the question of [frontier] delimitation will be entrusted to a special commission in which Hungary and the Succession States of the Austro-Hungarian Monarchy will be represented. The chairmanship of this commission will be assumed by a representative of the Ministry for Foreign Affairs of the French Republic.

The contemplated and possible frontier delimitations between Hungary and the Succession States of the Austro-Hungarian Monarchy are sketched on the map herewith attached.

The execution of the plans herein before outlined will take place by identical declarations of the French and Hungarian Governments. The French Government will endeavor to find a formula for making officially known to the Hungarian Government its willingness to intervene in favor of Hungarian interests. This would be followed by an exchange of notes between the Governments of France and of Hungary and by the constitution of a commisssion, composed of the representatives of the two Governments, to examine the points of view and to draw up the solutions necessary for the conclusion of a military and economic convention.

The present note will be submitted by the Hungarian Government for ratification to the National Assembly, and it will be only after this has occurred that the French Government will proceed to the execution of the plan described.

A comparison of the French note with the above summary of Halmos's memorandum indicates that the Quai d'Orsay accepted, by and large, the Hungarian proposals as the basis of the contemplated Franco-Hungarian agreement, but sought to limit its application for the time being to Rumania. To what extent this limitation was the result of the Hungarian suggestion designating Rumania as the neighbor with whom agreement appeared to be most desirable, or of the interest of France herself in conciliating Hungary and Rumania above all, it is impossible to say. It should also be noted that while the conversations which took place at the end of December, 1919, at Kassa, between Dr. Eck, Count Semsey, and Dr. Halmos envisaged a Hungarian-Czech alliance, directed more or less against Rumania, the French Foreign Office contemplated now, and as the first step, a reconciliation of Hungary and Rumania. The reasons for this change must also remain a matter of conjecture; it has been suggested that the desire to insulate Western Europe from bolshevik Russia may have been a consideration.[20]

From Hungary's point of view, the most important and in historical retrospect by far the most significant feature of this document is the clearly expressed willingness of Paléologue and of those French statesmen who stood behind him, including Prime Minister Millerand, to contemplate, in the interest of appeasement in Southeastern Europe, a substantial alteration of the territorial settlements approved by the Supreme Council. It is wholly immaterial that the extent to which the French were prepared to support Hungary's territorial claims may have fallen short of Hungarian expectations; the important factor is the principle involved. The territorial concessions outlined in the French memorandum fell short of Dr. Halmos's original suggestion, in that

[20] As has been indicated, *supra*, pp. 196–99, the Hungarian Government made efforts to reach some agreement with Czecho-Slovakia, at least in economic matters. There is some evidence that informal conversations with a view to possible territorial adjustments also took place in Prague during the month of Feb. The Minister for Foreign Affairs advised the Peace Delegation that an official of the Foreign Office, Consul General Edl, discussed confidentially and informally Hungarian-Czech relations with the chief of the Political Department of the Czech Foreign Office, Mr. Frederick Stepanek. The position of the Czechs seems to have been that they were prepared to negotiate with Hungary after the peace treaty was concluded, but not before; that territorial questions concerning Csallóköz, or Grosse Schütt Island, and the Little Lowland might be subject to bargaining, since the Czechs desired those territories merely because it gave them control over the river mouths. Ruthenia, according to this report, was considered important only as a possible bridge between Czecho-Slovakia and Russia. The willingness of the Czechs to negotiate with Hungary regarding the Csallóköz and Ruthenia was reasserted in a subsequent conversation between Consul General Edl and Mr. Stepanek. "Political Diary," entries of Feb. 21 and 23, 1920. It is not known whether these conversations had been in any way connected with the plans formulated at Kassa at the end of Dec., 1919, between Dr. Eck, Dr. Halmos, and Count Semsey. See *supra*, pp. 254–55.

the latter described more or less precisely Hungary's claims against all her neighbors, whereas the former was specific only with respect to the Hungarian-Rumanian frontier. In that respect the French memorandum adopted in all its essentials the Hungarian claims. As far as Czecho-Slovakia and Yugoslavia were concerned, the frontier adjustment was to be left to a commission presided over by a Frenchman, which presumably would have insured due consideration for Hungary's interests. The Hungarian claim for Ruthenia and Eastern Slovakia—a claim based on economic considerations—was passed over in silence; and the request for a plebiscite in Western Hungary was also ignored. In some respects, the bases proposed for the Hungarian-Rumanian settlement by the French were even broader than those set forth in the Halmos memorandum, although in all likelihood the issues there specified had been raised in one form or another by the Hungarians in the course of previous conversations. Thus the French note foresaw an equitable settlement of the question of dismissed, pensioned, or expelled Hungarian civil servants and of the retention by Hungary —apparently for economic reasons—of the important salt mines in the county of Máramaros, adjoining Ruthenia.

Like the Halmos memorandum, the French note did not specify the *quid pro quo* which Hungary was expected to give in exchange for French support, but for the first time it reveals that, in addition to preferences in economic matters, the conclusion of a military convention between Hungary and France was also in contemplation.

Finally, the note having been expressly addressed to the Hungarian Government—a postscript to the note specifically stated that it was presented to Count Andor Semsey for transmittal to the Hungarian Government—and having envisaged formal communications between the two governments and ratification by the Hungarian legislature, it definitely put an end to private, unofficial conversations and indicated that henceforth the negotiations were to be conducted through authorized plenipotentiaries.

Accordingly, while Count Semsey was returning to Hungary with the French note, Dr. Halmos wired to Budapest requesting the appointment of official Hungarian plenipotentiaries who were to come to Paris by the end of the following week. He reported that during a friendly conversation with M. Paléologue on the day following the presentation of the French note, the details of the contemplated agreement, including military questions, had been discussed; Dr. Halmos also advised

Budapest that the presentation of the final peace conditions had been delayed.[21]

While the government in Budapest was examining the French proposal and preparing instructions for its representatives, Dr. Halmos continued conversations in Paris. At a subsequent meeting with M. Paléologue, the latter conceded that the adjustment of territorial questions—which interested Hungary above all—was the most difficult of the problems. Dr. Halmos reported at the same time that several members of the French Government appeared to be in favor of the contemplated agreement.[22] He apparently also had further conversations on the economic questions with Count Saint-Sauveur, which, according to a communication to M. Paléologue dated April 23, were so satisfactory that Dr. Halmos thought that the options to the French "interest group" might be granted upon the arrival of the Hungarian representatives. In the light of such progress, Dr. Halmos proposed to M. Paléologue that an agreement could now be entered into between M. Paléologue, on behalf of the French Government and himself on behalf of the Regent of Hungary, concerning the conditions and extent of French support to be given to Hungary in the forthcoming negotiations with her neighbors.[23] This agreement would become effective when the French interest group received the options respecting the economic concessions to be granted by Hungary. The communication concluded with the assurance that once this agreement had been made, France could count definitely on Hungary and all the forces at her disposal.[24] Enclosed with this communication was a memorandum setting forth the main outlines of the contemplated political and eco-

[21] Mr. Praznovszky to Mr. Simonyi-Semadam, April 16, 1920. *HFR,* Vol. I, Doc. 227. On the same morning Lieutenant Colonel Henry told Mr. Praznovszky that the peace conditions would be handed to the Delegation on April 20 or April 21. "Political Diary," entry of April 16, 1920. In fact, the Allied reply and the final peace conditions were given to Mr. Praznovszky only on the evening of May 5. See *infra.* It is impossible to state whether this delay was due to M. Paléologue's influence or to the fact that the Allies, meeting at San Remo, were engaged in trying to solve other problems.

[22] Mr. Praznovszky to Count Teleki, April 20, 1920. *Ibid.,* Doc. 236.

[23] As appears from a subsequent document, Dr. Halmos had overstated his position when he claimed to be the representative of the Regent. See Count Emery Csáky's report to Count Teleki, dated May 3, 1920. *Ibid.,* Doc. 255.

[24] A copy of this communication was appended to Count Csáky's report to Count Teleki, cited in the preceding footnote. For the complete text see *ibid.,* Doc. 255(a). In the light of the instructions issued by the Hungarian Government to its plenipotentiaries (see *infra,* pp. 272–74), Dr. Halmos, by giving such an *assurance,* went beyond the limits which the government had set itself, for the time being.

nomic agreement. This memorandum followed closely the French note of April 15, quoted above.[25]

Meanwhile, the Hungarian Government, in possession of the Paléologue note, took formal notice of the heretofore informal conversations and appointed Count Bethlen, Count Emery Csáky—both, of course, members of the Peace Delegation—and Mr. Cornelius Tolnai, Director of the Hungarian State Railways, as special representatives of Hungary in the forthcoming formal negotiations.[26]

The Formal Negotiations with France

The carefully prepared instructions for the Hungarian plenipotentiaries referred to the first Halmos memorandum, summarized above, as the basis of negotiations.[27] As we have seen, this memorandum was also accepted in its main points in the Paléologue note. With respect to the economic concessions to be granted to France by Hungary, the proposals made by Dr. Halmos to Count Saint-Sauveur were indicated as the starting point. These heretofore-unspecified proposals related, as appears from subsequent documents, to a long-term lease of the Hungarian State Railways and of the Railway Locomotive Works and to the building of the commercial port in Budapest by the Schneider-

[25] A copy of the memorandum was appended to Count Csáky's report to Count Teleki, dated May 3, 1920. HFR, Vol. I, Doc. 255. For the complete text see ibid., Doc. 255(b). The principal difference—apart from slight stylistic changes—between the French note of April 15 and Dr. Halmos's memorandum of April 23 was that whereas the former referred specifically to modifications of the Hungarian-Rumanian boundary only, the latter spoke of such modification (pursuant to the principles set forth in paragraph 1 (1) of the French note) with respect to Hungary's frontiers generally. Moreover, while the French note envisaged a political and economic convention between France and Hungary only, Dr. Halmos's memorandum stated that Hungary would be prepared to enter into an alliance and even a military convention with one or more other states designated by France. Here again Dr. Halmos clearly ventured to go further than the point where he could count upon the support of the Hungarian Government.

[26] Count Teleki, who had just taken over the post of Minister for Foreign Affairs, addressed the following communication to Count Emery Csáky under date of April 22: "I am gratified to know that you are leaving, with Count Stephen Bethlen and Mr. Cornelius Tolnai, for Paris in order to continue the conversations initiated by Mr. Halmos relative to certain questions interesting France, Hungary and our neighbors. I approve fully the general line of these conversations about which I was informed by Mr. Halmos on the occasion of his last visit to Budapest. I shall therefore look forward with the greatest interest to your reports concerning your negotiations with the competent French authorities." Ibid., Doc. 240.

[27] See supra, pp. 264–66.

Creusot concern. Later, the French also asked for the transfer to a French capitalist group of control over the Hungarian General Credit Bank, which, in its turn, had a considerable hold on Hungarian industry. Pursuant to a telegraphic request of Dr. Halmos,[28] the instructions set forth Hungary's minimum territorial claims. Should it appear that the French would not negotiate on the basis of the original claims set forth in the Halmos memorandum, the plenipotentiaries were authorized to abandon, without prior consultation with the government, claims to Pozsony, Eastern Slovakia, and the part of the Bánát settled by Germans. On the other hand, the satisfaction of Hungarian claims to the following territories was specified as *conditio sine qua non* for any agreement: in the north, the Csallóköz (or Grosse Schütt Island), the Little Lowland, and parts of the counties of Hont and Nográd, which were regarded as essential for the strategic security of Budapest; in the east, Ruthenia; in the south, the county of Bácska north of the Francis-Joseph Canal and the triangle claimed by the Yugoslavs in the county of Baranya. Moreover, autonomy for Magyars and Saxons in those parts of Transylvania which were to be ceded to Rumania was also indicated as indispensable.

The Hungarian plenipotentiaries—apart from the exception above stated—were not empowered to commit their government without prior consulation and were to be guided, in the language of the instructions, by the principle of *do ut des,* or the principle of give and take. Concretely, this meant that sacrifices which Hungary would be required to make must be commensurate to the benefits she would obtain and that all agreements between Hungary on the one hand and either France or Hungary's neighbors on the other must be interdependent, so as to come into force simultaneously.

These instructions indicate clearly that the Hungarian Government entered into these negotiations without illusions and with their eyes open. They show that the government was aware of the danger which Hungary might incur by linking her fate to France and of the possible implications of an agreement with her neighbors, as far as territorial claims were concerned. The consideration which outweighed these disadvantages was stated as follows:

Whether or not it is commensurate with the internal strength of the French nation, it is undeniable that France is today the strongest continental power,

[28] Mr. Praznovszky to Count Teleki, April 20, 1920. *HFR,* Vol. I, Doc. 236.

due to the political situation created by the peace treaties. If such a powerful state shows willingness to improve substantially the grave situation of our unfortunate country, we are not justified in disregarding such an opportunity because of possible future dangers. Even if the negotiations should not bring results, securing France's goodwill in the present critical moment would still be for us of great importance.

Neither was the Hungarian Government unduly optimistic as to the ability of France—fully conceding the good intentions of her spokesmen—to induce Hungary's neighbors to consent to the contemplated adjustments, particularly to territorial concessions. For that reason the Hungarian representatives were instructed to inquire at the outset as to the means at the disposal of France for the accomplishment of the desired objectives and to seek some tangible evidence of their good will.[29]

Equipped with these instructions, the Hungarian representatives arrived in Paris on April 28 and were immediately informed by Dr. Halmos of the progress he had made since the delivery of the French note on April 15.[30] On the same day, the Peace Delegation was advised that the final peace conditions would be presented the following week;[31] this may explain why M. Paléologue expressed the hope to Dr. Halmos, when the latter notified him of the arrival of the Hungarian representatives, that the preliminary Franco-Hungarian agreement, following mainly the line of Halmos's memorandum and of the French note, might be concluded by the end of the week—that is to say, before the presentation of the final peace conditions.[32]

However, as appears from reports sent by Count Csáky to Budapest, a week passed before the Hungarian plenipotentiaries were allowed to meet M. Paléologue. The explanation given for the delay was that M. Millerand, having just returned from the San Remo Conference, was very busy. The Hungarians believed that the reason was rather the indecision of the Schneider-Creusot group with respect to the contemplated economic arrangements. But the principal difficulty seems to have been caused by the divergent objectives of the French and the Hungarian Governments respectively. As seen by the Hungarian plenipotentiaries, the French sought to reach an agreement with Hungary

[29] For the complete text of these instructions, dated April 23, 1920, see *HFR*, Vol. I, Doc. 242.

[30] Mr. Praznovszky to Count Teleki, April 28, 1920. *Ibid.*, Doc. 245.

[31] Mr. Praznovszky to Count Teleki, April 28, 1920. *Ibid.*, Doc. 246; cf. also "Political Diary," entries of April 28 and May 2.

[32] Mr. Praznovszky to Count Teleki, April 28, 1920. *Ibid.*, Doc. 247.

solely on the principles which would serve as a guide for the collaboration of the two countries and to leave the details until later; moreover, they wanted to accomplish this, quite understandably, without compromising France's political position with her allies, great and small. The Hungarians, on the other hand, were unwilling, again quite understandably, to commit themselves to a French orientation and to relinquish valuable economic assets without obtaining the desired *quid pro quo* in the form of some assurance that France would support Hungary's claims. In order to break this vicious circle, Count Csáky proposed in his report that the Hungarian representatives be empowered to grant to the French capitalist group options with respect to the contemplated economic objectives, as against an agreement of the French Government recognizing the justice of Hungary's claims. He also reported that the French regarded the phase of preliminary negotiations as ended and believed that the Hungarian delegates were empowered to sign any agreement reached without further authorization from their government.[33]

The first meeting between M. Paléologue and the Hungarian plenipotentiaries took place on May 5, after conversations with the Schneider-Creusot interests during the preceding two days had led to a general agreement on economic questions. The detailed report on the exchange of views on this occasion, sent by Count Csáky to Budapest,[34] indicated clearly that Hungary should not have had too sanguine hopes for amelioration of her position in the immediate future. M. Paléologue acquainted the Hungarian plenipotentiaries with the substance of a note which the French Government was planning to address to Hungary. Count Csáky summarized its contents in his report, drafted obviously with the utmost discretion, as follows:

The French Government is convinced that peace and order can be maintained in Central Europe only if the nations immediately concerned will mutually agree in a way satisfactory to all the interested parties.

Based on this conviction and loyal to the peace treaty and to the spirit of the accompanying note, the French Government is willing to use its good offices to bring about, and to support in every way, such agreements between Hungary and her neighbours provided that the general structure of the peace treaty should not be disturbed thereby ["sans toucher à la structure générale du traité de paix"]. In particular, the French Government is will-

[33] Count Emery Csáky to Count Teleki, May 3, 1920. *Ibid.,* Doc. 255.
[34] Count Emery Csáky to Count Teleki, May 5, 1920. *Ibid.,* Doc. 259.

ing to assist in the conclusion of agreements which aim at the alteration or revision of certain ethnical and economic injustices contained in the peace treaty. Furthermore, the French Government is willing to assist in the conclusion of agreements which aim at the restoration of complete freedom of communications, at the reconstruction of normal economic life, at the uniform administration of hydrographic questions, etc.

When the Hungarians tried to get a statement as to the extent to which M. Paléologue admitted the justice of the Hungarian claims set forth in the memoranda submitted by Dr. Halmos and as to the methods whereby and the limit to which the French Government could and would support such claims against Hungary's neighbors, the answer was evasive. M. Paléologue, pointing to France's delicate position in this matter, tried to impress upon the Hungarians the necessity of looking at the Franco-Hungarian *rapprochement* as a long-term enterprise. He repeatedly stated that France was then determined to base her policy in Southeastern Europe on Hungary and that therefore French policy would of necessity aim to strengthen Hungary both politically and economically; but, he said, the attainment of this objective, desired by both France and Hungary, would take a long time. M. Paléologue also informed the Hungarians that in his opinion the results of the negotiations up to that moment were embodied in three documents, namely: the note accompanying the final peace conditions; [35] Dr. Halmos's memorandum; [36] and the note which, as he had just stated, the French Government proposed to send to Hungary.[37] Count Csáky

[35] This reference is to the Covering Letter, signed by M. Millerand, with which the final peace terms were transmitted to the Hungarian Peace Delegation. The complete French text of this letter is in *HFR*, Vol. I, Doc. 265. Although it is dated May 6, it and the peace terms were handed to Mr. Praznovszky on the evening of May 5—the same day that the first meeting took place between M. Paléologue and the Hungarian plenipotentiaries—in order to expedite Mr. Praznovszky's return to Budapest. See "Political Diary," entry of May 5, 1920. Concerning this important Peace Conference document, see *infra*, Doc. 46, p. 551. As appears from Count Csáky's report of May 3, *supra*, n. 33, the Hungarian plenipotentiaries were informed confidentially a few days earlier—as proof of France's good faith—of the contents of the Covering Letter.

[36] It is not quite clear whether M. Paléologue referred to the first memorandum which Dr. Halmos presented to him on April 13 (see *supra*, pp. 264–66) or to the second memorandum, accompanying Dr. Halmos's communication to M. Paléologue of April 23 (see *supra*, pp. 271–72). It is believed, however, that the reference was to the later document.

[37] A declaration substantially similar to the summary of the draft outlined above was made on May 18 by the French High Commissioner in Budapest to Admiral Horthy, and the note was delivered to Count Teleki on June 24. See, on these developments, *infra*, pp. 288–89, 300–301.

inquired whether the French note was in the nature of a reply to Dr. Halmos's memorandum and therefore evidence that the French Government had taken cognizance of the Hungarian claims stated therein. Upon M. Paléologue's replying in the affirmative, Count Csáky stated that the proposed note would be acceptable as the basis of Franco-Hungarian coöperation.

That the Hungarians were not wholly satisfied with the noncommittal language of M. Paléologue's draft note is shown by the view expressed in this report that they felt it desirable to have in the final text an express recognition of the Hungarian claims by the French, that is, as these were set forth in Dr. Halmos's memorandum and as they would be amplified through subsequent conversations between M. Paléologue and the Hungarian plenipotentiaries. They outlined the procedure whereby they proposed to bring about such modification; but, as will appear later, their endeavors in this respect were unsuccessful. The course of the conversations indicated clearly that the French desired to move only with the utmost caution. M. Paléologue made it clear that negotiations between Hungary and her neighbors could be initiated only after the signature of the peace treaty and that any agreement between France and Hungary on details, or going beyond the broad policy outlined in the draft of the French note, would have to await such signature. Neither did the Hungarian plenipotentiaries succeed in obtaining information as to the means and methods whereby France could induce Czecho-Slovakia, Rumania, and Yugoslavia to come to terms with Hungary. The evasion of this issue may have been due to M. Paléologue's apprehension that France was, in fact, not so powerful as it appeared.

Despite the equivocal character of the interview with the French statesman, the Hungarian plenipotentiaries suggested to their government that they be empowered to extend the options to the Schneider-Creusot group, their validity being dependent on the consummation of the political agreement with the French Government.

The Final Peace Conditions and the Allied Reply

While the negotiations between France and Hungary made slow progress, the peace treaty between the Allies and Hungary reached a decisive point, with the presentation of the final peace terms to the Hungarian Delegation on the evening of May 5. As already stated, this occurred on the same day on which the meeting between M. Paléologue and the Hungarian plenipotentiaries, described above, took place —thus frustrating M. Paléologue's earlier expressed hope, doubtless shared by the Hungarians, that the Franco-Hungarian agreement might be concluded before the peace terms were submitted to Hungary.

Three documents were handed to the Hungarian Peace Delegation: (1) a lengthy memorandum, unsigned and undated, entitled "Reply of the Allied and Associated Powers to the Observations of the Hungarian Delegation on the Conditions of Peace"; [38] a "Covering Letter," dated May 6, 1920, addressed to the President of the Hungarian Delegation and signed by M. Millerand; [39] and the text of the peace terms which the "Covering Letter" designated as final and definitive.

As stated generally in the Covering Letter and in more detail in the Allied Reply, the voluminous arguments and proposals offered by the Hungarians had produced only a few, insignificant changes in the original peace terms, with one or two exceptions to be noted, which had been presented on January 15. According to the Covering Letter, the Allies had carefully examined the Hungarian observations—an assertion borne out by the detailed analysis of voluminous Hungarian documents, contained in the Allied Reply—but were unable to accept, in the overwhelming majority of instances, the points of view therein expressed. While admitting that the minute Hungarian criticisms were not answered point by point, the Covering Letter warned against any interpretation that would regard the absence of a specific reply as Allied acquiescence in the unanswered Hungarian arguments.

The essence of the Covering Letter related to the territorial question, which, as has been repeatedly pointed out, was the pivot around which the Hungarian argument revolved. On this vital issue, the Allies refused to permit any modification of the frontiers determined upon, on the ground that any such modification "would lead to disadvantages graver than those foreseen by the Hungarian Delegation." It was stated that the mixture of races in that part of Europe made it impossible to fix political boundaries which would coincide with ethnic lines and that this necessitated the subjection of Magyar populations to alien sov-

---

[38] English text in *HPN*, II, 551 ff.

[39] For the complete text see *infra*, Doc. 46, p. 551; the original French version is printed in *HFR*, Vol. I, Doc. 265.

ereignties. This, the Covering Letter stated, was regrettable, but, "a state of affairs, even when millennial, is not founded to exist, when it has been recognized as contrary to justice." The Hungarian plea for plebiscites was also rejected, with the explanation that "such a consultation, if carried out with all guarantees of complete sincerity, would not offer a result differing sensibly from those to which they [the Allies] have arrived after a minute study of the ethnographic conditions of Central Europe and of national aspirations." But one concession was made to the Hungarians, which subsequently became a focal point in Hungary's endeavors to obtain a peaceful revision of her frontiers. Admitting the possibility that the new frontiers might not always coincide with ethnic or economic requirements, the Covering Letter outlined a procedure whereby adjustments could be proposed in such cases by the Frontier Delimitation Commissions, to be established pursuant to the provisions of the treaty.

. . . when the Delimitation Commission will have commenced activity [reads the Covering Letter], should they find that the dispositions of the Treaty in some spot . . . create an injustice which it would be to [the] general interest to efface, it shall be allowable to them to address a report on this subject to the Council of the League of Nations. In this case the Allied and Associated Powers accept that the Council of the League may, under the same circumstances, at the request of one of the parties concerned, offer their services for an amicable rectification of the first delineation at the passages where a modification has been judged desirable by a Delimitation Commission. The Allied and Associated Powers are confident that the proceeding will furnish a convenient method for correcting in the delineation of the frontiers all injustice against which objections not unfounded can be raised.

The Covering Letter also referred to another territorial matter, namely to the question of Ruthenia, and, while rejecting the Hungarian suggestions, sought to give assurance that the treaty between the Allies and Czecho-Slovakia would suffice to insure autonomy for the Ruthenian people.

No satisfaction was given to Hungarian claims for more effective protection for minorities, because, in the opinion of the Allies, the minority treaties would amply safeguard the Magyars passing under alien sovereignties. The Covering Letter concluded by saying that the powers conferred on the Frontier Delimitation Commissions, together with the rephrasing of or amendments to several clauses of the original treaty draft, hereafter to be noted, marked "the extreme limit" of Allied concessions and it requested a declaration that the Hungarian Delegation be authorized to sign the treaty "as it is" within ten days.[40]

The other modifications—apart from purely stylistic changes—to which the Allies consented, as appears from their reply memorandum and a comparison of the original and the final treaty drafts, were as follows:

1. Articles 44 and 47 were each amended by a paragraph under which Yugoslavia and Rumania recognized and confirmed their obligations to agree to the insertion of appropriate clauses in their respective treaties with the Principal Allied Powers providing for the protection of minorities and for safeguarding the freedom of trade.[41]

2. Some of the military and naval clauses were slightly modified so as to give contingent concessions of no significance to the Hungarians. Specifically, Article 107, restricting the number of men in the police and customs service to the number similarly employed within the new boundaries in 1913, was amended to permit the Military Control Commission, to be established under the terms of the treaty, to recommend a slight increase; Article 115, confining the manufacture of arms and ammunition to a single factory, was modified to the effect that the Allies might authorize temporarily such manufacture in one or more other factories; Article 120, which originally permitted Hungary to maintain three police patrol boats on the Danube, now authorized the Control Commission to recommend an increase; and, finally, Article 122, providing for the destruction of all warships under construction, was amended to permit the preservation of some uncompleted mine tenders, subject to a finding of the Allied Naval Commission that utilization of these for commercial purposes was desirable.

3. Article 177 (in Part VIII on Reparations) was amended so as to enable Hungary to claim from Austria documents and objects of an

[40] A delay of ten additional days was sought in a communication, dated May 6, from Mr. Wettstein, the chargé d'affaires of the Hungarian Delegation, to the President of the Peace Conference. *HPN,* II, 511. M. Millerand answered this request on May 8, granting a delay of five days, thus giving Hungary time to answer by May 21. *Ibid.,* p. 514.

[41] No such amendment was added to Section IV, Part III of the treaty draft relating to Czecho-Slovakia, since that country had already ratified her treaty with the Allies, and this contained such clauses. See the Allied reply, *HPN,* II, 551.

artistic, historic, or scientific character which appertained to institutions formerly owned in common by the two partners in the Monarchy.[42]

4. Article 186, paragraph 2 (Financial Clauses), providing for the reapportionment by the Reparations Commission of the unsecured bonded debt of Hungary among the Succession States, was amended to allow the Commission to take into account certain financial arrangements which had existed, prior to the war, between Hungary and Croatia-Slavonia.[43]

5. Article 207, providing for special agreements between Hungary, Poland, and Czecho-Slovakia regarding the supply of coal, foodstuffs, and raw materials, was amplified by a provision for the negotiation of separate conventions between all the Succession States which would insure the continued exchange of goods across the new political boundaries.[44]

6. Article 250, prohibiting the retention or liquidation of property, rights, or interests of Hungarian nationals situated in the territory of the former Monarchy, was made more effective by an added provision that claims of such nationals arising under this article should be submitted to the Mixed Arbitral Tribunals to be established pursuant to the treaty.[45]

7. Finally, a new article—Article 293—was added, which, adopting the essence of an elaborately documented Hungarian proposal, provided for the establishment of a commission composed of representatives of all interested states, under a chairman to be named by the League of Nations Council, to supervise and insure the continued operation of the hydraulic system built up by Hungary for the middle Danube basin.[46]

---

[42] It may be noted that a like provision was contained in Article 156 of the Treaty of Peace of Saint-Germain, enabling Czecho-Slovakia, Poland, Rumania, Yugoslavia, and Italy to make similar claims against Austria. In other words, this amendment merely put Hungary vis-à-vis Austria in the same position as the other Succession States and can hardly be classified as a concession to Hungary. See, for the explanation of the amendment, the Allied reply in *HPN,* II, 557.

[43] See *ibid.,* p. 559. [44] See *ibid.,* p. 562.

[45] See *ibid.,* p. 566. It was on the basis of this amendment that the legality of expropriations, carried out in several of the Succession States, was brought before the various arbitral tribunals in the postwar years, and the contest as to the jurisdiction of these international courts over such claims constituted the *cause célèbre* for international lawyers throughout the 1920's.

[46] See *ibid.,* p. 570.

The Reception of the Final Peace Terms in Hungary

The practically unaltered final peace terms were received with bitter disappointment by the Hungarian people. The public was then wholly ignorant of the confidential negotiations in progress between France and Hungary and therefore could not console itself even with the meager hope that their successful conclusion might lead, in the future, to some improvement. The passage in the Covering Letter characterizing the thousand-year-old possession of the lands of the Holy Crown by Hungary as an "injustice," and its acceptance of resolutions passed by the self-appointed Czecho-Slovak, Rumanian, and Yugoslav national councils as satisfactory and conclusive expressions of the will of the peoples, in lieu of properly supervised plebiscites, were deeply resented as gratuitously insulting.[47] At the moment, even the authority granted to the Frontier Delimitation Commissions to recommend frontier rectifications and the reference to the League of Nations as the agency to be used to modify situations, if required by changed conditions, escaped attention.

In official circles the disappointment was somewhat tempered by the knowledge of the Franco-Hungarian negotiations and the belief that despite the difficulties revealed in Count Csáky's reports, ultimate success was still within the realm of possibility.[48] Also, the government had had a better understanding of the general situation than the mass of the people and had been less hopeful from the outset that the Hungarian arguments, however well-founded, could move the Allies to change the pattern into which Europe was already frozen.

The official Hungarian point of view regarding the peace terms was very evident in Count Teleki's address to Parliament on May 10 [49] and in the discussions which took place at the meetings of the Peace Delegation in Budapest held on May 10, May 12, and May 19.[50] Count Teleki

[47] See Count Teleki to the Hungarian Peace Delegation in Paris, May 7, 1920. *HFR*, Vol. I, Doc. 268. See also Count Teleki's references to these passages of the Covering Letter in his discussion of the final peace conditions before Parliament. *Records of the National Assembly* [in Hungarian], II, 403 ff.; English translation in *HFR*, I (Appendix III, No. 2), 958–59.

[48] The reports of May 3 and May 5 from the Hungarian plenipotentiaries in Paris, summarized above, reached the government at the same time as the final peace terms and the accompanying documents.

[49] *Records of the National Assembly* [in Hungarian], II, 403 ff.; English translation in *HFR*, I (Appendix III, No. 2), 953–71.

[50] The minutes of these meetings were incorporated in the "Political Diary."

devoted a considerable part of his address to an analysis of the Covering Letter, which indicates the importance which the Hungarian Government attached from the outset to that document. He noted the comparatively courteous tone of the communication as a sign of growing understanding in Allied circles and laid emphasis on the promise contained therein regarding the future adjustment of unjustly drawn frontiers by the Delimitation Commissions. Count Teleki declared that this promise, if conscientiously fulfilled, would be regarded by Hungary as truly significant.[51] As to the text of the treaty itself, Count Teleki analyzed dispassionately and in some detail the few changes made in the original terms and indicated that the establishment of the Hydraulic Commission might be regarded as the most important concrete success of the Peace Delegation. He did not try to put matters for the nation in a more favorable light than the facts warranted and, while paying tribute to the efforts of the Peace Delegation, he stated frankly that he regarded the treaty as very bad.

When the Peace Delegation met on the same afternoon to consider what action it should take, the opinion was well-nigh unanimous that despite the harshness of its terms, Hungary had no alternative but to sign on the dotted line. The only question was whether the Peace Delegation should carry on, or whether it should resign in protest and leave

[51] "I declare here," said Count Teleki, "that the Hungarian nation acknowledges this as a concession, but only if the frontier delimitation commissions use their privilege[s] and power whenever and wherever Europe's interests demand it; [only] if they will consider it their moral responsibility to exercise their rights whether it is in the material interest of Eastern Europe . . . or in the moral interest of Europe, which means that there should be no illegality or injustice committed or maintained. If this is their conception of Europe's interest, if the Peace Conference itself interprets it thus, if the frontier delimitation commissions will interpret and act accordingly, and if the League will interpret and execute it in the same spirit, then this paragraph of the Covering Letter is significant indeed." *HFR,* I (Appendix III, No. 2), 961. Count Apponyi also expressed the view at the Peace Delegation's meeting held on May 10 that the true significance of the Covering Letter would be revealed through its interpretation. "Political Diary," entry of May 10. At the last meeting of the Peace Delegation, held on May 19, Count Apponyi expressed the view that the harshness of the treaty was mitigated only by the Covering Letter and he minimized the value of those changes in the treaty text itself to which the Allies had consented because, in his opinion, these concessions did not in any way alter the character of the treaty. The essence of the treaty, he said, was the territorial question, and in this respect no change whatever had been made. "Consequently," he continued, "the modifications of the economic and financial clauses are completely worthless because their execution depends solely upon the good will of our neighbors." But, he said, the Covering Letter contained definite promises "which open the door for revision of the Hungarian peace treaty." "Political Diary," entry of May 19.

the government to attend to this painful but inevitable task through newly appointed representatives. The procedure to be followed was discussed for several days,[52] and finally the conclusion was reached that the Delegation must resign. The reasons leading to this decision were fully set forth in a letter, dated May 16, which Count Apponyi, as President of the Hungarian Peace Delegation, addressed to M. Mille-rand.[53] This letter referred to Count Apponyi's statement, when he addressed the Supreme Council on January 16, that the Delegation regarded the original peace terms, unless substantially modified, as unacceptable; and, pointing to the fact that the Allies had refused to apply the principle of self-determination, he gave notice to the President of the Peace Conference that the Delegation did not consider itself authorized to sign the practically unaltered treaty and had decided to resign.

In another communication to M. Millerand, dated May 17, the Prime Minister, Mr. Simonyi-Semadam, and Count Teleki, as Minister for Foreign Affairs, associated the Hungarian Government with the protests registered in Count Apponyi's letter, but stated that in view of the country's grave situation the Hungarian Government "do not consider themselves able to refuse to sign" the treaty of peace and expressed willingness to appoint plenipotentiaries to do so. This communication set forth in some detail the interpretation which the Hungarian Government put on the Covering Letter and indicated clearly that one inducement for signing was the hope that the promises contained therein would be fulfilled by the Allies.[54]

Both of these communications were delivered to the Secretariat of the Peace Conference on the afternoon of May 21 by Mr. Praznovszky, who had returned from Budapest on that morning, empowered by his government to make arrangements for the signature of the treaty.[55] M. Millerand, in a letter to Mr. Praznovszky dated May 22, acknowledged the receipt of the two documents, designating June 4 as the date of signature and stating the wish of the Allies that the treaty be signed

---

[52] See the minutes, "Political Diary," entries of May 10, 12, and 19.

[53] For the text, see *infra,* Doc. 47, p. 555.

[54] For the text see *infra,* Doc. 48, p. 558. Parliament was informed of the resignation of the members of the Peace Delegation and the decision of the government to sign the treaty, in a brief statement by Count Teleki on May 26. See *Records of the National Assembly* [in Hungarian], III, 84 ff.; English text in HFR, Vol. I, Appendix III, No. 3, p. 971.

[55] "Political Diary," entry of May 21, 1920.

by at least one member of the Hungarian Government.[56] The Hungarian plenipotentiaries, Dr. Ákos Benárd, Minister of Labor, and Mr. Alfred Drasche-Lázár, a diplomatic officer with the rank of envoy, reached Paris on the morning of June 3, accompanied by Count Stephen Csáky, who had served from the outset as the executive secretary of the Peace Delegation.[57] The treaty was signed at a formal ceremony on the afternoon of June 4 in the Grand Trianon Palace. The Hungarian delegates were treated courteously: the Allied representatives, already assembled, rose when the Hungarians entered; upon their leaving the Palace after the signature, a guard of honor presented arms. In the words of the Hungarian recorder of this event, "the sorrowful ceremony took place without any incident";[58] the peace treaty between the Allies and Hungary became a reality.

The Influence of the Franco-Hungarian Negotiations upon Hungary's Decision Regarding the Peace Treaty

The events just narrated, culminating in the signature of the Treaty of Trianon, can be fully understood only in the light of the influence which the Franco-Hungarian negotiations exerted on the Hungarian statesmen who had to chart the course for Hungary to follow. It must remain a matter of conjecture whether or not the treaty would have been signed, had there not been in the minds of those responsible for Hungary's decision at least a slight hope that an understanding with France might be arrived at in time to improve the country's situation. But that such a hope—whether or not justified is immaterial—was a decisive factor in their decision is borne out by the available record, and this is also confirmed by several of the principal actors in the drama—particularly by Count Apponyi, Count Teleki, and Count Stephen Csáky—whom the author has interviewed. While the reports from the Hungarian plenipotentiaries in Paris, which reached the government simultaneously with the final peace terms, were not conducive to undue optimism, and it may be said that neither Count Apponyi nor Count Teleki was likely to overlook realities, they were nevertheless indicative of an earnest willingness on the part of the French to give some support to Hungary. Rightly or wrongly, the

[56] Text in HPN, II, 532. Cf. Mr. Praznovszky to Count Teleki, May 23, 1920. HFR, Vol. I, Doc. 294.

[57] See "Political Diary," entry of June 3, 1920. [58] Ibid., entry of June 4, 1920.

Hungarian statesmen considered the Covering Letter, particularly its promise to correct territorial injustices by means of the Frontier Delimitation Commissions and the League of Nations, as concrete evidence of French good will. There is nothing to prove directly that the Covering Letter, or any part of it, was due to French influence; but it is a fact that throughout the negotiations with France the Hungarians always put the territorial question in the foreground and that the French did acquaint the Hungarians confidentially with the substance of the Covering Letter—particularly the paragraph relating to the authority of the Frontier Delimitation Commissions—when it was still in draft form and a closely guarded secret.[59] It is true that M. Paléologue was not precise in recognizing Hungarian territorial claims and was vague as to the time when and the methods whereby these aspirations would, in whole or in part, be satisfied; but it is a fact that the French note of April 15 did clearly and unmistakably envisage a Hungary with frontiers different from those laid down in the peace treaty and that in conversations with the Hungarian plenipotentiaries M. Paléologue did assume that territorial adjustments would be part and parcel of the contemplated politico-economic plan. Bearing in mind that the French spokesman was not an irresponsible person but the Secretary General of the French Foreign Office, acting, presumably, with the approval of his superiors and supported by powerful industrial and financial interests, it would seem reasonable that the Hungarian Government should regard these negotiations as an important factor to be considered in shaping its foreign policy. More particularly, the course of negotiations after the delivery of the final peace terms had justified the expectation that though the treaty should be signed, there might be revision of its terms before or even after ratification.

That the Hungarian Government was not unduly optimistic appears from its reaction to Count Csáky's first reports.[60] Pursuant to his suggestion, the Hungarian plenipotentiaries were authorized to grant the options to the French, with certain reservations,[61] and to sign the political agreement, but there was apprehension because of the indefiniteness of French commitments. In the opinion of the Hungarian Government, the value of the promised French support was substantially weakened by the anxiety of the French Government to

---

[59] *Supra,* p. 276 *n.*
[60] That is, the reports dated May 3 and 5, discussed *supra,* pp. 274–76.
[61] For example, the railway option was to safeguard the interests of employees.

preserve the "general structure" of the treaty and by the qualification that such support would be forthcoming "dans la mesure du possible" —a phrase appearing in the French note of April 15 and repeated in Dr. Halmos's memorandum of April 23. M. Paléologue's insistence that results might be expected only after long and sustained efforts was regarded in Budapest as evidence of French deference to the claims of Hungary's neighbors and of French inability to exert influence over them. Despite these discouraging considerations, Count Teleki wrote that in view of the exceedingly difficult situation of the country, "from which there does not seem to be any other way out," the negotiations must be continued. If nothing else should come of them, at least direct contact with the neighboring states might be made, leading perhaps to economic *rapprochement* after the signing of the peace treaty. To forestall possible misunderstandings, Count Teleki approved the suggestion that the Halmos memorandum of April 23, which M. Paléologue designated as one of three documents constituting the records of the negotiations, but which did not in all particulars coincide with the position of the Hungarian Government,[62] be replaced by a new memorandum, to be worked out in consultation with the French spokesmen, setting forth with more precision Hungary's claims and obligations.[63]

Following several conferences with M. Paléologue, such a memorandum was prepared by Count Csáky and Count Bethlen and presented to the French diplomat on May 12.[64] The introductory and concluding paragraphs of the new memorandum differed from those of the earlier memoranda prepared by Dr. Halmos;[65] but the basic

[62] The assurance that Hungary was prepared to enter into a military convention with one or more states designated by France was particularly objected to as committing Hungary further than the government deemed wise.

[63] See Count Teleki's dispatches to Count Emery Csáky, dated May 7, 9, and 11, 1920. *HFR*, Vol. I, Docs. 266, 274, 276.

[64] Text (in French) *ibid.*, Doc. 285.

[65] The opening paragraph set forth the aims of the Hungarian Government as follows: "Absolutely free to give her foreign policy a direction which appears best to safeguard her interest and conceiving that in this respect her interests and those of France are identical, Hungary is prepared to adopt a political and economic policy in conformity with this view. Led by the conviction that permanent peace in Central Europe, so necessary for the whole world, cannot be assured except by the reestablishment of satisfactory relations between Hungary and all of her neighbors and that such general appeasement would be greeted with satisfaction by the French Government whose interest thus would be particularly served, Hungary is prepared to enter into direct negotiations with all her neighbors with a view to an amicable settlement,

outline of the contemplated agreement, though amplified, remained practically unchanged. The following amplifications deserve notice: With respect to territorial readjustments, the memorandum of May 12 claimed specifically that Hungary should retain as much of her ancient territory as would supply her with the raw materials and the motive power indispensable to her economic life. The plebiscite which had been claimed in the earlier memoranda for the Swabian population, living in proximity to the new frontiers, was now also sought for that part of Western Hungary which the Allies had allotted to Austria.

Immediately after the delivery of this revised memorandum Count Csáky returned to Budapest to report orally to his government, then grappling with the difficult problems created by the Allied demand for the signature of the treaty. The French, disturbed by reports of the indignation aroused by the peace terms, an indignation then sweeping Hungary, and by rumors of the resignation of the Peace Delegation, came to the conclusion that some step was needed to counterbalance the disillusion manifest in Hungarian official circles and in public opinion. Accordingly the French High Commissioner in Budapest, M. Fouchet, was instructed formally to assure the Regent and the Hungarian Government of the good will of France, within the framework of the contemplated Franco-Hungarian agreement. M. Fouchet called on Admiral Horthy on May 18 and, in the presence of the members of the Hungarian Government, the President of the National Assembly, various members of the Peace Delegation, which had already resigned, and of Count Emery Csáky, read the following declaration:

The French Government is convinced that the peace and prosperity of Central Europe can be assured only through the coöperation of the interested States.

For this reason, the French Government is prepared to facilitate all effort and conversations between the Governments of Rumania, Czecho-Slovakia, and Yugoslavia on the one hand, and the Hungarian Government on the other, seeking a basis for such coöperation, which alone could guarantee a general peace.

As a faithful observer of the Peace Treaty, bearing its signature, the French Government draws inspiration from the Covering Letter when it

---

to the complete satisfaction of all parties concerned, of all pending questions." The concluding paragraph omitted reference to any military alliance and instead requested the French Government to facilitate the initiation of these negotiations and to lend support to Hungary in their course, as also before the various Allied and international committees having a part in the carrying out of the peace treaties.

offers its good offices to help to correct any ethnic or economic injustice in the peace conditions, to achieve the amplification and revision of the rights of minorities, and thus bring about the disappearance of all reasons for hostility, and reach agreements satisfactory to all parties concerned.

The French Government will assist the Hungarian Government in all efforts to reach agreements concerning the freedom of communications, railway problems, financial questions, the "régime" of waterways, and so forth, within limits compatible with the treaties bearing its signature.

The validity of this declaration is conditioned upon the signature of the Peace Treaty.[66]

Following the reading of this solemn declaration, which, in general, followed the draft of the French note as outlined by M. Paléologue to the Hungarian plenipotentiaries on May 5,[67] M. Fouchet stated informally that the French Government was in earnest about the promised support and he assured the Hungarian statesmen present that France was determined to base her whole future policy in Southeastern Europe on Hungary as the pivot.

It was in the light of these assurances that the decision to sign the peace treaty was taken, although the Hungarian Government felt far from satisfied with the results accomplished heretofore. This appears clearly in the instructions issued on May 30 to guide the Hungarian plenipotentiaries in the economic negotiations with the French.[68] In order to protect the Hungarian Government from a possible charge of bad faith, should the negotiations fail, the plenipotentiaries were instructed to lay Hungary's position frankly before the French and to point out the impossibility of obtaining parliamentary approval [69] for

[66] Original French text in *HFR*, Vol. I, Doc. 292.

[67] *Supra*, pp. 275–76.   [68] *HFR*, Vol. I, Doc. 301.

[69] Although the negotiations were then carried on in great secrecy, the Hungarian Government intended to submit the agreements reached to the National Assembly for ratification, in accordance with Hungarian constitutional law. This is shown clearly by the instruction to insert a clause in the options, conditioning their validity upon ratification by the legislature. Count Teleki to Mr. Praznovszky, June 2, 1920. *Ibid.,* Doc. 305. While the French did not agree to the insertion of such a clause, they recognized the necessity of ratification, in a separate written communication. See Count Csáky to Count Teleki, June 10, 1920. *Ibid.,* Doc. 343; Count Teleki to Count Csáky, June 12, 1920. *Ibid.,* Doc. 347. When the Regent addressed a communication to Count Teleki, affirming that the negotiations with France were being carried on with his knowledge and that the options relating to the railways and the Danube harbor were being extended with his approval, he stated that the government was in duty bound to submit the results of the negotiations to the National Assembly for its approval. Admiral Horthy to Count Teleki, June 8, 1920. *Ibid.,* Doc. 333.

either the French orientation of Hungarian foreign policy or for the economic agreements, which involved even heavier sacrifices than were anticipated, without some concrete and tangible concessions to Hungary. As has been repeatedly pointed out and as these instructions make clear, the Hungarians expected, above all, the satisfaction of their territorial claims, at least to the extent specified in the Hungarian memoranda presented to M. Paléologue. The granting of the options was conditioned upon some kind of guarantee from the French Goverment that the territories claimed would be returned to Hungary. Without such guarantee, the instructions explained, no Hungarian statesman or government could induce the nation to accept the sacrifices involved.[70]

Although the signature of the peace treaty was imminent, the conclusion of the Franco-Hungarian agreement was nowhere in sight. Indeed, new difficulties arose, which, for a time, threatened to lead to an impasse. This critical stage of the negotiations was reached during the week following the signature of the Trianon Treaty.

[70] This was stated unequivocally by Count Teleki in a communication to Count Csáky, dated June 10, 1920: "It would not be possible to obtain the ratification of Parliament for an agreement which would give control over our economic resources in exchange for a vague and theoretical declaration by the French Government." *Ibid.,* Doc. 339. Further to emphasize the interdependence of the political and the economic agreements, the Hungarian negotiators were instructed to deliver the options only upon receiving a written receipt from Count Saint-Sauveur for both the options and an accompanying letter setting forth the position of the Hungarian Government in this respect. Count Teleki to Count Csáky, June 1, 1920. *Ibid.,* Doc. 304. Count Saint-Sauveur agreed to give such a written receipt. Count Csáky to Count Teleki, June 6, 1920. *Ibid.,* Doc. 326.

VI. The Second Phase of the Franco-Hungarian Secret Negotiations and the Treaty of Trianon: From the Signing of the Peace Treaty, June 4, 1920, to the Resignation of M. Paléologue, September, 1920

The Period of Crisis

THE difficulties which delayed the conclusion of the Franco-Hungarian negotiations were due largely to differences in points of view as to the benefits and commitments of the contracting parties. Moreover, a reconciliation of the differing points of view was further complicated by extraneous considerations forced upon the two governments by reason of domestic politics and matters of international policy.

In the first place, the Hungarian Government desired to secure a precise statement as to the extent and character of the promised French support; it also sought to induce the French to commit themselves publicly to a policy friendly to Hungary, thus insuring that such support would, in fact, be forthcoming. The endeavors of the government to pin the French down followed logically upon the position it had taken from the outset and stated unequivocally in all instructions given to its plenipotentiaries—namely, that Hungary could consent to the sacrifices demanded only in exchange for equivalent political concessions. Moreover, the necessity of justifying the government's policy before public opinion in Hungary also became apparent at almost the same time. For despite the secrecy with which they were conducted, news of the negotiations had leaked out and rumors had begun to circulate in Budapest, toward the end of May, to the effect that, as a result, the Hungarian railways would be leased to France. The reaction not only of the uninitiated public, but also of responsible circles was definitely hostile; with the former, because France at that time was anything but popular in Hungary, while with the latter, the opinion was prevalent that even a guarantee of territorial integrity would not offset the loss of control over the country's lines of communication.

There was much doubt even in upper circles as to the wisdom of such a lease—especially when it was discovered that the French were, simultaneously, carrying on negotiations for similar leases with most of the Danubian states.[1] Nevertheless, the government still believed that for the moment Hungary's best and perhaps only chance was in securing French support; and, finding the opposition embarrassing, it sought to disarm it and also to mitigate the effect of the signature of the peace treaty on public opinion by trying to show some concrete results of its policy.

It will be remembered that M. Paléologue, in the first conference with the Hungarian plenipotentiaries on May 5, took the position that France could not discuss the Hungarian claims in detail and could not state precisely the extent of French support before the signing of the peace treaty. On the eve of the signing Count Csáky was instructed to press for such a statement, now that the treaty was about to be signed. He was further instructed to insist upon the necessity of informing Great Britain and Italy of the negotiations and of obtaining the consent of the French Government that the note to be sent to Hungary should be made public.[2] Accordingly Count Csáky had an interview with M. Paléologue on June 6, two days after the Treaty of Trianon was signed. He tried to impress M. Paléologue with the desirability of a reassuring gesture toward Hungary. He intimated that an expression of France's willingness to permit the Frontier Delimitation Commissions to settle the ultimate fate of Western Hungary, pursuant to its authority under the Covering Letter, would create a favorable impression in Hungary. M. Paléologue agreed to consider this suggestion, without, however, committing himself.[3] When Count Csáky in a subsequent interview again urged the necessity of concrete political results

---

[1] The idea behind the French plan seems to have been a grandiose politico-economic scheme, namely the establishment of a Danubian Federation, built on a centralized and unified railway system in Southeastern Europe and under French control. The Schneider-Creusot firm, which conducted the negotiations concerning the lease of the Hungarian railways, acted for a holding company, the *Société Anonyme du Matériel Roulant,* formed under the guidance of M. Loucheur and Count Saint-Sauveur for the carrying out of this plan. Cf. Count Teleki to Count Csáky, June 5, 1920. *HFR,* Vol. I, Doc. 314.

[2] See the dispatches of Count Teleki to Count Csáky and to Mr. Praznovszky, June 3 and 4, 1920. *Ibid.,* Docs. 307, 308, 310, 311.

[3] Count Csáky to Count Teleki, June 6, 1920. *Ibid.,* Doc. 324. The same suggestion, together with others, was again put forward a few days later when, shortly before the conclusion of the agreement, the necessity of giving concrete proof of France's good will was emphasized. Count Teleki to Count Csáky, June 17, 1920. *Ibid.,* Doc. 361.

in the immediate future, M. Paléologue conceded the reasonableness of the Hungarian position but evaded a direct answer, saying that he could not give more definite promises until he had sounded out the governments of the neighboring countries and had obtained a clearer picture of the possibilities. On the other hand, he could do this only after the agreement between France and Hungary had been concluded. But he told Count Csáky that preliminary inquiries had brought encouraging replies.[4]

A disclosure of France's new policy was also discussed at the interview which took place on June 6. Although the original plan had been to publish the results as soon as the negotiations were concluded, M. Paléologue now expressed his reluctance to permit such publicity for the time being, giving as his reason the internal political situation in France. He assured Count Csáky that Hungary's neighbors would be at once informed of France's new policy and stated that, subject to M. Millerand's approval—which was still to be obtained—there would be no objection on the part of the French Government to the publication of the French note in the Hungarian press.[5] A few days later M. Paléologue again stated that he saw no objection to the publication of the French note in Hungary; but he raised the question whether some delay would not be advantageous from the point of view of the Hungarian Government. Since the declaration of France's new policy had to be couched in vague terms, because of her delicate position in relation to her allies, M. Paléologue feared that the uninformed Hungarian public might find these vague terms disappointing.[6]

Budapest was not pleased with these developments. French hesitation to make public the understanding with Hungary and to make specific Paléologue's indefinite promises was regarded as an indication

[4] Count Csáky to Count Teleki, June 12, 1920. *Ibid.,* Doc. 349.

[5] Count Csáky to Count Teleki, June 6, 1920. *Ibid.,* Doc. 324. M. Paléologue's reluctance to make public the Franco-Hungarian understanding was doubtless due, in part, to apprehension over the growing opposition in France to the government then in power. Just as in Hungary, in France, too, news of the negotiations leaked out, and there were signs that M. Millerand's opponents planned to use rumors of the adoption of a friendly policy toward Hungary as affording an opportunity to attack the government. The Hungarians regarded the possibility of such an attack as rather favorable to their cause, because it would force the French Government to commit itself publicly. But there was apprehension in Hungarian quarters over the fact that this opposition in France could be traced, in part, to the efforts of Hungary's neighbors, including Austria, to prevent an understanding between France and Hungary. Count Csáky to Count Teleki, June 3, 1920. *Ibid.,* Doc. 309.

[6] Count Csáky to Count Teleki, June 14, 1920. *Ibid.,* Doc. 353.

of a changed attitude on the part of the French Government, which the Hungarian Government was inclined to attribute to the opposition and possibly the pressure of Hungary's neighbors.[7] The fear of Hungarian statesmen that France might be blocked by the opposition of the other Principal Allied Powers was heightened when the British High Commissioner in Hungary, Mr. (later Sir Thomas) Hohler, protested against the granting of any concessions to France and denied that any agreement in this respect had been reached between France and Great Britain.[8]

When the British protest was brought to M. Paléologue's attention, he was again evasive and sought to convey the impression that Paris had received no complaints. Conceding that opposition was to be expected from both Great Britain and Italy, he expressed his confidence that France would overcome such opposition.[9]

Another source of difficulty was the French demand for control of the Hungarian General Credit Bank. It will be remembered that originally the economic advantages sought by the French were confined to a long-term lease of the Hungarian railways and Railway Locomotive Works, and to the construction of the commercial port of Budapest. Subsequently, about the middle of May, the French put forward an additional demand, namely, that a group of French financiers should acquire a controlling interest in the General Credit Bank. The bank, which itself controlled a considerable part of Hungarian industry both within the new and the historic frontiers, was not wholly

[7] Count Teleki to Count Csáky, June 10, 1920. *Ibid.*, Doc. 339.

[8] The British protest was based on the Treaty of Trianon, which, it was claimed, reserved all of Hungary's assets as security for the Allies. See Count Teleki to Count Csáky, June 5, 1920. *Ibid.*, Doc. 315. Count Teleki at once informed the French High Commissioner in Hungary of the British protest, but M. Fouchet assured the Hungarian Foreign Minister that the difference between France and Great Britain would be settled. Subsequently the British informed Count Teleki that a protest had been lodged in France, against that country's having carried on negotiations with Hungary without any advice to the Allies. According to the British, M. Millerand had replied that the negotiations were in an embryonic stage and that France had made no promises to Hungary. See the dispatches of Count Teleki to Count Csáky, June 7, 1920. *Ibid.*, Docs. 327, 328.

[9] Count Csáky to Count Teleki, June 10, 1920 (two dispatches). *Ibid.*, Docs. 342, 344. The Hungarians seem to have had positive information that the British did, in fact, lodge a protest with the French Government. Cf. Count Teleki to Count Csáky, June 12, 1920. *Ibid.*, Doc. 346. For subsequent British and also Italian opposition to Franco-Hungarian *rapprochement* see *infra*, pp. 302–3.

averse to the proposal, but was not prepared to conclude a transaction of such importance too hastily. Accordingly one of the directors, Baron Kornfeld, was sent to Paris, with an authorization that was narrowly defined, to negotiate on behalf of the bank with the French financiers, but concurrently and in consultation with the plenipotentiaries of the Hungarian Government. In the course of the negotiations the French repeatedly made it clear that they regarded the Credit Bank transaction as an indispensable part of the Franco-Hungarian understanding.[10] Baron Kornfeld worked out an arrangement under which the bank would issue a certain number of new shares and would grant to the French capitalist group an option to take over 75 percent thereof at issue price; but the bank refused to agree, at least until the political issues between France and Hungary had been clarified.[11] The French interpreted the reluctance of the bank to accept the arrangement proposed by Baron Kornfeld as a sign that Hungary was no longer eager to conclude the agreement,[12] while the Hungarians, in turn, saw in the French insistence upon including the transaction a pretext for making a graceful withdrawal.[13]

As a matter of fact, these mutual suspicions were unfounded. The Hungarian Government was in no way responsible for the reluctance of the Credit Bank to accept the French proposals. As we have shown, the government was prepared, even before the peace treaty had been signed, to deliver to the French the options for the lease of the railways and for the construction of the commercial port of Budapest; and, the enterprises involved being state-owned, the granting of these options depended solely on the government. But the Credit Bank was a private institution over which the government had no direct control. Moreover, the Hungarian Government took the view that the Credit Bank affair was not included in the price which Hungary had originally been asked to pay for France's support and therefore it was not inclined to bring pressure on the bank directors.[14] This view appeared to be confirmed by a communication from the French High Commis-

[10] See the dispatches of Mr. Praznovszky and Count Csáky to Count Teleki, dated June 2, 3, 6, and 10, 1920. *HFR,* Vol. I, Docs. 306, 309, 323, 325, 341.

[11] Count Teleki to Mr. Praznovszky, June 4 and 8, 1920. *Ibid.,* Docs. 312, 330.

[12] Cf. Count Csáky to Count Teleki, June 9, 1920 (two dispatches). *Ibid.,* Docs. 337, 338.

[13] Count Teleki to Count Csáky, June 10, 1920. *Ibid.,* Doc. 339.

[14] Count Teleki to Mr. Praznovszky, June 4, 1920. *Ibid.,* Doc. 312.

sioner, requesting a written declaration from the Regent formally endorsing Hungary's commitments.[15] The absence of any reference to the Credit Bank transaction in this communication, which sought the Regent's guarantee in the matter of the railway and port options only, was, in the opinion of the Hungarian Government, inconsistent with the French insistence upon the conclusion of the Credit Bank proposal as an indispensable condition of the Franco-Hungarian agreement.[16] Neither were there any hidden motives behind the bank's reluctance to conclude the transaction. The truth of the matter was that its directors feared that they might be accused by public opinion, never particularly friendly toward banks, of engineering the whole unpopular arrangement with the French, in the interest of the Credit Bank itself.[17]

The French, for their part, had a perfectly plausible explanation for their insistence on the Credit Bank transaction. M. Paléologue claimed that French influence over the enterprises controlled by the Credit Bank, many of which were situated in territories to be detached from Hungary, would be a powerful weapon in the hands of France with which to exert pressure on Hungary's neighbors.[18]

Misunderstandings, although of minor importance, also arose in connection with the French request for the Regent's written guarantee, to which reference has already been made.[19] For constitutional reasons, the Regent could not address a communication directly to the French

[15] M. Fouchet to Count Teleki, June 5, 1920. *Ibid.,* Doc. 317. Concerning the complications which arose in this connection, see *infra,* p. 297.

[16] Count Teleki to Count Csáky, June 8, 1920. *Ibid.,* Doc. 332. The French explained this apparent inconsistency on the ground that they would not seek the Regent's guarantee for a transaction in the determination of which the Hungarian Government had no voice. Count Csáky to Count Teleki, June 10, 1920. *Ibid.,* Doc. 341.

[17] Count Teleki to Count Csáky, June 10, 1920. *Ibid.,* Doc. 339. As will be shown presently, the Hungarian Government had to give a clean bill of health in this respect before the bank finally agreed to satisfy the French demands. *Infra,* p. 298.

[18] Mr. Praznovszky to Count Teleki, June 15, 1920. *HFR,* Vol. I, Doc. 358. It was during this conference, which took place on June 14, that M. Paléologue explained the considerations which shaped his policy. According to Mr. Praznovszky's summary, M. Paléologue stated that Austria-Hungary had to be destroyed because of the threat which the Monarchy, allied with Germany, constituted for the Allies. But the French were not convinced that the Succession States could exist as independent units. Therefore, they ought to be brought together under French auspices. Recognizing the great antagonism among these new states, the French contemplated first economic *rapprochement* only, but hoped that later political collaboration would follow. Mr. Praznovszky warned his superiors in his report on this conversation not to expect the restitution of St. Stephen's Kingdom from the French, who were seeking to solve the problem of Southeastern Europe, rather than to restore Hungary's territorial integrity.

[19] See M. Fouchet to Count Teleki, June 5, 1920. *Supra,* note 15.

High Commissioner, as M. Fouchet suggested, and a way had to be found which, while keeping within the requirements of Hungarian public law, would give substantial satisfaction to the French. This was found, and the French request was met by a letter which the Regent addressed to the Hungarian Foreign Minister. This letter, referring to the declaration made by M. Fouchet on May 18,[20] stated that the Regent had full knowledge of the negotiations with France and of the "program for the reparation of certain injustices in the peace treaty with the assistance of France," presented to M. Paléologue by the Hungarian plenipotentiaries, and confirmed the options which they were authorized to extend.[21] This letter, countersigned by the Prime Minister, was then transmitted to the French High Commissioner,[22] who found it satisfactory and agreed to communicate it to his government.[23] But the fact that the Hungarian Government had searched two days to find the appropriate formula for the conveyance of the Regent's confirmation led M. Fouchet to believe, and so report to Paris, that this request of the French, like the Credit Bank transaction, was being used by the Hungarians as a pretext for the abandonment of the negotiations.[24] The delivery of Admiral Horthy's confirmation quickly disproved this pessimistic conclusion on the part of the French High Commissioner;[25] but no sooner had the needed confirmation reached the French Foreign Office than objection was raised to the Regent's reference to the "program for the reparation of certain injustices in the peace treaty." This passage in the Regent's letter referred to the memorandum which Count Bethlen gave to M. Paléologue on May 12 after the preliminaries described above.[26] M. Paléologue, in a conversation with Count Csáky, claimed that he had accepted this memorandum only in his private capacity and for his own information, although he admitted that its contents had been noted and the paper placed in the official files.[27] The French were obviously consistent in their refusal to

---

[20] *Supra*, pp. 288–89.

[21] Admiral Horthy to Count Teleki, June 8, 1920. *HFR*, Vol. I, Doc. 333.

[22] Count Teleki to M. Fouchet, June 9, 1920. *Ibid.*, Doc. 336.

[23] Count Teleki to Count Csáky, June 9, 1920. *Ibid.*, Doc. 335.

[24] Count Csáky to Count Teleki, June 9, 1920. *Ibid.*, Doc. 337. According to information given by Count Saint-Sauveur to Count Csáky, the difficulty in the Credit Bank transaction and M. Fouchet's reports caused both M. Millerand and M. Paléologue to take the view that the negotiations had failed.

[25] Cf. Count Teleki to Count Csáky, June 10, 1920. *Ibid.*, Doc. 340.

[26] See *supra*, pp. 287–88.

[27] Count Csáky to Count Teleki, June 12, 1920. *HFR*, Vol. I, Doc. 351.

make definite commitments, even by implication; for in the evening of
the conclusion of the Franco-Hungarian agreement M. Fouchet formally notified Count Teleki that the French Foreign Office accepted
Count Bethlen's memorandum setting forth the Hungarian claims
solely "à titre de simple information." [28]

Thus within a few days after the signing of the peace treaty a series
of mutual suspicions and misunderstandings had brought the negotiations to an impasse. M. Millerand was reported to have come to the
conclusion that the French had been "fooled" by the Hungarians,
while the Hungarian plenipotentiaries considered the situation so
hopeless that they deemed it advisable to prepare for a quiet withdrawal from the negotiations. [29]

At this moment, however, the Hungarian Government intervened.
It gave the Credit Bank its written assurance that the transaction was
in the national interest, and the directors of the bank finally agreed to
extend to the French financiers the desired option covering their acquisition of a controlling interest in the bank. [30] Since the Regent's
guarantee, requested by the French, had already been given, the Hungarian Government took the position that all outstanding issues had
now been satisfactorily solved and that there were no longer any obstacles to the conclusion of the agreement. [31] Accordingly the Hungarian plenipotentiaries in Paris received instructions to deliver to
Count Saint-Sauveur the railway and port options, coincidentally with
the delivery of the Credit Bank option to the French financiers by a
representative of the bank. The plenipotentiaries were to obtain from
the French Government an acknowledgement of the receipt of these
options and the much-discussed declaration of France's new policy
toward Hungary. Count Teleki again urged that some tangible evidence of French support was essential for gaining the sympathy of
Hungarian public opinion. He also desired to have M. Paléologue's attention called to the desirability of initiating negotiations, contemplated under the Franco-Hungarian understanding, with Hungary's
neighbors—particularly with Rumania—as soon as possible. [32]

[28] M. Fouchet to Count Teleki, June 20, 1920. *Ibid.*, Doc. 380.
[29] Cf. Count Csáky to Count Teleki, June 9 and 12, 1920. *Ibid.*, Docs. 337, 350.
[30] See the dispatches of Count Teleki to Count Csáky, June 15 and 17, 1920. *Ibid.*,
Docs. 355, 360, 361.
[31] Count Teleki to M. Fouchet, June 18, 1920. *Ibid.*, Doc. 366.
[32] Count Teleki to Count Csáky, June 17, 1920. *Ibid.*, Doc. 361. In addition to a
reassuring statement concerning Western Hungary, already proposed by Count Csáky

The good will which the Hungarian Government showed in the case of the French demand, when it brought pressure upon the Credit Bank, was reciprocated by concessions designed to end any doubt as to the true intent of the French Government. When Count Csáky informed M. Montille, M. Paléologue's chief of cabinet, that the Credit Bank had agreed to the option, M. Montille assured him that the Principal Allied Powers, as also Hungary's neighbors, would be notified of the Franco-Hungarian understanding. M. Montille again stressed the fact that France could not go far in publicly avowing her policy, lest her allies accuse her of assisting in the emasculation of a treaty forced upon Hungary only a few days before. But, he said, the Hungarians could tear that treaty to pieces whenever they were sufficiently strong; and, when that time came, Hungary could count upon the wholehearted support of France.[33]

Another concession secured at the last minute was the omission from the final text of the French note of the phrase "within the general structure of peace" which, as was pointed out above, caused apprehension to the Hungarians.[34] They feared that such a reservation might be relied upon by Hungary's neighbors to obstruct any change, and Count Csáky succeeded in bringing M. Paléologue around to the Hungarian point of view, M. Paléologue intimating that consent to the omission of the phrase was evidence of the willingness of the French Government, if necessary, to disregard, in Hungary's favor, the "general structure of peace."[35]

The Conclusion of the Agreement

All obstacles having been cleared away, the Hungarian plenipotentiaries in Paris delivered the options to Count Saint-Sauveur and the representatives of the French financial group on June 21.[36] At the same time M. Paléologue addressed a communication to the Hungarians in which he acknowledged the options granted to the Schneider-

---

in a conversation with M. Paléologue (see *supra,* p. 292), Count Teleki suggested that concrete proof of France's good will could be offered if it took the form of some concession in military matters, in French solicitude for the fate of the Hungarian population in the detached territories, or in the designation of Budapest as the headquarters of the International Danube Commission.

[33] Count Csáky to Count Teleki, June 18, 1920. *HFR,* Vol. I, Doc. 368.

[34] See *supra,* pp. 286–87.

[35] Count Csáky to Count Teleki, June 20, 1920. *HFR,* Vol. I, Doc. 378.

[36] Count Csáky to Count Teleki, June 22, 1921. *Ibid.,* Doc. 386.

Creusot concern—there was no reference to the Credit Bank transaction—and transmitted a copy of the French note, the original of which, he stated, would be delivered to the Hungarian Government by the French representative in Budapest. M. Paléologue characterized the note as proof of the desire of the French Government to see Central Europe rededicated "to order, to work and to prosperity." [37] Following the exchange of these documents, instructions were sent at once to French diplomatic representatives abroad to inform the governments to which they were accredited of the substance of the Franco-Hungarian understanding. Count Csáky, who was shown the text of these instructions, reported that they went into the economic agreement at great length, but were vague as to the political implications.[38] The French note which M. Fouchet presented to the Hungarian Foreign Minister on June 24 read as follows:

The French Government is convinced that the prompt re-establishment of prosperity in Central Europe, which constitutes an essential condition for the consolidation of peace in general, cannot be accomplished except through the mutual collaboration of the interested States. Therefore, the French Government is ready to facilitate all conversations which may take place between the Rumanian, Czecho-Slovak and Yugoslav Governments on the one hand and the Hungarian Government on the other hand, with a view to the creation among these States and Governments of the relations of trust and confidence which are the necessary bases of such collaboration.

Faithful observer of the Treaty of Peace which bears its signature, the French Government, inspired by the declarations contained in the Covering Letter addressed by the Allied and Associated Powers to the Hungarian [Peace] Delegation, is prepared to lend its good offices to all endeavors to reach a friendly agreement between Hungary and her neighbors aiming at the elimination of all causes of hostility between the interested parties to the mutual satisfaction of all.

These endeavors would have the purpose, under the conditions indicated in the Covering Letter above referred to, on the one hand, to correct certain economic or ethnic injustices, and on the other hand, to complete the provisions already made for the protection of minorities.

Specifically, the French Government is prepared to facilitate for the Hungarian Government the initiation of conversations with the neighboring Governments to seek equitable adjustment of their relations concerning freedom of their mutual trade, freedom of railway, postal and telegraphic

[37] M. Paléologue to Count Bethlen, Count Csáky, Dr. Halmos, and Mr. Kállay, June 21, 1920. *Ibid.,* Doc. 384.
[38] Count Csáky to Count Teleki, June 22, 1920. *Ibid.,* Doc. 387.

communications, financial questions, the regime of waterways, and so forth, to the extent that such agreements are compatible with the treaties in the making of which France has participated as one of the Principal Allied and Associated Powers.

This declaration shall be effective only from the day when the [economic] agreements concluded with the French group have been approved by the Hungarian legislature.[39]

A comparison of the final text of the French note, constituting the political agreement between France and Hungary, with the summary of its first draft, as indicated by M. Paléologue to the Hungarian plenipotentiaries on May 5,[40] and with the declaration of M. Fouchet made on May 18 [41] shows that the original French position was in all essentials maintained. A careful analysis of the text indicates that France's political commitment to Hungary consisted in a promise to assist Hungary in negotiating with her neighbors for friendly settlements. The required compatibility of these prospective settlements with the peace treaty was perhaps a less severe limitation than the original reservation concerning the "general structure of peace"; but the latitude to be allowed depended upon the interpretation of the Covering Letter, which was unequivocally designated as the framework within which French support would be confined. Despite these implied or expressed reservations and their general vagueness, the importance of the French commitments, from Hungary's point of view, in the light of conditions then prevailing in Europe, must be recognized. Assuming that the French Foreign Office was sincere in the protestation of its ultimate objectives, unexpressed and undefined in the note itself, Hungary's leaders could reasonably hope for an improvement of the country's position, however gradual and slow, considering the influence which France then exercised upon the Continent and presumably would continue to exercise for some time to come. The fact that the conclusion of the agreement with France was not much advertised in Hungary and that its text had not been published was due not to any failure of the government to appreciate its potentialities, but to wise caution

---

[39] M. Fouchet to Count Teleki, June 24, 1920 (in French). *Ibid.,* Doc. 393. With respect to the last paragraph of the declaration, it will be remembered that the Hungarian Government insisted upon the necessity of parliamentary ratification of the options. See *supra,* p. 289 n. While the French agreed to this, they in turn desired to condition the validity of their political declaration upon Hungarian legislative approval of the economic concessions. Cf. Count Csáky to Count Teleki, June 20, 1920. *HFR,* Vol. I, Doc. 378.

[40] *Supra,* pp. 275–76.   [41] *Supra,* pp. 288–89.

in refraining from claiming too much success in its foreign policy and from holding out hope in the face of an uncertain future. The Hungarian Government fully realized that only the first, halting step had been taken and that a long road had to be traveled before its efforts might bring fruit.

Caution was also counseled in view of the opposition of the other Allied Powers, particularly of Great Britain, but also of Italy, which had been brought forcibly to the attention of the Hungarian Government.

Reference has already been made to British protests lodged at the beginning of June.[42] Subsequently the Acting British Commissioner in Budapest, Mr. Athelstan-Johnson, read to Count Teleki a letter from Lord Curzon stating that the Franco-Hungarian agreement, being held to violate the peace treaty, was unacceptable to the British. The British Foreign Secretary suggested that the Hungarian Government inquire of the French whether they had informed the British and the Italians of the agreement, and, if so, whether these Powers had given their approval. Lord Curzon wrote that if French statesmen had made promises to Hungary, especially relating to territorial concessions, such promises could not correspond to the true intentions of the French Government, and, in his opinion, the French "have played a shady game with the Hungarians."[43] British dissatisfaction was further evidenced by misgivings which the British minister to Austria expressed, particularly regarding the railway lease, to the Hungarian chargé d'affaires in Vienna. And in that he had also been seconded by the Italian chargé d'affaires,[44] although at first there had been no evidence of Italian opposition.[45] But it had soon become evident that the Franco-Hungarian *rapprochement* was not pleasing to the Italians. The Italian High Commissioner in Budapest, Signor Cerruti, repeatedly warned Mr. Kánya, at the end of June and in early July, that this policy had created a bad impression in Italy and Great Britain and complained that earlier Hungarian attempts to win Italy's friendship

---

[42] *Supra,* p. 294.

[43] Memorandum on British representations concerning the negotiations with France, June 30, 1920. *HFR,* Vol. I, Doc. 409.

[44] Mr. Masirevich to Count Teleki, July 4, 1920. *Ibid.,* Doc. 420.

[45] Mr. Praznovszky reported, in the middle of June, a conversation with Count Vannutelli, a member of the Italian Peace Delegation in Paris, wherein the latter expressed satisfaction over the change of French policy toward Hungary. Mr. Praznovszky to Count Teleki, June 18, 1920. *Ibid.,* Doc. 369.

had not been followed up. Mr. Kánya pointed out that the Hungarian representative in Rome had not received encouraging replies to inquiries regarding possible Italian support and that he, Kánya, was unable to see why Italy and Great Britain need turn their backs on Hungary merely because of improvement in Franco-Hungarian relations. Why, he asked, could not Italy and France coöperate? Signor Cerruti replied that such coöperation, while conceivable in theory, was impossible in practice, because only *one* Great Power could have the decisive word. Italy's policy for maintaining the balance in Central Europe was based on Bulgaria, Rumania, and Hungary; and while Italy's hands were bound as far as Rumania was concerned, this did not preclude, despite Rumanian intransigence, autonomy for Transylvania, for which Italy would be willing to exert her influence.[46]

Despite these warnings, the Hungarian Government felt that it should persist in pursuing the policy of *rapprochement* with France. As Dr. Gratz explained to his British and Italian colleagues in Vienna, Hungary would have preferred British or Italian help, but had received a concrete offer of support only from France, which she felt compelled to accept, even though the *quid pro quo* admittedly entailed heavy sacrifices. It is interesting to note that both Mr. Lindley and Signor Biancheri expressed doubt as to the ability of the French to fulfill their promises and both questioned the wisdom of handing over to France the control of Hungary's railways.[47]

This brief review of British and Italian opposition to the Franco-Hungarian plans, although somewhat anticipating subsequent developments, should be kept in mind as the background against which the Hungarian Government sought to put into effect the agreement concluded with France.

The Steps Taken to Carry the Agreement into Effect

Following the exchange of the documents in Paris, the Hungarian plenipotentiaries submitted to M. Paléologue a memorandum setting

[46] Notes of the Secretary General of the Ministry for Foreign Affairs on his conversations with the Italian High Commissioner, July 3, 1920. *Ibid.*, Doc. 415.

[47] Dr. Gratz to Count Teleki, July 9, 1920. *Ibid.*, Doc. 433. The Italians continued to express misgivings over the railway lease, which, they said, would result in the impairment of Hungary's sovereignty. See the reports of the Special Representative of the Hungarian Government in Rome, Mr. Györgyey, to Count Teleki, Aug. 12, 17, and 27, 1920. *Ibid.*, Docs. 563, 581, 617.

forth certain matters in which, quite apart from direct negotiations with her neighbors, Hungary desired the support of France. The Hungarians sought: (1) the modification of the military clauses of the Treaty of Trianon (Articles 109–10) so as to permit her to maintain the army allowed under the treaty by draft, rather than by voluntary enlistment; (2) a postponement of the evacuation of Western Hungary, which the peace treaty allotted to Austria, pending the determination of the final boundary by the Frontier Delimitation Commissions; (3) the establishment of the headquarters of the International Danube Commission in Budapest; (4) the establishment of a Hungarian section of the Reparations Commission with its seat in Budapest; (5) supervision by French diplomatic and military agents of the treatment of Hungarian minorities in the detached territories; and (6) the prompt evacuation, under Allied supervision, of Pécs and other Hungarian territories within the Trianon frontiers still under Yugoslav or Rumanian occupation.[48]

The French position with respect to the issues raised by the Hungarian memorandum was conveyed orally to Count Csáky a few days later by M. Laroche, assistant director of the Political Department of the French Foreign Office, then in charge of Hungarian matters. His answers indicated the complications and difficulties attending the satisfaction of even these comparatively modest claims.

With respect to the military question, M. Paléologue was unable to promise immediate support and counseled patience until the issue might be raised under more favorable circumstances. It was explained that while the French disapproved on principle of the system of voluntary enlistment, they were unable to win over the British to this point of view. Since a similar request by Bulgaria had been rejected recently, Hungary would have very little chance of obtaining the same concession, especially as the Allies were reluctant to create a precedent for a change in the military restrictions imposed in any of the peace treaties, lest Germany should invoke it in her own favor. Concerning Western Hungary, M. Laroche promised that France would oppose any movement to enforce the surrender of this territory by Hungary prior to the ratification of the Treaty of Trianon, even though France, a signatory of both the Austrian and Hungarian peace treaties, could not openly advocate a radical alteration of their provisions. Unreserved support was promised with respect to the seat of the International Danube

[48] The French text of this memorandum is printed in full, *ibid.*, Doc. 405(a).

Commission and to a Hungarian section of the Reparations Commission. The French also agreed to instruct their representatives to interest themselves in the fate of Hungarian minorities living in Czecho-Slovakia, Rumania, and Yugoslavia and to bring about the early evacuation of Hungarian territories occupied by the Yugoslavs and the Rumanians. But M. Laroche confessed that the evacuation of Pécs and Baranya would not be a simple matter, because of an agreement between the Allies and Yugoslavia under which the Yugoslavs were not compelled to evacuate these territories until three months after the ratification of the peace treaty.[49]

However, these matters were of slight importance in comparison with the objectives Hungary hoped to accomplish through direct negotiations with her neighbors, negotiations which France agreed to facilitate. Apparently the French Foreign Office made inquiries immediately after the conclusion of the Franco-Hungarian agreement. The form and content of these inquiries is not known; but the Hungarians were informed early in July that the Czecho-Slovak and Yugoslav Governments were "enthusiastic" about the idea of direct negotiations with Hungary under French auspices.[50] The Rumanian reaction, in which Hungary appeared to be most interested,[51] was also reported to be favorable, although more reserved than the response of the two other governments, and it was accompanied by an expression of hope that France would not participate in the negotiations as Hungary's ally.[52] But the date when the opening of negotiations might be expected appeared to be distant. Indeed just about this time dark clouds began to gather on the European scene. The critical turn of the Polish-Soviet war inevitably affected diplomacy throughout Europe. With particular reference to Hungary, it lent immediate reality to the policy

---

[49] Count Csáky to Count Teleki, June 28, 1920. *Ibid.*, Doc. 405. This was the first that Hungary had learned of such an agreement between the Allies and the Yugoslavs. Mr. Praznovszky was instructed to ascertain whether such an agreement really existed (Count Teleki to Mr. Praznovszky, July 3, 1920. *Ibid.*, Doc. 416), but he did not succeed in obtaining precise information. Subsequent representations urging the evacuation of these territories were sidetracked by M. Paléologue, who claimed that the matter was within the jurisdiction of the Conference of Ambassadors. These evasions were felt to confirm assertions coming from Italian sources that the French in this respect supported the Yugoslavs. Mr. Praznovszky to Count Teleki, July 26, 1920 (two dispatches). *Ibid.*, Docs. 501, 506.

[50] Mr. Praznovszky to Count Teleki, July 3, 1920. *Ibid.*, Doc. 418.

[51] Cf. Count Teleki to Mr. Praznovszky, July 7, 1920. *Ibid.*, Doc. 426.

[52] Mr. Praznovszky to Count Teleki, July 14, 1920. *Ibid.*, Doc. 455.

of *rapprochement* which Hungary and Poland had cautiously pursued for some time;[53] and, for the time being, it became the controlling factor in Franco-Hungarian relations, based on the Paléologue agreement. It is at this point that the relationship between the Franco-Hungarian negotiations and the informal conversations of the Hungarian plenipotentiaries with the Polish Foreign Minister, which took place in Paris at the beginning of May, became relevant.

The Effects of the Polish-Soviet War

It will be remembered that one of the claims Hungary put forward, both through its Peace Delegation and in the course of the secret negotiations with France, was a demand for the relaxing of the disarmament provisions of the peace treaty. The Peace Conference had made no concessions in this respect, and France, as indicated, was reluctant to support the Hungarian aspiration for more and better armament than that allowed her by the peace treaty. This reluctance may have been due to a lack of faith in the Hungarians; or to fear that concessions granted to any of the former Central Powers might create an undesirable precedent that would be invoked by Germany; or to influences which outweighed that of M. Paléologue and his associates, who sought to base French policy in Southeastern Europe on Hungary; or to a combination of any of these factors. Hungary's insistence on this issue had been construed by her adversaries as evidence of her aggressive intentions to recover from her neighbors by force what she might fail to regain at the conference table. A more plausible explanation might be found in the state of Eastern Europe at that period—particularly the presence of a hostile bolshevik army in the vicinity of Hungary—and a feeling of insecurity among the Hungarians, which grew in proportion to the increasing armed strength of their unfriendly neighbors.

When the concrete question of Hungary's rearmament was raised in the course of a conversation between M. Paléologue and Dr. Halmos at the end of April, the French diplomat suggested that Hungary should seek the intervention of the Polish Government. Although at that time the Polish Army was advancing in the Ukraine, Poland was more immediately interested in securing support for her fight against bolshevism than were the other European powers; and M. Paléologue apparently proceeded on the theory that the French would have an

[53] *Supra,* pp. 201–3, 215–18.

easier task if the initiative for strengthening Hungary should come from a quarter which might actually need help. M. Paléologue, in fact, arranged a meeting between Mr. Patek, the Polish Foreign Minister, then in Paris, and Dr. Halmos,[54] as a result of which Count Bethlen and Count Csáky sought and obtained authority to enter into semi-official conversations with Mr. Patek.[55] The opportunity to discuss coöperation with Poland was welcomed by Budapest as one concrete benefit which Hungary had derived from the negotiations with France.[56] Conversations with Mr. Patek in Paris did not go beyond generalities, but he expressed a willingness to enter into negotiations with Hungary, and accordingly Count Csáky suggested that the ground should be prepared for the continuation of conversations in Warsaw.[57] This suggestion was followed, and as a result the Hungarian representative in Warsaw, Count Csekonics—who was recalled to Budapest for consultation—was, immediately after the signature of the Trianon Treaty, dispatched to Warsaw with a personal letter from the Regent of Hungary to Marshal Pilsudski, the President of Poland.

Admiral Horthy's letter called for the close coöperation of Poland and Hungary and expressed the hope of attaining a common frontier. To create the atmosphere necessary for such coöperation, the Regent frankly noted the existence of the common interests of Poland and Rumania, stated his willingness to compose differences between Hungary and Rumania in the interest of Polish-Hungarian friendship, and requested Marshal Pilsudski's good offices for the improvement of Hungarian-Rumanian relations.[58]

[54] Count Csáky to Count Teleki, May 3, 1920. *HFR,* Vol. I, Doc. 255.
[55] Mr. Praznovszky to Count Teleki, May 6, 1920. *Ibid.,* Doc. 260; Count Teleki to Count Csáky, May 7, 1920. *Ibid.,* Doc. 267.
[56] Count Teleki to Count Csáky, May 11, 1920. *Ibid.,* Doc. 276.
[57] Count Csáky to Count Teleki, May 12, 1920 (two dispatches). *Ibid.,* Docs. 281, 282.
[58] Admiral Horthy to Marshal Pilsudski, June 6, 1920. *Ibid.,* Doc. 321 (in French). This important letter reads, in English, as follows:
"At the end of the world crisis and at the dawn of the day on which Poland and Hungary have regained their independence, I hasten to convey to Your Excellency, together with my warmest greetings, the deep sympathy and affection of the whole Hungarian nation.
"Barely had Hungary recovered the control over her own destiny when her thoughts turned to the sister nation with whom, during the most brilliant period of our history, we were linked in intimate and unswerving friendship.
"I am convinced that this traditional friendship will persist in the future as it has in the past, for history itself imposes this unalterable necessity. Poland and Hungary

The instructions issued to Count Csekonics, entrusted with the delivery of the Regent's letter to the President of Poland, show conclusively that Hungary's offer to deal with Rumania originated in and related directly to the Franco-Hungarian negotiations, which, as we have seen, contemplated *rapprochement,* in the first place, between Hungary and Rumania. Count Csekonics was authorized to inform Marshal Pilsudski of the conditions under which, in the opinion of the Hungarian Government, relations between Hungary and Rumania could be put on a friendlier basis; these conditions followed basically those outlined in the course of the Franco-Hungarian conversations.[59] The Hungarian representative also was empowered to inform Marshal Pilsudski that he might have the use for bargaining purposes of a sum of nine billion crowns for which, the Hungarian Government understood, Rumania had been assessed by the Allies for the spoliation of Hungary.[60]

When Count Csekonics arrived in Warsaw, Poland was in the midst

---

having regained their independence, the community of interest which in times past bound them together, will be reborn.

"I am equally convinced that in the present political structure of Europe, close collaboration alone can assure to these two States the road of salvation. In such collaboration Poland will find the possibility of consolidating the position she has acquired, thanks to her brilliant and sustained efforts; Hungary, on her part, will seek to consolidate the bases of her national renaissance.

"United in feeling as in the past, our two nations have been forced to renounce their historic, common frontier. I firmly hope that justice will in the near future redress the wrong done to Hungary, by eliminating the artificial barriers between two nations whose hearts beat in unison.

"On the other hand, the diversity of relations which compose the lives of nations imposes on us the duty of respecting the particular interests of our friends.

"It is not a secret to me that in a number of questions relating to Eastern Europe the interests of Poland and Rumania are also to some extent analogous. In order to facilitate, in the field of general policy, collaboration between Poland and Hungary, the Hungarian Government is prepared to seek a satisfactory solution of the numerous difficulties which now separate Hungary and Rumania.

"I would be particularly grateful if Your Excellency's kind and doubtless effective intervention with the Rumanian Government should succeed in inducing that Power to adopt toward its citizens of Hungarian blood, as well as toward Hungary, a more friendly policy."

[59] Cf. Dr. Halmos's original memorandum, *supra,* pp. 264–66; M. Paléologue's note of April 15, *supra,* pp. 266–68; Dr. Halmos's memorandum of April 23, *supra,* pp. 271–72; and Count Bethlen's memorandum of May 12, *supra,* pp. 287–88, with the instructions to Count Csekonics, dated June 6, 1920. *HFR,* Vol. I, Doc. 322.

[60] Information regarding the assessment of Rumania was given to Count Csekonics by the Polish Foreign Minister just before he left Warsaw for Budapest at the end of May. It was only subsequently that Count Csekonics learned the source and authenticity

of a government crisis, but he was nevertheless received by the President on June 19 and he then presented the Regent's letter. According to Count Csekonics's report, Pilsudski appreciated the Regent's initiative and was particularly pleased with Hungary's realization of the importance of Rumania from Poland's point of view. Replying to the suggestion that Poland and Hungary ought to conclude a formal agreement, Marshal Pilsudski promised to support such a step, but stated that many difficulties might have to be overcome.[61] Count Csekonics also expressed Hungary's willingness to extend armed assistance to

---

of this information. During the presentation of the Regent's letter, Marshal Pilsudski stated that he had sent, a few weeks earlier, General Rozwadowski to Bucharest as his personal emissary to King Ferdinand, to intervene in Hungary's interest. The King had told Rozwadowski that the Allies had assessed Rumania for nine billion crowns for the damage caused to Hungary by requisitions during the occupation. While the Rumanians succeeded in obtaining an indefinite postponement of payment, they were eager to be relieved of this theoretical debt, if Hungary could be induced to abandon her claims. According to Marshal Pilsudski, the Allies intended to have these payments go to the reparations account, and for that reason Hungary was not even informed of the assessment. See Count Csekonics to Count Teleki, June 21, 1920. *Ibid.*, Doc. 383.

[61] The difficulties referred to undoubtedly related to Poland's dependence on the Principal Allied Powers. An indication of the extent to which Poland's policies toward the ex-enemy powers was governed by considerations of the attitude of the Great Powers can be found in her reluctance to extend *de jure* recognition to Hungary. Such a request was addressed to the Polish Government immediately after the signature of the peace treaty. Count Csekonics to Count Teleki, June 14, 1920. *Ibid.*, Doc. 354. Although Hungarian factories had been supplying Poland with war matériel for months (naturally with the permission of the Allies), the reply of the Polish Foreign Office was that the request must be examined. When Count Csekonics raised the issue with Prince Sapieha, the Foreign Minister of the newly formed Polish Government stated that while he would at once recognize Hungary, Poland was forced to take her cue from the Allies and hence could not extend recognition until the peace treaty was ratified. Count Csekonics to Count Teleki, July 10, 1920. *Ibid.*, Doc. 441. It is to be noted that the attitude of the Allies swayed not only countries in such a precarious position as Poland found herself, but also neutral European governments. The endeavor of the Hungarian Government to gain from neutral states formal recognition as an independent Hungary (see the instructions of Count Teleki to Hungarian representatives in Vienna, The Hague, and Copenhagen dated May 26, 1920. *Ibid.*, Doc. 298) had had immediate results only in the case of Spain. See the communication of the Spanish chargé d'affaires in Vienna to the Minister of Hungary in Vienna, July 19, 1920. *Ibid.*, Doc. 472. While Argentina expressed her willingness promptly to recognize Hungary (Dr. Gratz to Count Teleki, July 14, 1920. *Ibid.*, Doc. 454), the European neutrals delayed recognition, apparently in deference to the Allies, until much later. Thus Switzerland extended *de jure* recognition to Hungary only on Oct. 12 (Baron Bornemisza to Count Emery Csáky, Oct. 14, 1920. *Ibid.*, Doc. 713), the Netherlands on Nov. 13 (Mr. Máriássy to Count Csáky, Nov. 13, 1920. *Ibid.*, Doc. 794), and the Scandinavian States on Nov. 12 (Mr. Barcza to Count Csáky, Nov. 12, 1920. *Ibid.*, Doc. 792; Dr. Gratz to Count Csáky, Nov. 14, 1920. *Ibid.*, Doc. 796; Count Csáky to Dr.

Poland, within the limits of her own inadequate equipment. Marshal Pilsudski was much interested in this offer and in the collateral problem of the reëquipment of the Hungarian Army and asked the Hungarian representative to discuss the matter with the Polish Army's commander of reserves. The interview with General Sosnkowski took place two days later, and it appears from Count Csekonics's report that the General regarded Hungary as a potential ally. The possibility of a military convention was apparently discussed, and General Sosnkowski expressed his willingness to help to strengthen the Hungarian Army by placing orders for armament in Italy.[62] The receptive mood of Polish military circles can easily be understood, considering Poland's position. While the Russian offensive, launched on May 14, had been halted and the Poles had succeeded, about the end of June, in regaining the positions from which they had retreated under the first impact, their shortage of ammunition and supplies was acute. Indeed, on the eve of the second, almost fatal Russian attack, General Sosnkowski appealed urgently for delivery of munitions ordered earlier in Hungary and asked that the Hungarians expedite matters by delivering shipments to the Rumanian border.[63] On the following day, July 4, the Russians began their new onslaught, which brought the Soviet Armies in a little over a month's time to the gates of Warsaw. The break through of the Polish defense line was viewed with apprehension by Allied statesmen, just gathering for one of their periodical conferences at Spa; and with even greater dread by Hungary. In reply to the Polish appeal for more munitions, the Hungarian Government immediately put at Poland's disposal the whole accumulated ammunition reserve of the Hungarian Army and gave orders to the only munitions factory in operation in Hungary to devote its entire facilities for two weeks to the production of ammunition for Poland.[64] In compliance with an

Gratz, Nov. 16, 1920. *Ibid.,* Doc. 802). Finland, on the other hand, formally recognized Hungary on Sept. 10. See the communication of the Finnish Minister for Foreign Affairs, Mr. Holsti, to Mr. Barcza, Sept. 10, 1920. *Ibid.,* Doc. 648.

[62] Count Csekonics to Count Teleki, June 26, 1920. *Ibid.,* Doc. 401.

[63] Count Csekonics to Count Teleki, July 3, 1920. *Ibid.,* Doc. 417. One of the difficulties in supplying Poland was caused by the hostility or indifference of two of her neighbors. Although Germany and Czecho-Slovakia did not formally declare their neutrality until the latter part of July and early in August respectively, they both refused to coöperate with the Allies in their effort to assist Poland. In the case of Czecho-Slovakia, her unwillingness to let Hungary give assistance to Poland may have been due rather to her distrust of Hungary than to hostility to Poland. Cf. *infra,* pp. 319 ff.

[64] Count Teleki to Count Csekonics, July 8, 1920. HFR, Vol. I, Doc. 432.

earlier request of the Polish Government,[65] the Hungarian Government gave its consent to the transportation through Hungary of ammunition supplied to Poland by the Allies (these supplies came largely through Italy), under the supervision of Polish guards.[66] But by this time Poland was in need of more than supplies. While the Polish Prime Minister and Foreign Minister sped to Spa to appeal for Allied intervention on the side of Poland, Polish military authorities appealed to Hungary for a contribution of man power. The appeal was quite specific, asking for cavalry troops to the number of twenty to thirty thousand.[67] The Hungarian Government at once replied that while it was eager to help Poland, there were difficulties of a practical nature to be overcome. The cavalry desired by the Poles was for the moment not available, on account of the shortage of horses. But a smaller contingent of cavalry and other troops of strategic importance could be sent in a short time, provided that equipment could be obtained from the Allies. As to the feasibility of the suggestion that these troops might be transported through Rumania, the Hungarians expressed doubts, fearing that the Rumanians would interfere with their passage.[68] Hungarian military experts were immediately sent to Warsaw to discuss technical details of the assistance Hungary could render, while Polish diplomats began to explore the means whereby the Allies could be induced to make Hungary's help available.

The Boycott against Hungary

Lack of equipment and of Allied consent to equip an army were, however, not the only obstacles that kept Hungary from helping Po-

[65] Count Szembek to Count Teleki, June 20, 1920. *Ibid.,* Doc. 379.

[66] Count Teleki to Count Szembek, July 10, 1920. *Ibid.,* Doc. 437.

[67] Count Csekonics to Count Teleki, July 10, 1920. *Ibid.,* Doc. 438. This appeal was reinforced by a cordial reply by Marshal Pilsudski to Admiral Horthy's letter, quoted above. In this reply, the President of Poland assured the Regent that the Polish nation reciprocated the friendly feelings of the Hungarian people and that the Polish Government would do everything in its power to reconcile the differences between Hungary and Rumania, since the coöperation of these three powers would clearly serve the interest of peace in Eastern Europe. Marshal Pilsudski to Admiral Horthy, July 10, 1920. *Ibid.,* Doc. 440. Similar assurances had been given to Count Csekonics by the new Polish Foreign Minister, the day before. Prince Sapieha had told Count Csekonics that the only conceivable policy for Poland was an alliance with Hungary and Rumania, under French auspices. Count Csekonics to Count Teleki, July 10, 1920. *Ibid.,* Doc. 441. Concerning the background of the Polish request for military assistance see Count Csekonics to Count Teleki, July 24, 1920. *Ibid.,* Doc. 496.

[68] Count Teleki to Count Csekonics, July 13, 1920. *Ibid.,* Doc. 445.

land. An international boycott of labor organizations against Hungary, that had threatened since early spring, was put into effect about the time the Soviet Armies began to prepare their offensive. This boycott, one of the most astounding incidents in European postwar history, warrants a brief digression.

The boycott was organized by the International Confederation of Labor, commonly known as the "Second Internationale," with headquarters at Amsterdam, as a retaliation for the alleged persecution of labor by the Hungarian authorities.[69] The Confederation disclaimed all connection with the Communists, directed by the so-called "Third Internationale" with headquarters at Moscow; yet, by a curious coincidence, the boycott was put into effect just when it could render the greatest service to Soviet Russia. Attempts on the part of the Hungarian Government to avert the boycott were unsuccessful [70] and it went into effect on June 20.

Apart from disrupting the flow of needed raw materials from the

[69] The Bureau of the Confederation sent the Hungarian Government a resolution adopted early in March, 1920, threatening to boycott Hungary unless her alleged mistreatment of labor and the "white terror" ceased. For the text of the communication, dated March 10, 1920, and of the resolution see *ibid.,* Docs. 181, 181(a). The Hungarian Government, which from the outset took the position that it could not regard the Amsterdam organization as a sovereign agency, left this communication unanswered. A protest, apparently inspired by the Confederation, from the Parliamentary Committee of the British Trade Union Congress, dated March 12, 1920 (*ibid.,* Doc. 183) was, however, countered a few days later by an invitation from the Prime Minister to send an investigating committee to Hungary (*ibid.,* Doc. 190). No reply to this invitation can be found in the Hungarian archives.

[70] On May 1, 1920, Count Teleki invited the International Labor Office to send a fact-finding commission to Hungary; in acknowledging the invitation, the Director agreed to submit the matter to the next meeting of the Administrative Council. Mr. Albert Thomas to Count Teleki, May 25, 1920. *Ibid.,* Doc. 296. The offer of the I.L.O. Council to make an inquiry into the situation of labor organizations in Hungary was received in Budapest after the boycott had been put into effect. Mr. Thomas to Count Teleki, July 4, 1920. *Ibid.,* Doc. 421. The Hungarian Government took the view that an inquiry was then inopportune, in view of public opinion, irritated by the prominent part played by Austrian labor organizations in the boycott. As the commission proposed by Mr. Thomas included an Austrian labor leader, the government suggested that the inquiry be postponed. Count Teleki to Baron Bornemisza, July 31, 1920. *Ibid.,* Doc. 525. After the termination of the boycott, the Hungarian Government promptly gave its consent to the dispatch of a commission. Count Teleki to Baron Bornemisza, Sept. 2, 1920. *Ibid.,* Doc. 626. The Hungarian Government also tried in vain to enlist the assistance of the Allied Powers in averting the boycott. See the memorandum of the Prime Minister and of the Foreign Minister to the British, French, and Italian representatives in Budapest, dated June 15, 1920. *Ibid.,* Doc. 356.

west, the boycott put a further strain on the already unhappy relations between Hungary and Austria. The Hungarians suspected that the whole boycott movement was suggested to the Confederation by Austrian labor organizations, whose leaders, it was believed, were inspired by exiled Hungarian communists residing in Austria.[71] Whether or not this suspicion was justified, we do not know; but the prominent part played by Austrian labor in enforcing the boycott was noted in Hungary, and the somewhat equivocal position taken by the Austrian Government did not help to allay such suspicion.

Immediately upon the imposition of the boycott, Chancellor Renner offered to mediate, an offer which was accepted with reservation by Hungary.[72] Accordingly Dr. Renner proposed that meetings be held in Vienna;[73] this was accepted by the Amsterdam Bureau,[74] and the Hungarian Government authorized its minister in Vienna to furnish information to the representatives of the Confederation, without, however, entering into negotiations with them.[75]

The first meeting took place in Vienna on June 28, and, despite some difficulties,[76] several conversations took place, but without producing any results. Chancellor Renner sought to induce Dr. Gratz to make some concession, and apparently also requested the British minister in Vienna, Mr. Lindley, to prevail on the Hungarian representative, but without success. The Hungarian Government was unwilling to treat with the International Confederation of Labor on a basis of equal-

[71] Cf. Dr. Gratz to Count Teleki, July 7, 1920. *Ibid.,* Doc. 429.

[72] The original offer of Dr. Renner was mediation between the Hungarian Government and the leaders of the Hungarian trade unions. Dr. Gratz to Count Teleki, June 19, 1920. *Ibid.,* Doc. 372. This offer was declined by the Hungarian Government as unacceptable interference in domestic affairs; the government expressed its willingness, however, to furnish information on the situation in Hungary to representatives of the Confederation, which would make it plain that rumors giving certain reasons for the decision to boycott were unfounded. Dr. Gratz to Chancellor Renner, June 19, 1920; Count Teleki to Dr. Gratz, June 20, 1920. *Ibid.,* Docs. 375, 376.

[73] Dr. Gratz to Count Teleki, June 20, 1920. *Ibid.,* Doc. 377.

[74] Chancellor Renner to Dr. Gratz, June 24, 1920. *Ibid.,* Doc. 394.

[75] Count Teleki to Dr. Gratz, June 26, 1920. *Ibid.,* Doc. 399.

[76] The Secretary General of the Amsterdam Bureau handed to Dr. Gratz at the end of the first meeting a memorandum setting forth the "demands" of the Confederation. *Ibid.,* Doc. 406(a). Thereupon Dr. Gratz informed Chancellor Renner that he could no longer participate in the meetings. Dr. Gratz to Chancellor Renner, June 28, 1920. *Ibid.,* Doc. 406. The Chancellor succeeded in smoothing the matter over, and Dr. Gratz attended the afternoon meeting. Dr. Gratz to Count Teleki, June 29, 1920. *Ibid.,* Doc. 407.

ity and to abandon its intransigent position.[77] Thus the boycott continued, inflicting hardship not only on Hungary but also on the neighboring countries, particularly Austria. Indeed soon after the boycott was put into effect the Hungarian Government informed the Allied representatives in Budapest that it would resort to reprisals against neighboring countries which participated therein.[78] The closing of the Hungarian border against the movement of goods as well as of persons, which had been decreed by Budapest, primarily affected Austria, which was as much if not more dependent on the uninterrupted flow of foodstuffs from the Balkans as was Hungary upon the coal, salt, and other raw materials supplied from the west. The Austrian Government, disclaiming any responsibility for the participation of Austrian labor organizations in the boycott, immediately protested against these restrictive measures.[79] Hungary, invoking the right of self-defense, emphatically rejected the protest and replied to the disclaimer of responsibility by pointing out that employees of Austrian state-owned-and-operated enterprises, such as the railways, post, and telegraph, were playing a prominent part in the boycott.[80]

Hungary, on her part, protested to the Danube Commission against Austrian interference with international river traffic as violating the peace treaty and threatened to hold up food shipments from the Balkans to Austria unless the Austrians ceased to obstruct the down-river traffic.[81] The President of the Danube Commission, Admiral Troubridge, did attempt to prevent interference with international river

[77] See Dr. Gratz to Count Teleki, July 1 and 2, 1920. *Ibid.*, Docs. 411, 413.

[78] Count Teleki to the Allied representatives and the Commissioner of the United States in Budapest, June 22, 1920. *Ibid.*, Doc. 385.

[79] Chancellor Renner to Dr. Gratz, June 24, 1920. *Ibid.*, Doc. 394. This was followed by another protest against the closing of the Austro-Hungarian border to passenger traffic. The Austrian Legation in Budapest to the Hungarian Ministry for Foreign Affairs, July 5, 1920. *Ibid.*, Doc. 423.

[80] Dr. Gratz to Chancellor Renner, June 25, 1920. *Ibid.*, Doc. 398. Cf. the Hungarian Ministry for Foreign Affairs to the Austrian Legation at Budapest, July 13, 1920. *Ibid.*, Doc. 446. It may be noted that the Hungarian Government at no time accepted the contention that the Austrian Government was not responsible for the participation of Austrian labor organizations in the boycott. See Mr. Masirevich to Count Teleki, July 20 and 26, 1920, reporting on his interviews with Chancellor Renner. *Ibid.*, Docs. 474, 500. And cf. Count Teleki's statement to the Hungarian Parliament, July 22, 1920. *Ibid.*, Appendix 3, No. 5, p. 977.

[81] Count Teleki to Mr. Praznovszky, July 7, 1920. *Ibid.*, Doc. 427. There were also direct negotiations between Hungary and Austria, undertaken with a view to exempting Danube traffic from the boycott; but without success. Dr. Gratz to Count Teleki, July 7 and 15, 1920. *Ibid.*, Docs. 429, 458.

traffic.[82] But in the end he had to acknowledge that he had failed.[83]

By the middle of July it became evident that the boycott was far less effective than its devisers had been counting on. While it doubtless caused much inconvenience in Hungary, it failed fully to paralyze the country's economic activities. The hardships inflicted upon Austria's people indeed seemed to constitute the worst part of the boycott, and by that time Austrian labor organizations were reported to be urging Amsterdam to end it.[84] If the purpose of the boycott was, as many Hungarian officials believed, to keep Hungary from helping Poland, it must be held to have largely failed. It did not materially interfere with Hungarian deliveries to Poland and even less with Hungary's diplomatic activities, then seeking to enlarge the scope of the assistance that was to be extended to her friend.[85]

The French Attitude toward Hungarian Armed Assistance to Poland

Undisturbed by the above events and in view of the steady advance of the Soviet Armies, the Hungarian Government decided once more to bring up, in Paris, the question of rearmament. Reports from the Hungarian representative indicated that the French regarded Poland's situation as being very serious, and, as a result, the opposition to M. Paléologue's friendly policy toward Hungary had quieted down. In parliamentary circles particularly, the Soviet victories created consternation, and an appeal to the Czechs and Hungarians to join the

[82] Dr. Gratz to Count Teleki, July 7, 1920. *Ibid.*, Doc. 430. Count Teleki to Dr. Gratz, July 10, 1920. *Ibid.*, Doc. 436.

[83] In a communication requesting the Hungarian Government to refrain from reprisals, he stated that the Austrian Government was "incapable of contending" with the International Confederation of Labor. Admiral Troubridge to Count Teleki, July 16, 1920. *Ibid.*, Doc. 462. Two protests, lodged with the Conference of Ambassadors (see Mr. Praznovszky to Count Teleki, July 15. *Ibid.*, Doc. 459; Count Teleki to Mr. Praznovszky, July 27, 1920. *Ibid.*, Doc. 508), do not seem to have evoked any response.

[84] Dr. Gratz to Count Teleki, July 14, 1920. *Ibid.*, Doc. 453.

[85] The boycott formally collapsed on Aug. 8. See Count Teleki to Mr. Masirevich, Aug. 10, 1920. *Ibid.*, Doc. 551. It is interesting to note that the French minister in Vienna, M. Lefèvre-Pontalis, repeatedly endorsed the intransigent position of Hungary. The British minister in Vienna also was credited with disapproving generally, though perhaps less strongly, of the boycott movement. The Italian representative, Signor Biancheri, on the other hand, seems to have taken a noncommittal view. Cf. Dr. Gratz to Count Teleki, July 12, 1920. *Ibid.*, Doc. 444; Mr. Masirevich to Count Teleki, July 30 and Aug. 7, 1920. *Ibid.*, Docs. 520, 548.

fight against bolshevism was reported to be under consideration.[86] Upon receipt of these reports, Count Teleki instructed Mr. Praznovszky to call M. Paléologue's attention to the situation created by the Soviet victories and to inquire confidentially whether, in view of the dangers threatening Europe, the French Government had not changed its views, as expressed by M. Laroche at the end of June,[87] and whether it would not be willing to support Hungary's request for a relaxation of military restrictions. Specifically, Hungary was trying to obtain the assistance of the Allies in equipping seven infantry and one cavalry divisions, so as to be able to coöperate effectively with Poland in the struggle with Soviet Russia.[88]

When Mr. Praznovszky called upon M. Paléologue, he found that the French diplomat sympathized with Hungary's position, but was reluctant to express an opinion without discussing the matter with M. Millerand after the latter's return from Spa, where the possibility of Hungarian military assistance was also, in all likelihood, under discussion.[89] But the views of the French Government were not made known to Hungary until a week later, and, as before, the issue was evaded. Apparently expecting that the proposal of an armistice, made by the Spa Conference, would be accepted by Russia, M. Millerand's opinion, as conveyed through M. Paléologue, was that while Hungary's rearmament might be discussed in view of the bolshevik danger, the time had not yet arrived to do anything in this respect. M. Millerand did not seem to share the Hungarian and Polish view that the danger was imminent and that the situation called for prompt action. At any rate, M. Paléologue told Mr. Praznovszky that the Soviet Armies were worn out. Also Mr. Praznovszky was informed that in any event the whole matter had been referred to the special Anglo-French Mission sent to Warsaw and that the question of Hungarian assistance would be examined in the light of reports from this Mission.[90]

[86] Mr. Praznovszky to Count Teleki, July 11, 1920 (two dispatches). *Ibid.*, Docs. 442, 443. Cf. also Mr. Praznovszky to Count Teleki, July 24, 1920. *Ibid.*, Doc. 492.

[87] See *supra*, pp. 304–5.

[88] Count Teleki to Mr. Praznovszky, July 14, 1920. *HFR*, Vol. I, Doc. 451.

[89] Mr. Praznovszky to Count Teleki, July 19, 1920. *Ibid.*, Doc. 471.

[90] Mr. Praznovszky to Count Teleki, July 26, 1920. *Ibid.*, Doc. 501. In addition to trying to arrange an armistice between Poland and Russia, the British and the French statesmen agreed at Spa to send this joint commission to Warsaw. The principal members of the Mission were Lord D'Abernon, British ambassador to Germany; Major General Sir Percy Radcliffe, Director of Military Operations at the British War Office; M. Jusserand, from the Quai d'Orsay; and General Weygand, Marshal Foch's Chief

It would seem, however, that the Anglo-French Mission in Poland did not look with favor on Hungary's offer of assistance. The Poles, pressed hard by the advancing Soviet Army, pleaded in vain that their neighbor be allowed to come to their aid. A British member of the Mission was, in fact, reported to have been willing to accept Hungary's offer, only with the idea of discovering what equipment the Hungarian Army still possessed. Information confidentially conveyed to the Hungarian representative in Warsaw indicated that the negative attitude of the Czechs was influencing the views of the Mission and led him to report that "the Allies are more interested in Hungary's disarmament than in the help we can extend to Poland." [91] The importance of immediate military assistance was reiterated by the Polish Foreign Minister in an interview with Count Csekonics on July 31. The Polish Foreign Minister revealed to him that the reply to an inquiry sent to Paris by M. Jusserand, chairman of the Anglo-French Mission, was encouraging and that he intended to obtain, through the French, guarantees for the unhindered passage of Hungarian troops through Czecho-Slovakia.[92]

The Hungarians replied to this new appeal that they could participate in military operations beyond their frontiers only if the Allied countries or Poland would provide equipment for their troops.[93] Even without being urged on by Poland, the approach of the Soviet Army to

---

of Staff. The Mission, which reached Warsaw on July 25, traveled through Prague, where it conferred with Czech statesmen, whom it found not too friendly toward Poland and insistent on strict neutrality. Cf. D'Abernon, *An Ambassador's Diary,* I, 74–75.

[91] Count Csekonics to Count Teleki, July 28 (two dispatches) and 30, 1920. *HFR,* Vol. I, Docs. 509, 510, 518.

[92] Count Csekonics to Count Teleki, July 31, 1920. *Ibid.,* Doc. 526. A detailed report on this important conversation makes it plain that Prince Sapieha was trying to obtain precise information as to the help Hungary could extend to Poland and as to what was expected from Poland in exchange for past and prospective assistance. As to the first question, the Hungarian representative emphasized the point that Poland must obtain from the Allies a relaxation of the provision of the peace treaty, and, with it, equipment for the troops Hungary was willing to send to Poland; he also pointed out that their transportation could take place across Czecho-Slovakia only under Allied control of the railways. As to the second point, Count Csekonics stated that Hungary did not set a price upon her assistance, one of the axioms of her foreign policy being coöperation with Poland. The Polish Foreign Minister expressed doubt as to France's willingness to disregard the Czechs and, instead, to base her policy on Polish-Hungarian coöperation. Count Csekonics to Count Teleki, Aug. 4, 1920. *Ibid.,* Doc. 538.

[93] Count Teleki to Count Csekonics, Aug. 1, 1920. *Ibid.,* Doc. 528.

Lemberg increased the uneasiness in Hungary, and Mr. Praznovszky was again instructed to stress, to the French Government, the necessity of allowing Hungary to arm herself. Should Lemberg fall, the Russians would have a free passage to the Carpathians, then in the hands of the Czechs; and, the Hungarians feared, the Czechs and the Austrians would both join forces with the Soviets, thus converting the inadequately protected northern and northeastern borders of Hungary into a bolshevik front.[94]

The Hungarian Government, however, had one reason to hope that, apart from strategic considerations, its latest appeal for French support would be more sympathetically received, for there seemed now to be a promise of further progress toward the realization of the Franco-Hungarian agreement. Count Saint-Sauveur, representing the Schneider-Creusot interests, was returning to Paris at the end of July after an extended stay in Hungary, during which he had explored the ways and means whereby the Franco-Hungarian agreements might best be made operative. Budapest believed that he had been satisfied with the results of his mission and was returning with the intention of putting the agreements into operation.[95] When taking his leave, he had told Count Teleki that in order to accomplish this, he would have to solve three distinct problems in Paris: that of bringing about the beginning of negotiations between Hungary and Rumania; that of urging the necessity of Hungary's rearmament, in the interest of the struggle against bolshevism; and that of convincing the French that it was most urgent that both economic assistance and political support be extended to Hungary. The Hungarian Government thus hoped that Count Saint-Sauveur might end French hesitation, and Mr. Praznovszky was instructed to impress upon M. Paléologue the imminent danger in which Hungary would find herself, should Poland, unassisted, be unable to stem the Soviet onslaught.[96]

However, Hungarian expectations remained unsatisfied. Despite the continued advance of the Soviet Armies toward the Polish capital, the Franco-Hungarian agreement was not brought any nearer realization, and the problem of Hungarian armed assistance to Poland re-

[94] Count Teleki to Mr. Praznovszky, July 31, 1920. *Ibid.,* Doc. 523.

[95] An interview which Mr. Praznovszky held with Count Saint-Sauveur shortly after the latter's arrival in Paris confirmed the belief prevalent in governmental circles in Budapest that the French industrial leader had left Hungary favorably impressed. Mr. Praznovszky to Count Teleki, Aug. 7, 1920. *Ibid.,* Doc. 547.

[96] Count Teleki to Mr. Praznovszky, July 29, 1920. *Ibid.,* Doc. 512.

mained unsolved. The Hungarian representative in Paris attributed this lack of progress, in part at least, to a division of opinion in the French Foreign Office regarding French policy in Eastern and South-eastern Europe in general, and particularly in Hungary.[97] Another, perhaps even greater obstacle was the opposition of Hungary's hostile neighbors. The principal objector was beyond doubt Czecho-Slovakia, which, from the outset, adopted an attitude of aloofness in the Polish-Soviet war [98] and did everything in its power to prevent Hungarian collaboration with Poland.[99]

The reasons behind the attitude of the Czecho-Slovak Government were doubtless manifold. Exasperation, due to the controversy with Poland over Teschen, must have weighed heavily in the scale. Another consideration was perhaps the fact that some Czech statesmen, particularly Dr. Beneš, had strong pro-Russian sympathies and were fearful of jeopardizing a future alignment of Czecho-Slovakia with the Soviets.[100] At the same time, the conclusion is inescapable that Czecho-

[97] According to Mr. Praznovszky, M. Paléologue's Hungaro-phile policy was frowned upon by some officials occupying key positions, who were followers of M. Clemenceau and who opposed M. Millerand and his appointees for reasons of party politics and personal antagonism, rather than from any objective appraisal of the issues. Mr. Praznovszky also expressed the belief that some spokesmen of this opposition, naming MM. Berthelot and Laroche, were unfriendly to Hungary; he pointed out that it would be too much to expect support for a revision of the Hungarian peace treaty from the men who had helped to lay its foundations. Mr. Praznovszky to Count Teleki, July 26, 1920. *Ibid.,* Doc. 506.

[98] On Aug. 7 Czecho-Slovakia, invoking her neutrality, forbade the transportation of ammunition for Poland through Czecho-Slovakian territory. Cf. Mr. Tahy (the Hungarian representative in Prague) to Count Teleki, Aug. 10, 1920. *Ibid.,* Doc. 553.

[99] The Polish minister in Paris, Count Zamoyski, told Mr. Praznovszky that the French had been inclined to accede to the Hungarian suggestions for assistance to Poland, subject to the approval of Czecho-Slovakia and Rumania; however, these states had both refused their consent to any concessions in Hungary's favor in military matters. Mr. Praznovszky to Count Teléki, Aug. 4, 1920. *Ibid.,* Doc. 536. Also, according to Polish officials, the Czechs had refused to permit the passage of Hungarian troops. Prince Sapieha told the Hungarian representative in Warsaw that the Allies, not being able to prevail upon the Czechs, preferred to show intransigence toward Hungary, rather than admit their helplessness. Count Csekonics to Count Teleki, Aug. 10, 1920. *Ibid.,* Doc. 555. Cf. Count Teleki to Mr. Praznovszky, Aug. 13, 1920. *Ibid.,* Doc. 565.

[100] A historian, competent to speak on Czecho-Slovak foreign policy, explains Czecho-Slovakia's attitude toward the Polish-Soviet war as follows: "In the hour of Poland's greatest distress, Beneš had to make one of the major decisions of his diplomatic career. Public opinion in Czechoslovakia demanded a strong stand against Poland, or even military coöperation with Russia against her. Beneš, with the support of President Masaryk, determined to be strictly neutral: he wisely refused to heed either the domestic clamor or the rumor of a French request to help Poland. . . . Czechoslovak

Slovak policy was strongly, perhaps decisively influenced by fear that Hungary might strengthen her position, possibly at Czecho-Slovakia's expense, were she allowed to help Poland. Recurring and perhaps exaggerated rumors of a Franco-Hungarian *rapprochement* had already caused uneasiness in Prague and merely served to stiffen the government's determination to forestall any move which might conceivably impair Czecho-Slovakia's gains. Indeed, Dr. Beneš, beside opposing any military concessions to Hungary, had taken positive steps to render her harmless. Only in this light can the conclusion, at this moment, of a military alliance between Czecho-Slovakia and Yugoslavia be explained.

The Birth of the Little Entente

Although the idea of coöperation and alliance among the beneficiary Succession States of the former Monarchy was conceived at a much earlier date and although conversations looking to that end had taken place intermittently since the end of the war,[101] the first major step toward the realization of this plan was taken at the time when Hungary was believed to have a fair chance to improve her position. The accelerated pace of conversations between Prague and Belgrade would seem to coincide with Hungarian offers of armed assistance and with Polish efforts to secure Allied consent to the acceptance of these offers. Dr. Beneš's journey to Belgrade and the signature of the alliance a few days after Czecho-Slovakia declared her neutrality in the Polish-Soviet war can hardly be regarded as sheer coincidence, being evidently timed to counter diplomatic measures looking to Hungary's participation in the fight against the bolsheviks.

This conclusion is not affected by the fact that coincidentally with preparing the ground for the formation of the Little Entente, Dr.

---

labor organizations were particularly active in demanding a prohibition of arms shipments to Poland across Czechoslovak territories. . . . Apart from the dislike of becoming involved in a foreign quarrel, Beneš's policy was dictated by his desire to promote intra-Slavic solidarity, an ideal which had already been dealt a cruel blow by the Russo-Polish war and which he felt would be further injured by Czechoslovakia's participation on either side." Vondracek, *The Foreign Policy of Czechoslovakia, 1918–1935*, pp. 155–56.

[101] See *Documents diplomatiques relatifs aux conventions d'alliance conclues par la République tchécoslovaque avec le royaume des Serbes, Croates et Slovènes et le royaume de Roumanie.* Cf. Machray, *The Little Entente*, pp. 85 ff.

Beneš made what appeared to be a conciliatory gesture toward Hungary. On August 11, on the eve of his departure for Belgrade, he received Mr. Tahy, who presented his credentials as the *de facto* representative of the Hungarian Government in Prague. On this occasion Dr. Beneš assured Mr. Tahy that Czech policy was aimed at the development of friendly relations with all neighboring countries, including Hungary.[102] On the next day the Czecho-Slovak Foreign Minister entrained for Belgrade where, on August 14, 1920, the Czech-Yugoslav alliance was signed. The treaty was directed expressly and exclusively against Hungary, and with its signature the foundation of the Little Entente was laid.[103]

While Dr. Beneš did not succeed at this time in completing the ring of isolation around Hungary by securing Rumania's adhesion,[104] the conclusion of the Czech-Yugoslav alliance must be regarded as a major political event and as a decisive turning point in the diplomatic history of postwar Europe. Its significance was more or less understood in the European chancelleries concerned, including that of Hungary, despite contradictory interpretations. Dr. Beneš himself sought to exaggerate the magnitude of his accomplishment by also claiming to have come to a complete agreement with Rumania upon the Hungarian question, as a result of his visit to Bucharest.[105] At the same time he denied,

[102] Mr. Tahy to Count Teleki, Aug. 15, 1920. *HFR*, Vol. I, Doc. 573.

[103] For the text of the alliance see League of Nations Treaty Series, VI, 210.

[104] Following the signature of the treaty with Yugoslavia, Dr. Beneš journeyed to Bucharest, where he arrived on Aug. 17. There he found that while Rumania was willing to agree, without formal commitment, to reciprocal military assistance in case of aggression by Hungary, she was not yet prepared to join his plan for an alliance. Rumania's hesitation may have been due to several factors. First, it was not yet clear whether the Polish victory over the Soviets in the battle of Warsaw had definitely eliminated the bolshevik threat. Secondly, in view of this potential danger, Rumania appears to have been weighing the desirability of reaching, under French mediation, some sort of understanding with Hungary. See *infra*, pp. 324–25. Thirdly, the Rumanian Foreign Minister, Mr. Take Jonescu, had his own plans for the political organization of Eastern and Southeastern Europe, which differed from that of Dr. Beneš. See Machray, *The Little Entente*, pp. 117 ff.; Crane, *The Little Entente*, pp. 7, 105 ff. Cf. *HFR*, Vol. I, Docs. 650, 695.

[105] Cf. Count Teleki to Mr. Praznovszky, Aug. 23, 1920. *HFR*, Vol. I, Doc. 602. In fact, a treaty of alliance between Czecho-Slovakia and Rumania, similar to the Czecho-Slovak-Yugoslav treaty, was not concluded until Apr. 23, 1921, following King Charles's first unsuccessful attempt to reoccupy the throne of Hungary. League of Nations Treaty Series, VI, 215. The chain was completed with the alliance concluded between Rumania and Yugoslavia on June 7, 1921. *Ibid.*, LIV, 251.

especially as regarded Hungary, the exclusively anti-Hungarian character of the Czech-Yugoslav alliance,[106] although its tendency was obvious, both from its text and from the circumstances under which it was concluded.

The first reaction in France was not generally favorable, although Czech propaganda was very active in Paris.[107] M. Paléologue himself did not seem to attribute much importance to the Czech-Yugoslav alliance,[108] perhaps owing to the fact that Rumania did not join and in anticipation of a Hungarian-Rumanian *rapprochement*.[109] As will be shown presently, the chances for this appeared to be fair at that moment. But his optimism was not generally shared at the Quai d'Orsay. Count Emery Csáky, who had again been sent to Paris to press for the

[106] In a conversation with the Hungarian representative in Prague, Dr. Beneš claimed that the treaty aimed to safeguard peace and to strengthen economic relations among the Succession States. He assured Mr. Tahy that President Masaryk "ardently desired" to reach an agreement with Hungary. As evidence of good faith, Dr. Beneš expressed a desire to place diplomatic relations with Hungary on a *de jure* basis in the near future. Mr. Tahy to Count Teleki, Sept. 7, 1920. *HFR*, Vol. I, Docs. 641, 643 (two dispatches). Although Hungary agreed to this suggestion (Count Csáky to Mr. Tahy, Oct. 8, 1920. *Ibid.*, Doc. 700), relations remained on a *de facto* basis for some time. Cf. Dr. Beneš's account of the treaty and its objectives in his address before the Czecho-Slovak Parliament on Sept. 1, quoted at length in Machray, *The Little Entente*, pp. 126 ff.

[107] Mr. Praznovszky reported from Paris that the Czechs were carrying on strong anti-Hungarian propaganda and were working hard to draw a ring of isolation around Hungary. With this end in view, they were endeavoring to conciliate Italy and Yugoslavia. Mr. Praznovszky urged his government to reach an agreement with Rumania before Dr. Beneš completed his plans. Mr. Praznovszky to Count Teleki, Aug. 17, 1920. *HFR*, Vol. I, Doc. 582. Subsequently information was conveyed to the Hungarian Government that Italy had helped in the formation of the Little Entente, but this was categorically denied by the Italians. See Count Teleki's notes of his conversation with the Italian High Commissioner in Budapest, Signor Cerruti, Sept. 12, 1920. *Ibid.*, Doc. 649. It should be noted that in the late fall Italy concluded an agreement with Yugoslavia at Rapallo (Nov. 12, 1920), which settled a number of controversial political questions that were poisoning relations between the two countries. The fact that Italy promptly notified Czecho-Slovakia of the Rapallo Treaty and that Count Sforza simultaneously invited Dr. Beneš to visit Rome to discuss Italian-Czecho-Slovak political coöperation explains Hungary's reluctance to accept Italy's protestations of innocence, and likewise the perceptible cooling of Italo-Hungarian relations at the end of 1920. Cf. Mr. Kánya's notes on his conversations with the Italian minister in Budapest, Prince Castagneto, Dec. 24, 1920. *Ibid.*, Doc. 881.

[108] Mr. Praznovszky to Count Teleki, Aug. 28, 1920. *Ibid.*, Doc. 618.

[109] Another French diplomat, M. de Montille, also told the Hungarian representative that there was no ground for anxiety; were Hungary threatened, France would have been the first to advise her accordingly. Mr. Praznovszky to Count Teleki, Sept. 2, 1920. *Ibid.*, Doc. 629.

fulfillment of the Franco-Hungarian agreement, was warned by a high official of the Foreign Office that "the Czechs do everything in their power to bring about a Czech-Yugoslav-Rumanian alliance against Hungary to which Greece, Bulgaria and Poland also would later adhere"; and he was urged to seek an agreement with Rumania before she succumbed to Czech diplomacy.[110] At the same time there is some evidence—apart from an unfavorable reception in the daily press—that France did not, at the outset, approve Dr. Beneš's plans to encircle Hungary. The aggressive character of the Czech-Yugoslav alliance was freely admitted in French official circles, where the credit for Rumania's abstention was claimed to be due to French intervention. Such an admission was also implicit in the French endeavors to broaden the alliance by the inclusion of other states (particularly of Poland) and thus take away its anti-Hungarian character.[111] As will be shown, French foreign policy in this respect made a complete about-face, following the resignation of M. Paléologue; but even before this occurred, Czech opposition was influential enough to play an important role in frustrating progress toward the fulfillment of the Franco-Hungarian agreement in general or the securing of Allied approval for a limited reëquipment of Hungary's armed forces in particular.

The Last Stage of the Franco-Hungarian Rapprochement

In the critical days preceding the battle of Warsaw, the Hungarian Government, impatient with the procrastination of the French, decided to make one more bold attempt to obtain a decision. Accordingly Count Emery Csáky and Colonel Láng were dispatched to Paris with instructions to lay the whole question before M. Millerand and Marshal

[110] Count Csáky to Count Teleki, Aug. 25, 1920. *Ibid.*, Doc. 607.

[111] See Mr. Praznovszky's dispatch of Sept. 2 regarding his conversation with M. de Montille. *Ibid.*, Doc. 629. In a conversation with another official in the Foreign Office, M. Peretti told the Hungarian representative that the Little Entente might "almost" be regarded as directed against France. Mr. Praznovszky to Count Teleki, Sept. 4, 1920. *Ibid.*, Doc. 631. There is also some indication that the French tried to prevent the formation of the Czech-Yugoslav alliance. When they failed, they tried, for a while at least, to include other states not hostile to Hungary, so that Hungary's position vis-à-vis the Little Entente would be less pronounced. Cf. Mr. Praznovszky to Count Teleki, Sept. 13, 1920. *Ibid.*, Doc. 650. On the opposition point of view in France regarding the Franco-Hungarian *rapprochement*, Hungary's offer of assistance to Poland, and Hungary's relations with the Little Entente, see the enlightening remarks of M. Raymond Poincaré in *Revue des deux mondes*, LIX (6th ser.), 436 ff., especially 444–47.

Foch.[112] When informed of this, M. Paléologue, obviously embarrassed, requested that the visit of the Hungarian envoys be postponed. He told Mr. Praznovszky that France's delicate international position made it impossible for M. Millerand or Marshal Foch to receive special representatives from Hungary; such a visit would become known at once, would be likely to ruin everything, and would endanger the agreement between France and Great Britain, reached after much difficulty. Mr. Praznovszky was left with the impression that the question of Hungary's rearmament at least had been dropped completely by the French, even though the outcome of the battle in Poland still hung in the balance.[113]

The Hungarian envoys were already en route when the report on the French reaction to their visit reached Budapest; but the impasse which would have doubtless resulted from a refusal to receive them was averted by an unexpected suggestion from the Rumanian Government that direct relations with Hungary be established under French mediation. M. Paléologue, much pleased with this development, urged that Hungary should receive the mission Rumania proposed to send to Budapest and that she should reciprocate the gesture by appointing a corresponding mission to go to Bucharest. He told Mr. Praznovszky that he regarded this step as the first toward further negotiations and that on Hungary's prompt compliance with his suggestion might depend the success of such French mediation. Count Csáky, who had meanwhile reached Paris, also urged the acceptance of M. Paléologue's suggestions, with a view to facilitating the task of Colonel Láng and himself. Mr. Praznovszky was quick to utilize this turn of events and he sought and secured M. Paléologue's support for Count Csáky and Colonel Láng.[114]

[112] Count Teleki to Mr. Praznovszky, Aug. 9, 1920. HFR, Vol. I, Doc. 550.

[113] Mr. Praznovszky to Count Teleki, Aug. 11, 1920. Ibid., Doc. 559. It is to be noted that on the preceding day Dr. Halmos presented to M. Paléologue a memorandum on the status of Franco-Hungarian relations and proposals regarding them. M. Paléologue spoke very encouragingly to Dr. Halmos and said that he intended to discuss the matter with M. Millerand. Assurances given to Mr. Praznovszky from French official circles induced him to expect satisfaction of Hungarian claims, if the French view prevailed in a discussion of the Hungarian question said to be impending between M. Millerand and Mr. Lloyd George. Mr. Praznovszky to Count Teleki, Aug. 10, 1920. Ibid., Doc. 556.

[114] Mr. Praznovszky to Count Teleki, Aug. 14, 1920. Ibid., Doc. 568. Count Saint-Sauveur also intervened with M. Paléologue, who agreed to see the Hungarian envoys as soon as Hungary had accepted the Rumanian suggestion. Count Csáky to Count Teleki, Aug. 14, 1920. Ibid., Doc. 569.

The Hungarian Government promptly agreed to establish direct relations with Rumania and authorized its representatives in Paris to negotiate the matter with M. Paléologue.[115] Upon the receipt of this information, M. Paléologue had a long conference with Count Csáky and Colonel Láng on August 17. By this time the French had learned of both the Czech-Yugoslav alliance and the Polish victory over the Soviets—both having occurred on August 14—although the decisiveness of the latter was not yet clear. M. Paléologue attributed—it is believed correctly—the conciliatory advances of Rumania toward Hungary to the bolshevik threat. Admitting that Dr. Beneš's system of alliances was directed against Hungary, he expressed the belief that Rumania would not join such a bloc, which offered her insufficient protection against Russia. He urged the Hungarian representatives to make use of this favorable opportunity and to reach an agreement with Rumania, which, he said, would greatly facilitate France's task regarding Hungary's rearmament. In the absence of Marshal Foch and General Weygand, M. Paléologue referred the Hungarian representatives to the acting chief of the French General Staff, General Desticker, for a discussion of technical military questions.

This meeting took place on the same day. The Hungarians were cordially received and were told that the French High Command fully shared the Hungarian appraisal of the Russian situation. The possibility of an agreement with Rumania appeared to be uppermost in General Desticker's mind; he told Colonel Láng that France could send armament to Hungary only through Rumania.

The conversations with M. Paléologue and General Desticker were regarded by the Hungarian representatives as encouraging. Their impression was that the French were in earnest about rearming Hungary within the treaty limits, the main obstacle being the opposition of England and Italy. They did not believe that the Czechs could decisively influence France, but felt that an agreement with Rumania was essential.[116]

This favorable impression was strengthened by conversations on the following day regarding technical details with French staff officers designated by General Desticker. These conversations confirmed the impression gained by the Hungarian envoys that responsible French

[115] Count Teleki to Mr. Praznovszky, Aug. 15, 1920. *Ibid.*, Doc. 572.

[116] Count Csáky to Count Teleki, Aug. 18, 1920 (two dispatches). *Ibid.*, Docs. 590, 591.

political as well as military circles regarded bolshevism as serious a danger as did Hungary. Again the importance of an agreement with Rumania was emphasized by the French military experts, who promised a reply in a few days.[117] A further indication that the French still thought in those days in terms of M. Paléologue's policies was a request that the options granted on conclusion of the Franco-Hungarian agreement, which were to expire on August 29, be extended for another three months.[118] Finally, a basis for optimism was also found in the favorable comments in the French press on the impending *rapprochement* between Hungary and Rumania, which was claimed by the government to be a proof of the success in its foreign policy. Conversely, the attitude toward Dr. Beneš's diplomatic moves were, as already indicated, rather unfriendly; and it was reliably reported that France officially warned both Czecho-Slovakia and Yugoslavia.[119]

Despite these seemingly favorable developments, Hungarian expectations remained unfulfilled. As far as the military question was concerned, the victory of the Polish Army over the Soviets rendered the assistance offered by Hungary less valuable than it had appeared to be a few days earlier—at least in the opinion of French political circles. While French military experts were apparently inclined to continue making preparations to meet the Russian danger, and to lend assistance to Hungary's reëquipment as one part of such preparations,[120] the needed political endorsement was not forthcoming. M. Paléologue's attitude was reported to have changed as a result of the outcome of the battle of Warsaw; the bolshevik danger having been eliminated, he no longer felt that Hungary's rearmament was a pressing matter. In view of this changed attitude, the Hungarian envoys came to the conclusion

[117] Mr. Praznovszky to Count Teleki, Aug. 19, 1920. *Ibid.,* Doc. 596.

[118] Mr. Praznovszky to Count Teleki, Aug. 16, 1920. *Ibid.,* Doc. 577. The Hungarian Government readily agreed to the requested extension. Count Teleki to Mr. Praznovszky, Aug. 23, 1920. *Ibid.,* Doc. 601.

[119] Mr. Praznovszky to Count Teleki, Aug. 20, 1920. *Ibid.,* Doc. 597. M. Paléologue told Count Csáky that Messrs. Beneš and Pasić had laid the Little Entente plans before the Quai d'Orsay and had sought France's help to induce Rumania to join the alliance. The French Foreign Office disapproved of the plan and made it clear that the French Government would advise Rumania not to adhere. Count Csáky to Count Csekonics, Oct. 5, 1920. *Ibid.,* Doc. 695.

[120] General Desticker told Colonel Láng that the French Army was willing (1) to supply at once armament and equipment to the limits allowed Hungary under the peace treaty and (2) to arrange for additional supplies, should the Soviet Army move again. Mr. Praznovszky to Count Teleki, Aug. 27, 1920. *Ibid.,* Doc. 614.

that nothing could be accomplished and decided to return to Buda-pest.[121]

Equally inconclusive was the Rumanian gesture to which M. Palé-ologue first attributed such great importance. As we have seen, the French had repeatedly urged Hungary to reciprocate and Hungary had promptly acquiesced. Yet M. Paléologue was unable to arrange even a meeting between Count Csáky and the Rumanian minister to France, Prince Ghika, although he himself suggested that such a meeting should take place.[122] Within a few days the initial enthusiasm in the French Foreign Office for the expected Hungarian-Rumanian *rapprochement* gave way to an attitude of reserve and caution. M. Peretti, in a conversation with Mr. Praznovszky early in September, gave it as his advice that Hungary ought to make friends with Rumania on the basis of the Treaty of Trianon and ought not to seek revision until later. The change in attitude was in all likelihood due in part to increased pressure by Hungary's adversaries. M. Peretti admitted on the same occasion that Czech efforts to create distrust of Hungary

[121] Mr. Praznovszky to Count Teleki, Aug. 27, 1920. *Ibid.,* Doc. 613. Failure on this score should not, however, be attributed solely to the changed military situation on the Eastern front. Piecing together the course of events, one cannot fail to conclude that French policy was steeped in hesitation and equivocation. A striking illustration was disclosed to Count Csáky by M. Bignon, one of M. Millerand's associates and one of Hungary's true friends in France. He told Count Csáky that at a recent cabinet meeting the French Minister of War, uninformed of the Franco-Hungarian negotiations, had made a sharp attack upon Hungary, and the Prime Minister had had to defend her. In other words, not only the French public but even members of the government had been kept in the dark as to French foreign policy. It may be noted that this incident occurred before the decisiveness of the Polish victory became known, possibly even before the battle of Warsaw. Count Csáky to Count Teleki, Aug. 16, 1920. *Ibid.,* Doc. 578.

[122] Cf. Count Csáky to Count Teleki, Aug. 18, 1920; Mr. Praznovszky to Count Teleki, Sept. 4, 1920. *Ibid.,* Docs. 590, 631. The Hungarian Government was obviously fully prepared to carry out in good faith the proposed exchange of missions. Arrangements were made to send the Counsellor of the legation in Vienna, Mr. Masirevich, to Bucharest. The Hungarian Government even sought an "agrément" for Mr. Masirevich and was prepared to give him the same rank as that to be given to the Rumanian representative. Cf. Count Teleki to Dr. Gratz, Sept. 5, 1920; Dr. Gratz to Count Teleki, Sept. 6, 1920; Count Teleki to Dr. Gratz, Sept. 7, 1920. *Ibid.,* Docs. 632, 634, 637. As a matter of fact, the Rumanian mission did not reach Budapest until the beginning of Jan., 1921. With respect to the continued postponement by the Rumanians of the establishment of direct relations see Count Csáky to Mr. Tahy, Oct. 17, 1920; Mr. Tahy to Count Csáky, Oct. 31, 1920; Count Csáky to Mr. Praznovszky, Dec. 4, 1920; Mr. Parcher to Count Csáky, Dec. 7, 1920; Mr. Parcher to Count Teleki, Dec. 15, 1920. *Ibid.,* Docs. 722, 762, 846, 856, 870.

had begun to take effect and that the visit of Count Csáky and Colonel Láng in Paris had evoked violent displeasure among Hungary's neighbors, causing considerable embarrassment to the French Government.[123] The French press also, which in the middle of August had been decidedly adverse to the Little Entente and had commented favorably on the signs of Hungarian-Rumanian *rapprochement*, began to extoll Dr. Beneš's system of alliances, a result, according to the Hungarian representative, of Czech propaganda conducted "with tremendous expenditure of money."[124]

It was also at about this time that the French began to press Hungary for the ratification of the peace treaty, a step heralding the total collapse of the policy of M. Paléologue. Although on one or two previous occasions this issue had come up casually, it was stressed for the first time in the conversation between M. Peretti and Mr. Praznovszky referred to above.[125] Shortly thereafter another high official in the French Foreign Office, M. Laroche, urged on Mr. Praznovszky the necessity of early ratification. M. Laroche said that Hungary's failure to ratify the treaty in the near future would contribute to the distrust of her neighbors and would raise doubts, even among the Principal Allied Powers. It was on this occasion that Mr. Praznovszky first made clear, without diplomatic niceties, that Hungary was deeply disappointed because of France's failure to ease the pressure against Hungary; he said bluntly that, as seen from Budapest, Hungary had been cajoled into accepting, signing, and carrying out the peace treaty by promises which had never

---

[123] Mr. Praznovszky to Count Teleki, Sept. 4, 1920. *Ibid.*, Doc. 631. The Hungarians did not press for territorial adjustments as a condition for accepting the Rumanian step toward the establishment of direct relations. But they did inform the French that improvement in relations must be preceded by better treatment of Hungarian minorities by Rumania. The Hungarian representative was also instructed to inform the French that if they were embarrassed because of their Hungaro-phile policy, Hungary also had her difficulties, especially with Italy, because of her own *rapprochement* with France. Count Teleki to Mr. Praznovszky, Sept. 7, 1920. *Ibid.*, Doc. 638.

[124] Mr. Praznovszky to Count Teleki, Sept. 13, 1920. *Ibid.*, Doc. 650. With respect to the failure to solve satisfactorily the question of Hungary's rearmament, it should be pointed out that the failure of Hungarian-Rumanian *rapprochement* was not the result of any one single factor. Together with French procrastination and Czech pressure, an important element must also have been Rumania's diplomacy, which was appropriately described as trying to eat her cake and have it too. She had sought to find protection from Hungary through the Little Entente and from Russia by making some sort of deal with Hungary. Cf. Count Csáky to Count Csekonics, Oct. 5, 1920. *Ibid.*, Doc. 695.

[125] *Supra,* n. 123.

been fulfilled.[126] The day before the resignation of M. Paléologue, the Conference of Ambassadors formally requested the Hungarian Government to take steps for the prompt ratification of the peace treaty.[127] Thus the curtain rose on the concluding scene in the diplomatic history of the Treaty of Trianon.

[126] Mr. Praznovszky to Count Teleki, Sept. 21, 1920. *HFR*, Vol. I, Doc. 658.

[127] The Conference of Ambassadors to Mr. Praznovszky, Sept. 25, 1920. *Ibid.*, Doc. 669.

VII. The Third Phase of the Franco-Hungarian Secret Negotiations and the Treaty of Trianon: The Collapse of the Franco-Hungarian Rapprochement and the Ratification of the Trianon Treaty by Hungary

The Resignation of M. Paléologue

COUNT EMERY CSÁKY, who from the outset had been one of the chief participants in the negotiations with France, became Hungary's foreign minister on September 22, 1920. In all likelihood he was chosen to take over that post from Prime Minister Count Teleki in the hope that he would succeed, if anybody could, in overcoming the many and increasing difficulties which had postponed the realization of the Franco-Hungarian agreement. But, by the time he had dispatched a personal message to M. Paléologue expressing his hope and desire for the strengthening of relations with France, there had begun to circulate, in Paris, rumors of the imminent fall of the French diplomat.[1] On September 26 M. Paléologue resigned; his resignation marked a decisive change in French foreign policy. The completeness of this change was not immediately evident; indeed its ultimate consequences for Southeastern Europe, for European diplomacy, and for France herself were not fully understood until many years later, when Europe stood on the brink of another war.

The French themselves endeavored to assure the Hungarians, at any rate, that the change of personnel in the Foreign Office had not altered French policy.[2] But the evidence pointed in the opposite direc-

[1] Cf. Count Csáky to Mr. Praznovszky, Sept. 24, 1920; Mr. Praznovszky to Count Csáky, Sept. 24, 1920. *HFR*, Vol. I, Docs. 664, 666.

[2] The day following the shake up, Count Saint-Sauveur told Mr. Praznovszky that M. Paléologue would continue to exert influence as M. Millerand's adviser on foreign affairs. M. Paléologue himself assured the Hungarian representative that French foreign policy had not changed. Mr. Praznovszky to Count Csáky, Sept. 27 and 30, 1920. *Ibid.*, Docs. 674, 683. Identical assurances were conveyed to the Hungarian Government by M. Fouchet, upon express instructions from Paris. Cf. Count Csáky to Count Csekonics, Oct. 5, 1920. *Ibid.*, Doc. 695. Subsequently the new Prime Minister, M. Leygues,

tion and made it difficult for the Hungarians to take these assurances at face value, especially when it became known that M. Berthelot had succeeded M. Paléologue; for Hungarian circles regarded M. Berthelot as a great friend of the Czechs and an irreconcilable enemy of Hungary.[3]

Perhaps the most direct and immediate effect of M. Paléologue's dismissal was felt not so much in Franco-Hungarian relations as in the change in French views regarding the Little Entente on the one hand and Polish-Hungarian coöperation on the other. Although the Polish victory and the subsequent negotiations with Russia leading to the preliminary treaty of peace of Riga [4] rendered Hungary's armed assistance no longer a pressing necessity for Poland,[5] conversations with Hungary for the political stabilization of that area continued. Immediately preceding M. Paléologue's resignation, Marshal Pilsudski and Prince Sapieha were reported to be working, with French backing, for a Polish-Hungarian-Rumanian understanding, to counterbalance the Little Entente.[6] But no sooner did M. Paléologue leave the Quai

who also held the post of Foreign Minister, assured Dr. Halmos, who still sought to see the Franco-Hungarian agreement made an actuality, that no change had occurred in French foreign policy. But by that time, or less than a month later, M. Paléologue was reported to have lost all influence, so much so that M. Millerand was unable to have him appointed to the Conference of Ambassadors. Mr. Praznovszky to Count Csáky, Oct. 27, 1920. *Ibid.,* Doc. 755.

[3] There were rumors in French political quarters that M. Paléologue's elimination had been brought about in part by Czech agitation against his Hungaro-phile policy. See Mr. Praznovszky to Count Csáky, Oct. 8, 1920. *Ibid.,* Doc. 703. Meanwhile, reports of M. Berthelot's hostility to Hungary continued to reach Budapest. Cf. Mr. Praznovszky to Count Csáky, Oct. 27 and Nov. 16, 1920. *Ibid.,* Docs. 755, 805.

[4] For the text of the treaty concluded on Oct. 12, 1920, see League of Nations Treaty Series, IV, 8.

[5] In the darkest days of the war, when the fall of Warsaw had appeared imminent and when Allied procrastination had blocked direct aid by Hungary, Polish officials had begun to explore with the Hungarian experts sent to Warsaw a plan for the formation of Hungarian volunteer corps. Count Csekonics to Count Teleki, Aug. 10, 1920. *HFR,* Vol. I, Doc. 554. Under the plan, worked out by the Chief of the Polish General Staff, General Rozwadowski and Colonel Takács, of the Hungarian Army Command, Hungarian volunteers would travel singly through Czecho-Slovakia to assembly places behind the front, where they would be equipped and organized into units. Count Csekonics to Count Teleki, Aug. 19, 1920. *Ibid.,* Doc. 595. Later, the Rumanian Government expressed willingness to permit the passage of these Hungarian volunteers (Count Csekonics to Count Teleki, Aug. 30, 1920. *Ibid.,* Doc. 621), but the plan was abandoned after the conclusion of the Treaty of Riga. Cf. Count Csáky to Count Csekonics, Sept. 24 and Oct. 14, 1920. *Ibid.,* Docs. 665, 712.

[6] Mr. Praznovszky to Count Csáky, Sept. 24, 1920. *Ibid.,* Doc. 667. It was reported from Warsaw that the Czechs were active in seeking Poland's adherence to the Little

d'Orsay than the French minister in Warsaw was instructed to advise the Polish Government that contrary to her past attitude, France would thenceforth look with sympathy upon the Little Entente and would favor the establishment of friendly relations between Poland and Czecho-Slovakia.[7] The Polish Foreign Minister, apparently stunned by this sudden face about, assured the Hungarian representative that Poland nevertheless intended to stand by her friendship with Hungary; but, in view of Poland's continued dependence on the good will of France, the transformation of such an assurance into concrete terms was hardly to be expected.[8] In fact, pending the clarification of France's attitude, which, in turn, was bound to influence Rumania, Poland had no choice but to adopt a policy of watchful waiting.[9] The Poles hoped, during Mr. Jonescu's visit in Warsaw, to win over Rumania to Prince Sapieha's idea of a transversal bloc consisting of Poland, Hungary, and Rumania, made complete by an alliance with the Baltic states. This plan presupposed a common border between Poland and Hungary, which, the Hungarian Foreign Minister was assured, the Polish Government continued to regard as a matter of vital interest to Poland.[10] In opposition to this plan, Mr. Jonescu was the promoter of a Central-

---

Entente and in trying to induce her to abandon Hungary. Polish statesmen were for the most part disinclined to join the Little Entente. At the same time, they were just as unwilling to make an alliance with Hungary unless a reconciliation between Hungary and Rumania could be effected. Count Csekonics to Count Csáky, Sept. 25, 1920. *Ibid.,* Doc. 668.

[7] French support of the Little Entente was later confirmed from Paris. Mr. Praznovszky reported that the French were making every effort to bring the Czechs and Poles together, the aim being to set up a combination of powers that were against Hungary's revisionist aspirations. Mr. Praznovszky to Count Csáky, Oct. 17, 1920. *Ibid.,* Doc. 725.

[8] Count Csekonics to Count Csáky, Oct. 2, 1920. *Ibid.,* Doc. 689. Prince Sapieha attributed this change in French foreign policy to Mr. Jonescu's influence on M. Millerand, for the Rumanian Foreign Minister had stayed in France throughout September. See also Count Csekonics to Count Csáky, Oct. 9, 1920. *Ibid.,* Doc. 708. Mr. Jonescu himself, in a conversation with Count Csekonics during his visit in Warsaw, claimed credit for "having put an end" to France's friendship for Hungary. Count Csekonics to Count Csáky, Nov 3, 1920. *Ibid.,* Doc. 770. It is characteristic of Rumanian diplomacy that at the end of September circles close to Mr. Jonescu sounded out Budapest as to a *rapprochement,* intimating that Rumania would forego an alliance with Czecho-Slovakia for a bloc with Hungary and Poland. Cf. Count Csáky to Count Csekonics, Oct. 5, 1920. *Ibid.,* Doc. 695.

[9] Cf. Count Csekonics to Count Csáky, Oct. 23, 1920. *Ibid.,* Doc. 739 (reporting his conversation with Mr. Piltz, the new chief of the Political Department in the Polish Foreign Office).

[10] Notes of Count Csáky on conversations with Count Szembek, Nov. 1, 1920. *Ibid.,* Doc. 765.

European-Balkan bloc, consisting of Poland, Rumania, Czecho-Slovakia, Yugoslavia, and Greece and leaving out, for the time being,
Hungary, Bulgaria, and Turkey. In an interview which the Rumanian
Foreign Minister held with Count Csekonics while in Warsaw, he
frankly discouraged any expectation of a political *rapprochement* between Rumania and Hungary, although he did express a desire for improved economic relations. The reason given for his reserve in the
political field was that Rumania could not consider even the possibility
of any territorial revision.[11] It is not known how earnestly the Poles
pressed their guest for a less intransigent attitude on the Hungarian
question; but the fact is that Mr. Jonescu's visit to Warsaw ended without any visible results so far as Hungarian-Rumanian relations were
concerned. On learning the views expressed by Mr. Jonescu, Count
Csáky advised Prince Sapieha that the Hungarian Government realized the necessity of negotiating with Rumania on the basis of the
Trianon Treaty, exclusive of any revision of the territorial clauses. He
expressed the view that the adjustments sought by Hungary could be
made by merely applying the Covering Letter. Count Csekonics was
authorized to tell Prince Sapieha that there would be no objection to
the confidential communication of these views to the Rumanian
Foreign Minister.[12] Nevertheless, Poland did not succeed, then or later,
in effecting a reconciliation between Hungary and Rumania, a step
which would have made possible the harmonious coöperation of these
three states. On the other hand, the Little Entente was equally unsuccessful in inducing Poland to join; consequently, cordial relations
between Poland and Hungary remained unimpaired, even though
geography and the accidents of European political developments precluded the transformation of Polish-Hungarian friendship into a concrete and constructive collaboration in the interests of peace.

The End of the Franco-Hungarian Rapprochement

While the Hungarian Government had no illusions as to the probable consequences of M. Paléologue's resignation, it acted at the outset
on the assumption that the agreement concluded at the end of June
had remained unimpaired by the change of personnel in the French
Foreign Office.

Shortly after M. Berthelot's appointment as Secretary General at the

[11] Count Csekonics to Count Csáky, Nov. 3, 1920. *Ibid.,* Doc. 770.
[12] Count Csáky to Count Csekonics, Nov. 16, 1920. *Ibid.,* Doc. 803.

Quai d'Orsay, Mr. Praznovszky was instructed to assure him that Hungary was prepared to continue her policy in accordance with the Franco-Hungarian understanding; in particular, she was willing to establish friendly relations with her neighbors.[13] But before these instructions could be carried out, the Conference of Ambassadors made a second *démarche,* requesting an early ratification of the peace treaty.[14] This created a painful impression in Hungary. Mr. Praznovszky, in Paris, was instructed to stress the desirability of tangible concessions by France with regard to the moderate claims earlier put forward by Hungary, in order to give reality to and justification for Hungary's French orientation.[15] But, although relations with the French Foreign Office remained superficially friendly, inquiries as to the prospects for further conversations along the lines of the agreement brought only evasive replies.[16] When Dr. Halmos presented to Foreign Minister Leygues memoranda regarding the execution of the agreement, he was merely told that there was strong opposition—particularly British —to Hungary's military program. This, however, was only one of several issues which Hungary sought to settle,[17] without, as it turned out, any measure of success. M. Berthelot also received Dr. Halmos at the beginning of November and, while denying that he was opposed to M. Paléologue's policy in general, he admitted a disagreement as to details. His comments regarding the territorial adjustments envisaged in the Paléologue negotiations were reported to have been emphatically adverse.[18] There is no record in the Hungarian archives of any exchange of views with French officials following the presentation of these memoranda, which may, therefore, be regarded as the

[13] Count Csáky to Mr. Praznovszky, Oct. 17, 1920. *Ibid.,* Doc. 723.

[14] See *infra,* p. 336.

[15] Count Csáky to Mr. Praznovszky, Oct. 23, 1920. *HFR,* Vol. I, Doc. 737.

[16] Cf. Mr. Praznovszky to Count Csáky, Oct. 23, 1920. *Ibid.,* Doc. 738.

[17] Mr. Praznovszky to Count Csáky, Oct. 27, 1920. *Ibid.,* Doc. 755. For the French text of the two memoranda presented to Mr. Leygues see *ibid.,* Docs. 755(a), 755(b). The first analyzed the motivation and purpose of a political *rapprochement* between France and Hungary and gave a brief summary of the agreement reached. Admitting the difficulties of an integral carrying out of the whole program at once, the memorandum suggested that a start in carrying it out might be the settlement of problems of immediate concern to Hungary—specifically, the establishment of an independent section of the Reparations Commission in Budapest; the appointment of frontier delimitation commissions; and the approval of the reorganization of the Hungarian Army, as proposed by Hungarian military authorities. The second memorandum dealt with the economic agreement under three headings, French control over the Hungarian railways, over shipping on the Danube, and the acquisition of industrial plants.

[18] Mr. Praznovszky to Count Csáky, Nov. 7, 1920. *Ibid.,* Doc. 783.

last step taken by Hungary toward the carrying into effect of the understanding reached with M. Paléologue.

Similarly, the conversations for the reëquipment of the Hungarian Army, begun in August by Count Csáky and Colonel Láng,[19] ended in a deadlock. Colonel Láng, who remained in Paris, reported having arrived at a complete understanding with the French military spokesmen. But he recognized that the decision in this matter, one having political implications, did not rest with the military authorities and that the political preparation of the ground must be begun afresh.[20] The changed political atmosphere was unfavorable for Hungary and, following an unexplained misunderstanding with the French Army spokesmen, Colonel Láng left Paris without having accomplished anything, although his conversations had appeared to be proceeding favorably until the early part of November.[21]

Thus by the time Hungary had completed the ratification of the Trianon Treaty, the Franco-Hungarian understanding was rendered for all practical purposes meaningless.

Ratification of the Peace Treaty by Hungary

As already indicated, the Conference of Ambassadors formally requested Hungary, on September 25, to ratify the peace treaty.[22] The increase of pressure on Hungary by the Allies and the disappearance of Hungary's friend from the Quai d'Orsay coincided—perhaps not

[19] See *supra*, pp. 323–26.

[20] Colonel Láng to Count Csáky, Oct. 28, 1920. *HFR*, Vol. I, Doc. 757. When Colonel Láng was received by General Weygand, the latter intimated that, during the August conferences, General Desticker might have held out more encouraging prospects than were justifiable.

[21] Mr. Praznovszky to Count Csáky, Nov. 16 and 22, 1920. *Ibid.*, Docs. 805, 819. Attention may also be called to the rejection by the Conference of Ambassadors of Hungarian requests, relating to the modification of some of the military clauses of the peace treaty. It will be recalled that these requests were put forward at the time the agreement with France was brought to final form and related to the number of effectives and to the provisional organization of the army, as also to the substitution of the draft for recruiting. See *supra*, p. 304. With respect to effectives and the provisional organization of the army, the reply was wholly negative. As to the question of recruiting, the Allied reply insisted on the maintenance of the principle, but expressed a willingness to authorize temporary modification in procedure, following the precedent of a similar concession made to Austria. For the French text of the decision of the Conference of Ambassadors, given on Oct. 26, 1920, and the note of the representatives of the Principal Allied Powers in Budapest, dated Nov. 9, 1920, transmitting the decision, see *HFR*, Vol. I, Docs. 786, 786(a).

[22] *Supra*, p. 329.

wholly by accident. The Hungarian Government was confidentially informed that the Principal Allied Powers contemplated giving weight to the request of the Conference of Ambassadors by a collective *démarche* in Budapest.[23] In order to forestall this, the Hungarian Government dispatched a conciliatory reply stating that the bill to approve ratification had been prepared and would shortly be laid before Parliament.[24] While the promptness of this reply did avert a collective step, the British, French, and Italian representatives called individually on the Hungarian Foreign Minister on October 7 and, following the note of the Conference of Ambassadors, urged, in the name of their respective governments, early ratification by Hungary.[25] A few days later Mr. Praznovszky was instructed to assure both the Conference of Ambassadors and the French Foreign Office that the treaty would be ratified as soon as possible. At the same time he was to ask the French to facilitate the task of the Hungarian Government in gaining approval for an unpopular treaty, by pressing the neighboring states to improve the treatment of Hungarian minorities and by making preparations for the appointment of the frontier delimitation commissions referred to in the Covering Letter of May 6, 1920.[26]

On the same day that these instructions were issued the Conference of Ambassadors sent another note to Hungary. Although politely phrased, the note was in the nature of an ultimatum, in that it called for ratification by November 1. If Hungary should fail to comply, the Allies would no longer authorize the participation of Hungarian members in the work of various international commissions, including that of the Danube, set up under the peace treaties.[27] Budapest replied that Hungary intended to complete ratification as soon as constitu-

[23] In the Hungarian Foreign Office the view prevailed that the sudden solicitude of the Principal Allies for an immediate ratification by Hungary was the result of agitation by Czecho-Slovakia and Yugoslavia. Confidential information conveyed by Count Sforza at the beginning of September was to the effect that one of the consequences of the Czech-Yugoslav alliance would be a request to Hungary to ratify the peace treaty by the end of September, failing which the countries lined up against her would attack her. Cf. the notes of Count Teleki on his conversations with Signor Cerrutti, Sept. 12, 1920. *HFR*, Vol. I, Doc. 649.

[24] Count Csáky to Mr. Praznovszky, Sept. 29, 1920. *Ibid.*, Doc. 676.

[25] Count Csáky to Mr. Praznovszky, Oct. 8, 1920. *Ibid.*, Doc. 701.

[26] Count Csáky to Mr. Praznovszky, Oct. 18, 1920. *Ibid.*, Doc. 726.

[27] Conference of Ambassadors to Mr. Praznovszky, Oct. 18, 1920. *Ibid.*, Doc. 727. The time limit was subsequently extended to Nov. 15. Conference of Ambassadors to Mr. Praznovszky, Oct. 25, 1920. *Ibid.*, Doc. 746. Cf. the collective note of the Allied representatives in Budapest to the Foreign Minister, Oct. 26, 1920. *Ibid.*, Doc. 751.

tional requirements and parliamentary procedure would permit.[28] A few days later the bill was introduced into Parliament and referred to the appropriate committees. When informing the Conference of Ambassadors of this, Mr. Praznovszky requested the President of the Conference to have steps taken to compel Hungary's neighbors to respect the rights of minorities and to appoint the frontier delimitation commissions. Ambassador Cambon agreed to submit these requests to the next meeting of the Conference.[29] In a formal communication the Conference of Ambassadors replied that its intervention for the better treatment of minorities would be more effective after Hungary had given irrefutable proof of her peaceful intention by ratifying the peace treaty. Nevertheless, the Conference decided to call the attention of Hungary's neighbors to the minority treaties.[30]

Parliament voted on the ratification in a sober and solemn session on November 13. There was no debate, the legislators realizing that no other course was open to Hungary. A declaration, adopted unanimously by the House, indicated the attitude of the Hungarian people toward the treaty as a whole.[31] A motion by Prime Minister Count Teleki to make his responsibility for the disastrous treaty a matter for impeachment proceedings was tabled.[32]

The formalities were completed by the signature of the Regent on November 15, the date set by the Conference of Ambassadors, and the instrument of ratification was transmitted to Paris. When Mr. Praz-

[28] Count Csáky to Mr. Praznovszky, Oct. 23, 1920. *Ibid.*, Doc. 737.

[29] Mr. Praznovszky to Count Csáky. Oct. 29, 1920. *Ibid.*, Doc. 758. The complaints of the Hungarian Government regarding the treatment of minorities by Rumania, Yugoslavia, and Czecho-Slovakia were set forth in a lengthy note subsequently filed with the Conference. Mr. Praznovszky to M. Cambon, Nov. 8, 1920. *Ibid.*, Doc. 785.

[30] Conference of Ambassadors to Mr. Praznovszky, Nov. 5, 1920. *Ibid.*, No. 777.

[31] The text of this declaration is as follows: "The National Assembly, in deciding to assent to the ratification of the Trianon Treaty, declares before God, and appealing to the conscience of humanity, that it considers the peace document as being based on false data, unjust and contrary to the interests of humanity; that this treaty is not the result of an agreement reached through the bilateral examination of facts and interests, but is unilaterally imposed on us by alien forces; therefore, the National Assembly assents to its ratification solely because of this irresistible pressure. By its assent, under the circumstances, the National Assembly cannot impose any obligations on territories which are not herein represented. The National Assembly does not give up the hope that the return of normal conditions, after the passions now reigning have disappeared, will open the road to a rectification of the great injustice inflicted upon us under the guise of a peace treaty."

[32] The minutes of this meeting are printed, in an English translation, in *HFR*, I (Appendix 3, No. 8), 987 ff.

novszky informed the Conference of Ambassadors that Hungary had ratified the treaty, he asked the Allies to have the territories still occupied by Yugoslavia evacuated and repeated the request for more effective protection of Hungarian minorities.[33] With the depositing of the instrument of ratification in the French Foreign Office,[34] all the requirements for the execution of the Treaty of Trianon on the part of Hungary had been fulfilled.

[33] Mr. Praznovszky to M. Cambon, Nov. 24, 1920. *Ibid.,* Doc. 822. Cf. also Count Csáky to M. Cambon, Nov. 19, 1920. *Ibid.,* Doc. 813.

[34] Mr. Praznovszky to M. Leygues, Dec. 3, 1920; the French Ministry for Foreign Affairs to Mr. Praznovszky, Dec. 13, 1920. *Ibid.,* Docs. 843, 867.

PART FIVE

Conclusions

VIII. Conclusions: Retrospect and Prospect

THE ratification of the Treaty of Trianon by Hungary is an appropriate as well as a logical point at which to end this book. Our objective was a strictly limited one, an account of the making of the peace treaty with Hungary. The task of the Peace Conference, or more precisely the official committees which were its successors, as far as the making of the treaty was concerned, was accomplished when Hungary gave its final reluctant assent to the terms. Its acceptance by the other signatories, all direct or vicarious beneficiaries (or at least so they believed at that time) was a foregone conclusion, once Hungary, the only country asked to make sacrifices under it, accepted, however unwillingly, the place which the treaty assigned for her within the framework of postwar Europe.

The temptation is great to carry the story farther. The treaty did not become part of the public law of Europe for several months after its ratification by Hungary.[1] It may seem, therefore, that the coming into force of the treaty on July 26, 1921, would have been the appropriate place to stop. But the intervening months, however eventful and interesting, had no significance from the point of view of the making of the treaty. As already said, save for a compliance with formalities, the pattern had been designed by which Hungary's life, both in the society of nations, and—to some extent—internally, would be fashioned.

An even greater temptation was to follow the course of the treaty when in operation, at least in its beginnings. When Hungary completed ratification, the treaty was merely a blueprint; its articles became, with one major exception, a living reality only when the carrying out of its provisions began. This major exception was the territorial settlement, which, apart from insignificant details, had been fully carried out even before the treaty was signed. It was this fact which made the temptation so strong; for the territorial changes were

---

[1] Article 364 of the treaty provided for its coming into force upon its ratification by Hungary and by at least three of the Principal Allied Powers. The protocol registering compliance with this clause was not drawn up until July 26, 1921.

of such paramount importance in the case of Hungary that they were bound to influence decisively the subsequent execution of the economic, financial, military, and other clauses.

As an example of the difficulty in drawing a clear-cut line between what was to be included and what excluded from the present volume, the question of Western Hungary may be cited. The Peace Conference alloted this territory to Austria; but a final settlement of the issue was reached only after a year of protracted negotiations, guerilla warfare, Allied intervention, and a plebiscite which in fact substantially changed the frontier as determined by the treaty. Similarly, the story of the evacuation of the Hungarian territories occupied by Yugoslavia, which took place long after the treaty had come into force, might properly have been told here. Other incidents of a different character might have been included because of their origin in and their close inter-relation with the events herein unfolded. Perhaps the most striking illustration is the unsuccessful attempt of King Charles to regain the throne of Hungary in the spring of 1921. This incident set forces in motion which might have overthrown the painfully created treaty edifice, at that time not yet in force. In any event, it did have a decisive influence on Hungary's relations with her neighbors by nullifying a possible *rapprochement* attempted a few days earlier between Hungary and Czecho-Slovakia at the Conference of Bruck and by accelerating the consolidation of the Little Entente. This, in turn, made the political cleavage between Hungary and the Little Entente wider; and since the Porto Rose conference [2] later failed to bridge the economic cleavage

---

[2] The significance of the conference of the Succession States, held at Porto Rose, Italy, in Nov. 1921, seems to have escaped the attention of historians. The conference, which met largely through unofficial American initiative and effort, was one of the most important mileposts in European postwar history and may be regarded as the last step taken with a view to bringing order, along constructive lines, out of the chaos resulting from the disintegration of the Austro-Hungarian Monarchy. Had the conventions agreed upon by the participants been put into effect and carried out in good faith and mutual good will by each of the signatories, the history of Europe might have taken an entirely different turn. Yet the conference was practically unnoticed at that time, and one finds barely a reference to it in the relevant literature. The text of the agreements initialed by the delegates, together with a report of the American observer, Colonel Clarence Browning Smith, and a brief analysis by Professor Shotwell, are printed in *International Conciliation* No. 176 (July, 1922). Professor Shotwell himself attempted to give reality to the work of this conference through the coöperation of the Carnegie Endowment for International Peace with the International Chamber of Commerce, but failed, owing primarily to the opposition of the Czech members. Cf. Ridgeway, *Merchants of Peace*, pp. 156 ff.

separating the Succession States, it determined more or less the shape of things to come.

Yet these events have not been included in this narrative. It was felt that the execution of the treaty and the consequences both of its provisions and of the processes of their execution for Hungary, her neighbors, and Europe in general do not belong properly to the theme "Hungary at the Paris Peace Conference." They are most interesting and, as lessons of the past, vitally important, particularly today, when we look forward to another peace settlement. But they constitute a distinct chapter in history, though one for which this book, it is hoped, has laid a foundation which heretofore was lacking.

The student trying to assay the making of the Treaty of Trianon in the light of the record disclosed in the preceding pages has many pitfalls to avoid. The greatest difficulty lies in the inclination to make an appraisal in retrospect, in view of all the experiences of the intervening years, and then to apply the results as though the appraisal had been made contemporaneously. Whether praise for wisdom or criticism for lack of foresight, the judgment thus made assumes that the makers of the treaty, as well as those who opposed and sought to change it, possessed all the knowledge which, in the course of twenty years, has now become available to us.

Another difficulty is presented by the pragmatic approach, which unfortunately had been predominant for the last twenty-five years in all the social sciences, but quite particularly so in the field of international relations. The great drawback of the pragmatic approach lies in its oversimplification of causes; major movements in the evolution of society, national and international, and particularly the balance between peace and war, are compressed as though springing from single causes, such as the struggle for raw materials, or overpopulation. The economic factor is almost always predominant. Nowhere has this tendency been more evident and its results more overpowering than in the case of the peace treaties of 1919–20. The Germans, in particular, attributed all their ills solely and exclusively to the Treaty of Versailles, although Professor Shotwell demonstrated strikingly in his *What Germany Forgot* how misleading such an assumption was. Yet the thesis was accepted in Germany without reservation; and the Germans almost succeeded in convincing the rest of the world that the disintegration of Europe was caused largely if not exclusively by the inequities of the Treaty of Versailles. The Hungarians, who had to make sacrifices so much greater and whose national existence was so much more profoundly affected by the peace settlement than that of the Germans, have likewise regarded the Treaty of Trianon as the chief if not the only source of their sufferings and hardships since 1920.

Constructive criticism of the peace treaties must proceed on a broader basis. It should take into account the fact that the forces producing major transformations in society are too numerous and too complex to be identified with a single factor or phenomenon. As Professor Shotwell pointed out in the Foreword to this volume, the corrosive forces which destroyed European equilibrium were in operation long before the inadequacy of the peace treaties gave those forces greater striking power. Looking therefore at events in their historical perspective, Europe's bankruptcy must be attributed to something more fundamental and less tangible than the mistakes of the peace settlement.

Constructive criticism also should avoid basing conclusions on the letter of any treaty and should take account of the spirit and intent with which it is carried out. Even an imperfect treaty—and surely no political treaty was ever regarded by all of the co-contractants as perfect—could accomplish a desired end for the benefit of all, if applied wisely, with foresight and restraint. This is in no way different from the success or the failure of laws and institutions in the domestic life of nations, which depends not on the letter but on the spirit in which they are administered. Conversely, a treaty, or law, or institution, satisfying the highest standards of ethics or the most exacting principles of abstract justice, may bring disaster in its wake if its administration is characterized by inflexibility and shortsightedness. It is on this score that the peace treaties of 1919–20, and particularly the treaty with Hungary, can be subjected to severe criticism. But this is beyond the scope of our task.

With all these caveats in mind, there is still little praise for the Treaty of Trianon as an instrument of peace. In passing judgment, one need not adopt the bitterly critical point of view of the Hungarians. Their attitude was generated not only by the conviction that the provisions of the treaty—particularly the dismemberment of their country and the allocation of large numbers of Magyars to alien rulers—were unjust and inequitable. Their resentment was accentuated by the feeling that the treaty was made unilaterally, upon the presentation of *ex parte* evidence by Hungary's adversaries, and without adequate opportunity for rebuttal. So much for the Hungarian point of view.

Without necessarily subscribing to the Hungarian thesis in its entirety or to the charge of ill-will toward Hungary on the part of the framers of the treaty (a charge readily made in all sincerity by Hungarians), it must be conceded that the decisions incorporated in that document were arrived at by processes inconsistent with the rule of *audiatur et altera pars;* and that, in substance, they fell far short of the principles and objectives proclaimed by the Allies. To be sure, this conclusion is not to be confined to the Treaty of Trianon alone, but is equally pertinent in regard to all the peace treaties drawn up in 1919. The correctness of this conclusion may be tested by comparing the results of the treaties with Germany, Austria, Bulgaria, and Hungary— all completed by unilateral procedure—with those of the Treaty of Lausanne with Turkey, which was preceded by negotiations. In fairness it should be pointed out that the procedure followed at the Paris Peace Conference was not a preconceived one, for the original plan contemplated negotiations on the final peace terms with the ex-enemy states after the imposition of the armistice conditions and the establishment of a "preliminary" peace. Unless it is conceded that the Allies did envisage a negotiated peace, much of President Wilson's Fourteen Points would have to be regarded as meaningless. The great difference between the approach to the peace settlements as originally conceived and as actually practiced is strikingly illustrated by a confidential British document prepared, apparently, as a guide for the British peace negotiators.[3]

The introductory paragraphs of this document state that as regards the European Continent, Great Britain had no territorial ambitions or special commercial interests. "Our general object must be the establishment of a stable condition. . . . What we want is peace and order with open facilities for trade." Pointing out that general questions regarding Europe fell into two main categories, namely, territorial redistribution and guarantees for free international trade, the memorandum expressed the view that territorial questions were almost entirely confined to Eastern Europe, since boundaries in the West were settled permanently and satisfactorily after the question of Alsace-Lorraine had been adjusted. The memorandum then continues:

[3] This document, a photostatic copy of which is in the Library of Columbia University, cannot be precisely identified. It is undated and unsigned, but seems to have been prepared in the Foreign Office prior to the opening of the Peace Conference and certainly after the United States entered the war.

10. The East of Europe has not yet attained this condition; ultimately, this is one of the chief causes of the present war and no League of Nations can avoid future wars until this condition has been established there also. The establishment of this condition will, so far as it is possible, be the work of the Peace Conference. *In Eastern Europe, therefore, the territorial problem is that which will assume the first importance, and the future peace of the world will depend on the method in which this is settled. No settlement can be stable and permanent unless it is just. It is of the highest importance that no well-founded sense of injustice should be allowed to remain* and, to use President Wilson's words, "we must be just towards those to whom we should wish not to be just." The Germans in Bohemia and the Magyars must be treated on exactly the same principle as the Czechs and the Roumanians.[4]

Since England had no direct interest in these questions, the memorandum suggested that the British Government could exert a strong influence as a disinterested and impartial arbitrator. "Our object should be that when the whole transaction is concluded, all these nations, Czecho-Slovaks, Jugo-Slavs, Poles—we may perhaps add even Bulgarians, Magyars, and Germans—will feel that on the part of the British nation there has been an honest attempt to carry through a disinterested policy which has sought to represent the best interests of all, for, in the long run, the interests of each nation are not antagonistic to those of the other nations."

With respect to procedure, the memorandum counseled against taking the initiative and advocated intervention only if the parties directly concerned should not be able to agree:

14. The procedure to be adopted should . . . be that all the individual States concerned should be informed that the Allies would look to them to consider the frontiers which should be assigned to them in each case, and *to enter into negotiations with the other States* concerned. It is hoped that by negotiation and discussion a friendly agreement may be made. The final decision will, of course, be reserved for the Peace Conference. If an agreement has been arrived at by the States themselves, then presumably little would remain in such cases except for the Peace Conference to ratify the decision. If no agreement has been made, then the Peace Conference would consider the matter, and determine it in the form of an arbitration, but their determination would be final, and would, if necessary, be enforced by arms.[5]

No argument is necessary to show that the recommendations, whether substantive or procedural, contained in this British memoran-

---

[4] Italics added.   [5] Italics added.

dum have not been followed, although the assumptions upon which these recommendations were predicated were sound, as subsequent developments have proved. Failure to proceed according to the Wilsonian principles and the British suggestion may be explained but hardly excused by circumstances prevailing in 1919—the war-weariness in the Allied countries and the resulting pressure to "get done" with the peace settlement, the controversies between the Allies, the turn of sentiment in the United States which impaired the influence the Americans might otherwise have exercised, and other known factors which induced haste. The result was, as we know today and as thoughtful observers have realized for some time past, a settlement which was, at least in the eyes of large sections of Europe and elsewhere, not just and consequently not stable. The greatest dissatisfaction and the bitterest denunciation of the peace settlements came from the Hungarians, who looked upon the Treaty of Trianon, it seems, with a more intense feeling of injustice than that with which the Germans, Austrians, or Bulgarians received their respective treaties. The intensity of the feelings of the Hungarians was beyond doubt due largely to the magnitude of their losses—losses measured not merely in terms of square miles of territory but also in agricultural and industrial resources.

Yet, making full allowance for the Hungarians, the main criticism ought to be directed not against the injustices inflicted on the Hungarian people and not against the Treaty of Trianon as such, but rather toward the failure of the Peace Conference to deal realistically and constructively with the problem of European peace as an indivisible whole. Looking at the matter from this angle, the Treaty of Trianon becomes merely one of several pillars—though a rather important one—in a defective architectural plan; and the complaints of the Hungarians merely one of several outstanding examples of the results of the defects.

How can this failure be explained? Was the stature of the statesmen assembled in Paris smaller than of those who drew up, a century before, the Act of Vienna? I believe that such would be an unwarranted judgment. Had there been inadequate preparation? Never before had science and scholarship been called upon to contribute so much to the preparation of a peace treaty as in 1919; never before on such an occasion had statesmen been assisted by such an array of distinguished experts and technicians. The details were worked out painstakingly and in most instances, conscientiously; but how solid was the framework into which these details had to be fitted? How lasting the foundation upon which the framework itself was to rest?

In the past, treaties of peace were par excellence political treaties; the peace treaties at the end of the first World War were, with the exception of the Treaty of Lausanne, dominated by considerations of a moral character, in anticipation of an international society to be governed by a wholly new set of principles. The plan of President Wilson for the League of Nations which prefaced the peace treaties was devised and intended to embody this new international society. It was the most daring suggestion ever advanced for the orderly conduct of international relations; a suggestion which challenged the imagination of mankind as never anything before or since. The peace settlement was built on the fundamental assumption that it would operate in an international society, bound together in the League, and that the conduct of its members would be in conformity with the principles embodied in its Covenant. Inherent in and underlying this assumption was the expectation, at least on the part of the Americans, that inequities in the settlement would be gradually cured through the orderly processes of negotiations.

Unfortunately, the world was not ready for this revolutionary innovation. As far as Europe was concerned, the innovation, if successful, would have served as a substitute for the "balance of power." This system has always had a sinister implication for many people and, more particularly, for Americans, perhaps because their attention was focused on its dramatic failures, ignoring its less spectacular accomplishments. Nevertheless, the balance of power was more often than not a useful, indeed an indispensable instrument for the maintenance of Continental equilibrium in the face of constantly shifting forces. It had been the most constant political reality in European diplomatic history since the rise of the national state. Peace itself is of course nothing more, nor less, than a delicately balanced equilibrium of conflicting national interests—an equilibrium which insures that the forces on the side of stability, order, and peaceful evolution are evenly matched against single or concerted aspirations for revolutionary change. The balance of power, despite all its defects, was merely the application of this process to the peculiar conditions of the European Continent. It is true that with the disintegration of the Austro-Hungarian Monarchy one of the vital pillars supporting the balance disappeared; and that another vital arch in the system, Russia, engulfed in bolshevism, did not appeal to the Peace Conference as being an acceptable partner in the concert of Europe. Therefore the abandonment of the balance of power by the Peace Conference is in itself understandable.

A wholly different question is whether there was political realism in anticipating that the League of Nations could accomplish in a larger area what the balance of power could not do within the confines of Europe. The answer to this question, especially in relation to Southeastern and Eastern Europe, must be in the negative. In dealing with those areas the Peace Conference seems to have ignored two essential considerations. In the first place, the great importance of the Middle Danube basin in the interplay of European politics was overlooked. Whether from the economic or the strategic point of view, this importance could hardly be exaggerated. In the second place, no account was taken of the forces which would pit the small nations, successors of the Austro-Hungarian Monarchy, against each other—forces which were more likely to operate centripetally than centrifugally.

Even under the Monarchy these centripetal forces had been strong enough to prevent a genuine federalism and had been the cause of much factional dispute. It was therefore inevitable that if the framework of Empire and Kingdom was dissolved without some adequate substitute, there would be something approaching anarchy in the international relations of the Succession States. The framers of the peace treaties must therefore bear at least the initial responsibility for having brought about these conditions without an adequate safeguard against their consequences.

The political chaos which was bound to plague Europe, and perhaps the world, was foreseen by very few at that time. There is one notable exception: the distinguished French historian, Jacques Bainville, member of the *Académie française,* in a remarkable though little known book, published in 1920, pointed out the political shortcomings of the peace settlement and predicted, with uncanny accuracy, its political consequences.[6] M. Bainville, although concentrating primarily on the treaty with Germany, viewed the problems of the whole Continent.

[6] *Les Conséquences politiques de la paix.* The author stated in his preface that he did not write the book as an answer to Mr. Keynes's *Economic Consequences of the Peace,* which had appeared and had created a sensation a few months earlier. Nothing illustrates more clearly the a-political thinking of the period between the two world wars than the fact that M. Bainville's book, as prophetic in the political field as Mr. Keynes's in the economic, remained practically unnoticed.

He found the cardinal error in the fact that the Treaty of Versailles left German unity unimpaired, while the aggregate effect of the peace settlements was bound further to consolidate this unity internally and to open the road for further expansion externally by destroying and dissipating the barriers which could have stemmed such expansion.[7]

One of the important barriers in the past was the Austro-Hungarian Monarchy, which dissolved as a result of the war. Its disintegration was confirmed by the Peace Conference in the treaties with Austria and Hungary. Conceding that the Monarchy was too antiquated to justify resuscitation, the question still remains whether the Peace Conference should not have foreseen the necessity of a substitute, by some combination of the Succession States, which could serve as a politically, economically, and militarily equivalent heir to the defunct Monarchy, to bar the *Drang nach Osten*. Instead, after having concluded that a composite empire like Austria-Hungary ought not to exist, the Peace Conference created Czecho-Slovakia, surrounded on three sides by a compact mass of Germans and composed of five of the eight nationalities which lived in the former Monarchy. Instead, a truncated state of Germanic people was enjoined to lead an independent national existence under the name of Austria, although a little foresight should have made evident the irresistible appeal which the neighboring Reich would exert; should have shown that once Vienna became part of that Reich, Czecho-Slovakia was lost; and that having crossed the Carpathians, the road was open for the Germans down to the Black Sea and the Mediterranean, for neither Hungary, nor Yugoslavia, nor Rumania, nor Bulgaria could resist, either singly or even jointly.

The key to European peace had lain, at least since the Treaty of Westphalia, in the rule that no single nation ought to be allowed to dominate the Continent. True, wars had to be fought to enforce the rule; but these wars were decidedly on the decrease in the nineteenth century. As a matter of fact, adherence to this rule was one of the few immutable principles of the otherwise flexible and adaptable British foreign policy. It should have been a paramount consideration also at the Peace Conference, especially since the unification of Germany and its geographical position in the center of the Continent, together with

---

[7] M. Bainville's trenchant analysis of the consequences of the reorganization of Southeastern Europe is reprinted in an English translation, *infra,* Doc. 49, p. 560. The reader is urged constantly to keep in mind that his analysis was written in 1920.

the rapid growth of its population and its industrial development, made that country more than any other European power (with the possible exception of Russia) likely to impair the rule. Taking into account the political history of the nineteenth and early twentieth century, the unalterable geographic factors, and the lessons of trade and communications, then the vital importance of the Middle Danube basin as the corner stone of European equilibrium, whether threatened by Germany in the near future or by Russia in a somewhat more distant future, ought not to have escaped attention and should have received the most thoughtful examination of the statesmen assembled in Paris.

It is perhaps true that by an appreciation of the dangers which each of the new states in Southeastern Europe faced and through the application of wise statesmanship by the leaders of these states, much of the shortsightedness of the peace settlements might have been cured and many, if not all, of its tragic consequences avoided. It is possible that if the hope of a truly great statesman—that of the late President Masaryk of Czecho-Slovakia—had been possible of realization, the second world war could have been avoided. President Masaryk dreamed of a relationship between the new states in Southeastern Europe based on the principles of Jeffersonian democracy, transplanted from the United States to the banks of the Danube. How little the peoples of Southeastern Europe were ready to accept such principles in their dealings with each other is conclusively shown by the fact that the integral application and operation of them proved to be impossible, even in President Masaryk's own country. Thus the mistakes of the peace settlement, far from having been remedied in the succeeding years, as both President Wilson and President Masaryk had hoped and expected, were accentuated by the absence of sufficiently constructive statesmanship to restrain the forces of nationalism. The responsibility lies not so heavily on the individuals whose names are customarily connected with historic events as it does on the nations in whose names they have spoken and acted. Neither is such responsibility to be charged particularly to any one nation; all people, on both sides of the fence, ought to bear a share proportionate to the influence they wielded or could have wielded. It may be that neither individuals nor nations can profit much by past experience; yet it is hard to believe that the same mistakes would be committed twice by the same generation. For that reason, this book may be concluded with the sincere hope that whatever errors may mark the next peace settlement, they will not be repetitions of those which characterized the treaties of 1919–20. By looking not at the next elections but at the prosperity and happiness of the next generation, many of the pitfalls can be avoided.

PART SIX

Documents

DOCUMENT I

Terms of the Armistice between the Allied and Associated Powers and Austria-Hungary, November 3, 1918 [1]

I. MILITARY CLAUSES

1. All hostilities on land, at sea and in the air shall immediately cease.[2]

2. The Austro-Hungarian army shall be completely demobilised and the units in activity on the maritime front from the north to Switzerland shall be withdrawn at once.

In the Austro-Hungarian territories, within the boundaries fixed further below in Article 3, only 30 [3] army divisions, reduced to their pre-war, peace strength, at most, may be maintained as Austro-Hungarian armed force.

One half of the whole army corps and army division artillery material and of the equipment belonging to it, in the first place all that is to be found in the territory to be evacuated by the Austro-Hungarian Army, shall be collected at points to be fixed by the Allies and the United States of America, and shall be delivered up to them.

3. The territories occupied by Austria-Hungary since the beginning of the War shall be evacuated and the Austro-Hungarian Forces shall be withdrawn within the time to be determined by the Commanding Generals of the Allied Forces on the several fronts, behind the line traced as follows:

This line from the Pic Umbrail to the region north of the Stelvio follows the crest of the Rhaetian Alps as far as the source of the Adige and Eisack; then it passes over the Reschen and Brenner mountains and over the mountains of Oetz and Ziller.

Then it turns to the south, passes over the Toblach mountain and joins the present frontier running along the Carnian Alps. It follows this fron-

---

[1] *The Hungarian Peace Negotiations*, I, 344. Original French text in *British and Foreign State Papers*, CXI, 591. English and French text also in Temperley, *A History of the Peace Conference of Paris*, I, 481; the English translation printed in Temperley is slightly different from that printed above.

[2] The Supplementary Protocol to the Armistice containing the details and executive clauses of certain points of the Armistice (*Hungarian Peace Negotiations,* I, 346; Temperley, *op. cit.,* p. 487) provided, in Art. 1, for the cessation of hostilities on land, at sea, and in the air at all fronts of Austria-Hungary, at 3 o'clock in the afternoon (Central European time) of Nov. 4, 1918.

[3] According to the text printed in Temperley, *loc. cit.,* the number of army divisions allowed to Austria-Hungary was twenty.

tier as far as the Tarvis mountain, then beyond the Tarvis mountain the watershed of the Julian Alps over the Predil Pass, the Mangart mountain and the Tricorno (Terglou), the watersheds of the Podberdo, the Podlaniscam and the Idria passes. From this point onward the line follows a southeastern direction towards the Schneeberg, leaving outside the whole basin of the Save and its tributaries; from the Schneeberg the line descends to the shore so as to include Castua, Mattuglie and Volosca in the evacuated area.

Similarly it follows the present administrative boundary of Dalmatia, including in the north Lisarica and Trihania, and in the south an area delimited by a line starting at the shore at the Cape Blanca and following towards the east the peaks of the hills forming the watershed, so as to comprise in the area to be evacuated all valleys and water courses descending towards Sebenico, as the Cicola, the Kerka, the Butisnica and their affluents. It will also enclose all islands to the north and west of Dalmatia from Premuda, Selve, Ulbo, Scherda, Maon, Pago and Puntadura in the north to Meleda in the south; including Sant Andrea, Busi, Lissa, Lesina, Tercela, Curzola, Gazza and Lagosta, as well as the rocks and islets surrounding these islands, and Pelagosa, with the exception only of the islands of Great and Little Zirona, Bua, Solta and Brazza.

All territories thus evacuated will be occupied by the Allied Forces and by those of the United States of America.

In the territories to be evacuated all military and railway material of the enemy must be left behind.

All these materials (including the supplies of coal, etc.) shall be delivered up to the Allies and the United States, in accordance with the instructions in detail of the Commanding Generals of the Allied Forces at the several fronts.

The forces of the enemy shall refrain from any further destruction, plundering or renewed requisitioning in the territories to be evacuated by them and to be occupied by the Allied Forces.

4. The Armies of the Allied Powers will be given the means of free communication on all roads, railways and waterways of the Austro-Hungarian territories, as may be required.

The Forces of the Allied Powers are entitled to occupy at any moment any strategic points of Austria-Hungary, deemed by these Powers necessary in order to render any military operations possible or to maintain order.

The Forces of the Allied Powers are entitled, against payment, to effect requisitions in all the territories in which they find themselves.[4]

[4] The Supplementary Protocol, referred to *supra,* n. 2, contained in Art. 7 the following provisions:

"Regarding the railways, and the exercise of the right guaranteed to the Allied and Associated Powers in Art. 4 of the Minutes of the Armistice, we do herewith declare that the transportation of the troops, war material, food and other supplies

5. The German troops shall, within fifteen days, completely evacuate not only the Italian and Balkanic fronts, but all Austro-Hungarian territories as well.

All German troops that should not have left the Austro-Hungarian territories by the time specified shall be interned.

6. The evacuated Austro-Hungarian territories shall be provisionally administrated by the local authorities under the control of the troops of occupation of the Allied and Associated Powers.

7. Without reciprocity, all prisoners of war, all interned Allied nationals, and the civilian population of the evacuated territory shall be immediately repatriated, according to the conditions to be determined by the Commanders-in-Chief of the Armies of the Allied Powers at the fronts.

8. The sick and wounded incapable of being transported shall be cared for by the Austro-Hungarian personnel to be left behind for the purpose together with the requisite material.

II. NAVAL CLAUSES

1. All hostilities at sea must cease; and the position and movements of every Austro-Hungarian vessel shall be indicated with precision.

The Neutrals shall be advised that the navies and the mercantile fleets of the Allied and Associated Powers are free to navigate in all territorial waters, without the necessity of raising the question of neutrality.

2. Fifteen Austro-Hungarian submarines finished between the years 1910 and 1918, and all German submarines to be found in, or that might penetrate to, the Austro-Hungarian territorial waters, shall be delivered up to the Allies and to the United States of America. All other Austro-Hungarian submarines shall be completely disarmed and demobilised. These submarines shall remain under the supervision of the Allies and the United States of America.

3. Three battleships, three light cruisers, nine destroyers, twelve torpedo-boats, one mine-layer, six Danube monitors, armed and equipped, shall be delivered up to the Allies and the United States of America. The vessels to be handed up will be selected by the Allies and the United States of America. All other surface craft (including the river boats) shall be gathered together at the Austro-Hungarian bases of navigation to be indicated by the Allies and the United States of America; where they shall be completely demobi-

of the Allied and Associated Powers on the railway system outside the territories evacuated under the Armistice conditions, as well as the management and running of the railway system, shall be left to the employees of the Austro-Hungarian railway administration; however, under the control of Special Commissions to be appointed by the Allied and Associated Powers and by the military Railway Station Commands to be created according to the requirements."

lised and disarmed, and placed under the supervision of the Allies and the United States of America.

4. For all vessels belonging to the navies and the mercantile fleets of the Allied and Associated Powers there shall be free navigation on the Adriatic, including also the territorial waters, the Danube and its tributaries in the Austro-Hungarian territories.

The Allied and Associated Powers shall have the right of gathering up all mines and of destroying all obstruction, of which the location shall be indicated to them.

To ensure the freedom of navigation on the Danube the Allies and the United States of America are entitled to occupy or to dismantle all works of fortification or of defence.

5. The blockade by the Allied and Associated Powers shall be kept up according to the prevailing conditions, in such a fashion that the Austro-Hungarian ships encountered at sea shall be liable to capture. The exceptions shall be authorised by a commission to be appointed by the Allies and the United States of America.

6. All naval aerial craft shall be collected at the Austro-Hungarian bases indicated by the Allies and the United States of America, and immobilised.

7. The whole Italian shore and all ports occupied outside the national territory of Austria-Hungary shall be evacuated. All floating and naval material, and all equipment and stores required for navigation shall be left behind.

8. The Allies and the United States of America shall occupy the islands and the sea and land fortifications destined for the defence of Pola, the workshops and the Arsenal.

9. Austria-Hungary shall release all mercantile ships of the Allied and Associated Powers detained by her.

10. It is prohibited to damage the vessels and the material previous to evacuation, delivery or restitution.

11. Without reciprocity, all prisoners of war belonging to the Navies or mercantile fleets of the Allied and Associated Powers now in the hands of Austria-Hungary shall be returned.

DOCUMENT 2

Terms of the Armistice between the Allied and Associated Powers and Hungary, November 13, 1918 [1]

I. The Hungarian Government withdraws its troops to the north of the line traced by the upper valley of the river Szamos, Besztercze, Maros (village), the river Maros to its union with the Tisza, Szabadka, Baja, Pécs—in such a manner that these places remain unoccupied by the Hungarian troops —the course of the Drave to the junction of this river with the boundary of Croatia-Slavonia. The evacuation shall be effected within eight days.

The Allies will occupy with full right, and in accordance with the conditions to be fixed by the Commander-in-Chief of the Allied Forces, the territories evacuated. The civil administration in these territories shall remain in the hands of the present Government.

Within the zone evacuated only the police and gendarmerie forces indispensable for the maintenance of public order shall be left and those charged with securing the safety of the railway lines.

II. The Hungarian military and naval forces shall be demobilised, with the exception of six infantry divisions and two cavalry divisions, destined for the maintenance of public order, and with the exception of the fractions of police forces mentioned in Art. I.

III. The Allies are entitled to occupy all places or points of strategic significance, which it shall be the permanent right of the Commander-in-Chief of the Allied Forces to designate.

The Allied Armies have the right of passage and of sojourn in the whole of the Hungarian territory. They have the permanent right of using the railway or other rolling stock or the craft of navigation forming the property of the State or of private persons living in Hungary. The same applies to the beasts of traction or burden.

IV. The railway personnel and material doing duty, under normal conditions, in the area occupied (see Art. I.) shall remain in its place; besides which within one month a reserve stock of 2000 railway cars and 100 locomotives (standard gauge), and 600 railway cars and 50 locomotives (nar-

[1] *The Hungarian Peace Negotiations,* I, 343. A slightly different English text is printed in *British and Foreign State Papers,* CXI, 624, and in Temperley, *A History of the Peace Conference of Paris,* I, 491.

row gauge) shall be delivered up to the Commander-in-Chief for the requirements of the Allied Forces and to replace the Serbian losses of material following from the fact of the war. Part of this material may provisionally be taken from Austria. These figures are approximate.

V. The personnel and material of navigation doing duty normally in the area occupied shall remain in its place.

Besides which six monitors shall be at once delivered up to the Allies at Belgrade.

The remainder of the Danube flotilla shall be gathered for the purpose of disarmament into a Danube port to be designated at a later date by the Commander-in-Chief. Of this flotilla previously 10 passenger steamers, 10 steam tugs and 60 boats shall be surrendered within the shortest time for the requirements of the Allied Forces and to replace the Serbian losses of material consequent on the fact of the war. These figures are approximate.

VI. Within a fortnight a military railway detachment of 3000 men, supplied with the material required for repairing the railway lines of Serbia, shall be placed at the disposal of the Commander-in-Chief. These figures are approximate.

VII. Within 15 days sapper and telegraph detachments, supplied with the material required for repairing the Serbian telephone and telegraph lines shall be placed at the disposal of the Commander-in-Chief.

VIII. Within one month 25,000 horses and as much transportation material as shall be deemed necessary by him, shall be placed at the disposal of the Commander-in-Chief. These figures are approximate.

IX. The arms and the war material shall be stored at certain points to be designated by the Commander-in-Chief. Part of this material may previously be employed for the organisation of units placed under the command of the Commander-in-Chief.

X. The Allied prisoners of war and interned civilians shall be released at once, and collected at suitable railway stations, from where they shall be directed, for the purpose of repatriation, at times to be fixed by the Commander-in-Chief, to places to be designated by him. The Hungarian prisoners of war shall provisionally be further detained.

XI. The German troops are granted a space of fifteen days counted from the day of the signature of the Armistice Convention of General Diaz (November 4, 15 o'clock) for their passage through, and stoppage in, Hungary.

Any postal and telegraphic communications with Germany shall not be effected except under military control by the Allies. The Hungarian Government undertakes not to allow the transmission of military despatches to Germany.

XII. Hungary shall facilitate the approvisionment of the Allied troops.

Requisitioning is authorised provided it shall not be arbitrary; payments will be made at current prices.

XIII. The position of all Austro-Hungarian mines placed in the Danube and in the Black Sea shall be communicated at once to the Commander-in-Chief.

Besides, the Hungarian Government undertakes to stop all floating mines dropped above its boundary with Austria, and to remove those mines which are placed in its own waters.

XIV. The Hungarian post, wireless telegraph, telephone, telegraph and railway service shall be placed under the control of the Allies.

XV. A representative shall be delegated by the Allies to the Hungarian Minister for Public Approvisionment with a view to safeguarding the Allied interests.

XVI. Hungary undertakes to sever all relations with Germany; and to prohibit, unless expressly authorised by the Commander-in-Chief, all transports of troops and ammunition destined for the German forces of Roumania.

XVII. The Allies will not interfere with the internal administration of the Hungarian State.

XVIII. Hostilities between the Allies and Hungary are terminated.

Document 3

Report (Number 25) of Professor Archibald Cary Coolidge on His Mission to Hungary, January 19, 1919 [1]

No. 25.   Budapest,
                                                                    January 19, 1919.

The American Commission to Negotiate Peace,
4, Place de la Concorde,
Paris.

Geographic and Economic Unity of Hungary.

Sirs:

I have the honor to report that in support of their statements that the kingdom of Hungary forms a natural geographic and economic unity to a greater extent than any other state in Europe except Great Britain the Hungarians point to the following facts. The Hungarian state is made up of the basin of the middle Danube and its tributaries and of the surrounding hills and mountains. On the north, east and much of the south the frontiers of the wild Carpathians and of the Transylvanian Alps are about as good as could be desired. In the south until the loss of Croatia and Slavonia it has also been excellent. On the west, too, it is satisfactory. Hungary consists of flat, fertile plains and of the highlands about them. All the rivers (with some slight exceptions in Transylvania) ultimately flow into the Danube, which is thus the central artery reached by many tributaries. This great common river system now more than ever needs treatment as a whole. For instance, the Danube and its tributaries are subject to sudden rise and fall. What is needed is an elaborate storage system by which water should be preserved some times in one part, some times in another, and then used later in such measure as circumstances may require; but for such a system central management is necessary.

The Hungarian plains are rich, flat lands, which in former times were a natural resort of nomad or pastoral peoples like the Magyars, and the Huns and Avars before them. Today they are chiefly devoted to agriculture and produce fine crops, although these often suffer severely from drought. The Piedmont or region of the lower hills seems to integrate rather than to

[1] Printed from MSS.

separate the plains from the mountains, and it is here that many of the more important cities are to be found, cities which from their very position usually have a population belonging to several nationalities. In the more mountainous regions we find all the forests, all the mineral wealth and all the future considerable possibilities of the development of water-power, of which the war has here as elsewhere shown the need. As the Magyars have been men of the plains in the mountains we find predominating in numbers Slovaks, Ruthenians and Rumanians (except in the secklar [Szeckler] portion of Transylvania). The Germans have been numerous in the cities and are to be found scattered about in various places, but throughout the whole country the chief landowners have been Magyars, and they claim to have lived on good terms with the peasantry.

Thanks to this diversity in the character of its different regions, Hungary has been from the earliest times a singularly self-sufficing state. The plains have furnished the food, the hills have furnished the wood and the mineral wealth, the Danube and its tributaries have brought the people together. The different parts of the country have been attached to one another by the countless ties that come from having formed parts of the same unity through long ages. With the development of modern industry and communication the unity of the kingdom has been still further strengthened. In recent years mining has been carried on on a much larger scale, and many new manufactories have arisen and thrived. These establishments are to be found in the hill regions, that is, the borderlands, but they have been financed and managed from Budapest, which has grown in the last half century from a comparatively small town into one of the capitals of the world, with a population of nearly a million people before the war. Here is the center for the railroads, the seat of government, the winter home of people from every part of the country, the great focus of national life. Even distant Transylvania is and always has been economically found more closely connected with the central plain into which most of its waters flow than it has with Rumania on the other side of the mountains.

As a final argument the Hungarians point to the historic unity of their state, and say that it could never have been preserved through all the ups and downs of its history of a thousand years, despite the variety of nationalities that have lived in it, if its continuity had not been in the nature of things in obedience to geographic law.

We can understand then what a violent rupture in the economic life of the country has been produced by the occupation, whether temporary or not, of almost the whole Hungarian peripheral by the Czecho-Slovaks, the Rumanians and the Serbians, and in their severing of all relations between the lands they have occupied and the heart of the country. We can appreciate, too, the anguish of people here when they face the possibility of a Hungary reduced to the dimensions of the present unoccupied territory, without wood, without iron, without coal, without manufactories, nothing but an agricultural region and a great city condemned to certain ruin.

I have the honor to be, Sirs,

Your obedient servant,

[Signed] ARCHIBALD CARY COOLIDGE.

Document 4

Report (Number 26) of Professor Archibald Cary Coolidge on His Mission to Hungary, January 19, 1919 [1]

No. 26.   Budapest,
                                                         January 19, 1919.

The American Commission to Negotiate Peace,
4, Place de la Concorde,
Paris.

Sirs:

I have the honor to report that in the various conversations I have held in the last few days I have been able to gather certain impressions as to the general situation here, the position of the government and the strength of the various parties. I give these impressions, such as they are, leaving it to Mr. Storey to confirm or correct them when he has been there longer and has had time to study these matters more thoroughly.

The government of Count Karolyi is weak, its greatest asset being his own popularity and the difficulty of finding anyone to replace him. The aristocracy is bitterly critical of Count Karolyi. It accuses him of culpable weakness and declares he is leading the country to ruin and Bolshevism. They point out the small number of official adherents to the Socialist Party and say that Budapest is not Hungary or even a fair representative of it, that the present government is dominated by fear of the city mob and is steadily moving further and further toward the left. The military weakness of the government, as of the state, is only too evident. The troops returning in confusion from Italy and Serbia were sent to their homes by the War Minister without having to surrender their rifles and ammunition. This has had a demoralizing effect throughout the country. Later it was found necessary to have an army and after some hesitation five classes were called back to the colors. This produced dissatisfaction and the soldiers thus called proved unruly. Two classes were sent back, the other three having no wish to be as they were receiving good pay, had little to do and were under weak discipline. The councils of the soldiers (in which the officers take part) are already a power. Many people will tell one that against any revolutionary

[1] Printed from MSS.

attack there is practically no military force whatsoever. What the conservatives ask for, as is usual in such cases, is firmness, and they believe that they can rely on the support of the peasants. Many of the conservatives seem to reactionaries [sic] and would like to see the monarchy, (though hardly the recent emperor), restored. In general they appear to me not to realize how profoundly the situation has changed in the last three months and to lack constructive ideas.

The Social Democrats, among whom the Jewish element is strong, are well organized, in fact they have practically the only good organization that now exists in this country. Their leaders appear to be men of ability. They are planning all kinds of reforms in taxes, distribution of property and many other matters. There may be truth in the charge brought against them that they live in the domain of theory and not of fact. They are patriotic enough and dread the partition of their country as much as do the conservatives, though they admit errors in the past and appeal to the doctrine of self-determination rather than to history. They are suspicious and inclined to look on all conservatives as reactionaries plotting to restore the monarchy.

It is to be noted that one of the great weaknesses of Hungary is the absence of a strong middle class which might hold the balance between the main parties. Finance and industry are largely in the hands of the Jews and at present there is a strong Semitic feeling among the conservatives.

The government is conscious of its weakness and is trying to steer a middle course. It is based on a coalition and its members do not appear to get on harmoniously together. After a crisis which has lasted about ten days a new cabinet was announced this morning. Some members of the last one were retained, others left. I asked Count Karolyi if his new cabinet meant a step further to the left, he answered "a little, not much." There are now three socialists in it instead of two as before, but he pointed out that he had put in as a member a genuine peasant (whom I have met) to help counterbalance the power of the city democracy. Count Karolyi came in as the man who had opposed the war and who it was hoped might get better terms from the Entente. Since he has been in office he has not been able to get into communication with the Allies at all and he has seen a great part of his country overrun in a way not at all indicated by the armistice. The fact that this has happened and that the Magyars have attempted no resistance has tended to discredit and weaken the government and strengthen the power of its critics. Count Karolyi has an attractive personality, well educated, experienced, broad-minded. He realizes the difficulties of the situation and the futility of many of the plans proposed. He is doing his utmost under trying circumstances with not too great a confidence in the future. One feels attracted to him and sorry for him. He seems a very good fellow but nervous and permanently worried, which is perhaps not surprising.

The financial situation by all accounts is very bad. The expenses are enormous, a great number of pensioners and idle people are receiving what looks like high pay though it is not enough to keep them comfortably. Taxes do not come in. The economical life of the country has been disrupted by the occupation of the industrial portions by invading armies and I suspect that government finance is kept going chiefly with the aid of the printing press. The present reduced Hungary is being held responsible for the obligations imposed on the old larger one. Everybody says that any attempt to put on her an unfair share in the burden of the debt or in the currency or an indemnity will result in prompt and complete bankruptcy. Many people think this will come anyway.

As throwing light on the situation, I shall mention an incident which I witnessed yesterday. A band of students and others from the so called Szeckler portion of Transylvania who had gathered to protest against the incorporation of their country by the Roumanians, after proceeding to the hotel where I lived and cheering and singing the national hymn until I had to appear on the balcony, went on to the residence of the President where one of them made a speech and where I happened to be making my farewell call. The meeting, however, assumed an anti-socialist character and it was rumored that a demonstration would be made against the new Socialist Minister of War. When I left the palace and crossed the open place a Socialist guard (though I think that they were regular troops) was drawn in front of the residence with machine guns and others were coming to support them. I have been told that bloodshed was narrowly averted. In the evening there had been firing (without casualties) in one of the main streets through which I passed on my way to the station.

Still on the whole public order has so far been preserved and the Socialist leaders expressed themselves as being able to maintain it as long as the people have enough to eat and keep decently warm. The food qustion is not as bad here as it is in Austria, but the scarcity of coal is equally great and there is greater lack of material for clothes. If the absolute necessities of life give out no one can answer for anything. Mr. Boehm, the newly appointed Socialist Minister of War said to me "what we fear is not Bolshevism but anarchy."

I have the honor to be, Sirs,

Your obedient servant,

[Signed] ARCHIBALD CARY COOLIDGE.

Document 5

Excerpts from the Minutes of the Supreme Council, Held on January 31, 1919: the Presentation of Rumanian and Serbian claims to the Bánát [1]

. . . The question of Banat

2. M. Clemenceau then introduced the members of the Roumanian and Serbian Delegations, who would present their cases in regard to the question of the Banat.

M. Bratiano read the paper presenting the claims of Roumania to the Banat. (See Annexure "A.") [2]

M. Vesnitch stated that he had not a written memorandum to present, because he had only been informed of this meeting at eleven o'clock that morning. He had heard, with regret, that the Roumanian Delegation based their country's claim in part on the secret treaty of 1916. When this treaty was being negotiated, Serbia was fighting on the side of the Allies, without asking for any assurances, in the firm belief that after the war settlement would be made on the principles of justice, on the principles of the self-determination of nationalities, and in accordance with the promises of the Allies.

As in the past, so at the present, and in the future, Serbia desired to live in amicable relations with her neighbours, the Roumanians. Roumania and Serbia had existed side by side for ten centuries and no serious difficulties had arisen. As regards the Banat the Serbs based their claims solely on the principles recognised and proclaimed by all the Allies, and confirmed by the last nation to enter the war, the great democracy of America.

M. Clemenceau said that he was not aware that the Treaty of 1916 had been secret.

M. Vesnitch replied that not only had the Treaty never been published, but that as a representative of a power fighting with the Allies, he had several times asked here in the Ministry for Foreign Affairs to know terms of the Treaty. He had been told that the contents of the Treaty could not be divulged.

M. Bratiano stated that the discussion of the claims of Roumania had been begun in London in 1916, and had then been transferred to Petrograd,

[1] Miller, *My Diary*, XIV, 138 ff. (by permission).   [2] *Infra*, p. 375.

as a place where the examination of Eastern questions could be more conveniently carried on, especially in regard to Serbia.

M. PICHON then read the last paragraph of the Treaty, which required the maintenance of its secrecy to the end of the war.

M. VESNITCH, continuing, said that Serbia had no pretensions to the whole of the Banat. Serbia merely claimed that part to which she had a right on ethnological grounds, where their race had a majority over the Germans and Hungarians, and an absolute majority over the Roumanians. He did not mean to offend his Roumanian friends when he said that Germany and Hungary had always shown greater favour to the Roumanians than to the Serbians, and the Roumanians had been allied to the Central Powers for nearly thirty years.

Under the Hapsburgs this very part of Hungary had occupied a peculiar position. The boundaries of military districts had been arranged according to nationalities. The regiments raised in those districts had been recruited by nationalities, but no exact statistics were available. Moreover, while both Serbians and Roumanians belonged to the Orthodox Church, the Hapsburgs had insisted on their religious administration being carried out by nationality, and though this classification had been made by strangers the results showed the justice of the Serbian contention.

Furthermore, for forty years there had been Parliamentary elections in the Banat. These elections had always led to political contests between the Serbs and the Magyars; but there had never been any contests between the Roumanians and the Magyars.

MR. LLOYD GEORGE enquired whether any Serbian Members had ever been returned to Parliament, and for what districts?

M. VESNITCH replied in the affirmative to the first question and mentioned Werschebz [Versecz], Temesvar, Panesova [Pancsova], Seisskirchem [Weisskirchen, Fehértemplom], Kiknida [Kikinda], Banat Komlos, as electoral districts represented by Serbs at Budapest at the outbreak of the war. He added that in latter years the artificial means used by the Magyars to manipulate the elections had brought about a diminution in the Serbian representation.

MR. LANSING asked whether the Roumanians had returned any Delegates.

M. BRATIANO replied that violent political struggles had always occurred during the elections in the Banat in which the Roumanians had been involved, but he lacked any definite records as to the numbers of Roumanian Deputies returned. He thought, however, three million Roumanians were represented at Budapest by five Deputies, while the Serbians had only three. The violence of the Roumanian political struggles could not be measured by the number of Deputies sent to the Budapest, but by the number of Roumanian candidates in the prisons.

M. Vesnitch, continuing, said that as regards the violence of the political struggles they were in complete agreement. M. Bratiano's remarks applied equally to the Serbs and the Roumanians.

Since the Middle Ages the portion of the Banat claimed by Serbia had always been closely connected with the Serbian people. The manners, customs, aspirations, and traditions of the Serbs of the Banat and of the Serbs of Serbia were the same. At critical periods they had helped one another. When, in 1848, the Serbs had endeavoured to free themselves by siding with the Hapsburgs against the Magyars, the Hapsburgs had rewarded the Serbs by declaring the autonomy of a part of the Banat. A Voivoidia had been created with its own elected Voivod. As usual, the promises of the Hapsburgs had not been kept, but the territorial limits of the Voivoidia had been fixed, and the territory then demarcated was exactly the same as that which the Serbs now claimed. Historically, as the Isle of France was to France, and Tuscany to Italy, so was the Banat to Serbia. Serbian Renaissance had taken root in the Banat in the 17th Century; there Serb literature, art, theatre, etc., had reappeared; there the great Serbian ideal had been conceived. He, himself, entered political life there. In 1881 the young Serbians met there to discuss their new aspirations. The Banat had given birth to many Serbian leaders who had rendered service to the Allies, and carried their cause to a happy conclusion. He would merely mention such well known names as Pirdrik, Pashok, the greatest authority on financial questions, Nicholvitch, Porpish of Columbia University, and the present Rector of the University of Belgrade. As a further proof of the close attachment between Serbians of Serbia and the Banat, he called attention to the fact that the Royal Family, when exiled, had found an asylum there.

He submitted in addition two supplementary arguments. In his country, lying on the borderland between Christendom and Islam, the monasteries played a prominent part as a civilising agency, all of which were Serbian. Further, all real estates were still to this day in the hands of the Serbians, in spite of the efforts made by the Germans and Hungarians to dispossess them.

So far, he had presented merely the Serbian point of view, and he had not referred to the question of the frontiers. In dealing with this question both the interests of Serbia and the general interest must be considered. He was glad to say that from the Serbian point of view the two questions were identic. During the war the Serbian General Staff had realized that a successful offensive could only be made along the valley of the Morawa. As long as the Austrians had failed to attack along this line, the Serbians were able to resist successfully. But finally when the German General Staff assumed the leadership, and attacked down the Valley of the Morawa, further defence became impossible.

In conclusion he thought that if guarantees for future peace were required the proper protection of this feeble strategic point must be assured. He felt sure the Conference would consider favourably the just claims and aspirations of the Serbs, and coordinate these aspirations with the general interests of the world, and of civilisation, with which he felt confident they would be found to agree.

Mr. Balfour enquired whether the Serbian Representatives were in a position to give any figures. So far, only a general statement had been made but no statistics of populations by nationalities had been given.

M. Vesnitch replied that he was quite ready to supply the figures, but had not brought them with him.

M. Pashitch asked permission to lay on the table an official map dated 1853, prepared at the time when the Banat Voivoidia had been created. This map clearly showed the parts then belonging to Serbia and to Roumania. It would be seen that in the eastern portion, the population was chiefly Roumanian, whereas in the western part the Serbians were predominant. Between the two, the population was very mixed, because it had always been the policy of Austria to prevent the expression of national feeling by the introduction of emigrants. Notwithstanding this, it was extremely easy to find, between these two territories, the just line of demarcation, based on grounds of nationality. In conclusion, he would add that a paper setting forth the Serbian case had been prepared and would be submitted in due course.

M. Bratiano invited attention to the fact that though sentimental reasons, such as the statement that some great men had left one country to settle in another, deserved some recognition, it would, as a rule, be extremely unwise for statesmen to be influenced by such facts. It was with some emotion that he had heard the statement that the Royal Karageorgevitch family had taken refuge in the Temesvar. He thought that that hardly constituted a claim to the acquisition of that territory by Serbia, otherwise the whole of Roumania might as well be claimed by Serbia, since many of the members of the Royal families of Obrenovitch and Karageorgevitch had taken refuge in Roumania, and even M. Pashitch himself, when the situation in Serbia was somewhat dangerous, had made his home in Roumania. Furthermore, the convent question could establish no right, since the fact that many of the convents in the Banat were inhabited by Serbs was due to the religious leanings of the Slavs as a race. Thus, even in Roumania itself, many of the convents would be found to be occupied by more Serbs than Roumanians. Further, he wished to point out that the provisional partition of the Banat in 1848 by the granting of autonomy to the Voivoidia lasted theoretically for a period of ten years only. Moreover, Roumania had also taken part in the struggles for independence, but the tendency of the Hapsburg Government had always been to favour the Yugo-Slavs because they had stood by them in their wars against the Magyars.

Stress had been laid upon the secret character of the Treaty of 1916. Though the Treaty may have been secret its consequences were not secret, since that Treaty had permitted the maintenance at Salonika of an army of occupation, which had led to the results known by all.

M. Trumbitch asked permission to add a few words to M. Vesnitch's statement. As regards the secret Treaty he wished to declare most emphatically in the name of Serbia, as well as in the name of the Serbo-Croat-Slovene State, that the Treaty had been negotiated without Serbia's knowledge, and consequently Serbia refused to recognize it. Therefore, the problem must be discussed on another basis. In the first place, it was essential to define the objects of the discussion. Obviously there existed a territory which was in dispute between the Roumanians and the Serbo-Croat-Slovenes, namely, the Banat. M. Bratiano had talked about the whole of the Banat which included three comitats: Torontal, Temesver, and Krasnow(?). Now, the Serbians did not claim all three comitats: they merely claimed Torontal in the West of the Banat, Temosvar in the centre, and a small part of the Krasnow comitat. They were prepared to admit that all the Eastern part of the Banat was Roumanian. Therefore, he had nothing to say about that territory. The Serbs recognised Roumania's claims to that territory, which was inhabited by Roumanians, so that the principle of nationality could be applied. Consequently the question only dealt with two comitats, the claims of which were based on population and territory. As regards the population, everyone would agree that in those two comitats the inhabitants did not all belong to one nationality. There were Magyars, Germans, Serbs and Roumanians. The Magyars and Germans were enemies. The Germans were colonists living far from their own country and consequently they could possess no sovereign claims. Consequently it could positively be stated that the Germans must remain under the sovereignty of the country that would own that territory. The Magyars who inhabited the Banat were separated from Magyaria, and the Serbs and the Roumanians possessed the same rights and claims to ownership. In addition, he fully admitted that the wishes of all the people should be considered, not only those of the Serbs and Roumanians, but those of others also; because the question of future peace was involved and it was essential to ensure contentment to all the peoples. The Serbs thought that they were justified in claiming the two comitats not only on account of nationality, but also because the population itself would be pleased to form part of their State. The reason for this would also be made apparent by a study of the topographical situation. The Germans and the Magyars would obviously prefer to belong to a State which was situated along the Danube, whose Capital was on the Danube, and towards which river the people gravitated. Their economic and social interests were such that the Germans and the Magyars who were very numerous, would prefer to belong to Serbia, consequently the Serbs rested their claims not only on nationality, but also on the will of the people. Should the Great Powers decide to have a referendum on this question, Serbia would certainly agree.

The two comitats were bounded on the North by the River Maros, on the West by the River Theiss, on the South by the Danube and on the West by a line east of Temesvar and Werschetz. Hungarian statistics, which were never favourable to the Serbs, gave the following figures of population in the two comitats:

Roumanians 266,000
Germans 328,560
Magyars 251,000
Serbs 272,000

These were official statistics and they showed that the four nationalities were equally represented. The Serbs, however, were in the majority in the South and West, that is to say, in the territories of the Theiss, Danube and Maros. The above figures showed no great preponderance in favour of any nationality. Consequently the problem must be solved on other grounds than those of the principle of nationality. For this purpose, he thought, in the first place, the will and wishes of the people themselves should be considered, because the people were always fully alive to their own interests and were prepared to give them their full value.

The whole of the valley from the Maros to the Danube constituted the natural continuation of Serbia. That would explain why, in history, Serbs, when unhappy in Serbia, especially during the period of Turkish misrule, emigrated to the Banat and there created a new Serb centre of civilisation. When the Serbs began their struggle for independence it was the Serbs of the Banat who first fought for the cause of the first Karageorgo; and in 1849, when the Magyars attempted to crush the Serbs in the Banat, the Serbs of Serbia rushed to their rescue and they fought side by side, just as they had done in the last war. Though the Danube divided the territories into two, it did not divide the nationality, the civilisation, or the traditions of the Serbs on either side, and they could not now when victory had been achieved, after a struggle lasting so many centuries, abandon their brothers on the other side of the Danube.

The Serbs were anxious to establish good relations with the Roumanians. With the exception of the Banat problem, for which a solution must be found, the two countries had no differences. If the Roumanians wanted the Danube and the Theiss as their frontiers no agreement could possibly be reached. During this war of liberation Roumania had suffered bitterly, but it must not be forgotten that Serbia in particular and Yugo-Slavia in general, had also suffered heavy losses. And for this reason the Serbs insisted on the recognition of their claims to the two comitats. These claims meant no injustice to Roumania, for the Banat was a continuation of Serbia and Yugo-Slavia, whilst between Roumania and the Banat claimed by Serbia, stretched a chain of mountains the importance of which in the settlement of this question could not be overlooked.

M. BRATIANO apologised for having to address the meeting a third time. He was compelled to do so as the Roumanians had only two representatives to pit against the three representatives of Serbia. M. Trumbitch had explained the situation of the population in the Banat, and he had proposed to divide the territory into two parts, giving the mountainous portion with its mines and forests to Roumania, whilst allotting to the Serbs the industrial areas of Temesvar and the agricultural districts of Torontal. As regards the figures relating to the two comitats, given by M. Trumbitch, it would be remembered that the Germans and Magyars were twice as numerous as either the Serbs or Roumanians. The only possibility of applying the ethnical test was to consider the Banat as a whole, because on ethnical grounds it would be impossible to justify the placing of 580,000 Germans and Magyars under the control of 272,000 Serbs. Therefore, the Banat could not be divided into two for ethnical reasons. Similarly it would be easy to say that economically it would be unsound to separate the mines and forests from the commercial, industrial and agricultural regions. In the course of history the frontiers of the Banat had never been changed except on the Roumanian side because on that side no real frontier existed between the Banat and Wallachia. On the other frontiers no changes had ever occurred except during the ten years which covered the period of the existence in theory of the Voivoidia. Consequently, politically the Banat formed part of Roumania. Furthermore, the idea of separating the two fertile districts of the Banat from the mountainous one, where the population would be left without food resources, would be impossible, since the population of the latter would thereby be compelled to emigrate.

To sum up, for the populations inhabiting those regions, the work which the Conference was now called upon to carry out could be compared with that of an Inter-Allied Commission (had such a Commission then been possible) appointed in the time of Charlemagne to adjudicate on the question of the Rhine. Had the Commission at that time decided that the Rhine should form the boundary between Germany and France, what untold benefits might have been conferred on the world, what influence such a decision might have had on the events leading up to the present war. That Conference was now in the same way settling the future of Eastern Europe. The use of the Danube was essential for the development of civilisation. The

Danube could alone form the only real boundary of everlasting friendship. That being his conviction he would, in conclusion, invite the attention of the Great Powers to the dangerous situation now existing in the Banat which called for immediate action. The Serbian troops occupying the Banat were in open strife with the Roumanian population, and if the real wishes of the peoples must be known, the first step must be the removal of the Serbian troops and their replacement by Allied troops who could hold the scales evenly between the various peoples. This course was urgent, as serious developments might otherwise take place.

M. CLEMENCEAU enquired from M. Bratiano whether he would agree to the general principle of the referendum.

M. BRATIANO replied that he considered the question already settled. He had insisted on the Banat being dealt with as a whole, and he could not agree to any partition of the area. If a referendum were insisted on, he would require time for consideration, although at the moment he would not oppose the proposal.

M. VESNITCH expressed his regret that M. Bratiano had thought it necessary to raise the question of the actual occupation of the Banat by Serbian troops. If the French Commander-in-Chief of the Allied Armies in the East had ordered the Serbian troops to occupy that territory, the welcome that Army had received was sufficient proof that the decision taken had been a good one. At any rate, Serbia was not to blame if Roumania had not entered the Banat either now or in 1916.

(The Roumanian and Serbian Delegates then withdrew.)

The meeting adjourned until Saturday, 1st February, at 3:00 p.m.

Annexure "A" IC-129 (BC-19) The Question of the Banat

The task of setting forth Roumania's rights to the Banat is greatly facilitated by the fact that this question was considered by our three great European Allies during the weighty discussions which took place before the Treaty of Alliance of 17th August, 1916, and that this Treaty, which was signed by them, recognises the validity of our claim.

We have complete confidence in the support which the said Signatory Powers will grant in demonstrating our just claim to the two great non-European Powers who took no part in the examination of this question in 1916 and who may, therefore, be ignorant of the principles thereof.

The claims are based on the principle of ethnology, and are put forward in virtue of our right to national unity.

This principle should, however, be in accordance with other requirements of national life, which it is impossible to dissociate from the territorial conditions amongst which a nation has evolved.

Those desirous of assuring the future of Eastern Europe must face the problem of uniting these two principles. Our claims with regard to the Banat are based on the solution of this problem.

The Question of the Banat of Temesvar.

Nobody can think of denying Roumania the right to claim political union with a territory which has been inhabited for many centuries by Roumanians and where they number 600,000 as against less than 400,000 Germans, who settled in the district in the 18th century, and rather more than 300,000 Serbs, who immigrated in the 15th and especially in the 18th centuries, to mention only the ethnical units of most importance.

But it has been imagined that a distinction might be drawn in the Banat between the districts where the Roumanian population is absolutely in the majority and those in which it constitutes only a relative majority or an important minority; it has been thought that it might be possible to trace a State frontier line across the plain of the Banat between the Roumanians on the East, who would be reunited to the Kingdom of Roumania, and the non-Roumanians on the West, who would become subjects of the Serbian State; the Roumanian Government considers this a dangerous error.

The Banat is not a geographical term, it is a reality, a real geographical region and also a real political province forming at the present day, as it has done throughout the ages, a complete and indivisible whole. It is, in fact, difficult to conceive that any State can claim or accept one portion only of the country, and still more difficult to expect that, once in possession of that portion, it would be able to withstand the necessity of soon claiming the whole country.

The waterways which surround the Banat on three sides (the Maros, Theiss and Danube) form a natural frontier which bounds a region of plains on the West and a mountainous district to the East, which are closely interconnected. It is the plain of the Banat which yields the necessary food supplies for the inhabitants of the mountains; whilst the people of the hill country send the plain dwellers their wealth of timber and minerals. The rich plains, which are comparatively sparsely populated, draw their indispensable supplies of labour and settlers from the mountains; the plain and the mountains cannot exist apart from one another.

All the systems of communication, whether by road, rail, or water, are organised in the Banat for the whole province, and if a State frontier were drawn which would cut them asunder, all efforts made in this region since the 18th century to establish the means of communication indispensable to economic welfare, would be rendered ineffective.

The navigable rivers and canals traversing the plain carry the heavy produce of the mountains on the East to the Theiss and the Danube; a division of the Banat would leave the Roumanians the upper courses of the rivers and give the Serbs the lower reaches and the canals, which would result in ruining the very advantages of the natural situation of the Banat between its three waterways, by cutting off one entire part of the country from free access to the Danube and the Theiss.

Transylvania itself, where the Maros is the one great waterway intersecting the country and penetrating into the heart of its mountains, would be deprived of one of its most necessary outlets. The produce of its forests and mines normally descends the Maros and Theiss to the Danube and thence to the sea, but a Serbo-Roumanian frontier would stop its course below the Lower Maros.

No useful purpose would be served by solemnly affirming, or even guaranteeing *de facto,* freedom of navigation on all the waterways, streams, rivers and canals. Navigation requires something more than this—i.e., technical organisation, depots and warehouses, mechanical, commercial, and industrial installations—in order to preserve, manufacture, distribute, work up or convert the produce at the most suitable points and under the most favourable conditions.

The river trade of Transylvania and the Banat would naturally find all those advantages on the Roumanian banks of the Theiss and Danube; it would be useless to expect them from a foreign State for the products of another State.

But if, notwithstanding everything, the Banat were to be cut in two by a frontier on imaginary ethnographical lines, this would be impossible except by disturbing the necessary balance in every direction.

Even in the region where the Serbs are numerous, large groups of Roumanians are interspersed among them, as well as German colonies which cannot be reunited politically to any other State of the same nationality, but which there is no reason to join to Serbia and which could not, in any event, be annexed to that State because of their distribution throughout the centre of the Banat. These Germans (Suabians), so soon as they are at liberty to give public expression to wishes which are already known, will moreover refuse to allow their national numbers to be diminished by a division between Serbia and Roumania, and they will rally round the latter State.

The intermixture of these various nationalities in the West of the Banat is such that, in order to detach from Roumania the 200,000 Serbians inhabiting such region, it would be necessary, at the same time, to annex to Serbia double the number of non-Serbs, Germans, Magyars and Roumanians. And thus new hotbeds of Irredentism would be created.

In order that at least the Southwestern portion of the Banat might be wrested from Roumania, it is probable that the necessity for giving Belgrade a protective zone may be brought forward. The lessons of the last year of the war have resulted in an extraordinary diminution in the belief in the utility of such protection, and consequently of the importance of its corresponding argument.

Furthermore, Roumania replied to this contention in 1916, by inserting in her agreement with the Allied Powers a clause undertaking to leave a zone opposite the present capital of Serbia without military works or garrison.

This is a sufficient guarantee from the defensive point of view. But the creation, on the left bank of the Danube, of a protective zone in the nature of a Serbian political and military possession, would be a veritable bridgehead, or a military organisation less defensive than offensive.

Ever since the Serbian and the Roumanian States have adjoined each other on the Danube, history has furnished proofs of their active intercourse from the point of view of trade and civilisation, but has never had to record disagreements between them. The pacific feeling of both peoples has been greatly assisted by the fact that the Danube formed a well-defined and certain boundary between them, both as regards geography and interests.

The Roumanian Government has always been so persuaded of the Danube's importance as a peace-maintaining frontier, that it has never cast its eyes beyond this river, nor considered the possibility of uniting to that part of Roumania watered by the Northern Danube the many Roumanians settled in Serbia between the Timok and the Morava valleys.

It is persuaded that once the Danube is crossed, once a bridgehead is established on the further bank, yet wider territorial extensions in this direction will become of ever-increasing political and economic urgency. There would then be no end to the unappeasable disputes connected with more or less conventional frontiers. And those disputes, which Roumania has steadfastly refused to tolerate on the right bank of the Danube, could not fail to arise on its left bank with regard to a frontier line drawn across the plain of the Banat, for no nice adjustment could make it anything but ill-defined and inequitable.

Thus, the only results of allowing Serbia to cross the Danube in order to ensure that State a supposed ethnographical boundary, in the hope of finding in such concessions a guarantee for the organisation of international peace, would be economic disorganisation, arrested development of a whole region, and the certainty of future disputes.

It is hardly necessary to add that Roumania will ensure to all Serbs who may remain within her territory all the rights and guarantees ensured to Roumanian subjects by the Serbian State, in conformity with the principles which may be laid down by the League of Nations in the case of minorities.

Such were the general outlines of the arguments put forward by Roumania before the war, in order to justify the validity of her claims to the

Banat. The part played by Roumania in the war cannot fail to confirm such rights.

In order to appreciate what Roumania has done, without even calling to mind the conditions under which she was obliged to begin and continue her military action, one has only to remember the fact that the losses of the Roumanian army alone, not including even greater losses among the civilian population amount to a total of 335,000 men, and to trace on the map appended hereto the proofs of the influence of Roumania's military action on the general conduct of the war.

Document 6

Excerpts from the Minutes of the Supreme Council, Held on February 1, 1919: Rumanian Territorial Claims [1]

... Roumanian territorial claims

7. At this stage M. Bratiano and M. Misu, members of the Roumanian Delegation to the Peace Conference, accompanied by their experts, MM. A. Lapedatu and Constantine Bratiano, were admitted to the Conference.

M. Clemenceau asked M. Bratiano to put forward the Roumanian case.

M. Bratiano then read the following report on the situation in Roumania:

M. Bratiano [the first part of the report summarizing Roumania's attitude during the World War is omitted] . . .

The claims of Roumania, as recognised by her treaty of alliance, had never been of an imperialistic character. Her claims had only represented the manifestation of the national aspirations of the people and the desire of the Roumanians to be once more united on the ethnical territory assigned to them by history.

(b) Roumania's claims to Transylvania

A reference to the map would show in this corner of the world a mountainous district forming the central portion of Transylvania. This elevated region on the one side gradually sloped down to the rich plains of the Danube and the Dniester, whilst on the North it was bordered by the Carpathians and Galicia, and so constituted a well defined geographical area from every point of view. It was in this territory that the Roumanian nation had been constituted and formed; and all its aspirations for centuries had tended towards the political union of that territory.

At the outbreak of War, Hungary, with the Banat, constituted what might be called Transylvania, because from the political point of view Transylvania occupied the exact centre of the whole of that region. But in order to avoid mentioning different parts of that territory at every turn, in the term "Transylvania" would be included not only the Banat but all the countries extending as far as the Galician Carpathians and as far as the Theiss; the whole of that region having formed part of the late Kingdom of Hungary.

According to Hungarian statistics (the nature of which were such that

[1] Miller, My Diary, XIV, 162 ff. (by permission).

they could not be taken as basis for an accurate estimate), the Roumanians represented 55 per cent. and the Magyars 23 per cent. of the population.

M. ORLANDO enquired how many Hungarians there were in this district.

M. BRATIANO replied that, according to these same statistics, there were 1,000,000 Hungarians and 2,500,000 Roumanians in Transylvania, not including the Banat. It was, moreover, certain that these statistics were inaccurate. As a matter of fact, if one considers the increase in the Roumanian population according to these statistics, one finds fanciful figures, varying according to the political situation and the degree of acuteness of political struggles. Whilst the Roumanian population on the other side of the Carpathians had tripled and quadrupled, the Roumanian population of Transylvania remained stationary, according to the Hungarian statistics. If an exact census could be taken, 2,900,000 Roumanians and 687,000 Magyars or 72 per cent. and 15 per cent. respectively of the population would be found to be the exact figures. Whilst the Roumanian population represented 23 per cent. of the population of the towns and 72 per cent. of that of the villages, the Magyars only represented 40 per cent. of the urban population and 13 per cent. of that of the villages. The Magyars were chiefly officials and soldiers, but from the ethnical point of view they were far from representing the ethnical proportion that they claimed for themselves. The Magyar population formed a dominating class which had lived in the midst of the Roumanian population.

Transylvania also included, near the Moldavian frontier, a race related to the Hungarians and a Saxon population: the former numbering 450,000 and the latter 260,000.

On the whole, the great ethnical majority of the population was therefore Roumanian. There was one region that Roumania did not claim, although it included some Roumanian villages, namely the district of Debreczyn; but, in order to maintain the ethnical character of their claims, the Roumanians did not claim such an active Hungarian centre as this town constituted for the adjacent district.

At the beginning of the Armistice, the German colonies on the Wallachian and Moldavian frontiers joined Roumania, and the union of Roumania was accomplished with the greatest ease. The Saxon colonies even concluded a formal deed of union with the Kingdom of Roumania. The Roumanians of Transylvania immediately held a great meeting and constituted themselves into an Assembly, 150,000 men meeting for this purpose from all parts of the region; Roumania had already admitted into its Government three Ministers representing Transylvania and the Roumanian countries in Hungary. . . .

*(e) Present constitutional arrangements in Transylvania, Bukovina
and Bessarabia*

Mr. LLOYD GEORGE enquired whether the national assemblies formed
in these three countries, Transylvania, the Bukovina and Bessarabia had
demanded their return to Roumania and whether they had laid down any
conditions.

Mr. BRATIANO said that the three countries had made different constitutional arrangements. In Transylvania, the Roumanian representatives
formed themselves into a National Assembly, which the representatives
of the Saxon population joined: but the Hungarian population had refused
to do so. . . .

Transylvania had proclaimed complete union, but with provisional autonomy, in order to settle the legal conditions under which effect would
finally be given to such union. Transylvania had, as a matter of fact, different laws from those in force in Roumania and her representatives
wished to study these specially important questions and to refer the decision reached to the people before signing the final act of union.

Mr. LLOYD GEORGE enquired whether Roumania was asking the representatives of the Powers purely and simply to proclaim the annexation of
these different territories, or was she asking the Conference to declare that
in these various regions regularly constituted assemblies shall have power
definitely to declare for union and to settle the conditions? When the union
of Scotland with England had taken place, that union was only effected
after certain conditions imposed by Scotland had been carried out.

M. BRATIANO said that Roumania asked for the recognition of the union
of these provinces with Roumania, for that union had already been proclaimed and the latter had already sent three Ministers to the Roumanian
Cabinet. A Statute had even been arranged. The same remarks applied to
the Bukovina.

Mr. LLOYD GEORGE said that he had reason to believe that certain minorities had not taken part in the elections. It was important that the decision
should be made by assemblies representing the whole population.

M. BRATIANO said he could not quite follow the question put by the
Prime Minister of England. Roumania had fought in order to impose her
national will on the Hungarian minority in Transylvania. It was certain,
therefore, that if the Hungarians were asked to vote in favour of union
with Roumania, they could hardly be expected to do so. He did not think
a fresh election should be held at the present time. As regards the situation
created in Transylvania by the armistice, he considered that the question of
principle had been decided by the war, and that these territories must be
restored to Roumania. In their future political life, the rights of the minori-

ties would assuredly be respected and they would be granted the greatest possible freedom. But the vanquished could not now be expected willingly to unite themselves to a country, which for a thousand years they had sought to dominate.

Mr. LLOYD GEORGE agreed that the majority must be the final arbiters: but it was essential that the wrongs which had been imposed under Hungarian domination should not be perpetuated. It must not be possible for the minorities to be treated in future as were the Roumanians in the Hungarian State, who were deprived of their language, their traditions and their own life.

Roumania asks authorization to occupy immediately all territories claimed by her

M. BRATIANO expressed complete agreement on that point. In the Deed of Union with Transylvania it had been stipulated that the religious and political liberty of all the nationalities in Transylvania would be recognised, and that was the reason why the Saxon population had associated itself with the Union. The principle involved was one of general application, to be extended to all annexed countries without exception. But it would be an act fraught with serious consequences if the union with Transylvania were not to be declared now, at a time when her late masters were convinced that their cause was lost. There had been too much delay already; occupation of the territories must take place under the most favourable conditions, in the very interests of the nations who were to live together. For instance, the conditions were most satisfactory in the districts bordering on the Roumanian frontier which had been occupied before the signing of the armistice, even though Roumanians there actually formed the minority of the population, on the other hand, in the territories not occupied by Roumania, although Roumanians were in the majority, conditions were very serious owing to the enemy having organised a violent agitation on Bolshevik lines. The division of wealth and the abolition of rank had been promised; Wilson's policy had been proclaimed to be nothing but a capitalist policy; people had been told to kill officers and to do away with the governing classes. This propaganda had caused 100,-000 workpeople to strike and the news received from Transylvania was very disquieting. This state of affairs was largely due to the uncertainty of the future. Therefore, he would beg the Commission to come to an immediate decision on the practical questions arising out of the war, and to authorise Roumania to occupy these territories immediately. The Roumanian Government might still be able, without bloodshed, to make relations between the various nations possible and even fraternal. But if the present situation were allowed to drag on, a new animosity would be created and blood would flow once more. Roumania was in a condition of great exhaustion due to the trials she had undergone and to the Bolshevik propaganda which had spread from the Ukraine through Bessarabia. Roumania was in need of the moral support of the Allies, if she was to remain what she had been hitherto—a rallying point for Europe against Bolshevism. He did not know what decisions would be reached by the Conference with regard to Bolshevism; but it was not a political doctrine; it was a serious and contagious disease that must be fought. Roumania asked to be placed in a position to resist it. She asked this not only in her own interests, but in those of the whole of Europe and, without exaggeration, of the civilisation of the world.

MR. LLOYD GEORGE asked what troops were at present occupying Transylvania.

M. BRATIANO replied that the small tract bordering on the Roumanian frontier had been occupied by the Roumanians and that the remainder of the country, not being under any occupation, was a prey to anarchy. The Bukovina had been occupied by the Roumanians.

(f) Roumania asks for occupation of Banat and Dobrudja by Allied troops

Yesterday, at the close of the meeting with the Serbian representatives, he had ventured to request that the Banat should be evacuated by Serbian troops, and that these should be replaced by the Allied troops at present in that neighbourhood. In consideration of the nature and purpose of the meeting, he did not wish to enlarge upon the acts of violence which the Serbian Army were committing against the peoples of the Banat, and which might sow regrettable seeds of enmity. Whatever might be the decision of the Conference, it was most desirable that such occupation should be effected by Allied and not by Serbian troops. . . .

MR. LLOYD GEORGE expressed the view that the question of the Banat could not be discussed in the absence of the Serbs.

M. CLEMENCEAU thanked M. Bratiano for his statement with regard to Roumania's claims.

(The Roumanian Delegates then withdrew.)

MR. LLOYD GEORGE said that, speaking for himself and for many of those whom he had been able to consult, it was extremely difficult to decide questions of boundaries on statements, however lucid, made in the course of a conversation. He wished, therefore, to propose that in the first place experts of the five Great Powers should examine such questions, and, if possible, make a unanimous recommendation. It is quite possible that on many of the questions to be considered, the experts would agree. Naturally, these experts could not decide the problem, but they could clear the ground, and, in cases of disagreement, the representatives of the Great Powers would be compelled to argue out the case there in that Council Chamber. But there were many questions regarding which the Great Powers were perfectly impartial. For instance, they were quite impartial regarding the Roumanian claims on Hungary, to an exposé of which they had listened that day. He thought, therefore, that if a preliminary investigation was carried out by experts, it would greatly assist. He fully admitted that this procedure could not be introduced as a permanent arrangement, or be accepted as a precedent for universal application; but in the particular case of the Roumanian claims, in order to arrive at a decision, he hoped the experts would be allowed to examine the ground in the first instance, and the representatives of the Great Powers would eventually decide the question. He wished, therefore, to move the following Resolution:

It is agreed that the questions raised in M. Bratiano's statement on the Roumanian territorial interests in the Peace Settlement shall be referred for examination in the first instance by an expert Committee composed of two representatives each of the United States of America, the British Empire, France and Italy.

It shall be the duty of the Committee to reduce the questions for decision within the narrowest possible limits, and to make recommendations for a just settlement.

The Committee is authorised to consult the representatives of the peoples concerned.

PRESIDENT WILSON expressed the view, which he felt sure was shared by the mover of the Resolution, that only those aspects of the question, which did not touch the purely political side of the problem, should be examined by the experts. All other questions requiring the exercise of tact and compromise must necessarily be reserved to the representatives of the Great Powers, including the protection of minorities, etc. The experts, therefore, should merely consider the territorial and racial aspects of the case.

MR. BALFOUR thought that strategical questions might also be considered by the experts.

M. ORLANDO said he had a statement to make in reference to a matter of individual conscience, which he did not wish to force on his colleagues. But he felt himself bound to Roumania by a Treaty. In his opinion, the laws relating to public and civil rights only became valid after their promulgation. He did not wish to defend secret treaties which, indeed, were now out of fashion; but a treaty having been signed by Italy, France and Great Britain, he could make no distinction between a secret treaty and a public treaty.

M. CLEMENCEAU drew the attention of M. Orlando to the fact that the Roumanian Treaty had, by the common assent of the representatives of the Great Powers there in that room, been cancelled. It had been agreed that Roumania should, for reasons given, have proper representation at the

Peace Conference; but, it was distinctly understood that the grant of representation would not renew every clause of the Treaty, which she had broken by going out of the war . . .

Mr. Lloyd George also pointed out that Roumania was now claiming more than she had been granted by the secret treaty.

M. Orlando said he had no recollection of the incident quoted. But, in any case, the treaty of 1916 between Roumania and the Allies having been signed, did that fact tend to invalidate the Peace Treaty subsequently signed by Roumania with the Central Powers at Bucharest? If so, the previous treaty with the Allies was *ipso facto* annulled. In his opinion, Roumania was forced to sign the Peace Treaty with the Central Powers, and she had not been a free agent. Consequently, he did not consider the latter treaty to be valid, no more than he would consider himself bound by an agreement signed whilst a pistol was being held at his head.

M. Clemenceau remarked that he did not think such an argument really helped the case of the Roumanians.

M. Orlando said that, at any rate, he had given expression to a matter which had lain on his conscience. He turned now to Mr. Lloyd George's proposal and was glad to find that it was not to form a precedent. Therefore, some of his objections would fall to the ground. But, as regards the application of the proposal to the case under consideration, the decisive question to be settled was wholly and solely a political one. Being exclusively political, the whole responsibility for the settlement must rest with the representatives of the Great Powers.

Mr. Lloyd George's resolution said that specialists would be appointed. What kind of specialists? If it was intended to appoint specialists on the Roumanian question, he himself had none; and they would be difficult to find. But even then, he would ask: What branch of the Roumanian question should these specialists represent? Should they be geographical, historical, strategical or ethnographical specialists? The question was a very complex and mixed one, and its various aspects could not be separately examined. Consequently, the specialists who might be appointed though knowing their particular subject could not give good assistance in the final solution of the problem. Further, the resolution said that the Committee would consult the representatives of the people concerned. The experts would thus, in fact, become examining magistrates. Mr. Lloyd George's proposal thus became a very serious one, since the experts would constitute the Court of First Instance and the Delegates of the Great Powers, the Final Court of Appeal. He failed to see how such a procedure would expedite matters. In his opinion, it necessarily meant delay, especially if the experts decided that the enquiry must take place *in situ*. His proposals might not be acceptable to his colleagues: but he had felt obliged to put forward his views though he did not wish to press them. In his opinion, the procedure proposed by Mr. Lloyd George in this case had great inconveniences, and, if accepted, he noted with pleasure that it would not form a precedent.

M. Sonnino expressed the view that the experts might find themselves compelled to go to the spot to consult the representatives of the people concerned.

M. Lloyd George explained that the experts would carry out their work in exactly the same manner as their Committee on Teschen had done.

M. Sonnino replied that unfortunately in the case of the Roumanian claims, the representatives of the minorities (Hungarians, Ukrainians, Bolshevists), would have to be consulted, and they had no representatives in Paris. He did not see why the representatives of the Great Powers themselves should not first discuss the question with their own experts, and afterwards consult the Delegates of the countries concerned, who could give the most expert information available.

President Wilson agreed that perhaps it might be wise to omit the clause of the resolution which authorised the experts to consult the representatives of the people concerned. Ever since the United States of America had entered the war, he had had a body of scholars continuously studying such questions of fact as racial aspects, historical antecedents, and economic and commercial elements: the two latter being of very great importance in many of the questions under dispute, as had been realised in the case of the Banat. Furthermore, it must be remembered that however complete their confidence might be in the Delegates of Roumania, Serbia, and other countries, who would present claims, these Delegates were merely advocates, and they made opposite claims as to the right inferences to be drawn from facts. They did not represent their facts in the same way, and there would always be something that was not quite clear. As the United States of America were not bound by any of the treaties in question, they were quite ready to approve a settlement on a basis of facts. But the claimants did not always restrict themselves even to the limits set by Treaties and their claims frequently exceeded what was justified by the Treaties.

Mr. Lloyd George, in this connection, drew attention to the Roumanian claims on the Banat. The Roumanians now claimed the whole of the Banat, whereas the Treaty only gave them a part.

President Wilson, continuing, said that he was seeking enlightenment, and this would no doubt be afforded by a convincing presentation by the experts. If the resolution proposed by Mr. Lloyd George did not receive acceptance, he would find himself compelled to fight the question merely on the views expressed by the American experts; but he would prefer that these conclusions should be corrected by the views of the French, British and Italian experts.

M. CLEMENCEAU enquired from M. Orlando whether he still objected to the resolution.

M. ORLANDO said that he had already expressed his willingness to accept the resolution, provided it was not to create a precedent.

(It was agreed that the questions raised in M. Bratiano's statement on the Roumanian territorial interests in the Peace settlement should be referred for examination in the first instance by an expert committee, composed of two representatives each of the United States of America, the British Empire, France and Italy.

It shall be the duty of this Committee to reduce the questions for decision within the narrowest possible limits, and to make recommendations for a just settlement.

The Committee is authorised to consult the representatives of the peoples concerned.) . . .

Document 7

Excerpts from the Minutes of the Supreme Council, Held on February 5, 1919: Czecho-Slovak Territorial Claims [1]

. . . Czecho-Slovak territorial claims

2. M. BENES said that, before beginning to expound the Czecho-Slovak problem, he would like to declare what were the principles guiding Czecho-Slovak policy. The movement culminating in the formation of an independent Czecho-Slovak State had begun 3½ years ago. The agitation had been carried on by scattered exiles in the various Allied countries. There was, at that time, no Government and no organised political body. In 3 years these exiles had succeeded, with the help of the population remaining at home, in putting up a Central Government and a political organisation which was vital, and, with the help of the Allies, three armies in the field.

Before dealing with the question of the future frontiers of this new State, he would like to recall that the Czecho-Slovak people had shown a practical sense of politics which had won for them the recognition of the Allies. He would also like to recall that, in all these years, the Nation had been entirely united. It had never hesitated to side with the Allies in the interests of democracy. It had not fought for territory, but for the same principles as the Allied Nations. It had risen against a mediaeval Dynasty backed by bureaucracy, militarism, the Roman Catholic Church, and, to some extent, by high finance. The Nation had plunged into this struggle without asking for any guarantees or weighing the probabilities of success. All the Nation wanted was to control its own destinies. The Nation felt itself to be a European Nation and a member of the Society of the Western States.

In seeking now to shape the Czecho-Slovak State, the very same principles would be their guide. They would adopt the European and human point of view, and base their claims on the very principles the Conference was assembled to establish.

The Nation, after 300 years of servitude and vicissitudes which had almost led to its extermination, felt that it must be prudent, reasonable and just to its neighbours and that it must avoid provoking jealousy and re-

[1] Miller, *My Diary,* XIV, 211 ff. (by permission).

newed struggles which might again plunge it into similar danger. It was in this spirit that he wished to explain the territorial problem.

(i) The four provinces of Czecho-Slovakia

M. BENES, continuing, said that the first territorial question was that of the four provinces, Bohemia, Moravia, Austrian Silesia and Slovakia. These territories were claimed for ethnographical reasons. They contained 10 millions of the Nation.

(ii) Historical considerations

The first three had been one State from the sixth Century. The Czech Dynasty had lasted until 1747, when a unitary form of government had prevailed against federalist and national tendencies. In 1526, the Hapsburgs had been elected Kings of Bohemia, and, though, up to the present time they had *de jure* recognised Czech institutions, they had begun from that date to centralize power. Czech independence might be said to have lasted until 1747. Since then, though the juridical existence of the State continued to be acknowledged, it had no practical significance. Hence the Czech Insurrection in 1848 and that which had coincided with the beginning of this war.

Historical considerations, though not the predominant factor at the present time, must be accorded some weight, inasmuch as they very deeply affected public opinion. It was these old historical causes that armed the Czech people against the Germanic masses around them. Three times the Czech people had rebelled, not merely against Germanism but against a system of aristocratic and Roman Catholic privilege; three times the nation had been overwhelmed by the superior numbers of the German peoples. At the end of the 17th Century, after the great battle of the White Mountain, the Czech people had practically ceased to exist. It was reanimated only at the end of the 18th Century by the French Revolution. Since then the Nation had worked so hard that, at the beginning of the 20th Century, it was industrially, intellectually and politically, the most developed community in Central Europe. Throughout the 19th Century whenever the Czech people had attempted to free themselves it was always the appeal to history that had inspired them.

(iii) Exposed situation of Czecho-Slovakia

M. BENES said that he must draw attention to the exposed situation of the Czecho-Slovak nation. It was the advanced guard of the Slav world in the West, and therefore constantly threatened by German expansion. The Germanic mass, now numbering some 80 millions, could not push westwards as its road was blocked on that side by highly developed nations. It was, therefore, always seeking outlets to the south and to the east. In this movement it found the Poles and the Czechs in its path. Hence the special importance of the Czecho-Slovak frontiers in Central Europe. It might be hoped that the Germans would not again attempt forcible invasions, but they had done so in the past so often that the Czechs had always felt they had a special mission to resist the Teutonic flood. Hence the fanatical devotion of the Czechs which had been noticed by all in this war. It was due to the constant feeling of the Czechs that they were the protectors of democracy against Germanism, and that it was their duty at all times to fight the Germans. . . .

(viii) Slovakia

M. BENES said that Slovakia had at one time formed part of the Czecho-Slovak State. It had been over-run by the Magyars at the beginning of the 10th Century. The conquerors had attempted without success to magyarise the country. The population still felt Czech, and wished to belong to the new State. There was never any suggestion of separatism in Slovakia. The same language, the same ideas and the same religion prevailed. Slovak national enthusiasm had been bred by antagonism to the Magyars.

The Northern frontier of the Slovaks was formed by the Carpathians; their Southern frontier by the Danube. From the southward bend of the Danube to the River Theiss the frontier was partly natural and partly artificial. It was bound to include many Magyars, and this constituted a problem which must be solved by the Conference.

MR. LLOYD GEORGE expressed the opinion that no doubt existed about the claim to Slovakia proper. If this were so, he would suggest that Dr. Benes should confine his remarks to the doubtful points.

(It was generally agreed that the claim to Slovakia presented no difficulties, and that the only points requiring elucidation referred to the frontiers with Hungary.)

(ix) Danube Frontier

M. BENES, resuming, said that the Danube frontier was claimed as a matter of principle. Slovakia was a Danubian country. At the time of the Magyar invasion the Slovaks had occupied the whole of Pannonia. The Magyars had thrust the Slovak populations into the mountains, and after clearing them from the right bank of the Danube had come into contact with the Germans. On the left bank the Slav population had not been exterminated. They had remained on the land, though they had become more or less magyarised. The deepest strata of the population in the villages on the Northern side were Slovak. Only the upper strata artificially superimposed were Hungarian.

There was also a very cogent economic reason for the Danube frontier. The Czecho-Slovak State would have no direct access to the sea. It was surrounded on three sides by Germans and on the fourth by Magyars. It was an industrial country, and absolutely required some access to the sea. The Danube internationalised would afford them this access. It would become the base of the economic life of the State. This was a geographical necessity, and the new State could not survive without it.

MR. LLOYD GEORGE asked what percentage of Slovaks inhabited the Danubian regions.

M. BENES replied that in taking over this region the Czecho-Slovak State would be including some 350,000 Magyars. He again pointed out that the country had been forcibly magyarised. These figures applied to the area between Pressburg and Vaitzen [Vác]. He would add that on the other side of the river there were many scattered communities of Slovaks. For instance in the region of Budapest there were as many as 150,000. These would be abandoned in compensation for the Hungarians absorbed.

M. SONNINO asked what proportion the Slovaks represented as opposed to the Hungarians.

M. BENES replied that this varied according to the district. The districts on which statistics were based had been traced from North to South and thus made to comprise strong Magyar majorities. He estimated that in the districts to which he referred the Slovak population represented 60 per cent. but it was difficult to make a trustworthy estimate, as these areas had never been used as districts for census purposes.

PRESIDENT WILSON asked whether communal statistics could be obtained and whether it was a fact that the Slovak population only touched the Danube at Pressburg.

M. BENES replied that it reached the Danube also North of Budapest, but he admitted that the greater part of the riverain population was Magyar.

MR. LLOYD GEORGE asked whether the rivers passing through Slovakia were navigable.

MR. BENES replied that only the Vah [Vág] was navigable, but only half way up its course.

M. KRAMARTZ said that an attempt was being made to render the Morava navigable and a great development of canal communication was in project, which would connect the North Sea through the Elbe with the Black Sea through the Danube. These communications would pass through Czecho-Slovak territory.

MR. LLOYD GEORGE asked whether, if the territories claimed declared themselves Magyar, free access to the internationalised route of the Danube through the rivers of Slovakia would satisfy M. Benes.

M. BENES replied that these rivers were not at present navigable, with the exception of the Vah. The whole of Slovakia would be cut off from the Danube.

MR. LLOYD GEORGE asked whether, if Czecho-Slovakia obtained access by railway to fixed points on the Danube, this would satisfy them.

M. BENES replied that the valley and the uplands were so interdependent that great disorganisation would ensue on their separation. These territories lived by the exchange of industrial and agricultural necessaries. The uplands of Slovakia were industrial and the valley was agricultural.

(x) Frontier between Danube and Ung

M. BENES said that the claim for this frontier was dictated by railway communications. The mountains ran from North to South and there was little communication from East to West.

It was therefore necessary to include the only railway offering lateral communication. He admitted that a considerable Hungarian population would thus be brought in to the Czecho-Slovak State, but he would point out that the Hungarian census was even worse than the Austrian. As a whole, 250,000 Magyars would be included, while 350,000 Slovaks would be left out. In all, 650,000 Hungarians would become subjects of the new State, while 450,000 Czecho-Slovaks would remain within Hungary. Racial confusion in Hungary owing to the savage persecutions of the past, was very great.

The Slovaks had been particularly oppressed, and even Kossuth had said that the Slovaks could not be granted the franchise. Magyars freely said that the Slovaks were not men. Out of 2,300 officials in Slovakia only 17 had been Slovaks. Out of 1,700 judges only one had been Slovak, and out of 2,500 Collectors of Taxes only 10 had been Slovaks. In consequence nearly one-third of the Slovak population had emigrated to the United States of America. Others had left their homes and settled in places in Hungary where it was easier to make a living, which accounted for the 90,000 Slovaks found near Budapest, and the 80,000 round Debreczin.

(xi) Ruthenes in Hungary

M. BENES said that it remained for him to draw attention of the Conference to certain suggestions which were not to be considered claims made on behalf of Czecho-Slovakia.

The first of these suggestions related to the Ruthenes in Hungary. Next to the Slovaks and to the East of them, was a territory inhabited by Ruthenes. These Ruthenes were the same stock as the Ruthenes of Eastern Galicia, from whom they were divided by the Carpathians. They were close neighbours to the Slovaks, socially and economically similar to them, and there were even transitional dialects between their language and that of Slovakia. They did not wish to remain under Hungarian control and proposed to form an autonomous state in close federation with Czecho-Slovakia. They numbered about 450,000. It would be unjust to leave them to the tender mercies of the Magyars, and though Czecho-Slovakia made no claim on their behalf, he had undertaken to put their case before the Conference. If Eastern Galicia became Russian it would be dangerous to bring Russia South of the Carpathians. If Eastern Galicia became Polish, the Poles themselves would not wish to include this population. It follows, therefore, that this people must either be Hungarian or autonomous. If the latter, they wished to be federated to the Czecho-Slovak State. This would impose a burden on Czecho-Slovakia, but would afford them the advantage of a common frontier with the Roumanians . . .

(*xiii*) Communication with the Adriatic

M. BENES said that in order to free itself from the grip of the Germans and Magyars the Czecho-Slovak State wished to establish close relations with the Yugo-Slavs and with Italy. The nearest sea to the Czecho-Slovak territory was the Adriatic. He thought that by means of a small territory either under the Czech or Yugo-Slav Government, or under the League of Nations, means of communication would be best established. A railway line alone, with territory on either side of it would, he thought, be insufficient. He would suggest that this territory should be marked out on the confines of the Germans and the Magyars. It would thus furnish a corridor between Czecho-Slovakia and Yugo-Slavia.

This was merely a suggestion put forward for consideration with reference to the general principle adopted by the Conference.

The Czecho-Slovak Government had no wish to hamper the purposes of the Conference. They wished to do all in their power to assist a just and durable peace.

(The following resolution was then adopted:

That the questions raised in the statement by M. Benes on the Czecho-Slovak territorial interests in the Peace Settlement shall be referred for examination in the first instance to an expert Committee composed of two representatives each of the United States of America, the British Empire, France and Italy.

It shall be the duty of this Committee to reduce the questions for decision within the narrowest possible limits and make recommendations for a just settlement.

The Committee is authorized to consult representatives of the peoples concerned.)

(The Meeting then adjourned.)

DOCUMENT 8

Excerpts from the Minutes of the Supreme Council, Held on February 18, 1919: Yugoslav Territorial Claims [1]

STATEMENT OF CASE FOR YUGO-SLAVIA

M. CLEMENCEAU in opening the meeting asked the Serbian Delegation to make its statement.

M. VESNITCH said that he must begin by an apology. It had not, up to the present, been possible to supply the Conference with a full memorandum. There were certain difficulties due to distance, bad communications, etc., which had rendered this impossible. A memorandum giving general considerations had been supplied. Separate memoranda of a more technical order would be prepared subsequently.

(a) Causes of the Great War

In order to present the problem fully he wished first to draw the attention of the meeting to the origin of the war. This question had been dealt with publicly, but nevertheless he felt it must again be asserted before the Conference that the real cause of the war was the German tendency to expand towards Asia Minor and thereby to acquire dominion of the world. In its road this movement encountered a number of obstacles, the first of which was the Yugo-Slav people. Hence it was decided in Berlin and Vienna that this should be the first fortress to be taken.

(b) Eastward trend of German policy

The time-honoured German policy was well-known. Since 1848 and especially since 1878 Vienna under the direction of Berlin had sought to bring under its rule all the Serbians not yet included in the Dual Monarchy. This policy had involved the Great Powers. Since 1848, Great Britain, France and Italy had struggled to preserve the peace of Europe. One stage on this road to the East had been marked by the absorption of Bosnia and Herzegovina. Another critical moment was the Balkan War. Serbia issued from it victorious and became the centre of attraction for all the Yugo-Slav peoples. The enthusiasm shown in Bosnia, Croatia, Slavonia and the Banat was even

[1] Miller, *My Diary*, XIV, 487 ff. (by permission).

greater than that in Serbia proper. This had been carefully noted at the Ballplatz, where it was decided that the future must be secured as early as possible. This also was incontestably the reason which had rendered futile all the efforts of the Liberal Powers of Europe to find a peaceful diplomatic issue with the nations of Central Europe. The latter were determined to overcome the obstacle and to set forward on their march Eastwards in the quickest possible time. It had been impossible to stop them—hence the Great War.

(c) Action of Yugo-Slavs in the War

The Yugo-Slav troops of the Dual Monarchy from the very first day of the war began to hamper the purposes of the Central Powers. When other means failed, they surrendered in large numbers on the Russian and Serbian fronts, and at a later stage, on the Italian front. They felt that this was a war of extermination for their people. Encouraged by the promises made by the Great Liberal Powers, especially by the declaration that the war was waged for the liberation of oppressed peoples, they had contributed by every means in their power to the victory of the Allies. They were now inspired by the confident hope that their expectations of the fulfilment of the promises made by the victorious Allies would not be disappointed, and they felt that their services to the common cause had earned recognition.

(d) Principles for which the Allies fought

Since the very beginning of the war the Great Liberal Powers, France, Great Britain, and with them Russia, had proclaimed that they were not fighting for individual national advantages, but for certain principles. These principles were stated publicly and solemnly and were the three great principles of (1) Nationality, (2) the right of self-determination, and (3) freedom of the small Nations. After the signature of the first Armistice, M. Clemenceau, when welcoming the delegates of all the Allied Powers, had said that from that moment there was no difference between great and small nations, as the small nations had been as great as the greatest during the war. He wished to recall this expression to make clear the difference between the principles of the Allied Powers and those of the Central Powers. Before the war there had been a conversation between Herr Von Jagow and M. Jules Cambon. The former had declared that there was no more room in the world for small nations. This was fully in accord with the feelings of his nation. What M. Clemenceau had expressed to the Allies was the principle which had encouraged the Nations to group themselves and to bring about the triumph of something far higher than the self-interests of individual nations. It was in accordance with this spirit that the peace of Europe and the League of Nations must be brought about.

(e) *Attitude towards secret treaties*

Adhering to this spirit, the delegation he represented regarded the right of self-determination as an inviolable right. It could not recognise any treaty, public or secret doing violence to these principles, proclaimed by the Allies and latterly endorsed by the United States of America. The Delegation he represented therefore regarded as null and void any agreement disposing of the Yugo-Slav people without its consent. He felt obliged to make this declaration in the name of his Government and of his colleagues present in the room. Had he not made it, he would have betrayed his obligation to the Yugo-Slav people. It was not in the habits of this people to sing its own praises, but it must be declared that if this people had endured martyrdom to assist the Allies, it was because their leaders had assured them that these sufferings were absolutely necessary, that it was probably the last effort required of them, and that the open declarations of the Great Allied Powers were a complete guarantee of the future. The leaders of the people had made themselves responsible for the execution of these promises. The Yugo-Slav people, through them, had put complete trust in the Powers whom he now begged to do nothing which might cause disappointment to the legitimate hopes aroused, and thereby sow the seeds of future deplorable conflict.

(e) *Question of future frontiers of Yugo-Slavia*

M. VESNITCH, continuing, said that, if it was in order, he would approach the subject of the future frontiers of Yugo-Slavia. The Yugo-Slav people was in a peculiar situation. It had to delimit its territory with six or seven nations. On a former occasion explanations had been given concerning the problem to be solved with a friendly country. In tracing the boundaries separating them from enemy countries it was likely that no great difficulties would arise. But there was another friendly country with which there were problems to discuss. The Delegation would ask that it should be treated on a footing of equality with its Italian friends. He felt that in making this request he was not exceeding the limits of his rights and his duties. He hoped that the Allied and Associated Powers would consider this fair and practical and likely to ensure good understanding between two countries which were to be neighbours, and between which it was desirable that no germ of discord should arise.

(f) *Southern frontier*

M. VESNITCH explained, with the help of a map, what he proposed should be the future frontiers of Yugo-Slavia . . .

(h) Northeastern frontier

The Yugo-Slav arguments concerning the boundary to be drawn in the Banat had been heard on a previous occasion. Failing all other means of settlement, the Delegation for which he spoke was ready to allow the populations to make a free choice of allegiance. He would like to point out that all invasions of Serbia throughout history had come from that quarter. The latest examples furnished in the course of the late war were enough to prove his point. There were also ethnological, geographical and economic reasons. The divisions of the country made for administrative purposes by the common enemies of Serbia and Roumania were evidence in his favour. No less well-wishing judges could be found than the Magyars towards the Serbian people, nevertheless the division of the country made by them showed the Serbs to be in the majority.

(i) Northern frontier

In the North the Delegation proposed a frontier which corresponded not only to ethnic, but to geographical realities.

Dr. ZOLGER, continuing, explained that the proposed boundary with the Germans and Magyars was drawn in such a way as to include all the Croats, Serbs and Slovenes along the Drave . . .

AGENDA FOR FUTURE CONVERSATIONS

(b) Procedure regarding Yugo-Slav claims

Mr. BALFOUR said that the Council had now heard the evidence of the Yugo-Slavs. Similar evidence had been heard from other nationalities, and in most cases the problems raised had been referred for examination to a Committee, without power to decide on solutions, but with a Commission to report on the facts. In the case of the Yugo-Slav statement, he admitted that there were difficulties, especially by reason of the treaty commitments of some of the Powers present. He wished to ask what should now be done. Was the matter to be left just as it was?

M. SONNINO said that the subject was a difficult one. He wished to be quite frank. Italy could not take part in any Commission or in any discussion outside the Conference, or allow any Committee to make recommendations, regarding questions outstanding between Italy and the Yugo-Slavs. He would also oppose any Committee which was to examine collectively all questions raised by the statements heard that day. The question between the Yugo-Slavs and the Roumanians was already being sifted by a Committee. To this he had no objection.

Mr. BALFOUR then asked Baron Sonnino to state what procedure he did recommend. He understood that Baron Sonnino would raise no objection to a Committee on the subject of the Northern and Eastern frontiers of Yugo-Slavia. But he would refuse to be a party to any discussion of the frontiers between Italy and Yugo-Slavia outside the Conference. He would point out that the object of a Committee was to furnish the Council with facts, in order that the Council should be in a position to discuss the matter with full knowledge.

Baron Sonnino said that each Delegation was accompanied by its experts and he felt quite sure that at least eight members of the Council must have already consulted them.

M. Clemenceau asked Baron Sonnino whether he raised no objection to the formation of a Committee to investigate the other frontiers claimed by the Yugo-Slavs.

M. Sonnino said that he raised none, provided that the questions pending between Italy and Yugo-Slavia were excluded.

M. Clemenceau suggested that a Committee should be set up and that the Dalmatian Coast should be excluded from the terms of reference. He thought it impossible to entrust this question to any Committee or Commission, by reason of the commitments of the Powers and certain difficult political aspects of the question.

This question resembled that of the Rhine, which also could not be entrusted to a Committee. Such questions must be dealt with in the Council, which was not ill-supplied with the necessary statistics. In this matter, therefore, he agreed with Baron Sonnino. He proposed to name a Committee to deal with the problems raised, with the exception of those pending between Italy and the Yugo-Slavs.

Mr. Balfour then read the following draft resolution:

It is agreed:

That the questions raised in the statements made by MM. Vesnitch, Zolger and Trumbitch, on behalf of the Serbian Delegation on the Serbian territorial interests in the peace settlement (excepting only the question in which Italy is directly concerned) shall be referred for examination in the first instance to an expert Committee similar to that which is considering the question of the Banat.

It shall be the duty of this Committee to reduce the questions for decision within the narrowest possible limits and to make recommendations for a just settlement.

The Committee is authorised to consult representatives of the peoples concerned.

Mr. Lansing suggested that this question be referred to the same Committee as was dealing with the Banat.

M. Pichon said that some of the questions raised were different to the one under discussion in that Committee. It might, however, be convenient that the Committee on these other questions should be composed of the same members.

BARON SONNINO said that he supported Mr. Lansing's proposal as questions of reciprocal concession might arise.

(It was therefore decided that the above Resolution be adopted and that the Committee be the same as that appointed to deal with the Banat. . . .

DOCUMENT 9

Establishment of Neutral Zone between Hungarians and Rumanians

I. EXCERPTS FROM THE MINUTES OF THE SUPREME COUNCIL, HELD ON FEBRUARY 21, 1919 [1]

. . . 2. The first question to be discussed related to the creation of a neutral zone in Transylvania, and he [M. Pichon] would call on M. Tardieu, the Chairman of the Committee on Rumanian Affairs, to make a report.

M. TARDIEU said that the Committee on Rumanian Affairs had reached the conclusion that the question of Transylvania should be referred back to the Conference for settlement, for the following reasons. When the General Commander-in-Chief of the Allied Armies of the East had signed the Armistice with Hungary, Rumania had not yet re-entered the war and no reason had then existed for fixing a definite line of occupation between Rumania and Hungary. Hungarian troops, therefore, remained in occupation of Transylvania. These troops had been accused by M. Bratiano, in a report dated 9th February, 1919, of having committed acts of cruelty; and, consequently, Rumanian troops had moved forward with the intention of occupying the whole of that region up to the line fixed by the Treaty of 1916. On February 14th, 1919, General Franchet d'Esperey had cabled that the Rumanian troops were continuing their advance into Transylvania and had already reached the line: MARMARES-SZIGET, ZILAK, CZUEZA, NAGY-SZEBECS, ZAM.

Now, the final frontiers of Rumania had not yet been fixed by the Committee on Rumanian Affairs, who were still engaged in studying that question. But, owing to the advance of the Rumanians, it was possible that serious conflicts might take place at any moment between the Rumanian and Hungarian troops; an incident which would be doubly regrettable, seeing that the question in conflict was now under consideration. The Committee, therefore, had considered it expedient to report the situation to the Conference in order to avoid any conflict taking place in that region, and a proposal had been submitted four days previously, suggesting:

(1) The fixation of two lines at a certain distance from each other beyond which the Hungarian and Rumanian troops should not be permitted to advance, and

[1] Miller, *My Diary*, XIV, 506 ff. (by permission).

(2) The establishment of a neutral zone between the two proposed lines, to be occupied by Allied troops with a view to preventing the spreading of Bolshevism, which was prevalent in Hungary.

During the last two days, the Committee had received reports from General Alby, the French Chief of Staff, and from the military advisers of the Italian Peace Delegation in Paris. M. Bratiano had also forwarded a note on the subject, and, in addition, General Charpy, Chief of Staff to General Franchet d'Esperey, had just returned from those regions and submitted a report on the situation. Taking these facts into consideration, it was thought by the Committee that the military advisers of the Conference should be asked to fix the lines of extreme occupation above referred to and decide whether or not the intervening neutral zone should be occupied by Allied troops, in view of maintaining order against possible Bolshevist attempts.

Mr. Balfour enquired whether M. Tardieu's Committee had heard any military experts on the question under reference.

M. Tardieu replied in the negative, and explained that the Committee had merely read General Alby's report. They had purposely refrained from obtaining military advice, as the Committee might thereby have been led into a discussion of purely military questions, which were outside the terms of reference.

Mr. Balfour enquired how order would be maintained in the neutral zone if a neutral zone were constituted. Was that purely a military question?

M. Tardieu replied that in principle the maintenance of order in a neutral zone was not purely a military question, and for that reason the Committee had enquired into the matter. It had, however, been found that all sorts of military questions were involved—for instance: were Allied troops available for the occupation of the neutral zone? For that reason it had been decided to refer the question back to the Conference.

Lord Milner enquired whether it was intended that the question should be referred for report to the Military Representatives of the Supreme War Council at Versailles.

M. Tardieu replied that that was the intention of the Committee.

(It was decided to refer to the Military Representatives of the Supreme War Council at Versailles the questions raised in the following recommendation made by the Committee on Rumanian Affairs on February 17th, 1919:

The Commission on Rumanian Affairs beg to draw the attention of the Supreme Allied Council to the following situation:

(1) General Franchet d'Esperey sent a wire dated February 14th, 1919, saying that the Rumanian troops were continuing their advance into Transylvania and had already reached the line Marmaros-Sziget, Zilak, Czucza, Nagy-Szebecs, Xam.

(2) The Rumanian Government (letter from M. Bratiano to the President of the Peace Conference dated February 9th) justifies such advance by the acts of cruelty committed by the Hungarians in that region.

(3) The Commission on Rumanian Affairs is at the present time studying the line to be drawn as a frontier between Rumania and Hungary, and wishes that no armed conflicts should take place in that region.

For the above reasons the Commission on Rumanian Affairs asks the Supreme Council if the present situation does not seem to warrant the fixation of two lines beyond which the Hungarian and Rumanian troops should not go, a zone free of military occupation being thus established between the two proposed lines:

(A) 10 kilometres, west of general line running from Vasaros Nameny, point of confluence of the two Keres, Algyo north of Szegadin; as regards Hungarian troops.

(B) 10 kilometres east of line Szatmar-Nemeti, Nagy-Varad, Arad, as regards Rumanian troops.

It is for the Supreme Allied Council to decide whether or not the zone forbidden to Hungarian and Rumanian troops should be, in view of maintaining order against possible Bolshevist attempts, occupied by Allied troops.) . . .

II. COMMENTS OF DR. DAY AND HIS MEMORANDUM FOR GENERAL BLISS, FEBRUARY 17, 1919 [2]

Annex A to Agenda of Meeting of February 21, 1919

NEUTRAL ZONE BETWEEN MAGYARS AND RUMANIANS

Comment by Dr. Day, relative to Section No. 1, of Agenda

At Dr. Bowman's request I send you herewith copy of a memorandum which was sent to General Bliss, February 17th. We have no other document or report to offer. A report drawn up by M. Tardieu in the Committee was approved and left in his hands to be transmitted to the Supreme War Council.

At the session of the Committee yesterday it appeared that there were military objections to the plan which we had proposed as the limit of the Rumanian advance, namely a line ten kilometers south-east of the line Szatmar-Nemeti: Nagy-Karolyi: Nagy-Varad: Arad. It was asserted that it was necessary to allow the Rumanians to occupy those towns. The position of the Committee was that it had observed its functions in recommending that the area now under its consideration be protected from military occupation and armed conflict, and that it lay outside its province to make recommendation of a military nature.

[2] Miller, *My Diary*, XVII, 23 (by permission).

(Enclosure)   February 17, 1919.

Memorandum for General Bliss

At the meeting this morning of the Committee to consider Rumanian Territorial Claims, M. Tardieu interrupted the regular course of business to introduce the following matter:

When the Armistice was signed with the Central Powers, Rumania, which had made peace with them, was not a party to it. The Armistice line was drawn with reference to military, not to ethnical considerations, dividing Transylvania. The Rumanians, who, during the war, had advanced to the line Nagybania-Kolozsvai-Deva, have continued to advance to the line Maramaros-Sziget-Zileh-Csucsa, claiming all the territory to the limit accorded them by the Treaty of 1916.

Hungarian troops are now massed on the ethnic frontier which lies within the territory claimed by the Rumanians. General Franchet d'Esperey has no authority to stop the advance of the Rumanian troops, since they were not parties to the Armistice.

The French have been asked to send their troops to keep the two armies apart, but the French Foreign Office is naturally not inclined to assume the responsibility and the unpopularity of this action.

The members of the Committee agreed unanimously on a memorandum which will go at once before the Supreme War Council and which will aim to establish a neutral zone separating Rumanians and Hungarians. In the opinion of the members of the Committee, it is of direct interest to the prosecution of its work on territorial claims that districts within a debatable area should be preserved from armed occupation by either side. As the matter appears to be very urgent, we beg leave to bring it to the attention of the American Peace Commission through you in anticipation of the memorial which will very shortly be brought before the Supreme War Council.

III. EXCERPTS FROM THE MINUTES OF THE SUPREME COUNCIL, HELD ON FEBRUARY 26, 1919 [3]

. . . Creation of neutral zone in Transylvania

3. At M. Pichon's request, GENERAL BELIN read the following report:

REPORT ON THE CREATION OF A NEUTRAL ZONE BETWEEN HUNGARIANS AND RUMANIANS IN TRANSYLVANIA

The Military Representatives of the Supreme War Council
AFTER TAKING COGNISANCE of the decision reached by the Prime Ministers of

[3] Miller, *My Diary,* XV, 82 ff. (by permission).

the Allied and Associated Powers at their meeting on the 21st February, 1919, concerning the delimitation of a neutral zone in Transylvania between Hungarians and Rumanians;

AFTER HEARING IN SUCCESSION the Rumanian General Coanda on the general conditions, historical, moral, political and ethnographical relating to these questions;

The Rumanian Colonel Dimitresco on the strategical conditions required to place the Rumanian armies in a position to defend themselves against all eventual aggression by Hungarian troops;

Dr. Vaida, Rumanian Minister, on the general internal condition of Transylvania;

General Henrys, Commander-in-Chief of the French Army of the Orient;

General Charpy, Chief of Staff of the General Commanding-in-Chief of the Allied Armies in the East, on the possibility of the occupation by these Armies of the neutral zone to be defined;

AGREE:

On the principle that the proposals which they submit to the Conference of the Prime Ministers relate only to provisional measures of occupation, without prejudice in any manner to the final attribution of the occupied regions.

The Military Representatives

FURTHER CONSIDER:

That the advance of Rumanian troops to contact with Hungarian troops may have the consequence, among others, of causing serious conflicts between them;

That it is desirable to take all measures to avert such conflict as would impede the work of the Peace Conference and create between the peoples destined in the future to live side by side profound causes of hostility likely to disturb the peace.

The Military Representatives therefore conclude:

That it is desirable to create in Transylvania between Hungarians and Rumanians a neutral zone free from all Hungarian and Rumanian troops, the important points in which should be occupied by Allied troops (approximately 2 infantry battalions with some squadrons or 1 regiment of cavalry) with the mission of maintaining order and tranquility in this zone, with the assistance, if necessary, of inter-Allied Commissions whose function it will more particularly be to control the various administrative offices, the administration of the territories continuing to be carried out in accordance with the conditions fixed by the Armistice.

They propose that the zone should be defined as follows:

EASTERN OR RUMANIAN LIMIT: The main road from Arad to Nagyszalonta thence the railway Grosswardein (Nagy Varad)—Nagy Karoly, Szatmar Nemeti. All localities mentioned to be excluded from military occupation by the Rumanians but, together with the railway, to be available for the use of the Rumanian troops and inhabitants, under Allied control, for economic purposes.

NORTHERN LIMIT: The River Szimos.

WESTERN OR HUNGARIAN LIMIT: A line leaving the Theiss 5 Km. Northwest of Vasaros-Nameny passing then 5 Km. to the West of Debreczin to 3 Km. West of Deva-Vanya, and continuing to the West of Gyoma, 5 Km. West of Oroshaza,

Hotmezo, Vasarhely and Czegedin, then rejoining the Southern frontier to the South of Czegedin.

SOUTHERN LIMIT: The line of the River Maros, Arad and Szeged being occupied by Allied troops to the exclusion of both Rumanian and Hungarian troops.

GENERAL BELIN	CAVALLERO
Military Representative, French Section, Supreme War Council.	Military Representative, Italian Section, Supreme War Council.
C. SACKVILLE WEST	P. D. LOCHRIDGE
Major-General Military Representative, British Section, Supreme War Council.	Military Representative, American Section, Supreme War Council.

M. PICHON asked General Belin whether he felt sure that the Inter-Allied control could be organised.

GENERAL BELIN replied that this question had been put to General Charpy, who thought that General Berthelot's army could spare the two battalions required. There was not between the Hungarians and Roumanians any very notable tension, and a very small force would apparently suffice to maintain order. This had been found to be the case at Arad and at Szegedin, where one squadron of cavalry and one company respectively had been stationed. He had since heard that a report from General Pathé stated that General Berthelot could not furnish the two battalions. The Military Representatives, therefore, only stated that two battalions were required to keep order and left it to the Governments to find them. General Charpy, however, had told him that, if the Allied Governments decided to adopt the recommendations made by the Military Representatives, he felt sure General Henrys would contrive to ensure order.

MR. BALFOUR said that he would like to draw attention to a small point in the drafting of the report. The western limit of the zone was described as a line 5 kilometres west of the Treaty line of 1916. There had been a great deal of discussion as to whether this treaty had or had not been abrogated by the agreement made between Roumania and the enemy. This discussion had caused considerable excitement of public opinion in Roumania. It was perhaps desirable not to allude to it in such a document. He would suggest, therefore, that the geographical description of the line should be substituted for the description given.

(It was agreed that the draft should be altered accordingly.)

M. TARDIEU asked whether so small a force as that suggested would be able to occupy the railway effectually.

GENERAL BELIN explained that a company would be situated at each of the main junctions, together with a "Commission de gare" which would regulate the working of the line. The line would be used to furnish the necessary supplies to the Roumanian forces and to the local populations, under Allied control. Any trouble occurring between these occupied points could be dealt with rapidly by small flying columns. Very little trouble was anticipated. The same arrangements were contemplated on the Hungarian side, and a company would be stationed at Debroczen. In addition to the troops on the south, this force would be able to police the whole zone.

M. Salvago Raggi pointed out that mention was made in the document of an armistice with Hungary. He suggested that the words "with Hungary" be deleted.

(This was agreed to.)

He further suggested that in the last paragraph, for the words "the armistice line of November, 1918 (River Maros)," the words "the line of the River Maros" should be substituted.

(This was agreed to.)

(With the alterations noted above, the report of the Military Representatives was adopted.) . . .

The Military Representatives then withdrew. . . .

IV. COMMUNICATION OF GENERAL LOBIT, PROVISIONAL COMMANDER OF THE ALLIED ARMIES IN HUNGARY, TO COUNT KÁROLYI, PRESIDENT OF HUNGARY, MARCH 19, 1919 [4]

With a view to ensuring the avoidance of all conflicts in connection with its measures now in course, the Peace Conference in its sitting of February 26, 1919 has decided that it is necessary to create a neutral zone between the Hungarians and the Roumanians, which shall be entirely free of Hungarian or Roumanian troops, and the important places of which shall be occupied by inter-allied troops.

The Commander-in-Chief has charged me to solve, in mutual understanding with Your Excellency, all questions having a bearing on this decision of the Peace Conference.

I have therefore charged my representative at Budapest, M. Lieutenant-Colonel Vix, with the following:

1. to make known to you the above mentioned decision and the manner in which I have the intention of carrying it into effect;

2. to establish, in harmony with Your Excellency, the details of its execution;

3. to propose to me all those measures in which my intervention should appear necessary.

[4] *The Hungarian Peace Negotiations*, I, 393.

A) Boundaries of the neutral zone

The boundaries of the neutral zone to be occupied by the interallied troops are as follows:

Eastern boundary: The public road Arad—Nagyszalonta; the Nagy-szalonta-Nagyvárad-Nagykároly-Szatmárnémeti railway line in this wise that these towns cannot be kept occupied either by Hungarian or by Roumanian troops, while the lines of communication may be used by the Roumanian Army and by the civilian population, under interallied supervision, for purposes of economic traffic.

Northern boundary: The rivers Szamos and Tisza, to a point situated at 5 Kms to the north-west of Vásárosnamény.

Western boundary: This begins at the Tisza, at 5 Kms to the north-west of Vásárosnamény, and passes

at 5 Kms to the west of Debreczen,

at 3 Kms to the west of Dévaványa,

to the west of Gyoma,

and 5 Kms to the west of Orosháza, Hódmezövásárhely and Szeged.

Southern boundary: The Maros river, in this wise, that Arad and Szeged shall be occupied by interallied troops, to the exclusion of Hungarian and Roumanian troops.

The exact line of the boundary shall be fixed in detail later on.

B) Conditions of the evacuation and the occupation of the neutral zone

The withdrawal of the Hungarian troops to the west of the eastern boundary shall begin on March 23 and shall be terminated within 10 (ten) days.

During this time General Gondrecourt, whom I have charged with the Command of the neutral zone, will occupy it with interallied troops, and will supervise the evacuating movements of the Hungarian troops.

The Peace Conference has authorised the Roumanian troops to advance to the eastern boundary of the neutral zone; but they shall remain in their actual positions until the Hungarian troops shall have crossed the western boundary of the zone.

C) Materials and equipments

1. *War material.* The war material to be found in the territories to be occupied by the Roumanian troops, will be inventoried and guarded by French officers and soldiers. The Hungarians, however, are at liberty to carry it away, it constituting no war booty.

The war material to be found in the neutral zone is at the disposal of the Hungarian Government. It may carry it away, or leave it where it is, at its choice.

2. *Railway and agricultural material and equipment which is the property of the Hungarian State.* This material shall also be left where it is, until measures are taken regarding it. After its being inventoried, a mixed Hungarian-Roumanian commission presided over by General Gondrecourt shall submit proposals to me respecting its being taken in charge.

D) *Public administration*

The civil administration of the neutral zone shall remain in the hands of the Hungarian Government under the control of the Commander of the Interallied troops. The agents of the Hungarian police and gendarmerie shall maintain public order and tranquillity under the supervision of the Headquarters.

I beg Your Excellency within 48 hours to indicate to M. Lieutenant-Colonel Vix the day on which the withdrawing Hungarian troops shall have reached the western boundary of the neutral zone; considering that, as has been communicated above in paragraph B., the movements of the troops must begin on March 23, and must be terminated within 10 days at the latest.

The matter of the material and equipments cannot serve in any way as a pretext for a delay, since every provision has been made to deal with this matter after the evacuation.

V. COMMUNICATION OF COUNT KÁROLYI, PRESIDENT OF HUNGARY, TO LT. COL. VYX, CHIEF OF THE ALLIED MILITARY MISSION IN HUNGARY, MARCH 21, 1919 [5]

You were kind enough to direct a note to me, on behalf of General Lobit by which you notify the Hungarian Government of the decision of February 26, 1919, of the Peace Conference.

In behalf of the Government of the Hungarian Republic I beg to inform you that the Government finds itself unable to take note of this decision of the Peace Conference and to safeguard its execution.

This decision is entirely opposed to the Military Armistice Convention of November 13, 1918; and since it does not take into account the vital interests of the country, is only calculated to hinder them and to disturb the peace. The Hungarian Government, not being in a position to bear the responsibility for the execution of this decision, as it was not invited to the Peace Conference, and could not participate in taking this decision, found itself to-day obliged to hand in its demission.

In advising you of this I beg you, Sir, kindly to take measures that the

[5] *Ibid.,* I, 394.

Peace Conference might be informed as early as possible of this decision of the Hungarian Government.

I beg you, Sir, to accept the assurance of my deep regard.

VI. CODE TELEGRAM FROM GENERAL FRANCHET D'ESPEREY TO MARSHAL FOCH, MARCH 22, 1919 [6]

Constantinople, 22 March, 1919 3h15.

From: General Franchet d'Esperey.
To: War Ministry, Paris, and Marshal Foch, Paris.

(7228/3)   No. 746 to 748.

1. Decision Peace Congress having been notified to it 19 March, Hungarian Government resigned, declaring itself unable either to receive it or to prescribe measures to execute it. It requests that its decision be immediately communicated to the Peace Conference, at 19 h Colonel Vix has received from representatives of bourgeois party declaration proposing either an alliance with the Entente against Russian Bolshevists on condition that present lines of demarcation should be maintained and in that case the Allies should send 15,000 men to Budapesth to allow government to maintain order, or in case of refusal from the Entente they would make an alliance with the Bolshevists.

2. General commanding army in Hungary reports that Hungarian Government has given order to attack 18h this 21 March without front of attack being specified.

3. According to information received previously Hungarians have at their disposal on Transylvanian front about 25,000 men well disciplined and resolute.

4. General Berthelot has been notified as well as Voivode Mitchitch and General Pelle.

5. I am giving orders to army in Hungary and Voivode Mitchitch to group forces in the region about Belgrade and Banat so as to have 2 French infantry divisions and 3 Serbian infantry divisions ready for all events and to abstain, if not attacked, from all intervention until further orders.

6. I request instructions on the attitude to take, considering the advice which I expressed to you in 7200/3 of 12 March, Par. 5.

[6] Miller, *My Diary*, XVII, 281 (by permission).

Excerpts from the Report Submitted to the Supreme Council by the Committee on Czecho-Slovak Questions, March 12, 1919 [1]

I. CONSTITUTION AND COMPOSITION OF THE COMMITTEE

At their meeting of the 5th February last, the Supreme Council of the Allied and Associated Governments decided to appoint a Committee for the study of Tchecho-Slovak questions. This Committee was to consist of two Representatives of each of the following Great Powers—the United States of America, British Empire, France, and Italy. The Committee was directed to reduce the questions at issue to the narrowest possible limits and to present suggestions for an equitable solution.

In pursuance of this decision the Powers concerned nominated the following Delegates to represent them on this Committee:—

United States of America:
Dr. Charles Seymour.
Mr. A. W. Dulles.

British Empire:
The Right Hon. Sir Joseph Cook, G.C.M.G.
The Hon. Harold Nicolson.
Sir Eyre Crowe, K.C.B. (Technical Adviser).

France:
M. Jules Cambon.
M. Laroche.
General Le Rond (Technical Adviser).

Italy:
Marquis Salvago Raggi.
M. Stranieri.

The Committee selected M. Jules Cambon as Chairman and Marquis Salvago Raggi as Vice-Chairman, and appointed a special Sub-Committee to elaborate proposals for the future Tchecho-Slovak frontiers.

---

[1] Reprinted from the original Peace Conference Document. This was obtained from the files of Dr. James T. Shotwell, member of the American Commission to Negotiate Peace. Only parts of the Report affecting Hungary are reprinted.

This Sub-Committee was constituted as follows:

United States of America:

Mr. A. W. Dulles, assisted by Major Johnson.

British Empire:

The Hon. Harold Nicolson, assisted by Lieut. Col. J. H. M. Cornwall.

France:

General Le Rond.

Italy:

M. Stranieri, assisted by Captain Romagnoli.

The Sub-Committee, having appointed General Le Rond as its Chairman, held seven sittings. Dr. Benes was summoned as a witness before the Sub-Committee, and a report was eventually submitted to the Main Committee.

The conclusions reached by the Sub-Committee were unanimously adopted by the Committee.

II. CONCLUSIONS OF THE COMMITTEE

The Committee on Tchecho-Slovak questions, having performed the duty with which they have been charged, have the honor to present to the Supreme Council of the Allied and Associated Governments the following conclusions:

The Committee considered that the task entrusted to them consisted primarily in determining the frontiers, and consequently the territorial extent, of the new Tchecho-Slovak State. The Committee have been principally guided in their discussions by ethnical considerations, and it is upon these considerations that they have endeavored to base their conclusions as a whole.

The Committee have found it necessary, however, in certain cases to take into account certain important considerations other than those of nationality. It became evident, indeed, that whereas it was extremely desirable to give to the new Tchecho-Slovak State the greatest possible ethnic unity, it was above all essential to provide for the new State conditions which would satisfy its economic needs; and for this purpose it was considered important, on the one hand, not to destroy the existing unity of economic life, and on the other hand to assure to the Tchechs such means of communication as were indispensible to their economic development, as well as a frontier line providing the necessary guarantees for their national security.

The following recommendations have been based upon the above principles.

I. THE FRONTIERS OF TCHECHO-SLOVAKIA

(a) *Frontier with Hungary*

(i.) FROM THE POINT WHERE THE FRONTIER BETWEEN AUSTRIA AND HUNGARY MEETS THE DANUBE TO THE MOUTH OF THE EIPEL

Proposed Frontier

The *talweg* of the main stream of the Danube, as far as the confluence of the Danube and the Eipel (Ipoly).

Explanation

The Committee propose to attach the island of the Grosse Schutt to Tchecho-Slovakia, although the population is mainly Magyar. In making this proposal, the Committee were influenced by the consideration that the natural and economic relations of the Island are with the region to the north and not with that to the south of the main Danube.

(ii.) BETWEEN THE MOUTH OF THE EIPEL AND THE SAJO

Proposed Frontier

The *talweg* of the Eipel as far as a point about 10 kilom. south-south-west of Losoncz station.

A line following the watershed running from north-west to south-east; cutting the Salgo-Tarjan–Losoncz railway; continuing along the watershed towards the south-east, and then south as far as point 628, 7 kilom. east-north-east of Salgo-Tarjan.

Following the watershed, at first in a general north-easterly direction, and then, after reaching point 278 (south of the confluence of the Sajo and the Rima), in an east-north-easterly direction to meet the Sajo.

Explanation

The line of the Eipel has been adopted as the frontier, because it most nearly approaches the ethnic frontier.

In order, however, to give the Tchecho-Slovaks the free use of the railway following the Eipel Valley which connects the district of Rimaszombat with the Danube, the Committee decided to annex to the statement regarding this portion of the frontier the following protocol:—

The railway which follows the valley of the Eipel (Ipoly) between Losoncz and Csata, as well as the junctions of this line with the lines situated to the north and south, shall be administered under the ultimate supervision of the Allied and Associated Governments in such a manner as to assure to the neighboring interested States the free use of these lines during the period required for the construction in Tchecho-Slovak territory of the section linking up a continuous line of railway on the right bank of the Eipel.

The conditions of this supervision and the period during which the free use of the line shall be guaranteed equally to the nations interested shall be determined by the Allied and Associated Governments.

(iii.) BETWEEN THE SAJO AND THE BODROG

Proposed Frontier

A line cutting the Putnok-Losoncz railway at Banreve station (about 6 kilom. west of Putnok), so as to pass between the bifurcations of the two railways, leading, respectively, northwards to Pelsocz, and southwards to Borsodnadasd.

Following the watershed in a general north-north-easterly direction as far as a point 7 kilom. east of Pelsocz.

Following a general east-north-easterly direction and cutting the Torna-Edeleny railway at about 4 kilom. south-west of Torna.

Following in an easterly direction the ridge on the left bank of the Bodva, passing north of Kany and south of Buzita and Pereny, to meet the Hernad 6 kilom. north-east of Hidasnemeti, then following this river up-stream as far as a point just west of Nadasd.

Turning east and passing south of Nadasd, meeting and following the watershed between the Bozsva and Ronyva.

Meeting this latter river 8 kilom. north-north-west of Satoralja-Ujhely and following its *talweg* southwards.

Cutting the railway triangle south-east of Satoralja-Ujhely in such a way as to leave to the Tchecho-Slovaks the complete possession on their territory of the Kassa-Csap railway.

Crossing the Bodrog about 5 kilom. south-west of Bodrog-Szerdahely.

Explanation

As will be seen, the section of the railway Satoralja-Csap, which connects Tchecho-Slovakia with the district inhabited by the Ruthenes and with Rumania, is left entirely in Tchecho-Slovak and Ruthenian territory. On the other hand, the town of Satoralja, with its Magyar majority, is left to Hungary.

With respect to the line which runs from Torna to Putnok north of Miskolecz, the Committee decided to annex the following protocol to the definition of the frontier:—

The railway which runs from Torna by the valley of the Bodva to the junction situated 8 kilom. to the north of Miskolcz, and the railway which runs from this junction by the valley of the Sajo as far as the junction with the Pelsocz line, shall be administered under the ultimate supervision of the Allied and Associated Governments in such a manner as to assure to the neighboring interested States the free use of these lines during the period required for the construction in Tchecho-Slovak territory of a branch connection between the Kassa-Torna line and the Sajo valley line.

The conditions of this supervision and the period during which the free use of these lines shall be guaranteed equally to the nations interested shall be determined by the Allied and Associated Governments.

(iv.) BETWEEN THE BODROG AND THE FRONTIER OF THE RUTHENIAN TERRITORY SOUTH OF THE CARPATHIANS

Proposed Frontier

A line approximately parallel to and to the south of the Satoralja-Ujhely-Csap railway, passing north of Lacza and south of Perbenyik and Tarkany, to meet the Tisza (Theiss) east of the latter village.

Following the *talweg* of the Tisza up-stream to a point 2 kilom. east-south-east of Csap. This point is the junction of the frontiers of Tchecho-Slovakia, Hungary and the Ruthenian territory south of the Carpathians.

Explanation

The various economic and geographical considerations on which the Committee have based the above proposal will result in the inclusion of a considerable number of Magyar citizens within Slovakia.

The Committee consider that it will be necessary to obtain for these Magyars the same rights and guarantees as will be assured to other minorities included within the Tchecho-Slovak State.

(b) Frontier with the Ruthenian Territory South of the Carpathians

Starting from the point of junction of the frontiers of Hungary, the Ruthenian territory and Tchecho-Slovakia (2 kilom. east-south-east of Csap) northwards, the frontier between Tchecho-Slovakia and Ruthenian territory has been traced as follows:—

A line to the north-north-east, approximately parallel to the Csap-Ungvar-Perecseny railway.

The watershed between the basins of the Ung and the Latorcza, through points 978 and 992, then turning north.

Meeting the main chain of the Carpathians at a point of approximate position: 48° 56′ north; and 22° 53′ east of Greenwich.

This point is the junction of the frontiers of Galicia, Tchecho-Slovakia, and the Ruthenian territory south of the Carpathians. . . .

(f) Frontiers of the Ruthenian Territory South of the Carpathians

(i.) WITH TCHECHO-SLOVAKIA (see paragraph I(b) above)

(ii.) WITH EASTERN GALICIA

Starting from the point of junction between the frontiers of Galicia and Tchecho-Slovakia, in approximate position 48° 56′ N.; 22° 53′ E. of Greenwich.

A line running south-eastwards along the old frontier between Galicia and Hungary, following the crest of the Carpathians as far as point 1655 (47° 48′ N.; 24° 34′ E. of Greenwich), which is the point of junction of the frontiers of Galicia, Rumania, and the Ruthenian territory south of the Carpathians.

(iii.) WITH RUMANIA

Starting from the point 1655 westwards.

A secondary watershed in a general west-south-westerly direction, continuing to meet the Tisza north of its confluence with the Visso, then following westwards the *talweg* of the Tisza, so as to leave the Maramaros-Sziget-Borsa railway entirely in Rumanian territory, while affording to the Ruthenes adequate facilities to connect the line from Korosmezo to Alsoaspa and Huszt on the north bank of the river and wholly in Ruthenian territory.

Leaving the Tisza at a point 9 kilom. west of Alsoaspa.

Following the crest of the Avas-Hegyseg (between the Tisza and the Tur) as far as a point 2 kilom. south-west of point 805, and continuing to follow the watershed.

Cutting the Szatmar-Nemeti-Huszt railway, 3 kilom. north of Halmi station.

Running parallel to and 1 kilom. south of the Halmi-Tisza-Ujlak road, then following the Batar downstream to a point just east of Magosliget (about 7 kilom. south-south-east of Tisza-Ujlak). This is the point of junction between the frontiers of Rumania, Hungary, and the Ruthenian territory.

(iv.) WITH HUNGARY

Starting from the point of junction of the frontiers of Rumania, Hungary, and the Ruthenian territory north-westwards, following the *talweg* of the Batar as far as its confluence with the Tisza south of Tisza-Ujlak, then the *talweg* of the Tisza as far as a point west of Badalo.

A line in a general north-north-westerly direction as far as a point just north-east of Darocz.

Turning west and then reaching the Egerces which it follows north as far as a point 5½ kilom. south-east of Szaloka.

Turning north-west and meeting the Tisza south of Szaloka.

Following the *talweg* of the Tisza downstream to the point of junction of the frontier of Tchecho-Slovakia, 2 kilom. east-south-east of Csap. . . .

III. THE RUTHENES SOUTH OF THE CARPATHIANS

The Committee were of opinion that these Ruthenes at present constitute a population neither sufficiently numerous nor sufficiently developed from a political point of view to form an independent State. The Committee considered that the interests of the Ruthenes themselves required their union, under some form of autonomous government, with the Tchecho-Slovaks. This solution is further supported by the fact that the Ruthenes and the Slovaks speak almost identical language and live under similar economic and social conditions. This solution, which has been anticipated by certain elements of the Ruthenian population, will give to this population the best opportunity for economic and political development.

It will rest with the Supreme Council of the Conference to determine in what form this autonomy can be realized.

In view of the fact that the creation of a Ruthenian state or province attached to Tchecho-Slovakia might have as a consequence the economic severance of Hungary from Poland, the Committee held that it would be necessary to advise the Committee charged with the study of Means of Communication of this fact, drawing its attention to the importance of guaranteeing complete liberty of transit between Hungary and Poland.

IV. CONNECTION BETWEEN TCHECHO-SLOVAKIA AND YUGOSLAVIA

The Tchecho-Slovak Government has in one of its memoranda expressed the desire to free itself from the economic domination of the Central European States and to establish for the future close commercial relations with Yugo-Slavia and the Adriatic. It was not clearly laid down in this memorandum whether such relations should be established by a territorial corridor separating Austria and Hungary, or simply by the adoption of an international *régime* guaranteeing freedom of transit between Tchecho-Slovakia and the Yugo-Slavs.

The Committee were of opinion that they could not consider the solution of this question by the provision of a territorial corridor, but that on the other hand it was proper to inform the Committee which deals with the Internationalization of Railways and Waterways of the necessity of assuring by special conventions the economic communications of Tchecho-Slovakia with the Yugo-Slavs and the Adriatic. . . .

VI. GENERAL OBSERVATIONS

In conclusion, the Committee desired to submit the following observations:
1. The configuration of the Tchecho-Slovak State and its geographical position give a peculiar importance to the measures designed to assure communication between this State and neighboring countries.

The Committee desired to express the wish that this situation should be specifically submitted to the Committee charged with the study of questions affecting the international *régime* of ports, waterways and railways.
2. On the other hand, the Tchecho-Slovak State will include within its frontiers a very large proportion of alien population, and a considerable number of Tchechs and Slovaks will be left within neighboring States.

This situation, which it is impossible to avoid, appears to merit special consideration in the general study which will be made of the measures to be taken to ensure the protection of ethnic minorities. . . .
Paris, March 12, 1919.

JULES CAMBON (Chairman).
CHARLES SEYMOUR.
A. W. DULLES.
JOSEPH COOK.
HAROLD G. NICOLSON.
J. LAROCHE.
SALVAGO RAGGI.
AUGUSTO STRANIERI.

DOCUMENT 11

Excerpts from Report Number 1, Submitted to the Supreme Council by the Committee for the Study of Territorial Questions Relating to Rumania and Yugoslavia, April 6, 1919: Rumanian Frontiers [1]

RUMANIAN FRONTIERS

I.—FORMATION, MANDATE AND WORK OF THE COMMITTEE

The Supreme Council of the Allies, at its meeting of the 1st February, 1919, came to the following decision:—

The questions raised by the declarations of M. Bratianu on the territorial interests of the Rumanians in the Peace settlement shall be submitted for examination, in the first instance, to a committee of specialists composed of two Delegates for each of the following Powers: the United States of America, the British Empire, France and Italy. The duty of this Committee will be to study the questions to be settled, to condense them in as narrow limits as possible and to propose a solution for an equitable settlement. This Committee may hear Representatives of the peoples concerned. . . .

The Committee for the Study of Territorial Questions relating to Rumania (which subsequently became the Committee for the Study of Territorial Questions relating to Rumania and Jugoslavia) was composed as follows:—
United States:—
    Dr. C. Day.
    Dr. Seymour.
British Empire:—
    Sir Eyre Crowe.
    Mr. A. W. A. Leeper.
France:—
    M. Tardieu (*Chairman*).
    M. Laroche.
Italy:—
    M. de Martino (*Vice-Chairman*).
    Count Vannutelli-Rey.

[1] Reprinted from the original Peace Conference Document. This was obtained from the files of Dr. James T. Shotwell, member of the American Commission to Negotiate Peace. Only parts of the Report affecting Hungary are reprinted.

The following also took part in the work of the Committee:—
United States:—
Major Johnson.
Captain L. W. Perrin (*Secretary*).
Lieutenant Reuben Horchow (*Secretary*).
British Empire:—
Lieutenant-Colonel J. H. M. Cornwall.
Mr. C. M. Palairet (*Secretary*).
France:—
General Le Rond.
M. de Martonne.
M. Haumant.
M. Aubert.
M. de Saint-Quentin (*Secretary-General*).
M. Camerlynck (*Interpreter*).
Italy:—
General Cavallero.
Colonel Castoldi.
Major Mazzolini.
Major Rugio.
Count Vinci (*Secretary*).

On the 2nd March the Committee constituted a Sub-Committee which it entrusted with preparing various questions and with drawing up the detailed line of the frontiers of Rumania and Jugoslavia. The following took part in the work of the Sub-Committee:—
United States:—
Dr. C. Seymour.
Major Johnson.
British Empire:—
Mr. A. W. A. Leeper.
Lieutenant-Colonel J. H. M. Cornwall.
Lieutenant-Colonel T. G. G. Heywood.
Captain A. G. Ogilvie.
France:—
General Le Rond (*Chairman*).
M. de Martonne.
M. Haumant.
Major de Montal.
M. de Saint-Quentin (*Secretary*).
M. Camerlynck (*Interpreter*).
Italy:—
Count Vannutelli-Rey.

Colonel Castoldi.

Major Mazzolini.

Major Rugio.

The Committee held 20 meetings, and the Sub-Committee 10.

On the 22nd February the Committee received the Rumanian Delegation, composed of—

M. Bratianu (President of the Council of Ministers).

M. Vaida-Voevod (Minister of State).

M. Mishu (Rumanian Minister in London).

(Rumanian Delegates Plenipotentiary at the Peace Conference).

On the 25th February the Committee received the Serbian Delegation, composed of—

M. Pashich (former President of the Council of Ministers).

M. Trumbich (Minister for Foreign Affairs).

M. Veshnich (Serbian Minister in Paris).

M. Zholger.

(Serbian Delegates Plenipotentiary at the Peace Conference).

M. Tsviyich (Formerly Rector of the University of Belgrade).

General Peshich (Assistant Chief of the General Staff).

REPORT ON THE FRONTIERS OF RUMANIA

1. In accordance with the instructions given it on the 1st February by the Supreme Council of the Allies, the Committee has studied the territorial problems raised by the Rumanian claims.

After examining in succession the questions of Bessarabia, Bukovina, Transylvania, and the Banat, it has proposed the demarcation of the frontier of Rumania in these different regions. It has devoted to each question a short note explaining the principles and the facts on which the decisions taken have been based.

The description of the line adopted as a whole, according to the international map of 1–1,000,000; the detailed description of the frontiers of Rumania with Hungary, and Jugoslavia according to the Austrian map of 1–200,000; and statistical tables and maps, appear as Annexes to the report.

2. The Committee considered that it could not leave untouched certain questions which, though foreign to the territorial claims of Rumania, are still likely to present themselves in a critical aspect in the territories bordering on that kingdom, and might compromise the relations of Rumania with the neighboring States. . . .

3. The Committee has on several occasions indicated the necessity of provisions guaranteeing the rights of the ethnical or religious minorities in

Rumania. It has thought it well to draw the special attention of the Supreme Council to the Jewish question.

4. In conformity with the limited mandate entrusted to it, the Committee has been guided in its inquiries and conclusions by an examination of the facts and the justice of the case. It considered, in consequence, that it was not for it to pronounce on the juridical bases of the claims presented—bases the evaluation of which belongs to the Council of the Allies, and which in any case, are inapplicable in themselves to the sum of the demands at the present time submitted to the Conference. . . .

III. FRONTIER OF TRANSYLVANIA

1.—Principles

A. The Committee proposes to join to Rumania not only Transylvania proper but also the adjacent districts where the majority of the population is Rumanian. It has not, however, always been able to apply the ethnical principle to the sub-division of this zone, for the following reasons:—

(a) When on the linguistic frontier Magyar towns are found surrounded by Rumanian country districts, it appears to the Committee that the nationality of the country should be allowed more weight than that of the towns, where the Hungarian administration has created artificial majorities.*

(b) On the other hand, it would, in the opinion of the Committee, destroy the economic unity of Transylvania as a whole if Rumania were refused the outlets of the valleys in the plain, and a railway connecting these outlets with each other and with the Danube.

(c) Finally, the Committee considers it advisable, in the general interests of peace, to facilitate the junction of this railway with the railway systems of other Allied countries so as to make it a great connecting artery between those countries and the Danube.

B. The Committee has taken note of the declarations made by the Transylvanian Government and acquiesced in by the Rumanian Government, guaranteeing to the Magyar, Szekler, German or other minorities complete autonomy as regards local administration, education and religion. It considers that it will be advisable to obtain from the Rumanian Government the official confirmation of these engagements.

* The Italian Delegation maintains, on the other hand, the principle that the nationality of the towns, by reason of their great importance from the social, intellectual, and economic point of view, ought to outweigh that of the country districts.

Nevertheless, it has thought it right to depart from this principle as regards the Magyar towns situated on the railway from Arad to Maramaros-Sziget and to apply the other principle (equally maintained by it) that any line of railway essential to the economic life and the strategical security of a State must necessarily be comprised in the territory of that State, even if it traverses for a part of its distance a zone inhabited by alien populations.

2.—*Conclusions*

A—*Northern Frontier*

(a) The line proposed by the Committee for the northern frontier of Transylvania gives to the Ruthenes the valley of the Tisza and the railway following it, with the exception of the Rumanian centre of Maramaros-Sziget. Moreover, it leaves the Ruthenes free to re-establish the continuity of their railway by making a detour round that town.

(b) The Committee is of opinion that the railway from Tisza-Ujlak to Raho, as well as its connections with the railways situated on either side, should be operated under the supervision of the Allied and Associated Governments so as to ensure their free use by the neighboring States concerned during the time required for the completion of a continuous railway in Rumanian territory from Maramaros-Sziget to Szatmar-Nemeti and a continuous railway in Tchecho-Slovak territory on the northern bank of the Tisza. The conditions and duration of the supervision by the Allied and Associated Governments will be fixed by the said Governments.

(c) The Italian Delegation contended that in the interests of peace Western Transylvania ought to be placed in direct contact with Galicia and Poland without the interposition of a third State. It accordingly proposed to assign to Rumania the two railway lines running northwards from the Tisza, one to the west and the other to the east of Maramaros-Sziget.

The Committee feels unable to adopt this proposal, which would involve cutting in half the territory of the Hungarian Ruthenes and thus impede the homogeneous development of this people, whose destiny the Committee charged with considering their case has decided to entrust to the Tchecho-Slovak State.

B—*Western Frontier*

(a) The line proposed by the Committee for the western frontier of Transylvania would, if Rumania constructs a connecting railway-line between Kisjeno and Nagy-Szalonta, secure for her direct communication between the Danube and the region of the Upper Tisza via Arad, Nagy-Varad, Nagy-Karoly and Szatmar-Nemeti.

(b) The Committee is of the opinion that the railway from Nagy-Szalonta to Arad via Gyula and Békéscaba, as well as its connections with the railways situated on either side, should be administered under the supervision of the Allied and Associated Governments so as to ensure their free use by the neighboring States concerned during the time required for the completion of a continuous railway in Rumanian territory from Nagy-Szalonta to Kisjeno and Arad. The conditions and duration of the supervision by the Allied and Associated Governments will be fixed by the said Governments.

(c) The fact has not been overlooked that communication with the Tchecho-Slovak countries would be more naturally effected by the shorter railway-line from Nagy-Karoly to Csap. Nevertheless, taking into account the exclusively Magyar character of the regions traversed by the latter railway, the Committee decided on a line reaching the Tisza further to the east and yet permitting the improvement of the existing communications by an easily constructed railway between Halmi and Tisza-Ujlak.

IV. FRONTIER OF THE BANAT

1.—Principles

(a) The Committee has given the most serious attention to the arguments put forward by Rumania in favor of the indivisibility of the Banat.

Though it does not find them conclusive from the historical point of view, it recognizes their value from the economic point of view. It finds that no natural dividing line exists in the Banat, and that an artificial line, intersecting railways and waterways, is likely to disturb the economic system of the region.

(b) This consideration does not, however, appear so decisive as to allow the Committee to set aside the secular aspirations of the highly developed Jugoslav populations inhabiting the south-western portion of the Banat and closely connected with Belgrade.

(c) On the other hand, the Committee has come to the conclusion that the portion of the Banat situated in the neighborhood of the confluence of the river Maros and the river Tisza depends ethnographically and economically on the immediate surroundings of Szeged and should in consequence remain, with that town, in Hungarian territory.

2.—Conclusions

A.—The Committee has reserved a Hungarian zone to the south-east of Szeged. It has decided in favor of dividing the rest of the Banat between the Rumanians and the Jugoslavs, in such a way that a balance will be maintained as far as possible between the numbers of each of these two nationalities to be assigned to the other.

The line which it proposes leaves in the Banat approximately 75,000 Rumanians to Jugoslavia and approximately 65,000 Slavs to Rumania.

B.—This line also endeavors to assure, so far as possible, means of communication to each State in the zone assigned to it.

(a) It assigns to Rumania the course of the Maros, as far as the surroundings of Szeged, and gives her on the Danube the river-port of Bazias, which

she will be able to connect with the Arad-Temesvar railway, a prolongation /
of the main line of Western Transylvania.

(b) The Committee is of opinion that the railway from Vejté to Bazias,
as well as its connections with the railways situated on either side, should
be administered under the supervision of the Allied and Associated Governments so as to ensure their free use by the neighboring States concerned during the time required for the completion of a continuous railway in Rumanian territory from Vejté to Bazias. The conditions and duration of the
supervision by the Allied and Associated Governments will be fixed by the
said Governments.

(c) It gives Jugoslavia both banks of the Lower Tisza and railways connecting Nagy-Kikinda, Nagy-Becskerek and Versecz with Pancsova on the
Danube.

C.—The Committee, in view of the complexity of the problem and of the
intense partisan feeling which has been displayed, emphasizes the necessity
of reciprocal engagements to protect the minorities in conformity with the
provisions of the League of Nations. . . .

April 6, 1919.   A. TARDIEU (*Chairman*).
                                                  CLIVE DAY.
                                                  CHARLES SEYMOUR.
                                                  EYRE A. CROWE.
                                                  A. W. A. LEEPER.
                                                  J. LAROCHE.
                                                  G. DE MARTINO.
                                                  L. VANNUTELLI-REY.

Excerpts from Report Number 2, Submitted to the Supreme Council by the Committee for the Study of Territorial Questions Relating to Rumania and Yugoslavia, April 6, 1919: Yugoslav Frontiers[1]

FORMATION, MANDATE AND WORK OF THE COMMITTEE

. . . At its meeting of the 18th February, 1919, the Supreme Council of the Allies adopted the following resolution:—

The questions raised by the statements made by M. Vesnich, M. Trumbich and M. Zholger on behalf of the Serbian Delegation on the territorial interests of Serbia at the conclusion of peace, with the exception of the questions in which Italy is directly interested, shall be referred for a preliminary examination to the Committee of specialists charged with the examination of the Banat. It will be the duty of this Committee to reduce the questions on which a decision is to be taken to the narrowest limits possible and to present proposals for assuring an equitable solution. The Committee is authorized to consult the representatives of the peoples interested.

The Committee for the Study of Territorial Questions relating to Rumania (which subsequently became the Committee for the Study of Territorial Questions relating to Rumania and Yugoslavia) was composed as follows:—
[This part of the report is identical with Report Number 1, *supra,* Document 11.]

REPORT ON THE FRONTIERS OF YUGOSLAVIA

1. On the 18th February last the Supreme Council of the Allies entrusted the study of the questions raised by the territorial claims of Yugoslavia— "the questions in which Italy is directly interested being excepted"—to the Committee which had already, in its examination of the Rumanian territorial claims, been led to discuss the frontier between Yugoslavia and Rumania in the Banat.

The Supreme Council of the Allies, at its meeting of the 11th March, re-

[1] Reprinted from the original Peace Conference Document. This was obtained from the files of Dr. James T. Shotwell, member of the American Commission to Negotiate Peace. Only parts of the Report affecting Hungary are reprinted.

served for its own decision the Albanian territorial claims and, consequently, the question of the frontier common to Albania and Yugoslavia.

2. In conformity with the limited mandate thus conferred upon it, the Committee examined in succession the frontiers of the Yugoslav State with Bulgaria, Hungary and Austria. It pursued this last portion of its studies towards the west as far as the road running from Klagenfurt to Laibach. . . .

4. The Committee has taken into account in its labors all the elements of fact and all the considerations of equity which have come to its knowledge so far as ethnographical, historical, geographical, economic and political questions are concerned.

It considers generally that Yugoslavia and the neighboring States should enter into such reciprocal engagements as will guarantee the rights of minorities in conformity with the provisions of the League of Nations. . . .

II. FRONTIER BETWEEN YUGOSLAVIA AND RUMANIA (THE BANAT)

1. Principles

(a.) The Committee has given the most serious attention to the arguments put forward by Rumania in favor of the indivisibility of the Banat.

Though it does not find them conclusive from the historical point of view, it recognises their value from the economic point of view. It finds that no natural dividing line exists in the Banat, and that an artificial line, intersecting railways and waterways, is likely to disturb the economic system of the region.

(b.) This consideration does not, however, appear so decisive as to allow the Committee to set aside the secular aspirations of the highly developed Yugoslav populations inhabiting the south-western portion of the Banat and closely connected with Belgrade.

(c.) On the other hand, the Committee has come to the conclusion that the portion of the Banat situated in the neighborhood of the confluence of the river Maros and the river Tisza depends ethnographically and economically on the immediate surroundings of Szeged, and should in consequence remain, with that town, in Hungarian territory.

2. Conclusions

(A.) The Committee has reserved a Hungarian zone to the southeast of Szeged. It has decided in favor of dividing the rest of the Banat between the Rumanians and the Yugoslavs in such a way that a balance will be maintained as far as possible between the numbers of each of these two nationalities to be assigned to the other.

The line which it proposes leaves in the Banat approximately 75,000 Rumanians to Yugoslavia and approximately 65,000 Slavs to Rumania.

(B.) This line also endeavors to assure, so far as possible, means of communication to each State in the zone assigned to it.

(a.) It assigns to Rumania the course of the Maros, as far as the surroundings of Szeged, and gives her on the Danube the river-port of Bazias, which she will be able to connect with the Arad-Temesvar railway, a prolongation of the main line of Western Transylvania.

(b.) The Committee is of opinion that the railway from Vejté to Bazias, as well as its connections with the railways situated on each side of it, should be operated under the supervision of the Allied and Associated Governments so as to ensure their free use to the neighboring States concerned during the time required for the completion of a continuous railway in Rumanian territory from Vejté to Bazias. The conditions and duration of the supervision by the Allied and Associated Governments will be fixed by the said Governments.

(c.) It gives Yugoslavia both banks of the Lower Tisza and railways connecting Nagy-Kikinda, Nagy-Becskerek and Versecz with Pancsova on the Danube.

(C.) The Committee, in view of the complexity of the problem and of the intense partisan feeling which has been displayed, emphasizes the necessity of reciprocal engagements to protect the minorities in conformity with the provisions of the League of Nations.

III. FRONTIER BETWEEN YUGOSLAVIA AND HUNGARY

1.—Principles

(a.) The Committee has examined with the most benevolent attention the national claims of the Yugoslav populations inhabiting the Hungarian Comitats bordering on Serbia, Slavonia and Croatia.

(b.) It considers that in these regions, Serbs, Croats, Slovenes, Bunyevtsi and Shoktsi form, notwithstanding their divergences of language and religion, a mass which is homogeneous in tendency and will unite without difficulty with the Yugoslav State.

(c.) It attaches the greatest importance to avoiding the disturbance of the normal economic life of the populations. Its decisions have been dictated by this consideration in cases where the mixture and confusion of races made it impossible to define with certainty the ethnical frontier, or where that frontier could not be made to coincide with any natural frontier.

2.—*Conclusions*

(A.) IN THE BANAT

(See Section II dealing with the Banat.)

(B.) IN THE BACSKA

The Committee proposes to give to Yugoslavia the part of the Bacska situated to the south of a transversal line continuing the Yugoslav frontier in the Banat from a point southwest of Szeged to a point on the Danube north of Kiskoszeg.

This line gives to Yugoslavia:

(a.) A territory where the Yugoslavs of all categories are in a relative majority, if the official Hungarian statistics be properly corrected.

(b.) The large semi-urban and semi-rural districts of Szabadka and Zombor, places which possess an absolute majority of Slavs according to the rectified statistics, and which have been for centuries centers of Yugoslav civilization.

(c.) The railways and waterways necessary to the economic prosperity of the region: the canals known as "Francis" and "Francis Joseph" which connect the Danube and the Tisza, as well as the system of railways connecting the principal centres of population with each other and with the Danube and the Tisza.

(C.) IN THE BARANYA AND SOMOGY

The Committee proposes that the northern frontier of Yugoslavia should follow the course of the Danube to its confluence with the Drave, and then the course of the latter river to its confluence with the Mur.

(a.) This line leaves outside Yugoslavia, in the southern portion of the Comitats of Baranya and Somogy, only Yugoslav elements of a very scattered character and representing only a small minority in the district as a whole.

(b.) Gives Yugoslavia the economic and strategic advantages of an excellent natural frontier.

(c.) Satisfactorily assures the economic life of the Yugoslav districts bordering on the river Drave, this great navigable artery being connected with the south by a railway system.

The Committee considers that the railway from Kotor to Barcz, as well as its connections with the railways to the south, should be operated under the supervision of the Allied and Associated Governments so as to ensure their free use to the neighboring States concerned during the time required for the completion of a continuous railway in Yugoslav territory on the right bank of the Mur and the Drave. The conditions and duration of the supervision by the Allied and Associated Governments will be fixed by the said Governments.

(D.) MEDYUMURYE

The Committee proposes that after leaving the confluence of the Drave and the Mur, the northern frontier of Yugoslavia should follow the Mur till it meets the frontier between Hungary and Austria, to the east of Radkersburg.

The line leaves to Yugoslavia the region comprised in the angle formed by the confluence of the Drave and the Mur—a region known as the Medyumurye, which is inhabited by a population almost exclusively Yugoslav.

(E.) PREKOMURYE

The line indicated above excludes from Yugoslavia the Prekomurye, a region situated to the south of Szt. Gotthard between the Mur and the Raab.

The Committee, in taking this decision, does not dispute the fact that the Prekomurye includes in its southern portion a Slovene majority of clearly marked national aspirations. It considers, however:—

(a) That, owing to the mixture of races, it is impossible to establish a satisfactory ethnic frontier if the natural line of the Mur, the only geographical frontier, be abandoned.

(b) That it would be disadvantageous to the interests of the populations to assign to Yugoslavia a territory which would form a pronounced salient. . . .

April 6, 1919.

[Signatures as under Report Number 1, *supra,* Document 11.]

DOCUMENT 13

Modification of Frontiers between Hungary and Czecho-Slovakia

I. NOTES OF GENERAL SMUTS ON A CONVERSATION WITH PRESIDENT MASARYK, APRIL 9, 1919 [1]

In my conversation with President Masaryk at Prague on Monday, 7th April, the future frontiers of the Czecho-Slovak State were referred to. Under the Armistice terms, the Czecho-Slovak forces occupy the northern bank of the Danube from Pressburg to Komarom. The object, no doubt, in bringing the Czech occupation so far south was to give the future state a Danube frontier. But in order to do so it will have to include a very large purely Magyar population, which lives north of the Danube. I pointed out to President Masaryk the grave undesirability of this. He agreed, and said that he would prefer to waive all claims to this Magyar territory and withdraw the Czech frontier to the north, so as to leave all this ethnologically Magyar territory to Hungary. But on one condition: that in exchange Czecho-Slovakia should get a small strip of Hungarian territory south of the Danube at Pressburg towards Parndorf. This population here is more German and Croatian than Magyar. But the great advantage to Czecho-Slovakia of such an arrangement would be that the possession of both banks of the Danube for a short distance would enable the future state to build proper harbors and docks along both banks of the Danube. This it would be impossible to do on one bank only, when a possibly hostile power sits a few hundred yards off on the other bank. For this economic advantage Masaryk would be prepared to surrender his claim to a large area with an alien population.

With some millions of Germans already included in Bohemia in the north, the further inclusion of some 400,000 or 500,000 Magyars in the south would be a very serious matter for the young State, besides the grave violation of the principle of nationality involved. I would therefore press very strongly for effect being given to this exchange, as I am sure it would be both to the advantage of Bohemia, and immensely please the Hungarians, who already

---

[1] Miller, *My Diary*, XVI, 220 (by permission); also *op. cit.*, XVIII, 97. This memorandum formed Annex "B" to the minutes of the meeting of the Council of Foreign Ministers, held on May 3, 1919.

look upon this part of their Magyar population as lost to them. In fact the Great Powers thus obtain a valuable bargaining counter in any dealings with the Hungarian Government.

J. C. Smuts.

II. EXCERPTS FROM THE MINUTES OF THE COUNCIL OF FOREIGN MINISTERS, HELD ON MAY 3, 1919 [2]

. . . 3. M. Pichon said that the next question on the agenda paper (*i.e.,* the proposed modification of the frontier between Czecho-Slovakia and Hungary) had arisen from a report submitted by General Smuts, as a result of a conversation the General had had with President Mazaryk. (See Annex B.) He (M. Pichon) proposed that the question should in the first place be referred to the Interallied Commission dealing with Czecho-Slovakian affairs, for report.

Mr. Lansing concurred.

Lord Hardinge said that the British Delegation had prepared the following resolution, which he would submit for approval:

IT IS RESOLVED

THAT in view of the explanations furnished to General Smuts by the President of the Czecho-Slovak Republic, the general question of the southern frontier of Slovakia shall be referred for further examination to the Sub-Committee of the Czecho-Slovak Commission. This Committee shall proceed from the assumption that the island of the Grosse Schutt shall be excluded from Czecho-Slovak territory provided that in return a small enclave opposite Presbourg is ceded to the new Republic, and they shall consider whether the exclusion of this Magyar population renders it possible to modify in favour of Czecho-Slovakia the frontier proposed in the Eipol valley.

The Sub-Committee shall report at the earliest possible minute.

Mr. Lansing said he would agree to the first sentence of the draft resolution, but he would oppose the remainder of the text.

M. Pichon expressed his agreement with Mr. Lansing's point of view. In his opinion, the Council should not prejudge a case until it had received careful examination. He feared there had been some misunderstanding as to what President Mazaryk had said, and that the whole question required to be cleared up.

M. Laroche stated that Mr. Benes had formally stated that after obtaining cognisance of General Smuts' report of his interview with President Mazaryk, he had referred the matter to the President who had replied that General Smuts had seriously misunderstood what he had said. President Mazaryk in his interview with General Smuts had merely stated that cer-

[2] Miller, *My Diary,* XVI, 215 ff. (by permission).

tain parties in Bohemia held the view that the Island of Grosse Schutt might be exchanged for a small enclave opposite Presbourg. President Mazaryk himself, however, did not support that proposal. He maintained that the Island of Grosse Schutte was indispensable in order to ensure free navigation of the Danube. Furthermore, the President had received a deputation composed of the inhabitants of the Island of Grosse Schutte, imploring that the island in question should be attached to Czecho-Slovakia for the reason that the whole of the products of the island, including corn, were sent to Bohemia and not to Hungary. Under those conditions the Czecho-Slovak Delegation asked that the decision reached by the Commission on Czecho-Slovak affairs should be maintained.

M. Pichon held that the Interallied Commission on Czecho-Slovakia could alone throw light on this question. Furthermore, in his opinion, the question should not be referred to the Sub-Commission of the Czecho-Slovak Commissions, but to the Commission itself.

Mr. Lansing expressed his complete agreement with M. Pichon's views. He enquired whether Mr. Benes had submitted a written statement, giving President Mazaryk's explanation.

M. Laroche replied that he had had a personal interview with Mr. Benes, who had expressed his readiness to give evidence before the Commission. Dr. Benes would no doubt also be quite prepared to give a written statement if required.

Mr. Lansing thought that the Council could not do more for the present than to refer General Smuts' proposal to the Commission on Czecho-Slovak Affairs for investigation and report.

Lord Hardinge said that in view of what the Council had just heard, especially in regard to the misunderstanding which had occurred, the British Delegation would withdraw its resolution. It agreed that the whole question should be referred to the Czecho-Slovak Commission for report.

(It was agreed to refer General Smuts' proposal [see Annex "B"] to the Commission on Czecho-Slovak Affairs for investigation and report.) . . .

DOCUMENT 14

*Excerpts from the Minutes of the Council of Foreign Ministers,
Held on May 8, 1919: Frontiers of Hungary* [1]

REPORTS OF TERRITORIAL COMMITTEES ON FRONTIERS OF
AUSTRIA AND HUNGARY

(a) Question of secession of parts of Austria and Hungary

1. M. PICHON said that it would be convenient to begin with the frontiers
laid down for Roumania, and he would ask M. Tardieu to explain the finding of the Committee.

MR. BALFOUR thought that before examining the particular reports it
might be desirable to define what Austria and Hungary were to be, in terms
of territory. He instanced the case of Vorarlberg. Was it to be Swiss or
Austrian? In the former alternative, if Vorarlberg was allowed to split off,
how was the Conference to prevent other fractions of previous Austrian territory to follow suit, in order to alleviate the debt on the population or for
any other reason whatever? Before the Treaty could be made with Austria
or Hungary this question must be settled in principle.

BARON SONNINO said that as far as he was concerned, Vorarlberg was part
of Austria. He had no knowledge of this territory as an independent unit.
Its recognition as such would lead to the secession of other populations, and
result in endless confusion.

MR. BALFOUR said that if he understood Baron Sonnino aright, it was intended that the discussion should result in a definition of Austria.

BARON SONNINO said that it should result in a definition of Hungary as
well as Austria.

MR. BALFOUR agreed that the method of defining the frontiers by adopting
the results reached by the territorial committees might perhaps be the best.
The circuit would then be complete and the various difficulties arising on
the way could be considered.

MR. LANSING said that in his view the Council was dealing with the territory which in 1914 had been the domain of Austria and Hungary. It was
recognized that this territory was to be dismembered, that Austria and Hungary were to be made separate States, and that their lands were to be limited

[1] Miller, *My Diary*, XVI, 223 ff. (by permission).

by new States, whose frontiers were to be determined. No definition of Austria and Hungary, therefore, appeared necessary. The definition would arise automatically as a result of establishing the new States.

MR. BALFOUR said that the question still remained what would the Conference do if any other part of Austrian or Hungarian territory wished to split off like Vorarlberg?

MR. LANSING said that this question would have to come before the Conference when it arose. In his opinion the population could not be allowed to secede in order to avoid paying taxes.

MR. BALFOUR thought that in the Treaty there should be a clause covering such cases. He pointed out that there was to be a plebiscite in Vorarlberg in fifteen days, and that the Conference was doing nothing to stop it.

M. PICHON observed that the French Government had several times been informed by the Swiss Government that the adhesion of Vorarlberg was not desired. On the last occasion the Swiss Government had said that they would not welcome Vorarlberg, unless a crushing majority in the plebiscite practically forced their hands. The question, however, had not yet arisen, and it did not appear necessary for the Council to deal with it before it arose. He would therefore ask M. Tardieu to begin his explanation of the boundary adopted by the Committee for Roumania.

(After a short discussion it was decided not to consider the boundary of Roumania on the Russian side, but only to deal with its boundary on the Hungarian side.

MR. LANSING said that in his opinion when the delimitation of Roumania and Russia was made, it would be necessary that Russia should be represented. The Peace Conference could not adjudicate on territory belonging to a State with whom the Powers represented were not at war.)

(b) Hungarian frontier with Roumania

M. TARDIEU said that he would explain the finding of the Committee in respect of the Roumanian-Hungarian boundary in Transylvania. Referring to the map attached to Report No. 1 (W.C.P. 656), he explained that the red line indicated the demands of the Roumanian Delegation, and the blue line the recommendations of the Committee. There had been long discussions on the subject of the frontier in question, occupying no less than twelve meetings. He would explain in a few words the reasons which had prevailed with the Committee. Had the demands of the Roumanian Delegation been accepted without modification, a very large number of aliens would have been attributed to both sides. These numbers were halved by the recommendations of the Committee. Ethnologically, therefore, he thought that the results obtained were satisfactory. It had also been thought reasonable to keep within Roumanian territory a main line of communication running from Northeast to Southwest; from Szatmar-Nemeti to Nagy-Varad, while a parellel line connecting Szeged and Debreczen was left in Hungary.

Mr. Lansing asked where the proper ethnic line would be.

M. Tardieu said that the population was very mixed and that the blue line represented an equitable compromise. A truer line might perhaps in some cases be 20 kilometres east but on the whole, as he had explained, he thought the line would be satisfactory.

Mr. Lansing asked why a more accurate ethnic line could not be followed.

M. Tardieu explained that it would cut the railway line and suppress continuous communication.

Mr. Lansing asked if anywhere west of the line there could be found a preponderant Roumanian population.

M. Tardieu said that this might occur in certain isolated places.

In reply to further questions, M. Tardieu said that some 600,000 Hungarians would remain under Roumanian rule while some 25,000 Roumanians would remain within Hungary.

Mr. Lansing expressed the view that this distribution did not appear very just; in every case the decision seemed to have been given against the Hungarians.

M. Tardieu said that any other adjustment would have been all in favour of the Hungarians and correspondingly to the detriment of the Roumanians. The whole question had been discussed with the very greatest care—the solution had been adopted unanimously and represented, he thought, the best that could be done in very difficult circumstances. In some places where the Committee had thought it possible for new lines of communication to be built they had adhered more strictly to ethnographical considerations, but on the main part of the frontier, by reason of the mountainous ground, it was impossible to substitute new lines for those already existing. By reason of the way in which the Hungarians were grouped in Transylvania, it was absolutely impossible to avoid attributing large numbers of them to the future Roumanian State.

Mr. Lansing said that he appreciated the efforts of the Committee to make an equitable distribution. After further consideration, he withdrew his criticisms and made no objection to the recommendations of the Committee.

Mr. Balfour also stated that he raised no objection.

It was not possible for the Council to go over in detail the whole work of the Committee. As long as the Council was satisfied that the Committee had done the utmost to find an equitable solution, he felt that nothing could be done to improve the resolution, unless there had been disagreement within the Committee itself.

Baron Sonnino also expressed his agreement.

(No other objections being raised to the finding of the Committee, the frontier between Roumania and Hungary, as proposed by the Committee, from the former frontier of Russia at Khotin to the point of contact with the Danube was accepted.

It was decided that the frontier as between Roumania and Jugo-Slavia in the Banat should be reserved for future discussion.)

The hope was expressed that a solution of the latter question would be reached by agreement between the Roumanian and the Jugo-Slav Government.

(c) Frontier between Hungary and Jugo-Slavia

M. TARDIEU said that the eastern frontier of Hungary had now been determined. There remained the southern frontier between Hungary and Jugo-Slavia. Referring to the map attached to Report No. 2 of the Committee (W.C.P. 646) he pointed out that there was a very considerable variation between the demands of the Jugo-Slavs and the recommendations of the Committee. The Committee had certainly excluded a large number of Slavs from the area to be attributed to Jugo-Slavia, but they were not in sufficient numbers in the Committee's opinion to justify the line claimed by the Jugo-Slavs.

The Committee had therefore unanimously adopted the blue line from west of Mako to the point of intersection with the former boundary between Austria and Hungary.

M. PICHON asked if any criticisms of this line were forthcoming.

No criticisms were made and the boundary proposed by the Committee from the angle west of Mako to the point of intersection with the former boundary between Austria and Hungary was accepted.

(d) Boundary between Austria and Hungary

M. SONNINO asked whether anything had been done regarding the boundary between Austria and Hungary.

M. PICHON said that no Commission had been charged with this subject.

MR. LANSING questioned whether it was necessary to make any alteration in this boundary.

MR. BALFOUR said that it might possibly be necessary to do so, as he understood that there was a German population in Hungary which might wish to join Austria. If so, it might be desirable to be prepared to deal with this eventuality.

M. SONNINO pointed out that up to date neither Austria nor Hungary had raised the question.

Mr. Balfour said that the question did not greatly interest the Allies, unless the financial or economic terms were to differ as between Hungary and Austria. In that case, some trouble might arise.

M. Sonnino said that he could see no reason why any difference in the treatment of the two countries should be made.

Mr. Balfour said that if the Treaties in both cases were identic, it might not be necessary for the Conference to define the areas of the two states. In the other alternative, it might be desirable to do so.

M. Pichon thought it was unnecessary to deal with the question at once.

Mr. Lansing said that, in his view, certain economic questions might arise which, unless the frontiers had been adjusted, might cause difficulties. As these two countries were now to be separated, he thought it would be well to ask a Commission to make a report to the Conference as to whether the previous boundary lines required to be changed or not. The Conference would therefore be prepared beforehand to deal with any proposal that might be made either from the Austrian or from the Hungarian side.

M. Sonnino said that if either the Austrians or the Hungarians had raised the question, he would be inclined to agree. As neither had done so, he could see no reason for setting a Commission to work. As far as he was concerned, he accepted the old frontier. Should either side desire an alteration, he would then be prepared to recommend examination by a Commission.

Mr. Lansing observed that neither the Austrians nor the Hungarians were present to raise the question. He suggested that, as the Allies had so often been unready to deal with emergencies when they arose, they should in this case take steps to be prepared in advance.

M. Sonnino pointed out that full liberty had been left to the Serbians and the Roumanians to compose their differences. It was only should they disagree that the Conference would step in. He suggested that the same procedure be adopted regarding Austria and Hungary. He saw no reason for stirring them up. The Hungarians were not represented but had made a very considerable fuss about their frontier with Roumania. It appeared to him quite gratuitous to suggest to them that they should raise needless trouble. The two countries had not quarrelled for fifty years over this frontier; their present Governments were very insecure and the time seemed very inopportune for thrusting a controversy upon them.

Mr. Lansing said that his suggestion was that the question should be dealt with without rousing either the Austrians or the Hungarians.

M. Sonnino said that if it could be done without the knowledge of either he would not object.

M. Pichon said he understood the suggestion to be that a Committee should be asked to deal objectively with a possible rectification of boundary between Austria and Hungary.

(It was decided that a Commission be appointed to collect information regarding any possible rectification of frontier between Austria and Hungary which might be proposed by either of the parties concerned. The object of the investigation was to be to place the Council in a position to settle rapidly any trouble that might arise between Austria and Hungary on this subject. No action would be taken unless the question were to be raised by Austria or Hungary.)

(e) Frontier between Czecho-Slovakia and Hungary

M. LAROCHE explained that the finding of the Committee had been unanimous. From the point where the ancient boundary between Hungary and Austria met the Danube to the confluence of the Ipoli and the Danube, the frontier between Hungary and Czecho-Slovakia followed the stream. The reason for giving this frontier to Czecho-Slovakia was obvious. It was necessary to endow the new State with wide access to this important international waterway. A suggestion had been made to give up to Hungary the Gross Schutt in exchange for a bridge-head across the Danube at Pressburg. This solution had been unanimously rejected.

MR. LANSING asked whether the population of the Gross Schutt was Hungarian.

M. LAROCHE replied that it was partly Hungarian and partly German, but that this area was closely connected economically with the Czecho-Slovak hinterland. The people desired to maintain connection with the Czecho-Slovak State, in order to save their economic interests. The problems in this region were complicated and had been studied very carefully at a great number of sittings. The Committee had adopted what appeared to be the most reasonable solutions and unanimous agreements had been reached on all points.

MR. LANSING pointed out that, as a result of the findings of the two Committees, some two million Hungarians were to be placed under alien rule in Roumania and in Czecho-Slovakia.

M. LAROCHE observed that, as far as the Czecho-Slovak Committee was concerned, it had so reduced the claims of the Czechs that only 855,000 Hungarians instead of 1,300,000 would become subjects of Czecho-Slovakia. On the other hand, a great number of Czechs and Slovaks lived outside the boundaries of the new State. According to M. Benes, no less than 638,000 Slovaks would be left in Hungary. This figure might be exaggerated, but the number was considerable, and might be regarded as a guarantee for the good treatment of the Hungarian minority in Czecho-Slovakia.

(After some further discussion, the line proposed by the Committee, from the intersection of the former boundary between Austria and Hungary up to the angle formed by the meeting of the Roumanian and Ruthenian territory, was accepted as the Northern frontier of Hungary.)

(f) Ruthenia

MR. BALFOUR said that the problem of dealing with the Ruthenians was one which had not been settled. The Ruthenians had some affinity with the Slovaks, but not enough to be included without some precautions in the same State. Some kind of local autonomy had been suggested for them. The definition of the expression "some form of autonomy" was still to seek. There were, he was told, some 400,000 Ruthenians. They were considered too few to form an entirely separate State. On the other hand, it might be desirable to save them from the various annoyances arising from association with a larger and, to some extent, alien population in the same State. The precise means of dealing with this difficulty had not been thought out. A similar difficulty however, would arise not only in the peace with Austria and Hungary but elsewhere.

M. PICHON said that the Committee had referred the question of Ruthenian autonomy to the Supreme Council. He suggested that a Commission be asked to make recommendations as to the form of autonomy suitable to the Ruthenians.

MR. BALFOUR thought that the question might perhaps be referred to the Committee dealing with the rights of minorities.

M. SONNINO said that he had no knowledge of this Committee on which there was no Italian representative.

MR. LANSING said that he would prefer to name a new Commission with local knowledge of the area in question. He proposed that the question be referred to the Committee on Czecho-Slovakia.

MR. BALFOUR asked whether it was proposed to proceed in this manner whenever the question of autonomy should arise.

MR. LANSING said that he would support this, provided that the Council had the opportunity of examining the proposals, in order to ensure that contradictory principles were not applied in the various cases.

M. LAROCHE said that the Committee on Czecho-Slovak Affairs would ask the Czecho-Slovak Government for its proposals. Should these proposals not meet with the approval of the Committee experts could be consulted and the Ruthenians themselves could be asked to make their own suggestions. As far as the Treaty was concerned, all that need be stipulated was that the territory of the Ruthenians be ceded to the Allied and Associated Powers.

(It was then decided that the Committee on Czecho-Slovakia be asked to make recommendations regarding the future status of the Ruthenians in relation to the Czecho-Slovak State.)

AGENDA FOR THE FOLLOWING MEETING

2. The frontiers of Hungary having been defined by the above resolutions, it was decided that the question of the frontiers of Austria should be discussed on the following day.

(The meeting then adjourned.)

DOCUMENT 15

*Excerpts from the Minutes of the Council of Foreign Ministers,
Held on May 9, 1919: Blockade of Hungary* [1]

. . . Blocade of Hungary

6. M. SEYDOUX said that the Supreme Economic Council had for some time considered the question of the removal of the blockade restrictions on Hungary. It had been proposed to reopen relations with Hungary when the blockade restrictions on Austria had been removed. But on account of Bolshevik outbreaks in Hungary it had been found impossible on the 2nd April to give effect to this proposal. Indeed, it had been found necessary to insist on closing the frontier between Austria and Hungary. Now that the Government of Bela Kun was about to be upset, he thought steps could be taken to remove all commercial restrictions. Hungary was self-contained up to a certain point, but the supply of food and raw materials was becoming an urgent problem. It appeared, however, that a considerable quantity of breadstuffs and meat existed in the Banat and surrounding countries in excess of requirements of Greater Serbia, and was consequently available for export to Hungary. As a result of a study of this question the Supreme Economic Council had decided to enquire from the Council of Foreign Ministers whether the time had not now arrived for the lifting of the blockade on Hungary. Furthermore, the Eastern sub-Commission of the Blockade were taking measures to prevent the passing of food and other raw materials from Hungary into Russia.

MR. HOOVER pointed out that the proposal referred to by M. Seydoux had been reached by the Supreme Economic Council on the supposition that the Bela Kun Government would fall at once. So far that had not happened; but the Supreme Economic Council asked for a mandate to act as soon as that Government should disappear. The information available went to show that two days ago it appeared certain that the Bela Kun Government would be upset. Unfortunately, the invitation to Austria to attend the Peace Conference had been interpreted to include the Hungarian Government with the result that Bela Kun's Government had again been put on its feet.

MR. BALFOUR drew attention to the fact that no invitation had so far been delivered to the Hungarian Government.

[1] Miller, *My Diary*, XVI, 255 ff. (by permission).

M. PICHON expressed the view that the authority asked for by the Supreme Economic Council could be granted—that is to say that as soon as the political situation permitted, and order was reestablished in Hungary, the blockade should be removed.

M. SONNINO enquired what interpretation should be placed on the words "reestablishment of order." He enquired whether an unofficial notification could not be allowed to leak out that the blockade would be raised as soon as the Government of Bela Kun was overthrown.

MR. McCORMICK thought that if Bela Kun was put out of office the blockade could be removed. In his opinion the matter was one of the greatest importance, as Hungary was the last barrier that was still standing and preventing the reestablishment of normal economic conditions in Southern Europe.

MR. BALFOUR thought that the Supreme Economic Council and the General Staff should be the judges in regard to the reestablishment of order.

(It was agreed to authorise the Supreme Economic Council to take all preparatory measures to remove the blockade restrictions on Hungary without further reference to the Supreme Council as soon as the General Staff informed them that order had been reestablished in the country.)

(The meeting then adjourned.)

DOCUMENT 16

Excerpts from the Minutes of the Supreme Council, Held on May 12, 1919: Frontiers of Hungary [1]

... (c) Frontier between Austria and Hungary

PRESIDENT WILSON pointed out that it would be necessary to specify the frontier between Austria and Hungary in the treaty with the former. He reminded the meeting that it had been decided to set up a Commission to investigate this matter in order to prepare the Conference for the raising of the question by either of the parties interested. He was informed that the Austrians would raise the question, and that the Allied and Associated Powers would be called upon to decide it. He read the decision recorded in I.C.182 Para 1D,[2] and asked whether any nominations had been made.

(No nominations had been made.)

BARON SONNINO asked whether it would not be enough to require Austria to recognise the independence of Hungary, and Hungary that of Austria, without raising the frontier question at all.

PRESIDENT WILSON said that he was informed the Austrians would raise the question.

(After some discussion it was decided that Austria would be required to recognise the frontier of 1867 between Austria and Hungary, and that if any difficulty arose regarding this frontier, the Allied and Associated Powers might if necessary arbitrate.)

(d) Remaining frontiers of Hungary

After a short statement by M. Tardieu the frontiers of Hungary, as laid down in Annexure A, were accepted.

(The meeting then adjourned.)

[1] Miller, My Diary, XVI, 272 ff. (by permission).
[2] See supra, Document 14.

ANNEXURE "A" TO I.C.185.

AMENDED EDITION

ARTICLES REGARDING HUNGARIAN FRONTIERS PROPOSED BY THE
COUNCIL OF FOREIGN MINISTERS FOR INSERTION IN THE TREATY
OF PEACE WITH HUNGARY

Paris, 8th May, 1919.

In accordance with the instructions given to it by the Supreme Council
of the Allies, the Council of Ministers for Foreign Affairs studied the question of Hungarian frontiers at its meeting of 8th May.

It begs to suggest to the Supreme Council the adoption of the draft articles proposed:

1. *By the Committee on Czecho-Slovak questions in Annex III of its Report, relating to the frontier between the Czecho-Slovak Republic and Hungary* [3]

This frontier is fixed as follows:

(*1*) *From the point where the frontier between Austria and Hungary
meets the Danube as far as its confluence with the Eipel.*

The *Talweg* of the main stream of the Danube, as far as the confluence
of the Danube and the Eipel (Ipoly).

(*2*) *Between the confluence of the Eipel and the Sajo.*

The course of the Eipel as far as a point about 10 kilometers south-
south-west of Losonez [Losonc] station;

A line following the watershed running from north-west to south-east;
cutting the Salgo-Tarjan; Losonez railway; continuing along the watershed towards the south-east, and then south as far as point 628, 7 kilom.
east-north-east of Salgo-Tarjan.

Following the watershed, at first in a general north-easterly direction,
and then, after reaching point 278 (south of the confluence of the Sajo
and the Rima) in an east-north-easterly direction to meet the Sajo.

(*3*) *Between the Sajo and the Ung.*

A line cutting the Putnok-Losonez railway at Banreve station (about
6 kilometres west of Putnok) so as to pass between the bifurcations of the
two railways, leading respectively, northwards to Pelsocz, and southwards
to Borsodnadasd.

Following the watershed in a general north-easterly direction as far as
a point 7 kilometres east of Pelsocz.

[3] Cf. *supra*, Document 10.

Following a general east-north-easterly direction and cutting the Torna-Edeleny railway 4 kilometres southwest of Torna.

Following in an easterly direction the ridge of the left bank of the Bodva, passing north of Kany and south of Buzita, to meet the Hernad 6 kilometres north-east of Hidasnémeti, then following this river upstream as far as a point just west of Nádasd.

Turning east and passing south of Nádasd, meeting and following the watershed between the Bozsva and the Ronyva.

Meeting this latter river 8 kilometres north-north-west of Satoralja-Ujhely and following its *Talweg* southwards.

Cutting the railway triangle south-east of Satoralja-Ujhely, in such a way as to leave to the Czecho-Slovaks the complete possession on their territory of the Kassa-Csap railway.

Crossing the Bodrog about 5 kilometres south of Bodrog-Szerdahely.

(4) *Between the Bodrog and the frontier of Ruthenian territory.*

A line parallel to and to the south of the Satoralja-Ujhely-Csap railway, passing north of Lacza and south of Perbenyik and Tarkany to meet the Tisza (Theiss) west of the latter village.

Following the *Talweg* of the Tisza upstream to the point (2 kilometres east-south-east of Csap) where the frontier between Ruthenian territory and Hungary touches that river.

2. By the Committee on Roumanian and Yugoslav Affairs in Annex VI of its Report No. 1 relative to the frontier between Roumania and Hungary [4]

This frontier is fixed as follows:

Leaving the point of junction of the frontiers of Roumania, the Czecho-Slovak State (Ruthenian territory) and Hungary; the boundary between Roumania and Hungary runs in a general south-south-westerly direction, roughly parallel to and to the west of the railway Halmi; Szatmár-Nemeti; Nagy Károly; Nagy-Várad; Nagy-Szalonta.

Cuts the railway Nagy-Szalonta; Gyula about 12 kilometres from Nagy-Szalonta, passes between the two bifurcations formed by the junction of this railway and the railway Szeghalom-Erdögyarak.

Passes east of Kötegyan, east of Gyula, west of Ottlakan east of Kevermes, and east of Dombegyhaz, between Battonya and Tornya, where it

[4] Cf. *supra*, Document 11. While the Committee on Czecho-Slovak Questions incorporated into the body of its report the frontier line recommended by it, this Committee discussed the proposed frontier in the report in general terms only. The precise description of the line here recommended is identical, apart from insignificant stylistic changes, with that contained in the draft articles the Committee proposed for insertion in the peace treaty with Hungary. (Annex VI of the Report.)

meets the administrative boundary between the Comitats of Csanad and Arad.

Following this administrative boundary to its salient north-north-west of Nemet-Pereg, whence it runs towards the river Maros which it reaches about 1 kilometre south of Nagylak station, passing between the town and the railway station.

Follows the *Talweg* of the Maros downstream to a point about 3.5 kilometres upstream from the railway bridge on the line Makó-Szeged. Thence it runs west-south-west, following the *Talweg* of a backwater as far as the bend which it makes at a point about 1 kilometre south-east of point 84 and about 9 kilometres south-west of Makó, of approximate position 46° 10' North and 20° 22' East of Greenwich. This point is the meeting place of the three frontiers of Roumania, Hungary and Yugoslavia.

3. By the Committee for Roumanian and Yugoslav Affairs, in Annex VI of its 2nd Report, relative to the frontier between Yugoslavia and Hungary [5]

This frontier shall be fixed as follows:

Leaving the meeting place of the frontiers of Yugoslavia, Roumania and Hungary, 9 kilometres south-west of Makó.

A line running in a general north-westerly direction, passing between Szt-Ivan and Gyalo and meeting the main stream of the river Tisza.

Following downstream the *Talweg* of the main stream of the Tisza, and then following upstream that of its backwater, thus making a *détour* round the south of the island of Nagyret.

A line in a general E.W. direction, passing south of Roszke; cutting the railway line from Szabadka to Kishunhalas at about 3 kilometres to the south-east of the station of Kelebia.

A line in a general north-easterly-south-westerly direction, cutting the railway line from Szabadka to Baja at about 1.5 kilometres to the east of the station of Csikeria.

Meeting the river Kigyes at the bend which it makes 4 kilometres east-north-east of Dacsmadaras;

Following the *Talweg* of this river westwards;

Crossing the marshy region lying north and west of Rigyicza [Regöce] leaving this village to Yugoslavia, the exact trace to be determined on the ground by the Boundary Commission.

Rejoining the *Talweg* of the river Kigyos west of Rigyicza and following it to a point about 8 kilometres south-west of the railway junction at Rigyicza.

[5] Cf. *supra*, Document 12. See the preceding footnote.

Turning west-south-west, passing between the villages of Szantova and Bereg, reaching the main stream of the Danube at about 8 kilometres to the north of point 169 (Kisküszeg).

The *Talweg* of the main stream of the Danube southwards to its confluence with the river Drave.

The *Talweg* of the main stream of the Drave towards the north-west of its confluence with the river Mur.

The *Talweg* of the Mur to the point where the frontier between Hungary and Austria meets that river from the north.

In the region between Czecho-Slovak and Yugoslav territory, Hungary is coterminous with Austria.

DOCUMENT 17

Autonomy of Ruthenia

I. MEMORANDUM BY DR. BENEŠ ON THE STATUS OF THE RUTHENES TO THE SOUTH OF THE CARPATHIANS WHOSE TERRITORY FORMS PART OF THE CZECHO-SLOVAK STATE, MAY 17, 1919 [1]

[Translation.]

In order to give a special juridical status to the territory of the Ruthenes to the south of the Carpathians and to manifest the desire of the Tchecho-Slovak Republic to establish a just Government in that territory, the Tchecho-Slovak Republic, although possessing a common central legislature and administration, desire to accord to the Ruthenes to the south of the Carpathians a wide measure of autonomy. In order to provide guarantees of this autonomy the Tchecho-Slovak Republic might conclude a special Treaty with the Great Powers in this matter.

The following clauses represent the basis of this autonomy.

(1) The territory of the Ruthenes to the south of the Carpathians, within the whole region comprised by the frontiers delimited by the Great Powers, shall bear a special name to be determined on by agreement between the Tchecho-Slovak Republic and the Diet of the Ruthenes south of the Carpathians.

(2) The country of the Ruthenes south of the Carpathians shall possess a special diet. This diet shall enjoy legislative power in all linguistic, scholastic and ecclesiastical questions as well as in all other questions which the laws of the Tchecho-Slovak Republic may attribute to it in accordance with particular needs. The laws passed by this diet shall be approved by the President of the Tchecho-Slovak Republic and countersigned by the Governor of the country of the Ruthenes, who shall be responsible to the diet.

(3) As regards all other matters, the country of the Ruthenes to the south of the Carpathians shall share in the legislative power of the Legislative Assembly of the Tchecho-Slovak Republic, to which Assembly it will send deputies elected according to the constitution of the Tchecho-

[1] Miller, *My Diary*, XVI, 360–62 (by permission). For a slightly different translation of Dr. Beneš' memorandum, see *ibid.*, XIII, 93 ff.

Slovak Republic. These deputies will however not have the right of voting upon such legislative questions as will be attributed to the diet of the country of the Ruthenes.

(4) At the head of the administration of the country shall be placed a Governor nominated by the President of the Tchecho-Slovak Republic. This Governor shall represent the final authority, on the one hand in all linguistic, scholastic and ecclesiastical questions and on the other hand in matters affecting internal administration (political matters). For all other questions, the Ministers of the Tchecho-Slovak Republic shall be the supreme authority. In these Ministries special Ruthenian sections shall be established. The tribunals established in the territory of the Ruthenes south of the Carpathians shall be a part of the judicial organisation of the Tchecho-Slovak Republic. When, however, appeal is made to a higher court situated outside Ruthenian territory, the matter will be brought before a special Ruthenian Court.

(5) Government officials shall be appointed by the Governor up to the seventh class. Superior officials shall be appointed by the President of the Tchecho-Slovak Republic on the recommendation of the Governor or the Tchecho-Slovak Council of Ministers.

(6) The Ruthenes south of the Carpathians shall be represented upon the Council of Ministers of the Tchecho-Slovak Republic by a Minister without portfolio, who shall be a native of the Ruthenian territory and shall be chosen by the President of the Tchecho-Slovak Republic.

In order to demonstrate the extent of this autonomy it is necessary to give a general outline of the organisation which the Tchecho-Slovak Government proposes to establish in the other territories of the Republic.

The State is to be divided into departments.

At the head of the departmental administration there will be a Prefect who in all administrative questions will be subordinate only to the central authority.

In principle for each department any appeal shall be brought before a competent Ministry. The body (Departmental Council) which shall be constituted to assist the Prefect shall only enjoy administrative powers and the right of supervision. This body will in no case enjoy legislative power which shall be exclusively reserved for the Central Legislative Assembly.

II. REPORT OF THE CZECHO-SLOVAK COMMITTEE ON THE DEGREE OF AUTONOMY TO BE ACCORDED TO THE RUTHENES OF HUNGARY, MAY 20, 1919 [2]

At their meeting on the 8th of May, the Council of Foreign Ministers decided to invite the Territorial Committee on Tchecho-Slovak claims to

[2] Miller, *My Diary*, XVI, 358–60 (by permission). For the draft of this report, see *ibid.*, XIII, 91 ff.

submit recommendations as to the degree and form of autonomy to be granted by the Tchecho-Slovak Republic to the populations inhabiting the Ruthenian territory south of the Carpathians.

In pursuance of these instructions the Tchecho-Slovak Committee met on Thursday, the 15th of May, and invited Dr. Benes to lay before them the views and intentions of the Tchecho-Slovak Government regarding this question.

Dr. Benes explained that it was the general policy of the Tchecho-Slovak Government to encourage throughout the Republic a process of evolution towards some form of federal organisation. This evolution, however, could only be gradual, and it would be premature to introduce a complete scheme of decentralisation until the various provinces had attained to a greater degree of national consciousness and had reached a level of common cultural and economic development. This principle applied with especial force to the Ruthenes populating the districts south of the Carpathians: the country was poor and the population was backward: much money would be needed for the improvement of agriculture, communications and education: this money would be provided by the Central Tchecho-Slovak Government and would have to a great extent to be applied and administered by officials of the Central Government, since the Ruthenes themselves would not for many years be sufficiently developed adequately to cope with these problems.

Subject to the above descriptions Dr. Benes declared that his Government were anxious to give the Ruthenians all possible local autonomy.

The Committee, having taken note of Dr. Benes' arguments and having agreed with him as to the desirability, within the limits he had indicated, of granting to the Ruthenian populations a special status within the Republic, asked that they might be furnished by Dr. Benes with a written memorandum embodying the form of autonomy which the Tchecho-Slovak Government would themselves suggest.

The scheme accordingly furnished by Dr. Benes, which is given in the annex to this report,[3] was examined by the Committee at their meeting of the 17th May and was considered by them to be both adequate to the present needs of the population themselves and in harmony with the general principles which the Committee had themselves foreshadowed.

CONCLUSIONS

(1) The Committee are unanimous in recommending to the Council of Five that the scheme proposed by Dr. Benes should be adopted as the basis governing the future relations between the Ruthenians and the Tchecho-Slovak Republic.

[3] I.e., Dr. Beneš' memorandum printed *supra*, Document 17, I.

(2) They consider, therefore, that their report, if approved by the Council of Five, should be referred by them to the Special Committee on New States, who should be asked to embody Dr. Benes' proposals in such a form as may be in harmony with the general procedure adopted by them in other similar cases.

III. EXCERPTS FROM THE MINUTES OF THE COUNCIL OF FOREIGN MINISTERS, HELD ON MAY 23, 1919 [4]

. . . Autonomy for the Ruthenians

3. M. PICHON asked whether the conclusions in the report (see Annexure A [5]) were acceptable to the meeting.

MR. LANSING said that he wished to ask one or two questions. He referred to Article 5 providing for the nomination of functionaries. He suggested that the wish be expressed that these functionaries wherever possible be chosen from the Ruthenian population. The curse of these regions had been that their officials had hitherto all been Hungarians and the people had therefore never acquired the habit of self government.

M. PICHON suggested that Mr. Lansing's comment together with the report itself should be forwarded to the Commission on New States.

M. SONNINO said that Mr. Lansing, if he understood him aright, did not suggest that this proviso be applied to the Governor.

MR. LANSING said that what he had in his mind was that police and other minor officials should, wherever possible, be chosen from the local population.

M. LAROCHE said that the words "as far as possible" should be given prominence as the Ruthenians were an illiterate people and it might not be possible to find among them all the officials necessary.

MR. LANSING said that he had another question to ask. As the Ruthenians were to have a form of autonomy and nevertheless to be subject to a State, the majority of whose population would be alien to them, would it not be well to introduce a stipulation enabling them to appeal to the League of Nations in any case in which the sovereignty of the Czecho-Slovak Republic was exercised in a manner regarded by them as in conflict with their rights?

M. SONNINO said that he saw no objection to the principle but thought it might be dangerous to state it too openly. He thought it might be better for the League of Nations to intervene whenever necessary on its own initiative.

M. LAROCHE pointed out that the status of the Ruthenians was going to be settled by a Treaty between the Powers and the Czecho-Slovak Republic.

[4] Miller, *My Diary*, XVI, 348 ff. (by permission).
[5] I.e., the Report of the Czecho-Slovak Committee printed *supra*, Document 17, II.

The Treaty would give the former the right to intervene. Such a clause as that suggested by Mr. Lansing if put into the Treaty, might encourage immediate trouble in Ruthenia. There were already Ukrainians in Paris who laid claim to the territory of the Hungarian Ruthenians.

MR. LANSING said that this territory was to be put in a situation analogous to that of territory subject to a mandate.

MR. BALFOUR said that he thought he might assist or even perhaps terminate the discussion by calling attention to the work of the Commission on new States. This Commission had suggested a draft article with the object of safeguarding the rights of minorities in Poland. Mr. Balfour then quoted Article I of Chapter II of the second report of the Commission. He would therefore suggest that the question be deferred until the final report of the Commission.

M. PICHON said that as the proposals were in any case to be referred to this Commission, it would be the simplest procedure to refer them together with the record of the discussion.

(This was agreed to.) . . .

IV. DRAFT AND FINAL TEXT OF THE TREATY BETWEEN THE ALLIED POWERS AND CZECHO-SLOVAKIA

Draft of a Treaty Between . . . the Principal Allied and Associated Powers on the one hand, and Czecho-Slovakia on the other. (July 4, 1919) [6]

Treaty between the Principal Allied and Associated Powers and Czecho-Slovakia, signed at Saint-Germain-en-Laye, September 10, 1919.[7]

Art. 10. Czecho-Slovakia agrees to constitute the Ruthene territory south of the Carpathians within frontiers delimited by the Principal Allied and Associated Powers as an autonomous unit within the Czecho-Slovak State, and to accord to it the fullest degree of self-government compatible with the unity of the Czecho-Slovak State.

Art. 10. Czecho-Slovakia undertakes to constitute the Ruthene territory south of the Carpathians within frontiers delimited by the Principal Allied and Associated Powers as an autonomous unit within the Czecho-Slovak State, and to accord to it the fullest degree of self-government compatible with the unity of the Czecho-Slovak State.

Art. 11. The country of the Ruthenes south of the Carpathians shall possess a special Diet. This Diet shall enjoy legislative power in all linguistic,

Art. 11. The Ruthene territory south of the Carpathians shall possess a special Diet. This Diet shall have powers of legislation in all linguistic, scholas-

[6] Miller, *My Diary*, XIII, 245, 249–50 (by permission).

[7] *British Treaty Series*, No. 20 (1919).

scholastic, and religious questions, in matters of local administration, and in other questions which the laws of the Czecho-Slovak Republic may attribute to it. The Governor of the country of the Ruthenes, who shall be appointed by the President of the Czecho-Slovak Republic, shall be responsible to the Ruthene Diet.

Art. 12. Czecho-Slovakia agrees that officials in the country of the Ruthenes will be chosen as far as possible from the inhabitants of this territory.

Art. 13. Czecho-Slovakia guarantees to the country of the Ruthenes equitable representation in the legislative assembly of the Czecho-Slovak Republic, to which assembly it will send deputies elected according to the constitution of the Czecho-Slovak Republic. These deputies will not, however, have the right of voting in the Czecho-Slovak Diet upon legislative questions such as those attributed to the Ruthene Diet.[8]

tic and religious questions, in matters of local administration, and in other questions which the laws of the Czecho-Slovak State may assign to it. The Governor of the Ruthene territory shall be appointed by the President of the Czecho-Slovak Republic and shall be responsible to the Ruthene Diet.

Art. 12. Czecho-Slovakia agrees that officials in the Ruthene territory will be chosen as far as possible from the inhabitants of this territory.

Art. 13. Czecho-Slovakia guarantees to the Ruthene territory equitable representation in the legislative assembly of the Czecho-Slovak Republic, to which Assembly it will send deputies elected according to the constitution of the Czecho-Slovak Republic. These deputies will not, however, have the right of voting in the Czecho-Slovak Diet upon legislative questions of the same kind as those assigned to the Ruthene Diet.[8]

[8] Article 14 of the draft and of the treaty provided, as all the so-called minorities treaties concluded with the new states, that Czecho-Slovakia agreed that the stipulations of the preceding articles (including those above printed) constituted obligations of international concern, "so far as they affect persons belonging to racial, religious or linguistic minorities" and shall be placed under the guarantee of the League of Nations.

Document 18

Excerpts from the Minutes of the Council of Foreign Ministers, Held on June 12, 1919: Frontiers of Hungary [1]

BOUNDARIES OF HUNGARY WITH ROUMANIA AND CZECHO-SLOVAKIA

(a) *Communication of boundaries to the representatives of Roumania*

M. PICHON said that in a letter dated 11th June, 1919, the Supreme Council had referred certain definite questions to the Foreign Ministers, having reference to the meeting held yesterday. (I.C. 194). The first question was drawn up in the following terms:

First they think that some enquiry should be made as to why the frontiers between Roumania and Hungary, which were approved at a meeting of the Council of Ten on May 12th,[2] were never communicated to the representatives of Roumania, or presumably the other States concerned.

M. PICHON, continuing, said the answer to that question would be that the precedent applicable to all similar cases had been followed in regard to Roumania. For instance, the boundaries of Austria had been communicated to the parties concerned only on the day preceding the presentation of the Peace Treaty to Austria. The Council of Foreign Ministers had, therefore, been justified in supposing that the same procedure would, under normal conditions, have been followed in the case of Hungary.

MR. LANSING thought that the Foreign Ministers should go further and point out that even in the case of Germany, the frontiers fixed had not been communicated in advance to any of the parties concerned, except Belgium. Furthermore, the communication to the Belgian Government had been made by the Council of Four and not by the Foreign Ministers. It would appear, therefore, that the practice had become well established that the frontiers approved by the Supreme Council should not be communicated in advance to the parties concerned, except under instructions from the Council of Four.

M. TARDIEU asked the Council to consider what procedure would have

---

[1] Miller, *My Diary*, XVI, 386 ff. (by permission).
[2] *Supra*, Document 16.

been followed, in the ordinary course of events, in regard to the communication of the boundaries of Hungary, had not the present military operations occurred, which had made it desirable as an exceptional measure for some definite boundaries to be fixed. It was evident that the Hungarian Delegation would have been summoned to Paris, and the day before their arrival, the territorial clauses of the Treaty would have been communicated to the plenipotentiaries of the Allied and Associated Powers at a plenary secret meeting. Consequently, the question of principle had not in any way been altered, and it was only for special reasons that the Foreign Ministers had been instructed on this occasion to communicate the boundaries of Hungary with Czecho-Slovakia and Roumania to the Czecho-Slovak and Roumanian Delegates.

(At this stage, Lord Hardinge entered, and M. Pichon gave a summary of the statements recorded above.)

M. Sonnino said that in the reply to the Supreme Council, a rider should be added to the effect that in future, as soon as definite decisions were reached in regard to frontiers, these should forthwith be communicated to the parties concerned.

Lord Hardinge doubted whether it would always be advisable forthwith to communicate the decisions taken in regard to frontiers—for instance, in certain cases only one part of the frontiers might have been fixed whilst other parts still remained undetermined. He had in mind the case of Roumania, where the boundaries of Bessarabia and Dobrudja still remained unsettled. The same remark would probably also apply to Greece, when those frontiers came under discussion.

Mr. Lansing accepted M. Sonnino's recommendation that agreed frontiers should be communicated to the parties concerned with as little delay as possible. He thought, however, that the Council of Four should be responsible for determining the opportune moment for communicating the same to the interested parties, thus avoiding the danger of producing complications such as Lord Hardinge had contemplated.

Lord Hardinge expressed the view that Mr. Lansing's suggestions would cover the cases quoted by him.

(It was agreed to inform the Supreme Council that the established practice, heretofore approved by that Council, had been followed in the case of Roumania and Czecho-Slovakia, namely, that the boundaries of States should not, as a rule, be communicated in advance to the parties concerned, except under special instructions from the Supreme Council.

The Foreign Ministers also expressed the opinion that, in future, the boundaries of States should be communicated to the parties concerned, as soon as possible after a decision had been reached, on instructions to be issued by the Supreme Council.)

(b) Frontiers with Roumania. Views of M. Bratiano

M. PICHON said that the second question read as follows:

The Council would also like to be informed as to whether M. Bratiano gave any indication as to whether the proposed frontiers were acceptable or not, and whether he offered any criticism on the subject.

M. PICHON, continuing, said that M. Bratiano had raised certain objections. In the first place, he had definitely stated his inability to accept two portions of the proposed boundary line, namely, the portion between Csap and Nagykaroli and the portion between Nagyvarad and Szeged.

M. TARDIEU said that M. Bratiano had asked that the two bits of railway line in question should be included in Roumania. In addition to that, however, he had also invoked strategic reasons in support of his contention that the whole of the boundary line between Nagykaroli and Nagyvarad and onwards would be unacceptable, as it ran within two or three kilometres of an important railway line. As a result, he understood M. Bratiano to dispute the whole of the boundary line. M. Bratiano, on behalf of the Roumanian Government, had not definitely rejected the boundaries proposed, but he had asked to refer the whole question to Bucharest for examination and report.

MR. LANSING accepted the statement made by M. Tardieu. He thought, however, that the Foreign Ministers should, in addition, express an opinion to the effect that the boundaries proposed should be accepted without alteration.

(It was agreed to inform the Supreme Council, in regard to the boundaries of Hungary with Roumania, that M. Bratiano had expressed his inability to accept the frontiers proposed, or to discuss the same without first consulting his Government, for which purpose a period of 10 to 12 days would be required.

Further, the Foreign Ministers expressed the opinion that the boundaries, as approved by the Foreign Ministers and the Supreme Council, should be adhered to without alteration.)

(c) Frontiers with Czecho-Slovakia. Alterations proposed by Dr. Kramarcz

M. PICHON said that the third question referred to the Foreign Ministers by the Council of Four had reference to the alterations in the frontiers of Hungary with Czecho-Slovakia, namely:

The Council would be glad to receive, as early as possible, the recommendations of the Council of Foreign Ministers as to the alterations in the frontier asked for by the Czecho-Slovak Delegation.

M. CAMBON said that the Czecho-Slovaks had, in principle, accepted the proposed boundaries of Hungary with Czecho-Slovakia. Dr. Kramarcz had, however, asked for two slight modifications to be made.

The first modification related to a small strip of territory situated on the southern bank of the Danube, over against Pressbourg. The area in question, known as Edor, constituted a suburb of Pressbourg and the Magyars had been firing from there across the Danube into Pressbourg. The Commission on Czecho-Slovak Affairs were, however, unanimously agreed that the Danube formed an excellent boundary and that no reasons existed for any alterations to be made to the boundary proposed.

(It was agreed that no alterations should be made in the proposed boundaries of Czecho-Slovakia in the region of Pressbourg.)

M. CAMBON, continuing, said that the second request made by the Czecho-Slovakian Delegation related to the railway line running between Kalondo and Komoron [Komárom], which, in accordance with the decision reached by the Commission, would remain in the hands of the Hungarians including the railway junction Ipolysk [Ypolyság]. Should the demands of the Czecho-Slovak Delegates be accorded, a large number of Magyars would have to be included in Czecho-Slovakia. On the other hand the railway line running from Ipolysk to Horpona [Korpona] served an important stretch of Czecho-Slovak territory which was practically inaccessible except from the South, and the fact that the junction of this railway line (Ipolysk) had been allotted to Hungary would undoubtedly cause very grave inconveniences to the Czecho-Slovaks.

Under these conditions he would, as President of the Commission, strongly recommend that the proposed boundary line in the immediate vicinity of Ipolysk be slightly altered in order to place the railway junction inside the boundaries of Czecho-Slovakia.

BARON SONNINO understood that the boundary line accepted by the Commission had been the result of a compromise.

M. CAMBON agreed. He said that for that very reason the Commission had recommended that the boundary between Kalondo and Csap as a whole should not be altered. He had merely suggested that a very slight modification should be made at the railway junction, such a modification being really essential in order to obtain full use of the Horpona railway line which merely served Czecho-Slovak territory. No material alteration in the agreed boundary line was intended.

BARON SONNINO understood M. Cambon's proposals to be that a small corner of territory round the railway junction of Ipolysk should be transferred to Czecho-Slovakia. In this connection he invited attention to the following recommendation of the Committee on Czecho-Slovak Affairs:

The railway which follows the valley of the Eipel (Ipoly) between Losonez and Csata, as well as the junctions of this line with the lines situated to the north and south, shall be administered under the ultimate supervision of the Allied and Associated Governments in such a manner as to assure to the neighbouring interested States the free use of these lines during the period required for the construction in Tchecho-Slovak territory of the sections linking up a continuous line of railway on the right bank of the Eipel.

The conditions of this supervision and the period during which the free use of the line shall be guaranteed equally to the nations interested shall be determined by the Allied and Associated Governments.

He wished to enquire whether that recommendation still held good?

M. CAMBON replied that the stipulation in question would still remain.

(It was agreed that the boundaries of Czecho-Slovakia in the vicinity of the railway junction of Ipolysk should be so altered as to include the railway junction itself in Czecho-Slovak territory.

The Committee on Czecho-Slovak questions were asked to meet without delay and to submit definite proposals to this effect.

(d) Boundaries with Czecho-Slovakia. General Pelle's proposals

M. PICHON said that the last of the four questions, referred to the Foreign Ministers by the Supreme Council, read as follows:

Finally, they would also like to receive the recommendations of the Council of Foreign Ministers of the proposals of General Pelle. The Council of Foreign Ministers are, of course, at liberty to obtain any military or other expert advice they desire.

At the meeting held yesterday, the Council of Foreign Ministers had expressed the view that it would be undesirable from a political standpoint, to fix a military line of demarcation divergent from the frontier laid down by the Supreme Council, and accepted by the Czecho-Slovak Delegation. At the same time the Foreign Ministers had admitted that military reasons might exist which would necessitate the delimitation of a temporary line as suggested by General Pelle. He, personally, did not think that it would be necessary to take military advice, especially as the matter under reference appeared to be extremely urgent. He thought the Foreign Ministers could forthwith agree to the opinion expressed yesterday, namely, that the Hungarians should be asked to withdraw their troops forthwith to the permanent boundary line.

MR. LANSING enquired whether the Hungarians had crossed the permanent boundary line.

M. PICHON replied that the Hungarian forces were now a long way, about 40 miles, north of the permanent boundary line, and their advance continued. He added that General Pelle's line would be situated further in Hungarian territory than the proposed permanent line.

M. TARDIEU added that the line proposed by General Pelle possessed the further inconvenience that it coincided with the boundary originally claimed by the Czecho-Slovaks. He thought that fact made it imperative to avoid accepting General Pelle's proposal.

BARON SONNINO agreed. He understood that the boundary to be laid down would apply to both parties concerned. That is to say, the Hungarian forces would be ordered to retire to the permanent boundary line, and the Czecho-Slovaks would be similarly prevented from crossing that line.

(It was agreed to recommend that the permanent boundaries of Hungary with Czecho-Slovakia, as approved by the Council of Foreign Ministers and the Supreme Council, should forthwith be laid down, and that the Hungarian forces should be required forthwith to withdraw their troops within their own territory, as thus defined.)

(The meeting then adjourned.)

DOCUMENT 19

Frontiers of Hungary

I. EXCERPTS FROM THE MINUTES OF THE SUPREME COUNCIL, HELD ON JUNE 13, 1919 [1]

. . . *Military situation in Hungary*

12. (Mr. Balfour was introduced.)

MR. BALFOUR read the attached telegrams (Appendix V-A to F) which he had prepared at the request of the Council of the Principal Allied and Associated Powers. He explained that they consisted of the following:

1. A general telegram to be addressed to the Hungarian, Czecho-Slovak and Roumanian Governments. (V-A.)

2. Three additions attached to the general telegram and addressed respectively to each of the above Governments. (V-B, V-C, V-D.)

3. A separate telegram containing the frontiers between Hungary and Czecho-Slovakia and Hungary and Roumania respectively. (V-E, V-F.)

(Mr. Balfour's drafts were approved, and the Council thanked him for preparing them.)

(M. Clemenceau signed each of the telegrams and Sir Maurice Hankey was instructed to communicate them to the Secretary-General for immediate transmission, and for communication to the Roumanian and Czecho-Slovak Delegations in Paris.)

II. TELEGRAMS OF THE SUPREME COUNCIL TO HUNGARY, RUMANIA, AND CZECHO-SLOVAKIA, JUNE 13, 1919 [2]

TELEGRAM.   *APPENDIX V-A* to C.F.65.
                                 June 13th, 1919.

GENERAL

In their telegram of June 7th, the Allied and Associated Powers expressed their "firm determination to put an end to all useless hostilities." To this determination they adhere; and they expect and require all the Nations and Governments concerned to assist them in carrying it out.

They have reason to think that the chief motive animating those respon-

---

[1] Miller, *My Diary*, XVI, 399.   [2] *Ibid.*, XVI, 406.

sible for what would otherwise seem senseless bloodshed is the belief that the future frontiers of the New States will be modified by the temporary accidents of military occupation. This is not so. No State will be regarded for prolonging the horrors of war by any increase of territory; nor will the Allied and Associated Powers be induced to alter decisions made in the interests of Peace and Justice by the unscrupulous use of military methods.

They desire therefore to declare:

1. That the frontiers described in the accompanying telegram are to be the frontiers permanently dividing Hungary from Czecho-Slovakia and from Roumania.

2. That the armed forces of these States must immediately cease hostilities and return without avoidable delay within the national frontiers thus laid down.

The Allied and Associated Powers are aware that in certain places these frontiers cut railways necessary for the economic service of both the co-terminous States; and also that there are a certain number of small frontier adjustments which can only be finally settled by impartial investigation on the spot. Provision for both these cases is made in the Treaty of Peace; and in the meanwhile, they should not be allowed to stand in the way of the policy insisted on by the Allied and Associated Powers. With the smallest goodwill they are capable of local arrangements; and, if differences should arise, these should be referred to Allied Officers on the spot, whose award must be treated as binding until peace is finally declared.

TELEGRAM.   *APPENDIX V-B to C.F.65.*

HUNGARY (SPECIAL)

In accordance with these general principles the Hungarian Army now fighting in Czecho-Slovakia is required immediately to withdraw behind the assigned frontier of Hungary, within which all other Hungarian troops are required to remain. If the Allied and Associated Governments are not informed by their representatives on the spot within four days from mid-day on June 14th, 1919, that this operation is being effectively carried out, they will hold themselves free to advance on Buda Pesth, and to take such other steps as may seem desirable to secure a just and speedy peace.

The Roumanian troops will be withdrawn from Hungarian territory as soon as the Hungarian troops have evacuated Czecho-Slovakia. The Allied and Associated Powers must insist that, during this operation, the Roumanian troops shall be unmolested, and that no attempt shall be made to follow them across the Roumanian borders.

G. CLEMENCEAU.

TELEGRAM. *APPENDIX V-C* to C.F.65.

CZECHO-SLOVAKIA (SPECIAL)

In accordance with these general principles the Allied and Associated Governments have directed the Hungarian forces now in Czecho-Slovakia to retire behind the Hungarian frontier; and they have the fullest confidence both that the Czecho-Slovakian Government will see to it that this retirement is unmolested, and that when it is accomplished the Czecho-Slovakian forces shall remain within their own borders.

G. CLEMENCEAU.

TELEGRAM. *APPENDIX V-D* to C.F.65.

ROUMANIA (SPECIAL)

In accordance with these principles the Hungarian Army has been required to withdraw from Czecho-Slovakia, and the Hungarian Government have been informed that when this is accomplished the Roumanian Army will in its turn withdraw within the new Roumanian borders. It is unnecessary to add that this operation will not be interfered with by Hungarian troops, nor will the latter be allowed to invade Roumanian territory.

The Allied and Associated Powers feel confident that Roumania will carry out its share of this common policy, thus maintaining unimpaired the solidarity of the Alliance.

G. CLEMENCEAU.

APPENDIX V-E to C.F.65.

III. FRONTIER BETWEEN HUNGARY AND CZECHO-SLOVAKIA [3]

From point 123 (about 1.2 kilometres east of Magosliget in a north-westerly direction to the Batar about 1 kilometre east of Magosliget) thence the course of this river downstream, thence the Tisza downstream to just below Badalo and near this village;

thence north-north-westwards to a point immediately north-east of Darocz:—

a line leaving in Ruthenian territory Badalo, Csoma, Macsola, Asztely and Deda, and in Hungarian territory Bereg-Surany and Darocz;

thence north-eastwards to the confluence of the Fekete-Viz and the Csaronda:—

a line passing by point 179, leaving in Ruthenian territory Darui-Tn., Mezö Maszony [Kaszony], Lonyay Tn., Degenfeld Tn., Hetyen, Vorvathi

[3] Miller, *My Diary*, XVI, 409.

Tn. [Horvathi], Komjathy Tn., and in Hungarian territory Kerek Gorond Tn., Berki Tn. and Brabas [Barabas];

thence the Csaronda downstream to a point in its course above the administrative boundary between the Comitats of Szabolcs and Bereg;

from this point westwards to the Tisza where it is cut by the above mentioned boundary coming from the right bank:—

thence the Tisza downstream to the point about 2 kilometres east south-east of Csap where it is cut by the administrative boundary between the Comitats of Ung and Szaboles;

thence the Tisza downstream to a point just east south-east of Tarkany;

thence approximately westwards to a point in the Ronyva about 3.7 kilometres north of the bridge between the town and the station of Satoralja-Ujhely:—

a line leaving to Czecho-Slovakia Tarkany, Perbenyik, Örös, Kis-Kövesd, Bodrog-Szerdahely, Bodrog-Szog, and Borsig and to Hungary Damoc, Laca, Rozvágy, Pacin, Karos, Falso-Berecki, crossing the Bodrog and cutting the railway triangle south-east of Sátoralja-Ujhely, passing east of this town so as to leave the Kassa-Csap railway entirely in Czecho-Slovak territory;

thence upstream to point 125 about 1½ kilometres south of Alsomihalyi the course of the Ronyva;

thence north-westwards to a point on the Hernad opposite point 167 on the right bank south-west of Abaujnadasd:—

a line following approximately the watershed of the Ronyva to the east and the Bozsva to the west, but passing about 2 kilometres east of Pusztafalu, turning south-westwards at point 896, cutting at point 424 the Kassa-Sátoralja road and passing south to Abaujnadasd;

thence downstream to a point about 1½ kilometres south-west of Abaujvar:—

the course of the Hornad;

thence westward to point 330 about 1½ kilometres south-south-west of Pereny:—

a line leaving to Czecho-Slovakia the villages of Miglecznémeti and Pereny and to Hungary the village of Tornyosnemeti;

thence westward to point 291 about 3½ kilometres south-east of Jandk:—

the watershed of the Bodva to the north and the Rakacza to the south, leaving in Hungarian territory, however, the road on the crest south-east of Buzita;

thence west-north-westwards to point 431 about 3 kilometres south-west of Torna:—

a line leaving to Czecho-Slovakia Jano [Janok], Tornahorvati and Bodvavedegi [Bodvavendégi]; and to Hungary Tornaszentjakab and Hidegardo [Hidvégardó];

thence south-westwards to point 365 about 12 kilometres to south-south-east of Pelsboz [Pelsöc]:—

a line passing by points 601, 381 (on the Rozsnyo-Edeleny road) 557 and 502;

thence south-south-westwards to point 305 about 7 kilometres north-west of Putnok:—

the watershed of the Sajo to the west and the Szuha and Kelemeri to the east;

thence south-south-eastwards to point 278 south of the confluent of the Sajo and Rima:—

a line leaving Banreve station to Hungary while permitting if required the construction in Czecho-Slovak territory of a connection between the Pelsosz and Losonez railway lines;

thence south-westwards to point 485 about 10 kilometres east-north-east of Salgo-Tarjan:—

a line following approximately the watershed of the Rima to the north and the Hangony and Tarna rivers to the south;

thence west-north-westwards to point 727:—

a line leaving to Hungary the mines and villages of Salgo and Zagyva-Rona, and passing immediately south to Somos-Ujfalu station;

thence north-westwards to point 391 about 7 kilometres east of Litke:—

a line following approximately the crest bounding to the north-east the basin of the Dobrida [Dobroda] and passing point 446;

thence to a point on the Eipel 1½ kilometres north-east of Tarnocz:—

a line passing through point 312 and between Tarnocz and Kalonda;

thence downstream to the bend of the river 1 kilometre south of Tosmeg:—

the course of the Eipel;

from there west to a point on the course of the Eipel 1 kilometre west of Tesa;

a line passing 2 kilometres south of the junction of the railway of Korpona and immediately to the north of Berneczo and Tesa;

from there downstream to its confluence with the Danube;

thence upstream to a point to be chosen about 4 kilometres west of Pressburg, which is the point common to the three frontiers of Czecho-Slovakia, Hungary and Austria:—

the principal course of the Danube.

APPENDIX V-F to C.F.65.

IV. FRONTIER BETWEEN HUNGARY AND ROUMANIA [4]

From a point about 1 kilometre south-east of point 84 and about 9 kilometres south-west of Mako, of the approximate position 46′ 10″ north, 20′ 22″ east of Greenwich:—

east north-eastwards to a point on the Maros 3½ kilometres upstream from the railway bridge between Mako and Szeged:—

a line running:

thence south-eastwards to the salient of the administrative boundary between the comitats of Csanad and Arad north-north-west of Nomet-Pereg;

a line running between Nagylak and the railway station;

thence east-north-eastwards to a point half way between Battonya and Tormya [Tornya]:—

this administrative boundary, passing north to Nemet-Pereg and Kis-Pereg;

thence to point 123 (about 1.2 kilometres east of Magosliget) to a point common to the three boundaries of Hungary, Roumania and the Czecho-Slovak State (Ruthenian territory):—

a line running west of Nagy-Varjas west of Kis-Varjas and Forray-N-Itratos [Nagyiratos], east of Dombogyhaza, Kovermos and Elek, west of Ottlaka, Nagy-Pél, Gyula-Varsaud [Varsánd], Ant and Illye, east of Gyula-Vari and Kötegyán, cutting the Nagy-Szalonta-Gyula railway about 12 kilometres from Nagy-Szalonta and between the two bifurcations formed by the crossing of this line and the Szeghalom-Erdögyárak railway; passing east of Mehkerok west of Nagy-Szalonta and Marezihaza east of Geszt west of Atyas, Oláh-Szt-Miklós and Rojt, east of Ugra and Harsany, west of Koresszeg and Koros-Tarjan, east of Szakal and Berek-Böszörmény, west of Bors, east of Artand, west of Nagy-Szántó, east of Nagy-Kereki, west of Polbarthida [Pelbárthida] and Bihardiószeg, east of Kis-Marja, west of Csokály, east of Nagy-Léta and Álmosd, west of Ér-Selind, east of Bagamer, west of Er-Kenez and Er-Mihályfalva, east of Szt-György-Ábrány and Ponoszlck [Peneszlek], west of Szaniszlo, Bore-Csomakoz, Feny, Csanalos, Bervely and Domahida, east of Vallaj, west of Csengör-Bagos and Ovary, east of Csenger-Ujfalu, west of Dara, east of Csenger and Komlod-Totfalu, west of Pete, east of Nagy-Gecz, west of Szaraz-Borek, east of Mohtelek, Garbolez and Nagy-Hodos, east of Fortes-Almas, east of Kis-Hodos, west of Nagy-Palad, east of Kis-Palad and Magosliget.

[4] Miller, *My Diary*, XVI, 412.

DOCUMENT 20

Report by the Military Representatives, Supreme War Council, on Measures to Be Taken Regarding Hungary, July 8, 1919 [1]

SUPREME WAR COUNCIL
MILITARY REPRESENTATIVES.   SECRET
W.C.P. 1120
S.W.C. 438

REPORT ON THE MEASURES TO BE TAKEN REGARDING HUNGARY

On July 5th the Supreme Council of the Allied and Associated Powers charged the Military Representatives of the Supreme War Council:

(a) To examine from the military point of view the means at the disposal of the Allied and Associated Powers to comply with the conditions of the armistice accepted by her; *

(b) To give the Supreme Council information regarding the manufacture and the stocks of munitions at the disposal of the Hungarian Government.

In their Joint Note No. 43 of June 7th, 1919, the Military Representatives already considered the military measures to be taken eventually against Hungary in order to put an end to the Hungarian attacks against the Czecho-Slovaks.

At that time the greater part of the Hungarian forces was concentrated on the Czecho-Slovak front; the Hungarian Command had only left weak covering forces in the East (Rumanian front) and in the South (Franco-Serbian front).

The execution of the military operation set forth in its broad lines in the Joint Note above mentioned would seem therefore capable of realization without any great difficulties if it had been undertaken immediately.

Since the 7th June, however, the military situation in Hungary has appreciably changed.

---

[1] American Delegation, SH Bulletin 479, July 12, 1919. MSS.

* The Italian Military Representative said that he must repeat the declaration which he had already made before, namely that he could only consider the armistice of November 3rd, 1918 (Armistice of the Villa Giusti), as the military convention of General Franchet d'Esperey had not been recognized by the Italian Government.

DISPOSITIONS OF THE HUNGARIAN ARMY

On the intervention of the Supreme Council of the Allied and Associated Powers, the Government of Bela Kun agreed to stop its attacks against the Czecho-Slovaks, and moreover to order its troops to evacuate Czecho-Slovak territory under the conditions laid down by General Pelle in the name of the Allied and Associated Powers.

From the latest information received from General Pelle it would appear:—

That the evacuation of the above-mentioned territory by the Hungarian troops has been carried out within the time limit prescribed.

That the greater part of the Hungarian troops who were on the Slovak front and who had been liberated as a result of this evacuation, *are in process of concentration in the regions of Miskolcz (150 kilometers N.E. of Buda Pesth) Cegled and Kecskemet (80 to 100 kilometers S.E. of Buda Pesth)*, where they are in a position to threaten both the Rumanian and the Franco-Serb forces.

It appears also that the Government of Buda Pesth is at the present moment forming 2 new divisions of infantry, which will bring the total number of the Hungarian forces up to *8–10 divisions of infantry and 2 divisions of Cavalry,* or 100,000 to 120,000 combatant troops. Recent information points to these troops being disciplined, well-equipped, provided with numerous machine-guns and considerable artillery, and to their supplies of ammunition, though no precise information is forthcoming,* allowing them to offer considerable resistance; and lastly to their being animated by a very strong national feeling.

Under these conditions, and taking into consideration the force that the Hungarian Command would in the ordinary course of events be obliged to maintain on the Czecho-Slovak front, it does not seem an exaggeration that on the Rumanian and Franco-Serbian fronts alone the Armies of the Entente, in case of offensive action against the Hungarian Army, would have to fight a force of at least 90,000 to 100,000 good troops.

It must be added that Buda Pesth, the seat of the Hungarian Govern-

---

* From the latest returns received by the British and French Military representatives the Hungarian Army has at its disposal material and stocks of munitions from the old *Henved* [*Honvéd*], from the Mackensen Army, which was disarmed in Hungary, and an unknown quantity of arms and munitions which have been sent from Austria.

The possibility of manufacturing war material in Hungary is little known. A great effort would appear to have been made and 6 or 7 factories appear to be in full working order, of which

    1 is for the manufacture of guns,

    1 for the manufacture of small arms,

    2 for the manufacture of explosives (20,000 shells per day?)

    1 for the manufacture of aeroplanes,

    1 for the manufacture of monitors, gun-boats and material for river craft.

There is no indication of the manufacture of ammunition for infantry; this does not,

ment and the final objective of the Entente Armies, appears now to have been transformed into a veritable fortress provided with successive lines of defence extending to a great distance and a strong defensive organization, the capture of which would without doubt entail a great effort if the Hungarian Government had not beforehand asked for peace.

DISPOSITION OF THE ALLIED ARMIES

The Allied and Associated Powers could oppose to the Hungarian Army:—

(1) *Conditional on the agreement of the Rumanian and Serbian Governments*

6 Rumanian Divisions ⎱	
1 Rumanian Cavalry Division ⎰	60,000 men
2 French Divisions	16,000 men
1 Serbian Division	8,000 men

in all, 84,000 men of which two-thirds belong to the Rumanian Army.

It must moreover be noted that the Rumanian troops have been forced to evacuate after the initial success of the Hungarian offensive against the Czecho-Slovaks, the bridge-heads which they had occupied on the right bank of the Theiss, and are consequently in a disadvantageous position to undertake operations against the Hungarians.

(2) *Conditional on the agreement of the Government of Prague*

Such weak Czecho-Slovak forces as it has been possible to re-organise up to date after the reverses of last month, amounting to at the most:—

2 Divisions . . . . .20,000 men.

The remainder of the Czecho-Slovak Army will probably not be available for action for two months. In any case the Entente would have at its disposal for the proposed operation only a total force, including Czecho-Slovaks of

100,000 to 110,000 men

with which to oppose

100,000 to 120,000 Hungarians.

CONCLUSIONS

In consideration of the above, the Military Representatives are of the opinion that the proposed operation is possible, but presents a great ele-

---

however, appear to be deficient. Hungary is drawing from the mines of Salge-Tarjan [Salgótarján] and from the region of Miskolcz 550 wagon loads of raw material (lignite and iron) per day.

ment of risk if measures are not taken to ensure the reinforcement of the Allied forces in time.

The Military Representatives further consider they should draw the attention of the Supreme Council of the Allied and Associated Powers to the following points:—

(1) The possibility of undertaking this action depends absolutely on the consent of the Serbian, Rumanian and Czecho-Slovak Governments.

(2) Serious difficulties must be expected in the carrying out of the operation, viz:—

(a) Changes in the dispositions of the Hungarian Army in process of concentration between the Theiss and the Danube to the South of Budapest and in the region of Miskolcz.

(b) The loss by the Rumanian forces of the bridgeheads which they had occupied on the right bank of the Theiss.

(c) The defensive organisation carried out round Budapest.

(3) If the operation is contemplated it is of importance to postpone the retirement of the Rumanian troops from the region East of the Theiss.

With these reserves and if a military operation against the Hungarian Army is decided on by the Supreme Council in spite of the difficulties set forth above and the large expenditure involved, the general plan of operations contemplated by the Military Representatives in their Joint Note No. 43 of June 7th still appears capable of execution in its broad lines. It would be for the General Commanding-in-Chief the operating Armies to modify the plan as circumstances may dictate.

In any case the Military Representatives insist, if the success of the operation is to be assured, on the necessity of the operations being under the direction of one Commander accepted by the Rumanian, Serbian and Czecho-Slovak Governments. The General Commanding-in-Chief, the Allied Armies of the East is the sole Commander who appears for the moment to be in a position to make the necessary dispositions without loss of time and consequently to ensure the necessary co-ordination of action.

(sd) GAL. BELIN	(sd) C. SACKVILLE-WEST	(sd) UGO CAVALLERO
Military Representative, French Section, Supreme War Council.	Major-General Military Representative, British Section, Supreme War Council.	Military Representative, Italian Section, Supreme War Council.

(sd) TASKER H. BLISS

Military Representative,
American Section,
Supreme War Council.

DOCUMENT 21

Excerpts from the Minutes of the Council of Heads of Delegations (H.D. 9), Held on July 17, 1919: Military Operations against Hungary [1]

. . . The Council heard the report of Marshal Foch on the plan for military operations against Hungary. The Marshal estimated that in order to liberate Hungary from communism in one week a force of eight infantry divisions, one cavalry division, one hundred aeroplanes, and as many armored cars as possible would suffice provided that arrangements should be made for a single high command. It was also necessary that the high command should be informed of the desires of the Powers regarding the form of government which should be established by him and that steps should be taken to obtain for the Czecho-Slovaks the delivery of the arms in Austria and provisions made, for the delivery of material, equipment and supplies to Roumania as well as a plan for the revictualing of the civilian population in Hungary which must be arranged and controlled by the British forces on the Danube.

A lengthy discussion took place with reference to the passage in Marshal Foch's report alluding to the necessity of establishing in Hungary a Government with which the Entente could negotiate peace. M. Tittoni suggested that Allied agents be sent to get into touch with the Government at Szeged. M. Benes disapproved the negotiations being carried on with any Hungarian party. M. Kramarcz expressed the opinion that the Allied Armies must march under the banner of "respect for the Armistice." The Roumanian representative agreed with M. Kramarcz and M. Benes. General Bliss pointed out that if action was to be based on the pretext of a breach of the Armistice by Hungary the Allies must be quite clear that the fault was on the side of Hungary. The General then went on to show that there was a considerable question as to the soundness of the argument that the Hungarians had broken the Armistice. He thought that if the Allies would examine the matter carefully it would be found that the Hungarian Army had become reconstituted after considering violation of the Armistice by the Roumanians.

Mr. Balfour went on record as dissenting from the allegation made by

[1] Miller, *My Diary*, XVI, 494 (by permission).

General Bliss that the breach of the Armistice was merely alleged as a pretext for attacking the Communist Government of Hungary. He was not animated by any consideration of Hungarian internal politics little though he might approve of Bela Kun. He agreed with M. Kramarcz that the Allies must not allow the Hungarian State to become a military stronghold from which economic and political disturbances radiated over central Europe. After some further discussion it was decided that the Heads of Delegations would continue the discussion at the next meeting on the following morning.

DOCUMENT 22

*Rumanian Proposal for the Pacification of Hungary,
Submitted to the Peace Conference, July 31, 1919* [1]

[Translation]
Paris, July 31, 1919.

Thanks to an elevated spirit of sacrifice and discipline, and thanks also to its consciousness of duty, the Rumanian army has succeeded once more in repelling the attack of the Magyar Bolshevists.

However, like all the Allied armies, the Rumanian army, after the numerous sacrifices and sufferings endured, deserves to be demobilized, at least partially. A few young classes only would be maintained for the defense of the frontier of the Dniester against the Russian Bolshevists.

We then take the liberty of addressing to you, Mr. President, the respectful request to be good enough to be our interpreter and to make possible finally the pacification of Hungary. We should be able to achieve with our enemies of yesterday and today the Magyars, a situation of friendly neighborliness.

In relation to the innumerable cruelties of the Bolshevist reign of terror, and to the quantity of innocent blood unjustly shed by it, we all have the humanitarian and moral duty of making it possible for the Magyar people to determine freely its own fate.

From all these points of view, the pacification of Hungary is of a vital interest, as well for the Hungarian people as for all States bordering on Hungary and for all the Allied and Associated Powers.

In order to pacify Hungary, and to assure order and moral development within the country, the following measures should be taken immediately:

I. MEASURES OF A MILITARY NATURE

Immediate disarmament and demobilization of the Hungarian forces, with this end in view:

a) They must be made to give up all arms;
b) All munitions;
c) All arsenals;

[1] American Delegation, SH Bulletin 618, August 2, 1919. MSS.

d) All factories of munitions, fire-arms, cannon, etc., must be closed, machinery used in manufacture will be dismounted;

e) Will be put at the disposal of the Allies all means and lines of communication, telegraph and wireless stations.

The disarmament of the City of Budapest once completed, the same proceeding will be followed in what concerns the other cities, disarming in the shortest possible time the entire territory of Hungary.

In order to assure the execution of these measures, it would be necessary to occupy *provisionally* the country and its capital, which is its political and industrial centre. This occupation would be effected by the Allied troops bordering the frontiers of Hungary.

II. MEASURES OF A POLITICAL NATURE

1. At the time the order to advance is given, a manifesto to the Hungarian people must be published. This people must be assured that the Allied armies are coming to free it from the Bolshevist terror and not to impose upon it anew the military yoke of feudalism. The Magyar people will have the privilege of choosing its government in full liberty; it may establish its new constitution on democratic bases which it will determine itself. France and her Allies are willing generously to assure the liberty of all peoples, and also the liberty of the Hungarian people. The neighbors of the Magyars desire a happy and friendly Hungary, a free state among free States. This manifesto should be signed by Marshall Foch in the name of the Supreme Command of the Allied Armies. The name of the Marshal alone means: Victory. It gives to Allied Armies an irresistible enthusiasm; it gives them the feeling of assured success; it demoralizes the Bolshevists, but at the same time it fills the soul of the Hungarian people, oppressed by the Soviet regime, with confidence in the Allies.

Besides Marshal Foch, the commanders of the Allied Armies should also sign, to confirm in their turn their good and neighborly intentions.

2. After the provisional occupation of Budapest and during the execution of the disarmament, the formation of a ministry should be achieved. In order to avoid the mistakes of the past (the various civil and military representatives of the Allied, the Smuts Mission, etc.) it would be well to join to the Commander-in-chief and to each Allied Army, a commission of political counsellors (two or three for each army). The latter should be chosen from among the Czecho-Slovaks, the Rumanians, the Serbs, Croats and Slovenes *of former Hungary, from among men who know thoroughly, not only all the twists of the Hungarian intellect, and the institutions peculiar to Magyar law, but also all the Hungarian politicians, as well as the political shades of all parties.*

It is not admissible that the Allies should exercise an open and direct management in the formation of the new Hungarian Government. It is necessary to aid tactfully the elements likely to succeed and to prevent, on the contrary, the success of men and groups who might hinder a happy issue.

The new Government should be composed with the greatest care in order that its stability may be assured, even after the withdrawal of the Allied Armies. That is why care must be taken to put aside, as well the Bolshevist elements who are hoisting the mast of Socialism, as the reactionaries disguised as democrats in order to be able better to reconstitute thus former feudal Hungary.

The former would start up Bolshevism again; the latter would reawake in the Hungarian people hate for the Allies and would give it the impression that the Allies have fought only to throw Hungary into the feudal reaction of the regimes of the past.

Solely a government guided by sincere democratic convictions could satisfy at the same time the ends pursued by the Allies and the real interests of the Magyar peoples.

The formation of the Government will take place only once discreet negotiations with Magyar-Hungarian politicians have been favorably concluded, allowing the proper persons to convoke a great assembly. This assembly should acclaim its government. Up to that moment, no other assemblies will be allowed.

3. The new government will issue a manifesto in which it will assure the Hungarian people that as soon as the Allied armies have been withdrawn and the necessary administrative measures taken, new elections will be decreed for the Constituent Assembly, and will be accomplished as speedily as possible.

4. The new government will form a constabulary, necessary for the maintenance of order. The organization of a Hungarian army will be allowed only after the signature of the Peace Treaty by the Hungarian Delegates. Only after this signature recruiting and the organisation of units limited by the Peace Treaty will begin.

5. The Allies will decree and put into execution the arrest of dangerous Bolshevists, great and small. But in no case will they try them. The opening of judicial proceedings against these criminals, as well as the trial and execution of sentence, are in the province of the Hungarian Government, which will have the choice of time and of method for this measure.

6. The necessary expenses for the occupation of Hungary by the Allied armies will be charged to the Hungarian Government.

Before allowing and before making possible the formation of any government, the men judged capable of forming it should make a formal promise that they will accept all conditions imposed upon Hungary by the Allied Command and that they will sign and ratify the Peace Treaty without discussion.

Proclamation

To the Magyar People!

To save Hungary from certain ruin, the Allied Powers have decided to free it from the fear of anarchy. They have decided to prevent Hungary from committing suicide. The Allied Powers, although it is a question of an enemy country, have not been able to remain unmoved before the spectacle of a people martyrized by a band of criminals who are setting fire to the center of Europe.

The states neighboring upon Hungary, aggrandized through the decisions of the Peace Conference by territories claimed on the principle of national unity, desire a pacific Hungary, a national Magyar State, free and friendly among the other free national states.

The Allied Armies are bringing neither oppression nor the yoke to the Magyar people.

They have not in view the re-establishment of the feudal regime in coming to conquer disorder and anarchy.

Our armies have as mission to give to the Magyar people the most precious of blessings, which this people has vainly desired since its arrival in Europe a thousand years ago: liberty guaranteed by democratic institutions.

The Magyar nation may freely decide upon its fate, in full possession of the right of determining alone the organization of its state. It may freely take its place among the other national states.

The Magyar nation may accomplish if it so desires a new constitution, agrarian and financial reforms, as well as all the institutions and laws necessary for the exercise of the normal life of a state.

The Allied armies will not mingle in the internal affairs of the Magyar people. They will be withdrawn from the territories of this state, as soon as order has been re-established and in conformity with the provisions made to this end by the Peace Treaty.

All good citizens of Hungary should have confidence in the Allied Powers and in their representatives.

Our end is to make of a Hungary, oppressed and deceived by the feudalism of the collapsed oligarchy, of a Hungary martyrized by a band of irresponsibles, of a Hungary inimical to the Allies, a country satisfied, free and democratic.

DOCUMENT 23

Armistice Proposal by the Hungarian Government, August 1, 1919 [1]

[Translation]
Budapest, August 1, 1919.

To His Excellency
George Clemenceau, President of the Peace Conference, Paris.

The Hungarian Government of the Republic of Councils resigned to-day and has been replaced by a Government which has declared itself ready to accept the propositions of the Allied Powers agreed upon at Vienna on July 25th by Prince Borghese, Italian Minister, and Colonel Cunningham, head of the British Military Mission at Vienna.

The new Government has charged the undersigned, in his capacity as sole representative of the above-named Powers at Budapest, with conveying to the commanders of the opposing armies a proposal for an armistice. Awaiting the decision which Your Excellency may be good enough to make, I am taking the liberty of transmitting this proposal directly to the said commanders, with the view of preventing any further bloodshed. The propositions advanced are as follows:

1. Awaiting the decisions of the Supreme Council of the Allied and Associated Powers, to suspend all hostilities between the Allied armies and the Hungarian army with the shortest possible delay.

2. To stop, consequently, any forward movement of the Allied forces.

3. To conclude an armistice with the commander of the Hungarian army, holding the provisory lines of occupation, until the President of the Peace Conference has made known his decisions on this subject. The Hungarian Government earnestly requests that the armistice line for the Rumanian army shall be fixed at the Theiss.

The Commander of the Italian Military Mission.
LIEUTENANT COLONEL ROMANELLI.

[1] MSS in the Archives of the Hungarian Foreign Office. English translation as in American Delegation, SH Bulletin 680, Aug. 11, 1919, Annex V. MSS.

DOCUMENT 24

Reply of the Supreme Council to the Hungarian Armistice Proposal, August 2, 1919 [1]

[Translation]
Paris, August 2, 1919.

The President of the Peace Conference
to Lieutenant Colonel Romanelli, Budapest.

I have the honor to acknowledge the receipt of your radio of August 1st, announcing the resignation of the Government of the Republic of Councils, the formation of a new Hungarian Government and the declarations made by the latter, which have been brought to the knowledge of the Supreme Council.

The Council of the Allies believes it ought not to interfere in the internal politics of the Hungarian Republic and for this reason has not seriously considered the propositions suggested by the two members of the Allied missions at Vienna.

The only recognized bases of relations between the Allied and Associated Powers and Hungary are: (1) the armistice of November 3, 1918,[2] the conditions of which must be respected by the new Hungarian Government, particularly so far as the demobilization of the army is concerned; (2) the notification of the Peace Conference, under date of June 13th,[3] establishing the line on which the Hungarian troops were to be maintained along the frontiers of Czecho-Slovakia and Rumania.

The Council of the Allies will only request the Rumanian Government to stop its troops on the positions which they now occupy, as the result of the aggression of the Hungarian Army to which they have just been subjected, and will not ask them to retire to the line fixed June 1st, until the new Government at Budapest has conformed strictly to the terms of the armistice.

The Allied and Associated Powers rely upon the acts of the new Hungarian Government and hope that the succession of a Government which will execute its engagements and will represent the Hungarian people may hasten the re-establishment of peace and the resumption of regular economic relations.

[Signed] CLEMENCEAU

[1] American Delegation, SH Bulletin 633. Aug. 5, 1919. MSS.
[2] *Supra,* Document 1. [3] *Supra,* Document 19, III and IV.

Reply of Rumania to the Representations of the Supreme Council Relative to Hungary's Occupation, August 9, 1919 [1]

The Rumanian Government has been very painfully surprised by the communication received from the Peace Conference. It has deserved neither the reproaches nor the accusations contained in this communication. Rumania could not defy a Conference in whose decisions she is to participate as a result of her cooperation with the Allies in the work of justice which the victory of the Allies assures to the world, as well as the national claims that the Rumanians formulated precisely when they formed the entente with the Allies. Rumania has not changed her territorial claims according to the success of her army, but she does consider that the new military efforts that she has been constrained to make in order to throw back the Hungarian offensive, and the services that she has rendered to civilization by her sacrifices, give her a new title to claim her rights.

The Rumanian Government, at Budapest as elsewhere, intends to work in accord with the representatives of the Allied Powers. The Rumanian military command has received orders to collaborate with the military missions at Budapest, in order to fix together the measures necessary to facilitate the possibility of a Hungarian Government, which will assure order in the country and guarantee the security of peace relations on the Rumanian frontier. With this very object in view the Royal Government has instructed its High Commissioner, Monsieur Diamandy to go to Budapest, where, thanks to the order established by the victory of the Rumanian army, he will be able to meet the representative of the Allied Powers. Rumania is decided in her intention of acting in accord with the policy that the Conference may henceforth fix in regard to Hungary, as a result of the new order of things established by the intervention of the Rumanian army.

Concerning the attitude of the Rumanian Government and of the Command towards the decisions of the Conference concerning the occupation of Budapest, it is well known that the Rumanian troops were already there when the communication was made to the Royal Government, and that

[1] American Delegation, SH Bulletin 708, Aug. 14, 1919. MSS. This note also appears as App. "B" to the Minutes of the Council of Heads of Delegations, held on Aug. 14, 1919 (H.D. 31).

the other four were presented to it simultaneously, and not earlier than the afternoon of the ninth of August. Moreover this occupation, which does not imply the bloodshed that the Conference fears, is indispensable if it is desired to bring an end to the state of affairs that has troubled the center of Europe too long already. Previous events have proved this.

The Rumanian Government could not foresee that the Peace Conference would consider the Armistice of November, 1918, as still existant, after having received from it the invitation to cooperate in a military action against the Hungarian army. Still less could it foresee this attitude after having been the object of a general offensive on the part of this army.

Rumania could not conceive that, after the bloody combats which resulted in the surrender of all the enemy's organized forces to the Rumanian army, she would not have the right to take possession of the war material that the former had used to attack her, without being prevented by the situation created by the previous armistice. As to the other requisitions, they were levied only in proportions that assured, in addition to the needs of the population, large quantities for exportation, and did not compromise economic activity of the country.

Rumania was obliged to take such action as a result of the state of complete exhaustion due to the Hungarian and German invasions and by the fact that it was in these regions—now occupied by her—that the greater part of the spoils of war taken by the armies of the Central Powers were deposited. It would be difficult to conceive that this right should be denied to Rumania when other Allied Armies were able, without any obstacle on the part of the Conference, to completely drain and exhaust occupied territories, which should have been, according to the Peace, turned over not to a former enemy but to an Ally.

The Rumanian Government regrets that the Allies should have taken into consideration the slanderous accusations preferred by an unscrupulous enemy. Far from encouraging pillaging, the Rumanian troops, by their very presence, re-established order and checked anarchy and devastation. The presence of the Representatives of the Allied Powers at Budapest is a testimony to such a state of affairs. The Rumanian Command, from the very first days, adopted measures to insure the provisioning of the Hungarian Capital which he had found completely deprived of provisions. Railroad transportation was interrupted only temporarily in the strict interest of military security. Concerning the Governments which have succeeded Bela Kun, they have been neither established, nor replaced nor interfered with by the Rumanian troops.

The Rumanian Army has proved, in the midst of all the hardships which it has had to sustain, the high spirit with which it is animated and the discipline which reigns, and has never lost sight of the duties towards humanity and civilization which were incumbent upon it. The reception given to the army by the population in all the occupied territories is a brilliant proof of the equity of their actions. If the Rumanian military accomplishments, thanks to the direction of the operations and to the bravery of the troops, have developed and culminated so rapidly, Rumania has the clear conviction that she has rendered an eminent service towards the work of peace which is the object of the Peace Conference.

DOCUMENT 26

Telegram from the Supreme Council to the Rumanian Government, August 14, 1919 [1]

The Peace Conference, without referring to a certain number of points which would call for rectifications on its part, registers with satisfaction the declaration of the Rumanian Government "that it has decided to act in accord with the policy which the Conference shall fix regarding Hungary."

The Conference interprets this declaration as indicating that Rumania, in its quality as participating State at the Peace Conference, intends to conform to the decisions communicated through the intermediary of the Military Mission at Budapest delegated by the Supreme Council.

The directions forwarded on three occasions by the Conference to the Mission of Allied Generals and communicated to Bucarest defined in a detailed and explicit manner the policy of the Allied Powers regarding Hungary in the present situation ("disarmament of the Hungarian troops, maintenance of order with a minimum of foreign troops, provisioning of Hungary, abstention from all interference with interior politics, with reserve concerning the free expression of the national will.")

The Supreme Council insists on the fact that no definite recovery of war material, railroad material, agricultural supplies, or stock, etc., may take place at the present time.

It appertains, in accordance with the principles of the Conference accepted by all the Allied States and applied in particular in the Treaty with Germany, to the whole group of the Allied and Associated Powers only to determine the reparations to be furnished by Hungary and their distribution among the States concerned. Neither the Rumanian Army nor the Rumanian Government are authorized to themselves determine the share of Rumania, as the Hungarian possessions of every kind are alone the security in common of the Allied Powers.

[Signed] S. PICHON.

[1] American Delegation, SH Bulletin 1078, Oct. 16, 1919. MSS.

DOCUMENT 27

Note of Dr. Beneš to the President of the Peace Conference Relative to the Habsburg Question in Hungary, August 12, 1919 [1]

[Translation]

In accordance with the Prague Government, I consider it our duty to inform the Peace Conference on the official point of view of the Czecho-Slovak Government regarding recent events in Hungary, and the monarchical restoration which will not be long in coming about, if Archduke Joseph of Hapsburg continues to manage the affairs of Budapest and especially if he is supported either by the decisions of the Conference, or by measures inaugurated by one of the Allied Governments.

The Czecho-Slovak nation having called the Hapsburg by a free choice to the throne of Bohemia, in the 16th century, was not long in falling under the yoke of that family, which used Germans to subjugate it first and to try to exterminate it afterwards. For three centuries we engaged in a life and death struggle with this dynasty. It used every possible means to stifle every desire of independence in our nation. It succeeded only in almost completely attaining its end. It is a Germanic dynasty, it never will be anything else; it is a proud, absolutist and anti-liberal dynasty the very name of which is deeply hated because of all these events by every Czech.

The entire Czecho-Slovak nation is convinced that it will serve only Germanic ends, as for that matter the present war has proved. Further, certain of the archdukes, who were high military dignitaries during this war, have distinguished themselves by their cruelty toward Czechs and should rather be brought before a court as responsible either for having helped to bring on the war or for having acted against the principles of international law.

Every Czecho-Slovak entertains feelings of profound hostility toward everything which recalls the Hapsburg Monarchy and Dynasty. The accession of Joseph of Hapsburg has produced in entire Bohemia a feeling of astonishment, surprise and fright.

There is no doubt that the opposition of the Czecho-Slovak Republic to the Government of Bela Kun was not any greater than its opposition to Joseph of Hapsburg.

[1] American Delegation, SH Bulletin 708, Aug. 14, 1919. MSS.

In general, between the Czecho-Slovak Republic and Hungary, in which the restored Hapsburg Dynasty seems to be reigning, no peaceful collaboration would be possible. This is approximately the feeling today general in the Czecho-Slovak Republic. I consider it necessary to warn the Conference at the moment when it is taking up the affairs of Hungary. Indeed, the reasons for this hostility are not merely sentimental; for the Hapsburg Dynasty would never give up regions out of which it has been driven, even if it signed the Treaty; it would never give up Slovakia, as it believes itself heir to the throne of St. Stephen which should, according to its opinion, include entire former Hungary. Filled with Germanic spirit, it will try by every means to intrigue among the Germans in Czecho-Slovak Republic to make trouble for us and to unite again some day under its sceptre the territories of former Austria-Hungary. The same problem arises for the Transylvanians and for the Serbo-Croats in the south. If the Hapsburgs reign at Budapest, it will not be long before Vienna is undergoing the influence of the intrigues of this dynasty, and the policy followed by the Germans before the war to succeed in their pan-German plans, will again find an extremely favorable ground, troubling again the entire new political situation in Central Europe.

In this situation, the Czecho-Slovak Republic will never have any hope of arriving finally at the peace it so much desires and of a somewhat stable situation amongst its neighbors.

I repeat, Mr. President, what is at present occurring in Hungary, under the wing of Joseph of Hapsburg, is extremely dangerous for the peace of Central Europe. It will disturb the entire political situation not only in what concerns the external policy of the new states of Central Europe, but also in what concerns their internal situation.

You remember, Mr. President, that the point of view of the Czecho-Slovak Government has always been that the Peace Conference should intervene in Hungary in order, after having established a military governor at Budapest and after having imposed in an exact fashion the peace conditions enacted by the Conference for new Hungary, to be able to help the democratic elements of Hungary to set up a national democratic government. The Czechs have always been ready to aid the Entente in such a task and to put at its disposal, if necessity arose, all their troops. We had thought that such an attitude would have avoided a reaction like the present one and at the same time would have put down Bolshevism; if the policy of abstention is continued at present under the reign of Joseph of Hapsburg, the same result will be reached as under the Government of Bela Kun, that is, an extremely profound hostility of all the neighboring states towards Hungary. Under the influence of Joseph of Hapsburg, all the former Magyar imperialists, all the aristocrats compromised in the war: Apponyi, Windischgraetz, and Andrassy, etc., will return to take up their former policy toward their neighbor.

The Czecho-Slovak Government, having seen the hesitation of the Entente to intervene with the well-defined plan indicated above, in the affairs of Hungary, to be able to prevent both Bolshevist terrorism and imperialist reaction, had abstained at the critical moment from intermixing in affairs and from taking part in the expedition against Budapest. It feared that on the one hand its participation might have been misunderstood by the Allies, and that, on the other hand, unwillingness to adopt a clear attitude toward the evolution of Hungarian affairs might lead to a reaction for which it would not care to be responsible. But in view of the present situation, dangerous for all Hungary's neighbors and especially dangerous for the Czecho-Slovak Republic as well as for the future peace of entire Central Europe, I take the liberty of transmitting these few lines to the Conference that I may inform it quite simply on the point of view of the Czecho-Slovak Government.

The Czecho-Slovak Government is convinced of the necessity of not supporting in any way whatever the accession of the Hapsburg reaction in Hungary. It considers the accession of the Hapsburg Dynasty as an extreme danger for its own existence, and, in accord with the Allied Powers, it would like to do everything that events transpiring in Hungary may not be injurious to the vital interests of the Czecho-Slovak nation.

We therefore beg the Conference to take into consideration these remarks, not to support the regime which has just been re-established in Hungary, not to recognize the Government of Joseph of Hapsburg, and to do nothing which might strengthen the position of an archduke who, during the war, was one of the most violent enemies of all the Allied and Associated Powers and who on the day following the signature of peace will combine with all the former German pan-Germanists and imperialists to begin again the policy of revenge.

Please accept, etc.

DOCUMENT 28

Note of Mr. Pasić to the President of the Peace Conference Relative to the Habsburg Question in Hungary, August 15, 1919 [1]

[Translation]

The Serb-Croat-Slovene delegation is following with anxiety the most recent events in adjoining Hungary, and is looking with apprehension upon the Government of Archduke Joseph who seized power by means of the constabulary. The Archduke and those surrounding him are the most expressive representatives of Magyar Chauvinism. He is a member of the Hapsburg Dynasty, the head of which was Emperor and King Charles who —and this must be emphasized—has not yet renounced his rights as sovereign. Also, in our conviction, Archduke Joseph, in his role as "administrator" of Hungary, is proceeding with the first steps which are to lead to the restoration of the Hapsburg Government in the Danube countries. This fact represents a serious danger for our State, as well as for the other peoples who have liberated themselves from the Austro-Hungarian domination.

According to the testimony of representatives of the Great Allied and Associated Powers, former Austro-Hungarian [Monarchy] was menacing the peace of Europe by the subjugation of its non-German and non-Magyar people. During the war, it treated and hemmed them in at the instigation of Turkey. The Hapsburgs caused the world war by treacherously attacking Serbia. Their restoration would cause the rebirth of the hopes of their accomplices, the Hohenzollerns, and would inevitably restore the regime which bears the responsibility for the world conflagration.

All the preceding shows the danger which our State is running, as well as all the enfranchised peoples, and at the same time the rest of the world, from the restoration of reactionary elements in Hungary. Peace, liberty and civilization would gain nothing from the change from Bolshevism to the Hapsburgs. For these reasons, the Delegation of the Serbs-Croats-Slovene Kingdom desires to prove briefly why it considers that the Peace Conference should reject the request, sent to it by Archduke Joseph, for the recognition of this Government.

Today, when the situation created in Hungary permits the Allied and

[1] American Delegation, SH Bulletin 743, Aug. 21, 1919. MSS.

Associated Powers to have their decisions respected, it is a question of establishing order there and preventing Hungary from continuing to constitute a center of disorders and a danger for the neighboring peoples. As the present Delegation had already the honor to declare, our State would gladly receive such an aim and would furnish efficacious help.

To this end, we consider that the general-staff must first be dissolved and the Magyar army disbanded to such an extent that it will not be indispensable for the maintenance of internal order, and by means of democratic elements a Government, worthy of this name, must be formed, which will have as its task, under the permanent control of the Allies, the establishment of peace and order in the country, the satisfying of the needs of the people and, as soon as possible, elections for the National Assembly on the basis of democratic principles and free suffrage.

The preceding represents the point of view of the Delegation of the Serb-Croat-Slovene Kingdom as to the new relations formed by the coup-d'Etat of Budapest, a point of view to which it has the honor of drawing the kind attention of the Supreme Council.

DOCUMENT 29

Letter of the Assistant Secretary of State of the United States, Mr. Polk, to the President of the Peace Conference, Mr. Clemenceau, Relative to Rumanian Requisitions in Hungary, August 20, 1919 [1]

My dear Mr. Clemenceau:

It is confirmed by telegrams and by eye-witnesses, whose reports I have heard yesterday and today, that the Roumanian forces in Hungary are continuing the systematic and wholesale seizure of Hungarian assets. This procedure, although attempted to be justified as the securing of due reparation, in reality jeopardizes for all nations the securing of adequate reparation for damage, and operates to nullify the Treaty provisions to this end.

The Peace Conference found a situation where the immediately available assets of the enemy were utterly inadequate to afford compensation for the damage which the Allied and Associated Powers have suffered in varying degrees. Under these circumstances it was obvious to all who studied the reparation problem that indemnification would not be left dependent upon such factors as geographical proximity to enemy assets or upon the result of competition between Allied States in possessing themselves of such assets. An orderly scheme of reparation was essential to avoid flagrant injustice and serious discord. Accordingly the Treaty with Germany establishes certain fundamental reparation principles, among which are:

(1) The joint and several liability ("solidarity") of the enemy states and a consequent pooling of their assets in the common interest of all Powers entitled to reparation. It may be noted that even material received by France under the Armistice of November 11th is to be valued and the value placed in the common pool.

(2) A system of accounting is established so that all of the Allied States will participate in the common fund in proportion to approved claims after taking into account any agreed offsets against these claims.

(3) A central reparation commission is established as an exclusive agency of the Allied and Associated Powers for the collection and distribution of enemy assets by way of reparation.

[1] Minutes of the Council of Heads of Delegations, held on Aug. 21, 1919 (H.D. 35). Appendix "A." MSS.

The action of Roumania contravenes the principle of "solidarity" in that Roumania is appropriating to her exclusive use enemy assets which in reality are the common security of all of the Allies.

The action of Roumania involves a repudiation of the agreed principle of participation in enemy assets, in particular in that Mr. Antonesco, Roumanian Plenipotentiary on June 27th, agreed, subject to the approval of his Government, that a certain liability of Roumania should be discharged by offsetting the same against the first claim of Roumania to reparation, and that "no further payments on account of reparation shall be made until the other states to whom reparation is due shall have received payments on account of a like proportion of their approved claims for reparation."

The action of Roumania involves a repudiation of the agreed principle that the Reparation Commission should act as an exclusive agency of all of the Allied and Associated Powers in the collection of enemy assets by way of reparation.

Under these circumstances either Roumania must undo wholly and completely what she has done or the scheme of reparation established by the Treaty with Germany and draft Treaties with other States is wholly destroyed. If Roumania is allowed to retain Hungarian assets, it constitutes public notice to the world, including Germany, that the scheme of reparation established by the Treaty is a paper scheme only, which the Allied and Associated Powers have not the intent or the will to enforce. The collection of reparation will inevitably degenerate into individual and competitive action by the several Allied and Associated Powers, in the course of which injustices will be done and animosities will be created, and in the confusion of which the enemy will either evade, or be incapacitated from, making the maximum of reparation. The Reparation Commission is at once discredited, and it is difficult for me to believe that any Government would desire to be represented on a body the authority and usefulness of which is so nullified at its very incipiency.

I suggest that this important and urgent matter be given serious consideration at an early date, and am bringing copies of this letter to the attention of our Colleagues on the Council of the Heads of Delegations.

I am, my dear Mr. Clemenceau,

Faithfully yours
[Signed] FRANK L. POLK

Copies sent to Mr. Balfour
Mr. Tittoni
Mr. Matsui

DOCUMENT 30

Report of Marshal Foch to the Peace Conference Relative to the Situation on the Czech-Hungarian Boundaries, August 26, 1919 [1]

[Translation]

I. HISTORY OF THE EVENTS

In the beginning of July last, the Hungarian Red Army having, upon the injunction of the Allied and Associated Powers, evacuated the Czecho-Slovak territory north of the Czecho-Hungarian frontier fixed by the Peace Conference, a neutral zone comprising a stretch of 2 kms. on both sides of this frontier was established between the Czechs and the Hungarians. . . .

Later, during the Rumanian counter-offensive in the direction of Buda-Pesth, the Czecho-Slovak Army, pretending to act upon the request of the populations and of the local authorities, occupied certain points south of the above-mentioned neutral zone and especially the northern part of the mining basin of Salgo-Tarjan on Hungarian territory. . . .

This advance put the Czecho-Slovak troops in contact with the Rumanian troops. But General Pelle stated that after an agreement between the Czechs and the Rumanians a line of demarcation had been adopted between them. This demarcation, bordered on the south by a new neutral zone . . . leaves to the Czechs the territories which they have occupied south of their frontier.

General Pelle specified besides that this agreement was only provisional and could in no way affect the eventual decisions of the Interallied Commission of Buda-Pesth, to which the Czech Government was sending a Delegate.

In the meanwhile, however, the Interallied Commission of Buda-Pesth sent an order to the Czech Government to evacuate the territories occupied by its troops south of the frontier.

Under date of August 22, General Graziani stated that in spite of the injunctions of the Commission, the Czecho-Slovaks were still occupying the mining basin of Salgo-Tarjan.

[1] American Delegation, SH Bulletin 808, Aug. 30, 1919. MSS.

II

This situation requires the attention of the Supreme Council.

The problem raised by the occupation of Salgo-Tarjan is not only of a military and political order but also of an economic order: in the present time characterized by the lack of fuel, it is indispensable to insure the exploitation of the mines of that region on which depend all the Hungarian railroads.

The question is raised therefore to know whether or not the occupation of the mining basin of Salgo-Tarjan is necessary:

—Either as security or guarantee towards Hungary.

—Or to maintain order and insure the exploitation.

In the negative, the occupation by the Czecho-Slovaks not being justified, it seems that the Allied and Associated Powers should invite the Prague Government to have it cease.

In the affirmative, it would be well to fix the conditions and the mode of occupation and especially:

—The Forces of occupation,

—The Power entrusted to furnish them (Czecho-Slovakia or Roumania),*

—The destination to give to the coal furnished by the exploitation and, eventually, its distribution, being understood that the satisfaction of Hungary's needs should have priority.

In consequence, it would be advisable to invite the Interallied Commission to give information to the Peace Conference on these various points and to send to it proposals for the decisions to be made.

* It is certain that the substitution of the Rumanians to the Czechs would be hard to admit by the latter, by reason of the situation of the territory to be occupied as regards their frontier.

DOCUMENT 31

Declaration of the Supreme Council to the Rumanian Government, September 5, 1919 [1]

The Associated Powers have watched with the deepest concern the recent developments of Roumanian policy in Hungary, which seems to indicate a deliberate resolve of her rulers to separate themselves from their Allies and pursue an independent course of their own.

So long as the Soviet Government of Bela Kun were attacking or threatening to attack the Roumanian Army with forces in excess of those permitted by the Armistice, the Roumanian Government were able to allege that self-preservation required them to occupy a strong defensive line on Hungarian soil, notwithstanding that the Conference had requested them to retire within their own newly drawn frontier. Whatever apparent force this argument may have once possessed it has none now. Events have demonstrated the military impotence of Bela Kun as clearly as his political bankruptcy; and assuredly no considerations of national security can any longer be urged by the Roumanian Government in defence of their recent action. Even if Hungary under its Soviet Government, did not completely carry out the provisions of the Armistice, it was for the Associated Governments, by their collective action, to deal with the situation thus created, not for one of them in isolation to pursue a policy of its own devising. This however is exactly what Roumania has done, and in a manner which seems wholly without excuse. Hungary, suing for peace, already partially disarmed, in the throes of revolution, without allies and without food, has been overrun by troops, who under order from Bucharest, systematically strip it of every species of movable wealth, alive or dead, which seems worth the labour of transportation. Cattle, horses, agricultural implements, raw material, machinery, railway equipment, even the outfit of a children's hospital, choke the lines which lead from Buda Pesth to Roumania. Wherever there are Roumanian soldiers, and Hungarian prisoners to work for them, everything is being taken that can be taken, however necessary it may be to provide employment in the towns or to raise food in the country. The economic problem

[1] American Delegation, SH Bulletin 844, Sept. 5, 1919. MSS. This declaration was communicated to the Rumanian Government by Sir George Clerk, the special representative of the Supreme Council sent to Rumania on a temporary mission.

presented by Hungary, in any case difficult of solution, is thus becoming rapidly impossible.

The Associated Powers are well aware of the provocation which Roumania has received. They make no excuses for her enemies. She was abominably treated by Hungary and the allies of Hungary in their hour of triumph; and if she is now plundering on her own account, she has been herself most cruelly plundered. Doubtless the majority of her soldiers genuinely believe that, since they are only taking back what was once their own, their conduct needs no defense.

But though this may be true of the Roumanian soldiers, it cannot be true of the Roumanian Government. They must be well aware that this rough and ready method of exacting reparation is neither just to their allies nor expedient in the common interests. If indeed it did no more than impoverish Hungary and enrich Roumania it might be said, with truth, that both countries got what they deserved. But none know better than the Roumanian Government that the policy of the Associated Powers takes account of far wider issues and far more complicated interests; for in the framing of that policy Roumanian delegates took their share.

The decisions then arrived at assume the truth of two principles, both of which are violated by the action of the Roumanian authorities in Hungary. The first is that while enemy countries are justly liable for all and more than all they are able to pay, this amount will be diminished not increased if they are made the victims of exactions which utterly destroy their powers of production. The second is that as the war was a common undertaking, the funds obtained for reparations should be divided on a fixed scheme among the allies who suffered loss.

Now the Roumanian Government, when they organized the plundering of Hungary must have been well aware that they were violating both these principles. They must have known that they were reducing Hungary to a condition in which she was much more likely to be a charge upon Allied charity than to contribute to the reparation of Allied losses; and they must have known that what was taken from Hungary, belonged as of right to the general reparation fund and not to any single one among the belligerent Powers.

These considerations are so obvious in themselves, and have been so earnestly pressed upon the Roumanian Government, that the Associated Powers are reluctantly compelled to ask themselves whether Roumania still counts herself among their number. None of the events that have occurred during the last few weeks are of a nature to reassure them. Remonstrances addressed to Bucharest have remained without reply. Remonstrances addressed to Roumanian representatives at Paris have been of no effect. Remonstrances made in the name of the Conference by the Allied generals at Buda Pesth have been met with fair promises. But the promises have not been kept. Roumania has persistently treated Hungary as a conquered province, and herself as its conqueror, sole and irresponsible. There is no sign that she still deems herself a member of an Alliance, or that in her judgment the Five Great Powers who mainly won the war have any predominant claim to settle the terms of peace.

These are facts which the Conference note with the greatest regret. They acclaimed the entry of Roumania into the war; they rejoiced that after a succession of calamities which the Western belligerents were powerless to prevent, she was about to share to the full the fruits of their victory; they never doubted that she was to be counted among their Allies. Unhappily, they are forced against their will to doubt it now; and, in one way or the other, for good or for evil, their doubts must be resolved without delay.

They desire therefore a clear reply to the following questions:

Is Roumania prepared on a date to be fixed by the Conference to withdraw her troops from Hungary.

Is she prepared at once to cease appropriating to her account Hungarian property.

Is she prepared to surrender to the Reparation Commission the property already appropriated?

Is she prepared to cooperate loyally with the Associated Powers, and under their direction, in the task, of so restoring order in Hungary as to enable a responsible Government to negotiate terms of peace.

The Conference are most unwilling to believe that the Roumanian Government will hesitate to return an affirmative answer to all these questions. Their refusal would be an immeasurable misfortune. It would shatter the hopes of those who see in the unbroken cooperation of the Associated Powers the surest security for future peace; only those would be content who hold that in the hour of victory no alliance can stand the strain of competing national interests. Whether Roumania would gain by a severance of friendly relations with her Western Associates it is for Roumanian statesmen to determine. But the Conference must know, and know without delay, where they stand, and how they are henceforward to look upon a State they have been proud to call their Ally.

DOCUMENT 32

The Prime Minister of Hungary, Mr. Friedrich, to the Interallied Military Mission in Budapest, September 6, 1919 [1]

[Translation]

The present Government of Hungary, of which we insist on stating with pride and satisfaction that it enjoys the absolute confidence of the greater part of the population of the country—finds itself without the necessary support on the part of the Allied and Associated Powers as well as on the part of their representatives. This state of things has created a situation for which it is impossible for us to assume the responsibility, and it is a result of this situation that the Council of Ministers has considered putting the power at present in its hands, in the hands of the Mandatories of the Powers of the Entente.

Allow me, Gentlemen, to refer first of all to the requisitions of the Rumanian army of occupation, brutally interrupting the continuity of productive labor, leaving hundreds of thousands of workmen without bread. To its great regret, the government has not been able to come to the support of the masses of men out of work, seeing that its financial resources are completely exhausted. Therefore, it is obvious that the discontent of the masses unable to make a living will increase from day to day and will necessarily lead to outbreaks threatening public order and safety.

We must first of all insist on the fact of the requisitions of the Rumanian army, striking at the root of the rural economy and depriving the farmers of draught animals, seed, forage and farm implements to such a degree that even the harvest of next year is jeopardized. Now, if by these requisitions economy itself is deprived of the means of production, our country will no longer be able to support the public burdens and the feeding of the population will have to be effected by foreign importation. But as we also lack the financial means, it will be the Powers of the Entente who in the future will have to guarantee alone the public food supply. The stripping of the country of all means of communication by the Rumanian army makes it impossible to provide the capital with food, coal and wood, so that without effective intervention and urgent measures on the part of the Allied and Associated

[1] From MSS in the Archives of the Hungarian Foreign Office.

Powers the Hungarian Government absolutely can not assume responsibility in this matter.

What especially weighs upon the country is the fact that by reason of the occupation the Government can not use the public revenues that it would have at its disposal under normal conditions. The collection of taxes and contributions is suspended, the recovery of all public revenues is impossible, because of the difficulties of communication, as well as by reason of the seizure of the service of posts, telegraphs and telephones. Not being able to meet the most urgent expenses, the government is unable to pay the employees of the state and the public services. It is therefore in absolute need of benevolent aid from the Allied and Associated Powers, in order that the government may affirm its credit, may profit on this basis by the support of the Austro-Hungarian Bank, and finally stamp the notes of the bank.

However, the most urgent task is the holding of the elections. All the preliminary labors to this effect are completed; but so long as the Rumanian occupation lasts the elections can neither be called nor held.

We therefore take the liberty to request you, in accord with the Command of the Rumanian Royal army, to have that part of the country beyond the demarcation line evacuated, as well as to consent to the organization of an armed force necessary for the maintenance of order and public security.

According to our faith and belief, the elections will declare in favor of the present government, that is to say, the new national assembly will approve all the acts of the government.

With this absolute conviction, although under similar circumstances no government can arrogate to itself the favor of being recognized by the Allied and Associated Powers, we appeal to the High Representatives of the Allied and Associated Powers to kindly intervene with their governments in order that the mandatories of the Entente may enter into relations with this government which enjoys the full confidence of the country and to give the task favorable support, respectively lending assistance in order that, by the elections of the National Assembly, the country may come into possession of a legitimate government with power to establish a legal State.

We declare, therefore, in the name of a crushing majority of the Hungarian nation, that if certain political parties at this time absent from the theatre of our public life, shall henceforth enjoy the support of the Powers of the Entente and if by this fact it will be impossible for us to live up to the most elementary governmental duties relative to the consolidation of our country, the government will be obliged to abandon its place and to hand over its power to the Allied and Associated Representatives.

Accept, etc. . . .

DOCUMENT 33

Excerpts from a Note from the Rumanian Government to the Supreme Council, Transmitted on September 9, 1919 [1]

. . . The same is true of the frontier fixed by the Great Powers between Rumania and Hungary: neither the stipulations of the Treaty of 1916 nor the act of union have been taken into consideration, and this conventional line established without the cooperation of the Rumanian representatives takes account neither of the local economic conditions nor of the conditions of security necessary to the railway that skirts it.

This frontier even crosses the Marca [Maros] to separate its mouth from the rest of its course, and yet this river constitutes the more important way of communication for the center of the Kingdom.

It is behind this frontier line that the Great Powers had asked Rumania to withdraw her army without first proceeding to the disarmament of the Hungarian Bolshevist troops. This decision, contrary to the interests of order and stability in this part of Central Europe, changed Rumania's military situation in the most dangerous way.

It exposed to the danger of Bolshevist domination the territories and cities which the Rumanian occupation had freed from it, and encouraged and fortified the hotbed of anarchy in Budapest, the propagation of which threatened the entire center of Europe.

Recently the Great Powers have been in a position to understand that it is only by the occupation of Budapest that Central Europe could be pacified.

This new service rendered by Rumania to the cause of Peace and order should have constituted a new title before the Conference to do justice to the claims that were recognized by the Treaty of Alliance of 1916.

It is with the most painful surprise that Rumania saw diminishing the possibilities offered by her armed occupation of establishing and consolidating in Hungary, on democratic bases, a state of things which would at the same time insure order and peace to the center of Europe and friendly relations along the new frontiers of this country.

The Supreme Council has not wished to attain this end by friendly collaboration at Budapest; on the contrary, its action encouraged the disposition to hostility. It decided to impose, as existant in regard to Rumania,

[1] American Delegation, SH Bulletin 882, Sept. 11, 1919. MSS.

the Hungarian Armistice of November, 1918, after the latter had been twice violated against her by the Budapest Government, after the Conference itself had called for the cooperation of the Rumanian Army against Hungary and after the Hungarian forces, organized in spite of the prescriptions of this Armistice, had undertaken a general offensive against Rumania.

It is upon the basis of such an armistice that it is desired to consider the entire situation of Rumania in Hungary; it is also by virtue of its stipulations that the Rumanian Army is denied the right to appropriate the war and railway material taken from the enemy, which the latter used to attack her. Opposition is offered to Rumania's recovering a minimum part of the machinery and agricultural and industrial material of which the enemy during his occupation had totally deprived her and a great part of which had been delivered to Hungary. Yet the requisitions exacted by the Rumanian Command would not have reached a third of the assets, so as to respect the needs of the population and not to stop the economic life of the country.

This attitude of the Supreme Council towards Rumania must not make us forget the fact that other Allies were able, under the regime of this same Armistice of November 1918, and without being justified by new conflicts with the Hungarian Army, to drain dry regions not claimed by them, not only without opposition from the Great Powers, but with the effective cooperation of their representatives. It is true that these territories were to fall to an Ally, Rumania, and not to be returned to the enemy. . . .

Document 34

Memorandum by the American Representatives on the Organization Committee of the Reparations Commission on the Hungarian Situation and the Effect of Rumania's Appropriation of Values and Property in Hungary on the Other Allied and Associated Powers, September 23, 1919 [1]

Roumania has removed values and property from Hungary far in excess of her individual equity under the reparation and other policies laid down by the Allied and Associated Powers. Roumania has forcibly effected monetary exchanges in Hungary to her own benefit disregarding the reparation equity of her Allies in these same benefits. It results that Roumania has appropriated values and property belonging to Italy, Serbia, Czecho-Slovakia, Poland and other interested Powers. The latter, therefore have just claim against Roumania for compensation.

Roumania is reported to have stripped Hungary of all its seed grain, live stock, agricultural machinery, etc., with the result that the supplying of the minimum needs of the Hungarian population will shortly have to be borne by Roumania's Allies at considerable sacrifice and financial cost to their respective Governments and peoples. It would, of course, have been to the joint interest of all the Allies had sufficient seed grain, live stock, agricultural machinery, etc., been left in Hungary to take care of the minimum requirements of these people.

A substantial surplus of foodstuffs existed in Roumania, even before her appropriation of Hungarian foodstuffs. Under the ordinary working of the laws of supply and demand, Roumania is now in that curious position whereby she alone will benefit by supplying foodstuffs to her Allies (particularly Czecho-Slovakia and Poland), from stocks in which her Allies had a joint ownership. A similar situation with corresponding effects occur in the case of many other classes of property similarly appropriated by Roumania.

A portion of this same surplus foodstuff must go to Austria which is faced with a serious shortage in foodstuff for the coming year. The Supreme Council has decided, and the same intent is written in the Austrian Peace Treaty, that the "first preoccupation" of the Reparations Commission in

[1] American Delegation, SH Bulletin 1020, Oct. 7, 1919. MSS.

Austria is to set up finance to meet the minimum needs of the Austrian population during the coming year. The curious analogy is therefore presented of the Reparations Commission setting up finance, at the expense of Roumania's Allies, for the purchase of foodstuffs and other property which they in fact own in common with Roumania but for which Roumania alone will benefit.

The Allied and Associated Powers will shortly have to give the Reparations Commission with reference to Hungary, a similar "first preoccupation," they have already given it with reference to Austria. This would not have been necessary had Roumania waited the orderly workings of the Reparations Commission in securing her reparations. However, by her systematic stripping of Hungary, without preoccupation as to leaving the minimum necessities for the Hungarian population during the coming year, Roumania has improperly thrown this burden on her Allies. A similar curious analogy occurs in this case as already exposed in the Austrian case. In the Austrian case, however, the minimum necessities of the population did not exist. In the Hungarian case these necessities which actually existed in Hungary and which were appropriated by Roumania must now be replaced by necessities provided at the expense of the latter's Allies.

Roumania has taken values and property out of Hungary without the prior agreement or approval of her Allies and without their representation at the time of removal. Therefore, there exists no basis for determining which if any of these were due Roumania under the adopted policy of providing for "restitution of cash, animals, objects of every nature and securities seized and sequestrated." "which prove possible of identification." Under these circumstances and for accounting purposes, it is only possible at this time to assume that none of these come within the "restitution" categories and, therefore the full valuation of all must be charged to Roumania on her various reparation accounts. What part or parcel of these values or property now in Roumania as come within the definition of "restitution" consequently rests on Roumania to prove before the Reparations Commission before these charges can be properly cancelled.

As Roumania similarly failed to consider the interests of her Allies when taking over values and property not coming within the "restitution" categories, which she presumably considered to be her reparation equity, its valuation and the determination of the respective allies' reparation equities, including Roumania's can now alone be determined and reported to the Reparations Commission by the other interested allies.

A proposal, today, on the part of Roumania to abide, in the future, by the terms of her engagements with the Allied and Associated Powers could not be accepted as an equitable solution of this matter. An agreement to

*any such proposal would be to the sole interest of Roumania with an entire
disregard of the other Allied interests, as such agreement could only be
construed as a "quitclaim" or approval of all Roumania's appropriations of
Hungary's values and property to date. Any agreement entered into today
with Roumania should be predicated upon her admission of the right of her
allies to make a joint inquiry into what has happened in the past and to
fix their own and Roumania's interests in all Hungarian values and property in the manner hereinafter set forth.*

It is therefore, suggested that the Organization Committee of the Reparations Commission recommend to the Supreme Council the early adoption
of the following resolutions:

First: That a Special Commission, including representatives of the Allied and
Associated Powers having property and financial interests in Hungary under the
Reparation clauses, which interests have been either partially or wholly appropriated by Roumania, be established at once in Budapest for the purpose of listing
and valuing the property removed by Roumania in contravention of Roumania's
engagements with her allies and in contravention of the direct and specific instructions of the Supreme Council.

Second: That this Special Commission will establish the value of the various Allies'
equities in Hungarian values and property appropriated by the Roumanians, in
accordance with the reparation policies adopted by the Allied and Associated
Governments, and that these values will be at once reported to the Committee
on Organization of the Reparations Commission, so that upon the establishment
of the Reparations Commission, they may be appropriately entered against the
Roumanian accounts, under the various treaties of peace which have or are to be
formulated.

Third: That this special Commission investigate and report to the Supreme
Council the fiscal or other effect on Roumania's Allies of Roumania's appropriation of foodstuffs, grain seeds, live stock, agricultural machinery, etc., with
reference to its effect on future purchases by them of Roumanian food and other
surpluses and the similar direct or indirect effect of Roumania's action so far as
it affects benefits accruing to Roumania's Allies from Austrian and Hungarian
reparations.

Fourth: That this Special Commission is empowered to give proper credit to
Roumania for values and property returned to Hungary up until the time of the
closing out of its operations and to make appropriate cancellations on this account
on reports submitted to the Supreme Council or to the Organization Committee
of the Reparations Commission, as provided for in the preceding paragraphs.

It is recommended that the proposed Special Commission include representatives of the principal Allied and Associated Powers and representation
of Serbia, Czecho-Slovakia and Poland and that these Powers be requested
to at once designate their representatives on this Commission and to send
them to Budapest accompanied by such accountants, statisticians, etc., as

they may consider necessary, for the first meeting of the Special Commission which should be held at Budapest September 28, 1919.

It is further recommended that Chairmanship of the Commission rotate from day to day as between the Representatives of the Principal Allied and Associated Powers represented on it.

In view of the existing political situation in Hungary, it is recommended that for the time being this Special Commission be subordinated to the Allied Commission of Generals now in Budapest.

DOCUMENT 35

Report by Sir George Clerk on His Mission to Bucharest, October 7, 1919 [1]

The Supreme Council is already aware of the situation in Roumania up to September 24th last, on which date I sent Mr. Leeper to Paris with M. Bratiano's detailed views, and it is perhaps unnecessary to recapitulate anything before that date.

But in order to give a clear appreciation of the Hungarian situation, I must travel somewhat outside the actual object of my mission, as political developments in Roumania interact closely upon her attitude in Buda-Pesth.

When Mr. Leeper left, a pro-Bratiano Government had been formed under M. Manolescu but it collapsed that same day owing to the sudden refusal of the Transylvanian Ministers to participate. Bucharest is a small place, and in view of the general political excitement, which made it impossible for me to greet a Roumanian statesman without immediate rumours that the Supreme Council were supporting his party, I judged it best to withdraw to the country while waiting for the instructions which were to be sent to me after the meeting of the Council on September 25th.

On September 28th I received the telegram instructing me to proceed to Buda-Pesth, and I arranged to leave next morning. Meanwhile, after the collapse of the Manolescu Government, the King sent for M. Take Ionescu, who also spoke for General Averescu and M. Maniu, and agreed to their forming a joint Government, whose foreign policy was to be based on complete understanding with the Allies, including, in M. Take Ionescu's intention, acceptance of the Minorities Treaty, but with, if possible, modifications of some of the most obnoxious clauses. The same afternoon M. Bratiano had a long interview with the King, with the result that His Majesty suddenly formed a Government of six Generals, on the active list, under General Vaitoianu with M. Misu as Minister of Foreign Affairs. This Government took office next day, and was in being on my return to Bucharest. The King was under the impression that he has happily solved his difficulties by creating a neutral non-political Government that could hold the elections with complete freedom and impartiality, but in fact it is only a form of a Bratiano Government, for the President of the Council, who was Minister of War

[1] American Delegation, SH Bulletin 1027, Oct. 9, 1919. MSS.

under M. Bratiano, is bound by many ties to M. Constantinescu, who is the political shadow of M. Bratiano.

Before leaving for Buda Pesth on September 29th, I saw M. Bratiano and General Vaitoianu. Both assured me, as the King had repeatedly done, that Roumania intended to stay in the Alliance and to co-operate wholeheartedly with the Entente. The difficult point was the Minorities Treaty, to yield on which was impossible for Roumanian honour and independence, but the intention was to keep this burning question floating until the Roumanian people had pronounced upon it at a free election. I wondered what would happen if the Allies, who were perhaps less interested in the skillful moves of M. Bratiano's internal policy, could not keep their decision waiting for the Roumanian elections, which have, I think been successively postponed since last January, and should demand a definite answer from Roumania in the near future. Neither M. Bratiano nor General Vaitoianu—who told me he absolutely accepted M. Bratiano's foreign policy—could answer more than that a very serious situation would arise. On the other hand, both gave me the most satisfactory assurances as regards Hungary. All requisitions, beyond those of railway and war material, and food supplies for the army of occupation, had been stopped, and the Roumanian Government were most anxious, in their own interests to establish good relations with Hungary. It was only a question of finding a Hungarian Government with which both the Allies and Roumania could work in accord.

I left Bucharest on the morning of Monday, September 29th but only arrived at Buda Pesth on Wednesday morning, October 1st. I could not see the Allied Generals until the afternoon, so I visited M. Diamandy, the Roumanian High Commissioner, first. He repeated what M. Bratiano had said about the stopping of requisitions, and maintained that care had been exercised to leave the agricultural population supplies sufficient for their needs, and gave me the attached report on the supplying of Buda Pesth, to show what had been done for the inhabitants of the city. As regards the breaking up and removal of machinery, with the consequent loss of work and danger of disorder, he maintained that Roumania was justified in protecting herself against her enemy being able to manufacture masses of war material, and inevitably the Roumanian action was on a large scale, since practically every Hungarian factory turned out war material.

With respect to his relations with the Hungarian Government, he said that M. Friedrich would neither resign himself, nor accept colleagues in his Ministry from other political parties, so that a coalition Government, which alone gave the guarantee necessary for a free electoral choice of the Hungarian people, did not exist. M. Friedrich was, after all, the man who called the Archduke Joseph to take charge of the Government and stood for a reactionary and anti-Roumanian policy. M. Diamandy had been much impressed, during a recent visit to Vienna, by the anxiety with which M. Renner and the Austrian Government were watching developments in Hungary. They, and to some extent he too, professedly dread reaction and a White terror.

Lastly, M. Diamandy complained that he got but little help or support from the inter-allied Mission, though he recognised that this was largely due to the fact that they were soldiers, rigidly bound by, and adhering to, certain definitely limited instructions. He could therefore never get from them any wider political consideration, but he felt that while he, whatever differences there might be amongst ourselves, always tried to maintain outwardly the solidarity of the Allies, the Generals tended to look on themselves as the protectors of the Hungarians against the Roumanian oppressor —an attitude of which the Hungarian was not slow to avail himself.

Subsequently I attended a meeting of the Commission of the four (4) Allied Generals, of which a proces-verbal is attached. Their instructions from the Supreme Council were:—

1. to see that the conditions of the November armistice were properly carried out;
2. to protect such Hungarian property as would form the common reparation stock of the Allies and to prevent it from being taken out of the country;
3. to organize a Hungarian police and gendarmerie.

To these instructions they have rigidly adhered, but say that they have found nothing but obstruction from the Roumanians. They cannot get Roumanian officers detailed to help them in checking requisitions, they get promises, but nothing else, of rifles wherewith to organize the police, and they live in a cloud of polite lies. In view of the Roumanian attitude, it has been impossible for them to carry out their instructions, and their position in Buda Pesth is helpless until there is either an Allied Dictator, with force at his back which the Roumanians must respect, or the Roumanians evacuate. The first solution being improbable, the Generals strongly advocate immediate evacuation, the more so as they are confident that, whatever might have been the case 3 or 4 weeks ago, M. Friedrich could now keep order from the moment the Roumanians leave. But they urge strongly that they should have authority from the Conference to give the amount of support, which provisional recognition by the Conference would confer, to such a Government as they, with their experience of the situation, consider adequate for a temporary administration and for preparing the elections. Such recognition would both oblige the Roumanians to loosen the bands with which they have tied the Hungarian Government hand and foot, and would enable that Government to exercise real authority and so escape having to improvise it at the last moment.

As regards the question of requisitions, the Generals consider that the Roumanians, who were at first gratefully welcomed by the Hungarian people as their saviours from the Bolsheviks, have seriously if not irretrievably, spoilt their position by the persistence, extent and stupidity of their requisitioning, and they have further lost Hungarian sympathy by the way in which they have blocked all attempts of the Hungarian Government to administer the country.

The inter-Allied Mission has accumulated a mass of evidence which it is quite impossible to ignore on the subject of requisitions. I annex to this report some of the instances which the Mission have given to me. It is believed to be true that the Roumanian Government have given official orders to stop all requisitioning of private property and is requisitioning only railway material, war material, and food-stuffs necessary for the army of occupation. Indeed, the Roumanians are actually by way of sending back into Hungary, locomotives in excess of the thousand they have already taken. Now while the Roumanian idea of "war material" is very large, if these orders were rigorously applied, the Hungarians would at least know where they stand and could make a beginning of a fresh industrial and agricultural life. But the facts carefully compiled by the inter-Allied Mission leave little doubt that in practice requisitioning of all sorts is continued. Cases brought to the notice of the Roumanian authorities such as M. Diamandy, the High Commissioner or General Mardarescu, the Commander-in-Chief, are indeed dealt with at once by them and an order is immediately issued for investigation, reparation, and, if necessary, punishment. But the experience of the Allied Mission is that, with the writing of the order, the matter ends and the members of the Mission have neither time nor personnel to drive the Roumanians into full investigation of the large number of cases that are reported daily. In fact, the Roumanian, who is after all a Balkan and therefore an Oriental, and who has been pillaged and looted by the enemy and by his Russian ally, sees here, in the occupation of Hungary, an opportunity which he will consider himself a lunatic to forego. From the private soldier who "requisitions" the umbrella of a passenger leaving the station, to the officer who "requisitions" a motor car or a carpet to be sold for cash to a Jew and re-sold by the latter at a higher price to its original owner, they intend to leave this country with their pockets full. The Roumanian Government, and those responsible for the conduct of its affairs do realize that Hungary, stripped bare of all necessaries of life, is entirely contrary to the interests of Roumania, and are possibly sincere in their intention to take, with a little interest, only what they consider to be their lawful property, stolen from them, and to limit their requisitions to the quantities they have laid down. But unfortunately they have neither the authority nor the energy to suppress with a rigorous hand the mis-doings of their subordinates.

While it is hard to believe that the Roumanians can really have stripped the country to the extent presumed in the Memorandum of September 23rd, 1919 by the American Representatives on the Organisation Committee of the Reparation Commission [2]—after all, the Hungarian peasant is as good as others in hiding his possession from the looter, and the Roumanian has many more accomplished rivals in the art of looting—there is no shadow of doubt that the common property of the Allies has been diminished by Roumanian action, and that owing largely to that action, the Allies have the additional burden of helping Hungary to regain her economic existence.

I also had an interview with M. Friedrich, the head of the Hungarian Government. He is a young man, the son, I believe, of a small doctor, and not, I should say, a man of big political imagination. But he has shown strength and courage in holding on to an office which is neither lucrative nor comfortable, and he has by now probably more or less established himself in the opinion of a great mass of Hungarians. He is frankly against a coalition government, which in reality, according to him, really means giving a wholly disproportionate representation to the 8 or 10 per cent of Socialists among the workers of Buda Pesth. He admits that his strength does not lie in Buda Pesth, but claims that the country outside is wholly with him. In fact one reason why he has not resigned, in face of the impossible position in which he is kept by the Roumanians, is that, were he to do so, the peasants would see in it a Jewish manoeuvre and would start local retaliation, with fatal results. He is frankly anti-Roumanian: in fact, he is—like the leaders in all these countries in regard to their neighbors—pessimistic about the stability of all the new and aggrandized States of Southern and Central Europe, except Hungary, whose geographical position, command of the Danube, and industrial population ensure her recovery and eventual prosperity. But to recover, Hungary needs help, and M. Friedrich looks to the Western Powers to provide it. Hungary entered the war, not because she liked it nor for gain, but because in honour bound to Austria and Germany. She has lost and must pay the price, but now asks for help to win back her rightful place among the nations of Europe. For the moment, M. Friedrich does not ask the Supreme Council to grant him provisional recognition, for fear they should refuse, and thereby undermine such moral authority as he possesses. But he does ask that the Council should allow him to hold the elections, under the control and supervision of Allied officials, so that there may be no accusations of pressure or unfairness. The elections will provide a Government which Roumania cannot completely ignore, and will allow Hungary to make a beginning of her new life.

M. Friedrich further assured me that he could maintain order in Buda Pesth when the Roumanians left.

[2] *Supra*, Document 34.

I also received a visit from M. Garami, a leader of the Social Democrat party.

He said that Hungary had two pressing needs; social quiet and order at home, and an early peace with the Allies. M. Friedrich's Government was unable to secure one or the other. It was unrepresentative, for it included neither the commercial nor the industrial nor the working sections of the community. Its strength was among the peasants and it represented those who belonged to the three "Christian" parties who were well under 50 per cent of the population and the majority of the territorial magnates, but it did not even include the small land-holders, the strongest peasant organisation in Hungary. It was avowedly royalist, and M. Friedrich was merely keeping a place warm for the Archduke Joseph. Such a Government could not bring social quiet, nor did it correspond to the demand of the Peace Conference for a Government representing *all* parties. But so long as M. Friedrich was there, the way for any other Government was blocked. Therefore M. Friedrich must go.

There were two ways to effect this.

One, by a popular rising in Buda Pesth, but M. Garami, himself an avowed Social Democrat, would deplore this, for it would be a disaster for Hungary and Europe. Who could say where such a rising would end? And what would be the effect on the workers of Western Europe of the Hungarian proletariat, who had rejected Bolshevism, being driven back towards it as the only reply to the reactionary Government by which it was now replaced?

The other way, the only way, was for the Supreme Council to repeat to M. Friedrich the message they had sent to the Archduke. It was no longer possible to be rigid about nonintervention in the internal affairs of Hungary. The principle had already been broken in the case of the Archduke, and only intervention could save Hungary now.

All classes, if they knew that the Allies' view, as stated to the Archduke, held good for Friedrich, were ready to form a Government answering to those views. But it would want a week or ten days, and, in the absence of any international force, must therefore be done while the Roumanians were still in occupation. Otherwise, Admiral Horthy's force would come, and the incidents of Trans-Danubia would be repeated on a larger scale in Buda Pesth, until the workers, in self-defense, brought out *their* hidden arms, and revolution and anarchy broke loose.

Unless Hungary got a new Government, which the Allies would accept until the elections, or unless an *international* gendarmerie could be created to replace the Roumanians, Hungary was doomed.

M. Garami said that in such a representative Government the workers, about 20 per cent of the population, would not insist on having their members, and would in no case accept more than two offices, provided always that the basis of the Government was republican and democratic. Moreover, if, when the elections came, and provided they were really free, the result was a majority in favour of a monarchy, the workers would loyally accept the voice of the country, though they would continue to fight the decision with all possible legal and constitutional weapons.

M. Garami's practical proposal was that the "bourgeois" parties should visit the inter-allied Mission with a list of a coalition Government, corresponding to the demands of the Allies, for immediate communication to Paris. If the Supreme Council assented to the formation of such a provisional Government, it would come into being forthwith, provided the Roumanians were still in occupation to maintain order. The important thing was to obtain as soon as possible from the Allies a clear statement of their intentions and of how they viewed these suggestions. Otherwise, everyone in Hungary was working in the dark.

Before seeking to draw any conclusions from these various expressions of opinion and desire, I venture to submit that the general foreign policy of Roumania is also a factor that must be taken in account.

At present, the policy of M. Bratiano holds the field. That centers on refusal to accept the principle of the Minorities Treaty, and it is there that the Allies will have to apply most pressure. Their weapons are not many, and they cannot afford to dissipate them, and M. Bratiano is possibly counting on this. That is, he means to use his positions in Roumania to the utmost to extort the territorial concessions he has demanded. But if the Allies are firm, it is to be hoped that in his turn M. Bratiano will not carry his bluff so far as to break with the Allies over this Hungarian question. It would not pay him in the end.

The two problems in regard to the Hungarian question that have to be solved are:—

1. To stop the requisitions.

2. To find a Hungarian Government with which the Allies and Roumania can alike deal.

The Question of requisitions has again two sides to it:—

(a) Cessation.

(b) Restoration to the Allies of their common property or its value, and to Hungary of the means to live.

As regards (a), I fear that orders from the Roumanian Government however sincerely meant, will continue to be evaded, and that evacuation is the only real remedy. But it may be expected that the Roumanians, as their time draws to a close, will increase their activities, and it may be possible to put some check on this.

There are only the two roads from Hungary to Roumania over the Szolnok and Csongrad bridges.

At present, a French and Italian officer, with half a dozen men each, are doing most useful work in checking the trains as they go over, but they have no control over the contents of sealed wagons, of which over 6,000 have been sent across. These officers are there with the consent of the Roumanian authorities, and it would seem desirable to extend the system, *in collaboration with the Roumanians*. The officers and personnel should be largely increased and Roumanian officers must work with them. They should have a copy of the way-bill of every train, with full authority to verify the loads, and to open and inspect sealed wagons. This would at least check and put on record the depredations that are being committed; it would facilitate the making up of the bill against the Roumanians; it would be a test of the good faith of the Roumanian government; it might even, by exposures and their consequences, deter some of the looters from their proceedings.

It would, of course, be even better if such a commission could unload or detach trucks containing goods that should not have been taken, but I fear that difficulties of storing, and lack of sidings, make this impractical.

I may add that M. Diamandy expressed his personal assent to this suggestion, though he could not commit his Government, but pointed out a practical objection from the delay and blocking that inspection of sealed wagons might cause. It is an objection that would have to be over-ruled.

With respect to (b), the American Representatives on the Organization Committee of the Reparation Commission have, in a paper dated September 23rd last, suggested the establishment of a Special Commission at Buda Pesth to make out the bill against Roumania. So far as it goes, the proposal seems to be useful and practical, though more provisions might perhaps have been made for Roumanian collaboration. What the Roumanians feel, and feel very deeply, is that from the outset they have been pre-judged by their Allies as criminals and put into the dock. They ask for collaboration and co-operation, and, instead, are haled before the tribunal for sentence. This does not make them any more ready to sink their own interests in the common stock, and if they were treated more as Allies, who have fought and suffered, and less as criminals, things would probably go far more easily. They feel bitterly such implications as that their action alone has turned Hungary into a burden on the Allies. They ask that allowance should be made for other factors: Bolshevism, moderate harvest, the peasant's general mistrust of the future, the general dislocation of economic life in Europe; all these are factors in the Allies' disappointment at Hungary proving to be not self-supporting, but the whole sin is visited upon Roumania.

In any case, while the American plan provides a means for restoring common property, or its value, to the Allies, it contains no definite scheme for helping the Hungarians, though presumably it is to be inferred that the suggested Commission will study that aspect of the question, and no doubt make Roumania foot the bill. That would provide a solution, but if the Commission is to work under the Allied Generals, it will possibly be looked on by the Roumanians as absolutely anti-Roumanian, and they will continue their Oriental obstruction. The best chance is for an independent Allied and Roumanian Commission.

Even more difficult is the solution of the second problem, the discovery of a possible Hungarian Government.

I have set down, as faithfully and impartially as I can the views of those most qualified to speak. The Generals, disgusted by their experience of the Roumanians are on the whole for the recognition of M. Friedrich. The Roumanians themselves, and democratic Hungary, look sourly on Friedrich and hold that his recognition in any form by the Supreme Council would be a mortal blow to the moral influence of that body, after their action against the Archduke, for whom Friedrich is but the "Locum tenens."

It is for the Supreme Council to decide, and it is only with the greatest deference that I put forward any suggestions.

The first point seems to me to make clearly known to Roumania what the decision of the Supreme Council is in regard to the territorial adjustments asked for by M. Bratiano. Whether these requests be granted in whole or in part or refused altogether, the Roumanian Government should be informed at once, as it will then have no motive to coquet with various Hungarian parties, in the hope of getting the concessions out of them in return for recognition as a Government, and possibly even a separate Alliance.

It is, I think, the hope of finding a more pliant Hungarian administration that is a main cause of the Roumanian objections to Friedrich and one of their principal reasons for not leaving Hungary. If the Roumanians knew that they have nothing to hope for in this respect, they might be more ready to carry out immediate evacuation. The only plea the Roumanian Government could urge for remaining would be the maintenance of order, and that could be met by insisting on the provision of sufficient arms to the Hungarian Police.

The difficulty is, however, to decide what provisional Government is to control that police force and the choice must precede any steps that may be taken to ensure Roumanian evacuation. Though M. Garami's fears may be exaggerated, there is force in the case he makes against M. Friedrich from the point of view of the Peace Conference. On the other hand, the Generals believe in Friedrich and Horthy, and on the evidence before them have no fear of a white terror or reactionary excesses.

But could not M. Garami's proposal be applied to M. Friedrich first? He is, at present, opposed to widening the basis of his Ministry, but if he realised that only so could he comply with the Allies' conditions and secure recognition, he might accede. Pressure might have to be put on the other parties to come in, but if they are really moved by patriotism, a Coalition Government should not be an impossibility.

If M. Friedrich refuses, then the support of the Supreme Council might, as suggested by M. Garami, be offered to a Coalition Government without him, which would be prepared to meet the Allies' conditions.

There is also another alternative, which it might be worth while to consider. I believe that, technically, the Upper and Lower Houses of the Hungarian Parliament have never been abolished and still have a legal existence. The two Houses (or rather these members whose seats are included within the present frontiers of Hungary) might be summoned for the purpose of adding members from other parties to the Hungarian Ministry and of appointing dates for the elections and for a plebiscite as to the form of government which Hungary is to have. The objections seem to be (a) that such a Parliament has no real relation to the political feeling of Hungary to-day and (b) that the summons must be through the Hungarian Governmen and therefore provisional recognition of M. Friedrich is involved, though i would be confined to this one purpose alone.

None of these solutions may commend themselves to the Supreme Council, and other and better ones may be found, but I venture to submit the urgency of imposing some solution from the outside. On that point all parties are agreed: that Hungary can only be saved, if the Allies intervene and by their recognition of some Government, enable that Government to exhort the authority necessary to preserve the country from ruin and anarchy. This is an interest of all Europe.

DOCUMENT 36

The Rumanian Delegate to the Peace Conference, Dr. Vaida-Voivoda, to the President of the Peace Conference, Mr. Clemenceau, Concerning the Rectification of the Rumano-Hungarian Frontiers, October 10, 1919 [1]

[Translation]

Regarding the question of the frontiers proposed by the Commission for the delimitation of the frontiers between Rumania and Hungary, I have the honor to call your kind attention to the following circumstances:

1. The Maros is the principal waterway for the whole Rumanian region between the Carpathians and the Theiss.

It is true that the right bank of the mouth of the Maros, together with the city of Mako and the hinterland, is peopled in majority by the Magyars. But, taking into account the great number of Rumanians who, in the neighborhood of Debreczen remain in Hungary, the fact alone constitutes a sufficient compensation from the ethnic point of view.

On the other hand the benefit which, from the economic point of view, Hungary could obtain by the acquisition of that territory is very small in comparison with the immense losses which the economic, industrial and commercial interests of the whole Rumanian region situated between the Carpathians and the Theiss would suffer by the granting of said territories to the Magyars.

2. The Slovak and Rumanian population of the former Comitats of Bekes and Csanad has asked, by virtue of the right of self-determination, for the incorporation of their countries, in which even according to the official Hungarian statistics, notoriously falsified to their advantage, Hungarians form only an ethnic minority.

The Slovak deputation which came to Paris delivered through M. Benes a memorandum to the Conference asking for the incorporation with Rumania of the communes in majority Slovak and Rumanian of the Comitats of Bekes and Csanad, which form this well defined territory. Informed on that subject by M. Benes, the Rumanian Delegation answered that if the Supreme Council favored and approved the just demand of the non-Magyar population of said comitats, on her side Rumania would see their wish realized with

[1] American Delegation, SH Bulletin 1062. Oct. 14, 1919. MSS.

pleasure. In that case the Slovaks would enjoy broad legislative measures insuring their cultural and national development. Enclosed herewith is the original of the motion of the Great Assembly of the Delegates of the Communes of Bekes and Csanad held on July 13, 1919, at Bekescsaba, together with that of the representatives of the communes of the neighborhood of Pitvaros and Giula [Gyula].

3. The Consistory of the Rumanian-Greek Orthodox diocese of Oradea-Mare [Nagyvárad], in its plenary meeting of July 12, last, decided—enclosed herewith is a translation, which it addressed later to the Rumanian delegation at the Peace Conference with request that it be brought to the attention of the Supreme Council.

May we not be allowed, on this occasion, to ask your high solicitude for the seven Rumanian communes of Mehkerek, Kristor, Zsaka, Bawas, Yekeid, Szakal and Koues-Apato, who, just delivered from the Hungarian yoke, await with the greatest anxiety to be definitely incorporated to Rumania.

4. In 1912, on the request of the Magyar Government and of Emperor Francis-Joseph, after interventions which had lasted over 20 years, Pius X consented, through the Bull "Christifidels graeci de ritus catholici" that 46 Rumanian parishes of the Archdiocese of Albajulie and of Pajaras be incorporated to the newly created Hungarian diocese of Hajdudorogh. The Magyars in this way [wished] to denationalize these Rumanians. The victory of the Allies, however, saved them too. Pope Benedict—by papal letters of May 10, 1919, latin text appended, restituted to the Rumanian Greek Orthodox Church (unified) these 46 communes, which the Magyar intrigue and violence, as well as the hatred of the Rumanians which animated Francis-Joseph, had torn from it.

Over the fate of these Rumanians also hangs uncertainty. The Supreme Council will be kind enough to examine their special situation from a national and confessional point of view. To what diocese should they belong? How could they practice, if a part of these 46 parishes were given to the Hungarians? There are no Magyars of Greco-Catholic (Unified) confession. The language of the unified church is that of its flock: the Rumanian language. In what way could the ecclesiastical questions of these Rumanians be settled administratively? While on Rumanian territory all various Magyar confessions have their ecclesiastical organization, the autonomy of which was assured at Alba-Julia,—in Hungary the Rumanian Greek Catholics could nowhere find aid and protection unless a diocese of their own were created or it be also decided to leave for the future their parishes dependent on the Archdiocese of Alba-Julia and Fagaras. In either case, in order to come to a decision the Supreme Council would have to be in accord with the Papal Curia.

What complications would be avoided if again this time the Supreme

Council put on the scales a sympathetic consideration for the liberated Rumanians.

5. The Czecho-Slovaks have benefited, it appears, by the attribution of some Ruthenian and Rumano-Ruthenian communes on the left bank of the Theiss. I shall not invoke the Rumanian Treaty with her Allies, but it is my duty to call the attention of the Supreme Council to the fact that all the Rumanians of Transylvania and of Maramures have been deeply grieved to learn of this favor accorded to the Ruthenians on the left bank of the Theiss; there exist nevertheless on the right bank of the same river powerful Rumanian centres which the Rumanians on their side would like to see attributed to them, the communes of Apsa de sus, Apsa de jos, and Apsa de Mijloc, the cradle of illustrious Rumanian families such as the Mihale de Apsa. The Monastivea of Periis and important locality in the Rumanian history [sic].

The same historic arguments that our Serb Allies invoked in their claims relative to the Banat, can be more advantageously invoked by the Rumanians on the subject of the portion of the Maramures, starting from the crests of the mountains East of the river Taracs to the northern frontier northeast, east of Maramures. The toponymy is evident proof that this territory is Rumanian; Pietrosl-stony, Fransini-ash trees in Hungarian Karos-mezo—Koros —ash tree.

On the other hand, owing to the fact that the frontier of the 3 Apsa communes is determined by the mountains to the Carpathians,—that the Ruthenians are in this country Greco-Catholic like the Rumanians living there, —that the railroad Koros-Mezo-Maemaros-Bizet has not for the Czecho-Slovaks any very great importance, as they dispose of better connections with Galicia, while for the Rumanians, from an economic point of view as well as from a point of view of the superior political interest towards the neighboring and friendly Polish State, it is of a capital interest, we have full confidence that the Supreme Council, desiring to examine closely what has just been set forth, will not be unjust neither to the Czecho-Slovaks nor to the Ruthenians by incorporating to their fatherland the Rumanians inhabiting this piece of land situated on the right bank of the Theiss.

Mr. President,

I respectfully solicit your generous and enlightened support for our cause with the Supreme Council.

It is not imperialistic aims nor thirst for more territories which have induced me to address to Your Excellency the above set forth requests. We do not want our neighbors' property. We desire, on the contrary, on the territory of unified Rumania, the smallest possible number of foreigners.

But if the cruelty of late—fatal consequences of our geographic situation as well as of our historic past, determined by the struggles for conquest of the feudal oligarchies which surrounded us—tore from us piece by piece whole sections of Rumania, we are today in duty bound to make use of all our energies to the saving and keeping of as many Rumanians as possible for the fatherland.

How terrible is the despair which darkens the souls of those Rumanians who, having hardly caught a glimpse of liberty, again see themselves menaced with remaining in the future under the full domination of hatred of their millennial oppressors.

We desire to live, to be able to live in peace with all our neighbors. With the Hungarians, also. That is why we request your help to prevent the creation of a multitude of small Rumanian Alsaces.

The accomplished duty towards the Rumanian nation and country is the sentiment which animates me and which will find, I am sure, a strong echo in the generous heart of Your Excellency.

Please accept, etc.

DOCUMENT 37

Note from the Supreme Council to the Rumanian Government, October 11, 1919 [1]

[The] Supreme Council have received with great satisfaction the assurances of the Roumanian Government, reported by Sir George Clerk, that they have always intended, and still intend, to adhere firmly to the Alliance. The Supreme Council never doubted that such was the real wish of Roumania, and they are happy to think that the Mission of Sir George Clerk has only served to confirm the conviction they already held.

The Supreme Council feel however that recent events have once more demonstrated the necessity of avoiding, so far as possible, all ground for misunderstanding. Such has been the experience of all the Allies during the war, and perfect frankness on even the most difficult and delicate points of difference such as are bound to arise in the complicated relations and conflicting interests of a group of Allies has proved to be the only way to secure harmonious and successful progress.

The Supreme Council therefore desire to put before their Roumanian Allies their decisions on the three questions which form the principal subjects of divergence between Roumania and the Allies to-day. These decisions will be expressed quite definitely and frankly, but the Supreme Council trust that the Roumanian Government will realise that they have been taken, not with any desire to foster other interests at the expense of Roumania nor without the most sympathetic consideration of the Roumanian case, but because the Supreme Council firmly believe that they correspond most nearly to the general interests of peace and well-being.

The three points may be entitled 1. Territorial Frontiers. 2. The Minorities Treaty. 3. Hungary.

1. After renewing [sic] and careful study of the requests made by Monsieur Bratiano for both banks of the river Marosh up to its mouth, for Bekes-Ciabe, and for a frontier line 20 kilometres outside the Szatmar-Arad railway and of the arguments put forward by Monsieur Bratiano in favour of these modifications, the Supreme Council regret that they are unable to modify in favour of Roumania their original decision taken after the closest examina-

[1] American Delegation, SH Bulletin 1051, Oct. 13, 1919. MSS.

tion of all the relevant factors and made known as definite to all the parties interested.

2. The Allied Powers represented on the Supreme Council are absolutely united in their determination to uphold the principle underlying the Minorities Treaty. They feel that this principle is one of the vital elements in removing the causes of further wars and they intend to maintain it intact. It underlies the whole spirit which has led the world to accept a system of a society of Nations and it cannot be abandoned. This principle finds its expression, so far as Roumania is concerned, in Article 71 of the Treaty with Austria and in Article 13 of the Draft Treaty respecting minorities submitted to the Roumanian Government.

The Supreme Council feel that possibly these two Articles have been misinterpreted in Roumania. In the view of the Supreme Council there is nothing derogatory to the independence of Roumania. She is only asked, in common with other states, which like herself have, as the result of the war, profoundly altered the extent and nature of their dominions, to accept such obligations towards the Society of Nations as arise from membership of that body to which she is already pledged.

But as soon as the Supreme Council learn that the Roumanian Government is prepared to sign the Treaty with Austria without reservation, they, for their part, will be happy to consider in common with Roumania, such modifications of those clauses as affect Roumania individually, as apart from the general principle, in order to see whether it is not possible to meet the views of the Roumanian Government. The Supreme Council had the advantage, while the text of the Minorities Treaty with other Powers was being drafted, of the collaboration of representatives of other Powers, to the great advantage of both parties.

Hitherto this collaboration has been denied to them by the Roumanian Government, but the Supreme Council hope that if the Roumanian Government will now discuss the clauses with them, an equally satisfactory result may be reached.

Lastly the Supreme Council trust that their Roumanian Allies will announce their decision on this point forthwith. It is essential for the establishment of conditions of peace and for the renewal and restoration of economic life in Europe, that the treaties of peace with the enemy powers and the various agreements and arrangements arising out of those treaties, should be brought into force at once.

3. The Hungarian question has two main issues. The first is the question of requisitions by the Roumanian Army of Occupation. The general view of the Supreme Council with regard to the action of the Roumanian requisitioning for herself, without consultation and agreement with her Allies, supplies of material which should, by the agreement to which Roumania herself

is a party, form part of the common reparation stock of the Allies has already been expressed to the Roumanian Government. The Supreme Council have received and considered the Roumanian point of view as expressed by M. Bratiano, and it seems to them there is now no difference of opinion about the general principle. As regards the application of that principle, the Allies propose the following machinery for deciding what material shall be definitely allocated to Roumania and what part, or its value, assigned to the common stock. They are despatching an Inter-Allied Sub-Commission of the Commission on Reparation to Buda Pesth with authority from the Supreme Council to investigate and examine all the requisitions that have been made and to report on the distribution to be effected between Roumania and the Allies. The Supreme Council trusts that the Roumanian Government will appoint a representative with full authority to speak for them, to act on this Commission.

There is, however, an aspect of the question, which the Supreme Council feel that they cannot ignore. The Supreme Council recognizes that the Roumanian Government have given orders to confine their requisitions to those of railway materials, materials of war and supplies to the Army of Occupation. Unfortunately, the Supreme Council have in their possession a mass of evidence which leaves no room for doubt that the orders of the Roumanian Government to this effect are deliberately and continuously disobeyed. They do not question the good faith of the Roumanian Government, but on the other hand, they cannot suffer because the subordinates of that Government do not carry out the orders given to them. The Supreme Council accordingly propose that an Inter-Allied Organization, including Roumanian officials, should be established at once at the bridges of Szolnok and Czongrad to check and verify the way-bills of all trains passing over those two bridges into Roumania. This organization should have full powers to open sealed wagons and to remove all goods that have been improperly despatched to Roumania. At the same time, the Sub-Commission of the Commission on Reparation will have authority to receive all complaints already filed by the Inter-Allied Commission of Generals, or that may subsequently be made as to improper requisitions, and the Supreme Council has no doubt that the Roumanian Government will, in such cases as are definitely established, be prepared to make full reparation.

The other important point in the Hungarian situation is the establishment of a Hungarian Government which can maintain law and order, can hold the elections freely and impartially, and can negotiate peace with the Allies. The Government, of which M. Friedrich, as the titular Minister President of Hungary, is the head, does not, in the opinion of the Supreme Council, fulfill the conditions necessary to ensure these requirements. The Supreme Council consider that M. Friedrich should include in his Government representatives of the various political parties in Hungary, and should he be unwilling or unable to do so, the Hungarian people must realize that the Allies can only recognize and deal with a Government which fulfills these conditions. The Supreme Council are confident that this is also the view of their Roumanian Allies, since it appears that to them that what they desire is as much in the interests of Roumania as of the Allies generally.

Finally, the Supreme Council would be glad to receive assurances that the rifles for the Hungarian police and gendarmerie already promised by the Roumanian authorities in B. P. to the Mission of Allied Generals, will be immediately delivered and that the Roumanian forces will at once evacuate the country. They know that Roumania herself wishes to be relieved of this heavy charge upon her resources, and they consider that the burden which it also lays upon the impoverished State of Hungary should, in the interests of the Allies generally, be lifted as soon as possible.

DOCUMENT 38

Report of the Interallied Military Mission in Budapest, to the Supreme Council, October 13, 1919 [1]

Cold weather is setting in and a day's delay now more serious than would have been a week's delay two months ago. Inter-Allied Military Mission therefore desires to present the Supreme Council following statements of fact concerning conduct of Roumanians with request for prompt action. They have so thoroughly cleaned out country of rolling stock that there is not enough for transportation of local food and fuel requirements. Their administration has reduced food reserve in Budapest to one-third of what it was in September. According to report of Hungarian Food Minister, they have by unnecessary and cruel restrictions prevented food from going out of Budapest to neighboring suburbs, population of which estimated to be six hundred thousand. It is reported that during evacuation of Transdanubia, they released Bolshevists who had been detained, and in the city of Budapest they have repeatedly, by force and without, written orders taking Bolshevist prisoners out of jails. At Szolnok, where a Committee of this Mission was obtaining information of Roumanian exportation, they have arrested several of the Hungarian railway men who were aiding in our efforts. They have prevented university students from a continuation of their courses. On September 26 their Commander in Chief sent a letter to Mission stating that to cover needs of feeding Hungary, the zone between Danube and Theiss Rivers had been placed at disposition of Hungarian government; that no requisitions would take place in that zone except those necessary for actual feeding of troops; that especially for city of Budapest above zone would be extended to east of Theiss to boundary line fixed by said commander, despite which on October fifth the Roumanian Colonel Rujinschi seized thirty aeroplane motors at Budapest which can hardly be classified as food. On October tenth in Budapest from the firm of Schmitt and Társai they seized and removed machinery which put two thousand laborers out of work. A large number of similar cases with proof are on hand. In reply to letter from Mission that it was desired that objects in National Museum be not disturbed until acted

[1] Bandholtz, *An Undiplomatic Diary*, pp. 151–54 (by permission). This report forms Appendix "A" to the minutes of the Council of Heads of Delegations, held on Oct. 16, 1919 (H.D. 71). MSS.

upon by committee, they sent reply that they intended to take those objects and that the signers of letters, Mardarescu and Diamandi, assumed responsibility for such action, this being in effect an insult to nations represented on Inter-Allied Military Mission. That they did not take these objects was due to fact that doors were sealed and signed by the President of the Day at the time and they were afraid to go to extreme of breaking seals. Between five and six o'clock this morning they attempted to arrest Prime Minister Friedrich and did arrest two government officials, as result of which President of the Day in person delivered to General Mardarescu a memorandum from Mission, copy of which was telegraphed Supreme Council this date. They kept their Commander in Chief, General Mardarescu, and High Commissioner Diamandi absent in Bucharest a week, during which no representative was present with whom business could be transacted. Although they in August acknowledged the Inter-Allied Military Mission as representing their superior, they have with comparatively negligible exceptions carried out none of the instructions of this Mission and have always insisted on acting as though Roumania were equal or superior to nations represented on Mission. They have sent misleading reports to Paris placing themselves in attitude of saviors of Hungary and have censored the press in Hungary to such an extent that Hungarians could not refute any false statements. On the nineteenth of September their General Mardarescu wrote to the Mission that he had taken all necessary measures to make treatment of prisoners satisfactory, stating that especially from sanitary viewpoint according to report of his surgeon general conditions were very good. On October eleventh, Mission received communication from International Red Cross representative stating that his investigation at Arad resulted in discovery of conditions so opposed to conventions covering treatment of prisoners of war that he felt this Mission should take some action. His conclusions, which are as follows, concur with all reports concerning same except Roumanian reports:

"I find that these prisoners were not captured on the field of battle but many days after the cessation of hostilities; that the lodgings of the prisoners are unsanitary; that the army which captured them takes no care of them whatever, furnishes them neither food, clothing, medicine, covering, nor anything; that from the date of their captivity, the prisoners have had no funds and that the majority cannot purchase anything for even insufficient nourishment; that doctors are treated contrary to Article IX of Geneva Convention of 1906; that all these men are exposed to serious diseases if they are not promptly aided; that the order given to the Red Cross at Arad to take care of the prisoners' needs is entirely illegal and cannot be based upon any law or international convention."

Doctor Munro of the British Food Commission and the Swiss Captain Brunier of the International Red Cross have just returned from visiting the

following towns: Hatvan, Gyöngyös, Miskolcz, Sátoralja-Ujhely, Nyiregy-
háza, Debreczen, Szolnok, Nagyvárad, Békés-Gyula, Arad, Temesvár,
Szeged, all in permanent portion of Hungary, but now occupied by Roumanians, and have submitted signed statement from which following is ex-
tracted:

"In all towns occupied by Roumanians we found an oppression so great
as to make life unbearable. Murder is common, youths and women flogged,
imprisoned without trial, arrested without reason, theft of personal property
under name of requisition. Condition of affairs prevails difficult for Western
European to realize who has not seen and heard the evidence. People are
forced to take oath of allegiance to Roumanian King; if they refuse they
are persecuted. Experienced Hungarian Directors of Hospitals have been
replaced by inexperienced Roumanian doctors. Roumanian military authorities demand petition for every passport, request for coal or food. Petition
must be written in Roumanian language, Roumanian lawyer must be employed, and he charges enormous fees. Station master of Brad and the station master of Ketegyhaza have been most fearfully flogged. Last Good
Friday Roumanians advanced suddenly to Boros-Sebes and two hundred
fifty Hungarian soldiers were taken prisoners. They were killed in most
barbarous manner; stripped naked and stabbed with bayonets in way to
prolong life as long as possible. Roumanians have established custom-house
in every village. Delivery permits can only be obtained by payment of ridic-
ulously large sums. Commerce is impossible. People will soon starve. Deliberately and for no military and political reason apparent the hospitals are
not allowed transports for coal and wood which they have already paid for.
Very life of hospital hangs on coal. Hospitals will have to close down entirely
unless relieved immediately. Results will be disastrous. There will be outbreaks of all sorts of contagious epidemic diseases, such as typhus, typhoid,
etc."

An American officer and an Italian doctor, if Roumanians permit, will
accompany the International Red Cross representative on a thorough investigation of prisoner-of-war camps. In general Roumanian conduct has been
such that this Mission has been almost wholly unable to carry out its instructions and there is apparently no prospect of immediate improvement.
It is the unanimous opinion of the Mission that unless the Roumanians
immediately evacuate Hungary and make at least partial restitution in particular of rolling stock, machinery and much other property seized, there
will result in a very short time extreme suffering from lack of food and
fuel and a recrudescence of Bolshevism. This Mission is therefore of the
unanimous opinion that either the Roumanians should be forced to evacuate Hungary at once and make restitution as above outlined or that this
Mission should be relieved.

Document 39

M. Pichon, the French Minister for Foreign Affairs, to the French Representative in Belgrade, November 7, 1919 [1]

[Translation]

The Supreme Council has always affirmed its intention to conclude peace only with a Hungarian Government established by free elections. The concordant reports received from the military representatives and from Sir George Clerk have convinced the Supreme Council that an *immediate* evacuation of Hungarian territory by the Rumanian, Serb-Croat-Slovene, and Czecho-Slovak troops is essential before operating the vote.

Kindly, in the name of the Supreme Council, invite the Serb-Croat-Slovene Government to withdraw its troops beyond the frontiers indicated herein, and which are to be considered as final, at once:

a) for the Banat, the frontier as notified in a letter addressed to the President of the Serb-Croat-Slovene Delegation to the Peace Conference on June 30th.

b) for the Bacska, the frontier which was the object of a similar notification on August 5th.

c) for the Baranja and Somogy, a frontier outlined as follows:

From the point where the frontier between the Serb-Croat-Slovene State and Hungary in the Bacska cuts the principal arm of the Danube, about 8 kilometres to the North of Hill 169 (Kiskoszeg) and as far as hill 93, at about 3 kilometres to the Southwest of Baranyavar:

a line to be determined on the spot to run in a general South-westerly direction leaving to the Serb-Croat-Slovene State the Dalyck [Dályok], Foherczeglak, Baranyavar localities as well as the railway line uniting these two localities and the branch immediately to the North of Baranyavar, and to Hungary, the localities of Isabellafol with its railroad, Udvar, Sarch, Ivan Darda.

Starting from hill 93 to the West as far as the secondary arm of the Drava to a point to be chosen on the spot near hill 90, at about 10 kilometres to the East of Miholjacdl [Alsómiholjác]:

a line to be determined on the spot leaving to Jugoslavia the localities of Benge, Locs and Torjancz; and to Hungary, the localities of Illosska, Bere-

[1] American Delegation, SH Bulletin 1249, Nov. 10, 1919. MSS.

mend, Kassad and cutting the railway line immediately to the South of the Beremend station.

The secondary arm, then the thalweg of the principal arm of the Drava upstream as far as its junction with the Mur River.

This decision is in no wise prejudicial toward the solution which will be given by the Supreme Council relative to the requests recently received from the Serb-Croat-Slovene Delegation concerning the exploitation of the Pecs mines.

d) From the junction of the Drava and the Mur to the frontier between Hungary and Austria, the frontier as notified to the President of the S.C.S. Delegation to the Peace Conference on August 2nd.

DOCUMENT 40

Telegram from the Supreme Council to Sir George Clerk in Budapest, November 5, 1919 [1]

The Supreme Council has taken note of your various communications and is ready to adhere, in general, to your suggestions. It esteems that:

1st—The Rumanian troops must completely evacuate Hungary and withdraw beyond the frontiers fixed by the Conference; it is indispensable that the Hungarian elections be conducted with full liberty;

2nd—The Friedrich Ministry must withdraw to make room for a really different government comprising the democratic element. This Government would proceed with the elections, and you would be authorized to guarantee its recognition by the Allies.

The Council was presented with a suggestion tending to emphasize the necessity, in order to prevent the elections and the Hungarian Government being subject to the influence of the local police which is in the power of Friedrich, and by the small army of Admiral Horthy whose tendencies are openly reactionary, of replacing the Rumanian military force by an Allied military force capable of inspiring confidence in the population and strengthening the moral authority of the Commission of Generals and of the Conference itself. These facts appear to indicate that without material force their decisions are liable to remain non-executed.

On one hand, the fact that the Allies do not in any wise wish to impede the expression of the free will of the Hungarians must be clearly understood, but on the other hand they have decided to prevent the restoration of the fallen dynasty, in any form, either direct or indirect.

The Council would like to know if after consultation with the Commission of Generals, and having had recourse to all the authorized advice with which you are surrounded, you are convinced that the Rumanian forces ought to be replaced by Inter-Allied forces, or whether the assurances of Admiral Horthy and the guarantee of order represented by the Hungarian Gendarmerie can be trusted, which might perhaps be placed under the direct or indirect control of the Commission of Generals.

Another suggestion was made to the effect of entrusting the Commission

[1] American Delegation, SH Bulletin 1227, Nov. 6, 1919. MSS. This telegram forms Appendix "B" to the minutes of the Council of Heads of Delegations held on Nov. 5, 1919 (H.D. 84). MSS.

of Generals with the supervision of the organization of the Hungarian army, and to see that it is not employed for political purposes contrary to the views of the Allies. The Commission of Generals should also see that the occupation of the Capital and of the country be conducted without excesses and without disturbing public order.

The question of sending an Inter-Allied force presents the following difficulties: as the Great Powers have no effectives available, they would be envisaged with the sending of two divisions of Czech and Serbian *non-commissioned officers and soldiers,* commanded by English, Italian, American and French superior officers under the orders of an energetic General nominated by the Supreme Council.

The Italian Delegation objects to sending any Jugo-Slavs, owing to the state of mind of the Hungarian population. For that matter, all Delegations realize the inconveniences which might result from the presence of contingents from the small neighboring hostile countries of Hungary, even under a firm Allied Command. The main question is to ascertain whether the presence of a force at the disposition of the Allies is not necessary.

The Supreme Council, confident in your judgment and your local information, asks you for precise and prompt advice.

DOCUMENT 41

Telegram from Sir George Clerk to the Supreme Council, November 9, 1919 [1]

I venture to express my sincere opinion that decisions of Supreme Council in regard to evacuation by Roumanians, Czechs and Serbians and to action to be taken at Prague on question of coal will greatly help situation here. Atmosphere generally is much better than it was a fortnight ago and much uneasiness and mistrust has been dissipated. Most significant sign is that Admiral Horthy and leaders of extreme left met in my house two days ago and Admiral Horthy's declaration of impartiality and discipline of his army was fully accepted. There will always be a certain risk of incidents when Roumanians evacuate Budapest and Hungarians take over control but I had made up my mind as soon as I came here that such risk must be taken as nothing can really be done until Roumanians have left and I feel today danger is immeasurably less. Inter-Allied Mission of Generals, Admiral Troubridge and I have complete confidence in Admiral Horthy's loyalty and sincerity and there is every reason to believe his hold over army is really effective.

Question of police and gendarmerie is somewhat different. I had already discussed matter with Inter-Allied Mission and I feel that their authority over police and gendarmerie is a guarantee against latter abusing their power. It is scarcely possible for Allies to send troops or even police in sufficient numbers and my considered opinion is that we must trust to our influence over Hungarian troops, gendarmerie and police.

Inter-Allied Mission of Generals agree but we would suggest immediate despatch of 20 Allied officers rank of major and captain to be attached to various armies and police units would be valuable safeguard and assistance.

Political situation is developing satisfactorily though there are still many obstacles to be overcome before complete solution can be reached. It must be realised that great bulk of opinion mostly ignorant in country stands behind Friedrich. Pendulum has swung violently from left to right but is now beginning to come slowly towards centre. But allowance must be made for present state of populace and to some extent to natural prejudice and changes

[1] American Delegation, SH Bulletin 1267, Nov. 11, 1919. MSS. This telegram forms Appendix "E" to the minutes of the Council of Heads of Delegations held on Nov. 12, 1919 (H.D. 90). MSS.

of Government must be effected with as little disturbance of populace as possible.

All responsible politicians even these in Friedrich's cabinet now realise that coalition government must come and idea is becoming familiar to masses. Difficulties now are mainly reconciliation of personal interests and private political ambitions. I am not without hope of overcoming these difficulties only patience is required.

General sentiment of political leaders in country today so clearly recognises lines on which solution must be found and general atmosphere is so much better than it was a fortnight ago that I am fairly confident that law and order will be maintained. Impartiality of my mission is I think universally recognised as well as desire of Allies to help Hungary and confidence felt in mission of Generals and Admiral Troubridge is a moral factor of immense value.

It may take a little time to get satisfactory solution and Friedrich may resign and talk big but I am now much less anxious about internal peace and quiet here and Hungarian forces being used for reaction and oppression. While we are all here Hungarians will behave soberly.

Mission of Generals and Admiral Troubridge agree with terms of this telegram.

DOCUMENT 42

Telegram from Sir George Clerk to the Supreme Council, November 25, 1919 [1]

I have this morning given formal recognition of the Supreme Council to Hussar as provisional *de facto* administration of Hungary.

Recognition is subject to the condition that the provisional government undertakes to hold elections without delay, to maintain law and order in the country, to commit no aggressive action, to respect the provisional frontiers of Hungary pending the final definition in the Peace Treaty and to guarantee to every Hungarian national free civil rights including those of a free press, free right of meeting, freedom to express political opinions and a free secret, impartial and democratic election based on universal suffrage.

I have added that I have notified the Supreme Council that the Minister President is prepared to nominate delegates to attend the peace conference as soon as official invitation is received from Paris.

[1] American Delegation, SH Bulletin 1385, Nov. 28, 1919. MSS.

Document 43

Excerpts from the Report of Sir George Clerk to the Supreme Council on His Mission to Hungary, November 29, 1919 [1]

In pursuance of the instructions of the Supreme Council, I arrived in Budapest on October 23 last, in order to put before the Government of M. Friedrich the conditions under which the Supreme Council would be prepared to treat with the Hungarian Government.

The main condition was that such a Government must include representatives of the different political parties in Hungary. It also must be such as to satisfy the Supreme Council that it was able to maintain law and order, to hold elections based on universal suffrage, in a free, impartial and democratic manner, and be prepared to send delegates to Paris to negotiate the peace with the Allies.

It is unnecessary for me to give a long account of the tedious and difficult negotiations which were necessary before this result could be achieved, but it may be desirable to explain briefly the reasons why the negotiations were long and difficult.

Over four years of unsuccessful war, and the collapse of the whole administrative machine under the revolutionary Government of Michael Karolyi, followed by a communist regime, which again was immediately succeeded by the Roumanian occupation, had reduced the Hungarian spirit to a condition of apathy and depression which it required pressure from outside to rouse to action. On the other hand, the Communist Regime, of which the most prominent leaders were Jews, and its association with certain members of the Social-Democratic Party, had produced an inevitable re-action. Feeling throughout the country was excited to the highest pitch and very little would have led to an outburst of wild fanaticism. Moreover, M. Friedrich, the titular Minister-President, had become in the minds of the vast majority of the Hungarian people the symbol of this re-action against Jewish and Communist influence and anything that had the appearance of attacking or weakening his position was liable to be misinterpreted and to arouse an outburst of unreflecting but none the less dangerous, chauvinism.

Another element in the situation, which had to be taken seriously into

[1] American Delegation, SH Bulletin 1395, Dec. 1, 1919. MSS. This report forms Appendix "A" to the minutes of the Council of Heads of Delegations held on Dec. 1, 1919 (H.D. 103). MSS.

account, was the attitude of M. Friedrich, as expressed in the course of an interview which I had with him immediately on my arrival in Budapest. M. Friedrich asserted that during the three months for which his Government retained office, the whole country had rallied almost unanimously to his banner; the different Christian parties had fused together into a solid block which stood behind him. Personally he was ready to do his best to meet the desires of the Entente, but he was no longer a free agent, as he had been when he assumed power, but merely the trusted spokesman of the Christian National Block. He had already gone as far as possible in broadening the basis of his Government, but any attempt, even if made by himself, to introduce a Social-Democrat or a Jew, or any individual even remotely connected in the popular mind with the Communist regime, was foredoomed to failure. His followers simply would not hear of it, and his action must be guided by their will. If amalgamation with the Extreme Left were contemplated, then he preferred to hand over the Government of the country to the Allied and Associated Powers, failing which he would go into opposition to any Government which might take office, and the whole Christian Nationalist Block would follow him. Lastly, M. Friedrich sought to impress upon me the magnitude of the service he had rendered to the Entente by refusing repeated and tempting offers of direct negotiations with Roumania, and hinted that any other Government but his was likely to succumb to them.

It was, therefore, necessary to move carefully and to work so that the country gradually awoke to the fact that the wishes of the Entente were not directed against the feelings of the Hungarian people, but were solely intended that those sections of the Hungarian people who were all classed together as enemies of the State, should not suffer injustice when the elections came to be held.

But it was immediately clear to me that nothing effective could be done so long as the dead-weight of the Roumanian occupation lay upon the country. One after the other, leading Hungarians of independent views said the same thing to me—that it was useless to try to modify or reconstruct the Friedrich Government while the Roumanian occupation continued. To do so would inevitably involve disturbance and possibly worse, while, if a new Government resulted, which was in itself doubtful, that Government would lose its authority in a day, once it were seen that the Roumanians still remained. Moreover, it was obviously impossible to hold proper elections in any district still occupied by foreign troops. I had, therefore, no hesitation from the outset in urging the earliest possible withdrawal of the Roumanian troops upon the Roumanian authorities in Budapest. It was true that this involved a certain risk. In the unoccupied provinces, and to some extent in Budapest itself, there was much wild talk about the fate in store for the

Communists and Jews, and in the capital the Jewish and Social-Democratic sections of the people looked forward with great anxiety to the day when the Roumanians would leave and Horthy's "White" army come in. On the other hand, the organization of the gendarmerie and the police was under the supervision of the Inter-Allied Mission of Generals, who were sufficiently confident of the behaviour of these forces to confirm any intention to take the risk. There remained Horthy's army. Admiral Horthy came to see me at my request from his headquarters and in the course of a long conversation, I became convinced of his sincerity and patriotism, and above all of his complete recognition of the fact that it would be fatal for Hungary if disorders or abuses followed on the arrival of his troops in Budapest.

In taking this decision, I realized that I was throwing away the best lever with which to secure the withdrawal of M. Friedrich, for I could have used the departure of the Roumanians as a bargain and I could have easily brought about a change of Government. But I felt the gravest objections to putting the Roumanians in any way into a position which would enable them to say that their stay in Hungary was undertaken or prolonged at the request of the Allies. It would have been fatal to put the Allies under any obligation to Roumania. I, therefore, steadily pressed for their immediate evacuation.

Meanwhile, as it became clearer that the Roumanians were really going, the attitude of M. Friedrich and his immediate supporters stiffened. More than once I received assurances that once the departure of the Roumanians was definite he would be prepared to meet the wishes of the Allies in every way, and resign his office. But with that departure, there came an instantaneous change which, with the experience that I have acquired of M. Friedrich's character and political tactics, caused me no surprise. There was now, according to M. Friedrich, no reason why he should not remain in office, as desired by practically the whole country, and although the Allies certainly wanted peace, Hungary could quite well get along without it. Fortunately, there were in Hungary people of wider political experience and M. Friedrich was gradually forced to see that he must make an attempt to meet the wishes of the Allies. I cannot say that the attempt was undertaken very whole-heartedly. It ended with an invitation to the actual party leaders, sent on by M. Friedrich without my knowledge, to meet at my house in a conference, which was so arranged as to lead inevitably to a deadlock. M. Friedrich would then have been able to turn to me and say that I myself was a witness of how his best efforts were useless and that the only chance for the country was to retain a government which represented 80 or 90 per cent of the population. This Conference was to meet at 5 p.m. on November 18th. To checkmate this manoeuvre, I invited about 40 of the leading Hungarians to meet me informally at 3 p.m. on the same day, in order that I might put before them the situation in Hungary as I saw it. The Friedrich Party came to this meeting with the definite decision that M. Friedrich must remain Minister-President, or the whole Christian National Block would go into opposition. I spoke very plainly, and at least made the Friedrich party see that Hungary must have peace. I then left those present to discuss the position amongst themselves. The discussion lasted till late in the evening and swallowed up the proposed inter-party conference which M. Friedrich had called together. The position that evening was that Count Apponyi, nominated by the Extreme Left Social-Democratic Wing, was generally accepted by all parties outside the Christian National Block as the man who should form a Coalition Government corresponding to the wishes of the Allies. Even in the Christian National Block a large number of leading men were prepared to accept Count Apponyi, but the party as a whole insisted that if it was really impossible to keep M. Friedrich as their leader, the new Minister-President must at least come from the party. The Conference was resumed at my house next day and resulted in the agreement of all parties to accept M. Huszar, Minister of Education in the Friedrich Government, as Minister-President, provided that he could form a Government of all parties which would be acceptable to the country and agreeable to the Allies.

The hope and expectation of M. Friedrich and his immediate adherents was that the task would prove impossible, and would break M. Huszar's political neck, for he was by far M. Friedrich's most dangerous competitor for leadership. His rivals counted, soundly enough, on the fact that the Social-Democrats, who would have come in almost without terms under Count Apponyi, would exact so high a price from M. Huszar that the Christian National Party would be bound to refuse to pay it. Moreover, the five parties of the Left had formed themselves into a block and announced their intention of standing or falling as a whole.

However, in the end M. Huszar succeeded. . . .

M. Karl Huszar is still young, barely 40, I think, the son of very poor parents, and himself a village school teacher. He entered Hungarian political life as early as he could and has consistently upheld Democratic views and fought for the betterment of the working classes. His personal honesty is above suspicion and he enjoys respect among all political parties. He has great energy and force of character and is well fitted to lead Hungary through this troubled stage of its existence.

I think I should also place on record the fact that the final assent of all Hungarians to a Coalition Government was due more than anything else to the wisdom and influence of two men whose names would rather suggest re-action—Count Apponyi and Admiral Horthy.

Count Apponyi, who had withdrawn altogether from the political arena and was living in retirement on his estate near Pressburg, came to Budapest at my request. His arrival was the signal for a remarkable demonstration in the whole Hungarian press, which voiced the general feeling which was noticeable everywhere that, now that Count Apponyi had come, the solution would be found. By the irony of circumstances, Count Apponyi, who has never yet been Minister-President of Hungary, was proposed for this office on this occasion by his consistent and most bitter political opponents, the Social-Democrats—a striking testimony to their belief in his honesty and patriotism—and rejected by the Christian National Block, of whose policy he had been the accepted life-long exponent. Working solely for what he believed to be the interests of his country, Count Apponyi banished all personal feeling and it was his influence used on every party that more than anything else enabled M. Huszar to amalgamate the various resisting elements.

Admiral Horthy not only in every particular carried out the assurances that he gave me on the occasion of my first interview with him, but ever since his arrival with his troops in Budapest on the day the Roumanians left, he showed himself the leader of an army which is really national and a servant of the State, and used his full influence, at the moment greater than that of any man in the country, to make all Hungarians see that the only possible course for Hungary is to meet the wishes of the Allies. The extraordinary smoothness and absence of disorder which marked the departure of the Roumanians and the entrance of the Hungarians was due very largely to the arrangements carefully worked out by the Inter-Allied Mission of Generals and Admiral Troubridge with Admiral Horthy's staff, but most of all to the complete hold which Admiral Horthy had over the forces under his command . . .

The Government as now constituted is really representative of Hungarian opinion—in fact the left wing is proportionately more strongly represented in the Cabinet than its power in the country justifies—but the complete realization of the necessity for peace and the preliminary necessity to meet the wishes of the Allies had made possible the fusion, temporary though it be, of political opposites, the thought of which six weeks ago would have aroused utter incredulity in the minds of nearly every Hungarian.

I should like to testify to the extraordinary respect and attention which was paid to me personally by all the Hungarians, as well as by their Press. Even those who were hardest to convince and most profoundly disagreed with the object for which I was sent to Budapest, were agreed that my Mission served no personal end but was simply carrying out its duty as impartially as it could, and I received the most loyal assistance from nearly everyone.

I am also much indebted to the support and assistance of Admiral Troubridge and of the Inter-Allied Mission of Generals. I not only have to thank them for their great and ready help in all personal and departmental difficulties, but also for the fact that their influence was directed throughout to support my mission and to convince the Hungarians that the Allies were completely in unison.

But the real reason why my mission achieved its object was because the Hungarians themselves wished it to do so. During the time I spent at Budapest I heard the views of Hungarians of every shade of opinion, stated, I must admit, with great moderation. They realize that though they can claim, with justice, to be a great and civilized race, they allowed their foreign policy to be controlled in another, and to them a foreign capital, and largely by reason of that now find themselves deprived of large territories where, whatever their political behaviour towards their non-Magyar fellow nationals, they had built up a culture and a civilization, which it is difficult to deny, stands far higher than that of the neighbouring States, whose conduct has been in many respects deplorable.

They recognise, I think, the broad justice of the inclusion of peoples of one common stock in one State, but they feel that the Allies have, inevitably perhaps but unfortunately for Hungary, only heard one side of the case and have, in doubtful instances, naturally given the benefit to those who fought on their side. Moreover, the Hungarians plead for consideration of geographical and economic, as well as of purely national, factors.

The Allies certainly intend to be as just to their late enemies as to themselves, and to see that the small States, aggrandised through the war, do not, by abuse and oppression, cause the world to feel that the result of the war has after all only been to substitute one unrighteous system for another and to sow the seeds of inevitable future conflicts. It is because my experience in Hungary makes me feel that there is a serious danger of this occurring and being aggravated by a rupture of old economic ties and commercial relations, which affect the private citizen far more intimately than great political changes, that I venture to close my report with some observations on what is happening on the borders of Hungary and on the position of that country in general.

It is impossible to see a higher civilisation hopelessly mishandled by those who are still learners in the art of Government, without some sympathy for the victims and without some compunction for one's own share in what is happening. For instance, it seems unnecessary and uncivilised, and, I think, illegal, for the Roumanians to call for an oath of allegiance from university professors whose town and University have not yet been definitely handed over to them. But this is what the Roumanians did in the University of Kolosvar in May last. The professors very rightly said that they were still Hungarian subjects and could not consider themselves released from their duties as such until the Peace Treaty had definitely allocated Kolosvar to Roumania. The Roumanian answer was to turn the professors out of their posts, out of their houses, and to force them to work as labourers, to keep body and soul together. One distinguished Professor of Geography, who has a world wide reputation, was forced to hoe potatoes for a living and he gave his lectures to four pupils who hoed the rows on each side of him. He was then arrested, put in prison and made to clean the latrines. He was finally allowed to leave with his family in a cattle truck, but at the sacrifice of his personal possessions and of the fruits of his whole scientific life.

Another distinguished professor, over 70 years of age and an invalid, was arrested on an unfounded charge of Bolshevism, beaten, and put in prison, where he still remains.

Officers of the Hungarian army had been carried off in numbers for enquiry as to their behaviour during the Communist regime, and are confined in filthy barracks, doing manual work, under-fed, unpaid, with no clothes save those they have on, cut off from all outside communication. And so it goes on.

It is difficult to believe that the cause of Roumania is helped by this sort of thing.

In the territories occupied by the Serb-Croat-Slovene troops, abuses of all sorts are committed and it is credibly reported that the country is being stripped bare where it is being evacuated. I have already reported the instance of the unfortunate landowner who was shot dead with his small child and whose wife was seriously injured, simply because they happened to live in a house the contents of which appealed to the covetousness of the Serbian soldiers. In justice to the Serbians it must be added that the complaints about such abuses are directed far less against the authorities and forces of the old kingdom than against the new and imperfectly disciplined livies from the Serb, Croat and Slovene population of the absorbed territories.

In the district in the occupation of the Czechs there is a house of the Archduke Joseph. It is true that he is an Archduke and a Habsburg, but he cannot help either of these things, and he paid for this home 24 years ago out of his private funds and has spent the greater part of his life there. The Czechs continue to take away his private property in the house and are now proposing to sell by auction the wedding dress of his wife—a gift from the Empress Elizabeth whose wedding dress it had also been—and all her private family letters. The Church lands of the Archbishopric of Esztergom, now in Czecho-Slovakia, have been taken from Hungarian ecclesiastical authorities, and the educational and humanitarian institution which existed on the revenues of those properties have been ruined.

This form of ignoble persecution is unfortunately all too typical of the Allies whom we have made independent States.

It is for these and similar reasons that I have urged that Inter-Allied Commissions should be sent to see what is really happening in these lands which may eventually fall definitely to the lot of Roumania, Serbia, or Czecho-Slovakia, but are now suffering the fate of a village in debatable ground in Macedonia. It might be argued that the Allies cannot insist on sending a Commission into regions which have not been definitely assigned to those countries, but I venture to observe that where there is evidence that the authorities of those countries are anticipating and abusing the rights which the final Treaty of Peace may give them, the Allies owe it to themselves to see that their good name is not brought into disrepute. The danger of this is, unfortunately, serious and growing. In fact in my humble opinion there should be a Central High Commission for all these countries with real powers of inspection, and full authority to check abuses and outrages . . .

. . . It would be easy to multiply instances of the selfish and callous policy pursued by these newly created States, but what I wish to bring out is that the final result will inevitably be that the Great Powers, not only for humanity, but in order to prevent the recurrence of chaos in Europe, will be obliged to provide remedies out of their own resources at an infinitely greater cost and when bitter experience has so driven home to those who have suffered the futility of trust and confidence in the Allies that no amount of eleventh hour charity will restore that political balance which can alone be a guarantee for the peace of Europe.

[In an omitted paragraph, Sir George pleaded for creating an international commission to take charge of the water-control system of Hungary.]

In conclusion, I venture to submit, on the direct experience that I have now been privileged to have of Hungary and to some extent of Austria, that any idea of immediate payments on account of reparation from those countries must be abandoned. On the contrary, if we are not to condemn millions of human beings to misery and starvation, if we are not to be responsible for a catastrophe almost as great, and in its ultimate consequences possibly even greater, than the war itself, so far from exacting reparation, we have to find funds to keep Austria and Hungary alive . . .

Moreover, if the two countries feel that they have been able, through the help of the Allies, to avert the complete breakdown of their material and economic existence and to gain a foothold on the arduous path of recontruction, much will be done to diminish the likelihood of Austria seeking union with Germany as her one remaining chance of salvation, and to strengthen the Hungarians in their resolve to abjure for ever the German connection against which they have fretted for so many generations and from which they hope that they have now been finally released.

I can only say that . . . the neighboring States, our present Allies, need firm supervision and guidance to make them fit to enjoy the inheritance which has fallen to them through our sacrifice and effort.

DOCUMENT 44

Address of the President of the Hungarian Peace Delegation, Count Apponyi, to the Supreme Council, January 16, 1920 [1]

Gentlemen,

Allow me to repeat my thanks for the opportunity you have afforded us of expounding our point of view. What I really desired was to have a verbal discussion, because this is in my opinion the only way to an understanding and a clear comprehension of the complicated questions before us. The Supreme Council has, however, already fixed its intentions in this matter, and it is for me to bow to this decision. I accept the position in which I am placed and in order not to take up too much of your time I will straightway proceed to the object of my address.

In our eyes the present day differs from yesterday by the official knowledge of the peace-conditions we have gained since then. I am aware of the awful weight of responsibility falling to my share in this moment when the first word is to be pronounced on the part of Hungary as regards these conditions. I do not hesitate, however, openly to declare that the conditions of peace, as you have had the goodness to present them to us, are such as can not, without essential modifications, be accepted. I see clearly the dangers and difficulties likely to proceed from a refusal to sign the peace. Yet, should Hungary be placed in a position when she must choose between the acceptance or refusal of this peace, then, as a matter of fact, her choice lies in the question: should she commit suicide simply in order to escape a natural death?

Happily we are not yet reduced to this. You have called upon us to make our observations. Some of these we have ventured to hand in before receiving the conditions of peace. We feel sure that these observations already handed in and those to be presented hereafter will be subjected by you to the earnest and conscientious examination demanded by the gravity of the situation. And in this manner we hope to convince you. We hope this the more as it is not our intention either to-day or in the future to parade our sentiments or to adopt the exclusive standpoint of those interests which to defend is our task. We seek for a common basis on which we may achieve a mutual understanding. And, Gentlemen, this common basis we have already found in the great

[1] *The Hungarian Peace Negotiations,* I, 310 ff.

principle of international justice and the liberty of the peoples, so often proclaimed by the Allied Powers, and in the great common interest of peace, stability and the reconstruction of Europe.

It is from the point of view of these principles and these interests we will examine the conditions of the peace offered us.

In the first place we cannot conceal our astonishment at the extreme severity of the conditions of peace. This astonishment can easily be explained.

The conditions of the peace treaties contracted with the other belligerent nations, with Germany, Austria and Bulgaria, were certainly also severe. But not one of these contained such significant territorial changes inevitably affecting the national life, as those we are called upon to accept.

It is a case of Hungary losing two-thirds of her territory and almost two-thirds of her population, and of the remaining Hungary being deprived of almost every condition of her economic development. For this unfortunate country, i.e. the centre of the country, severed from its peripheries, would be deprived of the greatest part of its coal-ore-and saltmines; of its timber for building, its oil and natural gas-springs, a great part of its labour; it would be deprived of its Alpine pastures, which nourished the stock of cattle; this unfortunate centre of the country would be deprived of all sources and instruments of economic development at the very moment in which it is required to enhance its production. Faced by a position so difficult and so peculiar we inquire, which of the principles and interests quoted above required this special severity towards Hungary.

It is from the point of view of these great ideas and interests I wish now, as briefly as possible, to examine the question.

Can it be meant as a sentence passed against Hungary?

You, Gentlemen, whom victory has placed in the tribunal, you have pronounced guilty your former enemies, the Central Powers, and have decreed that the burden of the war should be cast upon those responsible for it. So be it; but in that case, I think, in dividing the burden, the measure of guilt should decide the proportion. Hungary being punished by the most severe conditions, threatening her very existence, one would think that of all nations she was the guiltiest. Gentlemen! Not entering into an elaborate discussion of this question—for the documents we shall hand in will do so—I must declare that such a sentence cannot be pronounced of a nation, which was, at the moment of war breaking out, not in full possession of its independence and was at most capable of exercising some degree of influence on the affairs of the Austro-Hungarian monarchy, an influence used, as is proved by documents lately come to light, to disapprove those steps which must of a certainty lead to war.

I cannot believe it is a sentence we are confronted by, for the pronouncing of a sentence would imply a preliminary process in which the parties would be given a hearing under equal circumstances, and having equal right to assert their arguments. Hungary, however, has till now been granted no hearing. It is therefore impossible, that the conditions of peace should have the character of a judgment delivered.

Or is it a question of administering the principle of international justice in a manner calculated to create, instead of polyglot states such as Hungary was, new States, settling the territorial differences between the different nationalities in a more equitable manner, ensuring their liberty more effectively? On reviewing facts I am constrained to doubt the present solution being brought about by such considerations.

In the first place, 35% of the 11,000,000 souls to be severed from Hungary are Hungarians, which means three and a half millions, even if we should take as basis the computation conforming least with our interest. The peace conditions sever, besides, one and a quarter of a million of Germans which, added to the percent of Hungarians, means 45%. These will not only not be benefited by the new application of the racial principle but will, on the contrary, suffer by it. Even allowing, what I am far from acknowledging, that this application of the nationality principle creates a situation more advantageous for the remaining 55% than was their portion in historic Hungary, still, this principle could not be applied to what is almost a half of the population to be severed, or, if applied, only in a contrary sense.

According to my view of the case if a principle be applied at all, it should be applied equally to all those who are affected by the orderings of the treaty.

But let us go on, and view the states aggrandised on the ruins of Hungary. We can asseverate that from a racial point of view they will be split into parts to the same degree, or even a higher degree, than Hungary formerly was.

I do not wish, Gentlemen, to fatigue you by an enumeration of facts which will certainly be contained in the documents we shall hand in on this question. Meanwhile, till you should have had time to get acquainted with these documents, I beg you to accept my statements, in order to follow the deductions I hope to make before you now.

I cannot see that the racial principle, the principle of national unity, would gain by the process of dismemberment. Only one consequence will evidently follow, which I beg leave to mention without meaning offence to anyone. I only wish to point out the fact that the consequence would be the transference of national hegemony to races at present mostly occupying a lower grade of culture.

To prove the truth of my words I would quote a few figures.

Among the Hungarians the number of those knowing to read and write touches on 80%; among the Germans of Hungary 82%; among the Roumanians 33%; among the Serbs 59 and some tenths, almost 60%.

On turning to the higher grades of society and considering those who have studied at the gymnasiums and passed the examination corresponding to the "baccalaureat" in France we shall find that the proportional number of

Hungarians among these who have finished these studies or passed an examination equivalent is 84%, though the Hungarians form only 54.5% of the total population; the proportion of Roumanians among those who completed these studies is 4%, whereas they form 16% of the total population; the Serbs 1% whereas their number in proportion to the total population is 25%.

I repeat that my remark is not made with the intention of affronting anyone. The situation is explained by the simple fact that these neighbouring people, owing to their unfortunate history, became members of the family of civilised nations later than we did. The fact, however, is there, and is undeniable. I should imagine that the transference of national hegemony to an inferior grade of civilisation could not be a matter of indifference to the great cultural interests of humanity. We have proofs of this already. Our neighbours desirous of appropriating part of our territories have actually obtained power over them at least a year ago; according to the Armistice Treaty they had the right of military occupation in these territories, but they appropriated the whole apparatus of government. The consequences are already visible. We will demonstrate in special notes what destruction has been worked to institutions of cultural value in one year. You will see from these notes, Gentlemen, how our two universities, answering the highest requirements of modern science, that of Kolozsvar, an ancient stronghold of Hungarian culture and the University of Pozsony, of recent foundation have both been ruined. The professors have been driven away and I wish you had means to know, who have been put in their places. I call upon you to send committees consisting of scholars and scientists to inquire into the true position of things so as to be able to make comparisons. Impossible that these universities and the faculties, each having a history of their own, could be replaced by anything of the same value. These great intellectual edifices cannot be replaced from one day to the other.

Circumstances are similar in the whole apparatus of administration, and among every grade of teachers.

Only in the territory occupied by the Roumanians more than two hundred thousands of children are growing up in the streets, because of a deficiency of teachers, as the Hungarian teachers have been ejected and the Roumanians are not capable of replacing them.

Gentlemen! From the point of view of the great interests of humanity I think the fact of national hegemony falling into the hands of races who, while offering the best hopes for the future, yet are to-day on a low level of civilisation, can be looked upon neither with indifference nor with satisfaction.

We have seen that the severity which punishes Hungary cannot proceed from the fact of judgment.

We have seen that the nationality principle would gain nothing from this solution.

Then perhaps this decision has been arrived at in the name of the liberty of the nations?

The starting point in this case would seem to be the supposition that the allogeneous races of Hungary would rather belong to a state upheld by a kindred race than to Hungary, where the hegemony of the Hungarians asserts itself.

This is, however, only a supposition; and, since we have now embraced the path of suppositions, I beg to observe that the same supposition can, in a contrary sense, be applied to the 45% of Hungarians and Germans now about to be attached to a new state, and of whom it is to be supposed that they would prefer to remain members of the Hungarian State. This argumentation leads to nothing but a placing of the advantages on the other side. But why should we take mere surmises to be the basis of our reasoning? Why should our starting point be a supposition when there are means at our disposal of ascertaining the truth, a simple and only way to that end, the use of which we loudly demand as being the only hope of seeing clearly in this matter. And this means is: a plebiscite.

In the name of the great principle so happily phrased by President Wilson, namely that no group of people, no population may be transferred from one State to the other without being first consulted,—as though they were a herd of cattle with no will of their own,—in the name of this great principle, an axiom of good sense and public morals, we request, we demand a plebiscite on those parts of Hungary that are now on the point of being severed from us. I declare we are willing to bow to the decision of a plebiscite whatever it should be. Of course we demand it should be held in conditions ensuring the freedom of the vote.

The plebiscite is all the more necessary as the National Assembly, to whom belongs the final decision in the matter of the Conditions of Peace will be incomplete. The inhabitants of the occupied territories will not be represented. No Government or National Assembly can be morally or legally authorised to settle the fate of those who are not even represented within that body. The Conditions of Peace themselves contain expressions calculated to raise difficulties. "Hungary renounces, so far as she is concerned" these are about the words of the Treaty of Peace. We should truly not consider ourselves authorised to dispose in matters either morally or legally binding that part of the population which will not be represented at the National Assembly.

I repeat, this is the principal request we have to submit to the Peace Conference.

If the arguments we are able to bring up in favour of our former territory, of historic Hungary, should not appear reasonable in your eyes or not sufficiently conclusive, we would suggest the consulting of the interested people themselves. We are ready in advance to submit to their verdict.

And if this be our standpoint, and if our enemies should not have the courage to submit their demands and aspirations to the popular sentence: in whose favour, I ask, may the supposition mentioned above incline?

There is still another point of view from which the peoples right of self-determination should be considered. A statement might be hasarded as to the rights of minority being more effectually assured on the territories of the new States than they were in Hungary.

I do not, on this occasion, wish to plead the case brought against Hungary relative to the alleged oppression of the non-Hungarian races. I will confine my words to declaring myself well pleased should our Hungarian brethren on the territories torn from our country enjoy the same rights and facilities as the non-Hungarian citizens of Hungary enjoyed.

We shall have occasion to return to this question. At the present moment I am not in the position to speak of this for one thing: because the necessary documents are not now at my disposal. But I am ready at any time for a comprehensive discussion on the matter. I may, however, already declare that had the nationalist policy of the one time Hungary been even worse than it was stated to be by our bitterest enemies, it was undoubtedly more favourable than the situation created by our neighbours and their troops on the occupied territories.

We will, Gentlemen, submit to you a whole series of papers relating more especially to recent events in Transylvania. We have strictly examined all notices coming to us in this matter; and though their authenticity is verified by the leading men of the three Christian churches of Transylvania: the Roman Catholic, the Calvinist and the Unitarian, we cannot demand our words to be accepted being, as they are, in full opposition to declarations coming from other quarters. We beg of you, however, to examine events on the spot, to send a committee of inquiry to the place of action before the final decision is arrived at, in order to obtain evidence as to the events happening on the aforesaid territory.

We are always the ones, Gentlemen, to demand that the darkness, obscuring the position of affairs should be dispelled, we are always the ones who ask for no other decision than what is based on a clear appreciation of the question. And, in the extreme case of territorial changements being forced upon us, we further beg the minorities right should be accorded a more efficacious and more clearly defined protection than are afforded by the Conditions of Peace handed to us. The projected assurances are, in our conviction, insufficient. We require more powerful assurances which we are quite ready ourselves to accord to the non-Hungarian population left to Hungary. In this matter we have come to a full understanding with their representatives. We believe, however, that it will be difficult to obtain more efficacious guarantees from the part of our neighbours, whose zealous care for the interests of their race is greater than ours. Recent experience compels us to expect tenacious opposition. In the matter of the withdrawal of the Roumanian Army of Occupation to the line of demarcation,—repeatedly requested by us and made a condition by our Government of sending a peace delegation to Paris,—the Allied Powers took such determined steps with the Roumanian Government as made it seem impossible that the demand of the Allied Powers should be disregarded. And yet that is precisely what happened. You will then understand, Gentlemen, the anxiety we feel for our brethren should they be subjected to this alien rule.

Having passed in review the whole series of principles, the principles of international justice, of nationality and of the liberty of the peoples, and not having found any application of these principles capable of throwing light on the motives of the Conditions of Peace offered us, I ask myself, were they then inspired by the great interests mentioned by me at the commencement of this expose, the interests of peace and stability and the reconstruction of Europe?

Gentlemen, the Hungarian problem is not so insignificant a portion of the general problem as bare statistics would have it seem.

The territory which belonged to Hungary, and which legally still belongs to her, for centuries played an extremely important part in preserving the peace and security of Europe, especially Central-Europe. The centuries preceding the Hungarian Conquest and the conversion of the Hungarians to the Christian faith were a period of trouble and unrest in that part of the world. Central-Europe was the battlefield of divers barbaric peoples. Security has only been established since the Hungarian line of defence was formed. For the sake of peace and stability it is most important that the whirl-pool of Eastern-Europe should not be suffered to extend, spreading unrest to the very heart of Europe. Historical evolution was impeded on the Balkan by Turkish conquest and the balance has not yet been reestablished. May the Heavens grant a speedy readjustment. But it is of signal importance that the unrest so often disturbing the peace of Europe, driving us repeatedly to the very threshold of war, should not be allowed to spread.

Historic Hungary fulfilled the duty of maintaining a State of balance and security, thus insuring the peace of Europe from imminent danger menacing from the East. This mission she fulfilled for ten centuries, qualified thereto by her organic unity. Allow me to quote the words of the great French geographer, Elisé Reclus, declaring this country to possess a geographical unity unrivalled in Europe. Its river and valley system, converging from the peripheries to the centre of the country, forms a unit governable only by a unified power. The economic interdependence of its parts is also perfect, the centre forming a powerful economic concern and the peripheries producing all the material necessary for economic progress.

Historic Hungary then forms a natural geographic and economic unit such as stands alone in Europe. Within its territories no natural boundaries can be drawn, and not one single part can be severed without the other parts suffering from it. This is the cause of their unity having been preserved by history for the length of ten centuries. You may refuse to recognise history as a principle in the building up of a juridical construction, but you cannot refuse her as a witness when she repeats the same evidence for ten centuries. It is no chance, it is the voice of nature speaking here. Hungary was in possession of every condition of organic unity with the exception of one: racial unity. But the states to be built up on the ruins of Hungary—according to the terms of the Treaty—will also lack racial unity, the one condition of unity missing in Hungary—nor, I may add, will they possess any other. The new states to be formed would cut through the natural geographical boundaries, would impede the most useful internal migration impelling the worker towards the more favourable offers of labour; would snap the thread of tradition binding in one common mentality those who have lived together for centuries, who have seen the same reverses, the same glory, the same progress and the same sufferings. Is not our fear then justified that instead of this well-tried pillar of stability seats of a new unrest will come into being? For we must not blind ourselves with illusions, these new state formations would be undermined by irredentism of a much more dangerous form than that reported by some to have been rife in Hungary, which did in fact exist in Hungary among certain parts of the educated classes but never permeated the great masses of the people. The new state formations, however, would be undermined by the irredentism of nations feeling not only the rule of a foreign power but also the hegemony of a nation of a civilisation inferior to their own. Here we must point to an organic impossibility: we may conceive the possibility of a national minority possessed of a higher standard of culture wielding a hegemony in the face of a majority of an inferior standard, but that a minority, or very small majority, whose cultural development has reached a lower level only, should be able to establish a hegemony, to attain a voluntary acknowledgement of their supremacy and a moral assimilation of a nationality of a culture superior to their own: this, Gentlemen, is organically impossible.

We are often accused of the intention of subversing by force any settlement of the question contrary to our desires. All such adventurous projects are far from us, Gentlemen. We put our hopes in justice, and the moral force of those principles on which we rest our arguments and what we may not be able to attain in the present we will expect from the peaceable methods of the League of Nations, one of whose tasks it will be to right such parts of the international position as menace the maintenance of peace. I make this declaration lest you might find in my words a menace as puerile as rain. But I also declare, Gentlemen, that with such artificial enactments as are contained in the Conditions of Peace the establishment of a peaceful political situation in this much-suffered part of Europe, so important from the point of view of general peace, is hardly possible. Only the stability of this territory is capable of guarding Central-Europe from dangers constantly menacing it from the East.

Europe is in need of economic reconstruction. Economic development will be, however, certainly frustrated by the new formations. I have shown how this circumstance will necessarily be brought about in the remaining Hungary. But the situation will be similar on the parts severed for the simple reason that they will be subjected to a lower standard of culture, and that, severed from the other parts of this organic unit in connection with which they could flourish again, they are doomed to stagnation or, probably, to decay.

Europe has need of social peace. You are better able to judge the dangers menacing this peace. You know better than myself how the consequences of the war have troubled and thrown off their balance the popular mind and the conditions of economic life. From past sad experience we know how the success of the subversive elements was due to the factors undermining the moral force of society, to everything calculated to enfeeble national feeling and to bring about the misery caused by lack of labour. If in this quarter of Europe, in near neighbourhood to the still burning fire of Bolshevism, the conditions of labour are made heavier, and the possibility of recommencing work impeded, the danger is fed which menaces social peace. Barriers are powerless to combat epidemics, especially moral epidemics.

Against all these fine theories you may bring up, as a factor clinching the argument, victory, and the rights of the victors. We are realistic enough in political matters to give due consideration to this factor. We are aware of our debt due to victory, and are ready to pay the ransom of our defeat. But can this be the one principle of reconstruction? Can violence be the sole foundation of the edifice? Can material violence be the single upholder of this construction, ready to collapse before its building is brought to a close? In this case the future of Europe were sad indeed. Gentlemen, we cannot believe this to be the mind of the victorious Nations. We do not find these principles in those declarations in which you advanced the ideas for whose victory you fought, and in which you defined the objects of the war.

We repeat, we cannot believe this to be the mentality of the great victorious nations. Pardon me if, beyond France, beyond England, beyond Italy, to mention only the victorious nations of Europe, I evoke the vision of that other France, always the vanguard of generous endeavour and the mouthpiece of great ideas; and of that other England, the mother of every political liberty, of that other Italy, cradle of the Renaissance, of the arts and of intellectual development. And if I acknowledge without murmuring the victor's right, to this other France, England and Italy I bow in gratitude, voluntarily accepting them as our masters and educators. Allow me, Gentlemen, to advise: do not endanger this great moral influence to which you have every right by insisting too much on the note of superior force, which is yours to-day, but is subject to change; guard in its fulness this, the finest part of your inheritance.

In spite of the difficulties besetting our path, in spite of misunderstanding and every hindrance some seek to pile up in our way, we have broached with confidence the road opened to us at last to enable us to take part in the work of peace; and this we do in absolute singleness of purpose. We believe in the sincerity of the principles declared by you. We should be doing you an injury should we think otherwise. We believe in the power of the moral factors with which we identify our cause, and I wish you, Gentlemen, that the glory of victorious arms should be surpassed by the glory of creating a peace worthy to be presented by you to the whole of humanity.

I have only a few more words to say, Gentlemen!

You will recognise the impossibility of my discussing the peace, offered us, in detail. I have spoken of the question of territory only, this question encompassing all the rest. I should, however, like to draw your attention to a few other points, the solving of which I consider especially urgent.

First of all we are faced by a matter of humanity, the question of the prisoners of war.

The terms of the conditions of peace make the return of the prisoners of war follow on the ratifying of peace. I beg you, Gentlemen, not to adhere to a formality which may cause suffering to so many innocent families.

In the cause of the unhappy prisoners of war detained in Siberia we have presented a special plea to the Supreme Council. In settling this matter I would appeal to your feelings of humanity; feelings which, even in time of war, must stand superior to policy. There is one more remark I wish to make regarding the financial clauses.

I do not think the conditions of peace sufficiently take into consideration the special position Hungary finds herself in. Hungary had to live through two revolutions, four months of the ragings of Bolshevism and several months of the Roumanian occupation. Under the circumstances it is impossible for us to carry out the financial and economical clauses imposed by the Treaty of Peace. Should the credit allowed us by the citizens of the victorious powers be made payable in the moment of signing the Peace, as is expressed in the conditions, this would involve insolvency, bankruptcy, the effects of which would inevitably be felt by the victorious nations. I admit, we have many creditors in your countries. The debts will be paid if we be granted time, but will not be capable of being refunded, should instant payment be demanded of us.

It is further demanded of us—and this goes to prove how much more expedient it would have been to grant us a previous hearing—it is demanded that we supply Austria with iron ore. As we ourselves are depending on the import of ore, we are incapable of fulfilling this condition.

The situation is the same in the matter of wood for building.

These are details which we would beg you to examine with the good will already promised us by your official representatives.

Before closing my words I express my gratitude to you, Gentlemen, for according me this opportunity of stating my point of view by word of mouth, and also for the considerate and persevering attention with which you have honoured me.

DOCUMENT 45

Declaration of the Conference of Ambassadors regarding the Restoration of the Habsburg Dynasty, February 2, 1920.[1]

TO THE PRESIDENT OF THE HUNGARIAN DELEGATION

Paris, February 2, 1920.

Sir:

I have the honour to inform you that the Conference of Ambassadors, have, in their sitting of the 2nd February accepted the following declaration.

The Principal Allied and Associated Powers consider it their duty to pronounce a formal denial of the rumours that are spread and are liable to lead public opinion astray; they being represented as ready to recognise or to favour the reëstablishment of the Habsburg dynasty on the Hungarian throne. The Principal Allied and Associated Powers consider that the restoration of a dynasty personifying, in the eyes of their subjects, a system of oppression and domination of other races, in alliance with Germany, would not be compatible with the principles for which they fought nor with the results the war has allowed them to achieve in the liberation of peoples bound hitherto to servitude. It is not the intention, as it cannot be looked upon as the duty of the Principal Allied Powers to interfere in the interior affairs of Hungary or to dictate to the Hungarian people the form of Government or constitution they should adopt; still, the Powers cannot allow the restoration of the Habsburg dynasty to be treated as a matter of interest to the Hungarian Nation alone. They therefore declare in this present that a restoration of this kind would be in contradiction to the fundamental principles of the peace and would be neither acknowledged nor tolerated by them.

I beg you, Sir, to accept the assurance of my high consideration.

A. MILLERAND

[1] *The Hungarian Peace Negotiations,* II, 469. Original French text in *Papers and Documents relating to the Foreign Relations of Hungary,* I, Doc. 114.

DOCUMENT 46

Covering Letter of the Reply of the Allied Powers to the President of the Hungarian Peace Delegation, May 6, 1920 [1]

Sir,

The Allied and Associated Powers have studied with the most scrupulous attention the Notes in which the Hungarian Delegation have set forth their observations on the subject of the Conditions of Peace communicated to them. In their examination they have been animated by the sole desire to come to decisions conforming with justice and those higher interests of which they are the guardians. If the result of this study is not, in its essential features, in accordance with the counter-propositions formulated by the Hungarian Delegation it is because the Powers have found it impossible to adopt the point of view taken by that Delegation.

The Allied and Associated Powers, while expressing their hope that the Hungary of the future will become an element of stability and peace cannot, indeed, as far as they are concerned, forget the portion of responsibility falling to Hungary as regards to the outbreak of the world-war and, in general, as to the imperialistic policy pursued by the Dual Monarchy.

The stipulations contained in the Conditions of Peace handed to them have been subjected to a minute criticism by the Hungarian Delegation. The replies to these observations the Principal Allied and Associated Powers have thought needful to make are here subjoined. If the arguments raised in the Notes presented by you to the Conference have not been taken up point for point to be refuted it is not because they are considered well-founded; the silence of the Allied and Associated Powers must not in any case be interpreted as approval. It must be clearly understood that an absence of reply is in no wise equivalent to an adherence to the thesis defended by you.

In particular the observations handed to you do not contain any remark concerning the numerous Memorials presented by the Hungarian Delegation relating to the frontiers of Hungary. They do not answer the propositions formulated in them on the subject of the institution of a plebiscite on the territories whose attribution to other States has been decided by the Powers. It is not without ripe reflection that the Allied and Associated Powers

---

[1] *The Hungarian Peace Negotiations*, II, 545 ff. Original French text in *Papers and Documents relating to the Foreign Relations of Hungary*, I, Doc. 265.

have adopted the standpoint of not modifying any point of the territorial clauses contained in the conditions of Peace. In coming to this resolution they have been guided by the consideration that any modification of the frontiers fixed by them would lead to inconveniences graver than those proclaimed by the Hungarian Delegation. The study to which they have devoted themselves have for the rest done nothing but confirm the conclusions previously arrived at by the Allied and Associated Powers on the examination of the documents of every kind liable to be invoked in support of the Hungarian thesis. The frontiers described in the Conditions of Peace handed to you have been traced on the basis of these conclusions.

The ethnographic conditions in Central Europe are such that it is indeed impossible for the political frontiers in their total extent to coincide with the ethnical frontiers. It follows from this—and the Allied and Associated Powers have not resigned themselves without regret to this necessity—that certain isles of Magyar population will pass under the sovereignty of another State. But no statement pretending that it would have been better not to modify the former territorial status can be based on this situation. A state of affairs, even when millennial, is not meant to exist when it has been recognised as contrary to justice.

It is true that the Hungarian Delegation argues from the fact that the Conditions of Peace do not provide for a plebiscite anywhere. If the Allied and Associated Powers have thought it unnecessary to have recourse to a popular vote of this nature, it has not been until acquiring the certitude that such a consultation, if carried out with all guarantees of complete sincerity, would not offer a result differing sensibly from those which they have arrived at after a minute study of the ethnographic conditions of Central Europe and of national aspirations. The will of the people was expressed in the October and November of 1918 at the collapse of the Dual Monarchy when the populations, oppressed for so long, united with their Italian, Roumanian, Yougo-Slav and Czecho-Slovak kindred. The events occurring since that epoch constitute so many proofs the more of the sentiments of the nationalities formerly subjected to the Crown of St. Stephen. The tardy measures taken by the Hungarian Government to satisfy the need felt by the nationalities for an autonomy is not able to create any illusion; they do not change at all the essentials of historic truth: notably, that during long years all the efforts of Hungarian policy were directed to stifling the voice of the ethnical minorities.

True to the spirit by which they were inspired in tracing the frontiers fixed by the Treaty the Allied and Associated Powers have nevertheless considered the case of the frontiers thus traced not corresponding precisely with the ethnical or economic requirements. An inquest held on the spot may, perhaps, make apparent the necessity of a displacement of the limits provided by the Treaty in certain parts. Such an inquest could not be actually pursued without indefinitely retarding the conclusion of a peace desired by the whole of Europe. But when the Delimitation Commission will have commenced activity, should they find that the provisions of the Treaty in some spot, as is stated above, create an injustice which it would be to general interest to efface it shall be allowable to them to address a report on this subject to the Council of the League of Nations. In this case the Allied and Associated Powers accept that the Council of the League may, under the same circumstances, at the request of one of the parties concerned, offer their services for an amicable rectification of the original demarcation at the passages where a modification has been judged desirable by a Delimitation Commission. The Allied and Associated Powers are confident that this proceeding will furnish a convenient method for correcting all injustice in the demarcation of the frontiers against which objections not unfounded can be raised.

In the case of Ruthenia the Principal Allied and Associated Powers have not made their decision without taking full account of the difficulties to be encountered. The union between Ruthenia and Czecho-Slovakia has been recognised by them in a Treaty with the last-mentioned State which contains special guarantees for the Autonomy of the Ruthenians. They have come to an agreement with Czecho-Slovakia that the provisions of this Treaty, inasmuch as they affect the ethnical, religious or lingual minorities should be guaranteed by the League of Nations. The Allied and Associated Powers believe that the Treaty with the Czecho-Slovak State signed by them provides the population of the autonomous province of Ruthenia with the means of making their desires publicly known. They will not fail to accord the most serious attention to the wishes to be formulated in the future by this population. For the rest, the pact of the League of Nations confers on every member of the Council of the League the right to draw the attention of the signatories of the Treaty concluded September 10, 1919, at Saint-Germain-en-Laye between the Principal Allies and Associated Powers and the Czecho-Slovak State to all questions relating to Ruthenia which shall deserve their examination.

Under these conditions the Powers consider the interests of the border population to be fully safeguarded. As to the isles of Magyar population passing under another sovereignty, the Treaties for the protection of minorities already signed by Roumania and the Serb-Croat-Slovene State and ratified by Czecho-Slovakia guarantee their entire safeguarding.

The Allied and Associated Powers register with satisfaction the adherence evinced by the Hungarian Delegation to the principles which are the basis of the Pact of the League of Nations. The League does not only protect the rights of all the signatories of the Treaty; it also institutes the organism with the help of which it will be made possible to intervene placably and by legal measures for all the arrangements that, in the regulation of the Peace, will be made necessary by novel circumstances. The loyalty with which Hungary shall acquit herself of the obligations imposed on her by the Treaty will serve to bring nearer the time at which she may be received into the League itself.

It has seemed impossible for the Governments of the Allied and Associated Powers to advance any further. The powers conferred on the Delimitation Commissions in regard to the territorial clauses, the touches given to different articles of the Treaty, regarding which the details are contained in the observations handed to you at the same time as this letter, mark the extreme limit of their concessions. The Conditions of Peace handed to you this day are, therefore, definitive.

Consequently the Allied and Associated Powers expect a declaration from the Hungarian Delegation within ten days counting from the date of the present communication giving them to understand that they are authorized to sign the Treaty as it stands. Measures will then be taken for proceeding to this signature.

I beg you, Sir, to accept the assurance of my highest consideration.

A. MILLERAND.

DOCUMENT 47

Letter from the President of the Hungarian Peace Delegation, Count Apponyi, to the President of the Supreme Council, M. Millerand, May 16, 1920 [1]

Sir,

The Supreme Council of the Allied and Associated Powers have with the date of May 6, 1920, conveyed to the Peace Delegation of Hungary their reply to the observations communicated to them by that Delegation on the subject of the Conditions of Peace proposed to Hungary as well as the definitive text of the Treaty; they have at the same time requested the said Delegation to declare within ten days whether they are authorised to sign the Treaty as it stands.

For the reasons set forth below the Hungarian Delegation do not consider they are able to assume the responsibility involved in an answer in the affirmative.

First and foremost we have the honour to remind you of the oral declaration made in the name of the Delegation by its President the day after the handing over of the Conditions of Peace at the sitting of the Supreme Council January 16, 1920. This is the text:

"I am aware of the awful weight of responsibility falling to my share in this moment when the first word is to be pronounced on the part of Hungary as regards these conditions. I do not hesitate, however, openly to declare that the conditions of peace, as you have had the goodness to present them to us, are such as can not, without essential modifications, be accepted."

Now the definitive text does not contain any essential modification of those presented to us in the month of January.

But we do not confine ourselves to this negative declaration. In the course of the same *exposé* the President of the Delegation indicated the solution of the territorial problem enjoined on us by the Treaty which would have shifted this problem on grounds we thought would be common grounds for all and conform to the principles proclaimed by the Allied Powers: namely to that imprescriptible right of the people of disposing of themselves. It was not Hungary's historical right to her ancient territory that we invoked: not that that right seemed to us debatable; not that we did not protest with all

[1] *The Hungarian Peace Negotiations*, II, 524–25.

the energy of our being against all assertions designating our millennial possession of that territory as an injustice; but it was the rights of the population interested that we insisted on, claiming a plebiscite for them as a means of asserting this right. We adopted this line of conduct as we wished to evade all possibility of a controversy, by indicating as a basis for the decisions to be taken a principle in itself indisputable and an action guaranteed to be impartial, for we at the same time declared our readiness to submit to the decisions the populations in question should arrive at by means of a plebiscite held amidst all guarantees of liberty of the vote. By acting in this manner we at the same time gave a positive disclaimer to the eternal accusation as to the oppression of the non-Magyar nationalities, constituting the very same people we were alleged to have oppressed as judges of the litigation. We it was who have proposed, we who have claimed and we who still claim this judgment which must be the best informed, the most competent, and certainly the most severe; it was our adversaries who wished to evade it; and by this sole fact, so it seems to us, the case is judged.

To our most painful surprise the Allied Powers refuse, in our case, the application of the principle proclaimed by them; this, however, does not release us from the obligation to remain bound to it. The moral force of this principle is indestructible; it is in no wise allowable for us to abandon it, for the natural right of millions of our citizens, and the question of human dignity are bound up in it. We are told, it is true, that the populations in question have already pronounced themselves in favour of the new ties imposed on them by the Treaty of Peace. But this is an error in fact easy to establish. Nothing of the sort has taken place. We do not think that similar manifestations have been attributed to the Magyars and Germans forming, after all, nearly the half of these populations, and as to the other half: there have been some demonstrations and some meetings which have enunciated decisions in the desired sense but there was no manifestation whatever of a representative character and no meeting authorised to speak in the name of any people whatever as a whole. The populations of the territories thus severed from Hungary would therefore be subjected to an act of constraint we have neither the right nor the power to sanction; and however great the loyalty with which we would fulfil all our obligations resulting from a treaty entered upon, the moral ties which bind us to them will never be broken. We shall never cease to be interested in their fate and if, as we have reason to fear, the persecutions they are suffering from persist in spite of the agreements relating to the protection of minorities which we cannot consider sufficient, we shall never cease to lay their complaints and sufferings before the League of Nations to the day when the nature of things, by pacific action, achieves a victory over the violence done to it. We are grateful for the account taken of some of our observations on economic and financial matters;

what remains of Hungary will be, however, none the less, reduced to desperate economic conditions. The natural outlets of the country are not assured neither in the direction of the Adriatic, the Aegean nor the Black Sea; it remains encumbered with financial obligations impossible to meet unless the Reparation Commission procures us an alleviation of the claims, which we are allowed vaguely to hope without receiving any guarantees concerning it. Even in this point of view nothing authorises us to alter our first opinion. But the decisive fact is the maintenance of the territorial provisions dismembering Hungary and the refusal of the plebiscite we requested for the interested populations in the name of their imprescriptible right to dispose of their own fate.

Under these circumstances our line of action is clearly traced. Not speaking of the injustice it contains towards our country the Treaty of Peace contains a breach of the imprescriptible right of the people, awarded to the new States without having been able to express their will. This is in evident contradiction of the principle of liberty that the Hungarian Delegation, expecting in this to be of one opinion with the Allied Powers, took for the basis of their action. Considered in itself, therefore, this treaty seems to us inacceptable and the Delegation, whose mandate extended only to its examination, do not consider themselves authorised to sign it.

We know, of course, that consideration of a different nature may exercise a decisive influence on the resolution to be taken. We are aware that it is a question of facing calmly and clear-sightedly the general situation of our country and so measuring the degree of pressure resulting therefrom, able to hamper the liberty of her decisions. At the same time we do not hesitate to acknowledge that the Covering Letter seems to open up a possibility of the reparation of certain injustices (we borrow the term from its text) to be found in the Treaty. But the weighing of these political points of view is beyond the province of the Delegation. Not the mandatories but the mandators are called upon to weigh their import and determine the influence they are to have on their decisions. We therefore relinquish our mandate into the hands of the Government from whom it was received, handing over to them the documents dispatched to us. Theirs it is to form the resolutions demanded by the conditions of the country; theirs it is to reply to your question concerning the signature of the Treaty.

I remain, Sir, . . .

DOCUMENT 48

Note from the Hungarian Government to the President of the Supreme Council, M. Millerand, May 17, 1920 [1]

Sir,

The Hungarian Delegation, as it appears from their letter of May 16 have relinquished their *pleins pouvoirs* into the hands of their mandators.

The Delegation have considered it morally impossible for them to sign a Treaty they have declared inacceptable and irrealisible and the provisions of which they have vainly essayed to modify. In their opinion only the compelling force of an exceptional situation can afford the motive of its signing but they do not consider it as within their competency to judge whether this constraint actually exists.

The Hungarian Government fully participate in the documentary objections and criticisms unceasingly raised by the Delegation as well as in the protest in general expressed in the course of the negotiations as well as in their present letter of demission. The Hungarian Government notably protest against the manifest breach of the principle of the right of a free self-determination for the people constituting the sole means of eliminating in advance all causes of trouble and upheaval. It is precisely in virtue of this principle that the Government thought possible to abstain from insisting on incontestable historic rights.

The Hungarian Delegation have meanwhile not omitted to point out certain passages in the Covering Letter of the Allied and Associated Powers seeming to be if not real guarantees at least formal promises of a nature to allow of some softening of the stipulations of the Peace Treaty in the near future.

The Allied and Associated Powers in their Covering Letter declare that it was impossible to alter the frontier they have, however, charged the Delimitation Commissions to propose the modifications judged necessary to rectify injustices brought about by the Treaty and which it is to general interest to efface. According to the Covering Letter the measures to be taken by these Commission[s] will fully safeguard the interests of the border population. We could not permit ourselves to doubt that the Allied and Associated Powers will see that the Reparation [Delimitation] Commissions should actually acquit themselves of their task in each case that an injustice is brought

[1] *The Hungarian Peace Negotiations*, II, 526–27.

to their knowledge and that they will insist that the Council of the League of Nations should use all its influence to cause all injustice and all iniquity to disappear. For Ruthenia the Covering Letter provides a broad autonomy placing it in a position to manifest its own will and, free of all constraint, to decide of its fate and of its appurtenance. The Allied and Associated Powers would certainly not have inserted these clear and categorical declarations in the Covering Letter if they had not the firm intention of assuring the Ruthenians the full freedom of their elections and of the functioning of their national assembly.

The Letter of Envoy finally approaches the moment in which Hungary shall be received on an equal footing in the League of Nations on the condition that she acquits herself loyally of the obligations binding her in the Treaty. The Allied and Associated Powers can certainly form a just idea of the burden of obligations weighing on Hungary whose loyalty cannot be called into question. But where the moral and material exactions of the Treaty overpass the limits of the possible, the will the most loyal must encounter insurmountable obstacles.

The gravity of the present moment, and the incontestable authority of the Allied and Associated Powers lend the promises inscribed in the very document in which Hungary is invited to sign the peace a most particular importance.

The impression to be gathered from the entirety of the formal promises is that of a *rapprochement* in the sense of the order of ideas we have attempted to assert. The Hungarian Government are convinced that this *rapprochement* whose commencement they seem to trace will assert itself in all the questions brought forward by the Treaty and will cause to disappear all the other injustices not expressly mentioned in the Covering Letter or not recognised as such.

Led by this supposition and fully conscious of the grave situation of the country, the Hungarian Government do not consider themselves able to refuse signing the Treaty of Peace.

By this resolution the Hungarian Government demonstrate that Hungary constitutes a valuable element in the political system of Central-Europe the consolidation of which is in the general interest of Europe.

I have the honour to inform you, Sir, that as soon as the exact date of the signature is known to the Hungarian Government, Hungary will not fail to appoint her delegates, furnished with *pleins pouvoirs,* for signing the Treaty of Peace.

I remain, Sir, your obedient servant

SIMONYI-SEMADAM M.P.
Prime Minister.
COUNT TELEKI M.P.
Minister of Foreign Affairs.

DOCUMENT 49

Excerpts from Jacques Bainville's "Les Conséquences politiques de la paix" (Paris, 1920), relating to Southeastern Europe, pp. 164–70.[1]

The instinct of self-preservation being the strongest, it will exert its influence also in the political arena. Peoples and governments, after having restored internal order, will be driven to the search of external stability; and the confusion resulting from an arbitrary distribution of states in Central and Eastern Europe will be felt as an international anarchy as noxious as the preceding one and likely to beget another. The integral application of nationality did not produce favorable results. By multiplying feeble and rival states, it had multiplied wars, both civil and international. To eradicate both scourges, another reorganization is called for. After having restored a social order, more similar to what we left behind than most of us would believe, Europe will be bound to reconsider the creation of states which are not viable or are the causes of incessant trouble because of their impotence to defend and to govern themselves. . . .

Several combinations, different from those created by the treaties are conceivable in Central and Eastern Europe. There are only two unlikely developments. One is that the structure created would outlive the conditions in which the new states have been created and their frontiers traced. When the Allies should no longer have the will or ability to oppose changes; when they should no longer agree in exercising supervision and guardianship over these divers peoples, it will not be long before all these peoples will obtain a new status. An equally unlikely development is that these peoples freely, from their own will and with the consent of all, would form something resembling the former Austria. Had not a few million Germans or even the Slovaks been included into the Czech state by command, they would not have joined it on their own accord. If they ought to be separated, they will do so only as a result of external force. For that reason the heirs of the Austrian Empire will not reunite on their own accord, however much it would be in their interest to live together. People believed for a long time in a Balkan federation which has never materialized. A Danubian federation which would spring up on its own power, simply because it would be the most reasonable

[1] Translation by the present author.

solution, is just as much a product of the imagination. In speaking of federation, one really means the federalizing factor. The Danube knew only one heretofore: it was the Habsburg. When the Emperor was chased from Vienna in 1848, the Empire would have disintegrated, had it not retained the army, Windischgraetz and Radetzky. . . . Another Habsburg fell in 1918. He retained neither the army nor its commanders. The theory that the sudden return of Charles I or any member of his family to the throne could reconstitute Austria solely by virtue of the principle of legitimacy cannot be taken seriously. This principle alone is as powerless to revive an empire as would be the ideal of republican federalism. Whatever advantages would inhere in bringing the people of the ancient empire again together, they would live in a state of hostility, forming changing coalitions until the appearance of a real federalizing force, imposing a federation, and this force will come from the most robust element, most capable of reassembling the others by dominating them. . . .

This analysis leads to the conclusion that if there ought to be a federation, the federalizing factor will be a nationality—not necessarily the largest but the most robust one, the one most imbued with the military spirit. There are only two of these: Yugoslavia and Hungary. And it seems that the second of the two possesses the necessary qualifications, despite her disaster. The Hungarians have a vigorous national consciousness and a fierce will. They have over their neighbors which have grown at their expense, the advantage —less paradoxical than it seems—that they do not have to assimilate new populations. Their unity is real. They can disturb the small and medium-sized states which surround them; and no great power has a direct interest in opposing their rise and progress. . . . Whether the counter-revolutionary tendency persists or we shall see a return of the revolution, whether a "white" Europe will clash with a "red" Europe, Hungary, as presently oriented, seems to be in a good position to crystallize the conservative elements in her surroundings,—even including the Germanic element. Thus the adumbration of a federation radiating as far as Bavaria is here conceivable.

But even if things should develop more or less according to imagination, it is by no means certain that this development will necessarily and inevitably serve our interests. Instead of detaching and reuniting the [lost] territories for herself, Hungary might well reassemble them for Germany; she may become herself an object of German aspiration and succumb to the attraction of a reorganized and vigorous Germany. . . . A Germany which restored quickly internal order would benefit thereby externally as well. Such a Germany would not only retain, instead of losing, the conservative elements in the South, but would also attract and absorb the heterogeneous elements around her, equally greedy for order, for preservation—and for revenge. As fifty years before, Berlin would become for the Hungarians the imposed itinerary. In that case, we should see Austria-Hungary reconstituted, in whole or in part, but for the benefit of and as appendage to the German Empire. Not to mention that the day the Austrian Republic is absorbed, the day the Germany of Berlin is installed in Vienna, will be the eve of her being also installed in Budapest and thus finally able to constitute the famous *Mitteleuropa*. All depends on the point of departure of the development. . . .

BIBLIOGRAPHY

I. *Documents of the Paris Peace Conference*

American Commission to Negotiate Peace.

Bulletins issued by the Secretariat of the Commission partially published in Miller, *My Diary at the Conference of Paris.*

Bulletins issued by the Information Section of the Commission. Unpublished.

Czecho-Slovak Delegation. Memoranda.

No. 1. The Czecho-Slovaks.—Their History and Civilization.

No. 2. The Territorial Claims of the Czecho-Slovak Republic.

No. 5. Slovakia. Territory Claimed.

No. 6. Problem of the Ruthenians of Hungary.

Peace Conference.

Minutes of the Meetings of the Council of Foreign Ministers. Partially published.

Minutes of the Meetings of the Council of Heads of Delegations. Partially published.

Minutes of the Meetings of the Supreme Council. Partially published.

Reports Presented to the Supreme Council of the Allies by the Committee for the Study of Territorial Question Relating to Rumania and Yugoslavia.

Report No. 1. Rumanian Frontiers.

Report No. 2. Frontiers of Yugoslavia.

Report Submitted to the Supreme Council by the Committee on Tchecho-Slovak Questions.

Rumanian Delegation. Memoranda.

La Roumanie devant le Congrès de la Paix:

1. Ses revendications territoriales.

2. Le Territoire revendiqué par les Roumains au nord-ouest de la Transylvanie proprement dite.

3. Actes d'union des provinces de Bessarabie, Bukovine, Transylvanie, Banat et des regions roumaines de Hongrie avec le Royaume de Roumanie.

Yugoslav Delegation. Memoranda on Territorial Questions.

1. Delimitation between the Serbians and the Roumanians in the Banat.

2. North Frontier. Delimitation between the Serbians and Magyars in the Batchka.
3. The Town of Riyeka (Fiume).
4. Memorandum Concerning the Claims of the Kingdom of the Serbians, Croatians and Slovenes.

II. *Government and Other Official Publications*

British and Foreign State Papers.

British Treaty Series.

Confidential Report on the Sopron Plebiscite. By Baron Frederic Villani, Hungarian representative to the Interallied Mission for Western Hungary. Budapest, 1923. In Hungarian. Printed for Government use only.

Documents diplomatiques relatifs aux conventions d'alliance conclues par la République Tchécoslovaque avec le Royaume des Serbes, Croates et Slovènes et le Royaume de Roumanie. Prague, 1922. Published by the Czecho-Slovak Ministry for Foreign Affairs.

Foreign Relations of the United States. Published by the Department of State.

Handbooks Prepared under the Direction of the Historical Section of the [British] Foreign Office. London, H. M. Stationery Office, 1920.

    No. 2. Bohemia and Moravia.

    No. 3. Slovakia.

Hansard, Parliamentary Debates.

Hungarian Peace Negotiations, The. 3 vols. and maps. Budapest, Viktor Hornyanszky, 1920–22. Published by the Royal Hungarian Ministry for Foreign Affairs.

Journal officiel de la République française. Débats parlementaires. (Chambre des députés.)

League of Nations Treaty Series.

Papers and Documents Relating to the Foreign Relations of Hungary. Vol. I, 1919–20. Edited by Francis Deák and Dezsö Ujváry. Budapest, The University Press, 1939. Published by the Royal Hungarian Ministry for Foreign Affairs. [This contains "The Political Diary of the Hungarian Peace Delegation".]

Publications of the Permanent Court of International Justice.

Recueil des documents diplomatiques concernant la question Jaworzyna, Décembre 1918—Août 1923. Warsaw, 1923. Published by the Polish Ministry for Foreign Affairs.

III. *Unofficial Documentation*

Almond, N., and R. Lutz. The Treaty of St. Germain. A Documentary History of Its Territorial and Political Clauses. Stanford University, Cal., Stanford University Press, 1935.

Lapradelle, G. de. Editor. La Documentation internationale: La Paix de Versailles. 12 vols. Paris, Les Éditions internationales, 1930–39.

Martens, F. de. Nouveau recueil général des traités, (3d ser.) Vols. X, XVII.

Miller, D. H. My Diary at the Conference of Paris. 21 vols. New York, Appeal Printing Co., 1924. Privately printed for the author.

IV. *General Works and Memoirs*

D'Abernon, Lord E. V. An Ambassador's Diary. 3 vols. New York, Doubleday, Doran and Co., 1929–31.

Andrássy, Count Julius. Diplomacy and the War. London, J. Bale Sons and Danielson, Ltd., 1921.

Ashmead-Bartlett, Ellis. The Tragedy of Central Europe. London, Thornton Butterworth, Ltd., 1923.

Aston, Sir George. The Biography of the Late Marshal Foch. New York, The Macmillan Co., 1929.

Bainville, Jacques. Les Conséquences politiques de la paix. Paris, Nouvelle libraire nationale, 1920.

Baker, Ray Stannard. Woodrow Wilson and World Settlement. 3 vols. New York, Doubleday, Page and Co., 1922.

Bandholtz, H. H. An Undiplomatic Diary. Edited by Fritz-Konrad Krüger. New York, Columbia University Press, 1933.

Benes, E. Aufstand der Nationen, der Weltkrieg und die tchechoslowakische Revolution. Berlin, Bruno Cassirer Verlag, 1928.

Burián, Count Stephen. Austria in Dissolution. London, E. Benn, Ltd., 1925.

Carrié, Albrecht-René. Italy at the Paris Peace Conference. New York, Columbia University Press, 1938.

Crane, J. O. The Little Entente. New York, The Macmillan Co., 1931.

Czernin, Count Ottokar. In the World War. New York and London, Harper and Bros., 1920.

Glaise-Horstenau, E. The Collapse of the Austro-Hungarian Empire. London, J. M. Dent and Sons, Ltd., 1930.

Gratz, G. The Era of Revolutions. [In Hungarian.] Budapest, Magyar Szemle Társ., 1935.

Gratz, G., and R. Schüller. The Economic Policy of Austria-Hungary during the War. English translation, by W. Alison Phillips. New Haven, Yale University Press, 1928.

—— Der wirtschaftliche Zusammenbruch Österreich-Ungarns. Wien, Hölder-Pichler-Tempsky, A. G., 1930.

House, E. M., and C. Seymour. Editors. What Really Happened at Paris: The Story of the Peace Conference, 1918–1919. New York, Charles Scribner's Sons, 1921.

Jászi, O. The Dissolution of the Habsburg Monarchy. Chicago, Chicago University Press, 1929.

Krofta, Kamil. A Short History of Czechoslovakia. London, Williams and Norgate, Ltd., 1935.

Lloyd George, D. Memoirs of the Peace Conference. 2 vols. New Haven, Yale University Press, 1939.

Macartney, C. A. Hungary. London, E. Benn, Ltd., 1934.

—— Hungary and Her Successors. London, Oxford University Press, 1937.

Machray, R. The Little Entente. London, Allen-Unwin, 1929.

Millin, Gertrude. General Smuts. 2 vols. Boston, Little, Brown and Co., 1936.

Nicolson, Harold. Peacemaking, 1919. Boston and New York, Houghton Mifflin Co., 1933.

Pap, Dezsö. Hungarian Social Policy in the World War. [In Hungarian.] Budapest, K. Grill, 1934.

Raschhofer, Hermann. Die tschechoslovakischen Denkschriften für die Friedenskonferenz von Paris 1919/1920. Berlin, C. Heymanns, 1937. Publication No. 24 of the Berlin Institut für ausländisches öffentliches Recht und Völkerrecht.

Ridgeway, George L. Merchants of Peace. New York, Columbia University Press, 1938.

Strong, D. F. Austria (October 1918–March 1919): Transition from Empire to Republic. New York, Columbia University Press, 1939.

Tardieu, André. The Truth about the Treaty. Indianapolis, Bobbs-Merrill, 1921.

Temperley, Harold W. V. Editor. A History of the Peace Conference at Paris. 6 vols. London, Frowde, 1920–24.

Thompson, Charles T. The Peace Conference Day by Day. New York, Brentano's, 1920.

Toynbee, A. J. Survey of International Affairs, 1920–1923. London, Humphrey Milford, 1925.

Vondracek, F. J. The Foreign Policy of Czechoslovakia, 1918–1935. New York, Columbia University Press, 1937.

V. *Articles*

Binkley, R. C., "New Light on the Paris Peace Conference," *Political Science Quarterly,* XLVI (1931), 509 ff.

Both, B. K., "La Tchécoslovaquie à la Conférence de la Paix: Les Cartes et mémoires Tchéchoslovaques présenté par la Délégation Tchéque," *Nouvelle Revue de Hongrie,* LVI (1937), 102 ff.

Szende, Zoltán, "Les Derniers Jours de l'armée austro-hongroise en 1918," *Nouvelle Revue de Hongrie,* LX (1939), 88 ff.

—— "Une Armée qui rentre et ne trouve pas sa patrie," *Nouvelle Revue de Hongrie,* LX (1939), 376 ff.

—— "La Guerre contre la Hongrie, après la guerre," *Nouvelle Revue de Hongrie,* LXI (1939), 181 ff.

Teleki, Count Paul, "A propos d'une carte ethnique," *Nouvelle Revue de Hongrie,* LVI (1937), 21 ff.

Temperley, Harold W. V., "How the Hungarian Frontiers Were Drawn," *Foreign Affairs,* VI (1928), 432 ff.

INDEX

Abernon, Lord d', 316*n*

Adriatic, corridor to, through H. suggested, 36; means of communication with, sought by Czecho-Sl., 394

Aerial navigation, H. note in reply to peace terms, 235

Agricultural questions, H. note in reply to peace terms, 234

Alby, General, French Chief of Staff (from Jan. 1919), 42*n*, 402

Alien Enemy Acts, 219

Allied Armies in the East, General in Command, *see* Franchet d' Esperay

Allied Danube Commission, told Rum. to keep hands off shipping on Danube, 127

Allied Powers

Allies and Hungary: requested H. troops not to resist Rum. occupation, 12; reply to protests against violations of armistice, 14; terms of Belgrade armistice between H. and, Nov. 13, 1918, 10-11, 355-61; armistice gave authority to occupy strategic points of Austria-Hungary, 9; secret treaty of Aug. 1916 with Rum., 30; regarded by Allies as canceled, 33; ultimate responsibility for new boundaries, 38; defiance of, by H. bolshevik govt., 57; blockade against Central Powers maintained after Nov. 1918, 61*n*; influence of small Allies, 84*n*; weigh possibilities of enforcing on H. respect for armistice conditions, 96; military action against H. contemplated, 97; fail to support Magyar patriots, 101; sought to end communist regime, 102; Rum. proposals for pacification of H. presented to, 106; rejected, 114; intervention in govt. of H. suggested, 151; preference for a coalition govt. in H., 156; provisional *de facto* recognition of new govt. in H., 166; dissatisfaction with handling of H. question expressed at meeting of Prime Ministers, 239; principles for which they fought, 396; draft and final text of treaty between Czecho-Sl. and, 453-54; question of replacing Rum. force in H. by Interallied force, 527; Interallied commissions to investigate

abuses in H. urged by Sir George Clerk, 537; danger of their good name being brought into disrepute, 538; Covering Letter of reply of, to president of H. Peace Del., 551-54

Conference of Ambassadors: functions of Supreme Council transferred to (*q.v., infra*), 211, 221; injection of dynastic question into peace negotiations, 227; request H. to ratify peace treaty, 329, 334, 335; rejection of H. requests re modification of military clauses, 335*n*; declaration re restoration of Habsburg dynasty, 550

Council of Foreign Ministers: re lifting blockade against H., 61*n*; recommendations of territorial commissions before Council of Four and, 63-72; request for recommendations re status of Ruthenians, 69; H.'s frontiers disposed of during a single meeting, 69; report approving H's future frontiers accepted, 71; final consideration by, of H.'s frontiers with Rum. and Czecho-Sl., 77-85; excerpts from Minutes, on modification of frontiers between H. and Czecho-Sl., 432-33; on frontiers of H., 434-41; on blockade of H., 442-43; articles re H. frontiers proposed by, for insertion in treaty of peace with H., 445; with Czecho-Sl., 445; Rum., 446; Yugosl., 447; excerpts from Minutes, on autonomy for the Ruthenians, 452; on frontiers of H., 455-60

Council of Four, *see infra*, Allied Powers, Supreme Council

Interallied Commission of Generals, *see infra*, Interallied Military Mission

Interallied Military Mission: Supreme Council's decision to send to Budapest, 109; tasks outlined, 110; request for suspension of execution of new armistice terms offered by Rum., 114; officers protest in person against excesses of Rum. occupation troops, 115; Yugosl. and Czecho-Sl. requested to withdraw behind demarcation line, 118; inability to obtain from Czechs the evacuation of neutral zone,

Budapest (*Continued*)
official announcement that Rum. troops would evacuate, 160; organization of police force, 165; evacuated by Rums.: entered by H. National Army, 165; building of commercial port by Fr. group, 272

Bukovina, constitutional arrangements in, 382

Bulgaria, defection of, 3

Burgenland, *see* Austria; Hungary, Western

Burian, Cnt. Stephen, Foreign Minister of Austria-Hungary, 6

Cambon, Jules, French diplomat, member French Peace Delegation, subsequently president of Conference of Ambassadors, 37, 186, 187, 204, 212n, 215n, 337, 396, 411, 418, 458; re Czech-H. frontier, 80, 81

Camerlynck, French scholar, member, Secretariat of the Peace Conference, 420

Castoldi, Colonel, Italian Army, 420, 421

Causey, Colonel William B., U.S. Army, member Interallied Commission on Relief of German-Austria, 113; report on food situation in Budapest, 117

Cavallero, General Ugo, Italian Military representative on Supreme War Council, 42n, 406, 420, 470

Cavendish-Bentinck, Lord H., British politician, member of Parliament, 243n

Cecil, Lord Robert, 220, 225n

Central Committee on Territorial Questions, 68n

Central Europe, confederation of states of, to check German influence, 18; warning to warring elements in, 40n; militarism, 244; unrest, 545; menaced from East, 547; ethnographic conditions, 552; position of H. in political system of, 559

Central-European-Balkan bloc, 333

Cermak, Bohumil, Czecho-Sl. minister to Rum. (1919–20), 200n

Cerrutti, Vittorio, Italian High Commissioner in Budapest (1919–20), 201n, 214n, 215n, 259n, 302

Charles, emperor of Austria and king of H., efforts to federalize Empire, 5; Manifesto transforming Monarchy into federal state, 5; effort to avert crisis, 6; Károlyi received appointment from, and was relieved of oath by, 7n, 8; Eckerstau declaration, 11; unsuccessful attempt to regain throne of H., 227, 342; rights as sovereign still claimed by, 486; *see also* Habsburgs

Charpy, General Charles, French Army chief of staff, Allied Armies of the East, 42, 402,

405; disapproval of demarcation line of neutral zone, 60n

Christian National Block, in H., 532, 534; Apponyi rejected by, 535

Clemenceau, George, 33, 40, 63, 77n, 82n, 109, 461, 478; requested cessation of hostilities in Northern H., 79; results of ultimatum to H. Communist Govt., 93; unequivocal promise to H., 99; Rum. proposals for pacification presented to, 108; reply, 108 f.; text of warning to Rum., 114n; view that conduct of Rum. could not be tolerated, 116; telegram to Intall. Mission in Budapest, 128; peremptory message to Rum., 131; instructions to Sir George Clerk, 134; asked to intervene to obtain release of interned H. experts, 173; reply to Apponyi, 186; greeting to H. Del., 206; defeated in Fr. presidential elections: resigned premiership and chairmanship of Supreme Council, 211; opposition of followers to Millerand, 319n; question of Bánát, 368, 375; Rum. territorial claims, 380, 384, 385, 387; Yugosl. territorial claims, 395, 396, 399

Clerk, Sir George Russell, British diplomat, 112n, 173, 492n, 517; sent to disentangle political situation in H., 129; mission to Rum., 134-51; documents illustrating failure of mission, 142, 143; excerpts, 144, 145; reports on his mission to Bucharest, 145, 148, 150n, 151, 503-12; assured that requisitions had been stopped, 146, 147; visit to Diamandi, 147; tribute to Friedrich, 148; Supreme Council's decision to send to Budapest, 154; mission to H., 155-70; telegraphic report of conclusions reached in Budapest, 157; telegram to Supreme Council concerning steps contemplated in Paris, 160; advised against sending Czech and Yugosl. contingents to H., 161; mission crowned with success, 166; telegram from Supreme Council to, 526-27; telegram to Supreme Council re evacuation of H. and political situation, 528-29; telegram to Supreme Council re recognition of Huszár, 530; excerpts from report to Supreme Council on his mission to H., 531-38

Coal shortage, in H., 94

Coanda, General Constantin, Rum. Army, and member of the Rum. Peace Delegation, 42, 405

Commission to Negotiate Peace (American), 181n, 184

Committee for the Study of Territorial Questions Relating to Rumania and Yugoslavia, 34, 40, 42, 164; discussion of Transylvanian